THE TREATY ON THE PROHIBITION OF NUCLEAR WEAPONS

The Treaty on the Prohibition of Nuclear Weapons (2017) sets out to challenge deterrence policies and military defence doctrines, taking a humanitarian approach intended to disrupt the nuclear status quo. States with nuclear weapons oppose its very existence, neither participating in its development nor adopting its final text. Civil society groups seem determined, however, to stigmatize and delegitimize nuclear weapons towards their abolition. This book analyzes how the Treaty influences the international security architecture, examining legal, institutional and diplomatic implications of the Treaty and exploring its real and potential impact for both states acceding to the Treaty and those opposing it. It concludes with practical recommendations for international lawyers and policymakers regarding non-proliferation and disarmament matters, ultimately noting that nuclear weapons threaten peace, and everyone should have the right to nuclear peace and freedom from nuclear fear.

Jonathan L. Black-Branch is the President of ISLAND – Foundation of International Society of Law and Nuclear Disarmament, a charitable foundation focusing on teaching, research and engagement activities regarding nuclear disarmament, non-proliferation and understanding and the human impact of living in a nuclear world.

Jonathan Black-Branch in this exhaustive study has delved, from an international legal perspective, into the complex details of the negotiation of the nuclear weapons prohibition treaty and its relationship to the current international security architecture that envisions the use and threat of use of nuclear weapons. The book provides an invaluable overview of the impact of the TPNW on the nuclear disarmament obligations under Article VI and how it could establish a *jus cogens* rule creating an *erga omnes* obligation for all NPT states parties. This thorough analysis of evolving law on nuclear disarmament, human rights and ecological security as reflected in the TPNW and its *travaux preparatoire* should be required reading for diplomats and policy makers before they casually discuss strategies for the use of nuclear weapons. It highlights traditional approaches, while exploring new perspectives on arms control and the limits of state sovereignty regarding defence. The community of international lawyers that produce legal opinions for their governments justifying the retention of nuclear weapons could be well served by the perusal of this *analysis legalis*. In a sense, this book provides the missing link, as Professor Black-Branch says, regarding the moral and legal arguments for disarmament; one that the drafters of the TPNW did not expressly state. It comes full circle from the dire warnings sounded by the inventors of atomic weapons all the way to the determined effort by the majority of the UN member states to finally establish the foundation of a legal norm against the possession and use of the deadliest weapons invented by humankind. The continuing survival of the human race and all other species on Planet Earth hang in the balance. A rules-based international order offers the best hopes for survival. In this regard the Treaty on the Prohibition of Nuclear Weapons could well close the loop, as Professor Black-Branch advocates, on outlawing the three existing categories of "weapons of mass destruction" and in the process advancing, as stated in the book's conclusion, a "right to nuclear peace."

Dr. Mohamed ElBaradei (Nobel Peace Prize winner 2005 and Former Director of the IAEA -International Atomic. Energy Agency)

Developing a broad and comprehensive understanding of the Nuclear Weapons Prohibition Treaty, this book is an invaluable resource that highlights how nuclear disarmament is a shared responsibility of all States in all regions of the globe, irrespective of their military capabilities or adherence to Alliances. It rightly points out that it is high time to overcome the existing schism between those forcing nuclear disarmament and those resisting it. Jonathan Black-Branch has gone a long way towards presenting professional legal and policy solutions that remain unexplored in too many States, who would benefit greatly from this timely and insightful work.

Dieter Fleck, Member of the Advisory Board, Amsterdam Center for International Law; former Director International Agreements & Policy, German Ministry of Defence

"This extremely well researched book on the TPNW will prove to be of great assistance to international lawyers for many years to come".

Dr. Konstantinos Magliveras
Faculty of Law, University of the Aegean,
Attorney at Law, Athens, Greece.

Professor Black-Branch demonstrates how the Treaty Prohibiting Nuclear Weapons challenges the status quo based on nuclear hierarchy, deterrence and fear. He not only provides a comprehensive legal evaluation of the Treaty, but also makes a cogent and powerful argument that is has the potential to change the world for the better.

Professor Nigel White, School of Law, University of Nottingham, UK
Co-Editor of the Journal of Conflict and Security Law
(Oxford University Press). Nottingham NG7 2RD United Kingdom

Jonathan Black-Branch offers a thought-provoking and timely contribution to one of the biggest threats that faces humankind today. He explains in a detail the paradigm shift that is taking place in this field, from a State-centred approach, focusing exclusively on the national security, towards a human and victim-centred logic at the forefront of the discussion. ...

One of the main achievements of the book is that it demonstrates that nuclear weapons are no longer a private matter or privilege of a handful of States but a global problem, an *erga omnes* concern.

He concludes by advocating the inspiring idea of a human right to nuclear peace and freedom from nuclear fear.

I have never seen a book that deals so comprehensively with all aspects of nuclear weapons, including environmental and economic concerns, humanitarian law and human rights. The book offers many fresh and valuable arguments to civil society and activists in their fight for a world without nuclear weapons.

Dr. Daniel Rietiker (PhD)
International Law Lecturer, Lausanne University

"Tremendous research work and passionate activism underlie this important and indeed all-inclusive book, which explores in depth the diplomatic, political, legal, technical, humanitarian and ethical aspects of nuclear disarmament. A most valuable instrument of study and an inspiring vision of a planet free from nuclear fear."

Gabriella Venturini, Professor Emerita, University of Milan, and President
to the Italian Branch of the International Law Association

Highly readable and intellectually stimulating, this book provides a fascinating analysis of the historical, legal and sociological aspects of the Treaty on the Prohibition of Nuclear Weapons (TPNW). Few scholars are better placed than Professor Jonathan Black-Branch, the Chair of the International Law Association's Committee on Nuclear Weapons, Non Proliferation and Contemporary International Law, to produce a comprehensive account of the TPNW and the complicated questions of nuclear non-proliferation and disarmament. This is an essential reference book for all who are genuinely interested in this matter of concern to all humankind.

Masahiko Asada, President of the Japanese Society of International Law
and Professor of International Law at Kyoto University

In his monograph, Jonathan Black-Branch ambitiously attempts to assess the synergies of the newly concluded Treaty on the Prohibition of Nuclear Weapons (TPNW) with the existing disarmament and nuclear legal architecture, as well as to explore its potential to challenge the nuclear status quo and provide an impetus for change. With its meticulous description and analysis of the TPNW, as well as its position within the (nuclear) disarmament regime and international law more generally, his monograph will be a must read for scholars and policy makers alike.

Dr. A.J.J. de Hoogh, Associate Professor in International Law
Department of Transboundary Legal Studies, section of
International Law
Faculty of Law University of Groningen,
The Netherlands

The Treaty on the Prohibition of Nuclear Weapons

LEGAL CHALLENGES FOR MILITARY DOCTRINES AND DETERRENCE POLICIES

JONATHAN L. BLACK-BRANCH

ISLAND - Foundation of International Society of Law
and Nuclear Disarmament

CAMBRIDGE
UNIVERSITY PRESS

University Printing House, Cambridge CB2 8BS, United Kingdom

One Liberty Plaza, 20th Floor, New York, NY 10006, USA

477 Williamstown Road, Port Melbourne, VIC 3207, Australia

314–321, 3rd Floor, Plot 3, Splendor Forum, Jasola District Centre, New Delhi – 110025, India

79 Anson Road, #06–04/06, Singapore 079906

Cambridge University Press is part of the University of Cambridge.

It furthers the University's mission by disseminating knowledge in the pursuit of education, learning, and research at the highest international levels of excellence.

www.cambridge.org
Information on this title: www.cambridge.org/9781108493055
DOI: 10.1017/9781108675307

© Jonathan L. Black-Branch 2021

This publication is in copyright. Subject to statutory exception and to the provisions of relevant collective licensing agreements, no reproduction of any part may take place without the written permission of Cambridge University Press.

First published 2021

A catalogue record for this publication is available from the British Library.

Library of Congress Cataloging-in-Publication Data
NAMES: Black-Branch, Jonathan L., author.
TITLE: The treaty prohibiting nuclear weapons : legal challenges for military doctrines and deterrence policies / Jonathan L. Black-Branch.
DESCRIPTION: Cambridge, United Kingdom ; New York : Cambridge University Press, 2019. | Includes bibliographical references and index.
IDENTIFIERS: LCCN 2020047468 (print) | LCCN 2020047469 (ebook) | ISBN 9781108493055 (hardback) | ISBN 9781108675307 (ebook)
SUBJECTS: LCSH: Nuclear disarmament. | Treaty on the Prohibition of Nuclear Weapons (2017 July 7) | Nuclear nonproliferation. | Nuclear arms control.
CLASSIFICATION: LCC KZ5675 .B53 2019 (print) | LCC KZ5675 (ebook) | DDC 341.7/34–dc23
LC record available at https://lccn.loc.gov/2020047468
LC ebook record available at https://lccn.loc.gov/2020047469

ISBN 978-1-108-49305-5 Hardback

Cambridge University Press has no responsibility for the persistence or accuracy of URLs for external or third-party internet websites referred to in this publication and does not guarantee that any content on such websites is, or will remain, accurate or appropriate.

Contents

Foreword		*page* xiii
Preface		xvii
Acknowledgments		xviii
List of Abbreviations		xix

1 Changing the Status Quo in Nuclear Arms Control Law: The Treaty on the Prohibition of Nuclear Weapons 2017 — 1

Introduction to the Book	1
A New Direction in International Disarmament Law	3
Toward Humanitarian Nuclear Disarmament	4
Legal Congruence with Existing Treaty Obligations	5
Universality under Customary International Law	6
Safeguards, Verification and Implementation	6
Nuclear Deterrence Policies and the Prohibition Treaty	7
Nuclear Defense Doctrines and Disarmament	7
A Bifurcated International Legal Infrastructure	8
Stigmatization Action	8
Toward Neo-Universalism	8
Obligations *Erga Omnes*	9
Conclusion: United We Stand, Divided We Fall	10

2 Adopting the Treaty on the Prohibition of Nuclear Weapons 2017: A New Dawn, a New Deal, a New Direction in Nuclear Disarmament Law? — 11

Introduction: The Evolution of Nuclear Disarmament Law	11
How and Why Did the New Treaty Arise?	12
The Process: Determined to Disarm	15
Outcome: The Treaty on the Prohibition of Nuclear Weapons 2017	41
Conclusion	44

3 Humanitarian Nuclear Disarmament: Challenging the Status Quo through New Approaches to Legal Process, Purpose and Provisions 46

Changing Times, Changing Voices? 47
TPNW Provisions Contrasted with the NPT 67
Impact on Nuclear Disarmament: Process, Purpose and Provisions 70
Conclusion: Impact on Nuclear Disarmament 72

4 Legal Congruence with Existing Treaty Obligations: Toward Complementary or Competing Interests? 74

A New Treaty toward Nuclear Nonproliferation? 74
Legal Congruence with Existing Treaty Obligations 75
Scope and Implementation of the CTBT: The Preparatory
    Commission for the Comprehensive Nuclear Test-Ban
    Preparatory Organization 86
Treaty on the Prohibition of Nuclear Weapons 2017 88
NATO's Position Is Not Inconsistent with ICJ Jurisprudence 101
Conclusion: Complementary or Competing Interests? 103

5 Customary International Law, *Opinio Juris* and State Practice Regarding the Treaty on the Prohibition of Nuclear Weapons 2017: Toward Universality? 105

Introduction: A New Direction in Nuclear Nonproliferation and
    Disarmament? 105
Universality 105
Wider State Participation, Treaty Legitimacy and Credibility 106
NATO and Allies against the Prohibition Treaty 114
Customary International Law, State Practice and *Opinio Juris* 116
Doctrine of the Persistent Objector 119
Nuclear-Weapon States: Disarmament and Ending the Arms Race
    or *vel non?* 127
Specially Affected States Doctrine 129
Legality of the Threat or Use of Nuclear Weapons, Advisory Opinion:
    Customary Law 131
Conclusion: Changing *Opinio Juris?* 134

6 Treaty Safeguards, Verification and Implementation: A Simple-Ban Approach and a Need for Oversight 135

Verification: Correctness and Completeness 135
The Scope of Prohibition of Nuclear Weapons and Explosive Devices 136
Verification under the TPNW 137
A "Simple-Ban" Humanitarian Approach 137

Contents ix

Verification Difficulties under the "Simple-Ban" Approach		138
Effectiveness of the Prohibition Treaty		139
Understanding Verification: Definition, Terms and Conditions		148
Effectiveness, Transparency and Confidence Building		150
Lessons Regarding Verification: Iran		151
Lessons from the Chemical and Biological Convention Verifications		155
The International Atomic Energy Agency Safeguards System and the Prohibition Treaty		156
A Competent International Authority: Authority to Disarm and Dismantle		162
Conclusions		166

7 Nuclear Deterrence Policies and the Prohibition Treaty: Disarmament Considerations 168

Nuclear Weapons and the Theory of Deterrence 168
Legal and Political Ramifications for NATO Members, Umbrella and Other States under the TPNW 177
Forcing Nuclear Disarmament in NATO and Umbrella States? 183
NATO, Umbrella and Other States 200
Other Arrangements: The CSTO and SCO 200
Analysis and Conclusions 201

8 Nuclear Defense Doctrines: Disarmament and Emerging Humanitarian Concerns 204

The Threat of Force and the ICJ Advisory Opinion 206
The Implementation of the TPNW and Its Potential for Change as to How Nuclear Weapons Are Perceived and Utilized around the World 226
Conclusions 234

9 Competition, Fragmentation and Polarization: A Bifurcated International Legal Infrastructure Regarding the Nuclear Architecture and Regulation? 236

The TPNW: Uniting Division 236
The TPNW in the International Context 237
Two Camps: Resolute States and Stalwart States 237
Stalemate between Resolute and Stalwart States 243
Nuclear-Weapon-Free Zones 266
How the TPNW and NWFZs Might Interact 273
The TPNW Creates a New NWFZ 276
Conclusion 278

x Contents

10 Stigmatization-Action and Changing Global Perceptions to Delegitimize and Eliminate Nuclear Weapons 280

Stigmatization and Moral Traction 280
Stigmatizing Nuclear Weapons 281
Nuclear Weapons: Stigmatize, Deligitimize, Eliminate 284
Conclusions: Stigmatize, Delegitimize, Eliminate 303
A Call to Action to Overcome the Growing Schism 304

11 Toward Neo-Universalism: Toward a New Reality in International Law? 306

Introduction 307
Toward Universal Acceptance of a Non-Nuclear World 307
Public and Government Support for Disarmament 309
State Support for the TPNW 310
Nuclear-Weapon States 310
Nuclear-Armed States 314
Non-Nuclear-Weapon States that Relinquished Nuclear Weapons 317
Nuclear-Weapon-Free Kazakhstan, Ukraine and Belarus 317
Africa: A Nuclear-Weapon-Free Zone 319
Latin America and the Caribbean: A Nuclear-Weapon-Free Zone 321
Non-Nuclear-Weapon States Living in Nuclear Fear 321
EU Member States 324
European Non-NWS NATO Members 324
Other EU NATO States 325
Anti-nuclear EU Members 326
Ambivalent EU States 328
Other States 329
Public and Government Support for Disarmament 332
A Shift from Realism to Universalism? 333
Conclusion: Changing the Status Quo through Neo-Universalism 338

12 Obligations *Erga Omnes*: The Missing Link for Nuclear Nonproliferation and Disarmament Compliance 340

What Are *Erga Omnes* Obligations? 341
Does the International Community Currently Recognize
   any *Erga Omnes* Obligations? 346
Why Are *Nuclear* Obligations Effective *Erga Omnes*? 348
How Should the International Community Enforce Nuclear
   Obligations *Erga Omnes*? 370

Contents

		xi
How do Obligations *Erga Omnes* Act as a Link between the Goals of the TPNW and a Binding Legal Framework that NWS already Adhere to?		374
Summary and Conclusion		376

13 The Treaty on the Prohibition of Nuclear Weapons within the Nuclear Nonproliferation and Security Architecture in International Law: From Grand Bargain to Grand Challenges with the Right to Nuclear Peace and Freedom from Nuclear Fear: Summaries and Conclusions   377

Toward New Approaches to Old Problems	377
From a Passive to an Active Role for TPNW States	384
The Nuclear Paradox	388
Human Rights Obligations to Peace and Freedom from Fear	392
Conclusions and Recommendations	404
Nuclear Declaration on the Right to Nuclear Peace and Freedom from Nuclear Fear 2028	412

Index   414

Foreword

The devastating power of the atomic bomb was recognized at the very beginning of the nuclear age by scientists working both in Germany and in the United States to develop a nuclear explosive device. These scientists understood early on the unique destructive power of atomic weapons and realized, albeit in different ways, the enormous responsibility on their shoulders of opening the "Pandora's Box" of nuclear fission. In fact, scientists such as Niels Bohr and Werner Heisenberg and their colleagues deliberately slowed their work on developing nuclear explosives for the regime in Germany and communicated their grave fears to their colleagues in the United Kingdom and United States. Robert Oppenheimer, the scientific lead of the Manhattan Project, lamented that he had become, "The Destroyer of Worlds," quoting from the *Bhagavad Gita*, on the successful detonation of the first atomic explosive device on July 16, 1945. The bombing by the United States of Hiroshima and Nagasaki, three weeks later, on August 6 and 9, 1945, affirmed his fears and demonstrated the horrific power of nuclear weapons.

In the aftermath of the destruction of Hiroshima and Nagasaki, Albert Einstein took full responsibility for the consequences of the letter of August 2, 1939, he and Leó Szilárd jointly sent to US President Franklin Delano Roosevelt warning against the dangers of Nazi Germany developing atomic weapons and recommending that the United States initiate a nuclear weapon development program – that led Roosevelt to commission the Manhattan Project. Einstein called it "the greatest mistake," and in 1947 he told *Newsweek* magazine "had I known that the Germans would not succeed in developing an atomic bomb, I would have done nothing." To atone for his mistake, Einstein joined with Bertrand Russell and other atomic scientists to issue the "Einstein-Russell Manifesto," on July 9, 1955; an ominous warning about the catastrophic humanitarian and environmental consequences of the use of atomic weapons and the first call to prohibit them:

> Shall we put an end to the human race; or shall mankind renounce war? ... It is stated on very good authority that a bomb can now be manufactured which will be 2,500 times as powerful as that which destroyed Hiroshima. Such a bomb, if

xiv *Foreword*

exploded near the ground or under water, sends radio-active particles into the upper air. They sink gradually and reach the surface of the earth in the form of a deadly dust or rain. It was this dust which infected the Japanese fishermen and their catch of fish. No one knows how widely such lethal radio-active particles might be diffused, but the best authorities are unanimous in saying that a war with H-bombs might possibly put an end to the human race. Although an agreement to renounce nuclear weapons as part of a general reduction of armaments would not afford an ultimate solution, it would serve certain important purposes.

The history of nuclear weapons has been one of dire warnings by all world nations and leaders of their impact on our very survival. It also has been a history of unfulfilled promises.

It is not without significance that the very first resolution adopted by the United Nations called for the "elimination of atomic weapons." On December 8, 1957, US President Dwight Eisenhower delivered his "Atoms for Peace" speech at the United Nations and warned against the devastating destructive potential of atomic weapons. He said that the world must not "accept helplessly the probability of civilization destroyed, the annihilation of the irreplaceable heritage of mankind handed down to us from generation to generation." At the same time Eisenhower held out the promise of applying "atomic energy to the needs of agriculture, medicine and other peaceful activities ... [and] to provide abundant electrical energy in the power-starved areas of the world."

Speaking four years later, on September 25, 1961, US President John Kennedy declared at the United Nations that, "Today, every inhabitant of this planet must contemplate the day when this planet may no longer be habitable. Every man, woman and child lives under a nuclear sword of Damocles, hanging by the slenderest of threads, capable of being cut at any moment by accident or miscalculation or by madness. The weapons of war must be abolished before they abolish us."

On July 1, 1968, the Treaty on the Non-Proliferation of Nuclear Weapons (NPT) was opened for signature; it entered into force on March 5, 1970. Today, the NPT has 191 states parties and remains the cornerstone of the global nuclear order; it establishes *inter alia* a clear legal obligation on the part of the five nuclear-weapon states party to eliminate all of their nuclear weapons. An obligation unanimously reaffirmed by the International Court of Justice on July 8, 1996.

Twenty-five years after John Kennedy's speech, on January 15, 1986, the President of the Soviet Union, Mikhail Gorbachev, called for a ban on all nuclear weapons by the turn of the millennium (2000), saying that "we propose that we should enter the third millennium without nuclear weapons."

States parties to the NPT in their agreed final documents of the review conferences of 1995, 2000 and 2010 issued calls to reduce nuclear weapons, affirmed an unequivocal undertaking by the nuclear-weapon states to eliminate nuclear weapons, and recalled the catastrophic devastation and humanitarian consequences of the use of nuclear weapons as noted in the preamble of the Treaty.

Foreword   xv

Three international conferences on the humanitarian impact of nuclear weapons were held, respectively, in Oslo (2013), Nayarit (2014) and Vienna (2016). At the Vienna conference, the "Austrian Pledge" endorsed by 125 states called on all "States parties to the NPT to renew their commitment to the urgent and full implementation of existing obligations under Article VI, and to this end, to identify and pursue effective measures to fill the legal gap for the prohibition and elimination of nuclear weapons."

This call then was taken up by more than 100 countries at the United Nations that set up an "Open-ended Working Group taking forward multilateral nuclear disarmament negotiations" and culminated in the decision by the General Assembly in December 2016 to "negotiate a legally binding instrument to prohibit nuclear weapons, leading towards their total elimination." On July 7, 2017, the Treaty on the Prohibition of Nuclear Weapons (TPNW) was adopted by 122 states. It is unfortunate that all nine nuclear-armed states, NATO members as well as a few other countries, all boycotted the negotiation of the TPNW and continue to oppose it, citing objections that do not appear credible or convincing.

During my time as Director General of the International Atomic Energy Agency, I repeatedly called for the creation of a peremptory norm of international law against the possession and use of nuclear weapons. I was heartened by Pope Francis' call at Hiroshima on November 11, 2019 in which he denounced not only the use, but also the possession of atomic weapons. This year, the *Bulletin of the Atomic Scientists* moved the Doomsday clock to 100 seconds, the closest to midnight than it has ever been in recognition of the heightened dangers and risks of nuclear weapons.

Jonathan Black-Branch in this exhaustive study has delved, from an international legal perspective, into the complex details of the negotiation of the nuclear weapons prohibition treaty and its relationship to the current international security architecture that envisions the use and threat of use of nuclear weapons. The book provides an invaluable overview of the impact of the TPNW on the nuclear disarmament obligations under Article VI and how it could establish a *jus cogens* rule creating an *erga omnes* obligation for all NPT states parties. This thorough analysis of evolving law on nuclear disarmament, human rights and ecological security as reflected in the TPNW and its *travaux preparatoire* should be required reading for diplomats and policy makers before they casually discuss strategies for the use of nuclear weapons. It highlights traditional approaches, while exploring new perspectives on arms control and the limits of state sovereignty regarding defense. The community of international lawyers that produce legal opinions for their governments justifying the retention of nuclear weapons could be well served by the perusal of this *analysis legalis*. In a sense, this book provides the missing link, as Professor Black-Branch says, regarding the moral and legal arguments for disarmament; one that the drafters of the TPNW did not expressly state. It comes full circle from the dire warnings sounded by the inventors of atomic weapons all the way to the determined effort by the majority of the UN member states to finally establish the foundation of a legal norm against the possession and use of the deadliest weapons invented by human-kind. The continuing survival of the human race and all other species on Planet Earth hang in the balance. A rules-based international order offers the best hopes for survival. In this regard the Treaty on the Prohibition of Nuclear Weapons could well close the loop, as Professor Black-Branch advocates, on outlawing the three existing categories of "weapons of mass destruction" and in the process advancing, as stated in the book's conclusion, a "right to nuclear peace."

Mohamed ElBaradei

Preface

The Treaty on the Prohibition of Nuclear Weapons was adopted at the UN General Assembly in July 2017, marking growing support for humanitarian efforts to take decisive action against nuclear weapons as a threat to peace and international security. It was endorsed by 122 UN Member States representing a wide range of political systems, economies and a significant percentage of the world's population. The Treaty is far from being universally accepted, however. The nuclear-armed states, including the five permanent members of the UN Security Council, refused to participate in its negotiations or accept the final Treaty text. Indeed, they do not support it, openly opposing its very existence. The treaty entered into force on 22 January 2021, since the writing of this book.

The purpose of this book is to examine the Treaty in relation to the international security architecture, providing an overview and its potential influence on disarmament commitments with reference to legal requirements under Article VI of the NPT and obligations *erga omnes*. Discussion outlines how the humanitarian approach advanced by the Treaty serves to challenge current deterrence policies and military defense doctrines in order to realign the status quo toward the elimination of nuclear weapons. The first treaty of its kind to ban nuclear weapons outright, it is meant to represent a clear disruptor within the existing disarmament framework. Civil society groups seem determined to stigmatize and delegitimize nuclear weapons for their complete abolition.

This book examines various legal, institutional and diplomatic considerations of how the Treaty aligns with existing commitments and its real and potential impact for both states acceding to the Treaty and those opposing it. It analyzes how the Treaty may affect the international security infrastructure regarding legal and institutional regulation over nuclear weapons and the governance of security assurances. It concludes by making a range of practical recommendations regarding nuclear nonproliferation and disarmament matters, ultimately noting that nuclear weapons do not protect peace but threaten it and everyone should have the right to nuclear peace and freedom from nuclear fear.

Acknowledgments

I would like to express my sincere gratitude and personal thanks to Dr. Dieter Fleck for all his encouragement and support over the past years. He has generously given me his time, wisdom and guidance.

A very special thanks is extended to Jason Poettcker, my research assistant in the initial stages of this work, for his unrelenting commitment to it.

I also wish to thank David G. Newman QC and Brenda Newman who dedicate their time and resources to peace advocacy and share my commitment to peace and disarmament.

Special acknowledgment is extended to Dr. Konstantinos Magliveras, Dr. André J. J. de Hoogh and Dr. Tariq Rauf who have offered their advice and invaluable suggestions.

Cambridge University Press has allowed me to publish this book and has assisted with patience. I am grateful to them for their interest in my work and professional diligence in supporting this important work regarding nuclear nonproliferation and disarmament.

A heartfelt thanks goes to all of you who work, aspire and advocate for a world without nuclear weapons and living with the right to nuclear peace and freedom from nuclear fear. I dedicate this book to you and those who have suffered the adverse effects of nuclear harm.

Abbreviations

AT	Antarctic Treaty 1959
CNBT	Comprehensive Nuclear-Test-Ban Treaty (1996)
CSTO	Collective Security Treaty Organization
CTBTO	Preparatory Commission for the Comprehensive Nuclear Test-Ban Preparatory Organization
DPRK	Democratic People's Republic of Korea
EU	European Union (2012)
GA	General Assembly (UN)
HRC	Human Rights Committee (UN)
IAEA	International Atomic Energy Agency
ICAN	International Campaign to Abolish Nuclear Weapons
ICCPR	International Covenant on Civil and Political Rights (1966)
ICESCR	International Covenant on Economic, Social and Cultural Rights (1966)
ICJ	International Court of Justice
ICRC	International Committee of the Red Cross
IHL	international humanitarian law
ILA	International Law Association
ILC	International Law Commission
NATO	North Atlantic Treaty Organization
NNWS	non-nuclear-weapon states
NPT	Treaty on the Non-Proliferation of Nuclear Weapons (1968)
NWFZ	nuclear-weapon-free zone
NWS	nuclear-weapon states
OST	Outer Space Treaty 1967
PNTT	Partial Nuclear Test Ban Treaty (1963)
SACT	Seabed Arms Control Treaty 1971
SC	Security Council

SCO	Shanghai Cooperation Organisation
TPNW	Treaty on the Prohibition of Nuclear Weapons (2017)
UK	United Kingdom
UN	United Nations
US	United States

1

Changing the Status Quo in Nuclear Arms Control Law: The Treaty on the Prohibition of Nuclear Weapons 2017

I can't believe that this world can go on beyond our generation and on down to succeeding generations with this kind of weapon on both sides poised at each other without someday some fool or some maniac or some accident triggering the kind of war that is the end of the line for all of us. And I just think of what a sigh of relief would go up from everyone on this earth if someday – and this is what I have – my hope, way in the back of my head – is that if we start down the road to reduction, maybe one day in doing that, somebody will say, "Why not all the way? Let's get rid of all these things."

Ronald Reagan, May 16, 1983[1]

INTRODUCTION TO THE BOOK

The Treaty on the Prohibition of Nuclear Weapons 2017[2] marks an important development in nuclear arms control law, diplomacy and relations between states. Adopted by the UN General Assembly on July 7, 2017, it was supported by 122 nations, representing a potential disruptor to the nuclear status quo. It is the first treaty to ban nuclear weapons outright, taking a clear humanitarian approach to disarmament. Despite its success in coming to fruition, however, it is not celebrated by all nations. The permanent members of the UN Security Council neither participated in its negotiations, nor adopted the final text. No state with nuclear weapons endorses the Treaty and indeed they openly oppose its very existence. That said, its adoption is supported by the vast majority of UN Member States, representing a wide range of geographical areas spanning the globe and consisting of a sizable proportion of the world's population. Furthermore, civil society groups seem determined to activate grassroots-level citizen support intended to change attitudes against the conventional nuclear stance toward meaningful change and calling for the complete abolition of nuclear weapons and explosive devices. While the real and practical impact of this Treaty remains to be seen, there is little doubt that it marks

---

[1] See www.thereaganvision.org/quotes/.

[2] Treaty on the Prohibition of Nuclear Weapons, A/CONF.229/2017/8 (July 7, 2017), available online: http://undocs.org/A/CONF.229/2017/8.

a fundamental departure from present-day affairs regarding nuclear arms control and armament matters.

The purpose of this book is to examine the Treaty on the Prohibition of Nuclear Weapons (TPNW) within the contemporary international context, exploring various legal, diplomatic and geopolitical issues emanating from its adoption at the UN General Assembly in 2017. The primary focus is to examine the Treaty against the existing legal infrastructure of the nuclear nonproliferation and disarmament framework; to see how it fits into the overarching legal and diplomatic international architecture.

It should be noted from the outset that this author is in favor of any agreement or development that advances nonproliferation and moves toward complete and verifiable nuclear disarmament. Any apparent criticisms are meant to be constructive and aimed at understanding outstanding gaps to be filled for full disarmament. Hence, this book is a foray into new territory following the advent of the 2017 Treaty, which by some accounts this author feels is the most important nuclear arms treaty since the atom bomb was created.

Discussion throughout this work grapples with the Treaty from many different perspectives: the historical development leading to this controversial agreement; the philosophical and sociological underpinnings of its foundations; legal implications regarding its real and potential impact within the global context for both states acceding to the Treaty and those that oppose it; as well as exploring its current and possible future effects on the international architecture (i.e., the legal, institutional and diplomatic framework that governs nuclear weapons and regulates nuclear capacity). This covers various perspectives, including its potential for good; its deficiencies; its effects on international relations; the new global humanitarian movement that the Treaty represents; and finally, suggestions for the future developments in the area of nuclear disarmament and nonproliferation law.

While first assessments have been published on the Treaty,[3] an in-depth discussion on these issues remains necessary in order to explore a wide range of issues from various perspectives. It is inevitable that a book of this nature will delve into possible options regarding the regulation of nuclear weapons, offering constructive observations. All discussion is meant in a positive spirit with the hope of identifying issues to address with a view to moving forward on what seems like an intractable "wicked problem"[4] facing humanity today: the nuclear conundrum regarding what this author would call "the nuclear trilemma: weapons, waste and war."

---

[3] See, e.g., Dieter Fleck, "The Treaty on the Prohibition of Nuclear Weapons: Challenges for International Law and Security," in: Black-Branch and Fleck (eds.) *Nuclear Non-Proliferation in International Law: Vol. IV Human Perspectives on the Development and Use of Nuclear Energy* (Asser Press/Springer, 2019), 395–415; Stuart Casey-Maslen, *The Treaty on the Prohibition of Nuclear Weapons. A Commentary* (Oxford University Press, Oxford Commentaries on International Law, 2019).

[4] First defined by design theorists Horst Rittel and Melvin Webber who introduced the term "wicked problem." See www.stonybrook.edu/commcms/wicked-problem/about/What-is-a-wicked-problem. With the hallmarks of a "super wicked problem" (Levin, K. B., Cashore, S. Bernstein and Auld,

A New Direction in International Disarmament Law

In essence, the primary aim of this book is to explicate the Treaty with a view to examining what it may mean for the international community as a whole, including what it has done and may do to the international nuclear legal infrastructure. In doing so, it is inevitable that an analysis of this nature will offer commentary as to whether this Treaty is a viable solution to solve the nuclear weapons problem, and what it has achieved and could still achieve within the contemporary global context.

A NEW DIRECTION IN INTERNATIONAL DISARMAMENT LAW

The TPNW brings together a commitment on the part of many nations and civil society groups to change the nuclear legal landscape and political status quo. Its origins, aims and aspirations highlight hope of a new way of looking at such destructive weapons that ultimately threaten peace and security. Treaty deliberations, negotiations and adoption at the UN present a new dawn in the field of nuclear disarmament, delivering a new deal calling for a reconfiguration of arms approaches based on humanitarian principles and ideals. Campaigners promote positive traction toward the abolition and elimination of nuclear weapons in a peaceful fashion. In order to fully understand the psychology leading up to and delivering the Treaty, it is appropriate to examine the thinking that went into the deliberations leading to such a Treaty and how proponents see its adoption as a natural step in the progression toward disarmament within the broader international context.

To that end, Chapter 2 explores the historical development of the TPNW; the context in which – how and why – the Treaty arose. It discusses how non-nuclear weapon states became frustrated with the lack of progress in the implementation of Article VI of the Treaty on the Non-Proliferation of Nuclear Weapons[5] (NPT)[6] which ultimately calls for disarmament. This growing discontent amongst non-nuclear weapon states prompted discussions that produced a Model Nuclear Weapons Convention,[7] to no avail. Concomitant to this, the NPT Review Conferences under the quintennial (five annual) review cycle failed to make progress, while parallel to this time frame three conferences on the *Humanitarian*

G. (2012). "Overcoming the Tragedy of Super Wicked Problems: Constraining our Future Selves to Ameliorate Global Climate Change." *Policy Sciences, 45,* 121–152.)

[5] Treaty on the Non-Proliferation of Nuclear Weapons (July 1, 1096), 729 UNTS 161.

[6] For a legal analysis of the NPT see Daniel H. Joyner, *Interpreting the Nuclear Non-Proliferation Treaty* (Oxford: Oxford University Press, 2011), with Foreword by Mohamed I. Shaker, author of *The Nuclear Nonproliferation Treaty: Origin and Implementation 1959–1979*, three volumes (London/Rome/New York: Oceana, 1980). See also 2010 Review Conference of the Parties to the Treaty on the Non-Proliferation of Nuclear Weapons, Final Document (NPT/CONF, 2010/50), 2–19.

[7] For the Nuclear Weapons Convention see UN General Assembly First Committee Resolution A/C.1/71/L.41 (October 14, 2017) on "Taking forward multilateral nuclear disarmament negotiations," and Report by the open-ended Working Group A/71/371 (September 1, 2016); see also, UN Doc A/62/650 (January 18, 2008), http://inesap.org/sites/default/files/inesap_old/mNWC_2007_Unversion_English_No821377.pdf.

4   *Changing Nuclear Arms Control Law*

Impact of Nuclear Weapons were held in Norway, Mexico and Austria[8] and an Open-ended Working Group was established by the General Assembly aimed to move "forward multilateral disarmament negotiations."[9] These conferences helped raise awareness of the humanitarian impact of nuclear weapons and built momentum and participation among a majority of states, the International Committee of the Red Cross and hundreds of NGOs which were led by the International Campaign to Abolish Nuclear Weapons (ICAN).[10] The negotiations for the Treaty began in 2015 within the United Nations General Assembly, leading to a report in 2016 that called upon states to create and conclude as soon as possible a legally binding instrument to prohibit nuclear weapons leading to their elimination. Ultimately, the Treaty was finalized and again endorsed by 122 countries in 2017.

Chapter 2 goes into detail explaining the key developments that helped build the foundation for the Treaty, including: (1) the Declaration of the Tenth Special Session of the General Assembly; (2) the United Nations Millennium Declaration;[11] (3) the secretary-general's five-point proposal on nuclear disarmament; (4) the 2010 Review Conference of the Parties to the Treaty on the Non-Proliferation of Nuclear Weapons;[12] (5) General Assembly Resolutions produced by the Open-ended Working Group; (6) the absence of concrete outcomes of multilateral nuclear disarmament negotiations within the United Nations framework for more than a decade; and (7) the urgency for substantive progress on priority disarmament and nonproliferation issues.

A look at the Treaty Working Group deliberations, in contrast with Secretary-General Ban Ki-Moon's proposal and earlier developments on nuclear disarmament, reveals the overwhelming complexity and divisiveness of the negotiations among states to create a treaty that would be explicit, contain effective measurable outcomes with strict timelines, have a strong verification and compliance regime and include as many nuclear and non-nuclear armed states as possible while making a bold and clear commitment to achieving and maintaining the elimination of nuclear weapons on a global scale. This chapter lays the foundation for the discussion throughout the rest of the book noting the unique development of the Treaty that has its strengths and weakness for now and in the future.

TOWARD HUMANITARIAN NUCLEAR DISARMAMENT

Humanitarian efforts have made great strides in recent years toward addressing the destructive force of weapons as well as protecting and providing remedial assistance

---

[8]   See www.bmeia.gv.at/en/european-foreign-policy/disarmament/weapons-of-mass-destruction /nuclear-weapons/vienna-conference-on-the-humanitarian-impact-of-nuclear-weapons/.

[9]   A/RES/67/56 (2012), www.un.org/disarmament/wmd/nuclear/tpnw/.

[10]   See overview at www.un.org/disarmament/wmd/nuclear/tpnw/.

[11]   UNGA Res 55/2 (September 8, 2000), www.ohchr.org/EN/ProfessionalInterest/Pages/Millennium .aspx.

[12]   2010 Review Conference of the Parties to the Treaty on the Non-Proliferation of Nuclear Weapons, Final Document, Vols. I–III (NPT/CONF.2010/50 (Vols. I–III)).

to individuals affected by them. Chapter 3 explores the development of the humanitarian nuclear disarmament approach that effectively mobilized civil society groups across the world in the fight to eliminate nuclear weapons and ultimately leading to the TPNW. Humanitarian disarmament refocuses the nuclear debate on preventing and remediating human suffering in all nations caused by nuclear weapons. Traditional disarmament in contrast has, since 1968, mostly hinged on states trying to control nuclear weapons to advance mainly their own state security and political interests. The humanitarian disarmament movement has also developed its own unique "processes, purposes and provisions" that stand in stark contrast to traditional disarmament techniques. The unique process was applied in 1997 with the Landmines Treaty and then in 2008 with the Convention on Cluster Munitions, both of which were primarily driven by groups and ordinary individual citizens and focused on the protection of civilians rather than states with the primary aim of reducing and restricting dangerous weapons and mitigating their effects. These citizens and civil society groups, along with the movers of the TPNW focused on criticizing nuclear weapons and exposing their devastating force and destructive human impact. Thus, treaty negotiations included some of the very people affected by nuclear weapons.

LEGAL CONGRUENCE WITH EXISTING TREATY OBLIGATIONS

The success of conceiving the TPNW, and its adoption at the UN level aside, its legal enforcement depends on treaty incorporation into domestic law at the national level. Which states will ultimately sign and ratify it within their respective home jurisdictions is yet to be seen. Moreover, questions remain regarding how Treaty implementation will occur and moreover, how it will affect other obligations under the current nuclear architecture. Chapter 4 analyzes the degree to which the Treaty on the Prohibition of Nuclear Weapons is legally compatible and congruent with existing laws and international obligations under the NPT[13] as well as the Comprehensive Nuclear-Test-Ban Treaty 1996 (CTBT).[14] It explores whether TPNW developments complement existing obligations or serve to compete with these same requirements, actually creating ambiguity and division, rather than harmony and legal certainty. Additionally, the chapter examines the legally binding nature of the Treaty, including the effect on those states that have neither signed nor ratified it, particularly regarding its enforceability within the various jurisdictions adhering to the NPT and those intending to adopt the CTBT. It begins with

[13] For a legal analysis of the NPT *see* Daniel H. Joyner, *Interpreting the Nuclear Non-Proliferation Treaty* (Oxford: Oxford University Press, 2011), with foreword by Mohamed I. Shaker, author of *The Nuclear Nonproliferation Treaty: Origin and Implementation 1959–1979*, three volumes (London/Rome/New York: Oceana, 1980). See also 2010 Review Conference of the Parties to the Treaty on the Non-Proliferation of Nuclear Weapons, Final Document (NPT/CONF, 2010/50), 2–19.

[14] Comprehensive Nuclear-Test-Ban Treaty (CTBT), adopted by General Assembly Resolution 50/245 (September 10, 1996), 35 *ILM* 1439.

6   *Changing Nuclear Arms Control Law*

summaries of the NPT, the Partial Nuclear Test Ban Treaty[15] (PTBT), the CTBT and the organizations that implement these treaties. It then explores the articles of the TPNW and its congruence with the CTBT and the NPT.

UNIVERSALITY UNDER CUSTOMARY INTERNATIONAL LAW

The TPNW aims to achieve universality. In that regard, there is little doubt that moves are afoot to alter the nuclear status quo relating to how politicians, diplomats and lawyers alike view such weapons with the intention of achieving a universal consensus for their elimination. Chapter 5 explores the question of whether the TPNW will be able to achieve universality through a shift in customary international law which changes according to state practice and *opinio juris*. It highlights the major challenges of achieving the ultimate goal of universality, including the opposition of nuclear-armed states as well as some non-nuclear-weapon states and comments on the lack of support from ICJ jurisprudence to that end. The discussion explains how customary international law develops and argues that the non-party states do not view the Treaty as imposing a legal obligation and show no sign of changing state practice to meet the Treaty obligations. Persistent objectors have already staked their claims and are not likely to budge in any manner, marking a fundamental challenge for Treaty supporters.

SAFEGUARDS, VERIFICATION AND IMPLEMENTATION

Aspirations for a world free of nuclear weapons provide new hope and meaning for many seeking their abolition. That said, full implementation requires complete and verifiable disarmament. Chapter 6 explores such issues, focusing on the text of the Treaty provisions and examining the specific wording in its various provisions. The fact that the Treaty lacks any distinct verification regime of its own raises important questions regarding measurable outcomes and credible enforcement mechanisms. The chapter discusses the verification deficiencies of the TPNW including problems with states self-declaring whether they own or have eliminated their nuclear weapons, different requirements for different states and the future role of the IAEA without having involved the organization in the Treaty negotiations. The chapter also draws lessons about the importance of strong verification regimes from the history of other weapons treaties and organizations including the NPT, the Biological Weapons Convention, the Chemical Weapons Convention and the IAEA. It explores how the Treaty could face challenges developing a competent international authority with expertise, capacity and staff.

---

[15] Treaty Banning Nuclear Weapons Tests in the Atmosphere, in Outer Space, and under Water (August 5, 1963), 480 UNTS 43.

NUCLEAR DETERRENCE POLICIES AND THE PROHIBITION TREATY

The TPNW challenges deterrence policies. Once promoted by nuclear-armed governments as a necessity to ward off would-be attacks, the Treaty calls for the absolute abolition of all nuclear weapons, including for deterrence purposes. Chapter 7 analyzes deterrence polices within a modern context, looking at the emerging position advanced through the Treaty and international activism. It explores how nuclear weapons have traditionally been promoted as effective deterrents by nuclear-weapon states and organizations such as NATO, examining various challenges to this hitherto accepted defense doctrine. The discussion focuses on the relationship between the TPNW and NATO and umbrella states as well as those of other defense alliances including the Collective Security Treaty Organization (CSTO) and the Shanghai Cooperation Organisation (SCO).

The TPNW clearly prohibits threats to use nuclear weapons which, this author argues, includes for deterrence purposes. This implies that the TPNW could be construed to be in direct conflict with the collective nuclear deterrence strategy of NATO, requiring states parties who aspire to accede to the TPNW and who are also members or umbrella states of NATO either to sever their relationship, or significantly alter it, depending on whether they possess or host nuclear weapons. Discussion focuses on the positions of states currently harboring weapons, and organizations promoting their role for deterrence purposes, noting that none of them show any sign of changing their policy any time soon toward adopting the TPNW in the near future.

NUCLEAR DEFENSE DOCTRINES AND DISARMAMENT

Defense doctrines predicated on nuclear arms and the use of nuclear weapons would be contrary to the spirit and intent of the TPNW. Chapter 8 discusses current defense doctrines and how they might interact with the TPNW and new developments in international humanitarian law. Discussion focuses on the ICJ 1996 *Advisory Opinion* which left open the possibility of using nuclear capacity in the event of extreme necessity and subject to IHL conditions. It suggests that a future court might decide differently given that there is now a treaty expressly banning nuclear weapons and the shift in how many states are now against the use of nuclear weapons. The Treaty also has important implications for international law under *jus ad bellum* and *jus in bello*, such that it may strengthen these norms and further restrictions on the use of nuclear weapons as reason to initiate war or to use during a war. The Treaty could also bolster norms that restrict the use of nuclear weapons found in the UN Charter and International Humanitarian Law.

A BIFURCATED INTERNATIONAL LEGAL INFRASTRUCTURE

Questions remain regarding the legal effect and impact the TPNW will have in a modern context. It remains to be seen just how it will fit within the existing nuclear architecture, or juxtaposed against the present legal structure. Chapter 9 explores how the Treaty may serve to challenge existing international legal infrastructure by establishing a different set of legal norms, principles and expectations that may further fragment an already divided global community. This author divides states into two main camps; Resolute States that will ratify the treaty and Stalwart States that may not be expected to do so. The chapter discusses how the Treaty may challenge the nonproliferation and disarmament framework, serving to disrupt current nuclear legal authority and organizational architecture. It explores relationships with: (1) the NPT; (2) the IAEA; (3) the CTBTO; (4) partners coordinating approaches regarding terrorism by non-state actors; and (5) the positions of NATO and umbrella states. The chapter examines the degree to which the TPNW may serve to fragment existing structures, forging a new international legal infrastructure regarding disarmament and nuclear nonproliferation law.

Additionally, the author explores the relationship between existing nuclear-weapon-free zones (NWFZ) and the obligations under the TPNW, concluding that NWFZ may serve to strengthen and further the goals of the Treaty and that such zones may create additional obligations on NWFZ states that will advance nuclear disarmament. However, the TPNW also has the potential to disrupt NWFZ states' relationships with NWS and break down the complex legal framework of the many NWFZ treaties.

STIGMATIZATION ACTION

Civil society groups are working toward the successive elimination of nuclear weapons through stigmatization action aimed at complete denuclearization. Chapter 10 explores how proponents of the Treaty employ scientific research; activism both within and outside governmental institutions, driven by civil society groups and nuclear survivors; legal and philosophical research; economic divestment of nuclear weapons; and advocacy to their cause. Their aim is to move citizens and states from a "nuclearist" stance to a "non-nuclearist" worldview. This shift is currently happening among lawyers, citizens, government leaders, corporations and banks, further contributing to the delegitimization of nuclear weapons and their eventual elimination.

TOWARD NEO-UNIVERSALISM

Beyond the goal of universality, the Treaty provides an opportunity to promote universalism within the spirit of its aspirations. Many proponents of the Treaty are concentrating their efforts on mobilizing collective action in order to change perceptions of how nuclear weapons are perceived and valued both locally and globally. As discussed in Chapter 11, effectively, a new form of universalism may change the current nuclear posture, igniting new forms of universal values based on what this author calls "nuclear peace without nuclear fear" (explored more fully in concluding Chapter 13).

Specifically, Chapter 11 examines how the TPNW, under the guidance of humanitarianism, may sow the seeds of new normative behavior within the global context ultimately contributing to an ideological shift from the current conventional armament stance based on realism to that of a humanitarian neo-universalism that shuns nuclear defense doctrines and the weapons that provide their very foundations. Whether or not states currently consent to the Treaty, at present there is an emerging move toward a united universal understanding of the risks and perils that such weapons pose. There is a growing shared fear of their effects and potential impact on political discourse, the environment and humanity as a whole.

OBLIGATIONS *ERGA OMNES*

A fundamental problem facing the TPNW is that the nine states with nuclear weapons openly defy its existence. Both states parties to the NPT – Russia, the United States, China, France and the UK – and non-NPT parties – India, Pakistan, Israel and North Korea –oppose it outright. They refused to participate in Treaty negotiations and contend that they will neither sign nor ratify it. Moreover, they have important backing from other states through various agreements such as NATO and umbrella alliances, as well as the CSTO and SCO. Consequently, it seems there is an important gulf between supporters of the TPNW and those opposing it. The dream of legally enforcing the Treaty seems more than remote; indeed, it seems nonexistent. The TPNW does not directly bind the NWS and it seems highly unlikely that they would ever join the Treaty or be bound under customary international law. At present there appears to be an intractable division between the positions of both camps.

In its 1996 Advisory Opinion relating to nuclear issues, the International Court of Justice (ICJ) referred to obligations *erga omnes*.[16] Chapter 12 explores these obligations relating to nuclear matters as universal norms applicable to all states and owed to the international community as a whole. It examines what is meant by *erga omnes* obligations, assessing their current recognition throughout the international community. It looks at why they are relevant to the area of nuclear disarmament discussions and how they may apply to current discussions. Moreover, discussion

---

[16] See also *Barcelona Traction, Light and Power Co. Ltd. (Belg. v. Spain)*, 1970 I.C.J. 3, 32 (February 5) at paras. 33–34.

pursues how they should be enforced, analyzing a link between the goals of the TPNW and binding nuclear legal obligations within a contemporary context.

CONCLUSION: UNITED WE STAND, DIVIDED WE FALL

In essence the TPNW has prompted much debate and speculation across the globe regarding its success as an arms control treaty, as well as its overall impact within the wider international community. The main purpose of the book is to examine a variety of issues emerging from the adoption of the Treaty in the UN General Assembly and to explore various implications pertaining to the Treaty. The concluding Chapter 13 will assess its real and potential impact, pointing to strengths and weaknesses, and thus illuminating how the Treaty could play out on the international stage. It ultimately calls for the right to nuclear peace and freedom from nuclear fear, concluding that nuclear weapons threaten peace and induce fear.

2

Adopting the Treaty on the Prohibition of Nuclear Weapons 2017: A New Dawn, a New Deal, a New Direction in Nuclear Disarmament Law?

The challenge of statesmanship is to have the vision to dream of a better, safer world and the courage, persistence, and patience to turn that dream into a reality.

Ronald Reagan[1]

INTRODUCTION: THE EVOLUTION OF NUCLEAR DISARMAMENT LAW

A legacy of the Cold War is that nuclear arms protect nations from attack; a stance that supporters of the TPNW wish to change. Indeed, this author would contend that nuclear weapons do not protect nations but actually threaten national, regional and global security. Many advocates of nuclear disarmament believe that the TPNW marks a new beginning; it was even celebrated with the Norwegian Nobel Peace Prize awarded to the International Campaign to Abolish Nuclear Weapons (ICAN),[2] at the time, a relatively newly formed civil society organization. The TPNW demonstrates international support to take decisive action to eliminate nuclear weapons and the threat they pose to international peace and security. This chapter traces the background discussions leading to the treaty, exploring some influencing factors as to how and why it arose, describing the process of the discussions, resolutions and negotiations that shaped the final document. The role and approach of civil society organizations in bringing negotiations for the treaty and their activism will be discussed in subsequent chapters.

The TPNW is undoubtedly a triumph for humanitarian efforts to ban nuclear weapons following a relatively short negotiation period. Indeed, it is considered somewhat unconventional in many respects. No state possessing nuclear weapons contributed to the deliberations. Moreover, those setting and dominating the

---

[1] From Reagan's Secret War by Martin and Annelise Anderson, see www.thereaganvision.org/quotes/.

[2] October 6, 2017. "The organization is receiving the award for its work to draw attention to the catastrophic humanitarian consequences of any use of nuclear weapons and for its ground-breaking efforts to achieve a treaty-based prohibition of such weapons," see www.nobelprize.org/nobel_prizes/peace/laureates/2017/press.html.

negotiations agenda and leading the discussions were largely a group of states and civil society groups frustrated by the lack of progress on disarmament issues over the past decades. Gaining momentum over the years, the movement toward a nuclear-weapons-free world, culminating in the adoption of the TPNW, is a definitive victory for civil society and humanitarian groups as well as many non-nuclear weapon states. To that end, July 7, 2017 marked a monumental day at the United Nations headquarters in New York, when 122 countries agreed to adopt this historic treaty, arriving at a time of growing fears regarding the escalation of North Korea's nuclear and ballistic missile program and mounting tensions with the United States, and nuclear modernization and war-fighting doctrines in both Russia and the United States.

Despite its adoption, under the strong support of human rights groups and civil activists, the TPNW faces strong opposition from nuclear-armed states and their Allies, maintaining a strategy of nuclear deterrence[3] and questioning the likelihood of achieving universal acceptance of the Treaty. Indeed, the determination of civil society groups to make the TPNW come into full force may be matched only by the defiance and opposition by its rivals for it not to be enforceable under international law. The diametrical polarization of these positions regarding disarmament is emblematic of the current and deepening division in the international community on the TPNW and denuclearization.

HOW AND WHY DID THE NEW TREATY ARISE?

Over time dissatisfaction surfaced regarding the lack of progress on disarmament as required under the Treaty on the Non-Proliferation of Nuclear Weapons 1968 (NPT).[4] Article VI requires that: "Each of the Parties to the Treaty undertakes to pursue negotiations in good faith on effective measures relating to cessation of the nuclear arms race at an early date and to nuclear disarmament, and on a treaty on general and complete disarmament under strict and effective international control."[5] Disappointment grew among the non-nuclear weapons states regarding the seemingly willful disregard by the nuclear-weapon states of the agreed NPT outcomes on nuclear disarmament under the NPT Review processes of 1995, 2000 and 2010.

General disillusionment in achieving these goals grew into impatience, especially in light of other countries developing nuclear weapons, directly contrary to nonproliferation requirements, and many nuclear-weapon states renewing their nuclear

---

[3] See D. Fleck, "*Legal Aspects of Nuclear Weapons Doctrines*," Chapter 17 in Jonathan L. Black-Branch and Dieter Fleck (eds.), *Nuclear Non-Proliferation in International Law: Vol. V Legal Challenges for Nuclear Deterrence and Security* (Berlin/Heidelberg: Springer/Asser Press, 2020).

[4] See also *A Perpetual Menace: Nuclear Weapons and International Order*, 1st Edition, by William Walker (Routledge, 2011).

[5] For a legal evaluation of Article VI NPT, see International Law Association, Report of the 76th Conference of the International Law Association held in Washington, DC, 2014, "Legal Aspects of Nuclear Disarmament."

How and Why Did the New Treaty Arise? 13

defenses instead of scaling them back. Further frustration has emerged because the Comprehensive Nuclear-Test-Ban Treaty (CTBT) remains not fully ratified, and still has not entered into force, over two decades later. The strict ratification process of the CTBT, involving the participation of specific states with nuclear capability or aspirations, has become a barrier to its coming into force. This was a condition that all participating states were fully aware of in making it a requirement, but nonetheless it has effectively thwarted its enactment.

Such setbacks are compounded by the ICJ ruling in the *Legality of the Threat or Use of Nuclear Weapons, Advisory Opinion* (1996)[6] which gave little hope to proponents of using existing international law and institutions to affect change. While the Court delivered some inspiration for change, there was little if any concrete legal authority to make it happen as a non-binding *Advisory Opinion*. Throughout the years there had been many discussions in the international community about a treaty toward banning and eliminating nuclear weapons, but no real action transpired. In 1996, three non-governmental organizations, IALANA,[7] INESAP,[8] and IPPNW[9] drafted a model Nuclear Weapons Convention (MNWC) "outlining what a nuclear weapons convention could look like and exploring the roads to a nuclear-weapons-free world." Costa Rica submitted the MNWC[10] to the United Nations secretary-general in 1997.[11] In April 2007, at the Preparatory Committee meeting of the Nuclear Non-Proliferation Treaty, together the three organizations launched a revised version of the MNWC,[12] which was introduced to the United Nations General Assembly by Costa Rica and Malaysia.[13] Their accompanying letter of December 17, 2007, explained that, "This revised model takes into account relevant technical, legal and political developments since 1997 ... It is submitted as a work in progress setting forth legal, technical and political elements for the establishment and maintenance of a nuclear-weapon-free world."[14] Such were the activities toward a global nuclear weapons convention, by this international consortium of lawyers, scientists and disarmament experts who drafted the Model Nuclear Weapons Convention, an eighty-one page document, in which it clearly defined obligations of states and persons, terms, declarations, phases for implementation, verification, implementation, rights and obligations of persons and agency, and gave clear direction for managing and controlling nuclear activities, material, facilities and weapons.[15] Needless to say, the Convention never materialized,

---

[6] *Legality of the Treat or Use of Nuclear Weapons, Advisory Opinion*, ICJ Reports (1996), p. 226, available online: see www.icj-cij.org/files/case-related/95/095–19960708-ADV-01–00-EN.pdf.
[7] International Association of Lawyers Against Nuclear Arms.
[8] International Network of Engineers and Scientists Against Proliferation, www.inesap.org/what-inesap.
[9] International Physicians for the Prevention of Nuclear War, www.ippnw.org/.
[10] See http://inesap.org/sites/default/files/inesap_old/publ_nwc_english.pdf.
[11] UN Doc. A/C.1/52/7.
[12] See http://inesap.org/sites/default/files/inesap_old/mNWC_2007_Unversion_English_N0821377.pdf.
[13] UN DOC A/62/650.
[14] See www.inesap.org/publications/nuclear-weapons-convention.
[15] UN DOC A/62/650.

and more time passed with further inaction. Whilst these developments were important in keeping the dream alive, nothing concrete materialized out of these efforts resulting in growing anger in relation to the seeming intransigence of the international community on these important matters.

To exacerbate matters, the quinquennial (five-annual) Review Conferences of the NPT (1995, 2000 and 2010) also produced very little change or concrete proposals on disarmament. The growing concern and significant disagreement among parties to the NPT about the failure to implement Article VI can be traced in the NPT Review Conferences.[16] Beginning at the 1975 NPT Review Conference, parties expressed their "serious concern that the arms race, in particular the nuclear arms race, is continuing unabated."[17] Such worries continued to plague the conferences until 2015, when disagreements ran deep and the negotiations were so contentious that the parties did not adopt an outcome.[18] Parallel to this, between 2013 and 2014, three inter-governmental conferences were held in Norway, Mexico and Austria which discussed the humanitarian impact of nuclear weapons and gained support from countries to address these concerns. Indeed, the United Kingdom and United States attended the Vienna Humanitarian Impact of Nuclear Weapons conference in 2014 where Austria issued a pledge which has been internationalized as a "humanitarian pledge" supported by more than 125 states.[19]

On April 24, 2014, the Republic of the Marshall Islands filed applications in the ICJ against the United Kingdom, India and Pakistan, the United States, France, Russia, China, Israel and North Korea, claiming they had violated their nuclear disarmament obligations both under the NPT and customary international law. The United Kingdom, India and Pakistan, had accepted the compulsory jurisdiction of the Court under Article 36 paragraph 2 of the Statute of the Court,[20] but the remaining six did not accept, refusing to argue the case on its merits before the Court.[21] During proceedings, the United Kingdom, India and Pakistan objected to the Court's jurisdiction to hear the case on the grounds that there was no justiciable dispute between them and the Marshall Islands, with which the Court agreed in 2016, finding there was insufficient evidence of a dispute, per se, and consequently it did not have jurisdiction as the respondents were not aware of the contentious issues. Needless to say, the Court was not in a position to answer important questions regarding disarmament and obligations pursuant to Article VI of the NPT.[22]

---

[16] See www.un.org/disarmament/wmd/nuclear/npt-review-conferences/.

[17] NPT/CONF/35/1, May 30, 1975, p. 8, online: see https://unoda-web.s3-accelerate.amazonaws.com /wp-content/uploads/assets/WMD/Nuclear/pdf/finaldocs/1975%20-%20Geneva%20-%20NPT% 20Review%20Conference%20-%20Final%20Document%20Part%20I.pdf.

[18] NPT/CONF.2015/50 (Part I), see https://undocs.org/NPT/CONF.2015/50(PartI).

[19] See www.bmeia.gv.at/en/european-foreign-policy/disarmament/weapons-of-mass-destruction /nuclear-weapons/vienna-conference-on-the-humanitarian-impact-of-nuclear-weapons/.

[20] Under Article 36(2) of the Statute of the Court.

[21] The RMI simultaneously filed a case against the United States in the US federal court in San Francisco.

[22] See Black-Branch, J., "International Obligations Concerning Disarmament and the Cessation of the Nuclear Arms Race: Justiciability over Justice in the Marshall Islands Cases at the International Court

Amid growing disappointment with the states possessing nuclear weapon and, especially the Security Council States leading the NPT Review, civil society groups, individual citizens and non-nuclear-weapon states began exploring new opportunities and avenues for dealing with the problem of nuclear weapons. As a result, Ambassador Elayne Whyte Gómez (Costa Rica) went to the UN to start negotiating a treaty and in 2015 the UNGA Resolution 70/33 established a working group to address concrete effective measures and legal provisions for maintaining a nuclear-free world.[23] In 2016, the Working Group of the UNGA produced a report recommending a legally binding instrument[24] followed by the UNGA resolution of November 2016 calling upon "States participating in the conference to make their best endeavours to conclude as soon as possible a legally binding instrument to prohibit nuclear weapons, leading toward their total elimination ... "[25] This led to the subsequent negotiation and adoption of the Treaty on the Prohibition of Nuclear Weapons in 2017.

THE PROCESS: DETERMINED TO DISARM

The direct process leading to the adoption of the Prohibition Treaty evolved over a relatively few years, under the successive work of Open-Ended Working Groups (2013–2014) as well as a wide range of states and civil society organizations in conjunction with the UN General Assembly. Developments were approved under General Assembly resolutions,[26] including 71/258 of December 23, 2016, where the General Assembly decided to convene in New York[27] a UN conference to negotiate a legally binding instrument to prohibit nuclear weapons, leading toward their total elimination with the participation and contribution of international organizations and civil society representatives. Following what has come to be known as a humanitarian negotiating process, they set a relatively tight time frame for negotiations from March 27 to 31 and from June 15 to July 7, 2017, along with a one-day organizational session in New York,[28] which was held on February 16, 2017,[29] resulting in the final text and the adoption of the Treaty on the Prohibition of Nuclear Weapons on July 7, 2017. Although there was a relatively short negotiating

---

of Justice," *Journal of Conflict & Security Law* Vol. 24, Iss. 3, Winter 2019, pp. 449–472. See https://academic.oup.com/jcsl/article-abstract/24/3/449/5563993; https://doi.org/10.1093/jcsl/krz020.

[23] Para. 1. GA Resolution 70/33. See http://undocs.org/A/RES/70/33.

[24] See www.unidir.org/files/publications/pdfs/the-2016-open-ended-working-group-en-660.pdf.

[25] Para. 12. United Nations. (2016). *General and Complete Disarmament: Taking Forward Multilateral Nuclear Disarmament Negotiations* (A/C.1/71/L.41).

[26] General Assembly Resolutions 67/56 of December 3, 2012; 68/46 of December 5, 2013; 69/41 of December 2, 2014; 70/33 of December 7, 2015 and Resolution 71/258 of December 23, 2016.

[27] Following the Rules of Procedure of the General Assembly unless otherwise agreed by the conference.

[28] Which was to be held as soon as possible after the adoption of the resolution.

[29] Report of the United Nations conference to negotiate a legally binding instrument to prohibit nuclear weapons, leading toward their total elimination. (United Nations General Assembly July 24, 2017 A/72/206), see http://undocs.org/A/72/206.

time frame, many of the same disarmament issues had been on various discussion tables over a number of years and had been looked at in great detail.

Indeed, the preamble of various resolutions between 2012 and 2015[30] made express reference, *inter alia*, to important developments regarding disarmament including: (1) the Declaration of the Tenth Special Session of the General Assembly; (2) the United Nations Millennium Declaration;[31] (3) the secretary-general's five-point proposal on nuclear disarmament; and (4) the 2010 Review Conference of the Parties to the Treaty on the Non-Proliferation of Nuclear Weapons.[32] Additionally they noted: (5) the absence of concrete outcomes of multilateral nuclear disarmament negotiations within the UN framework for more than a decade; and (6) the urgency for substantive progress on priority disarmament and nonproliferation issues. These developments are explored in detail below.

Declaration of the Tenth Special Session of the General Assembly

The focus of the Tenth Special Session of the General Assembly, held in May and June 1978, was disarmament. Indeed, this was the first special session devoted to disarmament matters, resulting in a Declaration where it was noted, "that all the peoples of the world have a vital interest in the success of disarmament negotiations and that all states have the right to participate in disarmament negotiations."[33] But despite these fine words, frustration remained regarding the lack of real or substantive progress on such matters. Nevertheless, those committed to disarmament kept it on the UN agenda.

United Nations Millennium Declaration

In 2000, some two decades later, the General Assembly approved the United Nations Millennium Declaration, emphasizing responsibility regarding threats to international peace and security in which the UN must play the central role. Here, the General Assembly adopted the Millennium Declaration at its 8th plenary meeting on September 8, 2000[34] where Part I of the Declaration highlights values and principles to which heads of state and government aspire in entering the new millennium,[35] including shared responsibility regarding "threats to international

---

[30] GA Resolutions 67/56 of December 3, 2012; 68/46 of December 5, 2013; 69/41 of December 2, 2014; 70/33 of December 7, 2015.

[31] Resolution 55/2.

[32] *2010 Review Conference of the Parties to the Treaty on the Non-Proliferation of Nuclear Weapons, Final Document*, Vols. I–III (NPT/CONF.2010/50 (Vols. I–III)).

[33] Resolution S-10/2, sect. II.

[34] 55/2. United Nations Millennium Declaration see www.un.org/millennium/declaration/ares552e.htm/

[35] At para. 1. 55/2. United Nations Millennium Declaration www.un.org/millennium/declaration/ares552e.htm/.

The Process: Determined to Disarm 17

peace and security."[36] Part II of the Declaration elaborates on this value[37] resolving: "To strive for the elimination of weapons of mass destruction, particularly nuclear weapons, and to keep all options open for achieving this aim, including the possibility of convening an international conference to identify ways of eliminating nuclear dangers."[38] Again, despite this important recognition, and wording, many advocates were skeptical of such developments without having a specific action plan, dismissing the Declaration as empty platitudes.

Secretary-General's Five-Point Proposal on Nuclear Disarmament

In terms of action, in 2008 in an address to the East-West Institute, the then secretary-general of the UN, Ban Ki-moon[39] unveiled a five-point proposal on nuclear disarmament entitled "The United Nations and security in a nuclear-weapon-free world."[40] Thanking the East-West Institute and its partner non-governmental groups for organizing the event on weapons of mass destruction and disarmament, Secretary General Ban Ki-moon described this challenge as "one of the gravest challenges facing international peace and security."[41] Commending the Institute for "its timely and important new global initiative to build consensus," Ban Ki-moon urged its leadership "to rethink our international security priorities in order to get things moving again," stating that "we need specific actions, not just words."[42]

He noted that one of his priorities as secretary-general was "to promote global goods and remedies to challenges that do not respect borders," highlighting that a "world free of nuclear weapons would be a global public good of the highest order," and hence the focus of his talk. He highlighted the "unique dangers and the lack of any treaty outlawing them" and the importance of achieving "a world free of all weapons of mass destruction."[43] He spoke from his own personal experience, coming from the Republic of Korea which had "suffered the ravages of conventional war and faced threats from nuclear weapons and other WMD." He noted the

[36] At para. 6. 55/2. United Nations Millennium Declaration www.un.org/millennium/declaration/ares552e.html/.

[37] Para. 8 states: "We will spare no effort to free our peoples from the scourge of war, whether within or between States, which has claimed more than 5 million lives in the past decade. We will also seek to eliminate the dangers posed by weapons of mass destruction."

[38] Para. 9. Resolution 55/2. United Nations Millennium Declaration. See www.un.org/millennium/declaration/ares552e.html/.

[39] See www.un.org/sg/en/formersg/ban.shtml.

[40] Secretary-General's address to the East-West Institute entitled "The United Nations and security in a nuclear-weapon-free world," October 24, 2008. www.un.org/sg/en/content/sg/statement/2008–10-24/secretary-generals-address-east-west-institute-entitled-united. See also the secretary-general's five-point proposal on nuclear disarmament "The United Nations and security in a nuclear-weapon-free world." See www.un.org/disarmament/wmd/nuclear/sg5point/.

[41] Ibid.

[42] Ibid.

[43] Ibid.

18 *Adopting the TPNW 2017*

"support throughout the world for the view that nuclear weapons should never again be used because of their indiscriminate effects, their impact on the environment and their profound implications for regional and global security."[44] While recognizing that states make the key decisions in this field, he claimed that the UN has important roles to play in which to provide a central forum wherein states can agree on norms to serve their common interests. Mr. Ban Ki-moon further emphasized that disarmament and the regulation of armaments are found in the UN Charter and that the very first General Assembly resolution, in London in 1946, called for eliminating "weapons adaptable to mass destruction" – goals he noted which have been supported by every secretary-general since, and indeed "the subject of hundreds of General Assembly resolutions, and have been endorsed repeatedly by all our Member States."[45]

He reiterated that "Nuclear weapons produce horrific, indiscriminate effects [... and] Even when not used, they pose great risks [... and indeed] Accidents could happen any time [... moreover] The manufacture of nuclear weapons can harm public health and the environment. And, of course, terrorists could acquire nuclear weapons or nuclear material." He noted that "[u]nfortunately, the doctrine of nuclear deterrence has proven to be contagious," indicating that this has made nonproliferation "more difficult, which in turn raises new risks that nuclear weapons will be used." In the *Legality of the Threat or Use of Nuclear Weapons, Advisory Opinion* (1996)[46] the International Court of Justice (ICJ) stated that nuclear deterrence is a "fact," effectively acknowledging the political reality. That said, it also stated, unanimously, that "[t]here exists an obligation to pursue in good faith and bring to a conclusion negotiations leading to nuclear disarmament in all its aspects under strict and effective international control."[47] Effectively, this may be seen as imposing a positive duty under Article VI of the NPT.

Against this backdrop, secretary-general Ban Ki-moon offered a five-point proposal for nuclear disarmament. To begin with, he urged all NPT parties to fulfill their obligation under the Treaty to undertake negotiations on effective measures leading to nuclear disarmament, as is required under Article VI. He particularly challenged the nuclear-weapon states to adhere to meeting such obligations. In that regard the secretary general suggested that they should agree to "a framework of separate, mutually reinforcing instruments." Or, alternatively, they should negotiate a nuclear-weapons convention; one that is backed by a strong system of verification, regarding which the aforementioned draft convention had been distributed as requested by Costa Rica and Malaysia.[48]

---

[44] Ibid.

[45] Ibid.

[46] *Legality of the Treat or Use of Nuclear Weapons, Advisory Opinion,* ICJ Reports (1996), p. 226, available online: see www.icj-cij.org/files/case-related/95/095–19960708-ADV-01–00-EN.pdf.

[47] Ibid., at 267.

[48] Secretary-general's address to the East-West Institute entitled "The United Nations and security in a nuclear-weapon-free world," October 24, 2008. See www.un.org/sg/en/content/sg/statement/2008–

Secretary-general Ban Ki-moon then suggested that the Security Council's Permanent Members commence discussions on security issues in the nuclear disarmament process, unambiguously assuring non-nuclear-weapon states that they would not be the subject of the use or threat of use of nuclear weapons. To this end, the Council could convene a summit on nuclear disarmament and non-NPT states should freeze their own nuclear-weapon capabilities and make their own respective disarmament commitments.[49]

The third initiative related to the "rule of law" in which the secretary-general noted in regard to a unilateral moratoria on nuclear tests and the production of fissile materials required as well as bring into force the CTBT, and that the Conference on Disarmament ought to begin negotiations on a fissile material treaty immediately and without preconditions. He also expressed his support for the entry into force of the Central Asian and African nuclear-weapon-free zone treaties and encouraged the nuclear-weapon states to ratify all the protocols to the nuclear-weapon-free zone treaties. He said he strongly supported efforts to establish such a zone in the Middle East and urged all parties to the NPT to conclude their safeguards agreements with the IAEA, and to voluntarily adopt the strengthened safeguards under the Additional Protocol. He stated the importance of not forgetting that "the nuclear fuel cycle is more than an issue involving energy or non-proliferation; its fate will also shape prospects for disarmament."[50]

The fourth proposal concerned issues of accountability and transparency. Highlighting that accounts submitted by the various nuclear-weapon states describing their efforts in this regard seldom reach the public, he invited the nuclear-weapon states to send such material to the UN Secretariat, and encouraged its wider dissemination, noting that the nuclear powers could expand the amount of information they publish about the size of their arsenals, stocks of fissile materials and specific disarmament achievements, stating that "the lack of an authoritative estimate of the total number of nuclear weapons testifies to the need for greater transparency."[51]

Fifthly, the secretary-general stated that a number of complementary measures are needed, including "the elimination of other types of WMD; new efforts against WMD terrorism; limits on the production and trade in conventional arms; and new weapons bans, including of missiles and space weapons."[52] He also noted that the General Assembly could also take up the recommendation of the Blix Commission for a "World Summit on disarmament, nonproliferation and terrorist use of weapons

---

10-24/secretary-generals-address-east-west-institute-entitled-united. He also urged the nuclear powers to actively engage with other states on this issue at the Conference on Disarmament in Geneva; the resumption of bilateral negotiations for arms reduction between the United States and Russian Federation; as well as for governments to also do more in verification research and development.

[49] Ibid.
[50] Ibid.
[51] Ibid.
[52] Ibid.

of mass destruction."[53] Acknowledging doubt that the problem of WMD terrorism could be solved, he noted that if they could achieve real and verified progress in disarmament, then the possibility of eliminating this threat would grow "exponentially" and "it will be much easier to encourage governments to tighten relevant controls if a basic, global taboo exists on the very possession of certain types of weapons." That is to say, "as we progressively eliminate the world's deadliest weapons and their components, we will make it harder to execute WMD terrorist attacks."[54] Ending his speech, the secretary-general stated that his proposals would seek a fresh start on disarmament and aim to strengthen international peace and security noting that "when disarmament advances, the world advances."[55]

This important five-point plan could be seen as a significant plea to the world to do something about the lack of movement on nuclear disarmament and the fear of inaction on these nuclear issues, concerns that would be examined further at the next NPT Review Conference.

2010 NPT Review Conference

On September 24, 2009 at an historic summit presided over by US President Obama and addressed by thirteen other heads of state and government, the Security Council pledged its backing "for broad progress on long-stalled efforts to staunch the proliferation of nuclear weapons and ensure reductions in existing weapons stockpiles, as well as control of fissile material."[56] Following on the aspirations and commitments of Secretary-General Ban Ki-moon, the outcome of the 2010 Review Conference of the Parties to the Treaty on the Non-Proliferation of Nuclear Weapons[57] included a series of action points as part of its conclusions and recommendations, worth noting in light of this discussion, including:

Action 1: "All States parties commit to pursue policies that are fully compatible with the Treaty and the objective of achieving a world without nuclear weapons."[58]
Action 2: "All States parties commit to apply the principles of irreversibility, verifiability and transparency in relation to the implementation of their treaty obligations."[59]

---

[53]　See https://ycsg.yale.edu/sites/default/files/files/weapons_of_terror.pdf.
[54]　Ibid. at 51.
[55]　Ibid. at 51.
[56]　Historic Summit of Security Council Pledges Support for Progress on Stalled Efforts to End Nuclear Weapons Proliferation (September 24, 2009), see www.un.org/press/en/2009/sc9746.doc.htm.
[57]　*2010 Review Conference of the Parties to the Treaty on the Non-Proliferation of Nuclear Weapons, Final Document*, Vols. I–III (NPT/CONF.2010/50 (Vols. I–III)).
[58]　Ibid. at p. 20.
[59]　Ibid.

The Process: Determined to Disarm

Action 3: "In implementing the unequivocal undertaking by the nuclear-weapon States to accomplish the total elimination of their nuclear arsenals, the nuclear weapon States commit to undertake further efforts to reduce and ultimately eliminate all types of nuclear weapons, deployed and non-deployed, including through unilateral, bilateral, regional and multilateral measures."[60]

Action 4: "The Russian Federation and the United States of America commit to seek the early entry into force and full implementation of the Treaty on Measures for the Further Reduction and Limitation of Strategic Offensive Arms and are encouraged to continue discussions on follow-on measures in order to achieve deeper reductions in their nuclear arsenals."[61]

Action 5: "The nuclear-weapon States commit to accelerate concrete progress on the steps leading to nuclear disarmament, contained in the Final Document of the 2000 Review Conference, in a way that promotes international stability, peace and undiminished and increased security. To that end, they are called upon to promptly engage with a view to, *inter alia*: (a) Rapidly moving towards an overall reduction in the global stockpile of all types of nuclear weapons, as identified in action 3; (b) Address the question of all nuclear weapons regardless of their type or their location as an integral part of the general nuclear disarmament process; (c) To further diminish the role and significance of nuclear weapons in all military and security concepts, doctrines and policies; (d) Discuss policies that could prevent the use of nuclear weapons and eventually lead to their elimination, lessen the danger of nuclear war and contribute to the non-proliferation and disarmament of nuclear weapons; (e) Consider the legitimate interest of non-nuclear-weapon States in further reducing the operational status of nuclear weapons systems in ways that promote international stability and security; (f) Reduce the risk of accidental use of nuclear weapons; and (g) Further enhance transparency and increase mutual confidence. The nuclear-weapon States are called upon to report the above undertakings to the Preparatory Committee at 2014. The 2015 Review Conference will take stock and consider the next steps for the full implementation of article VI."[62]

Action 6: "All States agree that the Conference on Disarmament should immediately establish a subsidiary body to deal with nuclear disarmament, within the context of an agreed, comprehensive and balanced programme of work."[63]

Action 7: "All States agree that the Conference on Disarmament should, within the context of an agreed, comprehensive and balanced programme of

---

[60] Ibid.
[61] Ibid. at pp. 20–21.
[62] Ibid.
[63] Ibid.

work, immediately begin discussion of effective international arrangements to assure non-nuclear-weapon States against the use or threat of use of nuclear weapons, to discuss substantively, without limitation, with a view to elaborating recommendations dealing with all aspects of this issue, not excluding an internationally legally binding instrument. The Review Conference invites the Secretary-General of the United Nations to convene a high-level meeting in September 2010 in support of the work of the Conference on Disarmament."[64]

Action 8: "All nuclear-weapon States commit to fully respect their existing commitments with regard to security assurances. Those nuclear-weapon States that have not yet done so are encouraged to extend security assurances to non-nuclear-weapon States parties to the Treaty."[65]

Action 9: "The establishment of further nuclear-weapon-free zones, where appropriate, on the basis of arrangements freely arrived at among States of the region concerned, and in accordance with the 1999 Guidelines of the United Nations Disarmament Commission, is encouraged. All concerned States are encouraged to ratify the nuclear-weapon-free zone treaties and their relevant protocols, and to constructively consult and cooperate to bring about the entry into force of the relevant legally binding protocols of all such nuclear-weapon free zones treaties, which include negative security assurances. The concerned States are encouraged to review any related reservations."[66]

Action 10: "All nuclear-weapon States undertake to ratify the Comprehensive Nuclear-Test-Ban Treaty with all expediency, noting that positive decisions by nuclear-weapon States would have the beneficial impact towards the ratification of that Treaty, and that nuclear-weapon States have the special responsibility to encourage Annex 2 countries, in particular those which have not acceded to the Treaty on the Non-Proliferation of Nuclear Weapons and continue to operate unsafeguarded nuclear facilities, to sign and ratify."[67]

Action 11: "Pending the entry into force of the Comprehensive Nuclear-Test-Ban Treaty, all States commit to refrain from nuclear-weapon test explosions or any other nuclear explosions, the use of new nuclear weapons technologies and from any action that would defeat the object and purpose of that Treaty, and all existing moratoriums on nuclear-weapon test explosions should be maintained."[68]

[64] Ibid.
[65] Ibid. at p. 22.
[66] Ibid. at p. 22.
[67] Ibid.
[68] Ibid. at p. 23.

Action 12: "All States that have ratified the Comprehensive Nuclear-Test-Ban Treaty recognize the contribution of the conferences on facilitating the entry into force of that Treaty and of the measures adopted by consensus at the Sixth Conference on Facilitating the Entry into Force of the Comprehensive Nuclear-Test-Ban Treaty, held in September 2009, and commit to report at the 2011 Conference on progress made towards the urgent entry into force of that Treaty."[69]

Action 13: "All States that have ratified the Comprehensive Nuclear-Test-Ban Treaty undertake to promote the entry into force and implementation of that Treaty at the national, regional and global levels."[70]

Action 14: "The Preparatory Commission for the Comprehensive Nuclear-Test-Ban Treaty Organization is to be encouraged to fully develop the verification regime for the Comprehensive Nuclear-Test-Ban Treaty, including early completion and provisional operationalization of the international monitoring system in accordance with the mandate of the Preparatory Commission, which should, upon entry into force of that Treaty, serve as an effective, reliable, participatory and non-discriminatory verification system with global reach, and provide assurance of compliance with that Treaty."[71]

Action 15: "All States agree that the Conference on Disarmament should, within the context of an agreed, comprehensive and balanced programme of work, immediately begin negotiation of a treaty banning the production of fissile material for use in nuclear weapons or other nuclear explosive devices in accordance with the report of the Special Coordinator of 1995 (CD/1299) and the mandate contained therein."[72]

Such admirable intensions were well received for the most part, but humanitarian advocates of change noted the absence of concrete outcomes of multilateral nuclear disarmament negotiations within the UN framework for more than a decade. There was growing impatience and a thirst for substantive progress on priority disarmament and nonproliferation issues. Action points on paper without action in practice were nothing more that lofty aspirations. As a result, civil society and humanitarian groups took to pursue their own agenda using the UN General Assembly as their forum.

General Assembly Resolutions

Failing to achieve concrete and meaningful disarmament through the NPT quinquennial review process, civil society groups and states committed to substantive

---

[69] Ibid.
[70] Ibid.
[71] Ibid.
[72] Ibid.

change took it upon themselves to move these matters forward. Over a relatively short period, between 2012 and 2017, they initiated negotiations on a treaty through the UN General Assembly, ultimately resulting in the TPNW. Momentum gathered with the 2012 General Assembly Resolution 67/409,[73] in which it was decided "to establish an open-ended working group to develop proposals to take forward multilateral nuclear disarmament negotiations for the achievement and maintenance of a world without nuclear weapons."[74] This resolution established that a working group would convene in Geneva in 2013 for up to fifteen working days, with contributions from international organizations and civil society.[75] The working group would submit a report on its work to the General Assembly at its sixty-eighth session.[76] It was agreed that the secretary-general would provide the support necessary to convene and support the working group and transmit its report to the Conference on Disarmament and the Disarmament Commission.[77] It would include a provisional agenda of the UN General Assembly sixty-eighth session as an item entitled "Taking forward multilateral nuclear disarmament negotiations."[78]

Building on from this, in 2013, General Assembly Resolution 68/46[79] noted with satisfaction that the Open-ended Working Group had commenced its work engaging in discussions in an open, constructive, transparent and interactive manner to address various issues relating to nuclear disarmament.[80] Welcoming the report of the Working Group,[81] it requested that the secretary-general seek the views of Member States on how to take forward such multilateral nuclear disarmament negotiations as well as submitting a report on such developments to the General Assembly at its sixty-ninth session,[82] with the view to including its provisional agenda of its sixty-ninth session.[83]

The subsequent 2014 General Assembly Resolution, 69/41,[84] welcomed the report of the secretary-general[85] which now contained the views of Member States regarding multilateral nuclear disarmament negotiations and requested the secretary-

---

[73] Of the 48th plenary meeting December 3, 2012 based on the report of the First Committee (A/67/409). See www.un.org/en/ga/search/view_doc.asp?symbol=A/RES/67/56.

[74] At para. 1. GARes. 67/56. See www.un.org/en/ga/search/view_doc.asp?symbol=A/RES/67/56.

[75] At para. 2. GARes. 67/56. See www.un.org/en/ga/search/view_doc.asp?symbol=A/RES/67/56.

[76] At para. 3. GARes. 67/56. See www.un.org/en/ga/search/view_doc.asp?symbol=A/RES/67/56.

[77] At para. 4. GARes. 67/56. See www.un.org/en/ga/search/view_doc.asp?symbol=A/RES/67/56.

[78] At para. 5. GARes. 67/56. See www.un.org/en/ga/search/view_doc.asp?symbol=A/RES/67/56.

[79] Taking forward multilateral nuclear disarmament negotiations, based on the report of the First Committee (A/68/411), adopted by the General Assembly 60th plenary meeting December 5, 2013. See http://undocs.org/A/RES/68/46.

[80] At para. 1. GA Resolution 68/46. See http://undocs.org/A/RES/68/46.

[81] At para. 2. GA Resolution 68/46. See http://undocs.org/A/RES/68/46.

[82] At para. 8. GA Resolution 68/46. See http://undocs.org/A/RES/68/46.

[83] Under the item entitled "General and complete disarmament," the sub-item entitled "Taking forward multilateral nuclear disarmament negotiations." At para. 11. GA Resolution 68/46. See http://undocs .org/A/RES/68/46.

[84] Taking forward multilateral nuclear disarmament negotiations, based on the report of the First Committee (A/69/440), adopted by the 62nd plenary meeting of the General Assembly December 2, 2014, GA Resolution 69/41. See http://undocs.org/A/RES/69/41.

[85] See www.undocs.org/A/RES/70/33. See also A/69/154 and Add.1.

The Process: Determined to Disarm

general to transmit that report to the Conference on Disarmament and the Disarmament Commission for their consideration.[86] In addition to this, it asked to review progress made in the implementation of the present resolution at its seventieth session and to further explore options on nuclear disarmament negotiations, including if necessary through the Working Group,[87] and to include it in the provisional agenda of its seventieth session.[88] Traction was clearly building toward adopting requirements for meaningful change regarding disarmament.

The aspiration for a nuclear disarmament treaty thus became an unstoppable movement in humanitarian disarmament. General Assembly Resolution A/70/33[89] in 2015 reiterated the universal objective of achieving and maintaining a world without nuclear weapons, emphasizing the importance of addressing issues relating to nuclear weapons in a comprehensive, inclusive, interactive and constructive manner, for the advancement of multilateral nuclear disarmament negotiations.[90] It reaffirmed the urgency of securing substantive progress in multilateral nuclear disarmament negotiations,[91] deciding that the Open-ended Working Group would also substantively address recommendations on other measures that could contribute to taking forward multilateral nuclear disarmament negotiations, including, but not limited to, (a) transparency measures related to the risks associated with existing nuclear weapons; (b) measures to reduce and eliminate the risk of accidental, mistaken, unauthorized or intentional nuclear weapon detonations; as well as (c) measures to increase awareness and understanding of the complexity of and interrelationship between the wide range of humanitarian consequences that would result from any nuclear detonation.[92] To that end, all Member States were encouraged to participate in the Open-ended Working Group,[93] which would convene in Geneva in 2016 for up to fifteen working days,[94] wherein participating states would make their "best endeavours to reach general agreement"[95] and the group would submit a report along with its agreed recommendations to the General Assembly at its seventy-first session, with a view to assessing progress on such developments.[96]

---

[86] At para. 1. GA Resolution 69/41. See http://undocs.org/A/RES/69/41.
[87] At para. 6. GA Resolution 69/41. See http://undocs.org/A/RES/69/41.
[88] Under the item entitled "General and complete disarmament," the sub-item entitled "Taking forward multilateral nuclear disarmament negotiations" at para. 8. GA Resolution 69/41. See http://undocs .org/A/RES/69/41.
[89] Taking forward multilateral nuclear disarmament negotiations, based on the report of the First Committee (A/70/460) at the 67th plenary meeting December 7, 2015. GA Resolution 70/33. See http://undocs.org/A/RES/70/33.
[90] At para. 1. GA Resolution 70/33. See http://undocs.org/A/RES/70/33.
[91] At para. 2. GA Resolution 70/33. See http://undocs.org/A/RES/70/33.
[92] At para. 3. GA Resolution 70/33. See http://undocs.org/A/RES/70/33.
[93] At para. 4. GA Resolution 70/33. See http://undocs.org/A/RES/70/33.
[94] At para. 5. GA Resolution 70/33. See http://undocs.org/A/RES/70/33.
[95] At para. 6. GA Resolution 70/33. See http://undocs.org/A/RES/70/33.
[96] At para. 7. GA Resolution 70/33. See http://undocs.org/A/RES/70/33.

The resolution requested that the secretary-general provide, within available resources, the support necessary to convene the Open-ended Working Group and to transmit the report of the working group to the Conference on Disarmament and the Disarmament Commission and to the international conference foreseen in paragraph 6 of Resolution 68/32.[97] It moved to include it in the provisional agenda of its seventy-first session, under the item entitled "General and complete disarmament," and the sub-item entitled "Taking forward multilateral nuclear disarmament negotiations."[98] Provided below is an overview and reproduction of the deliberations of the Working Group. These are worth noting both for a complete understanding of the deliberations and to provide insights to the humanitarian disarmament approach taken by many civil society organizations, which will be examined in greater depth throughout this book.[99]

2016 GA Resolution: Working Group on Multilateral Nuclear Disarmament Negotiations

As requested, the Working Group convened a series of open-ended deliberations regarding nuclear disarmament negotiations. The 2016[100] General Assembly Resolution 71/371, highlighted the work of the Group which held thematic discussions structured around various panel sessions.[101] Two panels were held from February 22 to 26, 2016, with Panel I focusing on addressing concrete effective legal measures and provisions and norms required to attain and maintain a world without nuclear weapons.[102] Panel II deliberations were aimed at addressing recommendations on other measures that could contribute to nuclear disarmament treaty negotiations, including: (i) transparency relating to the risks associated with existing nuclear weapons; (ii) reducing and eliminating the risk of detonating nuclear weapons, be it by accident, mistake, or unauthorized or intentional detonations; (iii) measures to increase awareness and understanding of the complexity of and interrelationship between the wide range of humanitarian consequences resulting from any nuclear detonation; and, (iv) other relevant measures.[103]

---

[97] At para. 8. GA Resolution 70/33. See http://undocs.org/A/RES/70/33.

[98] At para. 9. GA Resolution 70/33. See http://undocs.org/A/RES/70/33.

[99] While circumstances of the conclusion of a treaty, and its preparatory works, can be used as a supplementary means to the interpretation of a treaty under Article 32 VCLT, this is not the intention of this discussion. It is merely to understand the background and changing international environment and not interpretation of the TPNW, per se.

[100] GA Resolution 71/371 of September 1, 2016.

[101] The deliberations of the Working Group meetings.

[102] Para. 17(a) GA Resolution 71/371. Consisting of the following panelists: Gro Nystuen, International Law and Policy Institute, Rebecca Johnson, Acronym Institute for Disarmament Diplomacy, Kathleen Lawand, International Committee of the Red Cross (ICRC) and Louis Maresca, ICRC.

[103] Para. 17(b) GA Resolution 71/371. Consisting of the following panelists: Tariq Rauf, Stockholm International Peace Research Institute, Beyza Unal, Chatham House, Pavel Podvig, UNIDIR and John Borrie, UNIDIR.

The Process: Determined to Disarm 27

Discussions from May 2 to 4, and May 9 to 13, 2016 were structured around the six panels.[104] Panel I of this round of deliberations focused on measures to reduce and eliminate the risk of accidental, mistaken, unauthorized or intentional nuclear weapon detonations.[105] Panel II examined transparency measures relating to the risks associated with existing nuclear weapons.[106] Panel III assessed additional measures to increase awareness and understanding of the complexity of, and inter-relationship between, the wide range of humanitarian consequences that would result from any nuclear detonation.[107] Panel IV focused on essential elements that would comprise effective legal measures, legal provisions and norms that would need to be concluded in order to attain, and to maintain, a world without nuclear weapons.[108] Panel V examined possible pathways to take forward multilateral nuclear disarmament negotiations.[109] Lastly, Panel VI looked at other measures, including reviewing the role of nuclear weapons in the security and other contexts of the twenty-first century.[110]

During their substantive discussions the Working Group exchanged general views, *inter alia*, reaffirming "the resolve to achieve and maintain a world without nuclear weapons."[111] It emphasized the importance of addressing these issues relating to nuclear weapons in a comprehensive, inclusive, interactive and constructive manner in order to advance multilateral nuclear disarmament negotiations. The Working Group recalled the "unequivocal undertaking" by the nuclear-weapon states at the 2000 NPT Review Conference "to bring about the total elimination of their nuclear weapons,"[112] and noted the threat posed to humanity by "the existence of nuclear weapons."[113] Moreover, against these considerations the Working Group "noted with concern" that progress in multilateral nuclear disarmament had been slow highlighting the "serious challenges" faced by the existing UN disarmament machinery, including the fact that the Conference on Disarmament, had not been able to carry out negotiations pursuant to an agreed program of work in two decades, and that the UN Disarmament Commission had "not produced a substantive outcome since 1999."[114] In addition, it noted that the 2015 Review Conference of

[104] Para. 18 GA Resolution 71/371.
[105] Para. 18(a) GA Resolution 71/371. Consisting of Patricia Lewis, Chatham House.
[106] Para. 18(b) GA Resolution 71/371. Consisting of Piet de Klerk, International Partnership for Nuclear Disarmament Verification.
[107] Para. 18(c) GA Resolution 71/371. Consisting of the following panelists: Ira Helfand, International Physicians for the Prevention of Nuclear War, and Sara Sekkenes, United Nations Development Programme.
[108] Para. 18(d) GA Resolution 71/371. Consisting of Stuart Casey-Maslen, University of Pretoria.
[109] Para. 18(e) GA Resolution 71/371. Consisting of Nick Ritchie, University of York.
[110] Para. 18(f) GA Resolution 71/371. Consisting of the following panelists: James E. Cartwright, Global Zero Commission on Nuclear Risk Reduction, and Paul Ingram, British American Security Information Council.
[111] Para. 19 GA Resolution 71/371.
[112] Para. 19 GA Resolution 71/371.
[113] Para. 20 GA Resolution 71/371.
[114] Para. 21 GA Resolution 71/371.

the NPT Parties had "failed to reach an agreement on a substantive final document."[115]

In its work, the Working Group sought to identify areas where additional legal measures, provisions and norms required further elaboration or needed to be concluded[116] for a world without nuclear weapons. While many states expressed the view that "there is a legal gap in the current international framework for the prohibition and elimination of nuclear weapons,"[117] highlighting the need for "legal measures to be negotiated with urgency,"[118] a number of other states did not see such a gap in the current international disarmament infrastructure remarking that the Treaty on the Non-Proliferation of Nuclear Weapons, in conjunction with its review conferences, served as "an essential framework for the pursuit of nuclear disarmament."[119]

During the discussions, a number of states referred to the current international security environment, highlighting the role of nuclear weapons in existing security doctrines, noting the importance of taking these into account in the pursuit of any effective measures for nuclear disarmament, without which the participation of nuclear-armed states and other states relying on nuclear weapons in their security doctrines would be difficult.[120] Conversely, many other states stressed that collective security should be prioritized over national interests with respect to nuclear weapons. They argued that there was no contradiction between national security and collective security and noting that, in light of the transboundary and potential global impact, "the risk posed by nuclear weapons was too high and that the existence of nuclear weapons within a State does not increase but rather lowers the protection and security of its population."[121]

The Working Group considered that the best chance for achieving a world without nuclear weapons would be by involving all states that possess nuclear weapons.[122] To that end, a number of states noted the steps that had already been taken by nuclear-weapon states to reduce the overall number of nuclear weapons, as well as their role in security doctrines and negative security assurances.[123] Many states noted, however, that such steps had resulted in "only a partial reduction in the role of nuclear weapons while still leaving intact a capacity to hold entire societies at risk." To that end, they expressed concern regarding continued efforts by nuclear-weapon states toward "the qualitative improvement and modernization of their nuclear arsenals, as well as their continued reliance on nuclear weapons."[124]

---

[115] Para. 21 GA Resolution 71/371.
[116] Para. 22 GA Resolution 71/371.
[117] Para. 25 GA Resolution 71/371.
[118] Ibid.
[119] Para. 26 GA Resolution 71/371.
[120] Para. 27 GA Resolution 71/371.
[121] Para. 28 GA Resolution 71/371.
[122] Para. 29 GA Resolution 71/371.
[123] Para. 30 GA Resolution 71/371.
[124] Para. 31 GA Resolution 71/371.

Concern was also expressed regarding the "perceived weakening of norms relating to the use or threat of use of nuclear weapons."[125] The ICJ's ruling in the *Nuclear Weapons, Advisory Opinion*,[126] considering the threat or use of nuclear weapons in any circumstance permitted under international law, in para. 67 emphasized that it "does not intend to pronounce ... upon the practice known as the 'policy of deterrence,'" recognizing that the Members of the international community are profoundly divided on the matter of whether non-recourse to nuclear weapons over the past fifty years constitutes the expression of an *opinio juris*.[127] It decided, *inter alia*, that there was neither an authorization,[128] nor any comprehensive and universal prohibition[129] in either customary or conventional international law regarding the threat or use of nuclear weapons as will be discussed in more depth in subsequent chapters. With this in mind, some states emphasized the need to shift the focus from simply reducing the role of nuclear weapons to actually stigmatizing nuclear weapons. This would involve changing international and public attitudes regarding policies and practices that are premised on the acceptance of such weapons. They saw this paradigm shift to be consistent with the humanitarian pledge issued at the Vienna Conference on the Humanitarian Impact of Nuclear Weapons held in December 2014. This called for the prohibition and elimination of nuclear weapons, whereby subscribing states committed to the stigmatization, prohibition and elimination of nuclear weapons in light of their unacceptable humanitarian consequences, environmental impact and other associated risks.[130]

Working Group Outcomes: Legal Measures, Provisions and Norms for a World without Nuclear Weapons

The Working Group sought to identify concrete effective legal measures and provisions, as well as norms needed in order to attain and maintain a world without nuclear weapons. In examining the substantive elements, the Working Group affirmed that the development of any effective legal measures for nuclear disarmament would have to aim at strengthening the nuclear disarmament and nonproliferation regime, including implementing Article VI of the NPT.[131] It noted that in

---

[125] Para. 31 GA Resolution 71/371.
[126] *Legality of the Treat or Use of Nuclear Weapons, Advisory Opinion (GA Request)*, ICJ Reports (1996), p. 226, available online: see www.icj-cij.org/files/case-related/95/095-19960708-ADV-01-00-EN.pdf.
[127] See *Legality of the Treat or Use of Nuclear Weapons, Advisory Opinion (GA Request)*, ICJ Reports (1996), p. 226, available online: see www.icj-cij.org/files/case-related/95/095-19960708-ADV-01-00-EN.pdf.
[128] Unanimously.
[129] By eleven votes to three. In favor: President Bedjaoui; Vice-President Schwebel; Judges Oda, Guillaume, Ranjeva, Herczegh, Shi, Fleischhauer, Vereshchetin, Ferrari Bravo, Higgins; and Against: Judges Shahabuddeen, Weeramantry, Koroma.
[130] At Para. 32 GA Resolution 71/371.
[131] At para. 33 GA Resolution 71/371.

2017 a majority of states[132] expressed support for the commencement of such negotiations which would be open to all states, international organizations and civil society organizations. They would work toward agreeing a legally binding instrument that would prohibit nuclear weapons, leading to their complete elimination. It would establish general prohibitions and obligations as well as impose a political commitment to achieve and maintain a nuclear-weapon-free world.[133] Highlighted in these substantive talks were provisions that could be covered in such an instrument, including, prohibitions on the ownership, development and testing of devices, as well as prohibiting any use or training; or permitting nuclear weapons on national territory or having effective or passive control with a states' jurisdictional boundaries. Moreover, discussed were prohibitions on financing nuclear weapon activities or providing special fissionable material to any states that did not adhere to International Atomic Energy Agency (IAEA) comprehensive safeguards. Such an instrument should also address the rights of victims of nuclear fallout and provide environmental remediation where relevant.[134] It was noted that the elements and provisions to be included in any such instrument would be subject to its negotiation.

Against this backdrop, discussions focused on the approach for a legally binding treaty prohibiting nuclear weapons. Deliberations explored whether the instrument would be an interim or partial step toward nuclear disarmament. Discussion explored whether such an agreement should include measures for elimination and leave measures for the irreversible, verifiable and transparent destruction of nuclear weapons for future negotiations. At this point it would merely contribute to the progressive stigmatization of nuclear weapons.[135] In that regard, states supporting such an instrument considered it to be the most viable option for immediate action as it would not need universal support for the commencement of negotiations or for its entry into force. They stressed the importance of time suggesting that pursuant to

---

[132] Comprising, *inter alia*, members of the African Group (fifty-four states), the Association of Southeast Asian Nations (ten states) and the Community of Latin American and Caribbean States (thirty-three states), as well as a number of states from Asia and the Pacific and Europe.

[133] Such an approach was supported by representatives of civil society. At para. 34 GA Resolution 71/371.

[134] Specifically, subject to negotiations: "(a) prohibitions on the acquisition, possession, stockpiling, development, testing and production of nuclear weapons; (b) prohibitions on participating in any use of nuclear weapons, including through participating in nuclear war planning, participating in the targeting of nuclear weapons and training personnel to take control of nuclear weapons; (c) prohibitions on permitting nuclear weapons in national territory, including on permitting vessels with nuclear weapons in ports and territorial seas, permitting aircraft with nuclear weapons from entering national airspace, permitting nuclear weapons from being transited through national territory, permitting nuclear weapons from being stationed or deployed on national territory; (d) prohibitions on financing nuclear weapon activities or on providing special fissionable material to any states that do not apply International Atomic Energy Agency (IAEA) comprehensive safeguards; (e) prohibitions on assisting, encouraging or inducing, directly or indirectly, any activity prohibited by the treaty; and (f) recognition of the rights of victims of the use and testing of nuclear weapons and a commitment to provide assistance to victims and to environmental remediation. It was noted that the elements and provisions to be included in such an instrument would be subject to its negotiation." At para. 35 GA Resolution 71/371.

[135] Para. 36 GA Resolution 71/371.

The Process: Determined to Disarm

Resolution 68/32 of the General Assembly, they should convene a UN high-level international conference on nuclear disarmament no later than 2018 to review the progress made in achieving the objective of the total elimination of nuclear weapons.[136]

At this juncture, many states supported a comprehensive nuclear weapons convention, aimed at setting out general obligations, prohibitions and practical arrangements for time-bound, irreversible and verifiable nuclear disarmament, focusing on a process for negotiating such a convention and bringing negotiations to a conclusion as a phased program for the complete elimination of nuclear weapons within a specified time frame.[137] Indeed, such a convention would constitute a non-discriminatory and internationally verifiable legal arrangement that would give states assurances that nuclear weapons had been destroyed and that no new weapons were being produced, noting the technical difficulties in negotiating detailed provisions for the verified elimination of nuclear weapons without the involvement of states possessing nuclear weapons.[138] That said, while many states supported commencing immediate negotiations on a comprehensive nuclear weapons convention, it was again noted that such a convention could only be effective with the participation of those states which were in possession of nuclear weapons. Some participants supported the negotiation of a legally binding instrument to prohibit nuclear weapons.[139]

At this point some states proposed the option of a framework agreement which would comprise either a set of mutually reinforcing instruments dealing progressively with various aspects of the nuclear disarmament process, or a chapeau agreement followed by subsidiary agreements or protocols that would lead gradually to a nuclear-weapon-free world, providing greater flexibility and leaving room for confidence-building measures in order to allow for a smooth transition toward nuclear disarmament, simultaneously taking into account the concerns of all states.[140] This approach would not necessarily need a specific time frame for accomplishing the elimination of nuclear weapons, proposing that a first subsidiary agreement or protocol be negotiated regarding a prohibition on the use or threat of use of nuclear weapons.[141]

Also presented was a hybrid approach, which would include the immediate negotiation of a treaty prohibiting nuclear weapons that would be complemented by protocols relating to national declarations, national implementation, verification and phases of destruction, assistance and technical cooperation and a non-

---

[136] Ibid.
[137] Para. 37 GA Resolution 71/371.
[138] Ibid.
[139] Ibid.
[140] Para. 38 GA Resolution 71/371.
[141] Ibid.

discriminatory verification regime to be implemented following the complete elimination of nuclear weapons.[142] Those favoring this approach argued that it would provide a framework for the progressive inclusion of all States initially resistant to joining, thus reflecting the inclusiveness of the framework approach, while also providing for the same level of comprehensiveness and effectiveness as the nuclear weapons convention.[143]

A number of states expressed support for a "progressive approach,"[144] highlighting the relevance of the existing global regime, emphasizing the NPT, consisting of treaty-level commitments on the goal of eliminating all nuclear weapons, the framework within which both non-nuclear-weapon states and nuclear-weapon states needed to work together on the building blocks of the nonproliferation architecture, consisting of parallel and simultaneous effective legal and non-legal measures which can be of a multilateral, plurilateral, bilateral or unilateral nature, and which are mutually reinforcing.[145]

The progressive approach called for effective legal measures including the early entry into force of the Comprehensive Nuclear-Test-Ban Treaty and negotiating a verifiable and non-discriminatory treaty banning the production of fissile material for nuclear weapons or explosive devices. It would see the commencement of negotiations on a post-New Strategic Arms Reduction Treaty (START)[146] between the United States and the Russian Federation, as well as achieving universal adherence to the International Convention for the Suppression of Acts of Nuclear Terrorism[147] and promoting full implementation of the 2005 amendment to the Convention on the Physical Protection of Nuclear Material.[148] Furthermore, the progressive approach would provide support for the practical implementation of Security Council Resolution 1540 (2004), as well as strengthening nuclear-weapon-free zones and creating new nuclear-weapon-free zones and weapons-of-mass-destruction-free zones along with supporting and strengthening the IAEA safeguards system.[149] As significant as it would be to achieve this comprehensive set of developments, some participants felt that the progressive approach reflected existing

[142] Para. 39 GA Resolution 71/371.
[143] Ibid.
[144] Para. 41 GA Resolution 71/371.
[145] Para. 40 GA Resolution 71/371.
[146] Treaty between the United States of America and the Russian Federation on Measures for the Further Reduction and Limitation of Strategic Offensive Arms (The New START Treaty) and Protocol (April 8, 2010), www.whitehouse.gov/blog/2010/04/08/new-start-treaty-and-protocol, to expire on February 5, 2021, unless extended by Presidents Putin and Trump.
[147] International Convention for the Suppression of Acts of Terrorism (April 13, 2005), see https://treaties.un.org/Pages/ViewDetailsIII.aspx?src=TREATY&mtdsg_no=XVIII-15&chapter=18&Temp=mtdsg3&clang=_en.
[148] Convention on the Physical Protection of Nuclear Material was signed at Vienna and at New York on March 3, 1980, www.iaea.org/publications/documents/conventions/convention-physical-protection-nuclear-material.
[149] Para. 41 GA Resolution 71/371.

commitments that enjoyed consensus.[150] They needed to go beyond the status quo of aspirational goals that showed little sign of progress.

Also explored was the idea of an additional protocol to the Treaty on the Non-Proliferation of Nuclear Weapons, which would be negotiated as a separate instrument, keeping nuclear disarmament as an integral part of the Treaty.[151] Assessed by the Working Group during the substantive negotiations were criteria for evaluating the feasibility and effectiveness of the various approaches for nuclear disarmament with some states suggesting that such criteria could include the necessary scope and content and achieve the required membership and normative value and political viability to contribute to achieving and maintaining a world without nuclear weapons.[152] Others, however, felt that the scope of the adopted approach should be the only criterion that should be considered.[153]

It was noted that while different approaches would entail different types of legal instruments or sets of instruments, many elements were suggested that could form part of such legal instruments.[154] It was also noted that many of the elements discussed in the Working Group coincided with obligations undertaken by some states pursuant to their existing treaty-based commitments, including the NPT and the various nuclear-weapon-free zone treaties. Certain provisions were considered to be analogous with basic obligations contained within the Biological Weapons Convention and the Chemical Weapons Convention.[155] Moreover, some measures could only be pursued and implemented with the engagement and cooperation of the states possessing nuclear weapons.[156] The Working Group acknowledged that there is a variety of different manners by which nuclear disarmament could be achieved,[157] noting that various possible elements and provisions could be pursued under each of the various approaches and many could be pursued across more than one avenue.[158] To that end, possible elements and provisions vary in their connection to the process of disarmament and in their potential impact on efforts to achieve and maintain a world without nuclear weapons and that certain measures vary in their applicability to all states, nuclear-armed states, non-nuclear-armed states and other states that continue to maintain a role for nuclear weapons in their security doctrines.[159]

---

[150] Para. 40 GA Resolution 71/371.
[151] Para. 42 GA Resolution 71/371.
[152] Para. 43 GA Resolution 71/371.
[153] Ibid.
[154] Para. 44 GA Resolution 71/371.
[155] Para. 45 GA Resolution 71/371.
[156] Para. 45 GA Resolution 71/371.
[157] Para. 46 GA Resolution 71/371.
[158] Ibid.
[159] Ibid.

Working Group: Additional Measures for Multilateral Nuclear Disarmament Negotiations

In addition to the substantive issues discussed above, the Working Group considered other measures that could assist in multilateral disarmament negotiations, including transparency, risk reduction and awareness-raising. These measures are seen as important to achieving the verifiability and irreversibility of nuclear disarmament.[160] In particular, the Working Group discussed transparency measures relating to the risks associated with existing nuclear weapons along with the principles of irreversibility and verifiability, which are seen as crucial to the nuclear disarmament process.[161] They stressed the importance of ensuring access to information reported by the states possessing nuclear weapons for the general public as well as to states neighboring countries possessing nuclear weapons and other states as well.[162] The matter of public disclosure of information related to nuclear weapon programs and activities is seen as essential, of course, balanced by the need to protect sensitive information from malicious use by terrorists, criminals and non-state actors.[163] In doing so, the Working Group reviewed various transparency measures regarding risks associated with existing nuclear weapons and the standardization of information at regular intervals,[164] with an emphasis on the number, type and status of nuclear warheads within nuclear-state territories and deployed in the territories of other countries,[165] including delivery vehicles.[166] Such transparency and information should also apply to countries' measures to reduce the role and significance of nuclear weapons,[167] as well as the risk associated with nuclear weapons[168] and to de-alert or reduce operational readiness.[169] Openness, transparency and information would be required regarding systems dismantled and reduced in disarmament efforts,[170] the quantity of fissile material produced for military purposes[171] and plans, expenditures and facilities related to modernization efforts.[172] The Working Group felt that such standardized information should be provided to the secretary-general who should, in turn, make it available to Member States and to the public at large.[173] In that regard, many states suggested that states whose military and security link to nuclear weapons should also be encouraged to provide standardized

---

[160] Para. 47 GA Resolution 71/371.
[161] Para. 48 GA Resolution 71/371.
[162] Para. 49 GA Resolution 71/371.
[163] Para. 50 GA Resolution 71/371.
[164] Para. 51 GA Resolution 71/371.
[165] Para. 51(a) GA Resolution 71/371.
[166] Para 51(b) GA Resolution 71/371.
[167] Para 51(c) GA Resolution 71/371.
[168] Para 51(d) GA Resolution 71/371.
[169] Para 51(e) GA Resolution 71/371.
[170] Para 51(f) GA Resolution 71/371.
[171] Para 51(g) GA Resolution 71/371.
[172] Para 51(h) GA Resolution 71/371.
[173] Para 52 GA Resolution 71/371.

The Process: Determined to Disarm

information at regular intervals regarding, specifically, the number, type and status;[174] delivery vehicles;[175] and measures taken to reduce the role and significance of nuclear weapons.[176]

As for measures to reduce and eliminate the risk of accidental, mistaken, unauthorized or intentional nuclear weapon detonations, the Working Group concluded that the only way to eliminate such risk was by the complete elimination of nuclear weapons.[177] Risk would persist for as long as nuclear weapons were in existence.[178] Although it is difficult to predict the precise nature of the risks, given the lack of current transparency, the Group felt that a number of factors contribute to the present and growing nuclear risk including: increasing tensions both at international and regional levels; the vulnerability of nuclear-weapon command and control systems to cyberattacks as well as attacks by non-state actors; and the increasing automation of weapon systems.[179]

Indeed, many states expressed concern that high alert levels could significantly multiply the risks and the threat posed by nuclear weapons and negatively affect the process of nuclear disarmament, noting that measures to reduce the operational status of nuclear weapons systems would increase human and international security as an important interim step toward nuclear disarmament and the need to mitigate some of the risks associated with nuclear weapons.[180] The Working Group expressed support for the implementation of measures to reduce risks and increase safety, pending the total elimination of nuclear weapons, nevertheless it was emphasized that this does not imply support for the possession or the use of any nuclear weapons under any circumstances.[181]

Working Group: Reducing Risks

In the course of Working Group discussions, states suggested various measures for reducing the risk of accidental, mistaken, unauthorized or intentional nuclear weapon detonations, pending the total elimination of nuclear weapons. Specifically, states that possessed nuclear weapons and other relevant states should undertake further practical measures to reduce the number of deployed strategic nuclear weapons,[182] as well as non-strategic and non-deployed nuclear weapons.[183] They should reduce their designated surplus stockpiles[184] and rapidly move toward

[174] Para 53(a) GA Resolution 71/371.
[175] Para 53(b) GA Resolution 71/371.
[176] Para 53(c) GA Resolution 71/371.
[177] Para. 54 GA Resolution 71/371.
[178] Para. 54 GA Resolution 71/371.
[179] Para. 55 GA Resolution 71/371.
[180] Para. 56 GA Resolution 71/371.
[181] Para. 57 GA Resolution 71/371.
[182] Para. 58(a) GA Resolution 71/371.
[183] Para. 58(b) GA Resolution 71/371.
[184] Para. 58(c) GA Resolution 71/371.

an overall reduction of the global stockpile of all nuclear weapons.[185] Additional measures included reducing risks associated with such delivery vehicles, namely, nuclear-armed cruise missiles, and adopting measures to limit or prevent deployment and move to a ban on all nuclear-armed cruise missiles.[186] With this they must reduce, or at least freeze, the number of nuclear weapons held, until beginning and concluding plurilateral negotiations on nuclear weapons reductions.[187] This extends to reducing the role of nuclear weapons in military security doctrines and their reliance placed on nuclear weapons during military training.[188]

As for weapons launch systems, states should develop and implement nuclear weapons policies that would reduce and eliminate any dependence on early launch or launch-on-warning postures as well as refraining from increasing the alert levels of their nuclear forces.[189] They should conclude agreements to eliminate launch-on-warning from their respective operational settings, carrying out a phased stand-down of high-alert strategic forces.[190] The Working Group noted that states should start to develop a long-term formal agreement to lower the alert level for the use of nuclear weapons, taking measurable steps to be carried out within an agreed time frame,[191] as well as increasing the safety and security of nuclear weapon stockpiles[192] and to ensure the protection of nuclear-weapon command and control systems from cyber threats.[193]

Whilst waiting for the Comprehensive Nuclear-Test-Ban Treaty to enter into force, states should refrain from the development and use of new nuclear weapon technologies, as well as any action that would undermine the object and purpose of the CTBT including maintaining all existing moratoriums on nuclear-weapon-test explosions.[194] Pending the negotiation of a treaty banning the production of fissile material for nuclear weapons or other nuclear explosive devices, states should maintain and declare moratoriums on the production of fissile material for nuclear weapons purposes.[195] In that regard, they should dismantle, or convert for peaceful uses, facilities for the production of fissile material for use in nuclear weapons or other nuclear explosive devices.[196] Moreover, the Working Group felt that states should fully respect their commitments to security assurances, and extend such assurances if they had not already done so and withdraw reservations and interpretative statements on the protocols to the treaties establishing nuclear-weapon-free

---

[185] Para. 58(d) GA Resolution 71/371.
[186] Para. 58(e) GA Resolution 71/371.
[187] At para. 58(f) GA Resolution 71/371.
[188] At para. 58(g) GA Resolution 71/371.
[189] At para. 58(h) GA Resolution 71/371.
[190] At para. 58(i) GA Resolution 71/371.
[191] At para. 58(j) GA Resolution 71/371.
[192] At para. 58(k) GA Resolution 71/371.
[193] At para. 58(l) GA Resolution 71/371.
[194] At para. 58(m) GA Resolution 71/371.
[195] At para. 58(n) GA Resolution 71/371.
[196] At para. 58(o) GA Resolution 71/371.

The Process: Determined to Disarm 37

zones.[197] In addition, they should be more transparent regarding accidents involving nuclear weapons and steps taken in response to such accidents.[198]

Working Group: Humanitarian Consequences of a Nuclear Detonation

The Working Group focused on identifying additional measures that would increase awareness of issues and understanding the complexity of the wide range of humanitarian consequences that would likely result from any nuclear detonation. It noted the importance of promoting education regarding disarmament and nonproliferation issues, emphasizing the humanitarian consequences of using nuclear weapons, with a view to imparting knowledge and skills as well as empowering individuals to achieve concrete measures toward complete disarmament under effective international control.[199] In so doing, the Group recognized the importance of various players including Member States, the UN, international organizations and civil society organizations in enhancing public awareness about the threat of nuclear weapons. It also noted their respective roles regarding the nuclear impact on health and gender, sustainable development, climate change and the environment, as well as the protection of cultural heritage and human rights.[200] It stressed the importance of engaging young people, through special youth communicators and student peace ambassadors who could pass knowledge on to future generations.[201] Many states see public awareness regarding the humanitarian impact of nuclear weapons as central to creating a broadly informed citizenry.[202] In that regard, a variety of measures were suggested by various states, including measures that all states could take to increase awareness and understanding of the complexity of, and interrelationship between, the wide range of humanitarian consequences resulting from a nuclear detonation.[203] Such measures include disarmament and nonproliferation education,[204] especially in states that possess nuclear weapons.[205]

As part of school and university curricula, they should promote education and training on peace, disarmament, nonproliferation and international law, including international humanitarian law, with the objective of fostering critical thinking skills among youth on such matters.[206] Such training should be in history books and include information on the atomic bombings of Hiroshima and Nagasaki, as well as on the consequences of nuclear testing, including in the South Pacific and elsewhere.[207] In order to promote mutual understanding of security concerns and

[197]   At para. 58(p) GA Resolution 71/371.
[198]   At para. 58(q) GA Resolution 71/371.
[199]   Para. 59 GA Resolution 71/371.
[200]   Para. 60 GA Resolution 71/371.
[201]   Para. 61 GA Resolution 71/371.
[202]   Para. 62 GA Resolution 71/371.
[203]   Para. 63(a) GA Resolution 71/371.
[204]   Para. 63(a) GA Resolution 71/371.
[205]   Para. 63(a)(i) GA Resolution 71/371.
[206]   Para. 63(a)(ii) GA Resolution 71/371.
[207]   Para. 63(a)(iii) GA Resolution 71/371.

threat perceptions, the Working Group encouraged the employment of simulation and role-playing techniques,[208] as well as training in the use of open-source tools and technologies, such as geospatial imaging, 3D modeling and big data analysis as a means of promoting societal verification.[209] The various players should identify national disarmament and nonproliferation education focal points as a means to facilitate reporting on the implementation of the recommendations of the United Nations Study on Disarmament and Non-proliferation Education (A/57/124),[210] and support the establishment of youth peace ambassadors to share messages in national and international fora promoting peace and a world without nuclear weapons.[211]

In addition to understanding the humanitarian consequences of nuclear weapons,[212] the parties should promote efforts to raise grassroots level awareness about the consequences of the use of nuclear weapons across national borders and throughout generations.[213] Such activities should include interconnected issues such as sustainable development, the environment, climate change, the protection of cultural heritage, human rights, humanitarian action, children's rights, public health and gender.[214] They should ensure greater emphasis on the unique impact of nuclear weapons on the health of women and girls[215] as well as support the designation of atomic bomb survivors as special messengers for a world without nuclear weapons.[216] The various players should support efforts to raise awareness of the legacy of nuclear testing around the world, including through the commemoration of August 29 as the International Day against Nuclear Tests.[217] They should translate the stories of nuclear test victims and encouraging visits to former nuclear test sites[218] as well as support the translation of the testimonies of atomic bomb survivors into multiple languages.[219] World leaders, decision makers, diplomats and academics should be encouraged to visit Hiroshima and Nagasaki in order to experience first-hand the impact of nuclear weapons and to interact with survivors.[220] Convening additional international conferences on the humanitarian impact of nuclear weapons,[221] and supporting additional research and studies about risks and the long-term consequences associated with nuclear weapons would also assist building and

---

[208] Para. 63(a)(iv) GA Resolution 71/371.
[209] Para. 63(a)(v) GA Resolution 71/371.
[210] Para. 63(a)(vi) GA Resolution 71/371.
[211] Para. 63(a)(vii) GA Resolution 71/371.
[212] Para. 63(b) GA Resolution 71/371.
[213] Para. 63(b)(i) GA Resolution 71/371.
[214] Para. 63(b)(i) GA Resolution 71/371.
[215] Para. 63(b)(ii) GA Resolution 71/371.
[216] Para. 63(b)(iii) GA Resolution 71/371.
[217] Para. 63(b)(iv) GA Resolution 71/371.
[218] Para. 63(b)(iv) GA Resolution 71/371.
[219] Para. 63(b)(v) GA Resolution 71/371.
[220] Para. 63(b)(vi) GA Resolution 71/371.
[221] Para. 63(b)(vii) GA Resolution 71/371.

developing increased understanding and awareness.[222] Players should conduct outreach through various forms of media, including television, radio and printed materials and through social media.[223] There is a need to integrate nuclear disarmament with policymaking, including at the highest levels of global governance, and in all other areas which may have a global impact such as sustainable development, climate change, food security, cyberterrorism, human rights or gender considerations.[224] Local, regional and global players should use the International Day for the Total Elimination of Nuclear Weapons (September 26) to enhance public awareness about the threat of nuclear weapons, including the humanitarian consequences of any nuclear weapon detonation.[225]

Working Group: Other Considerations Regarding Negotiations

The above discussion encompasses an extensive list of considerations to be taken into account whilst negotiating a treaty to ban nuclear weapons. In addition to this comprehensive list, the Working Group identified further measures that would assist in disarmament efforts regarding multilateral nuclear disarmament. These included the need for the prompt and effective implementation of Article VI of the NPT which requires action to be taken in good faith, "on effective measures relating to cessation of the nuclear arms race at an early date and to nuclear disarmament, and on a treaty on general and complete disarmament under strict and effective international control."

The Working Group emphasized the importance of paragraphs 3 and 4(c) of the decision adopted at the 1995 NPT Review and Extension Conference.[226] In particular, paragraph 3 states:

> Nuclear disarmament is substantially facilitated by the easing of international tension and the strengthening of trust between States which have prevailed following the end of the cold war. [Unfortunately, circumstances may have changed, however, especially with respect to the Russian Federation. Although perhaps we are not in another Cold War situation, it does appear that there is a Cold Peace now.] The undertakings with regard to nuclear disarmament as set out in the Treaty on the Non-Proliferation of Nuclear Weapons should thus be fulfilled with determination. In this regard, the nuclear-weapon States reaffirm their commitment, as stated in article VI, to pursue in good faith negotiations on effective measures relating to nuclear disarmament.[227]

Paragraph 4 states:

[222]   Para. 63(b)(viii) GA Resolution 71/371.
[223]   Para. 63(b)(ix) GA Resolution 71/371.
[224]   Para. 63(b)(x) GA Resolution 71/371.
[225]   Para. 63(b)(xi) GA Resolution 71/371.
[226]   Entitled "Principles and objectives for nuclear non-proliferation and disarmament."
[227]   NPT/Conf.1995/32 (Part I), Annex Decision 2 Principles and Objectives for Nuclear Non-Proliferation and Disarmament. See https://unoda-web.s3-accelerate.amazonaws.com/wp-content/uploads/assets/WMD/Nuclear/1995-NPT/pdf/NPT_CONF199501.pdf.

The achievement of the following measures is important in the full realization and effective implementation of article VI, including the programme of action as reflected below: ... (c) The determined pursuit by the nuclear-weapon States of systematic and progressive efforts to reduce nuclear weapons globally, with the ultimate goals of eliminating those weapons, and by all States of general and complete disarmament under strict and effective international control.[228]

The Group noted the practical steps for achieving nuclear disarmament, which had agreed by consensus in the Final Document of the 2000 NPT Review Conference, as well as the conclusions and recommendations for follow-on actions agreed by the 2010 NPT Review Conference, with particular emphasis on the nuclear-weapon States, through concrete benchmarks and timelines.[229]

In addition to such unaccomplished past commitments, the Group also suggested various other measures to move forward with nuclear disarmament negotiations.[230] These included: a return to the substantive work in the Conference on Disarmament, including negotiations on the four core areas of (1) nuclear disarmament, (2) a treaty banning the production of fissile materials for nuclear weapons or explosive devices, (3) the prevention of an arms race in outer space and (4) effective international arrangements to assure non-nuclear-weapon States against the use or threat of use of nuclear weapons.[231] In addition, there was a need for further major reductions in nuclear arsenals.[232] Increasingly, it seems that instead of deterrence expiring with the Cold War it has become the status quo, despite Article VI obligations of the NPT as reiterated by the International Court of Justice. Indeed, there is a great risk of a renewed arms race between the United States and Russia, which will invariably draw China in as well, complicating matters further. Instead of increasing arms through state military doctrines and deterrence policies, there is a need for nuclear arms reduction with measurable outcomes and enforcement disarmament measures. There is also a need to improve the capability to detect nuclear explosions;[233] to strengthen nuclear-weapon-free zones as well as to establish new ones, with the Middle East as a priority.[234] States should cease all upgrades and modernization to existing nuclear weapons;[235] as well as support measures to minimize the use of highly enriched uranium on a voluntary basis and use low enriched uranium where technically and economically feasible.[236] They should also

[228] Ibid.
[229] Para. 64 GA Resolution 71/371.
[230] Para. 65 GA Resolution 71/371.
[231] Para. 65(a) GA Resolution 71/371.
[232] Para. 65(b) GA Resolution 71/371.
[233] In accordance with the resolution establishing the Preparatory Commission for the Comprehensive Nuclear-Test-Ban Treaty Organization (CTBT/MSS/RES/1). See para. 65(c) GA Resolution 71/371.
[234] As per the implementation of the resolution adopted at the 1995 Review and Extension Conference of the Parties to the Treaty on the Non-Proliferation of Nuclear Weapons on the Middle East. See para. 65 GA Resolution 71/371.
[235] Para. 65 GA Resolution 71/371.
[236] Ibid.

assess international legal obligations within the context of the use or threat of use of nuclear weapons.[237] Along with the above measures, there is a need for assessing the ethical dimensions of nuclear weapons in debates and conferences.[238]

OUTCOME: THE TREATY ON THE PROHIBITION OF NUCLEAR WEAPONS 2017

This extensive list of considerations set the backdrop for agreeing the text of the TPNW. In a monumental development, negotiating states agreed a legally binding multilateral treaty never in any circumstances to "develop, test, produce or manufacture nuclear weapons or other nuclear explosive devices."[239]

Moreover, they would never "otherwise acquire, possess or stockpile" such weapons or devices.[240] States agreed neither to transfer them or control over them, to any recipient,[241] nor receive the transfer or control over nuclear weapons or other nuclear explosive devices, either directly or indirectly.[242]

Under the TPNW parties will never "use or threaten to use nuclear weapons or other nuclear explosive devices,"[243] and will not "assist, encourage or induce, in any way, anyone to engage in any activity prohibited to a State Party under this Treaty."[244] They must never "seek or receive any assistance, in any way, from anyone to engage in any activity prohibited to a State Party under this Treaty."[245] They must not "allow any stationing, installation or deployment of any nuclear weapons or other nuclear explosive devices in its territory or at any place under its jurisdiction or control."[246]

The TPNW requires parties to submit declarations to the UN secretary-general regarding their individual state ownership, possession or control over nuclear weapons and the elimination of any nuclear-weapon program, including the presence of nuclear weapons or devices in their territory or under their jurisdiction or control that are owned, possessed or controlled by another state.[247] Stipulations are imposed for safeguard requirements regarding commitments to maintain International Atomic Energy Agency safeguards obligations and bring into force a comprehensive safeguards agreement (INFCIRC/153 (Corrected)).[248]

---

[237] Obligations under international humanitarian law, international human rights law and international environmental law. See para. 65 GA Resolution 71/371.

[238] Para. 65 GA Resolution 71/371.

[239] Article 1(a). See https://undocs.org/A/CONF.229/2017/8.

[240] Article 1(a). See https://undocs.org/A/CONF.229/2017/8.

[241] Article 1(b). See https://undocs.org/A/CONF.229/2017/8.

[242] Article 1(c). See https://undocs.org/A/CONF.229/2017/8.

[243] Article 1(d). See https://undocs.org/A/CONF.229/2017/8.

[244] Article 1(e). See https://undocs.org/A/CONF.229/2017/8.

[245] Article 1(f). See https://undocs.org/A/CONF.229/2017/8.

[246] Article 1(g). See https://undocs.org/A/CONF.229/2017/8.

[247] Article 2 Declarations. See https://undocs.org/A/CONF.229/2017/8.

[248] Article 3 Safeguards. See https://undocs.org/A/CONF.229/2017/8.

Adopting the TPNW 2017

A key aspect of the TPNW is the total elimination of nuclear weapons with specific requirements for various states, depending on their ownership or control status of nuclear weapons,[249] as well as the adoption of the necessary measures to implement treaty obligations at the national level.[250]

A special feature of the TPNW is its requirements regarding victim assistance and environmental remediation with respect to individuals affected by the use or testing of nuclear weapons.[251] In terms of victim assistance, states must provide age and gender-sensitive assistance, without discrimination, including medical care, rehabilitation and psychological support and to assist with social and economic inclusion of those affected.[252] Jurisdictions effected by testing or the use of nuclear weapons require appropriate environmental remediation action in the areas contaminated.[253] In relation to these and other treaty matters, reference is made to broader international cooperation and assistance in order to facilitate the implementation of the TPNW.[254] These include non-governmental organizations, the International Committee of the Red Cross, the International Federation of Red Cross and Red Crescent Societies, or national Red Cross and Red Crescent Societies.[255] To this end, parties have "the right" to seek and receive assistance from other states parties[256] and if feasible they must provide technical, material and financial assistance to parties affected by nuclear-weapons use or testing and to assist in the implementation of the treaty,[257] including to the victims of such harms.[258] Moreover, unique to this treaty, state parties that have used or tested nuclear weapons or devices are responsible for providing assistance to affected states parties, regarding victim assistance and environmental remediation.[259]

The treaty opened for signature on September 20, 2017[260] and requires ratification, acceptance, approval or accession to it,[261] with its entry into force ninety days after the fiftieth of such instruments being deposited.[262] While the present state of ratifications does not meet initial expectations and there are critical objections in some countries[263] as to the advisability of ratification, the entry into force may be

---

[249] Article 4 Towards the total elimination of nuclear weapons.
[250] Article 5 National implementation.
[251] Article 6 Victim assistance and environmental remediation.
[252] Article 6(1) Victim assistance and environmental remediation.
[253] Article 6(2) Victim assistance and environmental remediation.
[254] Article 7(1) International cooperation and assistance.
[255] Article 7(5) International cooperation and assistance.
[256] Article 7(2) International cooperation and assistance.
[257] Article 7(3) International cooperation and assistance.
[258] Article 7(4) International cooperation and assistance.
[259] Article 7(6) International cooperation and assistance.
[260] Article 13 Signature.
[261] Article 14 Ratification, acceptance, approval or accession.
[262] Article 15 Entry into force.
[263] See, e.g., Sweden (Inquiry into the consequences of a Swedish accession to the Treaty on the Prohibition of Nuclear Weapons, January 2019, www.regeringen.se/48f047/contentassets/ 55e89d0a4d8c4768a0cabf4c3314aab3/rapport_l-e_lundin_webb.pdf) and Switzerland (Federal Department of Foreign Affairs, Report of the Working Group to analyze the Treaty on the

expected in due time. The depositary is the UN secretary-general.[264] The implementation of the TPNW should not prejudice existing obligations.[265] Note that contracting parties' existing international agreements must be consistent with the obligations of the TPNW, since the Treaty demands that the parties' pre-existing obligations must conform to the Treaty. It does not allow for any reservations[266] and is of unlimited duration.[267] It does, however, provide for the right to withdraw if extraordinary events relating to the subject matter of the Treaty have jeopardized the supreme interests of a country.[268] Withdrawal will take effect twelve months following the receipt of the notification and subject to a party not being embroiled in an armed conflict.[269]

In the lead-up to its implementation, the parties of the TPNW agree to meet regularly regarding the implementation of the Treaty,[270] the first of which will take place within one year of its entry into force.[271] Other aspects of the Treaty refer to administrative and operational features including reference to the authentic texts of the Treaty[272] and the allocation and disbursement of costs.[273] Any disputes arising relating to the interpretation or application of the Treaty require the parties concerned to consult together with a view to the settlement of the dispute by negotiation or by other peaceful means of the parties' choice in accordance with Article 33 of the Charter of the United Nations.[274] The meeting of states parties may also contribute to the settlement of such disputes by offering its good offices or calling upon the parties to start a settlement procedure.[275]

The TPNW allows for amendments[276] and after its entry into force any state party may propose such amendments,[277] requiring a two-thirds majority.[278] Notably, it is hoped that this Treaty will achieve universality, under which "each State Party shall encourage" non-parties to accept and ratify the treaty with "the goal of universal adherence."[279] This requirement may seem curious to some, as it may raise the

Prohibition of Nuclear Weapons, June 30, 2018, www.eda.admin.ch/dam/eda/en/documents/aussen politik/sicherheitspolitik/2018-bericht-arbeitsgruppe-uno-TPNW_en.pdf).

[264] Article 19 Depositary.
[265] Article 18 Relationship with other agreements.
[266] Article 16 Reservations.
[267] Article 17(1) Duration and withdrawal.
[268] Article 17(2) Duration and withdrawal.
[269] Article 17(3) Duration and withdrawal.
[270] Article 8(1).
[271] Article 8(2).
[272] Article 20 Authentic texts.
[273] Article 9 Costs. See https://undocs.org/A/CONF.229/2017/8.
[274] Article 11(1) Settlement of disputes.
[275] Article 11(2) Settlement of disputes.
[276] Article 10 Amendments.
[277] Article 10(1) Amendments.
[278] Article 10(2) Amendments.
[279] Article 12 Universality "Each State Party shall encourage States not party to this Treaty to sign, ratify, accept, approve or accede to the Treaty, with the goal of universal adherence of all States to the Treaty."

44 *Adopting the TPNW 2017*

question as to whether states even have the right to approach third states and ask them to become parties. Some may argue that it would be different if this concerned asking signatory parties to ratify/approve a treaty, see e.g., Article 21(1) of the Oslo Convention on cluster munitions.

CONCLUSION

Over decades there have been various acknowledgments regarding the need for disarmament, such as in the United Nations Millennium Declaration,[280] the secretary-general's five-point proposal on nuclear disarmament, and in the preambles of various General Assembly resolutions.[281] Most notably nuclear disarmament language takes center-stage in the Declaration of the Tenth Special Session of the General Assembly, as well as in the action points of the 2010 NPT Review Conference.[282] Despite these admirable aspirations, the dream of a treaty banning nuclear weapons often seemed somewhat fleeting. Although continuously on the horizon, it was seemingly out of reach in light of strong resistance by nuclear-weapon states and their allies, as well as the nuclear ambitions of those states wishing to proliferate, thus complicating hopes of reaching a treaty. In essence, the political reality of heavily armed states, mixed with those developing nuclear weapons, compounded the hopes of reaching a treaty banning nuclear weapons.

Regardless, disarmament advocates, humanitarian groups and civil society organizations pressed on with the dream of a world without nuclear weapons. Failing to achieve substantive progress through the NPT quinquennial review process, these champions of disarmament funneled their efforts through the UN General Assembly, seeing successive development under General Assembly Resolution A/67/409 (2012),[283] "to establish an open-ended working group,"[284] followed by Resolutions 68/46 (2013),[285] 69/41 (2014)[286] and A/70/460 (2015).[287]

---

[280] Resolution 55/2.

[281] GA Resolutions 67/56 of December 3, 2012; 68/46 of December 5, 2013; 69/41 of December 2, 2014; 70/33 of December 7, 2015.

[282] *2010 Review Conference of the Parties to the Treaty on the Non-Proliferation of Nuclear Weapons, Final Document*, Vols. I–III (NPT/CONF.2010/50 (Vols. I–III)).

[283] Of the 48th plenary meeting December 3, 2012 based on the report of the First Committee (A/67/409). GARes. 67/56. Taking forward multilateral nuclear disarmament negotiations. See www.un.org /en/ga/search/view_doc.asp?symbol=A/RES/67/56.

[284] At para. 1. GARes. 67/56, www.un.org/en/ga/search/view_doc.asp?symbol=A/RES/67/56.

[285] Taking forward multilateral nuclear disarmament negotiations, based on the report of the First Committee (A/68/411), adopted by the General Assembly 60th plenary meeting December 5, 2013. See http://undocs.org/A/RES/68/46.

[286] Taking forward multilateral nuclear disarmament negotiations, based on the report of the First Committee (A/69/440), adopted by the 62nd plenary meeting of the General Assembly December 2, 2014, GA Resolution 69/41. See http://undocs.org/A/RES/69/41.

[287] Taking forward multilateral nuclear disarmament negotiations, based on the report of the First Committee (A/70/460) at the 67th plenary meeting December 7, 2015. GA Resolution 70/33. See http://undocs.org/A/RES/70/33.

Conclusion

Finally, at its sixty-eighth plenary meeting on December 23, 2016, the UN General Assembly adopted Resolution 71/258,[288] resolving to move forward with multilateral negotiations toward nuclear disarmament. In doing so, it made express reference to its previous resolutions[289] regarding treaty negotiations for achieving and maintaining "a world without nuclear weapons."[290] Resolution 71/258 was the result of the sheer tenacity and perseverance of campaigners and civil society organizations in keeping their goal of nuclear disarmament alive and, following a relatively brief negotiating period on July 7, 2017, 122 countries voted to adopt the Treaty on the Prohibition of Nuclear Weapons,[291] with many hoping to change the international nuclear disarmament landscape forever.

---

[288] See http://undocs.org/A/RES/71/258. The Resolution was based on the report of the First Committee (A/71/450) General and complete disarmament Report of the First Committee. See http://undocs.org /A/71/450.

[289] 67/56 of December 3, 2012, 68/46 of December 5, 2013, 69/41 of December 2, 2014 and 70/33 of December 7, 2015.

[290] See http://undocs.org/A/RES/71/258.

[291] See http://undocs.org/A/CONF.229/2017/8.

3

Humanitarian Nuclear Disarmament: Challenging the Status Quo through New Approaches to Legal Process, Purpose and Provisions

Nobody made a greater mistake than he who did nothing because he could do only a little.

Edmund Burke

The TPNW demonstrates growing support of humanitarian efforts to take action against nuclear weapons. It marks a fundamental shift by some states and individuals in the international community in their approach to addressing concerns regarding nuclear weapons and represents their willingness to challenge the status quo regarding the power of the nuclear states and their allies. Humanitarian disarmament efforts through civil society groups, in conjunction with a core group of like-minded states, have rallied together to outlaw nuclear weapons. The intention is to relegate them to the annals of history – eliminating them forever. The Armed Conflict and Civilian Protection Initiative notes that this approach to disarmament is intended to be "people-centered in substance and process," stating that "Humanitarian disarmament seeks to prevent and remediate arms-inflicted human suffering and environmental harm through the establishment and implementation of norms."[1] To some, the term itself, "humanitarian disarmament" may seem controversial. It may be perceived as undermining the existing arms control and nuclear architecture without replacing it with a viable defense infrastructure, hence leaving states vulnerable from a military perspective. The focus of this chapter is to examine the humanitarian approach under the mobilization of civil society groups to challenge conventional disarmament efforts, which has led to this significant development to ban nuclear weapons. Discussion highlights the growing support for such decisive action against these weapons noting a change from traditional negotiations to that of humanitarian disarmament under the participation of human rights centric groups and states supporting a treaty to ban nuclear weapons. The chapter demonstrates the emerging paradigm shift in the international community, marking a major challenge to the

---

[1] See https://humanitariandisarmament.org/about/.

Changing Times, Changing Voices? 47

nuclear status quo regarding traditional disarmament and the powers of nuclear states and their allies.

CHANGING TIMES, CHANGING VOICES?

The adoption of the TPNW marks an important departure from the conventional disarmament approaches taken post-World War II and during the Cold War whereby the five permanent members of the Security Council – the United States, the United Kingdom, France, Russia and China[2] – dominated debates and discussions regarding military security and armament matters. By and large, these five powers set and promoted the arms control agenda under which they were the central focus of discussions, serving to shape and direct nonproliferation and disarmament political discourse, diplomatic efforts and legal developments. As a result, other countries often felt they were neither given serious consideration, nor deemed to be legitimate participants in such discussions unless they were accepted and invited into the nuclear arms fold. When, and if, they participated in deliberations, some felt they were quickly marginalized and excluded from discussions if they did not adhere to conventional approaches regarding the arms control agenda, allowing them, at best, to formulate nuclear-weapon-free zones and be tolerated for their allegedly naïve stands. As evidenced from the TPNW, the tables have now changed and opposition is mounting against the nuclear powers, NATO and other states supporting nuclear weapons.

The humanitarian movement aims to challenge, and effectively change, the starting point of discussions regarding disarmament concerns under international law and diplomacy. The process of the humanitarian movement seeks to redress a perceived power imbalance between the nuclear states and countries that feel they were not heard, or listened to, on such matters. Many countries did not have license to speak on these issues and were marginalized for expressing views opposing the nuclear stance. Equally unique under this emerging approach is that it includes the voices and views of individuals who have been, or potentially may be, affected by nuclear testing or explosions. As documented in Chapter 2, the various panel hearings of the Working Group allowed for a wider array of issues to be aired and discussed throughout the negotiations process and considered in agreeing the final text of the TPNW. The humanitarian process outlines the rationale behind the need for the Treaty in order to achieve the aims to which it aspires. Its provisions are driven and determined by those participating in the discussions. Under this new reality, countries seeking full disarmament created a license to speak, not to be marginalized or ostracized for their views and their aspirations regarding desired treaty outcomes. To that end,

---

[2] Note that, until October 1971, Taiwan held the seat in the Council and not the PRC, and that the negotiations on and adoption of the NPT therefore involved the PRC not yet taking up that seat. See https://learning.blogs.nytimes.com/2011/10/25/oct-25-1971-peoples-republic-of-china-in-taiwan-out-at-un/.

they seek full disarmament and present themselves as legitimate participants in these important discussions. They reframe the dialogue, setting a new template for approaching nuclear armament talks. Nuclear weapons threaten humanity and should be eliminated. Nuclear weapons threaten peace and do not protect it. Here two worlds are clashing, creating a major challenge as to how to bridge them. The following discussion maps the development and rationale behind the humanitarian movement and this paradigm shift that challenges the conventional legal and political thinking on disarmament and nonproliferation, leading to the adoption of the TPNW.

Humanitarian versus Traditional Disarmament

Until recently most arms control agreements have been agreed under a traditional disarmament negotiating process. The TPNW, however, aims to reverse this stance, placing the emphasis on the humanitarian impact by highlighting the destructive force of nuclear arms. It represents a mind shift as to how nuclear weapons should be perceived and indeed challenged under principles of international humanitarian and human rights law.[3] In her article "A 'Light for All Humanity,'" Bonnie Docherty emphasizes that the TPNW is largely driven by humanitarian disarmament, which "seeks to prevent and remediate human suffering caused by indiscriminate or inhumane weapons through the establishment of legal norms."[4] Notably, this stands in contrast to traditional disarmament which has been largely "driven by states, which have engaged in efforts to control weapons largely to advance their own security."[5] To that end, there are significant differences between traditional disarmament and humanitarian disarmament. To begin with, humanitarian disarmament seeks to shift the emphasis away from the security of states, per se, which has conventionally formed the central focus of traditional disarmament, to that of the people themselves living within states and their overall security and personal well-being. Their participation is seen as central to the process in order to highlight their needs and concerns, as noted during discussions of the Treaty Working Group presented in Chapter 2.

Negotiations for humanitarian disarmament agreements can be differentiated by both the participants involved in the process and the approach itself to negotiations. They are more transparent and inclusive of a wide range of people who have been, or could be, harmed by such weapons which allows them to play a greater role in identifying relevant issues as well as proposing new solutions to actual problems. Effectively, these individuals are legitimate participants in the process wherein their

---

[3] See Daniel Rietiker, *Humanization of Arms Control. Paving the Way for a World Free of Nuclear Weapons*, Routledge 2018.

[4] Bonnie Docherty (2018), "A 'Light for all Humanity': The Treaty on the Prohibition of Nuclear Weapons and the Progress of Humanitarian Disarmament," *Global Change, Peace & Security*, DOI: 10.1080/14781158.2018.1472075 at 2, 3.

[5] Ibid.

Changing Times, Changing Voices?

49

experiences are valued and respected. Traditional disarmament methods are the opposite and hence criticized for lacking transparency in negotiations, often "dominated by diplomats, military experts, and select groups of scientific technical experts,"[6] and removed from the individuals most affected by such weapons. Moreover, they are seen as being exclusive, whereby civil society organizations wishing to participate are perceived as "outsiders"[7] and given little if any voice in the deliberations. Critics argue that taking a traditional approach largely removes important human perspectives from both negotiations and decisions being taken, invariably having a significant impact on the final provisions and desired outcomes of any agreements. Moreover, this affects the subsequent implementation and potential utility of any agreement reached purely on consensus and general agreement.

Aside from the actual participants in the process, another distinguishing feature of humanitarian disarmament is its approach which focuses on delivering an agreement within a set and often quick time frame. This requires the parties to focus on the overall intended aim, in this case: nuclear disarmament. As a result, the method calls for "speed, innovation and flexibility, which protects lives and limbs by ensuring tangible results in a timely fashion."[8] Conversely, traditional disarmament is often seen as more "bureaucratic, cumbersome and time-consuming"[9] and often falls victim to deadlock, delay and weaker results because it relies too heavily on consensus.[10] Needless to say, critics of the humanitarian approach call into question the effectiveness of focusing too much on final outcomes without broader consensus, which will be explored in greater depth in subsequent chapters.

Traditional disarmament may be subdivided into security disarmament and hybrid disarmament. Security disarmament aims to protect the interests of sovereign states rather than focusing on ending human suffering, per se. Hybrid disarmament attempts to address both security and humanitarian interests.[11] Docherty highlights that,

> Security disarmament, exemplified by the 1972 Biological Weapons Convention and the 1993 Chemical Weapons Convention, seeks to protect the interests of sovereign states, rather than end human suffering. Military powers generally dominate the consensus-based negotiations of such legal instruments. The instruments themselves contain prohibitions and stockpile destruction obligations, but they do not require remedial measures to address past and ongoing harm or incorporate cooperative approaches to implementation ...

---

[6] Docherty, 3.
[7] Ibid.
[8] Docherty, 6.
[9] Docherty, 3.
[10] Ibid.
[11] Docherty, 4.

50 *Humanitarian Nuclear Disarmament*

Hybrid disarmament, associated primarily with the 1980 CCW and its protocols, strives to address both security and humanitarian interests. 15 States parties to the CCW often claim that it is an appropriate forum for disarmament because it balances military necessity and humanitarian considerations and includes the major military powers, although they have undue influence because of the need for consensus.[12]

While traditional disarmament may at times be informed or motivated by humanitarian concerns, its defining feature is that it "generally prioritises state interests over those of the individual."[13] This can be reversed by taking a humanitarian approach whereby the negotiating focus is on the process, purpose and provisions of agreement, as was done with the TPNW.

Humanitarian Nuclear Disarmament: Processes, Purposes and Provisions

In recent years humanitarian initiatives have come to influence some arms control negotiations reaping successful results. For example, the Land Mine Ban Treaty, agreed in 1997,[14] was led by the International Campaign to Ban Landmines, seeking to end the use of antipersonnel landmines worldwide.[15] Commonly referred to as the Ottawa Convention, it opened for signature on December 3, 1997, and entered into force on March 1, 1999. To date, 164 countries have ratified the treaty, and it remains open to accession by other countries.[16] For example, one country harshly affected by nuclear testing, the Marshall Islands, has signed but not yet ratified and there remain some thirty-four non-signatories, including three nuclear States: United States, Russia and China, as well a few countries in "key regions of tension" such as in the Middle East and South Asia, opting not to participate.[17] As arms control treaties go, the Ottawa Convention is lauded as a great success and heralded as a major breakthrough by humanitarian groups.[18]

Following the success of the Mine Ban Treaty, the humanitarian movement continued in its work with the adoption of the Convention on Cluster Munitions[19] in 2008, referred to as the Oslo Process. Signed in Dublin on May 30,

---

[12] Docherty, 4.

[13] Docherty, 5.

[14] Convention on the Prohibition of the Use, Stockpiling, Production and Transfer of Anti-Personnel Mines and on Their Destruction. See www.un.org/Depts/mine/UNDocs/ban_trty.htm.

[15] See The Ottawa Convention at a Glance, by Daryl Kimball (updated by Sara Schmitt) January 4, 2018. See www.armscontrol.org/factsheets/ottawa.

[16] As of February 2019. See www.regjeringen.no/en/topics/foreign-affairs/humanitarian-efforts/mine ban/id467182/.

[17] See The Ottawa Convention at a Glance, by Daryl Kimball (updated by Sara Schmitt) January 4, 2018. See www.armscontrol.org/factsheets/ottawa.

[18] See http://natoassociation.ca/the-ottawa-process-two-decades-later/ and http://canadianlandmine.org /20-years-later-and-the-success-of-the-ottawa-treaty.

[19] See https://treaties.un.org/pages/ViewDetails.aspx?src=TREATY&mtdsg_no=XXVI-6&chapter=26&clang=_en.

Changing Times, Changing Voices? 51

2008, it prohibits the use, production, stockpiling and transfer of cluster munitions and requires the destruction of existing stocks and the clearance of remnants. The Convention requires states to provide assistance to survivors and communities affected by them as well as for contaminated lands to be cleared within ten years and to provide victim assistance to people affected by cluster munitions via effective victim assistance measures.[20] Entering into force on the August 1, 2010, as of April 2019, it has 121 signatories and 108 states parties.[21]

Daryl Kimball, the executive director of the Arms Control Association explains its origins. Under the agreement of the Convention on Certain Conventional Munitions (CCW) there were no express restrictions on the use of cluster munitions, a situation that a group of states initially sought to address by establishing a new protocol to the CCW banning cluster munitions. Following years of negotiations, the consensus-based forum failed to produce any such protocol.

> Frustrated with the slow-moving CCW approach, Norway at the November 2006 review conference announced an alternative effort to negotiate a [separate] treaty on cluster munitions. The inaugural meeting of that effort convened February 2007 in Oslo. Of the 49 governments attending the conference, 46 ultimately signed the "Oslo Declaration" to "conclude, by 2008, a legally binding instrument that will . . . prohibit the use, production, transfer, and stockpiling of cluster munitions that cause unacceptable harm to civilians."[22]

The humanitarian successes of the Mine Ban Treaty and the Cluster Munitions Convention[23] demonstrate that despite State military and defense positions regarding the necessity and utility of certain weapons from a defense position, there have been progressive and successive developments regarding legal protections through weapons bans based on humanitarian grounds. The mine and cluster munitions examples are founded on a humanitarian approach where the consensus approach of traditional disarmament failed to deliver an agreement. Both of these treaties were novel in that they were initiated and led and supported by citizens and like-minded governments and their provisions focus on the protection of civilians through the reduction of dangerous and highly destructive weapons, rather than on state defense and security. Docherty contends that the Mine Ban Treaty, in particular, revolutionized the field of disarmament because it was led by a global civil society coalition of ordinary

---

[20] See Cluster Munitions at a Glance, by Daryl Kimball (updated by Daria Medvedeva) December 10, 2017. See www.armscontrol.org/factsheets/clusterataglance.

[21] See www.stopclustermunitions.org/en-gb/the-treaty/treaty-status.aspx.

[22] See Cluster Munitions at a Glance, by Daryl Kimball (updated by Daria Medvedeva) December 10, 2017. See www.armscontrol.org/factsheets/clusterataglance.

[23] Additionally, the Arms Trade Treaty, although not a typical disarmament treaty, provides another expression of the hybrid approach, and adopted in similar vein when negotiations were being deadlocked. This landmark treaty regulates the international trade in conventional arms, ranging from small arms to battle tanks, combat aircraft and warships. It entered into force on December 24, 2014. See www.un.org/disarmament/convarms/arms-trade-treaty-2/.

people instead of states, which is not typical of the traditional disarmament model. The success of the Mine Ban Treaty paved the way for the Convention on Cluster Munitions, which followed a similar process and was successful in producing a comprehensive ban within fifteen months.[24] Docherty argues that, like the TPNW, these treaties are uniquely humanitarian in their respective "processes, purposes and provisions".

The unique features of the Landmine and the Cluster Munitions treaties taken together distinguish humanitarian approaches from traditional disarmament and demonstrate by their outcome that humanitarian-focused disarmament[25] can be successful in outlawing conventional weapons. Humanitarian disarmament is seen as a force to be reckoned with and is capable of accomplishing the same goals as traditional disarmament, and arguably at times more effective in achieving a positive outcome faster, as the Landmine and the Cluster Munitions treaties both demonstrate. As mentioned earlier the Cluster Munitions Convention was achieved within a relatively short period through humanitarian disarmament whereas traditional disarmament could not result in accomplishing a ban in either the CCW, per se, or a protocol to it after years of negotiations in this area based on the consensus model.

Unlike the Mines and Cluster Munitions treaties or the most recent Prohibition Treaty, critics feel that the Nuclear Non-Proliferation Treaty (NPT) which is widely recognized as "the cornerstone of global nuclear non-proliferation regime,"[26] is a prime example of traditional disarmament. In contrast to the humanitarian approach, the NPT focused on convincing other states to endorse the treaty by appealing to the protection of "their own security interests rather than to prevent the suffering of individuals."[27] Daniel Reitiker writes, "the NPT concluded in 1968, is considered more of a product of governments' calculations and security assessments than a response to pressure by civil society. Launched by Ireland in 1958, the NPT was pushed by major military powers (the United States and USSR) from 1965 onward, after they had realized that the value of their own nuclear forces would be at stake if many other States acquired nuclear capability."[28]

Since the signing of the NPT in 1968 some five decades on, civil society groups, international organizations and states have grown increasingly dissatisfied with the

---

[24] Human Rights Watch, *Meeting the Challenge: Protecting Civilians through the Convention on Cluster Munitions* (New York: Human Rights Watch, 2010), 1, www.hrw.org/sites/default/files/reports/arm sclusters1110webwcover.pdf (accessed June 13, 2018).

[25] Note that both the Landmines and CCW treaties were greatly aided by the humanitarian aspects of civilian casualties in countries affected by such weapons. This campaign was magnified by media and high-profile champions such as Diana, Princess of Wales, and others which eventually changed the dynamic and led states such as Norway and Canada to champion bans. It seems that Japanese examples assist, but no such situation exists regarding nuclear weapons since 6/9 August 1945.

[26] See 2015 NPT Review Conference. See www.un.org/en/conf/npt/2015/.

[27] Docherty, 8. See also: Bonnie Docherty, "Ending Civilian Suffering: The Purpose, Provisions, and Promise of Humanitarian Disarmament Law," *Austrian Review of International and European Law*, vol. 15, pp. 7–44 (2010).

[28] Daniel Reitiker, *Humanization of Arms Control: Paving the Way for a World Free of Nuclear Weapons*, Routledge, 2017, 126.

slow progress toward the implementation of Article VI, in particular, and the lack of consensus amongst the parties to the NPT regarding disarmament. Note, however, others might say that the formulation is too sweeping considering that most parties are fulfilling their obligations not to proliferate nuclear weapons, which constitutes the object and purpose of the NPT. Regardless of such a formulaic approach, as discussed in Chapter 2, it is noted that the NPT has produced limited progress toward disarmament, per se. Moreover, although the Conference on Disarmament in 1996 produced the CTBT, it has failed to enter into force. Annex 2 to the Treaty lists forty-four States that must ratify the Treaty in order for it to enter into force, with eight states still requiring ratification.[29] Further, critics note that the NPT's five-year quinquennial review conferences went from embracing total elimination of nuclear weapons to disagreement over a consensus outcome document. Echoing such sentiments, Docherty concludes that "states' implementation of their commitments under the NPT has been 'woefully inadequate.'"[30] David Jonas, maintains that the NPT parties have failed to meet the general and complete disarmament (GCD) requirement of Article VI.

> Since the NPT entered into force in 1970, *both* NWS and NNWS have shrunk from the lofty aspirations expressed in the GCD obligation, but at least NWS, most notably the United States and Russia, have terminated the nuclear arms race and have taken major steps in nuclear arms control, which certainly looks like GCD, while the NNWS have undertaken probably unintentional and only superficial measures toward GCD.[31]

Jonas also argues that parties' efforts toward general and complete disarmament have not gone far enough to constitute "negotiations in good faith" as required under Article VI of the NPT:

> In 2006, the [United Nations General Assembly] UNGA established another [Open-Ended Working Group] OEWG on [Special Session on Disarmament] SSOD-IV and charged it with the same goals as in 2003, bearing in mind "the ultimate objective of general and complete disarmament under effective international control." This Working Group also did not result in any final agreement on the issues.
>
> The GCD obligation requires states to "pursue negotiations in good faith." This requires more than merely hosting several SSODs over forty years since the NPT's entry into force. Moreover, the SSODs and other efforts at disarmament have been focused primarily on nuclear disarmament rather than GCD and, so defined, these efforts do not meet the states' obligations. While paying lip service to the ultimate goal of GCD, the NNWS were probably not pursuing negotiations related to a treaty on GCD as much as pursuing their interest in NWS disarmament.[32]

---

[29]   See www.ctbto.org/the-treaty/treaty-text/.
[30]   Docherty, 9.
[31]   David S. Jonas, "General and Complete Disarmament: Not for Nuclear Weapons States Anymore," 43 *Geo. J. Int'l* 587, 634 (2012) at 624.
[32]   Jonas 2012, 627–628.

He also contends that because Article VI calls for a *single comprehensive treaty* on general and complete disarmament, current conventional disarmament treaties which only aim at partial measures do not constitute negotiations as required for general and complete disarmament.[33] Further, according to Stockholm International Peace Research Institute (SIPRI) global military spending has also increased over the last decade.[34]

Tillman Ruff, one of the founders of ICAN, also points out the dissatisfaction of states without nuclear weapons regarding the NPT.

> [T]he harsh reality is that none of the nuclear-armed states are serious about fulfilling their obligation to disarm, and in fact they are all doing the opposite – arguing that conditions are not right to disarm, planning to retain their nuclear weapons indefinitely, and investing over US$100 billion per year in modernising their nuclear arsenals, making them more accurate, deadly and "usable." So the game-changing breakthrough needed must come from the states without the weapons, most of them alarmed and frustrated about being held under a nuclear sword of Damocles, with no end in sight, by governments that refuse to fulfil a legally binding disarmament commitment they made under the NPT since 1970.[35]

Partly in response to the perceived lack of progress made by the NPT Review Conference in 2010, proponents of a nuclear weapon ban treaty decided to reframe the issue as a humanitarian matter rather than of state security.[36] Speaking to the Geneva diplomatic corps, then president of the International Committee of the Red Cross, Jakob Kellenberger said, "The currency of this debate must ultimately be about human beings, about the fundamental rules of international humanitarian law, and about the collective future of humanity."[37] From 2010 to the eventual signing of the TPNW in 2017, states and organizations including the International Red Cross, Red Crescent Movement, ICAN and UN agencies endeavored to refocus the debate regarding nuclear weapons toward more humanitarian concerns. This was achieved in part by holding a series of conferences known as the Humanitarian Initiative.[38] Docherty feels that reframing the debate as humanitarian concerns was helpful to breaking down barriers to diplomatic action both by raising awareness of the human consequences of a nuclear explosion as well as by treating nuclear weapons like other inhumane weapons, rather than as viewing them as unique strategic tools necessary for deterrence purposes.[39] This fundamental shift allowed advocates to point out the potential "unacceptable harm" that would be caused by

[33] Jonas, 629.

[34] Jonas, 631.

[35] Tillman Ruff (2018), "Negotiating the UN Treaty on the Prohibition of Nuclear Weapons and the Role of ICAN," *Global Change, Peace & Security*, DOI: 10.1080/14781158.2018.1465908, 7.

[36] Docherty, 9.

[37] Quoted from Docherty at 9.

[38] Docherty, 10.

[39] Docherty, 10–11.

Changing Times, Changing Voices?

nuclear weapons arguing on legal, ethical, moral as well as political grounds. This helped rally a majority of the world's nations to act, culminating in the UN General Assembly agreeing to convene an Open-Ended Working Group in 2016 and eventually passing a resolution to negotiate a legally binding ban on nuclear weapons.[40] With this development, finally on July 7, 2017, 122 states adopted a global nuclear ban on nuclear weapons. Despite the lack of participation of nuclear weapon states and their allies, the success in adopting of the TPNW could be attributed to its unique humanitarian process, purpose and provisions.[41]

Humanitarian Disarmament Treaty Process

The process of how parties approach negotiating a treaty invariably shapes its focus and determines the final text and desired legal outcomes. The Cambridge dictionary defines process as "a series of actions or events performed to make something or achieve a particular event."[42] The actions taken following the humanitarian model, certainly proved most effective in "making" and creating both the Mines and Cluster Munitions treaties, achieving the coming into force of the policy objectives of these respective legal instruments. The humanitarian disarmament approach to negotiating treaties follows a different process to traditional disarmament methods under the NPT and CTBT. It involves different participants as well as employing a relatively short time period, focusing on the negative impact caused by weapons, as well as addressing real or potential humanitarian consequences of their use.

The Mine and the Cluster Munitions treaties seek to address the destructive nature of the weapons in these respective conventions, criticizing the harm they cause and emphasizing the injuries inflicted by their use. Hence, the focus of negotiating these treaties was to prevent further damage as well as to ensure redress and assistance to those adversely affected by such weapons. The impetus for initiating these treaties was to address the catastrophic impact of such weapons on civil populations post-conflict, particularly on children, highlighting the adverse effects which often continue for years beyond their initial deployment. Therefore, the processes of treaty negotiations were inclusive of civilians, survivors and a variety of states, civil society organizations, agencies and independent groups holding meetings outside of the UN. The negotiations were intensive, quickly responding to urgent humanitarian problems by adhering to strict deadlines for adopting a final treaty text.[43]

---

[40] Report of the Open-Ended Working Group Taking Forward Multilateral Nuclear Disarmament Negotiations, A/71/371, September 1, 2016, para. 67. Opponents to this recommendation preferred "practical steps" that addressed "national, international, and collective security concerns." Ibid. Quoted in Docherty, at 11, n. 67.

[41] As argued by Docherty.

[42] See https://dictionary.cambridge.org/us/dictionary/english/process.

[43] Docherty, 6.

Under the humanitarian disarmament model process, the TPNW was also "inclusive, independent, and intensive",[44] in order to enhance the humanitarian impact of the intended objectives. The TPNW process included the voices and concerns of persons and states who could be affected by nuclear weapons and not simply focusing on the interests of states that had the potential to use them.[45] This process was not universally accepted, however. Many of the nuclear states and their allies refused to cooperate with such a process. Treaty supporters such as Docherty seem unfazed by the boycotting of the nuclear armed and umbrella states who did not participate in the deliberations. They emphasized that the focus was on the humanitarian process and the impact of the results was vital to achieving the final text of the TPNW. Ruff argues that the boycott of all the nuclear armed states also reveals "the gap in their sincerity, consistency and good faith to deliver on their NPT Article VI obligation 'to pursue negotiations in good faith on effective measures relating to cessation of the nuclear arms race at an early date and to nuclear disarmament.'"[46] The TPNW process nevertheless included a wide range of states, including "developed and developing countries, states affected by use and testing, and states with no direct connection to nuclear weapons, states with high-tech militaries and those with limited military power" or ownership over the final product.[47] It is felt that gaining the support of such diverse states will assist in promoting the aspiration toward universalization of the treaty as well as increasing its overall impact, regardless of whether or not the nuclear armed states become parties. The fact that those driving the humanitarian initiative believed they did not need the approval of nuclear armed states in order to ban nuclear weapons, was to Docherty, a major breakthrough for this process. In the past, the NWS have dominated the debate on nuclear weapons and focused on state security, deterrence, and mutual compliance.[48] Tilman Ruff puts it this way:

> [T]he process leading to the negotiation and adoption of this Treaty [the TPNW] was managed and led by states without nuclear weapons. This changed the status quo of nuclear disarmament steps being almost solely in the hands of the states that claim a special right to threaten all humanity with indiscriminate nuclear violence; and the rest of the world being sidelined to wait for whatever crumbs of tweaks of nuclear weapons numbers or policy the nuclear-armed states might deign to offer from time to time.[49]

---

[44] Docherty, 12.

[45] Docherty, 12.

[46] Ruff 2018, 4.

[47] Docherty, 12.

[48] Alexander Kmentt, "The Development of the International Initiative on the Humanitarian Impact of Nuclear Weapons and Its Effects on the Nuclear Weapons Debate," *International Review of the Red Cross* 97 (2015): 682: Austrian Ambassador Alexander Kmentt argues, "the nuclear armed states and their allies consider nuclear weapons the backbone of a security policy that is based on nuclear deterrence as the 'ultimate security guarantee' and as a means to maintaining a strategic – albeit precarious – stability between them," quoted in Docherty, 8.

[49] Ruff 2018, 2.

Changing Times, Changing Voices?

Effectively, the process of the movement altered which countries have license to speak on such matters, changing the starting point of the discussions from that of a conventional armament approach to more of a humanitarian-focused process.

An important and unique aspect of the TPNW process is the involvement of the UN General Assembly in the negotiation and adoption of the treaty which allowed them to avoid the consensus requirements of the UN Conference on Disarmament and the Convention on Conventional Weapons. Notably, this also prevented any of the five nuclear armed members of the Security Council from potentially vetoing the final treaty decision. The UN General Assembly process also proved to be efficient. It moved from "negotiating mandate to adopted text in just eight months, with only four weeks of face-to-face negotiations," which is tighter than both the Oslo and Ottawa Processes.[50] Ruff who was deeply involved in the negotiations notes, "In over three decades of working for the eradication of nuclear weapons, I have never previously witnessed such a level of commitment of governments in a decision-making forum about nuclear weapons."[51]

It may seem surprising that some parties do not apparently care that the NWS failed to participate in the development of this treaty.[52] Indeed, that might be their precise point; a movement driven by moral conviction and humanitarian concern does not wait for, or depend upon the powerful buying in or participating. Docherty highlights:

> These positive obligations, modelled on humanitarian disarmament precedent, give the TPNW the power to have an immediate humanitarian impact. Their implementation does not depend on nuclear armed states, which are likely to remain outside the treaty for the near future. Instead affected states parties bear primary responsibility for the TPNW's remedial measures, and all other states parties must support them.

Finnis, Boyle and Grisez echoed a similar point in their earlier 1987 work, *Nuclear Deterrence Morality and Realism*, when they wrote: "The norm which forbids intending to kill the innocent forbids the nuclear deterrent. To maintain the deterrent pending mutual disarmament, is to maintain the murderous intent which the deterrent involves."[53] Their conclusion easily applies to the current nuclear climate: "Moreover, mutual disarmament is not even remotely in sight, and there are good reasons to think that the priority at present given deterrence is inconsistent with its [mutual disarmament] coming about. Finally, the very advice to keep the deterrent but to disavow any intention to use nuclear weapons pending

---

[50] Ruff, 3.

[51] Ruff, 3.

[52] Indeed, it would seem that they already knew that the NWS would not take part, thus they were even more motivated to go around the NWS and take charge of the negotiation. The NWS and their allies, on the other hand, believed that they were deceived by the HINW supporters who had led the NWS to believe that the HINW process was not aiming to get a NWC/TPNW.

[53] Finnis, 1987, 326.

mutual disarmament tends to weaken whatever disposition there might be to join in seeking that goal."[54] At the time those authors called on our nations to *renounce nuclear deterrence at once*, even though "their unilateral initiated renunciation would almost certainly go unreciprocated by the Soviets (who would retain a nuclear arsenal preferring to enjoy the resulting immense increase in their own security and power)."[55] They admit that "unilateral renunciation of the deterrent," is an inherently risky decision – "a public social act" – without a guaranteed outcome, but it is nevertheless required by the moral prohibition of intending to kill the innocent.[56] One can detect a similar tone in the TPNW, which completely denies any possibility of maintaining a deterrent under any circumstances. Nobuo Hayashi advocates that nuclear weapons should be rejected, "not because they fail to serve the purposes that their proponents say they do, but because their use and threat are inherently immoral."[57]

The main difference between the argument advanced by Finnis, Boyle and Grisez and the new TPNW is that they are specifically calling on and appealing to the NWS – Britain, Russia, France, China and the United States – as well those with nuclear weapons – Israel, India, Pakistan, North Korea – to unilaterally disarm their nuclear weapons. While advocates of the TPNW call on all nuclear-armed states and nuclear umbrella states to eventually sign and ratify the treaty. Article 12 aspires for universality with the goal of adherence of all states to the Treaty.[58] The TPNW Working Group did not wait to get the approval or participation of the NWS in the negotiations, thus the legal, moral and political demands it makes effectively remain outside the circle of decision makers to whom they apply: those who possess nuclear weapons. While the aim of the TPNW is a noble one, as noted elsewhere in this work and by some critics, if it does not affect the decision makers who possess nuclear weapons, it is not likely to fully accomplish its goal.[59] This is not to say that the only way to affect the decision makers is to convince them to sign the treaty immediately. Instead champions of the TPNW intend to actively lobby nuclear-armed states

[54] Finnis 1987, 326, 328.
[55] Finnis 1987, 328–329.
[56] Finnis 1987, 337.
[57] Docherty quotes Nobuo Hayashi at a 2015 NPT Review Conference.
[58] Article 12, Treaty on the Prohibition of Nuclear Weapons, A/CONF.229/2017/8: "Universality Each State Party shall encourage States not party to this Treaty to sign, ratify, accept, approve or accede to the Treaty, with the goal of universal adherence of all States to the Treaty."
[59] See G. Perkovich, "The Nuclear Ban Treaty: What Would Follow?," Carnegie Endowment for International Peace, May 31, 2017, see http://carnegieendowment.org/2017/05/31/nuclear-ban-treaty-what-would-follow-pub-70136; A. Mount and R. Nephew, "A Nuclear Weapons Ban Should First Do No Harm to the NPT," *Bulletin of the Atomic Scientists*, March 7, 2017, http://thebulletin.org/nuclear-weapons-ban-should-first-do-no-harm-npt10599; and P. Izewicz, "The Nuclear Ban Treaty and Its Possible Ramifications," *IISS Voices*, November 1, 2016, www.iiss.org/en/iiss voices/blogsections/iiss-voices -2016-9143/november-27c6/the-nuclear-ban-treaty-and-its-possible-ramifications-36fc. For a comprehensive response, see K. Egeland, T. Graff Hugo, M. Løvold and G. Nystuen, "A Ban on Nuclear Weapons and the NPT: Ambiguity, Polarization and the Fear of Mass Withdrawal," International Law and Policy Institute, March 2017.

Changing Times, Changing Voices? 59

directly and indirectly by stigmatizing nuclear weapons and those who support them. The TPNW process challenges conventional wisdom on disarmament by ignoring the objections and the boycott of the nuclear-armed states and pushing forward to arrive at a robust treaty that enshrines strong demands based on humanitarian concerns. Ruff makes a similar point that the Treaty's process and substance, "represents a seismic shift in bringing global democracy to nuclear disarmament, and in asserting the interests of shared humanity. It bodes well for other negotiations that might be undertaken in the UNGA. This disruption of the hegemony of nuclear-armed states is no doubt one of the reasons why these states oppose the treaty so vociferously."[60]

To sum up, the process by which the parties approached the issue in question was to give license to a group with different perspectives from those involved in conventional treaty negotiations. It focused on criticizing the weapons themselves and the destructive force of nuclear explosives, including their catastrophic impact. Hence, negotiations needed to include a wide range of participants, including civilians, states, agencies and civil societies in order to achieve its principal purpose.

Humanitarian Disarmament Treaty Purpose

The process and approach taken during any negotiations will undoubtedly affect the outcome of any treaty text, invariably influencing its intended purpose of what the parties wish to achieve as final outcomes. The main purpose of humanitarian disarmament is to focus on addressing the adverse effects caused by weapons of war and armed conflict, highlighting that the destructive force and the nature of injuries caused by using such weapons far outweighs any military benefit. Their use is oppressive and barbaric. From a defense perspective these weapons may be valued for achieving specific military objectives, but proponents argue any utility comes at far too high of a cost to humanity. They are indiscriminate in their focus and cause superfluous suffering, as will be discussed in subsequent chapters in reference to rules and principles of International Humanitarian Law. Humanitarian disarmament seeks to address the real and potential consequences of their use. The Mine and the Cluster Munitions treaties focused on the destructive nature of the weapons, criticizing the harm they cause and the damage inflicted with the purpose of preventing further damage while ensuring remedial assistance to those harmed by such weapons. Specifically, the destruction caused by mines and unexploded bomblets (duds) from cluster munitions formed the emphasis and listed as de facto ticking time bombs, killing and maiming innocent civilians for years beyond the actual hostilities or conflict. In addition, such weapons rendered wide swaths of fertile land inaccessible and unusable due to the number of unexploded ordinance lying latent. These two conventions note the importance of clearing these explosive devices as a part of community redevelopment and

---

[60] Ruff, 3.

60   *Humanitarian Nuclear Disarmament*

reconciliation. They recognize the cost, time and effectiveness of clearing efforts wherein the main parts of these treaties are celebrated as being humanitarian-focused.[61]

The purpose behind negotiating a treaty outlines the rationale behind it, outlining the importance of taking forward the humanitarian issues at hand. The TPNW has a distinct purpose: preventing human suffering through the elimination of nuclear weapons. The process and text of TPNW stands in stark contrast when compared to the language of the NPT and statements made during negotiations which focus on national security. Indeed, as Docherty points out, during the NPT drafting and negotiations the United States said that the burden of new treaty obligations would be "far outweighed by the degree to which it will *serve our national security and our national interests.*"[62] The United States continued: "We fully expect that every sovereign State represented here, in deciding its own attitude, will measure the treaty by the same yardstick: *its own enlightened national interest and its national security.*"[63] To be fair, the framers of the NPT included the purpose of protecting all human beings in the preamble: "Considering the *devastation that would be visited upon all mankind* by a nuclear war and the consequent need to make every effort to avert the danger of such a war and to take measures to *safeguard the security of peoples.*"[64] The key difference, however, is that it only links the devastation of humanity with *nuclear war*, not the existence of nuclear weapons, per se. The TPNW goes a step further and draws the causal link between human suffering and the *existence and use of* nuclear weapons.

Contrast the above NPT preamble with the language of the TPNW preamble which brings the actual and potential human cost of nuclear weapons to the forefront, alongside national and international security:

> Deeply concerned about the *catastrophic humanitarian consequences* that would result from *any use of nuclear weapons* and recognizing the *consequent need to completely eliminate such weapons,* which remains *the only way to guarantee that nuclear weapons are never used again under any circumstances,*
>
> Mindful of the risks posed *by the continued existence of nuclear weapons,* including from any nuclear-weapon detonation by accident, miscalculation or design, and emphasizing that *these risks concern the security of all humanity* ...
>
> Cognizant that the catastrophic consequences of nuclear weapons cannot be adequately addressed, transcend national borders, pose *grave implications for*

---

[61] Victim assistance comprises six pillars: "emergency and continuing healthcare; physical rehabilitation; psychological and psycho-social support; economic inclusion; data collection; laws, regulations, and policies." See www.icbl.org/en-gb/finish-the-job/assist-victims/six-pillars-of-victim-assistance.aspx.

[62] Statement of United States to First Committee Meeting on Non-Proliferation of Nuclear Weapons, UN General Assembly Official Records, A/C.1/PV.1556, New York, April 26, 1968, 3, quoted in Docherty, 8.

[63] Statement of United States to First Committee Meeting on Non-Proliferation of Nuclear Weapons, UN General Assembly Official Records, A/C.1/PV.1556, New York, April 26, 1968, 3, quoted in Docherty, 8.

[64] Treaty on the Non-Proliferation of Nuclear Weapons (NPT), preamble.

human survival, the environment, socioeconomic development, the global economy, food security and the health of current and future generations, and have a *disproportionate impact on women and girls,* including as a result of ionizing radiation,

Acknowledging the ethical imperatives for nuclear disarmament and the urgency of achieving and maintaining a nuclear-weapon-free world, which is a global public good of the highest order, *serving both national and collective security interests,*

Mindful of the *unacceptable suffering of and harm caused to the victims* of the use of nuclear weapons (hibakusha), as well as of those affected by the testing of nuclear weapons,

Recognizing the *disproportionate impact of nuclear-weapon activities on indigenous peoples,* [emphasis added].[65]

An ordered outline of the logic of the preamble's argument might look something like the following:

1. The use of nuclear weapons can and has caused unacceptable human suffering, and environmental and economic destruction: for example, hibakusha survivors and nuclear test victims and accidents.
2. The risks posed by the continued existence of nuclear weapons concern the security of all humanity, and essentially the survival of life as a whole.
3. The catastrophic consequences of the use of nuclear weapons are unmanageable, affect all nations and have negative implications for every aspect of human existence.[66]
4. The potential for human suffering, multifaceted destruction, and risks to the security of all humanity as listed above are caused by the continued existence of nuclear weapons.
5. Any use of nuclear weapons is likely to violate principles and rules of international law and may be contrary to the principles of humanity and the dictates of the public conscience.
6. Achieving and maintaining a nuclear-weapons-free world is a global public good and an ethical, moral imperative, as well as an *erga omnes* obligation.
7. The only way to prevent the use of weapons – which violate international law, principles of humanity and are an affront to the public conscience, the continued existence of which works against a global public interest, violates the ethical and moral imperative for nuclear disarmament, threatens human security and rights and increases the risks of superfluous human suffering, and destruction of the environment, the risk on nuclear terrorism and causing adverse economic ramifications – is to completely eliminate them.
8. Therefore, all nuclear weapons must be completely eliminated.

---

[65] Treaty on the Prohibition of Nuclear Weapons, A/CONF.229/2017/8.
[66] The bombing of Hiroshima and Nagasaki induce nuclear fear in people inhibiting our ability to live in nuclear peace.

Humanitarian Nuclear Disarmament

Each premise supports the conclusion which is the means of accomplishing the purpose of the treaty; preventing human suffering caused by nuclear weapons. The complete elimination of all nuclear weapons is the necessary and sufficient condition for preventing the use of nuclear weapons. Those who want to criticize this treaty must either attack the truth of the premises or the validity of the argument. Most criticisms to date have dealt with the practical implications and feasibility of accomplishing the goal.

Others in favor of the deterrent, attack premise 4, arguing that the continued existence of nuclear weapons – in the possession of the 5 NWS – is necessary to protect the security of states and the international community and to decrease the risks associated with nuclear weapons falling into the wrong hands. This would be a consequentialist argument that deterrence is the best way to prevent human suffering caused by nuclear weapons. This view is supported by history: it could be argued that deterrence prevented the Soviets and the United States from using nuclear weapons, and more recently, that Donald Trump and Kim Jong Un successfully used deterrence to avoid a nuclear war – so far. Arguably, deterrence of this nature involves threatening to use nuclear weapons, which could be classified as a violation of international law if the threat violated principles of necessity, proportionality and non-combatant immunity. Specifically, as will be discussed later in this book, threatening the use of nuclear weapons is contrary to Article 1(1) (d) of the TPNW. The framers of the Treaty would argue that the use of most nuclear weapons would violate international humanitarian and international human rights law, and the moral prohibition against intending to indiscriminately kill the innocent. Thus, they would also argue that deterrence should be viewed as a violation of international law, an affront to morality, and it poses a great risk to the security of humanity.[67] They conclude that the only way to eliminate that risk is to eliminate nuclear weapons completely. A violation of international law may also be at stake if threatening to use nuclear weapons would constitute an unlawful threat of force under Article 2(4) of the Charter; i.e., when use would be contemplated in circumstances that would not allow for the invocation of self-defense as a justification,[68] as will be discussed in subsequent chapters.

The NPT, in contrast, presents a different scenario, the logic of which is outlined in the NPT preamble and can be put like this:

1. A nuclear war would cause the devastation of all mankind.
2. The proliferation of nuclear weapons increases the danger of nuclear war.
3. There is a need to make every effort to avert the danger of nuclear war and to safeguard the security of peoples.
4. The best way to avert the danger of nuclear war and safeguard the security of peoples is to prevent wider dissemination of nuclear weapons – which implies

---

[67] See Finnis, 1987, 326.
[68] See Nuclear Weapons Advisory Opinion paras. 47–49.

Changing Times, Changing Voices? 63

allowing nuclear weapon states to keep their nuclear weapons for now – create and follow safeguards for all nuclear activities, declare an intention to stop the nuclear arms race, move in the direction of nuclear disarmament, and to urge the cooperation of all states in attaining this goal.

5. Therefore, states must not share nuclear weapons, they must follow safeguards, intend to stop the nuclear arms race, and cooperate with each other to move toward nuclear disarmament; at their own determined pace.

The overall purpose of the NPT is to place restrictions on nuclear weapons in order to *avoid nuclear war* and *protect the security of peoples*. When one compares the NPT logic with that of the TPNW, it becomes clear that the goal of the NPT is weaker and more ambiguous than the TPNW because avoiding nuclear war and protecting the security of peoples can be achieved through nuclear deterrence which requires the continued existence of nuclear weapons. Declaring an *intention* to stop the arms race and to *move in the direction* of disarmament and *expressing a desire* to ease international tension and strengthen trust between states in order to *facilitate* the cessation of the manufacture of nuclear weapons, eliminating their existing stockpiles, nuclear weapons, and the means of their delivery, all sounds uncommitted, vague and unenforceable because there are no clear-cut obligations for states to meet.[69] Indeed, the NPT is inherently contradictory in that it both accepts that nuclear weapons exist, according legal legitimacy to them in that the NWS are permitted to possess them,[70] while at the same time the treaty calls for nonproliferation and ultimate disarmament effectively delegitimizing them. Can it be that the treaty that accepts them also rejects them? Is this not an inherent irony; a contradiction in terms? This may be seen as self-imploding and the inherent contradiction allows the world to continue to drift without decisive action which results in the growth and proliferation of nuclear armament; the very end that the NPT is meant to curb. The sad twist is that the very treaty that is meant to eliminate nuclear weapons is actually perpetuating them.

Looking only at the preamble, one could characterize the NPT and traditional disarmament in general as an approach built on the assumption of the Hobbesian state of nature, which is national self-interest and perpetual war among states, *Cold* or otherwise. This state of nature requires parties to appeal to self-interest of nations and their governments in order to come to any agreement or covenant that recognizes the authority of a sovereign legislative office.[71] Thus, the framers of the NPT

---

[69] Treaty on the Non-Proliferation of Nuclear Weapons (July 1, 1968) 729 *UNTS* 161, Preamble, which was effectively the gist of the Atoms for Peace initiative.

[70] As per Article IX, a nuclear-weapon state is one which has manufactured and exploded a nuclear weapon or other nuclear explosive device prior to January 1, 1967.

[71] Davide Orsi, *Michael Oakeshott's Political Philosophy of International Relations Civil Association and International Society*, 2016, Palgrave Macmillan, Switzerland, at 103: "As for Hobbes, in civil association there is no external criterion that may provide the ground for the authority of the legal order. Law is authoritative neither because of its expected outcomes, nor because of the approval by the members

had to appeal to the risk of global nuclear war which would destroy individual states, in order to get states to agree to restrictions on their freedom to use, share and develop nuclear weapons to maintain their own security.

Alternatively, the TPNW narrows in on how nuclear weapons have violated and could potentially violate the human rights of individuals and groups of peoples, irrespective of what nation they belong to. It also radically personalizes and humanizes the effects of nuclear weapons so that they can no longer be seen as an effective utilitarian measure or a necessary evil for maintaining national and international peace and security. By personalizing the effects of nuclear weapons, the framers are able to base the obligations of the Treaty on ethical imperatives, fundamental goods, principles of international humanitarian and human rights law, the principles of humanity and the dictates of the public conscience, rather than only on individual national security.[72] The preamble of the TPNW not only cites legal sources for the obligation to disarm, it also takes a strong position on how they apply to nuclear weapons. The most controversial is the statement that any use of nuclear weapons would be contrary to rules of international humanitarian law, which arguably conflicts with the majority ICJ decision in the 1996 *Advisory Opinion* that the use of nuclear weapons could be legal. The Court found that the threat or use of nuclear weapons would generally be contrary to the rules of international law applicable in armed conflict but could not conclude definitively whether the threat or use of nuclear weapons would actually be lawful or unlawful in an extreme circumstance of self-defense, in which the very survival of a state would be at stake.[73] That said, one must not ignore the dissenting views in the *Opinion* which supported their illegality.[74]

In summary, the purpose of the TPNW seeks to reduce the adverse human impact and environmental effects caused by nuclear testing and explosive devices focusing on a uniquely humanitarian perspective. In so doing it highlights a purpose based on ethical and moral imperatives, as well as *erga omnes* obligations to disarm.

Humanitarian Disarmament Treaty Provisions

There are three essential components to treaty success: (1) the text of the treaty provisions; (2) treaty implementation; and (3) enforcement. Central to achieving such goals lie the actual provisions themselves regarding the intended policy

---

of the association. In Hobbes, it is through the covenant that individuals recognize the authority of a sovereign legislative office as the sole author of valid laws, renouncing the possibility of other sources of moral obligation (Oakeshott 1991, 284)." Also see Mónica García-Salmones Rovira, *The Politics of Interest in International Law EJIL* (2014), Vol. 25 No. 3, 765–793 at 767.

[72] Treaty on the Prohibition of Nuclear Weapons, A/CONF.229/2017/8.

[73] International Court of Justice, "Legality of the Threat or Use of Nuclear Weapons," Advisory Opinion, July 8, 1996, para. 105(2)(E).

[74] See dissenting opinions. See www.icj-cij.org/files/case-related/95/095–19960708-ADV-01–00-EN.pdf. See also Marshall Islands cases.

intentions (i.e., the outcomes, agreed in the treaty). The process taken in approaching negotiations combined with the fundamental purpose of the treaty will inevitably shape the text and outcome in terms of the provisions agreed.

Provisions of the Mine and the Cluster Munitions treaties aim at both preventative obligations and provisions for remedial reparations to assist victims caused by the destructive forces of these weapons. The treaties seek to incorporate cooperative approaches to treaty implementation whereby states parties to the treaties agree to help each other to meet their legal responsibilities and they are encouraged to work collaboratively to promote full and complete compliance with their obligations. Emphasis is placed on remediation including clearance of contaminated areas and again, assisting victims and those adversely affected.

Needless to say, the provisions of any treaty or instrument are fundamental in setting expectations as well as its purpose and legal objectives. The humanitarian approach influenced the content of the TPNW's provisions making it a rather unique amongst humanitarian disarmament treaties. It is the first binding instrument to, *inter alia*, ban nuclear weapons. Indeed, its unique provisions come in three main categories: (1) preventative obligations; (2) remedial measures; and (3) cooperative approaches toward implementation.[75]

Preventative Obligations

There is no doubt that the best action against harm, injury or damage is to avert its occurring in the first place. Taking firm and decisive steps to stop the use of nuclear weapons is at the heart of the purpose of the TPNW and definitively reflects the policy intention of those participating in the negotiations process. The preventative obligations under the TPNW include strong prohibitions against nuclear weapons which are intended to be universal in its implementation.[76] Article 1 stipulates its prohibitions apply under "any circumstances" and are comprehensive, covering creation to production, acquisition and transfer, possession, use and threat of use, and assisting, encouraging or inducing anyone to engage in any of these activities.[77] Moreover, the TPNW includes strong prohibitions and steps toward the complete elimination of nuclear weapons including stockpile destruction.[78] The TPNW also prohibits states parties from depending on or hosting weapons for another state that possesses nuclear weapons. The steps toward elimination and enforcement are meant to be strict, defined and immediate – "as soon as possible"[79] – and all require transparency, verification and reporting to the UN Secretary-General.[80] The TPNW

---

[75] See Docherty, 15.
[76] Article 12. See https://undocs.org/A/CONF.229/2017/8.
[77] See https://undocs.org/A/CONF.229/2017/8.
[78] See https://undocs.org/A/CONF.229/2017/8.
[79] The words used in Article 4(2) and (4), see https://undocs.org/A/CONF.229/2017/8.
[80] See https://undocs.org/A/CONF.229/2017/8.

allows states that currently possess or host nuclear weapons to join and subsequently work toward disarmament. Such an approach advances elimination of nuclear weapons promoting the intended goal of universalization. That said, for some it may be difficult to square with Article 1(g) TPNW, as they seem somewhat incongruent.

Remedial Measures

The preamble of the TPNW makes reference to the unacceptable suffering and harm caused by the use and testing of nuclear weapons.[81] Humanitarian disarmament aims to go beyond state security matters, focusing on the victims of nuclear weapons, such as the mention of the "hibakusha" in the preamble.[82] Article 6 stipulates that each state also must take remedial measures and imposes positive obligations to actually assist victims and those affected by the use or testing of nuclear weapons. They must "adequately provide age- and gender-sensitive assistance, without discrimination, including medical care, rehabilitation and psychological support, as well as provide for their social and economic inclusion."[83] Moreover, states must clean up areas of the environment affected by any use or testing.[84] This ensures that affected states are held responsible for protecting the rights of its people, which goes beyond military security and recognizing the importance of remedial obligations.

Cooperative Approaches toward Implementation

In conjunction with assisting victims, Article 7 applies cooperative approaches to treaty implementation by requiring states to help and to facilitate each other to meet their respective obligations.[85] In particular, it imposes duties for states to assist victims of nuclear weapons, even if their state has not joined the treaty.[86] Indeed, each state has the right "to seek and receive assistance,"[87] including "technical, material and financial assistance"[88] where feasible. Notably, a states party "that has used or tested nuclear weapons or any other nuclear explosive devices shall have a responsibility to provide adequate assistance to affected States Parties, for the

---

[81]   See https://undocs.org/A/CONF.229/2017/8.
[82]   Ibid.
[83]   Article 6(1). See https://undocs.org/A/CONF.229/2017/8.
[84]   Article 6(2). See https://undocs.org/A/CONF.229/2017/8.
[85]   Article 7(1). Treaty on the Prohibition of Nuclear Weapons, A/CONF.229/2017/8, Art. 7(4). See https://undocs.org/A/CONF.229/2017/8.
[86]   Article 7(4). Treaty on the Prohibition of Nuclear Weapons, A/CONF.229/2017/8, Art. 7(4). See https://undocs.org/A/CONF.229/2017/8.
[87]   Article 7(2). Treaty on the Prohibition of Nuclear Weapons, A/CONF.229/2017/8, Art. 7(4). See https://undocs.org/A/CONF.229/2017/8.
[88]   Article 7(3). Treaty on the Prohibition of Nuclear Weapons, A/CONF.229/2017/8, Art. 7(4). See https://undocs.org/A/CONF.229/2017/8.

TPNW PROVISIONS CONTRASTED WITH THE NPT

purpose of victim assistance and environmental remediation."[89] Such remedial and cooperative measures serve as powerful provisions in terms of their humanitarian focus on those effected by nuclear testing and use of weapons. It clearly demonstrates that the provisions agreed in a treaty are largely influenced by both the negotiating participants and the policy objectives intended to achieve.

TPNW PROVISIONS CONTRASTED WITH THE NPT

In contrasting TPNW's provisions with those of the NPT there is a stark difference. The positive obligations regarding victim assistance, remedial support and environmental rehabilitation under the TPNW aim at grassroots level reparations that will assist both individuals and communities to move forward in the aftermath of being affected. The NPT, however, imposes a different sort, and arguably a more limited and one-dimensional set of obligations. Specifically, states parties are to cooperate in relation to uses of nuclear energy for peaceful purposes. Article IV recognizes the "inalienable right" to develop research, and to produce and use of nuclear energy.[90] In relation to this states "undertake to facilitate, and have the right to participate in, the fullest possible exchange of equipment, materials and scientific and technological information for the peaceful uses of nuclear energy."[91] States that are able "to do so shall also cooperate in contributing alone or together with other States or international organizations to the further development of the applications of nuclear energy for peaceful purposes" especially in regard to territories of non-nuclear-weapon states and giving due consideration for "the needs of the developing areas of the world."[92] Note, that these cooperative obligations are fundamentally different both in their intended scope and their reach to assist community development.

More telling is the specificity of the treaty language. Beyond remedial assistance,[93] the TPNW calls for the complete elimination of nuclear weapons and devices, proactively aiming to halt any further damage or destruction. According to Article VI NPT each party *undertakes to pursue negotiations in good faith* in a treaty on general and complete disarmament. Each qualifier that comes before "complete and general disarmament" effectively weakens the obligation and creates barriers to accomplishing the principal goal. One can undertake to do something and never accomplish it; one can pursue something and never attain it; one can also negotiate without ever coming to an agreement; and one could try to negotiate but give up because the other party is said not to be acting in good faith.

---

[89] Article 7(6). Treaty on the Prohibition of Nuclear Weapons, A/CONF.229/2017/8, Art. 7(4). See https://undocs.org/A/CONF.229/2017/8.

[90] Article IV(1). See www.un.org/disarmament/wmd/nuclear/npt/text.

[91] Article IV(2). See www.un.org/disarmament/wmd/nuclear/npt/text.

[92] Article IV(2). See www.un.org/disarmament/wmd/nuclear/npt/text.

[93] UNSC Resolution 984 calls for "Security assurances against the use of nuclear weapons to non-nuclear-weapon States that are Parties to the Treaty on the Non-Proliferation of Nuclear Weapons." See http://unscr.com/en/resolutions/doc/984.

68 Humanitarian Nuclear Disarmament

Obligations of conduct versus obligations of result.[94] Critics may say that parties to the NPT have several easy escapes from fulfilling their obligations, because the objectives set out therein have allowed for them to make excuses for not reaching the goal of general and complete disarmament. Countries can place qualifiers on joining treaties such as "I will not give up our nuclear weapons and disarm until other states do." "I will not join the CTBT until other states sign and ratify."

The TPNW, on the contrary, may be seen as more absolute in its intentions, perhaps accounting for its unpopularity with some states. The TPNW is unambiguous, non-amorphous, leaving very little room for interpretation. It is clear, definite, and perhaps somewhat radical, to some, in its ultimate goal: to eliminate nuclear weapons. An outcome which is supported by all of the disturbing consequences to human beings and is followed up with strict obligations that require immediate action toward disarmament.[95] Article VI of the NPT is somewhat vague and has no definite time line, effectively imposing no clear obligation or time frame. This is demonstrated by the fact that when states have tried to appeal to Article VI as a way of calling on another state to meet their obligation to disarm, the ICJ has allowed states to escape that obligation by arguing that fulfilling it depends on other NWS being a part of the negotiations.

In *Marshall Islands v. United Kingdom*, the Republic of Marshall Islands argued that the United Kingdom breached Article IV of the NPT, "by failing to pursue in good faith and bring to a conclusion negotiations leading to nuclear disarmament in all its aspects under strict and effective international control; . . . [as well as] by taking actions to qualitatively improve its nuclear weapons system and to maintain it for the indefinite future, and by failing to pursue negotiations that would end nuclear arms racing through comprehensive nuclear disarmament or other measures."[96] The ICJ quotes from the *Legality of the Threat or Use of Nuclear Weapons, Advisory Opinion, I.C.J. Reports 1996 (I)* pointing out that "[t]his twofold obligation to pursue and to conclude negotiations formally concerns [all] States parties to the [NPT], or, in other words, the vast majority of the international community," adding that "any realistic search for general and complete disarmament, especially nuclear disarmament, *necessitates the co-operation of all States*" (ibid., para. 100). One of the United Kingdom's objections is that other nuclear weapon states needed to be involved in the proceedings in order for the claim to be valid, at para 23.[97]

---

[94] See Nuclear Weapons Advisory Opinion, paras. 98–103.

[95] Treaty on the Prohibition of Nuclear Weapons, UNDOC A/CONF.229/2017/8 Article 4 requires "each State Party that owns, possesses or controls nuclear weapons or other nuclear explosive devices shall immediately remove them from operational status, and destroy them as soon as possible but not later than a deadline to be determined by the first meeting of States Parties, in accordance with a legally binding, time-bound plan for the verified and irreversible elimination of that State Party's nuclear-weapon programme, including the elimination or irreversible conversion of all nuclear-weapons-related facilities."

[96] See *Marshall Islands v. United Kingdom*, October 5, 2016, at para. 11.

[97] See *Marshall Islands v. United Kingdom*, October 5, 2016, and Legality of the Threat or Use of Nuclear Weapons, Advisory Opinion, I.C.J. Reports 1996 (I).

It would seem that according to this ruling, under the NPT, states can always argue that they are not obligated to initiate a negotiation because it depends on another state being willing to negotiate and the obligation only requires one to *pursue* negotiations not to actually come to agreement. They argue that the five-annual NPT review conferences and the various meetings and activities supporting this process represent their acting "in good faith" toward "effective measures relating to cessation of the nuclear arms race" and measures toward nuclear disarmament "under strict and effective international control" as required by Article VI. Their various agreements amount to attempts of "a treaty on general and complete disarmament." A treaty does not necessarily have to mean one all-encompassing document but could be a series of successive steps which they are trying to achieve. The TPNW, however, would not allow for the same level of creative compliance or varied interpretation afforded under the NPT. Moreover, those adopting it seem to be truly committed to its goals and not simply signing it to gain certain benefits – access to nuclear energy – without the burdens – nonproliferation and disarmament.

Article 4 of the TPNW requires states parties that possess nuclear weapons to come up with their own plan for disarmament which must be approved by all the states parties. This helps correct the power imbalance of the NPT which "effectively allows nuclear armed states to dictate the timetable and process for disarmament."[98] The TPNW would not allow for the same level of individual interpretation regarding meeting its goals and time lines on disarmament. The collective decision making is another way that the TPNW contrasts traditional disarmament because it both respects the individual voices of states parties, whether or not they have nuclear weapons, while demanding strict adherence to definite prohibitions and positive obligations to disarm and remedy the effects of nuclear weapons with tight deadlines.

As for enforcement *stricto sensu* or on dispute settlement, Article 11 addresses the settlement of disputes between two or more states parties relating to the interpretation or application of this Treaty.[99] In that respect the parties are required to consult together with a view to settling the dispute by negotiation or by other peaceful means, in accordance with Article 33 of the Charter of the United Nations. While some may see Article 11 as a weak procedure, this is standard for the purposes of interpretation, particularly regarding potential ambiguity. Article 31(1) of the VCLT states that, "A treaty shall be interpreted in good faith in accordance with the ordinary meaning to be given to the terms of the treaty in their context and in the light of its object and purpose."[100]

---

[98] Docherty, 18.
[99] Article 11. Treaty on the Prohibition of Nuclear Weapons, A/CONF.229/2017/8, Art. 7(4). See https://undocs.org/A/CONF.229/2017/8.
[100] See https://treaties.un.org/doc/Publication/UNTS/Volume%201155/volume-1155-I-18232-English.pdf.

70   *Humanitarian Nuclear Disarmament*

In summary, the provisions of the treaty aim to establish absolute preventative obligations which obliges states to adopt remedial measures to assist victims as well as to incorporate cooperative approaches to treaty implementation.

IMPACT ON NUCLEAR DISARMAMENT: PROCESS, PURPOSE AND PROVISIONS

The TPNW focuses on criticizing nuclear weapons and their destructive force. Its purpose is to eliminate nuclear weapons and explosive devices as well as to reduce the adverse human impact whilst establishing absolute preventative obligations. Despite these honorable intentions, some argue that the TPNW will be ineffective because it was boycotted by nuclear armed and umbrella states, crucially lacking their support. Regardless, supporters contend that overall humanitarian disarmament has accomplished more than traditional disarmament, pointing to the Mine and Cluster Munition treaties as concrete examples of successes, saying the same will prevail under the TPNW. Notably, over two decades on, the CTBT has still not entered into force,[101] and the NPT has failed to achieve its full objectives over a half a century on from its agreement and coming into force. The TPNW goes much further than existing international law governing nuclear weapons. Indeed, for the first time there is a treaty banning nuclear weapons and explosive devices. Docherty says:

> Despite longstanding moral outrage about nuclear weapons, until 2017, the international law dealing with nuclear weapons consisted only of partial prohibitions or restrictions. The NPT prohibited proliferation but did not require an immediate end to possession or use. The 1963 Partial (or Limited) Test Ban Treaty applied only to testing in outer space, underwater and the atmosphere; 104 as of April 2018, the CTBT had not entered into force. The nuclear-weapon-free zone agreements outlawed many nuclear weapon-related activities, but their legal effects were confined to certain regions.[102]

Needless to say, there are many reasons to celebrate the successes of the TPNW. Its advocates and negotiators are to be congratulated on their perseverance in getting this through the General Assembly and keeping the momentum going toward its eventual implementation. One amongst the many successes, it is a triumph for the humanitarian disarmament movement defying conventional armament approaches on such nuclear matters. "The TPNW challenges conventional wisdom that the road to nuclear disarmament should respect states' reliance on nuclear deterrence policies and proceed gradually ... By delegitimising nuclear deterrence policies, the TPNW removes a key obstacle to eliminating nuclear weapons." "The TPNW also rejects the premise that progress toward a world free of nuclear weapons should

---

[101] Note, however, that the CTBTO monitors compliance with the non-binding treaty.
[102] Docherty, 20.

Process, Purpose and Provisions 71

proceed incrementally ... The TPNW thus shows the feasibility of an expedited negotiating process and time-bound obligations for nuclear disarmament."[103]

It challenges conventional approaches to negotiating armament treaties as well as engages a wide range of participants in the process, extending a voice and legitimacy to non-traditional participants. Such a direct stance against conventional arms control without the support or participation of the powerful Security Council members or NATO could be seen as a rare triumph that defies power politics. In addition, the positive obligation imposed on states under the TPNW to address the humanitarian harm that is caused by nuclear weapons and testing is a firm departure from NPT obligations.[104] It addresses environmental concerns and the needs of victims affected.

> The imposition of positive obligations regarding victim assistance and environmental remediation constitutes a major development in the law governing nuclear weapons. Because previous treaties focused on security rather than humanitarian concerns, they did not seek to reduce the harm already caused by nuclear weapons, whether through use or testing. Certain states established compensation regimes, but they were national or bilateral, were not human rights based and sometimes required the establishment of legal liability.
>
> These positive obligations, modelled on humanitarian disarmament precedent, give the TPNW the power to have an immediate humanitarian impact. Their implementation does not depend on nuclear armed states, which are likely to remain outside the treaty for the near future. Instead affected states parties bear primary responsibility for the TPNW's remedial measures, and all other states parties must support them. Therefore, implementation can and should begin as soon as the treaty enters into force.[105]

Such successes are not to be understated in a contemporary global arms control context. Moreover, the greatest triumph for the TPNW is that it renders nuclear weapons illegal under an international treaty. Docherty contends that "[t]he TPNW makes nuclear weapons illegal as well as immoral ... By making nuclear weapons clearly and comprehensively unlawful, the TPNW not only limits the actions of states parties, but also increases the weapons' stigma, pressuring those outside the treaty to abide by its rules."[106]

There is little doubt that the process by which this treaty came about along with its purpose and provisions have raised questions amongst states relying on nuclear weapons for defense. There is evidence that this Treaty has disturbed the status quo in questioning the domination of the nuclear armed states over disarmament negotiations. As the humanitarian initiative progressed, the United States, France, Russia and the United Kingdom were said to have pressurized and made increasingly serious threats to states supporting the treaty. Specifically, Ruff reports:

---

[103] Docherty, 19.
[104] See Docherty, 19.
[105] Docherty, 21.
[106] Docherty, 20.

This pressure was coordinated and at times regionally allocated, and included diplomatic demarches and political, economic and aid threats. For example, the US reportedly threatened one heavily land-mined least developed country with the withdrawal of its funding support for clearance of landmines (mostly laid by the US) if the country voted in support of an UNGA resolution supporting banning nuclear weapons . . . In four[107] of the regions covered by nuclear-weapon-free zones – Africa, Latin America, Southeast Asia and the South Pacific – where support for disarmament and the Treaty is most widespread, pressure from nuclear-armed states forced some states not to vote or to abstain.[108]

While the actual impact the TPNW has had to date is difficult to measure, given its relative age, it is safe to say that its adoption at the UNGA has changed the disarmament world forever. The number of states who actually finally ratify the treaty remains to be seen but it has disturbed the status quo throughout the international community. The wider legal impact and political influence of the TPNW remains to be explored as will be discussed throughout this book.

CONCLUSION: IMPACT ON NUCLEAR DISARMAMENT

The humanitarian focus on process, purpose and provisions regarding the TPNW has led to a powerful result. Together, the aim of criticizing the harm caused by nuclear weapons, along with emphasizing the human suffering and humanitarian consequences of such weapons and devices have produced a significant set of provisions aimed at banning and eliminating nuclear weapons and addressing their adverse effects. This is a significant achievement, one that cannot be easily ignored or dismissed by its critics.

Considering the unique aspects of the TPNW that distinguish it from traditional disarmament approaches, it becomes clear that the humanitarian disarmament movement that gave rise to the TPNW is changing the way of conducting negotiations in the nuclear world. Firstly, humanitarian disarmament has taken a fresh path by building its argument on preventing suffering, and ensuring the safety, and security of human beings affected by nuclear weapons, rather than relying on state security and national self-interest. Secondly, humanitarian disarmament has exposed the alleged hypocrisy of nuclear armed states who say they are moving toward disarmament while at the same time they are building and modernizing their nuclear weapons. The TPNW has also changed the dialogue and leveled the playing field by including civil society groups, non-nuclear weapon states, and those that have been directly affected by nuclear weapons in the negotiation process, operated transparently, and redistributed power by ignoring the threats, grand-standing, and boycotts of the nuclear weapon states who refused to negotiate if they could not be in charge. In addition, the humanitarian disarmament process employed by the drivers

[107] Five regions with Central Asia.
[108] Ruff, 4.

Conclusion: Impact on Nuclear Disarmament 73

of TPNW was efficient and effective, producing a radical treaty that creates an absolute obligation to completely eliminate all nuclear weapons.

In conclusion, the starting point under the NPT was for the five NWS to be in control of the process and substance of any negotiations of a treaty to eliminate nuclear weapons under Article VI. They would drive the agenda thus placing them firmly at the center of any nuclear arms discussions. The NPT five annual quintennial review conferences served to solidify their position, squarely rendering them at the focal point of developments, setting and controlling the nuclear-arms control agenda and affirmed their places as the sole drivers of any progress on disarmament matters. The NPT effectively elevated the *Big Five* to a special elite status, allocating them a privileged position as the legitimate, and indeed, only negotiators. The TPNW process reversed this. It conversely removes the NWS from the heart of the discussion, reaching out to include those states that have acquired or aspired toward possessing nuclear weapons. The TPNW process has effectively realigned the status quo regarding who is driving and influencing the nuclear arms agenda on these matters. The purpose, process and provisions of the TPNW reversed this position. By creating and convening a separate forum and involving different players with different voices and views as to how to achieve the intended outcome of nuclear disarmament, the TPNW process has disrupted the status quo effectively creating a new normal, a form of disruptive innovation; a situation to which many NATO countries and umbrella states had grown accustomed and may now be in somewhat of a state of either disbelief or denial that the TPNW has been agreed. Adopted by a majority 122 countries, who, even though they do not have nuclear weapons, still count for a huge number of human beings against nuclear weapons, representing a significant percentage of the world's populations, we are perhaps reminded of the old adage, that the pen is mightier than the sword.

4

Legal Congruence with Existing Treaty Obligations: Toward Complementary or Competing Interests?

A NEW TREATY TOWARD NUCLEAR NONPROLIFERATION?

The text of the TPNW was agreed during a relatively short negotiation period. It includes comprehensive prohibitions regarding participation in any nuclear weapon activities, including undertakings not to develop, test, produce, acquire, possess, stockpile, use or threaten to use nuclear weapons. The Treaty prohibits the deployment of nuclear weapons on national territory and requires states parties to prevent and suppress any prohibited activity by persons within or on their territory or under their jurisdiction or control.[1]

On the face of it, it would seem that such a development would be welcomed in a world where there is an increasing fear of detonating nuclear devices. The negotiations surrounding the TPNW, however, were marked by the absence of all of the nuclear-weapon states, including those from NATO and states under nuclear-umbrella alliances, as well as states harboring nuclear ambitions. While the TPNW does not intend to prejudice existing international agreements or obligations undertaken by states parties,[2] important questions remain regarding the Treaty's relationship with existing treaties under international law. The purpose of this chapter is to assess the extent to which the TPNW is legally compatible and congruent with existing law and international obligations under the NPT and the CTBT. Note that an analysis regarding customary international law and the TPNW will follow in Chapter 5. This chapter will explore whether developments under the TPNW complement existing obligations or indeed may actually serve to compete with existing obligations, creating ambiguity and division, rather than legal harmony. Furthermore, discussion will examine the legally binding nature of this treaty, including to those states that have neither signed nor ratified it, particularly regarding its enforceability within the various jurisdictions adhering to the NPT and those intending to accept the CTBT.

---

[1] Article 5.
[2] Article 18.

LEGAL CONGRUENCE WITH EXISTING TREATY OBLIGATIONS

According to the Oxford dictionary, the word congruence means "agreement or harmony; compatibility."[3] The Cambridge dictionary lists the meaning as, "congruent ... similar to or in agreement with something, so that the two things can both exist or can be combined without problems ... there is no conflict."[4] The term is not normally used in a legal environment, but is often used in a business context, in particular to measure performance or opportunity gaps.[5] In the current discussion, the issue is whether there is agreement, harmony or compatibility between obligations set out in the TPNW and existing international treaty obligations. Specifically, the question to be addressed is whether the Treaty is similar to current systems, so the two sets of law can both exist or be combined without problems, such that there is no conflict.[6] Indeed, Article 18 stipulates that the TPNW "shall not prejudice obligations ... with regard to existing international agreements."[7] This indicates that any such obligations should be consistent with the Treaty.[8]

Relevant Nuclear Treaties and International Institutions in International Law

Following World War II, the world has witnessed the development and growth of nuclear weapons, which has raised significant concerns for military and human security throughout the international community.[9] Parallel to these developments have been successive and progressive attempts to limit and regulate the proliferation and use of nuclear explosives and devices on a global scale. To date, primary nonproliferation obligations are covered under comprehensive treaty regulations governing nuclear activities including the PTBT and the NPT. Such obligations require verification and enforcement guidelines through a variety of institutions and organizations working in a supervisory role to monitor nuclear activities including through the International Atomic Energy Agency (IAEA) and the European Atomic Energy Community (EURATOM) engaged in various aspects of enforcing treaty obligations as well as a variety of NGOs involved in supervising aspects of

---

3 See https://en.oxforddictionaries.com/definition/congruence.
4 See https://dictionary.cambridge.org/dictionary/english/congruent.
5 See Michael L. Tushman and Charles A. O'Reilly III, *Managerial Problem Solving: A Congruence Approach Excerpted from Winning through Innovation: A Practical Guide to Leading Organizational Change and Renewal* (Boston: Harvard Business School Press, 2007).
6 Other meanings include: accord, accordance, acquiescence, adjustment, affinity, agreement, coherence, coincide, common feature, compatibility, compliance, concert, conformance, conformity, congeniality, congruity, consensus, consistency, correspondence, harmony, likeness, oneness with, parallelism, relevance, similarity, understanding, uniformity, unison, unity.
7 Article 18.
8 Another reading, based on the rules applicable to successive treaties on the same subject matter, is that that already assumed obligations will continue to have to be observed notwithstanding the obligations assumed under this Treaty.
9 An estimated 95 percent of all nuclear arms are in the custody of the United States and Russia.

76   *Legal Congruence with Existing Treaty Obligations*

enforcement.[10] Complementing these developments is the CTBT, which is yet to come into legal force, with many of its obligations already being monitored by the Preparatory Commission for the Comprehensive Nuclear Test-Ban Treaty Organization (CTBTO).[11] The following discussion explores the significance of each of these treaties, setting the stage for an examination of their congruence with the TPNW.

Treaty on the Non-Proliferation of Nuclear Weapons (1968)

The NPT remains the cornerstone of nuclear nonproliferation obligations to prevent the spread of nuclear weapons and to promote cooperation in the peaceful uses of nuclear energy.[12] It recognizes (implicitly) five nuclear-weapons states under international law, namely the United States, Russia (formerly the Soviet Union), the United Kingdom, France and China. Article IX(3) states that, "a nuclear-weapon State is one which has manufactured and exploded a nuclear weapon or other nuclear explosive device prior to 1 January, 1967."[13] All remaining states parties are considered non-nuclear-weapon states for the purpose of the Treaty. Note that non-

---

[10] The wide range of relevant institutions may best be characterized by the following non-exhaustive list: International Atomic Energy Agency (IAEA), www.iaea.org; Preparatory Commission for the Comprehensive Nuclear-Test-Ban Organization (CTBTO), www.ctbto.org; UN Disarmament Commission (UNDC), www.un.org/Depts/ddar/discomm/undc.html; United Nations Office for Disarmament Affairs, www.un.org/disarmament/HomePage/about_us/aboutus.shtml; United Nations Institute for Disarmament Research (UNIDIR), unidir.org/html/en/home.html; International Law Commission (ILC), www.un.org/law/ilc/; Pugwash Conferences on Science and World Affairs, www.pugwash.org/about.htm; The Nuclear Threat Initiative, www.nti.org; the Arms Control Association, www.armscontrol.org; Acronym Institute, www.acronym.org.uk; World Institute for Nuclear Security (WINS), www.wins.org/index.php?article_id=61; the World Nuclear Association, www.world-nuclear.org; International Nuclear Law Association (INLA), www.nlain.org; Global Zero, www.globalzero.org; the Verification Research, Training and Information Centre (VERTIC), www.vertic.org; International Campaign to Abolish Nuclear Weapons (ICAN), www.icanw.org; The *Carnegie Endowment*, carnegieendowment.org; James Martin Center for Nonproliferation Studies, *Nonproliferation Review*, www.nonproliferation.org/research/nonproliferation-review; National Defense University's *Center for the Study of Weapons of Mass Destruction*, Washington, DC, wmdcenter.ndu.edu; Center for Energy and Security Studies (CENESS), Moscow, ceness-russia.org/engl; PIR Center. The Russian Center for Policy Studies, www.pircenter.org/en; the Landau Network based in Como (Italy), www.centrovolta.it/landau; the Insubria Center on International Security (University of Insubria, Italy), http://eeas.europa.eu/delegations/iraq/press_corner/all_news/news/2010/20100829_01_en.htm; Istituto Affari Internazionali, www.iai.it; Stiftung Wissenschaft und Politik, www.swp-berlin.org; Stockholm International Peace Research Institute SPRI; and the American Physical Society, www.aps.org/meetings.

[11] Comprehensive Nuclear Test-Ban Treaty Organization, see www.ctbto.org. See Sabine Bauer and Cormac O'Reilly, "The Comprehensive Nuclear Test Ban Treaty Organization (CTBTO): Current and Future Role in the Verification Regime of the Nuclear Test-Test-Ban Treaty," in Black-Branch and Fleck (eds.) *Nuclear Non-Proliferation in International Law: Vol. II Verification and Compliance* (Asser Press/Springer, 2016), 131–150; Jenifer Mackby, "Still Seeking, Still Fighting." 23 Nos. 3–4 *Nonproliferation Review* (2016), 261–286.

[12] Treaty on the Non-Proliferation of Nuclear Weapons (July 1, 1968, entered into force January 1, 1970), 729 *UNTS* 161.

[13] Article IX(3). Treaty on the Non-Proliferation of Nuclear Weapons (July 1, 1968), 729 *UNTS* 161. See www.un.org/disarmament/wmd/nuclear/npt/text.

Legal Congruence with Existing Treaty Obligations 77

parties are not bound by the NPT and general international law does not regulate possession of (nuclear) weapons.[14] Contrary to the spirit of the NPT, Israel,[15] India,[16] Pakistan[17] and the Democratic People's Republic of Korea (DPRK or North Korea) are understood to possess nuclear weapons. Of these states, Israel, India and Pakistan have never acceded to the NPT.[18]

Democratic People's Republic of Korea

North Korea became a Party to the NPT on December 12, 1985; it declared its withdrawal on March 12, 1993. Announcing its withdrawal, North Korea cited the resumption of joint US–South Korean military exercises, as a reason for its withdrawal, claiming such activities amounted to a nuclear war rehearsal against the DPRK. It also alleged a lack of impartiality on the part of the IAEA in dealing with its nuclear issues. The withdrawal was to enter into force on June 12, 1993 but one day before the withdrawal was to take effect the DPRK reached an agreement issuing a joint statement on June 11, 1993, announcing its suspension of the withdrawal. Since there is no rule for suspending the entering into force of a withdrawal notice under the NPT or under the general law of treaties, North Korea's status still remains somewhat obscure, effectively concluding that the IAEA could no longer oblige it to carry out its work under the comprehensive safeguards agreement, as required under the NPT.

With its history of strained relations regarding its nuclear program, on January 10, 2003 North Korea announced its decision to revoke its suspension of its 1993 notice of withdrawal stating that its formal withdrawal from the NPT would come into effect the next day, January 11, 2003. This was based on its original numerical calculation of having already fulfilled the withdrawal notice period minus one day. Given there is no system for suspending a withdrawal, or reinstating

[14] See *Nicaragua* case, Merits, para. 207 and in particular 269: "... in international law there are no rules, other than such rules as may be accepted by the State concerned, by treaty or otherwise, whereby the level of armaments of a sovereign State can be limited, and this principle is valid for all States without exception."

[15] Unconfirmed estimates for Israel's nuclear weapons stockpile range around eighty intact nuclear weapons and additional inventories of fissile materials of 0.3 tonnes highly enriched uranium (HEU) plus 0.84 ± 0.13 tonnes of separated plutonium, see Philip Schell and Hans M. Kristensen, "Israeli Nuclear Forces" and Alexander Glaser and Zia Mian, International Panel on Fissile Materials, "Global Stocks and Production of Fissile Materials, 2012," in *SIPRI Yearbook 2013* (Oxford: Oxford University Press, 2013) at 321–322 and 326–331. See also reports by the Federation of American Scientists (FAS), available online: www.fas.org/nuke/guide/israel/nuke and see Avner Cohen, *Israel and the Bomb* (Columbia University Press, 1998).

[16] See Security Council Resolution 1172 (1998); Agreement for Cooperation Between the Government of the United States of America and the Government of India Concerning Peaceful Uses of Nuclear Energy (October 10, 2008), available online: https://2001-2009.state.gov/p/sca/c17361.htm.

[17] See Security Council Resolution 1172 (1998); Agreement between the Government of Islamic Republic of Pakistan and the Government of Republic of India on Reducing the Risk from Accidents Relating to Nuclear Weapons (February 21, 2007), available online: www.stimson.org /agreement-on-reducing-the-risk-from-accidents-relating-to-nuclear-weap.

[18] See www.armscontrol.org/act/2005-05/features/npt-withdrawal-time-security-council-step.

78   *Legal Congruence with Existing Treaty Obligations*

a notice period, per se, legal analysis was required regarding the legality of North Korea's position. The IAEA treated the suspension as a revocation of the notice. In October 1994, the United States and North Korea concluded the Agreed Framework,[19] whereby Pyongyang undertook to freeze the operation and construction of nuclear reactors suspected of being part of a covert nuclear weapons program, in exchange for two proliferation-resistant nuclear power reactors. In addition, the United States agreed to supply North Korea with fuel oil pending construction of the reactors. The agreement was to be implemented under an international consortium called the Korean Peninsula Energy Development Organization.[20] After North Korea tested the Taepodong missile in 1998, the Clinton administration proceeded to take action, which was eclipsed by President Bush's election. A centrifuge program pursuing technology for a uranium enrichment program that could produce material for nuclear weapons was then revealed, leading to the ultimate abandonment of the Agreed Framework.[21] On January 10, 2003 North Korea declared an "immediate effectuation of its withdrawal from the NPT."[22] Some states did not receive the official notice lifting the suspension on January 10, 2003, nor was there a clear statement provided for reinstating the withdrawal notice.

State status is stipulated under Article IX(3) of the NPT whereby "a nuclear-weapon State is one which has manufactured and exploded a nuclear weapon or other nuclear explosive device prior to 1 January, 1967."[23] Being a non-nuclear weapon state, it must accept comprehensive safeguards as set by the International Atomic Energy Agency (IAEA) as per Article III(4), which states that non-nuclear-weapon states party to the Treaty shall conclude agreements with the IAEA to meet their Treaty requirements, either individually or together with other states in accordance with the Statute of the IAEA. North Korea gave notice on March 12, 1993 that it intended to withdraw from the NPT in accordance with Article X which provides that a party in exercising its national sovereignty has the right to withdraw from the Treaty, "if it decides that extraordinary events ... have jeopardized the supreme interests of its country."[24] A three-month notice of withdrawal period is required

---

[19] See www.iaea.org/sites/default/files/publications/documents/infcircs/1994/infcirc457.pdf.

[20] See Kelsey Davenport. The US-North Korean Agreed Framework at a Glance (July 2018). See www.armscontrol.org/factsheets/agreedframework.

[21] See Kelsey Davenport. The US-North Korean Agreed Framework at a Glance (July 2018). See www.armscontrol.org/factsheets/agreedframework.

[22] See www.atomicarchive.com/Docs/Deterrence/DPRKNPTstatement.shtml.

[23] Note that nuclear-weapon states are under an obligation not to transfer nuclear weapons or other nuclear explosive devices, or control over such weapons or devices, to any recipient whatsoever (Treaty on the Non-Proliferation of Nuclear Weapons – NPT (July 1, 1968), 729 *UNTS* 161 (Art. I)). Also, nuclear-weapon states are under an obligation not to transfer nuclear weapons or other nuclear explosive devices, or control over such weapons or devices, to any recipient whatsoever (Treaty on the Non-Proliferation of Nuclear Weapons – NPT (July 1, 1968), 729 *UNTS* 161 (Art. I)).

[24] Article X states: 1. "Each Party shall in exercising its national sovereignty have the right to withdraw from the Treaty if it decides that extraordinary events, related to the subject matter of this Treaty, have jeopardized the supreme interests of its country. It shall give notice of such withdrawal to all other Parties to the Treaty and to the United Nations Security Council three months in advance. Such notice shall include

Legal Congruence with Existing Treaty Obligations

under Article X, which must be submitted to the United Nations Security Council, as well as including a statement of the extraordinary events it regards as having jeopardized its supreme interests. Generally, it is a matter for the law of treaties to determine whether a state is a party to a valid treaty, and whether the treaty is in force for that state. The DPRK maintains that it has withdrawn from the NPT. It wants to be recognized as a nuclear-weapon state party, but, Article IX(3) stipulates that, "a nuclear weapon State is one which has manufactured and exploded a nuclear weapon or other nuclear explosive device prior to 1 January, 1967."[25]

The United Nations Security Council has requested North Korea to retract its withdrawal and to abandon all nuclear weapons and nuclear programs in a complete, verifiable and irreversible manner.[26] SC Res 1718 expressed its "firm conviction that the international regime on the nonproliferation of nuclear weapons should be maintained" and recalled that "the DPRK cannot have the status of a nuclear-weapon State in accordance with the Treaty on the Non-Proliferation of Nuclear Weapons."[27]

Iran

Iran, as a state party to the NPT, has not been compliant with applicable safeguards according to the IAEA[28] and has disregarded relevant Security Council resolutions.[29] In 2015, however, a Joint Plan of Action (JCPOA) adopted by the "EU3+3" and Iran,[30] which provides for a comprehensive solution, was endorsed by SC Res 2231.[31] The United States unilaterally withdrew from the JCPOA in May 2018. Starting in

---

a statement of the extraordinary events it regards as having jeopardized its supreme interests. 2. Twenty-five years after the entry into force of the Treaty, a conference shall be convened to decide whether the Treaty shall continue in force indefinitely, or shall be extended for an additional fixed period or periods. This decision shall be taken by a majority of the Parties to the Treaty."

[25] Note that nuclear-weapon states are under an obligation not to transfer nuclear weapons or other nuclear explosive devices, or control over such weapons or devices, to any recipient whatsoever (Treaty on the Non-Proliferation of Nuclear Weapons – NPT (July 1, 1968), 729 *UNTS* 161 (Art. I)).

[26] See Security Council Resolutions 1718 (2006), 1874 (2009), 2050 (2012), 2087 (2013) and 2094 (2013). See Jonathan D. Pollack, *No Exit. North Korea, Nuclear Weapons and International Security* (Routledge/IISS 2011).

[27] Security Council Resolutions 1718 (2006).

[28] See IAEA Report GOV/2013/40 of August 28, 2013, available online: www.iaea.org/sites/default/files/gov2013-40.pdf. The Committee will focus on the legal aspects of verification in its forthcoming Third Report.

[29] See Security Council Resolutions 1696 (2006), 1737 (2006), 1747 (2007), 1803 (2008), 1835 (2008), 1929 (2010) and 1984 (2011). It should be noted that many Security Council Resolutions have been challenged by a practice of non-compliance. See also Shannon N. Kile (ed.), *Europe and Iran: Perspectives on Non-Proliferation* (Oxford: Oxford University Press/SIPRI, 2005).

[30] Joint Plan of Action adopted by the "EU3+3" and Iran (November 24, 2013), available online: see www.treasury.gov/resource-center/sanctions/Programs/Documents/jpoa.pdf. See also Joint Statement by EU High Representative Catherine Ashton and Iran Foreign Minister Zarif (November 24, 2013), available online: www.europarl.europa.eu/meetdocs/2009_2014/documents/d-ir/dv/joint_st_ashton_zar/joint_st_ashton_zarif.pdf.

[31] See Dirk R. Haupt, "Legal Aspects of the Nuclear Accord with Iran and Its Implementation: International Law Analysis of Security Council Resolution 2231 (2015)," in Black-Branch and Fleck

80   *Legal Congruence with Existing Treaty Obligations*

May 2019, Iran stepped out of certain limitations on its enrichment activities and, in November 2019, acting director general of the IAEA, Cornel Feruta advised Iran to cooperate fully with the Agency in order to resolve outstanding issues: "As I reported to the Board on November 7th, the Agency has detected natural uranium particles of anthropogenic origin at a location in Iran not declared to the Agency. ... We have continued our interactions with Iran since then, but have not received any additional information and the matter remains unresolved."[32]

UNSC Resolution 2231[33] confers tasks on the Security Council relating to the implementation of the resolution. Operative paragraph 11 of the resolution provides that, acting under Article 41 of the Charter of the United Nations, within 30 days of receiving a notification by a JCPOA participant State of an issue that the JCPOA participant State believes constitutes significant non-performance of commitments under the JCPOA, it shall vote on a draft resolution.[34] Nevertheless, this has not triggered the reinstatement of Security Council sanctions yet. But if Iran persists in its alleged breaches, the parties to the JCPOA might insist on doing so.

Partial Nuclear Test Ban Treaty (1963)

The PTBT came about after a long effort involving the United Kingdom, the United States and the USSR in the late 1950s to end nuclear testing, which following a moratorium in 1960 and the Cuban missile crisis of October 1962, finally led to the breakthrough to achieve it. The PTBT was signed by the original parties[35] in August 1963 and entered into force on October 10, 1963. Despite the achievement, it did not prohibit underground tests as this was a bridge too far. Underground nuclear testing, therefore, continues to raise concerns regarding the need to further limit the testing of nuclear explosives and devices on a broader, more comprehensive, scale. Also, France was conducting atmospheric tests well into the 1970s. These were taken to the ICJ as will be discussed in subsequent chapters.[36]

Nuclear-Weapons-Free Zones and Regional Non-Nuclear Commitments

As will be discussed further in Chapter 9, today, there are five recognized NWFZ treaties and three others Treaties of interest, all of which have officially come into force. These are as follows: (1) Treaty of Tlatelolco 1967 (Latin America and the

---

(eds.) *Nuclear Non-Proliferation in International Law: Vol. III Legal Aspects for the Use of Nuclear Energy for Peaceful Purposes* (Asser Press/ Springer, 2016), 403–469.

[32] Acting Director General Urges Iran to Fully Cooperate with IAEA. Reported by Kendall Siewert. See www.iaea.org/newscenter/news/acting-director-general-urges-iran-to-fully-cooperate-with-iaea.

[33] See www.undocs.org/S/RES/2231(2015).

[34] See www.undocs.org/S/RES/2231(2015).

[35] The Union of Soviet Socialist Republics, the United Kingdom of Great Britain and Northern Ireland and the United States of America.

[36] See ICJ, *Nuclear Tests Cases* 1974.

Caribbean NWFZ); (2) Treaty of Rarotonga 1985 (South Pacific NWFZ); (3) Treaty of Bangkok 1995 (Southeast Asia NWFZ); (4) Treaty of Pelindaba 1996 (African NWFZ); (5) Treaty on a NWFZ in Central Asia 2006 (Central Asian NWFZ); (6) The Outer Space Treaty 1967; (7) The Antarctic Treaty; and (8) The Seabed Arms Control Treaty 1971.[37] Note that these NWFZs have a unique relationship with the NPT. To date, there is no treaty to establish a nuclear-weapon-free zone in the Middle East.

The Antarctic Treaty 1959

The Antarctic Treaty[38] was signed in Washington on December 1, 1959 and protects the Antarctic region including ice shelves. Originally signed by the twelve countries whose scientists had been active in and around the continent,[39] it has now been signed by fifty-three parties.[40] It prohibits any testing of any type of weapons,[41] including nuclear explosions,[42] or military use whatsoever,[43] peaceful and non-peaceful. It also bans all forms of storage of nuclear waste.[44] Enforcement of the Treaty is carried out by designated observers, who have authority to inspect any ships and aircraft in port and inspect all areas within the Antarctic region.[45] This Treaty does not use IAEA safeguarding for enforcement and verification.

The Outer Space Treaty 1967

The Outer Space Treaty, formally known as the Treaty on Principles Governing the Activities of States in the Exploration and Use of Outer Space, Including the Moon and Other Celestial Bodies (1967),[46] was concluded by the Legal Subcommittee in 1966 and adopted in the General Assembly that December and later entered into force in October 1967.[47] It is based largely on the Declaration of Legal Principles Governing the Activities of States in the Exploration and Use of Outer Space, adopted previously by the General Assembly in 1963, including new provisions.[48]

---

[37] UNODA, "Nuclear-Weapon-Free Zones" (accessed May 27, 2018), available online: see www.un.org /disarmament/wmd/nuclear/nwfz/.
[38] See www.ats.aq/e/antarctictreaty.html.
[39] See www.ats.aq/index_e.html.
[40] NWFZ Chart, Also see The Antarctic Treaty, December 1, 1959 (entered into force June 23, 1961), available online: Secretariat of the Antarctic Treaty www.ats.aq/e/ats.htm.
[41] Article I, Antarctic Treaty.
[42] Article V, Antarctic Treaty.
[43] Article I, Antarctic Treaty.
[44] Article V, Antarctic Treaty.
[45] NWFZ Chart.
[46] See http://disarmament.un.org/treaties/t/outer_space/text.
[47] UN General Assembly Resolution 2222 (XXI), December 19, 1966. See www.unoosa.org/oosa/en/ ourwork/spacelaw/treaties/outerspacetreaty.html.
[48] UN General Assembly Resolution 1962 (XVIII), December 13, 1963. See www.unoosa.org/oosa/en/ ourwork/spacelaw/principles/legal-principles.html.

82   *Legal Congruence with Existing Treaty Obligations*

The Treaty has 110 parties (as at June 2020), while several others have signed but not ratified.[49] The Treaty provides a basic framework regarding international space law[50] noting that, the exploration and use of outer space is to be carried out for the benefit and in the interests of all countries and shall be the province of all mankind.[51] Outer space is not subject to national appropriation by claim of sovereignty, by means of use or occupation, or by any other means;[52] and in the interest of maintaining international peace and security.[53]

Most notable for the purposes of this discussion, states shall not place nuclear weapons or other weapons of mass destruction in orbit or on celestial bodies or station them in outer space in any other manner.[54] Specifically, Article VI states:

> States Parties to the Treaty undertake not to place in orbit around the earth any objects carrying nuclear weapons or any other kinds of weapons of mass destruction, install such weapons on celestial bodies, or station such weapons in outer space in any other manner.
>
> The moon and other celestial bodies shall be used by all States Parties to the Treaty exclusively for peaceful purposes. The establishment of military bases, installations and fortifications, the testing of any type of weapons and the conduct of military manoeuvres on celestial bodies shall be forbidden. The use of military personnel for scientific research or for any other peaceful purposes shall not be prohibited. The use of any equipment or facility necessary for peaceful exploration of the moon and other celestial bodies shall also not be prohibited.

Again, the Treaty specifically prohibits Parties from placing objects carrying nuclear weapons in orbit around the earth, as well as any other kind of weapons of mass destruction. Moreover, they undertake not to install such weapons on celestial bodies, or to station them in outer space in any other manner. Although the mention of weapons of mass destruction is left open to interpretation with no definition and leaving potential for a broad and non-exhaustive list, nuclear weapons are expressly prohibited.

There is no reference the use of nuclear weapons in outer space, per se. This leaves questions regarding the use of ICBMs – intercontinental ballistic missiles – that may enter the jurisdiction of outer space, albeit for only a short period of their journey.

Within the solar system there is the sun with a range of celestial objects bound to it by gravitational pull, including planets (and dwarf planets) and their respective 169 known moons as well as comets, asteroids, meteors and meteorites. Article VI

---

49   See http://disarmament.un.org/treaties/t/outer_space.
50   See *United Nations Treaties and Principles on Outer Space*, UN Publication ST/SPACE/11, p. vi. See also International Space Law: United Nations Instruments 2017. www.unoosa.org/res/oosadoc/data/documents/2017/stspace/stspace61rev_2_0_html/V1605998-ENGLISH.pdf.
51   Article I.
52   Article II.
53   Article III.
54   Article IV.

contains provisions relevant to *jus ad bellum* in that the moon and other celestial bodies shall be used exclusively for peaceful purposes. In that regard, it prohibits the establishment of military bases, installations and fortifications. The Treaty bans testing any type of weapons, beyond nuclear and weapons of mass destruction, including conventional, and also forbids military maneuvers on celestial bodies. Notably, there is no direct reference to the right to self-defense, presumably not interfering with the inherent right under Article 51 of the UN Charter, and of course subject to international humanitarian principles and obligations.

Additionally, the Moon Agreement, formally known as Agreement Governing the Activities of States on the Moon and Other Celestial Bodies,[55] was adopted by the General Assembly in 1979[56] and entered into force in 1984. It reaffirms and elaborates on the Outer Space Treaty as it relates to the moon and other celestial bodies to be used exclusively for peaceful purposes; their environments should not be disrupted; and the United Nations should be informed about any stations built on such bodies.

The Seabed Arms Control Treaty 1971 – Prohibiting the Emplacement of Nuclear Weapons

The Seabed Arms Control Treaty 1971, is an arms control treaty with enforcement measures formally known as the Treaty on the Prohibition of the Emplacement of Nuclear Weapons and Other Weapons of Mass Destruction on the Sea-Bed and the Ocean Floor and in the Subsoil Thereof,[57] advancing important legal principles is intended to prevent the nuclear weapons and related conflict spreading to the seabed and ocean floor.[58] The Treaty was opened for signature on February 11, 1971 and entry into force May 18, 1972 and has ninety-four states parties and other signatories as of June 2020.

In its preamble it recognizes the common interest of mankind in the exploration and use of the seabed and the ocean floor for peaceful purposes. Notably, as an arms control Treaty it highlights that "the prevention of a nuclear arms race on the seabed and the ocean floor serves the interests of maintaining world peace, reduces international tensions and strengthens friendly relations among States."[59] It is meant to constitute a step toward the exclusion of the seabed, the ocean floor and the subsoil thereof from the arms race with an emphasis on nuclear. Indeed, it expressly states that it is "a step towards a treaty on general and complete disarmament under strict

---

[55] See www.unoosa.org/oosa/en/ourwork/spacelaw/treaties/intromoon-agreement.html.
[56] General Assembly Resolution 34/68. See www.unoosa.org/pdf/gares/ARES_34_68E.pdf; www.unoosa.org/oosa/en/ourwork/spacelaw/treaties/moon-agreement.html.
[57] See http://disarmament.un.org/treaties/t/sea_bed/text.
[58] See www.armscontrol.org/treaties/seabed-arms-control-treaty.
[59] Preamble.

84   *Legal Congruence with Existing Treaty Obligations*

and effective international control, and determined to continue negotiations to this end."

In particular, Parties undertake not to implant or emplace on the seabed and the ocean floor and in the subsoil thereof beyond the outer limit of a seabed zone, any nuclear weapons or any other types of weapons of mass destruction as well as structures, launching installations or any other facilities specifically designed for storing, testing or using such weapons.[60] Under Article II, the Treaty defines the outer limit of the seabed zone as coterminous with the twelve-mile outer limit of the zone referred to in part II of the Convention on the Territorial Sea and the Contiguous Zone.[61]

To ensure compliance with the objectives of the Treaty, states parties have the right to verify through observation the activities of other states parties on the seabed and the ocean floor and in the subsoil thereof beyond the agreed zone, without interfering with such activities.[62] Doubts regarding compliance require consultation toward removing such doubts. If, after which, such doubts remain, the state party with such doubts will notify the other states parties, and the parties concerned will cooperate on such further procedures for verification as may be agreed, including appropriate inspection of objects, structures, installations or other facilities that reasonably may be expected to be of a kind meant to be covered by the Treaty. Parties in the region of such activities, including any coastal state and other parties requesting, are entitled to participate in consultations and cooperation, following which a report will be circulated regarding the completion of further procedures for verification by the party that initiated such procedures.[63]

In the event that the state responsible for the activities giving rise to the reasonable doubts is not identifiable by observation of the object, structure, installation or other facility, the state party having such doubts will notify and make appropriate inquiries of states parties in the region of the activities and of any other state party. When the state party responsible for the activities is identified, cooperation and consultation will follow the above-mentioned procedure to deal with the matter from that point forward. If a state cannot be identified through these lines of inquiry regarding responsibility for the activities in question, then further verification procedures, including inspection, may be undertaken by the inquiring state party, inviting participation of the parties in the region of the activities, including any coastal state, and of any other party desiring to cooperate.[64]

---

[60]   Article I(1).

[61]   Signed at Geneva on April 29, 1958, and to be measured in accordance with the provisions of part I, section II, of that Convention and in accordance with international law (Article II). Such undertakings also apply to the sea-bed zone, except to the coastal State or to the sea-bed beneath its territorial waters (Article I).

[62]   Article III(1). Seabed Treaty 1971.

[63]   Article III(2). Seabed Treaty 1971.

[64]   Article III(3). Seabed Treaty 1971.

Legal Congruence with Existing Treaty Obligations 85

Where consultation and cooperation have not been able to remove the doubts concerning the activities and serious questions concerning the fulfillment of the Treaty obligations remain, a state party may refer the matter to the Security Council for consideration.[65]

Any state party may undertake verification using its own means, or with the full or partial assistance of any other state party, or through appropriate international procedures within the framework of the United Nations and in accordance with the UN Charter.[66] Any verification activities cannot interfere with activities of other states parties and must be conducted with due regard for rights recognized under international law, including the freedoms of the high seas and the rights of coastal states with respect to the exploration and exploitation of their continental shelves.[67]

Again, this is an arms control treaty, with enforcement measures, prohibiting the emplacement of nuclear weapons on the seabed and the ocean floor and in the subsoil thereof. The Treaty expressly left the promise of further developments. Specifically, Article V stipulates that the parties undertake to continue negotiations in good faith concerning further measures in the field of disarmament for the prevention of an arms race on the seabed, the ocean floor and the subsoil thereof.

Comprehensive Nuclear-Test-Ban Treaty (1996)

In January 1994, the Conference on Disarmament[68] began negotiating a comprehensive nuclear-test-ban treaty under an ad hoc committee to achieve this aim, after previous false starts since the mid-1970s.[69] Two working groups were established on February 16, 1994. Working Group 1 was to address issues of verification, while Working Group 2 would consider legal and institutional aspects of the Treaty.[70] In June 1996, a final draft treaty was presented to the Conference on Disarmament with an overwhelming majority of member states expressing their readiness to support the draft treaty. Only India opposed the adoption of the CTBT text at the Conference on Disarmament. This led Australia to take the CTBT for adoption by the UNGA. Only India voted against the enabling resolution. The CTBT was consequently adopted by the General Assembly and opened for signature in September 1996.[71] The basic obligations of this Treaty are outlined in Article 1, which commits States Parties "not

---

[65] Article III(4). Seabed Treaty 1971.
[66] Article III(5). Seabed Treaty 1971.
[67] Article III (6). Seabed Treaty 1971.
[68] See www.un.org/disarmament/wmd/nuclear/ctbt/. The Conference was "established in 1979 as the single multilateral disarmament negotiating forum of the international community, following the first Special Session on Disarmament (SSOD I) of the United Nations General Assembly held in 1978. The Director-General of UNOG is the Secretary-General of the Conference on Disarmament as well as the Personal Representative of the UN Secretary-General to the CD." See www.unog.ch /80256EE600585943/(httpHomepages)/6A03113D1857348E80256F04006755F6?OpenDocument.
[69] See www.ctbto.org/the-treaty/history-1945-1993/1977-94-renewed-test-ban-commitments/.
[70] See www.ctbto.org/the-treaty/1993-1996-treaty-negotiations/1993-95-prelude-and-formal-negotiations.
[71] By resolution General Assembly Resolution 50/245; see www.undocs.org/A/RES/50/245.

86   *Legal Congruence with Existing Treaty Obligations*

to carry out any nuclear weapon test explosion or any other nuclear explosion, and to prohibit and prevent any such nuclear explosion at any place under its jurisdiction or control."[72] In addition, they are "to refrain from causing, encouraging, or in any way participating in the carrying out of any nuclear weapon test explosion or any other nuclear explosion" and establish an international test monitoring and verification system.[73]

The CTBT[74] will enter into force 180 days following the ratification by the forty-four specific states listed in Annex 2, of which the vast majority have deposited their respective instruments of ratification.[75] The following eight states have not yet ratified the Treaty, as required under Article XIV: China, Democratic People's Republic of Korea, Egypt, India, Iran (Islamic Republic of), Israel, Pakistan and the United States.[76] China, Egypt, Iran, Israel and the United States have signed but not ratified; while the DPRK, India and Pakistan have yet to sign.

Article XIV of the CTBT specifies that if the Treaty has not entered into force three years after the date of the anniversary of its opening for signature, a conference may be held upon the request of a majority of ratifying states in order to facilitate the entry into force of the Treaty. The purpose of such conferences is to examine the extent to which the requirements for entry into force have been met, as well as to decide on measures to accelerate the ratification process. Conferences have been held for this purpose in 1999, 2001, 2003, 2005, 2007, 2009, 2011, 2013, 2017 and 2019.[77]

SCOPE AND IMPLEMENTATION OF THE CTBT: THE PREPARATORY COMMISSION FOR THE COMPREHENSIVE NUCLEAR TEST-BAN PREPARATORY ORGANIZATION[78]

The preamble of the CTBT notes the opportunity "to take further effective measures toward nuclear disarmament and against the proliferation of nuclear weapons in all its aspects" and stresses "the need for continued systematic and progressive efforts to reduce nuclear weapons globally, with the ultimate goal of eliminating those weapons, and of general and complete disarmament under strict and effective

---

[72]   Article I of the Comprehensive Nuclear-Test-Ban Treaty.
[73]   Article II of the Comprehensive Nuclear-Test-Ban Treaty.
[74]   As per Article XIV.
[75]   Algeria, Argentina, Australia, Austria, Bangladesh, Belgium, Brazil, Bulgaria, Canada, Chile, Colombia, Democratic Republic of the Congo, Finland, France, Germany, Hungary, Indonesia, Italy, Japan, Mexico, Netherlands, Norway, Peru, Poland, Romania, Republic of Korea, Russian Federation, Slovakia, South Africa, Spain, Sweden, Switzerland, Turkey, Ukraine, United Kingdom of Great Britain and Northern Ireland and Vietnam.
[76]   For a data sheet regarding signatures and ratifications see Daryl Kimball, *The Status of the Comprehensive Test Ban Treaty: Signatories and Ratifiers*, available online: www.armscontrol.org /factsheets/ctbtsig.
[77]   In reference to the most recent conference, see www.armscontrol.org/pressroom/2017-09/civil-society-leaders-renew-action-bring-ctbt-into-force. Update.
[78]   For a history of the CTBT as well as the CTBTO, see www.ctbto.org/the-treaty.

Scope and Implementation of the CTBT

international control."[79] Further, the preamble states that the Treaty will be an effective measure of nuclear disarmament and nonproliferation by "constraining the development and qualitative improvement of nuclear weapons and ending the development of advanced new types of nuclear weapons."[80] The Treaty prohibits all parties from conducting "any nuclear weapon test explosion or any other nuclear explosion."[81] To achieve this end, the Treaty establishes the Comprehensive Test Ban Treaty Organization (CTBTO),[82] consisting of a Conference of States Parties, an executive council, and a technical secretariat based in Vienna (also the home of the IAEA). The CTBTO will implement and enforce the Treaty while providing a forum for consultation and cooperation. The technical secretariat will implement verification procedures of the treaty, supervise the operation of the international monitoring system, and also receive, process, analyze and report on the data collected. The secretariat will also manage the international data[83] and be involved with on-site inspections.[84] The verification protocol sets out measures for the CTBTO to ensure compliance with the Treaty,[85] consisting of four main aspects: the international monitoring system, consultation and clarification, on-site inspections, and confidence-building measures.[86] The verification process will become operational when the CTBT enters into force.

Effectively, the CTBTO Preparatory Commission is an international organization established by the states signatories to the Treaty to *prepare* the Treaty for entry-into-force. It is an international organization, akin to an assembly of signatory states. While the Treaty is not yet in force, the CTBTO is making the necessary preparations for the implementation of the Treaty with a view to establishing a global verification regime, building upon a relationship agreement between the United Nations and the CTBTO which was adopted in 2000 by the UN General Assembly.[87] The TPNW arguably reinforces the CTBT's non-testing norm by indicating that states parties may not "test" nuclear weapons or other nuclear explosive devices.[88] In UN Security Council Resolution (UNSCR) 2310

---

[79] Comprehensive Nuclear-Test-Ban Treaty (CTBT), adopted by General Assembly Resolution 50/245 (September 10, 1996), 35 *ILM* 1439.

[80] Ibid.

[81] As per Article I.

[82] Article II.

[83] Union of Concerned Scientists, "Comprehensive Test Ban Treaty Summary," available online: www .ucsusa.org/nuclear-weapons/us-nuclear-weapons-policy/comprehensive-test-ban-treaty.html#bf-toc-4.

[84] For On-Site Inspection see Edward Ifft, On-Site Inspections under the Comprehensive Nuclear-Test-Ban Treaty1, available online: http://aip.scitation.org/doi/pdf/10.1063/1.5009217.

[85] Article IV.

[86] Union of Concerned Scientists, "Comprehensive Test Ban Treaty Summary," available online: www .ucsusa.org/nuclear-weapons/us-nuclear-weapons-policy/comprehensive-test-ban-treaty.html#bf-toc-4.

[87] Resolution A/RES/54/280.

[88] Arms Control Association, "Civil Society Leaders Call for Renewed Action to Bring Nuclear Test Ban Treaty Into Force at UN Conference" (September 20, 2017), available online: www.armscontrol.org /pressroom/2017-09/civil-society-leaders-renew-action-bring-ctbt-into-force.

88   *Legal Congruence with Existing Treaty Obligations*

on the CTBT of September 23, 2016 the Security Council called for early entry into force of Nuclear-Test-Ban Treaty, specifically for ratification by eight Annex 2 states that are yet to accede in what is referred to as the "Hold-Out States." Marking the twentieth anniversary of the call for signatures of the CTBT, the Security Council called upon the "hold-outs" to ratify the instrument and for all states to refrain from and maintain their moratoriums on nuclear-weapon tests or any other nuclear explosions.[89] Resolution 2310 (2016) was adopted by a vote of fourteen in favor to none against, with one abstention (Egypt). The Council further encouraged all state signatories to promote the instrument's universality, affirming that its early entry into force would help enhance international peace and security.[90] That said, the failure to actually bring the CTBT into force contributed to the frustration that invariably built momentum for the movement to create and adopt the TPNW.

TREATY ON THE PROHIBITION OF NUCLEAR WEAPONS 2017

The TPNW undoubtedly seeks to address perceived deficiencies in the existing nuclear nonproliferation and disarmament legal infrastructure, including those discussed above. In December 2016, the United Nations General Assembly[91] agreed to convene a Conference[92] to negotiate a legally binding instrument to prohibit nuclear weapons with a view to their total elimination, encouraging all UN Member States to participate, with the participation and contribution of various international organizations and civil society representatives.[93] The resolution to convene the Conference followed the recommendation of the Open-ended Working Group on taking forward multilateral disarmament negotiations, convened pursuant to resolution 70/33, which reported in September 2016[94] that "a legally binding instrument to prohibit nuclear weapons would establish general prohibitions and obligations as well as a political commitment to achieve and maintain a nuclear-weapon-free world. There was also an earlier open-ended working group of 2014 that was in part motivated by the three international conferences on the humanitarian consequences of nuclear weapons held in Oslo

---

[89]   Adopting Resolution 2310 (2016), Security Council Calls for Early Entry into Force of Nuclear-Test-Ban Treaty, Ratification by Eight Annex 2 Hold-Out States. www.un.org/press/en/2016/sc12530.doc.htm.

[90]   Ibid.

[91]   Resolution A/RES/71/258, adopted by the General Assembly on December 23, 2016.

[92]   United Nations Conference to Negotiate a Legally Binding Instrument to Prohibit Nuclear Weapons, Leading Towards Their Total Elimination.

[93]   Conferences were held in New York from March 27 to 31 and from June 15 to July 7, with a one-day organizational session in New York on February 16, 2017.

[94]   Report of the open-ended working group on taking forward multilateral nuclear disarmament negotiations, A/71/371 (September 1, 2016), available online: http://undocs.org/A/71/371.

Treaty on the Prohibition of Nuclear Weapons 2017

in 2013, Nayarit in 2014 and Vienna 2014.[95] The primary mandate of the Treaty open-ended working group was to address concrete effective legal measures, legal provisions and norms that would need to be concluded to attain and maintain a world without nuclear weapons."[96] This decision arrived at a time of growing fears regarding the escalation of North Korea's nuclear and ballistic missile program and mounting tensions with the United States. It should be noted that all nine states with nuclear weapons and states in nuclear alliances boycotted the negotiations; only the Netherlands attended due to a parliamentary edict but then voted against adoption of the Treaty at the very end.

The TPNW includes a comprehensive set of prohibitions on participating in any nuclear-weapon activities, including undertakings not to develop, test, produce, acquire, possess, stockpile, use or threaten to use nuclear weapons. The Treaty also prohibits the deployment of nuclear weapons on national territory and the provision of assistance to any state in the conduct of prohibited activities. States parties will also be obliged to prevent and suppress any activity prohibited to a state party under this Treaty undertaken by persons or on territory under their jurisdiction or control. Moreover, it obliges states parties to provide adequate assistance to individuals affected by the use or testing of nuclear weapons as well as to take necessary and appropriate measures regarding environmental remediation in areas under its jurisdiction or control contaminated as a result of activities related to the testing or use of nuclear weapons. To become a party, a state must ratify, accept, approve or accede to the Treaty and deposit an instrument for this purpose with the secretary-general of the United Nations.[97]

Article 18 of the new Treaty specifies that "[t]he implementation of this Treaty shall not prejudice obligations undertaken by States Parties with regard to existing international agreements, to which they are party, where those obligations are consistent with the Treaty."[98] It is important to note that no other multilateral nuclear weapons treaty of this nature has been adopted since the NPT in 1968. Note that the Treaty on the Prohibition of Nuclear weapons in Latin America and the Caribbean (Tlatelolco Treaty) of 1967 was the first to prohibit nuclear weapons, albeit in a specified region. Questions remain about what this means regarding its position in terms of treaty law generally but also how specific articles will, if at all, inter-relate to one another. Specifically, Article 1 of the TPNW provides:

---

[95] See www.unog.ch/80256EE600585943/(httpPages)/160EB2DDE30CCE6BC1257B10003A81A9? OpenDocument.

[96] "United Nations Conference to Negotiate a Legally Binding Instrument to Prohibit Nuclear Weapons, Leading Towards Their Total Elimination: Background information" (2017), available online: www.un.org/disarmament/tpnw/index.html.

[97] See "Treaty on the Prohibition of Nuclear Weapons: Signature and Ratification," available online: https://s3.amazonaws.com/unoda-web/wp-content/uploads/2017/08/Treaty-on-the-Prohibition-of-Nuclear-Weapons-information-kit-on-signature-and-ratification.pdf.

[98] Article 18. See https://undocs.org/A/CONF.229/2017/8.

Each State Party undertakes never under any circumstances to:

(a) Develop, test, produce, manufacture, otherwise acquire, possess or stockpile nuclear weapons or other nuclear explosive devices;
(b) Transfer to any recipient whatsoever nuclear weapons or other nuclear explosive devices or control over such weapons or explosive devices directly or indirectly;
(c) Receive the transfer of or control over nuclear weapons or other nuclear explosive devices directly or indirectly;
(d) Use or threaten to use nuclear weapons or other nuclear explosive devices;
(e) Assist, encourage or induce, in any way, anyone to engage in any activity prohibited to a State Party under this Treaty;
(f) Seek or receive any assistance, in any way, from anyone to engage in any activity prohibited to a State Party under this Treaty;
(g) Allow any stationing, installation or deployment of any nuclear weapons or other nuclear explosive devices in its territory or at any place under its jurisdiction or control.[99]

The Treaty's Congruence with the CTBT

While one may not think that the CTBT would be in conflict with the TPNW as the CTBT imposes a comprehensive ban on nuclear testing, nevertheless concerns are expressed. The prohibition on testing was a most controversial element included in the draft text of the TPNW. There was a fear that it might undermine the CTBT. From the outset, this author notes the risk that observers and negotiators may unnecessarily confuse matters pertaining to the TPNW and the CTBT. It is essential to note that each is a separate multilateral instrument with its own unique obligations and restrictions; the CTBT does not need to be affirmed by the TPNW or any other treaty. The CTBT prohibits all nuclear tests and parties to the CTBT are legally bound by its terms. The TPNW in its Preamble states that: *"Recognizing* the vital importance of the Comprehensive Nuclear-Test-Ban Treaty and its verification regime as a core element of the nuclear disarmament and non-proliferation regime"; thus it gives recognition to the CTBT. In its Article 1(a), the TPNW prohibits nuclear tests meaning that there is no incompatibility or incongruence with the CTBT. Thus, various discussions that the TPNW "reinterprets" other treaties could be seen as unwarranted or incorrect.

During negotiations of the TPNW, there was disagreement around whether or not the Treaty's prohibitions under this section should actually include nuclear testing.[100] However, the majority supported the reaffirmation of the CTBT's

---

[99] Treaty on the Prohibition of Nuclear Weapons, A/CONF.229/2017/8 (July 7, 2017), available online: http://undocs.org/A/CONF.229/2017/8.

[100] See Gaukhar Mukhatzhanova, "Nuclear Weapons Treaty, Negotiation and Beyond" (September 2017), *Arms Control Today*, available online: www.armscontrol.org/act/2017-09/features/nuclear-weapons-prohibition-treaty-negotiations-beyond.

importance in the preamble, which states that the states parties to this treaty do in fact recognize its importance and especially its verification regime, a key element regarding nuclear disarmament and nonproliferation.[101] While some believed that such an inclusion of testing in Article 1 might be redundant because of the existence of the CTBT, others thought it might serve to undermine efforts to bring the CTBT into force. Nevertheless, the majority of states involved in the negotiations supported the reaffirmation of the CTBT's importance in the preamble.[102] However, what this "reaffirmation" of the CTBT's importance actually means remains to be seen. Would its inclusion in the preamble mean that those who ratify the TPNW have to comply with the CTBT as well? And, even if they are not contracting parties to the CTBT themselves? Or does it simply mean that the treaty just recognizes the CTBT as being important and nothing more?[103]

Austria and Mexico contended that testing would be covered by a development ban. Further, they said, a separate testing prohibition would raise issues of consistency with the CTBT.[104] Although the TPNW drew on language from the CTBT regarding the prohibition on testing in Article 1, some say that the text failed to address the relationship of the two treaties, as it did for the NPT. Also, it did not specify that adherence to the CTBT is required in order to ensure compliance with a prohibition on nuclear weapons testing.[105] Noting such concerns among some of the member states and signatories that the TPNW is actually in conflict with the CTBT, Alexander Marschik, the political director of the Austrian Foreign Ministry, said that the TPNW's text "recognizes the vital importance of the CTBT and its verification regime as a core element of the nuclear disarmament and non-proliferation architecture." He added that the Treaty's "formulations regarding testing were very carefully drafted to ensure they are fully compatible with the CTBT. Moreover, there is reason for hope that the success of the new prohibition treaty negotiations will create a positive impulse for our common objective here: the entry into force of the CTBT and the cessation of nuclear testing."[106] Even after Marschik's statements, however, there

remained uncertainty for some observers as to the precise relationship between

---

[101] See Preamble of the Treaty on the Prohibition of Nuclear Weapons, A/CONF.229/2017/8 (July, 7 2017), available online: http://undocs.org/A/CONF.229/2017/8.

[102] See Gaukhar Mukhatzhanova, "Nuclear Weapons Treaty, Negotiation and Beyond" (September 2017), *Arms Control Today*, available online: www.armscontrol.org/act/2017-09/fea tures/nuclear-weapons-prohibition-treaty-negotiations-beyond.

[103] Ibid.

[104] See John Burroughs, "Key Issues in Negotiations for a Nuclear Weapons Prohibition Treaty" (2017) *Arms Control Today*, available online: www.armscontrol.org/act/2017-06/features/key-issues-negotiations-nuclear-weapons-prohibition-treaty.

[105] See William C. Potter, "Disarmament Diplomacy and the Nuclear Ban Treaty," (2017) 59:4 *Survival* at 75–108, DOI: 10.1080/00396338.2017.1349786.

[106] See Shervin Taheran, "Trump Administration Silent on CTBT" (October 2017) *Arms Control Today*, available online: www.armscontrol.org/act/2017-10/news/trump-administration-silent-ctbt.

the TPNW and the CTBT. Again, while many would see them as separate treaties with their obligations and restrictions; others would not. For TPNW supporters, however, both the CTBT and the TPNW are viewed as "effective measures," as called for in NPT Article VI.

In particular, one could be concerned about the TPNW's effects on monitoring. The prohibition of testing of nuclear weapons in the draft text does not include a reference to the CTBT's International Monitoring System (IMS), a global network of sensors which detect nuclear explosions. Arguably, duplicating the language of the CTBT – which bans nuclear testing – without making any direct reference to the IMS might be seen as undermining that treaty.[107] Explicit reference is made to the CTBT, but no mention is made to clear or precise monitoring, verification or other compliance issues, whereas other treaties such as the CTBT have such a provision. This has raised a great deal of concern throughout the international community. According to John Burroughs, the treaty does safeguard fissile materials and the detection of nuclear explosive testing. However, verification of a development prohibition probably will not be possible in the near future. As such, monitoring will now have to be done through peer review among states parties, national intelligence, civil society monitoring and whistleblowers, who ideally would be protected by the treaty.[108] These issues of monitoring appear to set the TPNW apart from the language of the CTBT and the monitoring processes of the IMS. Others may say that such discussion raises moot points on little relevance or substance.

Furthermore, the TPNW envisages a broader disarmament process, seeking to consider how to ensure that signatories comply with commitments for three classes of states (i.e., established non-NWS that join the treaty, transitional NWS that commit to eliminate their weapon stockpiles when joining the treaty, and legacy NWS with latent capabilities after having joined the treaty).[109] This distinction is not present in the CTBT.

As discussed, there are potential areas of conflict between the TPNW and other international legal obligations. In addition, disagreement regarding the interplay between the CTBT and the TPNW was clear during deliberations relating to the Treaty. Mexico, the Netherlands, Sweden and Switzerland expressed concerns about harming the CTBT. In an attempt to mitigate potential damage, Switzerland, supported by the Netherlands and Sweden, suggested adding "in

---

[107] See Alicia Sandres-Zakre, "Ban Talks Advance with Treaty Draft" (June 2017) *Arms Control Today*, available online: www.armscontrol.org/act/2017-06/news/ban-talks-advance-treaty-draft.

[108] See John Burroughs, "Key Issues in Negotiations for a Nuclear Weapons Prohibition Treaty" (2017) *Arms Control Today*, available online: www.armscontrol.org/act/2017-06/features/key-issues-negotiations-nuclear-weapons-prohibition-treaty.

[109] Zia Mian, "Addressing Verification in the Nuclear Ban Treaty" (2017) *Arms Control Today*, available online: www.armscontrol.org/act/2017-06/features/addressing-verification-nuclear-ban-treaty.

accordance with the CTBT" to the text on testing, but this proposal was not taken up.[110] Algeria, Cuba and Iran, among others, however, tried to broaden the scope of the testing prohibition, apparently with a view to "fixing" perceived loopholes in the CTBT. They argued for a specific reference to subcritical tests and computer simulations and objected to the use of the CTBT formulation prohibiting "any nuclear test explosion or any other nuclear explosion." One such loophole may relate to the issue of subcritical tests. Additionally, the question of dual purpose, for both peaceful and weapons goals, also raises concerns. Furthermore, Egypt and Iran opposed any mention of the CTBT's importance in the preamble of the prohibition treaty.[111]

Gaukhar Mukhatzhanova points out that the uneasy compromise ultimately devised by Ambassador Whyte Gómez of Costa Rica, who chaired negotiations, was to include "test" among the core prohibitions under Article 1(a), so that states parties to the TPNW would undertake "never under any circumstances to . . . test . . . nuclear weapons or other nuclear explosive devices." This broad formulation did not fully satisfy either side of the debate. States such as Cuba, Iran and Nigeria announced that they would interpret this text as encompassing "all forms" of nuclear testing, including subcritical testing, although that does not constitute an agreed interpretation of the TPNW. The broader interpretation means little in practical terms because there is no verification in place for subcritical testing and computer simulations, and the nuclear-armed states are not joining the TPNW in the foreseeable future. Yet, the TPNW's ambiguous language[112] could exacerbate the criticism that the Treaty reinterprets or otherwise undermines existing instruments.[113,114]

Subcritical nuclear tests are a component of the US Department of Energy's Science Based Stockpile Stewardship Management Program, intended to show whether nuclear weapons components such as plutonium and uranium will

[110] See "Compilation of Amendments Received from States on the Revised Draft Submitted by the President Dated 30 June 2017; A/CONF.229/2017/CRP.1/Rev.1" (June 30, 2017), available online: https://s3.amazonaws.com/unoda-web/wp-content/uploads/2017/06/CRP1_rev1_compilation_30-June-1-2_8pm.docx.

[111] See Gaukhar Mukhatzhanova, "Nuclear Weapons Treaty, Negotiation and Beyond" (September 2017), *Arms Control Today*, available online: www.armscontrol.org/act/2017-09/features/nuclear-weapons-prohibition-treaty-negotiations-beyond.

[112] Some may say that the TPNW prohibits nuclear tests period and it is not within its ambit to define a nuclear test (just as the CTBT does not define a nuclear test or explosion).

[113] See Gaukhar Mukhatzhanova, "Nuclear Weapons Treaty, Negotiation and Beyond" (September 2017), *Arms Control Today*, available online: www.armscontrol.org/act/2017-09/features/nuclear-weapons-prohibition-treaty-negotiations-beyond.

[114] Documents generally referred to are: "Compilation of Amendments Received from States on the Revised Draft Submitted by the President Dated 30 June 2017," A/CONF.229/2017/CRP.1/Rev.1 (June 30, 2017), available online: https://s3.amazonaws.com/unoda-web/wp-content/uploads/2017/06/CRP1_rev1_compilation_30-June-1-2_8pm.docx and "Compilation of Amendments Received from States on the Revised Preamble," A/CONF.229/2017/CRP.1/Rev.1 (June 29, 2017), available online: https://s3.amazonaws.com/unoda-web/wp-content/uploads/2017/06/CRP1_rev1_compilation_29-June-2.docx.

develop problems as they age. In these instances, the blasts will not produce a nuclear chain-reaction explosion and are referred to as "subcritical" because they never reach "critical mass."[115] Some antinuclear peace activists claim that such subcritical tests violate the spirit of the CTBT and could introduce a new round of the nuclear arms race. Questions remain as to whether the TPNW includes subcritical tests, this author would hope that they are implicitly included in the treaty, although not explicitly. Others would say that the CTBT defines its prohibitions and verification; sub-critical tests were not banned as prohibition of these cannot be verified, hence there is no benefit in reopening this discussion with in the TPNW context.

The Treaty's Congruence with the NPT

Beyond issues of interrelations with the CTBT, the TPNW's preamble also mentions the NPT, reaffirming: "the full and effective implementation of the Treaty on the Non-Proliferation of Nuclear Weapons, which serves as the cornerstone of the nuclear disarmament and non-proliferation regime, has a vital role to play in promoting international peace and security."[116] While advocates of the TPNW may have held the draft as a clear and strong basis for a nuclear-weapons prohibition, treaty skeptics raise important questions about the text's uncertain relationship to existing nonproliferation treaties.[117] In an effort to allay concerns that the TPNW might contradict the NPT, the draft text declares that the ban treaty will not influence the "rights and obligations" of states under the NPT. Some experts, however, claim the NPT "allows for temporary and limited nuclear possession, and thus a treaty prohibiting nuclear weapons altogether would inherently infringe upon the NPT rights of nuclear-weapons states" and even "advocates counter that the NPT does not allow for the indefinite possession of nuclear weapons and therefore the two treaties are compatible."[118] This debate will play out in further discussions. Note that the TPNW is binding only on those states that sign and ratify it, not on non-signatories. Hence, it could be argued that there is no abridgement of rights of NWS if they do not adhere to the TPNW, based on the view that each treaty is free-standing and has its own obligations and *travaux preperatoires*. To do otherwise may presuppose a hierarchy of treaties or a primacy function which do not exist.

---

[115] See www.nuclearfiles.org/menu/key-issues/nuclear-weapons/issues/testing/subcritical-what-is-st.htm.

[116] See Preamble of the Treaty on the Prohibition of Nuclear Weapons, A/CONF.229/2017/8 (July 7, 2017), available online: http://undocs.org/A/CONF.229/2017/8.

[117] See Alicia Sandres-Zakre, "Ban Talks Advance with Treaty Draft" (June 2017) *Arms Control Today*, online: www.armscontrol.org/act/2017-06/news/ban-talks-advance-treaty-draft.

[118] Ibid.

Addressing Situations of Incongruence under International Law

The 1969 Vienna Convention on the Law of Treaties (VCLT) addresses situations involving successive treaties relating to the same subject matter.[119] Article 30 suggests that when a treaty specifies that it is subject to – or that it is not to be considered as incompatible with an earlier or later treaty – the provisions of that other treaty will prevail. The apparent incongruence between the TPNW and previous treaties is not an unprecedented phenomenon. As Mark E. Villiger has observed,

> Conflicts of norms, "in particular of treaty provisions," are a common feature of international law in view of its decentralised structure, the concomitant absence of common norm-setting agencies, the rise of international cooperation and, as a result, the considerable number of new treaties concluded by the international community each year.[120]

Article 18 of the TPNW would require consistency. Article 18 indicates that the Treaty "shall not prejudice obligations ... with regard to existing international agreements," but such obligations have to be "consistent" with the TPNW. That said, it would appear that some of the provisions do not actually align and thus are not consistent with the NPT. For example, some would see it as the NPT, allowing[121] some states (specifically, NWS) to possess nuclear weapons whereas the TPNW does not permit this distinction.[122] By not permitting such variations and by focusing on a uniform ban, the overall intent of the TPNW is different. In addition, the TPNW explicitly prohibits states from allowing "any stationing, installation or deployment" of nuclear weapons on their respective territories, which could be said to be inconsistent with the NPT which may be seen to do so – although not explicitly stated following a strict interpretation of Article II. That is, some non-NWS, under NATO and allied arrangements, have weapons within their respective territories, albeit under the direct control of the United States as will be discussed in Chapter 6.

The major hurdle facing the TPNW now is implementation. The manner by which treaty law becomes binding in nature requires the express consent of a state, or it will not be legally enforceable under international law against that state.

---

[119] For a broader discussion on Article 30, see Alexander Orakhelashvili, "Article 30 of the 1969 Vienna Convention on the Law of Treaties: Application of the Successive Treaties Relating to the Same Subject-Matter" (May 1, 2016) 31:2 *ICSID Review – Foreign Investment Law Journal* at 344–365, available online: https://doi.org/10.1093/icsidreview/siw003.

[120] See overview of Mark E. Villiger, "Article 30: Application of Successive Treaties Relating to the Same Subject-Matter," in *Commentary on the 1969 Vienna Convention on the Law of Treaties* (2008) at 395–412 (E-ISBN: 9789004180796), available online: http://booksandjournals.brillonline.com/content/books/b9789004180796_036.

[121] Others would say that it does not "allow" them, per se, but merely defines a NWS for the purposes of the NPT and it is a misbegotten view that the NWS are "allowed" nuclear weapons.

[122] See Carlo Trezza, "The UN Nuclear Ban Treaty and the NPT: Challenges for Nuclear Disarmament" (September 9, 2017) *Instituto Affari Internazionali*, available online: www.iai.it/en/pubblicazioni/un-nuclear-ban-treaty-and-npt-challenges-nuclear-disarmament.

Treaty Law Requires Express Agreement

For issues of congruence to become relevant for NWS, the TPNW must actually be accepted by those states. The starting point for any discussion regarding the enforcement of any treaty begins with its ratification status. Is the TPNW legally binding law for the state in question? In examining how states might be bound by the Treaty, a helpful starting point is to return to the basic sources of public international law. Specifically, Article 38(1) of the Statute of the International Court of Justice provides that in deciding a dispute, in accordance with international law, the Court shall apply,

> a. international conventions, whether general or particular, establishing rules expressly recognized by the contesting states;
> b. international custom, as evidence of a general practice accepted as law;
> c. the general principles of law recognized by civilized nations;
> d. subject to the provisions of Article 59, judicial decisions and the teachings of the most highly qualified publicists of the various nations, as subsidiary means for the determination of rules of law.[123]

Any treaty – be it the TPNW, the NPT, or the CTBT – has been agreed to under a negotiating process. A state would be required to consent to the TPNW in order to be bound by it, in accordance with Article 38(1)(a). In relation to treaty law, the most recent version on the *International Court of Justice Handbook* states that,

> The expression "international conventions" in Article 38, paragraph 1, is a broad one, covering not only bilateral and multilateral treaties and conventions formally so called, but also all other international understandings and agreements, even of an informal nature, provided that they establish rules recognized and accepted by the States parties to the dispute. The ICJ has emphasized that manifest acceptance or recognition by a State of a convention is necessary before the convention can be applied to that State.[124]

Article 16 of the TPNW allows for no reservations. Any interpretation must be considered in relation to Articles 11–17 and 34–37 VCLT. Once ratified, Article 31(3)(c) of the VCLT stipulates that, in interpreting a treaty, "any relevant rules of international law applicable in the relations between the parties" would have to be taken into account. Furthermore, Article 26 of the VCLT requires that every treaty in force is binding upon the parties and is to be performed in good faith, *pacta sunt servanda*. Without ratification, approval or accession, however, a treaty is not enforceable.

---

[123] Notably, under paragraph 2, "This provision shall not prejudice the power of the Court to decide a case ex aequo et bond, if the parties agree thereto." See http://legal.un.org/avl/pdf/ha/sicj/icj_statu te_e.pdf and see also www.icj-cij.org/en/statute.

[124] See Registry ICJ, *International Court of Justice Handbook*, 6th ed. (Maubeuge, France: Triangle Bleu, 2014) at 96, available online: www.icj-cij.org/files/publications/handbook-of-the-court-en.pdf.

Treaty on the Prohibition of Nuclear Weapons 2017

Notably, the TPNW is not an enforceable convention for those states refusing to accept it. Although having been negotiated through a legitimate process with UN General Assembly approvals throughout the process, questions remain regarding its wider acceptance. In a joint press statement from the Permanent Representatives to the United Nations of the United States, United Kingdom and France, the Representatives state:

> We do not intend to sign, ratify or ever become party to it. Therefore, there will be no change in the legal obligations on our countries with respect to nuclear weapons. For example, we would not accept any claim that this treaty reflects or in any way contributes to the development of customary international law. Importantly, other states possessing nuclear weapons and almost all other states relying on nuclear deterrence have also not taken part in the negotiations.[125]

Given this opposition to the TPNW by the NWS, and other nuclear-armed states such as India[126] and Pakistan[127] making similar statements,[128] the TPNW will not become legally enforceable under international law for them. In their joint statement they emphasize that,

> This initiative clearly disregards the realities of the international security environment. Accession to the ban treaty [TPNW] is incompatible with the policy of nuclear deterrence, which has been essential to keeping the peace in Europe and North Asia for over 70 years. A purported ban on nuclear weapons that does not address the security concerns that continue to make nuclear deterrence necessary cannot result in the elimination of a single nuclear weapon and will not enhance any country's security, nor international peace and security. It will do the exact opposite by creating even more divisions at a time when the world needs to remain united in the face of growing threats, including those from the DPRK's ongoing proliferation efforts. This treaty offers no solution to the grave threat posed by North Korea's nuclear program, nor does it address other security challenges that make nuclear deterrence necessary. *A ban treaty also risks undermining the existing international security architecture which contributes to the maintenance of international peace and security.* [Emphasis added][129]

---

[125] "Joint Press Statement from the Permanent Representatives to the United Nations of the United States, United Kingdom and France Following the Adoption of a Treaty Banning Nuclear Weapons 7 July 2017" (July 7, 2017), *United States Mission to the United Nations*, available online: https://usun.state.gov/remarks/7892.

[126] See India not participating in UN talks on nuclear weapons ban. https://economictimes.indiatimes.com/news/defence/india-not-participating-in-un-talks-on-nuclear-weapons-ban/articleshow/57873885.cms?from=mdr.

[127] See Pakistan says not bound by treaty on prohibition of nuclear weapons. See https://economictimes.indiatimes.com/articleshow/59955068.cms?utm_source=contentofinterest&utm_medium=text&utm_campaign=cppst.

[128] See https://southasianvoices.org/a-joint-india-pakistan-initiative-on-the-humanitarian-impact-of-nuclear-weapons/.

[129] "Joint Press Statement from the Permanent Representatives to the United Nations of the United States, United Kingdom and France Following the Adoption of a Treaty Banning Nuclear

Legal Congruence with Existing Treaty Obligations

This is the nub of the problem: rejection of deterrence by many NNWS and reliance on deterrence by NWS and their allies. Thus, considering that nuclear deterrence is not illegal, per se, the argument is not necessarily a legal one for them, but political. They would say that they are forced to reconcile idealism with reality. Indeed, the Pakistani delegation made this point to the UNGA First Committee in 2017, stating that "this initiative faltered by ignoring the fundamental security considerations that underpin nuclear disarmament. While we empathise with the sense of disappointment that propelled its proponents, it only led us to the conclusion that the launch of such initiatives outside the CD, on a non-consensus basis and without all the key stakeholders on board, no matter how well intentioned and justified, would not lead to any real change on ground."[130]

Whilst some may admire the sentiment behind the concept of humanitarian disarmament, as advocated by civil society groups and the Armed Conflict and Civilian Protection Initiative, to ban nuclear weapons under a "people-centered" approach, the political and military reality remains. What will fill the deterrence void that would be created in removing the nuclear architecture? What is an adequate replacement? To that end they contend:

> We reiterate in this regard our continued commitment to the Treaty on the Non-Proliferation of Nuclear Weapons (NPT) and reaffirm our determination to safeguard and further promote its authority, universality and effectiveness. Working towards the shared goal of nuclear disarmament and general and complete disarmament must be done in a way that promotes international peace and security, and strategic stability, based on the principle of increased and undiminished security for all.
>
> We all share a common responsibility to protect and strengthen our collective security system in order to further promote international peace, stability and security.[131]

The NWS took an adamant stance against the negotiations. Their absence of engagement throughout the process, and their refusal to accept the final TPNW text cannot be overstated. Together with other nuclear-armed states, it is unlikely they will accede and give express consent to a treaty that they have not negotiated, and especially one that seems diametrically opposed to their current military defense positions.

Weapons 7 July 2017" (July 7, 2017), *United States Mission to the United Nations*, available online: https://usun.state.gov/remarks/7892.

[130] Pakistan, statement to the UNGA First Committee (October 13, 2017). www.reachingcriticalwill.org /images/documents/ Disarmament-fora/1com/1com17/statements/13Oct_Pakistan.pdf.

[131] "Joint Press Statement from the Permanent Representatives to the United Nations of the United States, United Kingdom and France Following the Adoption of a Treaty Banning Nuclear Weapons 7 July 2017" (July 7, 2017), *United States Mission to the United Nations*, available online: https://usun.state.gov/remarks/7892.

Treaty on the Prohibition of Nuclear Weapons 2017

The Relationship of the Treaty on the Prohibition of Nuclear Weapons with NATO

NATO[132] itself has stated that the TPNW is at "odds with the existing non-proliferation and disarmament architecture" and risks undermining the NPT raising questions regarding congruence with the IAEA Safeguards regime which supports it.[133] Moreover, NATO called on its "partners and all countries who are considering supporting this treaty to seriously reflect on its implications for international peace and security, including on the NPT."[134] It seems that NATO will preclude its members and umbrella states from ratifying the Treaty as it currently stands. NATO allies are interdependent with the organization for security matters and they are unlikely to defy the organization's position against the Treaty.[135] Unless something changes in the future whereby there is a shift of NATO members' policy position on this, it is unlikely that NATO members will ratify the Treaty.

The Netherlands, in particular, expressed its intention to explore restoring a "shared sense of purpose to the disarmament and non-proliferation regime" and working toward strengthening and implementing the NPT, including moving toward "effective disarmament measures under Article VI and utilizing their valuable experience gained as Chair of the 2017 PrepCom."[136] It stressed that notwithstanding positive aspects of the TPNW movement, and while it had negotiated in good faith, it simply could not sign an instrument that was "incompatible" with its commitments to NATO. The Netherlands stated that it had attempted to address this within the spirit of the treaty by introducing a temporality clause,[137] but most delegations would not agree based on their views of a nuclear weapons ban.

---

[132] Also see "NATO and the Non-Proliferation Treaty: Fact Sheet" (March 2017), available online: www .nato.int/nato_static_fl2014/assets/pdf/pdf_2017_03/20170323_170323-npt-factsheet.pdf. For a more comprehensive version of NATO's position on the Test Ban Treaty, see Michael Ruhle, "The Nuclear Weapons Ban Treaty: Reasons for Scepticism" (May 19, 2017), *NATO Review*, available online: www .nato.int/docu/review/2017/Also-in-2017/nuclear-weapons-ban-treaty-scepticism-abolition/EN/index.htm.

[133] That said, one may ask for evidence to support such claims.

[134] "North Atlantic Council Statement on the Treaty on the Prohibition of Nuclear Weapons" (September 20, 2017), available online: www.nato.int/cps/en/natohq/news_146954.htm.

[135] See www.nato.int/cps/ua/natohq/news_146954.htm.

[136] "Explanation of Vote of the Netherlands on Text of Nuclear Ban Treaty" (July 7, 2017), available online: https://s3.amazonaws.com/unoda-web/wp-content/uploads/2017/07/Netherlands-EoV-Nuclear-Ban-Treaty.pdf.

[137] "Article 1 is not compatible with our commitments as a member of NATO, should Article 1 not narrow its scope. We therefore propose the following text proposal to be added as a paragraph 1.3 in order to bring the text in line with security policies that combine a role for nuclear weapons with the goal of complete nuclear disarmament. In addition, the paragraph would strengthen the ties between this instrument and the NPT." "The text of this paragraph would read: 'The obligations in paragraph 1 of this article may be held in abeyance for a State Party to this Convention provided this is in conformity with their rights and obligations under the NPT. Any State Party wishing to do so must deposit a declaration to this end at the time of signature, ratification, acceptance, approval of or accession to the Convention and shall withdraw

In addition to NATO obligations, the Netherlands said that the non-verifiable nature of the Treaty was problematic and "harms its credibility," expressing concern for the "inadequate verification provisions." It also suggested that the TPNW failed to incorporate sufficient flexibility for future developments and to encourage its members to participate in verification-related initiatives. Moreover, it noted that the TPNW's safeguards standard was not sufficient for the IAEA to draw a conclusion about the absence of undeclared nuclear activities.[138] Note that the TPNW is not intended to replicate IAEA safeguards, and further the Additional Protocol has not been mandated by the Agency's board of governors as compulsory. It remains voluntary.

In addition to its incompatibility with NATO obligations and the verification concerns, the Netherlands raised issues of discrepancies between the TPNW and the NPT. It argued during negotiations that the Treaty should "strengthen and complement the NPT," as reflected by Resolution 71/258. That said, the Dutch position is that the current text "does not do that." Instead, it argued that it actually "places the treaty above the NPT and sets up a comprehensive parallel review mechanism, to which it assigns a mandate that at least partially overlaps with that of the NPT." It noted that this formulated "a recipe for competition and fragmentation" when "efforts on disarmament should be concentrated," highlighting that the NPT contains the only disarmament obligations binding the P5 (the five permanent members of the UN Security Council) and is the "primary framework for pursuing a world without nuclear weapons."[139] Some may say, however, that no evidence is provided by the Dutch to substantiate this assertion. Nevertheless, this notes potential incongruence, as discussed above. In the end, the Netherlands could not sign the TPNW as it is both "incompatible" with its NATO and other obligations and "undermines" the Non-Proliferation Treaty,[140] a view echoed by other NATO countries. D Tytti Erästo, concludes, differently however:

> It would be difficult to make the case of legal incompatibility between the TPNW and the NPT, as the former so clearly builds on NPT Article VI on disarmament. Instead, the perceived incompatibility between the two treaties mainly has to do with the indirect negative consequences that the TPNW could potentially have on the NPT's non-proliferation objectives. While it is indeed possible that some non-nuclear weapon states could withdraw from the NPT and umbrella states might lose faith in extended deterrence, the TPNW is unlikely to be the sole or even primary trigger for such developments.

such declarations as further progress is made on the full and effective implementation of Article VI of the NPT, but no later than the point at which the complete, verifiable, and irreversible elimination of nuclear weapons has been achieved.'" See www.nuclearabolition.info/index.php/archive/1052-amendment-to-the-treaty-on-the-prohibition-on-nuclear-weapons.

[138] Explanation of vote of the Netherlands on text of Nuclear Ban Treaty (July 7, 2017), available online: https://s3.amazonaws.com/unoda-web/wp-content/uploads/2017/07/Netherlands-EoV-Nuclear-Ban-Treaty.pdf.

[139] Ibid.

[140] Ibid.

Essentially, the dispute over the TPNW is based on political disagreement regarding how to advance nuclear disarmament. While the NPT reflected the need to prioritise non-proliferation over the long-term goal of disarmament, the TPNW represents the view that – half a century after the adoption of the NPT – progress on disarmament is long overdue.[141]

Japan and Australia demonstrated solidarity with the American NATO position in their public comments. Then foreign minister of Japan Fumio Kishida (whose birthplace is Hiroshima) stated that Japan would not sign the agreement due to differences in "view" and "approach" which are aimed at achieving total and general nuclear disarmament through "concrete and practical measures."[142] These measures include working through the existing avenues of the NPT and the CTBT as well as finalizing the Fissile Material Cut-off Treaty.[143] Australia's position reiterates the criticisms expressed by the United States, France and the United Kingdom, albeit in more measured terms.[144] An Australian government statement indicates "Australia will continue to push hard to build that political will, and to promote the practical steps that will be necessary to bring about the elimination of nuclear weapons."[145] Canada expressed a similar position, with Prime Minister Justin Trudeau wanting something more "tangible" and "concrete," and with the state reiterating its support for a Fissile Material Cut-off Treaty.[146]

NATO'S POSITION IS NOT INCONSISTENT WITH ICJ JURISPRUDENCE[147]

The International Court of Justice jurisprudence, which emanates from its 1996 *Advisory Opinion*, demonstrates legal positions toward attaining goals of disarmament

[141] The NPT and the TPNW: Compatible or conflicting nuclear weapons treaties? www.sipri.org /commentary/blog/2019/npt-and-tpnw-compatible-or-conflicting-nuclear-weapons-treaties.

[142] Thu-An Pham, "Reading G20 Reactions to the Nuclear Weapons Ban Treaty" (January 17, 2018), *Carnegie Endowment for International Peace*, available online: http://carnegieendowment.org/2018/ 01/17/reading-g20-reactions-to-nuclear-weapons-ban-treaty-pub-75279.

[143] See www.unidir.org/files/publications/pdfs/fissile-material-cut-off-treaty-elements-of-the-emerging-consensus-en-650.pdf.

[144] Thu-An Pham, "Reading G20 Reactions to the Nuclear Weapons Ban Treaty" (January 17, 2018), *Carnegie Endowment for International Peace*, available online: http://carnegieendowment.org/2018/ 01/17/reading-g20-reactions-to-nuclear-weapons-ban-treaty-pub-75279.

[145] See "Australia's Nuclear Non-Proliferation and Disarmament Policy" (2018), *Australian Government Department of Foreign Affairs and Trade*, available online: http://dfat.gov.au/international-relations/ security/non-proliferation-disarmament-arms-control/nuclear-weapons/Pages/australias-nuclear-non-proliferation-and-disarmament-policy.aspx.

[146] See Marie-Danielle Smith, "Opposition Seek Actions from Liberal Foreign Policy as Trudeau Shuns 'useless' Disarmament Talks" (June 7, 2017), *National Post*, available online: https://nationalpost.com /news/politics/opposition-seek-actions-from-liberal-foreign-policy-as-trudeau-shuns-useless-disarmament-talks.

[147] Except perhaps on one issue: namely, on negotiating on (nuclear) disarmament. More generally, while one must understand the difficulty involved in making negotiations contingent upon the will and good faith of individual states (parties), it does appear to that one cannot expect such negotiations

and nonproliferation. On December 15, 1994, the UN General Assembly adopted a resolution[148] to submit to the ICJ for an advisory opinion, noting concerns expressed during the 1990 NPT Review Conference that insufficient progress had been made toward the complete elimination of nuclear weapons at the earliest possible time. The question of concern was posed as: "Is the threat or use of nuclear weapons in any circumstance permitted under international law?"[149] The resolution requested that the Court render its opinion "urgently." Consequently, the Court received written statements from twenty-eight states, with written observations on those statements presented by two states, followed by oral proceedings in which twenty-two states presented oral argument.[150] On July 8, 1996, the Court delivered its *Legality of the Threat or Use of Nuclear Weapons, Advisory Opinion*[151] which ruled that "no comprehensive and universal prohibition of the threat or use of nuclear weapons exists." That said, the Court stated that there is an "obligation to achieve a precise result – nuclear disarmament in all its aspects." The ICJ found, *inter alia*,[152] that there is no treaty-based or customary international law specifically authorizing the threat or use of nuclear weapons. Nuclear weapons may not be used or threatened in a manner contrary to Article 2(4) or not otherwise in fulfillment of all the requirements under Article 51 of the UN Charter. Furthermore, a threat or use of nuclear weapons is subject to the international law applicable in armed conflict, as well as in relation to

---

    to be pursued without the NWS (*de jure* and *de facto*) being involved; this is the Achilles heel of the TPNW. Note that it is inaccurate to use *de jure* and *de facto* here: under international law generally all NWS are *de jure* possessors; it is only under the NPT that a distinction is made and this does not bind non-parties (Article 34 VCLT).

[148] See "General and Complete Disarmament," Resolution 49/75 of the General Assembly (December 15, 1994), available online: www.un.org/documents/ga/res/49/a49r075.htm.

[149] *Legality of the Treat or Use of Nuclear Weapons, Advisory Opinion*, ICJ Reports (1996), p. 226, available online: www.icj-cij.org/files/case-related/95/095-19960708-ADV-01-00-EN.pdf.

[150] Ibid.

[151] Ibid.

[152] As stated at paras. 105(2) (A)–(F) at 266–267 of the *Advisory Opinion*: "A. There is in neither customary nor conventional international law any specific authorization of the threat or use of nuclear weapons (Unanimously); B, There is in neither customary nor conventional international law any comprehensive and universal prohibition of the threat or use of nuclear weapons as such (By eleven votes to three …); C. A threat or use of force by means of nuclear weapons that is contrary to Article 2, paragraph 4, of the United Nations Charter and that fails to meet all the requirements of Article 51, is unlawful (Unanimously); D. A threat or use of nuclear weapons should also be compatible with the requirements of the international law applicable in armed conflict, particularly those of the principles and rules of international humanitarian law, as well as with specific obligations under treaties and other undertakings which expressly deal with nuclear weapons (Unanimously); E. It follows from the above-mentioned requirements that the threat or use of nuclear weapons would generally be contrary to the rules of international law applicable in armed conflict, and in particular the principles and rules of humanitarian law; However, in view of the current state of international law, and of the elements of fact at its disposal, the Court cannot conclude definitively whether the threat or use of nuclear weapons would be lawful or unlawful in an extreme circumstance of self-defense, in which the very survival of a State would be at stake (By seven votes to seven, by the President's casting vote …); F. There exists an obligation to pursue in good faith and bring to a conclusion negotiations leading to nuclear disarmament in all its aspects under strict and effective international control (Unanimously)."

other treaty obligations and undertakings dealing expressly with such weapons. Moreover, there is an obligation to pursue in good faith, and bring to conclusion, negotiations leading to nuclear disarmament in all its aspects, which the parties to the TPNW would say they were fulfilling while the NWS and their allies are not. For the most part, the most worrying aspect of the judgment concerns the Court's ruling regarding extreme self-defense whereby the Court effectively would not declare decisively on the illegality of nuclear weapons leaving the question open and sparking diametrically opposed interpretations of the ruling on extreme self-defense, with little legal certainty as to where treaty law stands on the issue. The legality of using any particular weapon is not regulated by the *jus ad bellum* (other than under necessity and proportionality requirements) and whether nuclear weapons were used in self-defense or by an attacking state makes no difference (with the caveat that in principle uses of weapons by an attacking state are unlawful generally; but this feature is not particular to nuclear weapons, since it applies to all weapons). Indeed, it may be time for the UNGA to adopt another resolution requesting a new advisory opinion in view of developments during the last twenty-five years including the conclusion of the TPNW. These matters will be explored in more detail in Chapters 7 and 8.

CONCLUSION: COMPLEMENTARY OR COMPETING INTERESTS?

This chapter sought to discuss the TPNW, from a generalist perspective, against existing treaty obligations in international law, to gauge whether there is compatibility and the degree to which there may be legal congruence, or incongruence, with existing obligations. It could be noted that a ban on testing is compatible with the CTBT, that many of the prohibitions of the TPNW are compatible with the NPT (at least for NNWS). Moreover, there appears in large part to be congruence and complementarity to the Partial Test Ban Treaty.

Legal congruence focuses on compatibility, agreement or harmony, so that the two systems can both exist or be combined without problems or conflict regarding existing international treaties.

The TPNW must also be viewed in relation to the other legal infrastructure and in conjunction with the manner by which treaty law becomes binding in nature. Without the express consent of a state, it will not be legally enforceable under international law, nor necessarily under domestic law assuming that, for example, an NGO would like to press a government to comply with TPNW obligations. This will be especially difficult given the opposition of both the NWS and the allied non-NWS. The five *de jure* NWS that include the United States, the United Kingdom, France, China and Russia did not participate in the negotiation sessions or vote in favor of the TPNW; neither did important other states, including Israel, India, Pakistan and North Korea, which have demonstrated no intention to sign or ratify the treaty. Furthermore, many states have raised important concerns regarding conflicting obligations under the TPNW. Their determination not to partake in the negotiations, compounded with realistic concerns, make it highly unlikely they will ever adopt the TPNW, particularly in view of the fact that NATO will effectively preclude its members from ratifying the TPNW as it currently stands. The ICJ jurisprudence emanating from the *Legality of the Threat or Use of Nuclear Weapons, Advisory Opinion* provides little assistance to legally attain the goals of the Treaty. At present, states are opposing such a legal position and ICJ jurisprudence effectively affirmed their stance.

In view of all these factors, contemporary international law does not appear to be aligned with the aspirations of the TPNW. Indeed, the Netherlands note that the TPNW formulates "a recipe for competition and fragmentation."[153] Others may dismiss such worries pointing to the five NWFZ treaties that prohibit and outlaw nuclear weapons in their respective regions. They are not held to compete with the NPT or to fragment the arms control framework, rather they are regarded as complementary to the NPT. Similarly, the CTBT and the TPNW are means of implementing NPT Article VI, as would be an FMCT and other future treaties. Nevertheless, others would contend that the TPNW is substantially different from the NWFZ treaties which do not aim for universality in the same form and the overall focus and intent is fundamentally different in its scope. The degree to which TPNW development complements existing obligations needs some time to play out. That said, this preliminary analysis indicates that the TPNW may not easily complement existing treaty obligations, in crucial respects, and apparently competes with exiting components of the current legal architecture and infrastructure, thus creating ambiguity. The TPNW may not be in legal harmony but rather in discord with some existing international obligations, and actually serves to compete with, rather than complementing existing treaties.

---

[153] "Explanation of Vote of the Netherlands on Text of Nuclear Ban Treaty" (July 7, 2017), available online: https://s3.amazonaws.com/unoda-web/wp-content/uploads/2017/07/Netherlands-EoV-Nuclear-Ban-Treaty.pdf.

5

Customary International Law, *Opinio Juris* and State Practice Regarding the Treaty on the Prohibition of Nuclear Weapons 2017: Toward Universality?

INTRODUCTION: A NEW DIRECTION IN NUCLEAR NONPROLIFERATION AND DISARMAMENT?

The adoption of the Treaty on the Prohibition of Nuclear Weapons (TPNW)[1] at the United Nations General Assembly and its movement toward ratification raises both hopes amongst some and fears amongst others regarding the development of customary practice under international law. Although the TPNW purports to strive for universality, significant questions remain regarding the Treaty's aims and achieving legal unity within the international legal order. The purpose of this chapter is to explore these and other issues regarding the TPNW's prospects of achieving universality under customary international law and *opinio juris*.

UNIVERSALITY

The TPNW strives toward achieving "universality." Article 12 stipulates that each state party will encourage states that are not party to the TPNW "to sign, ratify, accept, approve or accede to" it, working toward "the goal of universal adherence of all States" to the TPNW. This provision is commendable and indeed important for states who ratify the treaty in order to encourage broad acceptance of it within the international community. After all, the true worth and strength of the TPNW would be diminished without full and universal application toward its end goals.[2] But also, if states are truly committed to such ends, this should require an actual civic duty to promote the goal of disarmament. That aside, a more telling question is the degree to which such an endeavor is actually possible. Is universality a realistic goal? Or, were the parties so determined to get a result (i.e., achieve a treaty), that they lost sight of the broader mission expressed in the NPT and the CTBT, namely the

---

[1] Treaty on the Prohibition of Nuclear Weapons, A/CONF.229/2017/8 (July 7, 2017), available online: http://undocs.org/A/CONF.229/2017/8.

[2] For an interesting read in this area see Brunno Simma, "Universality of International Law from the Perspective of a Practitioner" (April 2009) 20:2 *European Journal of International Law* at 265–297, available online: https://academic.oup.com/ejil/article/20/2/265/500839.

106   *TPNW 2017: Toward Universality?*

acceptance of measurable and verifiable nuclear disarmament? Moreover, is universality a realistic prospect?

At first glance, achieving the goal of universality could be problematic in terms of sources of international law. As discussed in the previous chapter, it is unlikely to happen by treaty due to lack of accessions of nuclear-weapon states (NWS) and a number of non-nuclear-weapon states (NNWS) not wishing to adopt it at this stage. Under general principles of law it is unlikely, because of the difficulty of establishing recognition of "civilized" nations and because of the character of general principles of law: the principle of good faith does not impose obligations that otherwise do not exist, as articulated by the ICJ in Armed Actions between *Nicaragua and Honduras* 1988. Movement by binding decisions of the UN Security Council seems impossible considering the vetoes of the NWS permanent members and their respective positions on the TPNW at this point in time. This leaves the focus of customary international law which will be discussed in this chapter as the only remaining source possibly guaranteeing universality, since all states may in principle be bound. This would, however, require inclusion of specially affected states (NSCSC) and barring persistent objection (as discussed in the *Norwegian Fisheries Case*[3]), which is however likely to occur as will be discussed in turn.

In regard to achieving universality, it is fitting to examine what is actually meant within the context of the TPNW. It may be that "universality" is to be defined for the present purposes as all 193 UN Member States becoming contracting parties to the Treaty; or, it may be its acceptance by the vast majority of states to qualify as having achieved universality. Either way the TPNW faces a number of serious challenges. Firstly, the opposition of the NWS to the Treaty as well as a sizable number of NNWS prevents full and universal acceptance. Their resistance to and non-attendance at treaty negotiations, combined with their refusal to accept the final Treaty text renders it unlikely that universality could be achieved under customary international law, which takes into account both state practice and *opinio juris*. Moreover, the International Court of Justice jurisprudence, emanating from the 1996 *Legality of the Threat or Use of Nuclear Weapons, Advisory Opinion*, further demonstrates legal difficulties in attaining customary goals. At present, states are opposing such a legal position and ICJ jurisprudence effectively affirmed their stance.

WIDER STATE PARTICIPATION, TREATY LEGITIMACY AND CREDIBILITY

Negotiations for the TPNW may be heralded as a major success story for civil society organizations. As noted, participation from a wide range of humanitarian and human rights groups demonstrated a groundswell of popular international support

---

[3]   See www.icj-cij.org/files/case-related/5/005–19491109-ORD-01–00-EN.pdf.

for the spirit of the Treaty (i.e., the elimination of nuclear weapons). That said, the TPNW's negotiations and general reception within the wider global family of nations, however, lacks endorsement from some important countries. The five nuclear-weapon states, namely, the United States, the United Kingdom, France, China and the Russian Federation were conspicuously absent from the negotiation process, including UN General Assembly debates, formal treaty negotiations, as well as agreement on the final treaty text. Also missing were important de facto nuclear-weapon states, with Israel, India, Pakistan and North Korea failing to cooperate with the treaty conference. These states are known, or believed, to possess nuclear weapons, raising important questions regarding the TPNW's potential universality or effectiveness. That said, Iran, which was thought to be developing nuclear weapons, participated in the negotiation of the Treaty and voted in favor of its adoption in July 2017, but is still yet to sign the Treaty.[4]

Whilst the open-ended working group that preceded the negotiation of the TPNW, was open to all states, only 124 of the 193 UN Member States participated in the conference, with 122 states voting for adoption. The Netherlands voted against its adoption, and Singapore abstained. The remaining states elected not to participate in the prohibition negotiations. In their report, *The TPNW: Setting the record straight*, Gro Nystuen, Kjølv Egel and Torbjørn Graff Hugo of the Norwegian Academy of International Law address whether a treaty without all the nuclear-armed states on board would be better than a treaty without any of them involved, concluding that "it clearly would." They note in their report, however, that:

> One key reason why a nuclear ban treaty was believed to have merit even without the support of the nuclear-armed states (and their allies) was that such an agreement could advance international humanitarian law and disarmament law – fill a legal gap – by placing nuclear weapons in the same legal category as other weapons of mass destruction, that is, as fundamentally unacceptable means of war. The ban treaty also came to be seen as a tool for delegitimizing and stigmatizing nuclear weapons. The ban was conceptualized as a normative instrument that could translate the growing impatience of the non-nuclear-armed states – the vast majority of the UN membership – into political and normative pressure for progress. The inspiration for this approach was drawn, in large part, from the successful campaigns to ban anti-personnel landmines and cluster munitions.[5]

The TPNW will enter into force ninety days after the fiftieth instrument has been deposited.[6] This is standard procedure but notably different from the CTBT[7]

---

[4] "Positions on the Treaty" (as of October 1, 2018) *ICAN*, available online: www.icanw.org/why-a-ban/positions.

[5] The TPNW: Setting the Record straight Gro Nystuen Kjølv Egeland Torbjørn Graff Hugo, at pp. 3–4. See http://intlaw.no/wp-content/uploads/2018/10/TPNW-Setting-the-record-straight-Oct-2018-WEB.pdf.

[6] Article 15.

[7] As per Article XIV.

approach to entry into force with expressly listing some forty-four specific states that must ratify the treaty[8] in order for it to be of force or effect. Notably, however, even without entering into force, the CTBT together with the CTBTO plays an important role internationally and retains an important position globally. This ratification requirement has undoubtedly made entry into force of the CTBT fraught with problems. That said, such a high threshold has ironically given it legitimacy as it requires buy-in from the main players in the nuclear arena and once it is finally launched, the CTBT will play a significant role in nonproliferation. Without similar inroads, the TPNW may face irreconcilable issues of credibility and legitimacy, sowing seeds of cynicism regarding its final goals. Despite issuing these criticisms, this author emphasizes commitment to arms reduction and nuclear disarmament and supports progressive and verifiable steps toward those ends.

At the outset of the Treaty negotiations, the US ambassador to the United Nations, Nikki Haley, stated that they, along with some forty countries, would "not join talks on a nuclear weapons ban treaty," saying instead that the United States is "committed to the Non-Proliferation Treaty."[9] In a press conference, she stated that, as a mother and as a daughter, there was nothing more that she would like to see than a ban on nuclear weapons, but that the United States had to be realistic.[10] She stated that, "[i]n this day and time we can't honestly . . . say we can protect our people by allowing the bad actors to have them and those of us that are good, trying to keep peace and safety, not to have them."[11]

Notably, other nuclear-weapon states and permanent members of the UN Security Council issued similar comments, with the deputy French UN ambassador Alexis Lamek stating that "the security conditions were not right for a nuclear weapons ban treaty. In the current perilous context, considering in particular the proliferation of weapons of mass destruction and their means of delivery, our countries continue to rely on nuclear deterrence for security and stability."[12] The United Kingdom's UN ambassador Matthew Rycroft added: "The UK is not attending the negotiations on a treaty to prohibit nuclear weapons because we do not believe that those negotiations will lead to effective progress on global nuclear disarmament."[13] Note that this refusal to commence negotiations toward a treaty was very different from the reception given to the CTBT, which was led by the United States with its full participation. Indeed, the United States was the first to sign

---

[8] As required under Article XIV and listed in Annex II.

[9] Michelle Nichols, "US, Britain, France, Others Skip Nuclear Weapons Ban Treaty Talks" (March 27, 2017) *Reuters*, available online: www.reuters.com/article/us-nuclear-un/u-s-britain-france-others-skip-nuclear-weapons-ban-treaty-talks-idUSKBN16Y1QI.

[10] Paraphrased from Michelle Nichols, "US, Britain, France, Others Skip Nuclear Weapons Ban Treaty Talks" (March 27, 2017) *Reuters*, available online: www.reuters.com/article/us-nuclear-un/u-s-britain-france-others-skip-nuclear-weapons-ban-treaty-talks-idUSKBN16Y1QI.

[11] Ibid.

[12] Ibid.

[13] Ibid.

the CTBT in 1996, albeit ratification remains outstanding. The United Kingdom has both signed and ratified the CTBT.[14]

One question relates to what some see as an insufficient negotiation time allotted to the TPNW, and whether there should have been a longer negotiation period in order to get more countries on board as well as to have more time to explore the various issues under consideration. A relatively short negotiation time frame and the lack of a preparatory process, along with the absence of a number of states normally active in disarmament and nonproliferation fora of this nature, may have influenced the process and substance of the talks.[15] Negotiations were constrained by severe time limitations and the fact that the negotiators could not benefit from the work of preparatory committees or specially designated expert groups.[16] Mukhatzhanova highlights that the need for additional technical expertise, for example, was evident during the work on safeguards and nuclear weapons elimination provisions.[17] In contrast, the CTBT took more than two years of intensive negotiations before a final draft treaty was presented.[18]

With this in mind, it was not only states with nuclear interests or ambitions that expressed reluctance to enter into negotiations. Others generally in favor of complete nuclear disarmament highlighted their misgivings. For example, Canada did not participate in the negotiation of the TPNW. The Minister of Foreign Affairs, Chrystia Freeland, presented a vision for Canada that focused on participating as actively as possible in multilateral forums, yet Canada would not partake in the Treaty negotiations.[19] Freeland said that, "Canada is actively pursuing inclusive nuclear disarmament initiatives. However, the negotiation of a nuclear weapons ban without the participation of states that possess nuclear weapons is certain to be ineffective and will not eliminate any nuclear weapons. If anything, it may make disarmament more difficult."[20] Prime Minister Justin Trudeau questioned the benefit of the negotiations because they were boycotted by states that possess nuclear weapons.[21]

[14] Signed on the September 24, 1996 and ratified on the April 6, 1998. www.ctbto.org/the-treaty/status-of-signature-and-ratification/.

[15] Gaukhar Mukhatzhanova, "Nuclear Weapons Treaty, Negotiation and Beyond" (September 2017), *Arms Control Today*, available online: www.armscontrol.org/act/2017-09/features/nuclear-weapons-prohibition-treaty-negotiations-beyond.

[16] Ibid.

[17] Ibid.

[18] "Comprehensive Nuclear-Test-Ban Treaty: History of the Treaty," *United Nations Office for Disarmament Affairs*, available online: www.un.org/disarmament/wmd/nuclear/ctbt.

[19] See Marie-Danielle Smith, "Opposition Seek Actions from Liberal Foreign Policy as Trudeau Shuns 'useless' Disarmament Talks" (June 7, 2017), *National Post*, available online: https://nationalpost.com/news/politics/opposition-seek-actions-from-liberal-foreign-policy-as-trudeau-shuns-useless-disarmament-talks.

[20] "Canada's Absence from UN Nuclear Weapon Ban Negotiations Unacceptable, Says Advocate" (March 28, 2017) *CBC Radio*, available online: www.cbc.ca/radio/thecurrent/the-current-for-march-28-2017-1.4042750/canada-s-absence-from-un-nuclear-weapon-ban-negotiations-unacceptable-says-advocate-1.4042752.

[21] See Marie-Danielle Smith, "Opposition Seek Actions from Liberal Foreign Policy as Trudeau Shuns 'useless' Disarmament Talks" (June 7, 2017), *National Post*, available online: https://nationalpost.com

Canada's other political parties were not unanimous in support of the governing party's refusal to join the movement toward the treaty. The New Democratic Party (NDP) sought the government's support for a motion, urging Canada to participate in the international nuclear disarmament negotiations. "It is well-meaning, as the NDP often are," Prime Minister Trudeau said, but less "tangible" and "concrete" than what the government is doing in its support for a Fissile Material Cut-off Treaty, which would essentially limit ingredients for weapons but not weapons themselves.[22] Canada voted against the UN General Assembly resolution in 2016 that established the mandate for nations to negotiate the treaty, claiming that US nuclear weapons are essential for Canadian security.[23] Canada ultimately voted against the final TPNW text in July, 2017.[24] In contrast, urged by its Parliament, the Netherlands participated in the negotiations, expressed its positions and ultimately voted against adoption of the TPNW.

In a joint statement of explanation, several other non-nuclear countries who did not participate (Albania, Australia, Belgium, Bulgaria, Canada, the Czech Republic, Denmark, Estonia, Germany, Greece, Hungary, Italy, Latvia, Lithuania, Luxembourg, Montenegro, Poland, Portugal, Republic of Korea, Romania, Slovakia, Slovenia, Spain and Turkey), indicated their "shared vision of attaining global zero" but noted "significant differences" regarding "how best to take forward multilateral nuclear disarmament negotiations."[25] They stressed the premature nature of starting a process toward a nuclear weapon prohibition treaty, "without the support of nuclear weapon states and a large number of other countries with specific security interests."[26] These twenty-four nations noted that such a treaty would "be ineffective in eliminating nuclear weapons; have potentially adverse consequences for regional and global security; not advance implementation of Article VI of the NPT; and impact negatively on the NPT review process, making a consensus outcome in 2020 all the more difficult."[27] Some of such comments will be explored in greater depth in subsequent chapters, namely: 6 on Safeguards, 7 on

---

/news/politics/opposition-seek-actions-from-liberal-foreign-policy-as-trudeau-shuns-useless-disarmament-talks.

[22] Ibid.

[23] "Positions on the Treaty" (as of October 1, 2018) *ICAN*, available online: 23, www.icanw.org/why-a-ban/positions.

[24] "Voting on UN Resolution for Nuclear Ban Treaty" (December 2016) *ICAN*, available online: www.icanw.org/campaign-news/voting-on-un-resolution-for-nuclear-ban-treaty/.

[25] "Taking Forward Multilateral Nuclear Disarmament Negotiations – Explanation of Position on Behalf of the Following States: Albania, Australia, Belgium, Bulgaria, Canada, Czech Republic, Denmark, Estonia, Germany, Greece, Hungary, Italy, Latvia, Lithuania, Luxembourg, Montenegro, Poland, Portugal, Republic of Korea, Romania, Slovakia, Slovenia, Spain and Turkey," available online: http://reachingcriticalwill.org/images/documents/Disarmament-fora/1com/1com16/eov/L41_Poland-etal.pdf.

[26] Ibid.

[27] Ibid.

Deterrence, 8 on Defense and 9 on Fragmentation. In its current form it would only engage states which are already bound by the NPT, simply mirroring existing obligations without providing mechanisms to ensure compliance with the new treaty obligations. They concluded their letter of explanation by stating that such a treaty needs to be effective and verifiable with irreversible nuclear disarmament, requiring all states "to work in unison."[28]

Switzerland, which actually participated in the negotiating conference and voted yes on the adoption of the TPNW, also echoed such concerns. It expressed its commitment to the process and ideals of the Treaty as well as confirming its aspirations for "the goal of a world free of nuclear weapons."[29] Switzerland noted, however, "substantial concerns" including the lack of broader state participation and reiterated many of the anxieties expressed by other nations.

The Swiss permanent representative, Sabrina Dallafior, highlighted uncertainties for universality of the TPNW. Firstly, the Swiss delegation found the TPNW to be "deficient in the sense that some of its provisions are not effectively verifiable," constituting a departure from the principle agreed to in the NPT framework that "nuclear disarmament should be both irreversible and verifiable."[30] Secondly, Switzerland felt that some of the Treaty provisions "bear risks for existing norms, instruments and fora," causing fear that "the generic reference to nuclear testing could undermine the CTBT norm as well as efforts for its early entry into force."[31] Switzerland's explanation adds that "provisions related to IAEA safeguards might erode efforts to strengthen standards in this domain."[32] Furthermore, it felt that "tasks given to the meeting of states parties could duplicate or even contradict efforts undertaken in other fora" and, "treaty provisions could also challenge the centrality of the NPT" as the cornerstone of the nuclear disarmament and nonproliferation regime.[33] Switzerland also expressed its "regret" that it had not been possible to have a "more inclusive negotiation process," noting that "key concerns of States who had question marks about this negotiating process, whether they finally took part in it or not, were for the most part not taken into account."[34] The country noted that a number of treaty provisions "lack clarity" which "may give rise to different legal interpretations and therefore create some confusion and uncertainties." Indeed,

---

[28] Ibid.
[29] Submission of Sabrina Dallafior, Permanent Representative of Switzerland to the Conference on Disarmament, "Explanation of Vote" at the United Nations Conference to Negotiate a Legally Binding Instrument to Prohibit Nuclear Weapons (July 7, 2017), available online: https://s3 .amazonaws.com/unoda-web/wp-content/uploads/2017/07/Swiss-Explanation-of-Vote2.pdf.
[30] Ibid.
[31] Ibid.
[32] Ibid.
[33] Ibid.
[34] Ibid.

Switzerland itself in its letter raised issues of the "effectiveness of the treaty" as well as potential "universalization" concerns, concluding that it sees risks that this treaty may "weaken existing norms and agreements and create parallel processes and structures which may further contribute to polarization rather than reduce it."[35]

It should be noted that the 122 nations that voted to adopt[36] the Nuclear Prohibition Treaty and the various civil society organizations and humanitarian groups leading the charge, demonstrate the multitude of states as well as individual citizens wanting this development. Liechtenstein, for example, cited this as an "historic day, for the United Nations and the peoples around the world," commenting that the TPNW represents "a crucial contribution" to nuclear disarmament efforts.[37] Liechtenstein's statement notes that the Treaty would be complementary to and a political reinforcement of the NPT and the CTBT and was "a significant milestone."[38] Other countries, some of which belong to the G20, strongly promoted and supported the TPNW. For example, Argentina, Brazil, Indonesia, Mexico, Saudi Arabia and South Africa voted in favor of the treaty in the General Assembly.[39] Several months passed, however, before the Brazilian and South African heads of state made public remarks about the agreement, and when they did, they simply echoed their ambassadors' support for the treaty. In an article in the *Folha de S. Paulo*,[40] a major Brazilian daily newspaper, Foreign Minister Aloysio Nunes Ferreira greeted the Treaty's approval in celebratory terms, calling it a "victory of humanity in the search for a world free of the absurdity of nuclear weapons."[41] When asked about "resistance from nuclear weapons states," Ferreira argued that "the new Treaty is an important complement to Article VI of the Treaty on the Non-Proliferation of Nuclear Weapons (NPT), which established the obligation of nuclear disarmament."[42] Mexico was the only supporter of the TPNW amongst the

---

[35] Ibid.

[36] As of September 21, 2019, seventy states have signed: https://treaties.un.org/Pages/ViewDetails.aspx?src=TREATY&mtdsg_no=XXVI-9&chapter=26&clang=_en. See also Report of the Working Group to analyze the Treaty on the Prohibition of Nuclear Weapons (June 30, 2018).

[37] Georg Sparber, "Statement by Liechtenstein upon Adoption of a Treaty on the Prohibition of Nuclear Weapons" at the United Nations Conference to negotiate a legally binding instrument to prohibit nuclear weapons, leading toward their total elimination (July 7, 2017), available online: https://s3.amazonaws.com/unoda-web/wp-content/uploads/2017/07/2017-07-06-NWBT-Statement-upon-adoption_final.pdf.

[38] Ibid.

[39] Thu-An Pham, "Reading G20 Reactions to the Nuclear Weapons Ban Treaty" (January 17, 2018), *Carnegie Endowment for International Peace*, available online: http://carnegieendowment.org/2018/01/17/reading-g20-reactions-to-nuclear-weapons-ban-treaty-pub-75279.

[40] Aloysio Nunes Ferreira, "Towards a World Free of Nuclear Weapons" (July 17, 2017) *Brazil Ministry of Foreign Affairs*, available online: www.itamaraty.gov.br/en/speeches-articles-and-interviews/minister-of-foreign-affairs-articles/16886-rumo-a-um-mundo-sem-armas-nucleares-folha-de-s-paulo-17-7-2018.

[41] Thu-An Pham, "Reading G20 Reactions to the Nuclear Weapons Ban Treaty" (January 17, 2018), *Carnegie Endowment for International Peace*, available online: http://carnegieendowment.org/2018/01/17/reading-g20-reactions-to-nuclear-weapons-ban-treaty-pub-75279.

[42] Ibid.

Gɜo to issue a press release.[43] Mexico's Ministry of Foreign Affairs welcomed the adoption of the Treaty by the UN General Assembly, observing that it was the first Treaty ever adopted that globally prohibits nuclear weapons.[44] The statement further noted that the TPNW is consistent with Mexico's historic diplomatic tradition of supporting nuclear nonproliferation and disarmament.[45] It has signed and deposited its instrument of ratification with the UN secretary-general on January 16, 2018.

Sweden[46] and the Netherlands[47] expressed individual concerns regarding the Treaty, highlighting *inter alia*, the status and role of the NPT in juxtaposition to the TPNW. Sweden participated in the negotiations feeling obliged to do so due to its obligations under Article VI of the NPT and voted in favor of adopting the TPNW, despite some misgivings. Sweden saw a significant achievement in the "reaffirmation of the fundamental importance of the humanitarian perspective with regard to nuclear weapons" feeling that any use of them would be "catastrophic to humanity, as well as to the environment."[48] It noted nuclear weapons as the only weapon of mass destruction not hitherto prohibited.[49] Despite endorsing the TPNW, Sweden recognized that it had failed to address the delegation's aims. For example, Sweden wanted a firmer and more articulate stance on the effect that the NPT would remain the cornerstone of nuclear disarmament and nonproliferation, a view not shared by all delegations, in spite of declarations made in the First Committee and during the first session of the Conference.[50] Among other matters, Sweden did not subscribe to the language which aims at describing international law as it stands today, but instead maintained the view taken by the International Court of Justice in the *Nuclear Weapons Advisory Opinion* of 1996 that the threat or use of nuclear weapons would generally be contrary to the rules of international

---

[43] Ibid.

[44] "Mexico Welcomes Adoption of the Treaty on the Prohibition of Nuclear Weapons" (July 8, 2017) Press Release 264, *Government of Mexico Secretaria de Relaciones Exteriores*, available online: www.gob.mx/sre/en/prensa/mexico-welcomes-adoption-of-the-treaty-on-the-prohibition-of-nuclear-weapons?idiom=en.

[45] Note that Mexico's Alfonso García Robles, as then state secretary in the Secretariat of Foreign Affairs, is often credited as the father of the 1967 Treaty of Tlatelolco, which established the world's first nuclear-weapon-free zone over Latin America and the Caribbean. See Thu-An Pham, "Reading Gɜo Reactions to the Nuclear Weapons Ban Treaty" (January 17, 2018), *Carnegie Endowment for International Peace*, available online: http://carnegieendowment.org/2018/01/17/reading-g20-reactions-to-nuclear-weapons-ban-treaty-pub-75279.

[46] "Negotiations on a Legally Binding Instrument to Prohibit Nuclear Weapons, Leading towards Their Total Elimination – Concluding Statement by Sweden" (July 7, 2017), available online: https://s3.amazonaws.com/unoda-web/wp-content/uploads/2017/07/170707-EoV-Sweden.pdf.

[47] "Explanation of Vote of the Netherlands on Text of Nuclear Ban Treaty" (July 7, 2017), available online: https://s3.amazonaws.com/unoda-web/wp-content/uploads/2017/07/Netherlands-EoV-Nuclear-Ban-Treaty.pdf.

[48] Ibid.

[49] Ibid.

[50] Ibid.

law applicable in armed conflict, and in particular, the principles and rules of humanitarian law.[51]

Further Swedish criticisms of the TPNW include, as noted in its concluding statement, a strong preference not to have nuclear testing in the TPNW, since the CTBT has established a norm respected by all countries but one. Moreover, on verification Sweden was "disappointed" not to have the Additional Protocol, INFCIRC 540,[52] as the standard of verification of the TPNW, stating it believed it would have "strengthened the credibility of the treaty" and allowed for "sufficient verifications" of states parties' compliance with key elements of the general obligations.[53] Sweden also took exception to the language in Article 18, noting its strong preference to delete the words after the last comma which says existing obligations shall not be prejudiced "where those obligations are consistent with the Treaty." Sweden noted that the NPT and CTBT are to remain fully applicable even after the TPNW enters into force. Its position was that nothing in this Treaty "can be interpreted as reducing the obligations of states parties to the NPT and CTBT."[54]

NATO AND ALLIES AGAINST THE PROHIBITION TREATY

All NATO countries with the exception of the Netherlands were outside the negotiations. In relation to the prevailing international security environment, NATO[55] noted that:

> [s]eeking to ban nuclear weapons through a treaty that will not engage any state actually possessing nuclear weapons will not be effective, will not reduce nuclear arsenals, and will neither enhance any country's security, nor international peace and stability. Indeed it risks doing the opposite by creating divisions and divergences at a time when a unified approach to proliferation and security threats is required more than ever.[56]

NATO goes on to state that in its view, the TPNW is at "odds with the existing non-proliferation and disarmament architecture" and risks undermining the NPT

---

[51] "Negotiations on a Legally Binding Instrument to Prohibit Nuclear Weapons, Leading towards Their Total Elimination – Concluding Statement by Sweden" (July 7, 2017), available online: https://s3.amazonaws.com/unoda-web/wp-content/uploads/2017/07/170707-EoV-Sweden.pdf.

[52] See www.iaea.org/sites/default/files/infcirc540c.pdf.

[53] Ibid.

[54] Ibid.

[55] Also see "NATO and the Non-Proliferation Treaty: Fact Sheet" (March 2017), available online: www.nato.int/nato_static_fl2014/assets/pdf/pdf_2017_03/20170323_170323-npt-factsheet.pdf. For a more comprehensive version of NATO's position on the Test Ban Treaty, please see Michael Ruhle, "The Nuclear Weapons Ban Treaty: Reasons for Scepticism" (May 19, 2017), NATO Review, available online: www.nato.int/docu/review/2017/Also-in-2017/nuclear-weapons-ban-treaty-scepticism-abolition/EN/index.htm.

[56] "North Atlantic Council Statement on the Treaty on the Prohibition of Nuclear Weapons" (September 20, 2017), available online: www.nato.int/cps/en/natohq/news_146954.htm.

NATO and Allies against the Prohibition Treaty

and the IAEA safeguards regime with the "crisis caused by North Korea," underlining the importance of preserving and enhancing the existing framework of the NPT. Moreover, the TPNW "fails to take into account these urgent security challenges." NATO also notes that its fundamental purpose of nuclear capability is to "preserve peace, prevent coercion, and deter aggression," whereby the Allies' goal is to "bolster deterrence as a core element of our collective defence and to contribute to the indivisible security of the Alliance." According to NATO,

> [a]s Allies committed to advancing security through deterrence, defence, disarmament, non-proliferation and arms control, we, the Allied nations, cannot support this treaty. Therefore, there will be no change in the legal obligations on our countries with respect to nuclear weapons. Thus we would not accept any argument that this treaty reflects or in any way contributes to the development of customary international law.

Calling on its partners and all countries that might be considering supporting the TPNW, NATO has asked them "to seriously reflect on its implications for international peace and security, including on the NPT."[57] In that regard, Japan and Australia demonstrated support for this stance with then foreign minister of Japan, Fumio Kishida, saying that Japan would not sign the agreement due to differences in "view" and "approach." Australia emphasized the criticisms expressed by other countries including the United States, France and the United Kingdom.[58] As mentioned earlier, Canadian Prime Minister Justin Trudeau questioned the value of the TPNW because negotiations were boycotted by states that possess nuclear weapons.[59]

Similarly, the Netherlands did not sign the Treaty, calling it "incompatible" with its NATO and other obligations. As previously mentioned above, unlike other non-signatories, the Netherlands actually took part in the negotiations, but found the final text contained "inadequate verification provisions" and served to undermine the NPT. These concerns were shared by other NATO states. Having tried during the negotiations process to reconcile these factors by introducing a temporality clause, most delegations were against such a proposal leading to no tangible outcome. As the TPNW currently stands, the Netherlands maintained that its non-verifiable nature is vital, harming its overall "credibility," failing to incorporate sufficient flexibility for future developments, or encouraging its members to

---

[57] "North Atlantic Council Statement on the Treaty on the Prohibition of Nuclear Weapons" (September 20, 2017), available online: www.nato.int/cps/en/natohq/news_146954.htm.

[58] Thu-An Pham, "Reading G20 Reactions to the Nuclear Weapons Ban Treaty" (January 17, 2018), *Carnegie Endowment for International Peace*, available online: http://carnegieendowment.org/2018/01/17/reading-g20-reactions-to-nuclear-weapons-ban-treaty-pub-75279.

[59] See Marie-Danielle Smith, "Opposition Seek actions from Liberal Foreign Policy as Trudeau Shuns 'useless' Disarmament Talks" (June 7, 2017), *National Post*, available online: https://nationalpost.com/news/politics/opposition-seek-actions-from-liberal-foreign-policy-as-trudeau-shuns-useless-disarmament-talks.

participate in verification-related initiatives. The Netherlands also noted insufficient safeguards standards in order for the IAEA to draw a conclusion about the absence of undeclared nuclear activities.[60]

During the negotiations, the Netherlands argued that a treaty of this nature should "strengthen and complement the NPT," as per resolution 71/258. It stated that the current text "does not do that," and as such the Netherlands contended that it actually "places the treaty above the NPT and sets up a comprehensive parallel review mechanism, to which it assigns a mandate that at least partially overlaps with that of the NPT."[61] As a result, it said that this formulated "a recipe for competition and fragmentation" when "efforts on disarmament should be concentrated." The Netherlands maintained that the NPT contains the only disarmament obligations binding the five permanent members of the UN Security Council and is the "primary framework for pursuing a world without nuclear weapons."[62]

Such comments are important as the Netherlands was the only state participating in the negotiations that subsequently voted against the Treaty's adoption in July 2017. This significance cannot be underestimated in terms of the development of customary law, as this state is clearly not in favor of the TPNW despite offering suggestions for its overall improvement and effectiveness.

CUSTOMARY INTERNATIONAL LAW, STATE PRACTICE AND *OPINIO JURIS*

In questioning whether the TPNW may become enforceable under customary international law, it is useful to examine similar movements to the Ottawa Convention on Landmines and the Oslo Convention on Cluster Munitions.[63] While every clause of these documents is not necessarily binding on states not party to the agreement, there is speculation that the general prohibition against use either is, or could become, part of customary international law and thus, binding. The majority of states have adopted the 1997 Ottawa Convention, with the United States as a notable exception, and it has seen widespread compliance with respect to the non-use norm.[64] Based on the dramatic global reduction in the

---

[60] "Explanation of Vote of the Netherlands on Text of Nuclear Ban Treaty" (July 7, 2017), available online: https://s3.amazonaws.com/unoda-web/wp-content/uploads/2017/07/Netherlands-EoV-Nuclear-Ban-Treaty.pdf.

[61] Ibid.

[62] Ibid.

[63] See Carlo Trezza, "The UN Nuclear Ban Treaty and the NPT: Challenges for Nuclear Disarmament" (September 9, 2017) *Instituto Affari Internazionali*, available online: www.iai.it/en/pubblicazioni/un-nuclear-ban-treaty-and-npt-challenges-nuclear-disarmament.

[64] See, e.g., Adam Bower, "Authority in the Breach? Assessing the Influence of the Anti-Personnel Landmine Ban Over Non-Party States" (2011) *Annual Convention of the Canadian Political Science Association*, available online: www.cpsa-acsp.ca/papers-2011/Bower.pdf, which also cites Susan Benesch et al., "International Customary Law and Antipersonnel Landmines: Emergence of a New Customary Norm" (1999), available online: http://archives.the-monitor.org/index.php/publications/.

production, transfer, and use of landmines, the "trend of state practice" appears to be leading toward a norm whereby any use of landmines is in violation of customary international law.[65] Similar possibilities have been raised with respect to the more recent Convention on Cluster Munitions, which has seen a "large number of signatories, including several NATO states" and is thus "likely" to be accepted as customary international law in the future.[66] This author, however, would suggest that neither movement is analogous, nor directly applicable to the case at hand. Many states that became party to these conventions possessed such weapons, which they then moved to eliminate.[67] Thus, the political will to dispose of the weapons concerned seems (to have been) far greater than appears to be the case for states possessing nuclear weapons.

With respect to customary international law, the object of this discussion is to explore various rules to consider how the TPNW could potentially, and indeed the likelihood of whether it would, establish customary international law. Within this context, it seems that a nuclear weapons ban would mean that a rule prohibiting possession of nuclear weapons would require consistent state practice. This is important, because it matters to determine consistent and inconsistent state practice (omissions v. actions in case of prohibitive rules). From the outset of this discussion, as a general comment, one must separate the inquiry clearly with respect to state practice and to *opinio juris*. In this respect, the issue of specially affected states was broached by the International Court of Justice with respect to state practice and that is particularly relevant to this discussion regarding persistent objection. While divergent practice has a role to play, objection must primarily relate to *opinio juris* (a belief by the objecting state that it is not legally bound by the purported rule in development). In examining whether states might be bound, presently or in the future without ratifying the Treaty, one must examine Article 38(1)(b) of the Statute of the International Court of Justice which recognizes "international custom, as evidence of a general practice accepted as law."[68]

A similar pronouncement on landmines is made in Jaume Saura, "On the Implications of the Use of Drones in International Law" (Spring 2016) 12 *J Int L and Int Relations* 120 at 129.

[65] See Ryan Kocse, "Final Detonation: How Customary International Law Can Trigger the End of Landmines" (2013) 103:3 *Georgetown L J* 749 at 796, available online: https://georgetownlawjournal.org/articles/54/final-detonation-how-customary/pdf.

[66] Daniel Joseph Raccuia, "The Convention on Cluster Munitions: An Incomplete Solution to the Cluster Munition Problem" (2011) 44 *Vanderbilt J of Transnational Law* 465 at 485–486, available online: www.vanderbilt.edu/wp-content/uploads/sites/78/raccuia-cr.pdf.

[67] See Carlo Trezza, "The UN Nuclear Ban Treaty and the NPT: Challenges for Nuclear Disarmament" (September 9, 2017) *Instituto Affari Internazionali*, available online: www.iai.it/en/pubblicazioni/un-nuclear-ban-treaty-and-npt-challenges-nuclear-disarmament.

[68] Notably, under para. 2, "This provision shall not prejudice the power of the Court to decide a case ex aequo et bond, if the parties agree thereto." See http://legal.un.org/avl/pdf/ha/sicj/icj_statute_e.pdf and see also www.icj-cij.org/en/statute.

Unlike express agreement under treaties, the rules of customary international law do not originate from expressly negotiated outcomes, and consequently they do not require any domestic act of ratification to become binding as would be the case under treaty law. A state would be required to sign and ratify the TPNW in order to be bound by it in accordance with Article 38(1)(a); it would be bound by Article 18 VCLT and unlikely to take actions to defy its purpose. In the absence of an express intention to ratify the TPNW, given the right circumstances, a state instead may be bound legally under customary rules of international law listed in 38(1)(b) above. Customary international law refers to international obligations arising from established state practice, as opposed to obligations arising from formal written international treaties (as per Article 38(1)(a)). Note that *opinio juris* and state practice are separated (following the two elements approach).

Ian Brownlie identifies four elements to consider: duration; uniformity (described as consistency of the practice); generality of the practice; and *opinio juris sive necessitatis.*[69] Derived from the Latin phrase *opinio juris sive necessitatis* meaning "an opinion of law or necessity,"[70] it involves a subjective element, in that the state in question accepts and is bound by the law in question. Note that neither is actually mentioned in Article 38(1)(b). Applying the Brownlie formula to the TPNW, it seems unlikely that non-party states would be bound under customary international law. Effectively, "customary international law" results from a general and consistent practice of states whereby they follow the said practice from "a sense of legal obligation."[71] After all, the statements from non-party states set out above show they do not view the TPNW as imposing any such sense of obligation.

In relation to arguing a case to enforce customary international practice, the International Court of Justice Handbook states that, "[t]he Court's practice shows that a state which relies on an alleged international custom practised by States must, generally speaking, demonstrate to the Court's satisfaction that this custom has

---

[69] See Ian Brownlie, *Principles of Public International Law*, 7th ed. (Oxford University Press, 2008) at 7–10. See https://files.pca-cpa.org/pcadocs/bi-c/2.%20Canada/4.%20Legal%20Authorities/RA-58%20-%20Principles%20of%20Public%20International%20Law,%20Brownlie,%207th%20edition,%20Sources%20of%20Law.pdf. Note the more recent *Brownlie's Principles of Public International Law*, 8th ed. by James Crawford (Oxford University Press, 2012). For a good overview of the general principles of international customary law, see International Law Association, "Statement of Principles Applicable to the Formation of General Customary International Law" (2000), available online: www.law.umich.edu/facultyhome/drwcasebook/Documents/.Documents/ILA%20Report%20on%20Formation%20of%20Customary%20International%20Law.pdf. Also: Draft conclusions on identification of customary international law, with commentaries (2018), adopted by the International Law Commission at its seventieth session, in 2018, and submitted to the General Assembly as a part of the Commission's report covering the work of that session (A/73/10), http://legal.un.org/ilc/texts/instruments/english/commentaries/1_13_2018.pdf.

[70] "Opinio juris (international law)," *Cornell Law School*, available online: www.law.cornell.edu/wex/opinio_juris_%28international_law%29.

[71] "Customary International Law," *Cornell University Law School*, available online: www.law.cornell.edu/wex/Customary_international_law. See Malcolm N. Shaw, *International Law*, 5th ed. (Cambridge, 2003) at 80.

become so established as to be legally binding on the other party."[72] The Handbook illustrates this point through case examples citing the *North Sea Continental Shelf* cases in which the ICJ stated, with respect to customary international law, "[n]ot only must the acts concerned amount to a settled practice, but they must also be such, or be carried out in such a way, as to be evidence of a belief that this practice is rendered obligatory by the existence of a rule of law requiring it." In other words, a state's frequent or habitual performance of certain actions does not, by itself, establish *opinio juris*; there must be "a belief" that such a practice is obligatory.[73]

The Handbook goes on to offer further clarification on customary international law. It explains that, in the case concerning the Continental Shelf (Libyan Arab Jamahiriya/Malta), "the material of customary international law is to be looked for primarily in the actual practice and *opinio juris* of States." Further, in the case concerning Military and Paramilitary Activities in and against Nicaragua, the Court found that while it could not deal with complaints based on certain multilateral treaties owing to a reservation accompanying the declaration recognizing the compulsory jurisdiction of the Court, that reservation did not prevent it from applying the corresponding principles of customary international law. The Court explained that the fact that these principles "have been codified or embodied in multilateral conventions does not mean they cease to exist and to apply as principles of customary law, even as regards countries that are parties to such conventions." Furthermore, such principles "continue to be binding as part of customary international law, despite the operation of provisions of conventional law in which they have been incorporated."[74] As these statements show, the actual practice of states is a critical element of any argument that an international custom has become legally binding.

DOCTRINE OF THE PERSISTENT OBJECTOR

As discussed above, *opinio juris* is a primary element, along with state practice, in order to establish a legally binding international custom under Article 38(1)(b) of the Statute of the International Court of Justice. In the *Continental Shelf* case, the ICJ explained the concept of *opinio juris*, in that,

> for a new customary rule to be formed, not only must the acts concerned "amount to a settled practice," but they must be accompanied by *opinio juris sive necessitatis*. Either the States taking such action or other States in a position to react to it, must have behaved so that their conduct is evidence of a belief that the practice is

---

[72] See *International Court of Justice Handbook*, 6th ed. (Maubeuge, France: Triangle Bleu, 2014) at 97, available online: www.icj-cij.org/files/publications/handbook-of-the-court-en.pdf.

[73] *North Sea Continental Shelf, Judgment of the ICJ (Germany v. Denmark; Germany v. Netherlands)*, ICJ Reports (1969) p. 3, available online: www.icj-cij.org/files/case-related/51/051–19690220-JUD-01–00-EN.pdf.

[74] See *International Court of Justice Handbook*, 6th ed. (Maubeuge, France: Triangle Bleu, 2014) at 97, available online: www.icj-cij.org/files/publications/handbook-of-the-court-en.pdf.

120 TPNW 2017: Toward Universality?

rendered obligatory by the existence of a rule of law requiring it. The need for such belief ... the subjective element, is implicit in the very notion of *opinio juris sive necessitatis*.[75]

In other words, for a State to be bound as a source under Article 38(1)(b), the practice in question must be "accepted as law" in order to be applied. "Whether the practice of a State is due to *a belief* that it is legally obliged to do a particular act is difficult to prove objectively."[76]

The subjective requirement of *opinio juris* is even more difficult to establish if the state in question has been a persistent objector to the practice in question. The doctrine of persistent objector generally requires that the objection be persistent. The objection must normally have occurred during the formation of the norm and especially prior to the crystallization of the customary practice or behavior in question.[77] In this regard, it seems that acts and deeds could suffice as legitimate "objections" and do not necessarily require words, written or spoken, per se.

The concept of persistent objector first emerged as a characteristic of public international law in the 1950s, emanating from jurisprudence of the ICJ in the *Asylum* and *Fisheries* cases. In the *Asylum* case, the Court found that no actual custom existed regarding the rule concerning unilateral and definitive qualification of offenses eligible for asylum in a dispute between Colombia and Peru over Colombia's decision to grant diplomatic asylum to a Peruvian citizen who had been charged by Peru with the crime of "military rebellion." The Court stated that,

> even if it could be supposed that such a custom existed between certain Latin American States only, it could not be invoked against Peru which, far from having its attitude adhered to it, has, on the contrary, repudiated it by refraining from ratifying the Montevideo Conventions of 1933 and 1939, which were the first to include a rule concerning the qualification of the offence in matters of diplomatic asylum.[78]

Note that, the Court's argument here may be questioned, since failure to ratify a treaty can hardly be said to be a rejection per se of any particular rule contained within the treaty.[79] That said, the relevant practice in question must also be

---

[75] *North Sea Continental Shelf, Judgment of the ICJ (Germany v. Denmark; Germany v. Netherlands)*, ICJ Reports (1969) p. 3 at para. 77, available online: www.icj-cij.org/files/case-related/51/051–19690220-JUD-01-00-EN.pdf.

[76] "Opinio juris (international law)," *Cornell Law School*, available online: www.law.cornell.edu/wex/opinio_juris_%28international_law%29.

[77] See also Curtis A. Bradley and Mitu Gulati, "Withdrawing from International Custom" (2010) 120 *The Yale Law Journal* 202, available online: https://documents.law.yale.edu/sites/default/files/Bradley %20.

[78] *Colombian-Peruvian Asylum Case, Judgment of 20 November 1950*, ICJ Reports (1950) p 266 at 277–278, available online: www.icj-cij.org/files/case-related/7/007–19501120-JUD-01-00-EN.pdf.

[79] See in this respect André de Hoogh, "Regionalism and the Unity of International Law from a Positivist Perspective," 2012, pp. 60–61, footnote 65. www.researchgate.net/publication/256043234_Regionalism _and_the_Unity_of_International_Law_from_a_Positivist_Perspective.

consistent and uniform to show an expression of a right belonging to one state and a duty incumbent on another. In this instance, Colombia failed to prove consistent and uniform usage of the alleged custom by relevant states, thus not proving the existence of a regional custom. The various fluctuations and contradictions in state practice meant that the norm did not amount to a uniform usage. The ICJ held that,

> [t]he Party which relies on a custom of this kind must prove that this custom is established in such a manner that it has become binding on the other Party ... (that) it is in accordance with a (1) constant and uniform usage (2) practiced by the States in question, and that this usage is (3) the expression of a right appertaining to the State granting asylum and (4) a duty incumbent on the territorial State (in this case, Peru). This follows from Article 38 of the Statute of the Court, which refers to international custom "as evidence of a general practice accepted as law."[80]

A year later, in the *Fisheries* case, in relation to the ten-mile rule for the closing lines of bays, the Court stated that it "would appear to be inapplicable as against Norway inasmuch as she has always opposed any attempt to apply it to the Norwegian coast."[81] Both cases deal with the cementing into place – in other words, the crystallization – of customary practice into international law.

Years later, in the *North Sea Continental Shelf* cases, the Court highlighted the difference between custom (i.e., habits), and customary law, stating:

> [n]ot only must the acts concerned amount to a settled practice, but they must also be such, or be carried out in such a way, as to be evidence of a belief that this practice is rendered obligatory by the existence of a rule of law requiring it. The need for such a belief, i.e., the existence of a subjective element, is implicit in the very notion of the *opinio juris sive necessitatis*. The States concerned must therefore feel that they are conforming to what amounts to a legal obligation. The frequency, or even habitual character of the acts is not in itself enough. There are many international acts, e.g., in the field of ceremonial and protocol, which are performed almost invariably, but which are motivated only by considerations of courtesy, convenience or tradition, and not by any sense of legal duty.[82]

This often-cited passage shows that demonstration of a subjective belief is a key component of customary international law. It follows that a state which demonstrates its opposition to the practice is less likely to satisfy the *opinio juris* requirement. Along these lines, Ted Stein highlights that,

---

[80] *Colombian-Peruvian Asylum Case, Judgment of 20 November 1950*, ICJ Reports (1950) p. 266 at 276–277, available online: www.icj-cij.org/files/case-related/7/007-19501120-JUD-01-00-EN.pdf.

[81] *Fisheries Case, Judgment of December 18th, 1951*, ICJ Reports (1951) p. 116 at 131, available online: www .icj-cij.org/files/case-related/5/005-19511218-JUD-01-00-EN.pdf.

[82] *North Sea Continental Shelf, Judgment of the ICJ (Germany v. Denmark; Germany v. Netherlands)*, ICJ Reports (1969) p. 3 at para. 77, available online: www.icj-cij.org/files/case-related/51/051-19690220-JUD-01-00-EN.pdf.

[m]ainstream accounts of the principles governing the formation and application of rules of customary international law typically include reference to the principle of the "persistent objector." According to that principle, a state that has persistently objected to a rule of customary international law during the course of the rule's emergence is not bound by the rule. The principle thus permits individual states to opt out of new and otherwise universal rules of international law. Simple in statement and dispositive in effect, the principle of the persistent objector seems to present few of the notorious problems of judgment and degree that pervade inquiries into the existence *vel non* of any given rule of customary international law.[83]

In the abstract of his book *The Persistent Objector Rule in International Law*, James Green highlights:

[t]he persistent objector rule is said to provide states with an "escape hatch" from the otherwise universal binding force of customary international law. It provides that if a state persistently objects to a newly emerging norm of customary international law during the formation of that norm, then the objecting state is exempt from the norm once it crystallises into law. The conceptual role of the rule may be interpreted as straightforward: to preserve the fundamentalist positivist notion that any norm of international law can only bind a state that has consented to be bound by it.[84]

Similarly, Jonathan I. Charney in his article on universal international law, highlights that arguments supporting the persistent objector rule are based on the view that international law is the product of the consent of states.[85] With these understandings in mind, it becomes difficult to see how it could be interpreted that any of the five nuclear-weapon states, or the others not participating in the conference deliberations, or voting on the final text of the TPNW could be seen as agreeing to it either *de facto*, let alone *de jure*. In another case addressing a state which was similarly silent on a treaty, the *Namibia* Advisory Opinion,[86] the ICJ held that the silence of a treaty cannot be interpreted to exclude the invocation of a right (in that case to invoke a material breach as a ground for termination) originating outside of the treaty in general international law.

Olufemi Elias writes that:

[a]ccording to established doctrine, once a rule of customary international law has been established and is binding on a State (States), that State cannot exempt itself unilaterally from the obligations imposed by that rule. To avoid the applicability of

---

[83] Ted L. Stein, "The Approach of the Different Drummer: The Principle of Persistent Objector in International Law" (1985) 26 *Harv Int LJ* 457 at 458.

[84] Abstract of James A. Green, *The Persistent Objector Rule in International Law* (Oxford University Press, 2016). Note that Green also points out that in reality there are numerous unanswered questions regarding the manner that the rule actually works in practice. (Perhaps these unanswered questions might challenge the existence of the rule at all.)

[85] Jonathan I. Charney, "Universal International Law" (1993) 89 *American J Int L* 529 at 54.

[86] ICJ Reports (1971) p. 16, at p. 47 (para. 96).

Doctrine of the Persistent Objector

that rule to itself, the rule must be replaced by a different rule, and in order for a different rule to come into being, other States must recognize that new rule as being applicable. The question then is whether a State that does not want to be bound by a rule can exempt itself from the operation of the rule.[87]

The idea that non-consenting states might be bound under customary international law would be unlikely under contemporary customary law. To begin with, the NPT expressly recognizes the existence and legality of a nuclear-weapon state, defining it as, "one which has manufactured and exploded a nuclear weapon or other nuclear explosive device prior to 1 January, 1967."[88] As a result, as it stands today and throughout the negotiations of the TPNW, the United States of America, the Russian Federation, the United Kingdom, France and China are in fact nuclear-weapon states under this international treaty. In that regard, nuclear-weapon states are under a strict obligation not to transfer nuclear weapons or devices to any recipient whatsoever, and non-nuclear-weapon states are not to receive such weapons under any circumstances. Specifically, Article I of the NPT stipulates that nuclear-weapon state parties are "not to transfer to any recipient whatsoever nuclear weapons or other nuclear explosive devices or control over such weapons or explosive devices directly, or indirectly; and not in any way to assist, encourage, or induce any non-nuclear-weapon state to manufacture or otherwise acquire nuclear weapons or other nuclear explosive devices, or control over such weapons or explosive devices."[89] Nuclear-weapon states may argue that their legitimate position is well-established by international law, specifically under the NPT.

Moreover, given the refusal of various states to participate in the deliberations or vote on the TPNW, in conjunction with the international jurisprudence emanating from the ICJ, compounded by the rule of persistent objectors, it would seem that the sum total of all these factors means that it is nearly impossible for them to be held to the TPNW. Thus, any binding requirements or universal application of the Treaty are quelled. The Netherlands, for one, is on record as voting against the Treaty demonstrating an explicit lack of full consensus among the negotiating participants. Furthermore, over thirty countries refused to participate in the negotiations in any form, with some such as India, the United Kingdom, France and the United States, explicitly denouncing the Treaty.[90] Such objections cannot be ignored.

---

[87] Max Planck Encyclopedia of International Law, https://opil.ouplaw.com/view/10.1093/law:epil/9780199231690/law-9780199231690-e1455.

[88] Article IX(3) of the Treaty on the Non-Proliferation of Nuclear Weapons (July 1, 1968) 729 *UNTS* 161, available online: https://unoda-web.s3-accelerate.amazonaws.com/wp-content/uploads/assets/WMD/. Nuclear/pdf/NPTEnglish_Text.pdf.

[89] Article I of Treaty on the Non-Proliferation of Nuclear Weapons (July 1, 1968) 729 *UNTS* 161, available online: https://unoda-web.s3-accelerate.amazonaws.com/wp-content/uploads/assets/WMD/Nuclear/pdf/NPTEnglish_Text.pdf.

[90] See Carlo Trezza, "The UN Nuclear Ban Treaty and the NPT: Challenges for Nuclear Disarmament" (September 9, 2017) *Instituto Affari Internazionali*, available online: www.iai.it/en/pubblicazioni/un-nuclear-ban-treaty-and-npt-challenges-nuclear-disarmament.

124 TPNW 2017: Toward Universality?

That said, beyond the five nuclear-weapon states recognized under the NPT,[91] the first pillar of the Treaty requires nonproliferation of nuclear weapons, whereby non-nuclear-weapon states agree not to import, manufacture or otherwise acquire nuclear weapons or other nuclear explosive devices, prohibiting horizontal proliferation in that non-nuclear weapon states are not to acquire nuclear weapons. Nuclear-weapon states are under strict obligations not to transfer nuclear weapons or devices to any recipient whatsoever under Article I, effectively restricting their activities. Furthermore, Article II requires non-nuclear-weapon state parties "not to receive the transfer from any transferor whatsoever of nuclear weapons or other nuclear explosive devices or of control over such weapons or explosive devices directly, or indirectly; [as well as] not to manufacture or otherwise acquire nuclear weapons or other nuclear explosive devices; and not to seek or receive any assistance in the manufacture of nuclear weapons or other nuclear explosive devices."[92] The NPT is clear in the nonproliferation obligations it imposes upon non-nuclear-weapon states. Moreover, the signatories expressly agree to these terms.

Aside from some of the non-nuclear-weapon states accepting the terms of the TPNW, many of them have not yet accepted their obligations under the NPT. Charney highlights that nations often "forge new law by breaking existing law," thereby leading the way for other nations to follow such practices.[93] In this sense, it could be argued that many states are in fact establishing their persistent objections not only to the TPNW, but also the NPT, the very foundation and cornerstone of nuclear nonproliferation. Indeed, of late, this seems to be the case regarding some countries wishing to acquire nuclear-weapon state status under international law. Beyond the five nuclear-weapon states recognized under the NPT, some de facto nuclear-weapon states, namely North Korea, Israel,[94] India[95] and Pakistan,[96] seem to assert their defiance of existing norms and treaty obligations. Despite these NPT

[91] As per Article IX(3) of the NPT which states that, "a nuclear weapon State is one which has manufactured and exploded a nuclear weapon or other nuclear explosive device prior to 1 January, 1967." This acknowledges that United States, Russia, the United Kingdom, France and China are nuclear-weapon states under international law.

[92] Article II of the NPT.

[93] Jonathan I. Charney, "The Persistent Objector Rule and the Development of Customary International Law" (1985) 56 *Brit YB Int L* 21.

[94] Unconfirmed estimates for Israel's nuclear weapons stockpile range around eighty intact nuclear weapons and additional inventories of fissile materials of 0.3 tonnes highly enriched uranium (HEU) plus 0.84 ± 0.13 tonnes of separated plutonium, see Philip Schell and Hans M. Kristensen, "Israeli nuclear forces" and Alexander Glaser and Zia Mian, International Panel on Fissile Materials, "Global Stocks and Production of Fissile Materials, 2012," in *SIPRI Yearbook 2013* (Oxford: Oxford University Press, 2013) at 321–322 and 326–331. See also reports by the Federation of American Scientists (FAS), available online: www.fas.org/nuke/guide/israel/nuke and see Avner Cohen, *Israel and the Bomb* (Columbia University Press, 1998).

[95] See Security Council Resolution 1172 (1998); Agreement for Cooperation between the Government of the United States of America and the Government of India Concerning Peaceful Uses of Nuclear Energy (October 10, 2008), available online: https://2001-2009.state.gov/p/sca/c17361.htm.

[96] See Security Council Resolution 1172 (1998); Agreement between the Government of Islamic Republic of Pakistan and the Government of Republic of India on Reducing the Risk from

stipulations and other obligations, they have now acquired nuclear devices. This highlights a serious problem for nonproliferation enforcement. Given that they are not parties to the NPT and in light of the problem at hand, it may have been beneficial for the TPNW to tackle these matters directly.

Perhaps the most serious acts of defiance of the NPT have come from the Democratic People's Republic of Korea (North Korea), which has withdrawn from the NPT. All the more worrying is that one would think North Korea must have been preparing to build a nuclear weapon for some time before it sent its notification of withdrawal from the NPT. At this point it is not merely a persistent objector, but in breach of NPT obligations. In response, the United Nations Security Council called on it to recall its withdrawal and to abandon all nuclear weapons and existing nuclear programs.[97] To that end, Resolution 1718 makes it clear that North Korea cannot have the status of nuclear-weapon state, "[e]xpressing its firm conviction that the international regime on the nonproliferation of nuclear weapons should be maintained and recalling that the DPRK cannot have the status of a nuclear-weapon state in accordance with the Treaty on the Non-Proliferation of Nuclear Weapons."

This is stated in the preamble and it adds "in accordance with the Treaty on the Non-Proliferation on Nuclear Weapons." As such, the resolution is rather ambiguous, since demanding a retraction of the withdrawal seems to suggest that DPRK might no longer be a party to the NPT, and if not a party, consequently it may possess nuclear weapons. Indeed, one could challenge the DPRK's notification of withdrawal as ineffective stating that there were no extraordinary circumstances. The Resolution decided that North Korea must,

> abandon all nuclear weapons and existing nuclear programmes in a complete, verifiable and irreversible manner, [and] shall act strictly in accordance with the obligations applicable to parties under the Treaty on the Non-Proliferation of Nuclear Weapons and the terms and conditions of its International Atomic Energy Agency (IAEA) Safeguards Agreement (IAEA INFCIRC/403) and shall provide the IAEA transparency measures extending beyond these requirements, including such access to individuals, documentation, equipments and facilities as may be required and deemed necessary by the IAEA.[98]

To date, North Korea continues to defy UN Security Council orders, maintaining that it is not a party to the Treaty and therefore remains outside the NPT.[99] For

---

Accidents Relating to Nuclear Weapons (February 21, 2007), available online: www.stimson.org /agreement-on-reducing-the-risk-from-accidents-relating-to-nuclear-weap.

[97] See Security Council Resolutions 1718 (2006), 1874 (2009), 2050 (2012), 2087 (2013) and 2094 (2013).

[98] Security Council Resolution 1718 (October 14, 2006) at para. 6, available online: www.un.org/ga/ search/view_doc.asp?symbol=S/RES/1718%20%282006%29.

[99] "[T]he status of the Democratic People's Republic of Korea (DPRK) remains ambiguous as it offers a substantively different interpretation from the UN position. The DPRK became a party to the NPT on 12th December 1985 as a non-nuclear weapon State but on 12th March 1993 gave notice to withdraw in accordance with Art. X of the NPT. The DPRK cited the resumption of joint US-South Korean military

126   *TPNW 2017: Toward Universality?*

different reasons Israel,[100] India[101] and Pakistan[102] do not feel bound by the NPT as they had never signed or ratified the Treaty in the first instance. Iran, a state party to the NPT, was said to be in breach of its obligations in relation to applicable safeguards[103] and UN Security Council resolutions.[104] Now, under an historic Joint Comprehensive Plan of Action (JCPOA) adopted by the E3/EU+3 (China, France, Germany, the Russian Federation, the United Kingdom and the United States, with the High Representative of the European Union for Foreign Affairs and Security Policy) and the Islamic Republic of Iran,[105] the latter is implementing a comprehensive binding political accord, which is not a legally binding agreement.[106] Again, in May 2018 the United States unilaterally

> exercises as its reasons in its three month notice of withdrawal to all other State Parties to the Treaty and the United Nations Security Council (UNSC), claiming those exercises amounted to a nuclear war rehearsal against the DPRK and also alleging the IAEA's lack of impartiality in dealing with its nuclear issues. The withdrawal was to enter into force on 12th June 1993, but before this date the DPRK suspended its withdrawal after reaching an agreement one day before the withdrawal was due to come into effect. Given that there is no rule for suspending the entering into force of a withdrawal notice under the NPT, or under the general law of treaties, the DPRK status remained somewhat obscure. It declared a unique status under the NPT, effectively concluding that the IAEA could no longer oblige it to carry out its work under the comprehensive safeguards agreement, which is an obligation under the NPT." And, for further discussion as to why this author argues that North Korean is technically a party to the NPT, see Jonathan Black-Branch, "Nuclear Terrorism by States and Non-State Actors: Global Responses to Threats to Military and Human Security in International Law" (2017) 22:2 *Journal of Conflict & Security Law* 1 at 7-8.

[100]   See n. 99.

[101]   See Security Council Resolution 1172 (1998); see also Agreement for Cooperation between the Government of the United States of America and the Government of India Concerning Peaceful Uses of Nuclear Energy (October 10, 2008), available online: https://2001-2009.state.gov/p/sca/c17361.htm.

[102]   Ibid.

[103]   See IAEA Report by the Director General, "Implementation of the NPT Safeguards Agreement and the Relevant Provisions of the Security Council Resolutions in the Islamic Republic of Iran" (August 28, 2013), GOV/2013/40, available online: www.iaea.org/sites/default/files/gov2013-40.pdf. The Committee will focus on legal aspects of verification in its forthcoming Third Report.

[104]   See Security Council Resolutions 1696 (2006), 1737 (2006), 1747 (2007), 1803 (2008), 1835 (2008), 1929 (2010) and 1984 (2011). It should be noted that many Security Council Resolutions have been challenged by a practice of non-compliance. See also Shannon N. Kile (ed.), *Europe and Iran: Perspectives on Non-Proliferation* (Oxford: Oxford University Press/SIPRI, 2005).

[105]   See https://undocs.org/S/RES/2231(2015); Resolution 2231 (2015) on Iran Nuclear Issue (www.un.org /securitycouncil/content/2231/background) and www.undocs.org/S/2015/544. See also: Joint Plan of Action adopted by the "EU3+3" and Iran (November 24, 2013), available online: www.treasury.gov /resource-center/sanctions/Programs/Documents/jpoa.pdf. See also Joint Statement by EU High Representative Catherine Ashton and Iran Foreign Minister Zarif (November 24, 2013), available online: www.europarl.europa.eu/meetdocs/2009_2014/documents/d-ir/dv/joint_st_ashton_zar/join t_st_ashton_zarif.pdf.

[106]   Arguably, it could be seen as soft law, given the reference to good faith and the setting up of a Joint Commission to monitor the implementation of the near-term measures and to address issues that may arise. See also Dirk Roland Haupt, "Legal Aspects of the Nuclear Accord with Iran and Its Implementation: International Law Analysis of Security Council Resolution 2231 (2015)," in Black-Branch and Fleck (eds.), *Nuclear Non-Proliferation in International Law*, Vol. III, (Berlin/Heidelberg, 2016), 403–470.

withdrew from the JCPOA and in May 2019, Iran stepped out of certain limitations on its enrichment activities. In November 2019, acting Director-General Cornel Feruta of the IAEA, advised Iran to cooperate fully with the Agency in order to resolve outstanding issues.[107] With these points related to the universality of the NPT in mind, it is difficult to see how universality of the TPNW will be achieved.

As a general observation, one must distinguish a persistent objection from widespread opposition to a purported rule and its existence in the first place. In this case, there are at least nine states with nuclear arms (in fact), five of whom have the backing from a relatively large number of other states (allies). This suggests the latter situation is a more accurate description of reality than the former. That said, one must bear in mind that persistent objections cannot be used, however, to invalidate or ignore peremptory norms of *jus cogens*. Neither can such obligations be overridden by treaty law,[108] or obligations *erga omnes* which will be discussed in greater detail in Chapter 12.

NUCLEAR-WEAPON STATES: DISARMAMENT AND ENDING THE ARMS RACE OR *VEL NON*?

In addition to other requirements, pursuant to the third pillar of the NPT, nuclear-weapon states are required to move toward disarmament which arguably could be interpreted by supporters of the TPNW not to increase their stockpiles of weapons. Specifically, Article VI of the NPT requires that all parties undertake "to pursue negotiations in good faith on effective measures relating to cessation of the nuclear arms race at an early date and to nuclear disarmament, and on a treaty on general and complete disarmament under strict and effective international control."[109] Many states embrace this obligation. Even though the TPNW echoes support for Article VI obligations amounting to significant support, many states do not see this particular treaty, the TPNW, as the one to achieve this outcome. During the UN General Assembly's efforts to move the TPNW treaty process forward in October 2016, it was passed by a vote of 123 states in favor, but with 38 against and 16 abstaining. No further support was gained throughout the rest of the process leading to the final text being adopted in July, 2017. This is an important consideration whilst examining issues of *opinio juris* and persistent objectors in relation to the formulation of customary law and universality. In addition, in the *Namibia* Advisory

---

[107] Acting Director General Urges Iran to Fully Cooperate with IAEA. Reported by Kendall Siewert. See www.iaea.org/newscenter/news/acting-director-general-urges-iran-to-fully-cooperate-with-iaea.

[108] Gordon A. Christenson, "Jus Cogens: Guarding Interests Fundamental to International Society" (1987) 28 *Virginia J of Int L* 585, available online: https://scholarship.law.uc.edu/cgi/viewcontent.cgi?article=1161&context=fac_pubs.

[109] Article VI of the Treaty on the Non-Proliferation of Nuclear Weapons (July 1, 1968) 729 *UNTS* 161, available online: https://unoda-web.s3-accelerate.amazonaws.com/wp-content/uploads/assets/WMD/Nuclear/pdf/NPTEnglish_Text.pdf.

Opinion cited above,[110] the ICJ held that the silence of a treaty cannot be interpreted to exclude the invocation of a right originating outside of the treaty in general international law.

Even though for the most part, General Assembly resolutions are not legally binding, in the *Nuclear Weapons* case the ICJ highlighted that such resolutions can be important for either establishing the existence of a rule of customary law, or in order to establish the emergence of an *opinio juris*,

> it is necessary to look at its content and the conditions of adoption; it is also necessary to see whether an *opinio juris* exists as to its normative character. Or a series of resolutions may show the gradual evolution of the *opinio juris* required for the establishment of a new rule
> ... several of the resolutions under consideration in the present case have been adopted with substantial numbers of negative votes and abstentions; thus, although those resolutions are a clear sign of deep concern regarding the problem of nuclear weapons, they still fall short of establishing the existence of an *opinio juris* on the illegality of the use of such weapons.[111]

Two decades later, a similar lack of an *opinio juris* is still apparent among many states. A joint press statement from the Permanent Representatives to the United Nations of the United States, the United Kingdom and France stated:

> We do not intend to sign, ratify or ever become party to it. Therefore, there will be no change in the legal obligations on our countries with respect to nuclear weapons. For example, we would not accept any claim that this treaty reflects or in any way contributes to the development of customary international law. Importantly, other states possessing nuclear weapons and almost all other states relying on nuclear deterrence have also not taken part in the negotiations ... A ban treaty also risks undermining the existing international security architecture which contributes to the maintenance of international peace and security.[112]

India made a similar statement wherein its minister of external affairs indicated in a press release that it "cannot be a party to the Treaty, and so shall not be bound by any of the obligations that may arise from it. India believes that this Treaty in no way constitutes or contributes to the development of any customary international law."[113]

---

[110] ICJ Reports (1971) p. 16, at p. 47 (para. 96).

[111] *Legality of the Treat or Use of Nuclear Weapons, Advisory Opinion*, ICJ Reports (1996), p. 226 at 255, available online: www.icj-cij.org/files/case-related/95/095-19960708-ADV-01-00-EN.pdf.

[112] "Joint Press Statement from the Permanent Representatives to the United Nations of the United States, United Kingdom and France Following the Adoption of a Treaty Banning Nuclear Weapons 7 July 2017" (July 7, 2017), *United States Mission to the United Nations*, available online: https://usun.state.gov/remarks/7892.

[113] "Response by the Official Spokesperson to a Media Query Regarding India's View on the Treaty to Ban Nuclear Weapons" (July 18, 2017) *Government of India Ministry of External Affairs*, available online: www.mea.gov.in/media-briefings.htm?dtl/28628.

Specially Affected States Doctrine

These explicit pre-emptory rejections of customary international law bolster the case that several states could be considered persistent objectors to the TPNW.

SPECIALLY AFFECTED STATES DOCTRINE

As has been established, there is widespread agreement that customary international law consists of two elements: state practice and *opinio juris*.[114] In relation to the crystallization of *opinio juris* and practice into binding customary law, one must also bear in mind the ICJ's decision regarding states "whose interests" have been "specially affected" as per the *North Sea Continental Shelf* case.[115] In this case, the Court examined the delimitation of the continental shelf areas in the North Sea in relation to Germany and Denmark as well as between Germany and the Netherlands, looking beyond the partial boundaries which had been previously agreed upon by the parties. Specifically, the parties to the dispute requested the Court to issue principles and rules of international law to be applied to the delimitation of the continental shelf delimitation because they disagreed on the applicable principles or rules of delimitation.[116] In its decision, the Court listed criteria necessary in order to establish state practice, highlighting that the practices of those states whose interests were "specially affected" by the custom were especially relevant in the formation of customary law. There must be uniform and consistent practice and the belief that such state practice is a legal obligation.[117]

---

[114] "Practice and Customary Law in Military Operations, Including Peace Support Operations," *Congress of the International Society for Military Law and the Law of War* (2009), available online: http://ismllw.org/congres/General%20Report%20Congress.pdf.

[115] *North Sea Continental Shelf, Judgment of the ICJ (Germany v. Denmark; Germany v. Netherlands)*, ICJ Reports (1969) p. 3 at para. 74, available online: www.icj-cij.org/files/case-related/51/051-19690220-JUD-01-00-EN.pdf.

[116] Specifically, the case examined "What principles and rules of international law applied to the dispute regarding the delimitation of the continental shelf between the Federal Republic of Germany and Denmark on the one hand, and between the Federal Republic of Germany and the Netherlands on the other, and then how to delimit the area on that basis. Whether the delimitations at issue were required to be carried out according to the principle of equidistance as defined in Article 6 of the 1958 Geneva Convention on the Continental Shelf or apportionment (dividing the area into equal shares). Whether the delimitations at issue were to be carried out according to equitable principles, and if so, how these principles applied in this case." See *North Sea Continental Shelf, Judgment of the ICJ (Germany v. Denmark; Germany v. Netherlands)*, ICJ Reports (1969) p. 3, available online: www.icj-cij.org/files/case-related/51/051-19690220-JUD-01-00-EN.pdf.

[117] Separate from this point, see for more specific discussions regarding the case: Nikiforos Panagis and Antonios Tzanakopoulos, "The North Sea Continental Shelf Cases: Landmark or High Watermark?" (April 18, 2017) in Eirik Bjorge and Cameron Miles, (eds.), *Landmark Cases in Public International Law* (Hart Publishing, 2017) at 283–306; available online: https://ssrn.com/abstract=2954626; and see Shelly Aviv Yeini, "The Specifically-Affecting States Doctrine" (April 2018) 112:2 *American Journal of International Law* 244-253; available online: www.cambridge.org/core/journals/american-journal-of-international-law/article/speciallyaffecting-states-doctrine/A77B3C2A4BC4E8B632A3004B498DA10F.

The Court went on to indicate that while there is no specific amount of time required for establishing customary practice,[118] an indispensable requirement would be state practice, including amongst those whose interests are "specially affected."[119] Applying this point to the discussion at hand regarding nuclear-weapon states, both *de jure* and *de facto*, their respective interests would be specially affected by any evolving norm under the TPNW. Accordingly, any change of state practice would have to be both "extensive and virtually uniform" in regard to disarmament obligations. Moreover, it would require on their part, an acceptance of a general recognition that a rule of law has been invoked or that a legal obligation was necessary in order for the provision to be invoked.

Note that the "specially affected" relates to practice; as such, they would have to participate in the practice of not possessing nuclear weapons.

The Court also noted in regard to specially affected States:

> [t]he essential point in this connection – and it seems necessary to stress it – is that even if these instances of action by non-parties to the Convention were much more numerous than they in fact are, they would not, even in the aggregate, suffice in themselves to constitute the *opinio juris*; – for, in order to achieve this result, two conditions must be fulfilled. Not only must the acts concerned amount to a settled practice, but they must also be such, or be carried out in such a way, as to be evidence of a belief that this practice is rendered obligatory by the existence of a rule of law requiring it. The need for such a belief, i.e., the existence of a subjective element, is implicit in the very notion of the *opinio juris sive necessitatis*. The States concerned must therefore feel that they are conforming to what amounts to a legal obligation. The frequency, or even habitual character of the acts is not in itself enough. There are many international acts, e.g., in the field of ceremonial and protocol, which are performed almost invariably, but which are motivated only by considerations of courtesy, convenience or tradition, and not by any sense of legal duty.[120]

[118] "As regards the time element, the Court notes that it is over ten years since the Convention was signed, but that it is even now less than five since it came into force in June 1964, and that when the present proceedings were brought it was less than three years, while less than one had elapsed at the time when the respective negotiations between the Federal Republic and the other two Parties for a complete delimitation broke down on the question of the application of the equidistance principle. Although the passage of only a short period of time is not necessarily, or of itself, a bar to the formation of a new rule of customary international law on the basis of what was originally a purely conventional rule ... " (para. 74).

[119] "Although the passage of only a short period of time is not necessarily, or of itself, a bar to the formation of a new rule of customary international law on the basis of what was originally a purely conventional rule, an indispensable requirement would be that within the period in question, short though it might be, State practice, including that of States whose interests are specially affected, should have been both extensive and virtually uniform in the sense of the provision invoked; – and should moreover have occurred in such a way as to show a general recognition that a rule of law or legal obligation is involved." *North Sea Continental Shelf, Judgment of the ICJ (Germany v. Denmark; Germany v. Netherlands)*, ICJ Reports (1969) p. 3 at para. 74, available online: www.icj-cij.org/files/case-related/51/051-19690220-JUD-01-00-EN.pdf.

[120] *North Sea Continental Shelf, Judgment of the ICJ (Germany v. Denmark; Germany v. Netherlands)*, ICJ Reports (1969) p. 3 at para. 77, available online: www.icj-cij.org/files/case-related/51/051-19690220-JUD-01-00-EN.pdf.

Legality of the Threat or Use of Nuclear Weapons 131

So even if the nuclear-weapon states were to speak of the importance of disarmament and perhaps actually express their intentions to disarm, even on numerous occasions, it would not suffice to constitute the requisite *opinio juris* to establish state practice. In order for a specially affected state to be bound by the TPNW, two conditions must be fulfilled. The acts concerned must amount to a settled practice, as evidenced by both a belief that this practice is "obligatory by the existence of a rule of law requiring it" and the state's act of exercising the practice in question. Applying the above requirements to the TPNW, it would seem that attempts to force nuclear-weapon states to disarm pursuant to evolving norms under customary international law, argued to be consistent with the terms of the TPNW, would be contrary to established ICJ jurisprudence and would be thwarted accordingly. Nuclear-weapon states would be specially affected by this change of practice and accordingly, before they would be required to acquiesce to such new norms, they would have to demonstrate uniform and consistent practice as well as hold the belief that their state practice amounts to a binding legal obligation to be bound by it. The current statements and actions by these states show that neither of these two components have been fulfilled and are unlikely to be in the foreseeable future. State practice under both treaty law and customary practice consistently and uniformly obliges nonproliferation and disarmament, including through Security Council resolutions.

LEGALITY OF THE THREAT OR USE OF NUCLEAR WEAPONS, ADVISORY OPINION: CUSTOMARY LAW

In considering the development of customary practice in relation to nuclear weapons, one must also bear in mind the ICJ's *Legality of the Threat or Use of Nuclear Weapons, Advisory Opinion* (1996).[121] The main question before the Court was: "Is the threat or use of nuclear weapons in any circumstance permitted under international law?"[122] On July 8, 1996, the Court delivered its *Advisory Opinion* in which it found, *inter alia*:

"A. There is in neither customary nor conventional international law any specific authorization of the threat or use of nuclear weapons;[123]
B. There is in neither customary nor conventional international law any comprehensive and universal prohibition of the threat or use of nuclear weapons as such;[124]

---

[121] *Legality of the Treat or Use of Nuclear Weapons, Advisory Opinion*, ICJ Reports (1996), p. 226, available online: www.icj-cij.org/files/case-related/95/095-19960708-ADV-01-00-EN.pdf.
[122] Ibid.
[123] Unanimously.
[124] By eleven votes to three. In favor: President Bedjaoui; Vice-President Schwebel; Judges Oda, Guillaume, Ranjeva, Herczegh, Shi, Fleischhauer, Vereshchetin, Ferrari Bravo, Higgins; and Against: Judges Shahabuddeen, Weeramantry, Koroma.

C. A threat or use of force by means of nuclear weapons that is contrary to Article 2, paragraph 4, of the United Nations Charter and that fails to meet all the requirements of Article 51, is unlawful;[125]

D. A threat or use of nuclear weapons should also be compatible with the requirements of the international law applicable in armed conflict, particularly those of the principles and rules of international humanitarian law, as well as with specific obligations under treaties and other undertakings which expressly deal with nuclear weapons;[126]

E. It follows from the above-mentioned requirements that the threat or use of nuclear weapons would generally be contrary to the rules of international law applicable in armed conflict, and in particular the principles and rules of humanitarian law; However, in view of the current state of international law, and of the elements of fact at its disposal, the Court cannot conclude definitively whether the threat or use of nuclear weapons would be lawful or unlawful in an extreme circumstance of self-defence, in which the very survival of a State would be at stake;[127]

F. There exists an obligation to pursue in good faith and bring to a conclusion negotiations leading to nuclear disarmament in all its aspects under strict and effective international control."[128]

In other words, one sees that no customary or treaty-based international law specifically authorized the threat or use of nuclear weapons and that there is no comprehensive and universal prohibition of the threat or use of nuclear weapons. In addition, nuclear weapons may not be used or threatened in a manner contrary to Article 2(4) or not otherwise in fulfillment of all the requirements under Article 51 of the UN Charter. Moreover, a threat or use of nuclear weapons is subject to the international law applicable in armed conflict, as well as in relation to other treaty obligations and undertakings dealing expressly with such weapons. Beyond this, there is an obligation to pursue in good faith and conclude negotiations leading to nuclear disarmament in all its aspects and achieve effective international control as per Article VI of the NPT, which the parties to the TPNW would say they were fulfilling.

One of the most worrying aspects of the judgment concerns the Court's ruling regarding extreme self-defense. Essentially, the Court left the question unresolved sparking debate on both sides of the divide. Despite this, ICJ President Bedjaoui addressed those "who will inevitably interpret [this] as contemplating the possibility of States using nuclear weapons in exceptional

---

[125] Unanimously.

[126] Unanimously.

[127] By seven votes to seven, by the President's casting vote. In favor: President Bedjaoui; Judges Ranjeva, Herczegh, Shi, Fleischhauer, Vereshchetin, Ferrari Bravo; and Against: Vice-President Schwebel; Judges Oda, Guillaume, Shahabuddeen, Weeramantry, Koroma, Higgins.

[128] Unanimously. See *Legality of the Treat or Use of Nuclear Weapons, Advisory Opinion*, ICJ Reports (1996), at pp. 226–227, paras 105(2)(A)–(F), available online: www.icj-cij.org/files/case-related/95/095-19960708-ADV-01-00-EN.pdf.

circumstances,"[129] stating: "I feel obliged in all honesty to construe that paragraph differently, a fact which has enabled me to support the text." This statement did not add clarity, leaving the question regarding the illegality of nuclear weapons unresolved. As a result, those favoring nuclear weapons claim that international law authorized them to threaten or use nuclear weapons in some circumstances, invariably contrary to the outcome sought by those seeking the advisory opinion. Given these two diametrically opposed interpretations of the ruling on extreme self-defense, it is unlikely that the TPNW objectives will actually prevail as emerging customary law.

The position of the international community today appears relatively similar to the time of the 1996 *Advisory Opinion*, with tensions and doctrinal differences preventing the development of customary international law under Article 38(1)(b). In a specific examination of whether a prohibition of the threat or use of nuclear weapons flowed from customary international law, the ICJ in a Court overview states:

> [n]oting that the members of the international community were profoundly divided on the matter of whether non-recourse to nuclear weapons over the past 50 years constituted the expression of an *opinio juris*, it did not consider itself able to find that there was such an *opinio juris*. The emergence, as *lex lata*, of a customary rule specifically prohibiting the use of nuclear weapons as such was hampered by the continuing tensions between the nascent *opinio juris* on the one hand, and the still strong adherence to the doctrine of deterrence on the other.[130]

When determining the existence of customary international law, the International Law Commission (ILC) offered a non-exhaustive list of various materials in which "Evidence of Customary International Law"[131] could be found. Such materials include, but are not limited to, treaties, decisions of both national and international courts, national legislation, diplomatic correspondence, opinions of national legal advisers and finally the practice of international organizations. See also the current ILC project: 16 draft conclusions on the identification of customary international law, with commentaries (2018), submitted to the General Assembly (A/73/10),[132] and ways and means for making the evidence of customary international law more readily available, A/CN.4/710 (January 12, 2018).[133]

---

[129] Declaration of President Bedjaoui at para. 10. See *Legality of the Treat or Use of Nuclear Weapons, Advisory Opinion,* ICJ Reports (1996), p. 226, available online: www.icj-cij.org/files/case-related/95/095-19960708-ADV-01-00-EN.pdf.

[130] At para. 73. *Legality of the Treat or Use of Nuclear Weapons, Advisory Opinion,* ICJ Reports (1996), p. 226, available online: www.icj-cij.org/files/case-related/95/095-19960708-ADV-01-00-EN.pdf.

[131] Yearbook of the International Law Commission, vol. II, 1950, Report of the International Law Commission to the General Assembly, document A/1316, p. 368.

[132] See http://legal.un.org/ilc/texts/instruments/english/commentaries/1_13_2018.pdf.

[133] See http://legal.un.org/docs/index.asp?symbol=A/CN.4/710&referer=http://legal.un.org/ilc/sessions/70/docs.shtml&Lang=E.

The ICJ have recognized the validity of verbal acts of states when determining the customary law on a certain area, for example in the *Fisheries Jurisdiction* where it referred to conference debates as the basis of state practice from which the customary law on the fishery zone and the "preferential rights of fishing in adjacent waters" for the coastal state evolved. Also, in the *Asylum* case the ICJ regarded the "official views" as well as the "exercise of diplomatic asylum" in determining whether the usage was constant and uniform. In the *Nuclear Tests* case the court recognized unilateral acts of declarations, concerning legal situations, as having an effect on legal obligations and their creation. Crucial to any recognition is the state's intention to be bound, with no strict requirement on form, per se. Any changes to NATO or umbrella state policies may contribute to the emergence of normative practice and the evolution of customary international law in respect to the TPNW, but for now it would seem that the status quo will prevail.

CONCLUSION: CHANGING *OPINIO JURIS*?

The TPNW seeks to address disarmament concerns, in part raised by the apparent absence of clear progress on nuclear disarmament as required under Article VI of the NPT. Indeed, the TPNW aspires to achieve universality in international law. Despite the ground-breaking success in agreeing on the Treaty, however, as discussed the five nuclear-weapon states (the United States, the United Kingdom, France, China and Russia) were absent from the process and refused to ratify the TPNW. Non-nuclear-weapon states known, or believed to possess nuclear weapons,[134] as well as NATO umbrella countries, also refuse to cooperate with its implementation, invariably raising important questions regarding the Treaty's potential universality or even its limited effectiveness as an arms control treaty under international law. That aside, civil society organizations contend that the failure of those states to partake in treaty negotiations does not reduce the legitimacy of the process, maintaining that the TPNW is an important milestone that serves to delegitimize nuclear weapons. Regardless, as discussed, it would seem that non-consenting states would not be bound by the Treaty under customary law, based on contemporary *opinio juris* and state practice. Universality, at this point, is an unlikely dream, despite the move to stigmatize and delegitimize nuclear weapons on a global scale.

---

[134]   Israel, India, Pakistan and North Korea.

6

Treaty Safeguards, Verification and Implementation: A Simple-Ban Approach and a Need for Oversight

VERIFICATION: CORRECTNESS AND COMPLETENESS

The success of any arms control treaty generally depends on its ability to achieve its primary objectives and intended outcomes. At the heart of measuring such success are effective compliance criteria and verification mechanisms. This includes the ability to apply metrics to assess tangible outcomes and measurable outputs and benchmarks of achievement, including on-site visits. In relation to nuclear issues, this also means that verification of both the non-diversion of nuclear material from declared peaceful activities (i.e., correctness of conduct), and the absence of undeclared or clandestine nuclear activities in a particular state (i.e., completeness in following treaty terms). For example, in 1987 the United States and the Soviet Union signed the Treaty on the Elimination of Intermediate-Range and Shorter-Range Missiles (INF)[1] under which they agreed to eliminate specific nuclear and conventional ground-launched ballistic and cruise missiles[2] as well as to participate in extensive on-site inspections for verification purposes.[3] As many as 2,692 missiles were destroyed under the implementation process.[4]

At present, the TPNW lacks any distinct verification regime of its own, raising important questions regarding measurable outcomes and credible enforcement mechanisms. For states without nuclear weapons, it makes explicit reference to existing supervisory oversight by the International Atomic Energy Agency (IAEA) and for those States possessing nuclear weapons, it makes a somewhat open and amorphous reference to a "competent international authority" without providing

---

[1] See www.state.gov/t/avc/trty/102360.htm.

[2] With ranges of 500 to 5,500 kilometers (310–3,400 miles).

[3] Not covered by the Treaty were air- or sea-launched weapons, including the American Tomahawk and Russian Kalibr cruise missiles which are launched from ships, submarines or airplanes and which could fly similar distances.

[4] Note that in December 2018, US Secretary of State Michael Pompeo gave Russian President Vladimir Putin sixty days to return to full compliance of INF obligations or the United States would also cease to honor its terms. On February 2, 2019, President Putin announced that Russia, too, would suspend the INF and start work on creating new weapons. See https://ee.usembassy.gov/remarks-by-secretary-pompeo/.

135

Treaty Safeguards, Verification and Implementation

any further details or criteria on which to evaluate or to confirm compliance or to activate enforcement measures. The seeming lack of clarity on explicit safeguards and verification oversight raises important questions regarding the implementation and enforcement of the TPNW. The Treaty makes express reference to the IAEA in Articles 3 and 4. Whilst this is a progressive step, an opportunity may have been missed, to strengthen the IAEA's role regarding international nuclear security and safety. Note, however, that the IAEA was not involved in the Treaty negotiations.

The basic concept of the TPNW is to take "a simple-ban" approach, whereby it explicitly prohibits nuclear weapons activity outright.[5] The TPNW does not contain elaborate provisions for verification and dismantlement and lacks complex details regarding Treaty compliance or decommissioning and monitoring systems. The Treaty requires a simple reporting mechanism whereby states self-assess and report.[6] The purpose of this chapter is to examine this approach in light of existing international infrastructure under the IAEA in conjunction with the Nuclear Non-Proliferation Treaty (NPT), specifying what this may mean regarding compliance, safeguards and verification. Discussion begins by focusing on verification difficulties under the "simple-ban approach," and then examining how the TPNW relates to the existing verification system. It then explores legal oversight and emerging irreversible nuclear expectations under the TPNW, before exploring what this may mean regarding Treaty implementation, compliance and effectiveness.

THE SCOPE OF PROHIBITION OF NUCLEAR WEAPONS AND EXPLOSIVE DEVICES

The central focus of the TPNW is nuclear prohibition. Article 1[7] requires that each state party undertakes "never under any circumstances" to develop,

---

[5] See "Why Nuclear Weapon Ban Treaty Is Unlikely to Fulfil Its Promise," Michal Onderco, *Global Affairs* (2017), 3:4–5, 391–404. See www.tandfonline.com/doi/full/10.1080/23340460.2017.1409082.

[6] For example, in the case of a state that possessed nuclear weapons, it "shall submit to the Secretary-General of the United Nations a final declaration that it has fulfilled its obligations" once it has done so (as per Article 4(3)).

[7] Prohibitions "Article 1. Each State Party undertakes never under any circumstances to: (a) Develop, test, produce, manufacture, otherwise acquire, possess or stockpile nuclear weapons or other nuclear explosive devices; (b) Transfer to any recipient whatsoever nuclear weapons or other nuclear explosive devices or control over such weapons or explosive devices directly or indirectly; (c) Receive the transfer of or control over nuclear weapons or other nuclear explosive devices directly or indirectly; (d) Use or threaten to use nuclear weapons or other nuclear explosive devices; (e) Assist, encourage or induce, in any way, anyone to engage in any activity prohibited to a State Party under this Treaty; (f) Seek or receive any assistance, in any way, from anyone to engage in any activity prohibited to a State Party under this Treaty; (g) Allow any stationing, installation or deployment of any nuclear weapons or other nuclear explosive devices in its territory or at any place under its jurisdiction or control."

test, produce, manufacture, acquire, possess or stockpile nuclear weapons or explosive devices.[8] Each will "never" transfer,[9] receive,[10] use or threaten to use[11] nuclear weapons or other nuclear explosive devices. States will neither assist, encourage or induce,[12] nor seek or receive assistance[13] to engage in prohibited activities. States parties agree not to allow any stationing, installation or deployment of any nuclear weapons or explosive devices in their territory or within their jurisdiction or control.[14]

VERIFICATION UNDER THE TPNW

The TPNW makes reference to the Comprehensive Nuclear-Test-Ban Treaty, recognizing its importance as well as "its verification regime as a core element of the nuclear disarmament and non-proliferation regime"[15] within the global community. Indeed, the TPNW draws on wording from the CTBT regarding the prohibition on testing. That said, the TPNW's text fails to address the relationship between these two treaties regarding compliance with prohibiting the testing of nuclear weapons as it has done with regard to the NPT. Additionally, it does not specify that adherence to the CTBT is a requirement for ensuring compliance with a prohibition of nuclear weapons testing.[16]

A "SIMPLE-BAN" HUMANITARIAN APPROACH

Negotiations for the TPNW took a simple-ban approach. This humanitarian disarmament method of agreeing a treaty allowed the negotiating parties to conclude an agreement on the intended outcomes in a relatively short period of time. The main focus was to conclude a treaty with the desired end result of eliminating nuclear weapons. The text of the Treaty was the main policy objective from an ultimate ends-driven perspective. This humanitarian approach was taken and deemed highly successful in the cases of the Land Mines Convention in 1997, as well as the Convention on Cluster Munitions in 2008. Needless to say, explicit intricate details, especially relating to safeguards,

---

[8] Article 1(a).
[9] Article 1(b).
[10] Article 1(c).
[11] Article 1(d).
[12] Article 1(e).
[13] Article 1(f).
[14] Article 1(g).
[15] "Recognizing the Vital Importance of the Comprehensive Nuclear-Test-Ban Treaty and Its Verification Regime as a Core Element of the Nuclear Disarmament and Non-Proliferation Regime." Preamble at: http://undocs.org/A/CONF.229/2017/8.
[16] See William C. Potter (2017) "Disarmament Diplomacy and the Nuclear Ban Treaty, Survival," 59:4, 75–108, DOI: 10.1080/00396338.2017.1349786.

verification and enforcement were not included by its very design. This was not an oversight on the part of the framers, but simply a realistic consideration in order to achieve a result within a specific and short time frame. Supporters of the TPNW would see this as a strength of the Treaty and not a shortcoming, as they would argue that such a humanitarian approach has resulted in achieving the TPNW, whereas approaches under other traditional disarmament mechanisms have failed. That said, now that the Treaty has been concluded and open for signatures, questions arise pertaining to the next steps of implementation.

VERIFICATION DIFFICULTIES UNDER THE "SIMPLE-BAN" APPROACH

The concept of a simple-ban approach makes it relatively straightforward to gain consensus during treaty negotiations. While this humanitarian approach to negotiating such treaties achieves the desired objective in a theoretical sense, it also leaves the difficult task of compliance and enforcement to follow. The issue of verification is especially difficult. As Michal Onderco highlights, "verification of dismantlement is key for preventing the nuclear ban turning into a nuclear nightmare."[17] The very existence of the prohibition creates normative pressure on NWS to reconsider their nuclear armament activities. This was the approach allowed for by the UN General Assembly (UNGA) resolution of November 2016 calling upon "States participating in the conference to make their best endeavors to conclude as soon as possible a legally binding instrument to prohibit nuclear weapons, leading toward their total elimination."[18] Following this simple format, the TPNW does not contain elaborate provisions for verification and dismantlement.[19] On the one hand, the benefit is that such a straightforward and simple approach makes it easier to agree on an outcome in a relatively quick and timely fashion. On the other hand, for many states such as members of NATO, it raises, *inter alia*, security and verification issues that would make it difficult, if not impossible, for them to accede to the treaty. This became increasingly evident during the negotiating process whereby many states rejected it at the UNGA, also refusing to take part in negotiations.

The humanitarian approach meant that during discussions, negotiators were not bogged down with complex details regarding verification and monitoring.

---

[17] Michal Onderco, "Why Nuclear Weapon Ban Treaty Is Unlikely to Fulfil Its Promise," www .tandfonline.com/doi/full/10.1080/23340460.2017.1409082.

[18] UNGA Res 71/258 (December 23, 2016) Taking forward multinational nuclear disarmament negotiations, para. 12.

[19] Caughley, T. and Mukhatzhanova, G. (2017). *Negotiation of a Nuclear Weapons Prohibition Treaty: Nuts and Bolts of the Ban.* Retrieved from www.unidir.org/files/publications/pdfs/nuts-and-bolts-en-684.pdf.

They required a simple monitoring mechanism whereby states would self-assess and report. Again, concerns remain that the prohibition of testing nuclear weapons does not include an express reference to the CTBT's International Monitoring System (IMS), including the global network of sensors to detect nuclear explosions. Indeed, participating countries argued for a specific reference to subcritical tests and computer simulations and objected to the use of the CTBT formulation prohibiting "any nuclear test explosion or any other nuclear explosion."[20] Yet, such a reference did not find its way into the TPNW's final text.

Verification mechanisms are key to the success of an arms control treaty or convention, but the basis on which these are to be measured makes negotiating effective metrics very difficult. Practitioners of arms control negotiations openly acknowledge that the issue of verification is often complex for both sides of the negotiations and is amongst the most crucial elements, and the most difficult to negotiate.[21] Verification and monitoring compliance are central for determining whether an arms control law is effective.[22] Without effective verification measures, uncertainty prevails. This may explain why "most of the accounts of the nuclear disarmament and abolition spend significant amount[s] of space on the discussion about the need for verification."[23] With this in mind, questions remain regarding the utility of a TPNW that hosts a variety of enforcement deficiencies, and that some critics may argue is near impossible to enforce.

EFFECTIVENESS OF THE PROHIBITION TREATY

The overall effectiveness of the TPNW must be assessed in relation to the inter-dependence of Article 2, requiring self-declarations, and Article 3 regarding safeguards. Article 4 pertains to the complete elimination of nuclear weapons and Article 5 addresses implementation of the Treaty. These will be discussed in turn.

---

[20] See Gaukhar M. (2017). *Nuclear Weapons Treaty, Negotiation and Beyond (2017), Arms Control Today,* online: www.armscontrol.org/act/2017–09/features/nuclear-weapons-prohibition-treaty-negotiations-beyond.

[21] Graham, T. (2002). *Disarmament Sketches: Three Decades of Arms Control and International Law.* Seattle: Institute for Global and Regional Security Studies, University of Washington Press.

[22] Hart, J., and Fedchenko, V. (2009). "WMD Inspection and Verification Regimes: Political and Technical Challenges." In N. E. Busch and D. Joyner (eds.), *Combating Weapons of Mass Destruction: The Future of International Nonproliferation Policy* (pp. 95–117). Athens: University of Georgia Press.

[23] Perkovich, G. and Acton, J. M. (eds.). (2009). *Abolishing Nuclear Weapons: A Debate.* Washington, DC: Carnegie Endowment for International Peace as quoted from "Why Nuclear Weapon Ban Treaty Is Unlikely to Fulfil Its Promise," Michal Onderco. See www.tandfonline.com/doi/full/10.1080 /23340460.2017.1409082.

States Declarations

Article 2[24] requires self-declaration in which each state party must submit within thirty days after the Treaty enters into force, a declaration[25] as to "whether it owned, possessed or controlled nuclear weapons or nuclear explosive devices and eliminated its nuclear-weapon program, including the elimination or irreversible conversion of all nuclear-weapons-related facilities," prior to the TPNW coming into force.[26] Each state party is also required to "declare" whether it continues to own, possess or control any nuclear weapons or other nuclear explosive devices.[27] And, it must declare whether there are any nuclear weapons or other nuclear explosive devices "in its territory or in any place under its jurisdiction or control that are owned, possessed or controlled by another State."[28] All such information will be shared with other states parties.[29] This requires voluntary reporting in good faith. Critics may worry about issues of correctness and completeness of this reporting, pointing to deception and clandestine activities of some states as in the past situation in Iran and the current scenario with North Korea,[30] both of which highlight the need for monitoring. Without verification, a state could falsify declarations and have a covert nuclear weapons program. In other words, monitoring and verification are essential components of confidence-building in this delicate area. Minimal surveillance and safeguards are required regarding the non-diversion of nuclear material from declared peaceful purposes and the absence of undeclared nuclear activities.

Different Requirements for Different States

The TPNW sets out different requirements for different states. Under Articles 3 and 4, there are three categories of states, namely (1) those that never owned, possessed or controlled nuclear weapons; (2) those that did but have since relinquished them;

[24] Declarations "Article 2: 1. Each State Party shall submit to the Secretary-General of the United Nations, not later than 30 days after this Treaty enters into force for that State Party, a declaration in which it shall: (a) Declare whether it owned, possessed or controlled nuclear weapons or nuclear explosive devices and eliminated its nuclear-weapon program, including the elimination or irreversible conversion of all nuclear-weapons-related facilities, prior to the entry into force of this Treaty for that State Party; (b) Notwithstanding Article 1 (a), declare whether it owns, possesses or controls any nuclear weapons or other nuclear explosive devices; (c) Notwithstanding Article 1 (g), declare whether there are any nuclear weapons or other nuclear explosive devices in its territory or in any place under its jurisdiction or control that are owned, possessed or controlled by another State. 2. The Secretary-General of the United Nations shall transmit all such declarations received to the States Parties."

[25] Article 2(1).
[26] Article 2(1)(a).
[27] Article 2(1)(b).
[28] Article 2(1)(c).
[29] Article 2(2).
[30] See Jonathan L. Black-Branch, "The Effectiveness of UN Sanctions in the Case of North Korea Nuclear Disarmament and Non-Proliferation in International Law," in I Caracciolo and M Pedrazzi (eds.) *Nuclear Weapons: Strengthening the International Legal Regime* (Den Haag: Eleven International Publishing, 2015), 23–32.

and (3) those that still own, possess or control nuclear weapons or participate in prohibited activity.

Firstly, Article 3 refers to the first category whereby a state has never owned, possessed or controlled nuclear weapons or other nuclear explosive devices. Article 4 refers to a second classification of States those that may have owned, possessed or controlled nuclear weapons or other nuclear explosive devices, but have since "eliminated their nuclear-weapon program, including the elimination or irreversible conversion of all nuclear-weapons-related facilities, prior to the entry into force of the Treaty."[31] A third classification refers to the situation of a state that currently "owns, possesses or controls nuclear weapons or other nuclear explosive devices,"[32] whereby they are required to "immediately remove them from operational status, and destroy them as soon as possible but not later than a deadline to be determined by the first meeting of States Parties."[33]

From a safeguards and verification perspective, this third classification may create confusion and a lack of uniformity of results in an area of international regulation that demands transparency and clarity of outcomes. In some manner this third category seems to effectively recognize an ability to own nuclear weapons under the proviso that the State in question moves toward immediate disarmament. This, of course, would take time to accomplish, leaving practical questions regarding the full withdrawal or removal of weapons, and moreover the need for a surveillance and monitoring systems during such a process. There does not appear to be a succession plan in place regarding procedures or time frames. By inadvertently accepting that a state could possess nuclear weapons in some form, albeit for a short period of time, this classification arguably goes against one of the central purposes of the TPNW itself: non-ownership possession of nuclear weapons. After all, allowing them to exist for even the shortest length of time diametrically conflicts with the intent of the Treaty. This begs the question as to whether this was done intentionally or was simply an oversight on the part of the drafters, because they were attempting to complete negotiations promptly. This author feels it was done deliberately to encourage accession to the Treaty by the widest possible number of states. In so doing, however, it creates an inherent paradox. An alternative system may have been to allow full Treaty participation only after a period of verified disarmament under a transparent plan listed in the TPNW itself under a successive integrated approach.

Safeguards for States that Never Owned or Controlled Nuclear Weapons

Article 3 requires that each state party that never owned, possessed or controlled nuclear weapons or other nuclear explosive devices "at a minimum," maintain its safeguard obligations in relation to IAEA oversight in force at the time of the

---

[31] Article 4(1).
[32] Article 4(2).
[33] Article 4(2).

TPNW's entry into force, and "without prejudice to any additional relevant instruments that it may adopt in the future."[34] This reference serves to highlight the importance of the IAEA as the central authority on safeguard issues, which is consistent with the text of the NPT. In the event that a state party in this category has not yet concluded a comprehensive safeguards agreement[35] with the IAEA, that state party must begin negotiations for such agreement within 180 days of the Treaty entering into force, with the agreement coming into force no later than eighteen months from the entry into force of the Treaty for that state party.[36] After this, each such state party must "maintain such obligations, without prejudice to any additional relevant instruments that it may adopt in the future."[37]

The IAEA is the primary organization for verification oversight and indeed was already operative for several years before the NPT was adopted. There is no doubt that legal issues relating to different and interrelated nuclear verification regimes and their associated organizations are often complex. Despite general consensus regarding its role, however, controversies arise relating to the Agency's mandate to verify both the non-diversion of nuclear material from declared activities in terms of its correctness, and the absence of undeclared nuclear activities in the state regarding the completeness. Given the nature of a treaty intended effectively to ban nuclear weapons, arguably the TPNW should have required a higher threshold with deeper monitoring and supervisory oversight along with specific reporting and enforcement requirements. Article 3 is nothing more than the status quo as to what is currently required of states. Marc Finaud seems to accept this view, saying that states becoming party to the TPNW will be bound under Article 3 to maintain "at least" the same level of existing safeguards against any activity incompatible with the Treaty obligations. He notes that the fear of some hesitant countries, that the Treaty could be used as a loophole to escape their verification obligations under the NPT and with the IAEA safeguards,[38] is unfounded.[39]

Again, according to Burroughs, the Treaty safeguards both fissile materials and the detection of nuclear explosive testing. He suggests, however, that verification of the prohibition on development probably will not be possible over the short term, and that monitoring will be done through a peer-review process among states parties, national intelligence networks, monitoring efforts by civil society groups, and whistleblowers.[40] Many of these details, however, are yet to be established and agreed upon.

[34] Article 3(1).
[35] See INCIRC/153 (Corrected).
[36] Article 3(2).
[37] Article 3(2).
[38] See www.iaea.org/topics/safeguards-and-verification.
[39] Marc Finaud (2017) "A Treaty Prohibiting Nuclear Weapons: What For and What's Next?," online (www.gcsp.ch/News-Knowledge/Global-insight/A-Treaty-Prohibiting-Nuclear-Weapons-What-For-and-What-Next).
[40] John Burroughs (2017), "Key Issues in Negotiations for a Nuclear Weapons Prohibition Treaty," Arms Control Today, online: www.armscontrol.org/act/2017-06/features/key-issues-negotiations-nuclear-weapons-prohibition-treaty.

The absence of a tangible verification regime is viewed by critics as a definite drawback of the Treaty. There are two ways of looking at this issue. Firstly, it could be viewed as a weakness of the Treaty, conveniently leaving the hard task of verification out of the way. Secondly, this could be perceived as a strength, as the Treaty is not creating a separate regime that could further complicate already complex negotiations and verification processes. The Treaty leaves the task to the IAEA experts to do what they do best, and not try to replicate the existing regime or impose another, different compliance model wherein it might create forum shopping. Consequently, this means that in theory all parties to the TPNW must also participate in the IAEA. As a result, if a party to the TPNW does not participate, then under Article 8, of the Treaty, measures regarding enforcement may be taken to extend authority to IAEA experts. Again, Article 8 calls for meeting of states parties stating that they "shall meet regularly in order to consider and, where necessary, take decisions in respect of any matter with regard to the application or implementation" of the Treaty, including "measures for the verified, time-bound and irreversible elimination of nuclear-weapon programs, including additional protocols to this Treaty," as well as "any other matters pursuant to and consistent with the provisions" of the Treaty.[41] In future, they may even choose to agree bilateral safeguards agreement with the IAEA.

If they are to go in this direction, it may have been prudent to have the IAEA fully on board throughout the negotiation process to align the organization in this new domain of prohibition verification. Including stronger terms may also have been better to further clarify and perhaps strengthen the verification role of the IAEA, particularly regarding nuclear safety and security issues[42] for those states adhering to the TPNW. Jonathan Herbach observes that the legal frameworks for safety and security are quite different, as the framework for nuclear safety is much more developed than that for security. For instance, the 1994 Convention on Nuclear Safety provides a very robust peer-review process where states compile extremely detailed technical reports and share their processes in their safety regimes. Those

---

[41] Article 8. See https://undocs.org/A/CONF.229/2017/8.

[42] IAEA Safety Glossary, *Terminology Used in Nuclear Safety and Radiation Protection*, 2007 Edition (IAEA, Vienna): www-ns.iaea.org/standards/concepts-terms.asp?s=11&l=90. As noted in this Glossary under the definition of the term *(nuclear) security*, "There is not an exact distinction between the general terms safety and security. In general, *security* is concerned with *malicious* or negligent actions by humans that could cause or threaten harm to other humans; *safety* is concerned with the broader issue of harm to humans (or the environment) from *radiation*, whatever the cause. The precise interaction between *security* and *safety* depends on the context" (133). The Glossary further states that "*Safety* and *security* synergies concern, for example, the regulatory infrastructure; engineering provisions in the *design* and *construction* of *nuclear installations* and other *facilities*; *controls* on access to *nuclear installations* and other *facilities*; the categorization of *radioactive sources*; *source design*; the *security* of the management of *radioactive sources* and *radioactive material*; the recovery of *orphan sources*; *emergency response* plans; and *radioactive waste management*. *Safety* matters are intrinsic to *activities*, and transparent and probabilistic *safety analysis* is used. *Security* matters concern *malicious* actions and are confidential, and threat based judgement is used" (134).

144 *Treaty Safeguards, Verification and Implementation*

reports are then reviewed by other states. On the other side, security is still legally underdeveloped, and Herbach suggests it is worth exploring how the IAEA could be more explicitly mandated by states to play a specific role in supervising nuclear security.[43] The TPNW does not address the rising concerns regarding nuclear safety, as well as ambiguities regarding nuclear security. In 2021 there will be a review conference for the primary nuclear security treaty – the 1979 Convention on the Physical Protection of Nuclear Material (CPPNM) as amended. The 2021 conference will offer an opportunity to shape the interpretation of that Convention, because the review mechanism is broad and leaves open a number of possibilities to discuss a range of important points. For the purposes of this chapter, it is sufficient to say that the TPNW left continued uncertainties in this area of international law.

Toward the Total Elimination of Nuclear Weapons

Where Article 3 addresses safeguard matters in relation to states that never owned or controlled nuclear weapons or explosive devices, Article 4 focuses on moving states that, either in the past owned nuclear weapons or still today continue to own nuclear weapons, toward their total elimination. To be concise, Article 4 aims to achieve the total elimination of nuclear weapons.

States that Owned or Controlled Nuclear Weapons

Article 4(1) refers to states that "owned, possessed or controlled nuclear weapons or other nuclear explosive devices and eliminated its nuclear-weapon programme."[44] This includes "the elimination or irreversible conversion of all nuclear-weapons-related facilities,"[45] which was done prior to the TPNW entering into force as well as "the elimination or irreversible conversion of all nuclear weapons related facilities."[46] These states must "cooperate with the competent international authority"[47] for "verifying the irreversible elimination of its nuclear-weapon programme," whereby the "competent international authority"[48] will report to the states parties.

States that owned or controlled nuclear weapons are also required to conclude a safeguards agreement with the IAEA which will be "sufficient to provide credible assurance of the non-diversion of declared nuclear material from peaceful nuclear activities and of the absence of undeclared nuclear material or activities in that state party as a whole."[49] Under Article 4, similarly these states must begin negotiations of

---

[43] Jonathan Herbach, *Preventing Nuclear Terrorism. International Law and Nuclear Security Governance* (Academisch Proefschrift, Universiteit van Amsterdam, 2019), 141–160.

[44] Article 4(1).

[45] Article 4(1).

[46] Again prior to the Treaty coming into force. Article 4(1).

[47] Pursuant to para. 6 of Article 4.

[48] Article 4(1).

[49] Article 4(1).

Effectiveness of the Prohibition Treaty

such an agreement within 180 days from the TPNW's coming into force to enter into force no later than eighteen months from the TPNW's entry into force.[50] Once in force, the state must maintain these safeguards obligations – at a minimum.[51]

States that Currently Own or Control Nuclear Weapons

A state that currently "owns, possesses or controls nuclear weapons or other nuclear explosive devices"[52] is required to immediately remove such weapons and devices from "operational status, and destroy them."[53] This is to be done "as soon as possible" but not later than a deadline to be determined by the first meeting of states parties under "a legally binding, time-bound plan for the verified and irreversible elimination" of its nuclear-weapon program, including "the elimination or irreversible conversion of all nuclear-weapons-related facilities."[54] No later than sixty days after the TPNW's coming into force, they must "submit this plan to the States Parties or to a competent international authority designated by the States Parties."[55] The plan must then be "negotiated with the competent international authority, which shall submit it to the subsequent meeting of States Parties or review conference, whichever comes first, for approval in accordance with its rules of procedure."[56]

Like states that formerly held nuclear weapons, as discussed above, states that *currently* own or possess nuclear weapons must conclude a safeguards agreement with the IAEA.[57] The agreement must be "sufficient to provide credible assurance of the non-diversion of declared nuclear material from peaceful nuclear activities and of the absence of undeclared nuclear material or activities in the State as a whole."[58] Negotiations of such an agreement shall begin no later than the date upon which implementation of the plan is completed,[59] and the agreement will enter into force no later than eighteen months after the date of initiation of negotiations.[60] Additionally, the state must maintain these safeguards obligations, at a minimum.[61] Once this agreement has entered into force, it must submit a final declaration to the secretary-general of the United Nations stating that it has fulfilled its obligations as required.[62]

---

[50] Article 4(1).
[51] Again, without prejudice to any additional relevant instruments that it may adopt in the future. Article 4(1).
[52] Article 4(2).
[53] Article 4(2).
[54] Article 4(2).
[55] Article 4(2).
[56] Article 4(2).
[57] Article 4(2).
[58] Article 4(3).
[59] Article 4(2).
[60] Article 4(2).
[61] Again, without prejudice to any additional relevant instruments that it may adopt in the future. Article 4(3).
[62] Article 4(3).

Removal of Nuclear Weapons

Article 4(4) further requires[63] that a state with any nuclear weapons or other nuclear explosive devices in its territory or in any place under its jurisdiction or control that are owned, possessed or controlled by another state shall ensure their prompt removal.[64] Such removal is to be done as soon as possible but not later than a deadline to be determined by the first meeting of states parties.[65] Upon removal, the state must submit a declaration of such to the secretary-general of the United Nations.[66] Each state must submit reports to meetings of states parties at review conferences regarding progress toward implementing its obligations under Article 4, until they are completed in full.[67]

Designate a Competent International Authority

Both classes of states pursuant to Article 4, those that eliminated their nuclear-weapon program[68] and those that currently own, possess or control nuclear weapons or explosive devices,[69] must designate a "competent international authority or authorities" to negotiate and verify the irreversible elimination of their respective nuclear-weapons programs, including the elimination or irreversible conversion of all nuclear weapons-related facilities.[70] If designation to a competent international authority "has not been made prior" to the TPNW's entry into force,[71] the secretary-general of the United Nations will convene an extraordinary meeting of states parties to take decisions on what may be required[72] in order to achieve full compliance with the obligations under Article 4.

Article 4(1) pertains primarily to states that possessed nuclear weapons after 2001 but will have since eliminated them before the TPNW enters into force for those states. This clause does *not* cover Belarus, Kazakhstan and Ukraine, the former Soviet states that eliminated their arsenals before 2001. Article 4 appears to have different standards for different states which Thakur labels "a recipe for confusion and angst."[73] He feels that "[c]ountries that have resisted the more stringent

---

[63] Notwithstanding Article 1(b) and (g).
[64] Article 4(4).
[65] Article 4(4).
[66] Article 4(4).
[67] Article 4(5).
[68] Article 4(1).
[69] Article 4(2).
[70] As per Article 4(6) and in accordance with paras. 1, 2 and 3 of Article 4.
[71] To which para. 1 or 2 of this Article applies.
[72] Article 4(6).
[73] Ramesh Thakur (2018) "Nuclear Turbulence in the Age of Trump," *Diplomacy & Statecraft*, 29:1, 105-128, DOI: 10.1080/09592296.2017.1420531 (116) To link to this article, see https://doi.org/10.1080/09592296.2017.1420531.

safeguards requirements could go forum shopping. It is better to insist on the highest standards possible for all parties."[74]

Reference in Article 4 to a "competent international authority" may be seen as somewhat vague. The TPNW specifically calls upon the IAEA to handle compliance for states without nuclear weapons. In so doing, it did not assign the IAEA the primary role in verifying the elimination of nuclear weapons and the irreversible conversion of nuclear weapons-related facilities in those countries that now have nuclear weapons. Instead, this role was allocated to "competent international authority" without further elaboration. Sharon Squassoni states: "One imagines that the next 10 years could be spent figuring out how to set up such an authority to be competent without revealing security information that countries consider highly confidential."[75] Agreeing a treaty under a simple-ban approach does not make the difficult task of achieving complete and verifiable disarmament any easier; it merely delays the inevitable. That said, the momentum from the success of the TPNW may create a greater sense of purpose and inspire leaders to move quickly on the importance of establishing a competent authority.

National Implementation

Each state party must adopt the necessary measures to implement the Treaty obligations.[76] It must take all "appropriate" legal, administrative and other measures toward full implementation including imposing penal sanctions against individuals on its respective territory or under its jurisdiction or control in order to prevent and suppress activities prohibited under the TPNW.[77] Needless to say, these requirements are open to interpretation. To begin with, one may question what "necessary measures" would include. Does this require international cooperation and coordination? It suggests there are other effective measures relating to nuclear disarmament that are not covered by Article 4[78] of the TPNW. Who is to determine what such measures are and who is to oversee this and evaluate that which might constitute an "effective measure"? As for subparagraph 2, what actually constitutes "appropriate" legal and administrative measures? What would imposing "penal sanctions" require and in what ways might this lead to inconsistencies between state parties? Since negotiating states were most likely fully aware that such a monitoring system could have been included in the Treaty but none was included, one can infer that they did not wish to have one. For clarity, it may have been better to have a monitoring system with a governing body issuing guidelines and model-laws. Evidently, this must be

---

[74]   Ibid, 114.

[75]   See Sharon Squazzoni (2017), "A Controversial Ban and the Long Game to Delegitimize Nuclear Weapons," online: https://thebulletin.org/controversial-ban-and-long-game-delegitimize-nuclear-weapons10934.

[76]   Article 5(1).

[77]   Article 5(2).

[78]   Toward the total elimination of nuclear weapons.

148   *Treaty Safeguards, Verification and Implementation*

open for discussion and consideration at future meetings of states parties or at review conferences. Might this complement or conflict with existing mechanisms for nonproliferation, such as the Global Initiative to Combat Global Terrorism (GICNT)?[79] Again, taking a simple-ban approach leaves the difficult decisions for later, as well as keeping options open.

Perhaps Additional Protocols will allow for answers to some of these questions. Article 8 requires states parties to "meet regularly" to decide on, *inter alia*, "measures for the verified, time-bound and irreversible elimination of nuclear-weapon programs, including Additional protocols to this Treaty." Further, Article 10 allows for amendment to the TPNW with the approval of a majority of states. These mechanisms may allow for some enhanced certainty in the area of national implementation, among other areas. Still, it seems that there was a missed opportunity to address real gaps and pressing concerns regarding nuclear safety and security and to move toward a tighter regulatory framework with clear international oversight.

UNDERSTANDING VERIFICATION: DEFINITION, TERMS AND CONDITIONS

Under the TPNW, it becomes clear that many questions arise regarding safeguards and verification. Nuclear verification remains a highly problematic area within the international community, generally. Ambiguity and lack of clarity causes confidence to dissipate, insecurity to creep in, and distrust to take hold, leading to negative tendencies and potential adverse consequences. Indeed, the *Third Report*[80] of the Committee on Nuclear Weapons, Non-Proliferation and Contemporary International Law of the International Law Association (ILA)[81] was devoted to *Legal Issues of Verification of*

---

[79] See www.gicnt.org.

[80] Third Report of the Committee on Nuclear Weapons, Non-Proliferation and Contemporary International Law of the International Law Association 2016 at p. 4. See www.ila-hq.org/index.php /committees.

[81] The Committee mandate is "to consider competing legal approaches to non-proliferation and regulating nuclear weapons within the contemporary context." The Committee is engaged in a process of assessing the three pillars of the 1968 Nuclear Non-Proliferation Treaty – i.e. nonproliferation of nuclear weapons; the right to develop research, production and use of nuclear energy for peaceful purposes; and nuclear disarmament – with a special focus on controversial issues and existing interdependencies between those pillars. A preliminary report on key elements of the practice regarding nuclear energy, nonproliferation and the regulation of nuclear weapons was presented at the ILA Sofia Conference 2012. The Second Report, which was discussed at the Washington Conference 2014 (ILA Committee on Nuclear Weapons, Non-Proliferation and Contemporary International Law, Second Report: Legal Aspects of Nuclear Disarmament (Washington, DC 2014), www.ila-hq.org/en/committees/index.cfm/cid/1025) has concluded that steps toward fulfilling nuclear disarmament obligations and providing appropriate access to peaceful uses of nuclear energy may substantially influence compliance with nuclear nonproliferation obligations. It has underlined that effective nonproliferation may not only support developments toward nuclear disarmament, but also help to improve security and safety of peaceful uses. The Committee will have to keep this in mind when developing "options for future legal cooperation in this field," which is expected under the Committee Mandate. A first set of draft elements of the envisaged ILA *Declaration on Legal Issues of*

Nuclear Non-Proliferation Commitments. Specifically, it examined verification in a wider context, comprising general legal aspects of compliance control, dispute settlement and enforcement, thus reflecting legal controversies as discussed in the literature[82] as well as current state practices.[83]

To assist in a legal analysis of the TPNW one should refer to the rules of Articles 31–32 of the Vienna Convention on the Law of Treaties (VCLT)[84] and the identical Articles 31–32 of the Vienna Convention on the Law of Treaties between states and International Organizations or Between International Organizations (VCLTIO).[85] In the absence of specific treaty definitions, relevant terms should be used according to their ordinary meaning and common understanding. TPNW interpretations should adhere to the general UN terminology and principles which are especially relevant within this context.[86] There is general consensus that, verification consists of a specific assigned process aimed at establishing whether a states party is complying with its obligations under an agreement. This process involves a wide range of activities and analysis including the collection of specific information relevant to the obligation in question as listed under the arms limitation and disarmament agreement. Based on this, an analysis of the information and data collected is measured against the intended prohibition or limitation. Conclusions are drawn by reaching a judgment as to whether the stipulations and terms of the agreement are being met or adhered to. The specific context in which such verification exercises occur pertains to the sovereign right of the state in question to conclude such an arms control agreement and its respective obligation to implement any arms limitation or

---

Nuclear Weapons, Non-Proliferation and Peaceful Uses of Nuclear Energy was included in the Second Report. It comprises not only existing principles and rules, but also desirable new rules. This list has been expanded as shown in the Annex to this report, but there are gaps still to be filled. A comprehensive commentary of all principles and rules will accompany the final Declaration.

[82] See e.g. Oliver Meier and Christopher Daase (eds.), *Arms Control in the 21st Century. Between Coercion and Cooperation* (London: Taylor and Francis, 2012); Oliver Meier (ed.), *Technology Transfers and Non-Proliferation. Between Control and Cooperation*, Routledge Global Security Studies (New York: Routledge 2013); Geir Ulfstein (ed.), *Making Treaties Work. Human Rights, Environment and Arms Control* (Cambridge University Press, 2007), 243–272.

[83] A research project, conducted in November 2014 by the Committee Rapporteur in cooperation with the Institute of International Peace and Security Law at the University of Cologne and sponsored by the *Fritz Thyssen Stiftung für Wissenschaftsförderung* was of particular support for raising contentious issues, reviewing arguments and counter-arguments, and exploring possibilities for consensus solutions. The results of this research project have been published in Jonathan L. Black-Branch and Dieter Fleck (eds.), *Nuclear Non-Proliferation in International Law: Vol. II Verification and Compliance* (Berlin/Heidelberg: Springer/Asser Press, 2015).

[84] Vienna Convention on the Law of Treaties (May 23, 1969) 1155 *UNTS* 331, in force since January 27, 1980.

[85] Vienna Convention on the Law of Treaties between States and International Organizations or Between International Organizations (March 21, 1986), not yet in force.

[86] See United Nations Department for Disarmament Affairs, *Study on the Role of the United Nations in the Field of Verification*, New York 1991, www.un.org/disarmament/HomePage/ODAPublications/DisarmamentStudySeries/PDF/SS-20.pdf.

Treaty Safeguards, Verification and Implementation

disarmament agreement. To this end, verification refers to the relevant conduct of the states parties to adhere to such agreement as per the measure or metrics agreed.[87]

Accordingly, credible disarmament efforts under the TPNW require a process which establishes verification that the states parties are actually complying with their respective treaty obligations under the agreement. Such a process must include the collection of relevant information regarding the elimination of nuclear weapons and devices; stringent analysis by credible independent individuals and organizations; and reports submitted by non-partisan subject experts concerning adherence to treaty objectives. This must be done in an independent and transparent manner and subject to open scrutiny. As discussed above, the immediate lack of such specifics in the TPNW raise concerns regarding its effectiveness and credibility as an arms control treaty.

The five NWS (the "P5") established a dedicated Working Group in 2011 to establish a Glossary of Key Nuclear Terms under the leadership of the People's Republic of China, in conjunction with the other members.[88] The resultant *P5 Glossary of Key Nuclear Terms*, describes "design information verification" (DIV) as follows:

> Activities carried out by the IAEA at a facility to verify the correctness and completeness of the design information provided by the State. An initial DIV is performed on a newly built facility to confirm that the as-built facility is as declared. A DIV is performed periodically on existing facilities to confirm the continued validity of the design information and of the safeguards approach. The IAEA's authority for performing a DIV is a continuing right throughout all phases of a facility's life cycle until the facility has been decommissioned for safeguards purposes.[89]

To the extent that these UN and P5 documents do not fall within one of the specific elements set out in Article 31 of the VCLT and Article 31 of the VCLTIO, one may argue that they are authoritative as per Article 32 VCLT (Article 32 VCLTIO).

EFFECTIVENESS, TRANSPARENCY AND CONFIDENCE BUILDING

The question is whether the verification process serves its purpose in effectively assessing all relevant facts and establishing compliance with the obligations undertaken under existing treaty law and customary law and within the given context of the specific Treaty, in this case the TPNW. Within this assessment, one must not only consider existing legal obligations but also take into consideration emerging best

---

[87] Ibid., para. 12.

[88] Regular meetings of the Working Group were held along with various exchanges amongst P5 experts.

[89] *P5 Glossary of Key Nuclear Terms*, www.china-un.org/eng/chinaandun/disarmament_armscontrol/npt/P020150429800995728299.pdf, p. 135.

practices in the area. To that end, it is essential to establish specific metrics of verification, leaving no room for uncertainty with regard to acceptable standards which can be both measured from an objective standpoint as well as be transparent to the international community. The TPNW Working Group also emphasized the importance of transparency regarding vital information. Moreover, there must be enforcement mechanisms under an appropriate regime with clear and transparent processes along with definable and effective sanctions and actions for non-compliance with specified obligations.

One of the primary goals of verification is to build confidence amongst the parties to comply, in good faith, with their respective obligations. This requires that in a case of breach, state parties support effective enforcement mechanisms whereby the standards and criteria are expressly stated and followed. This includes an information-gathering process where they work toward amassing authentic, detailed and accurate information relating to the treaty requirement in a complete and timely fashion. The relevant standard for this exercise is not the same as the tests for what might be applied, for example regarding admissible evidence in a court of law, and no burden of proof rule would apply for cooperative efforts to maintain or restore confidence.[90] Specific practices have developed over time, however, that may be considered unique for a successful implementation of arms control agreements. Needless to say, such considerations are essential for the credibility of the TPNW.

LESSONS REGARDING VERIFICATION: IRAN

Verification and confidence lie at the heart of meaningful and trusting relationships. Lessons from the past illustrate the importance of complete and verifiable enforcement measures. Iran is a case in point regarding the immense challenges with verification. For an extended period of time the Islamic Republic of Iran was found not to be complying with its nuclear nonproliferation obligations under IAEA safeguards[91] and was consequently subjected to a wide range of comprehensive UN Security Council sanctions.[92] Following protracted negotiations, a cooperative solution was finally agreed between the E3/EU+3 (China, France, Germany, the Russian Federation, the United Kingdom and the United States of America, with the High Representative of the European Union for Foreign Affairs and Security Policy) and Iran.[93] The difficulties posed by the Iran problem highlight the importance of clear and unambiguous safeguards criteria.

---

[90]   See Michael Bothe, "Verification of Facts," in Rüdiger Wolfrum (ed.), *Max-Planck-Encyclopedia of Public International Law*, 10 vols. (Oxford University Press, 2012), para. 62, online edition www .mpepil.com (*MPEPIL*).

[91]   See IAEA Report GOV/2013/40 (August 28, 2013), www.iaea.org/Publications/Documents/Board/2013/ gov2013-40.pdf.

[92]   SC Res 1696 (2006), 1737 (2006). 1747 (2007), 1803 (2008), 1835 (2008), 1887 (2009), 1929 (2011), 1984 (2011), 2049 (2012).

[93]   See Joint Statement by EU High Representative Federica Mogherini and Iranian Foreign Minister Javad Zarif, and Joint Comprehensive Plan of Action (JCPOA) with Annex I Nuclear related

152 *Treaty Safeguards, Verification and Implementation*

Indeed the conclusion of this agreement was so significant that it went to the Security Council,[94] where it was unanimously endorsed.[95] Specifically, Iran must adhere to the safeguards regime associated with the Additional Protocol between Iran and the IAEA for the purpose of the implementation of Article III.1 and III.4 of the NPT, whereby IAEA inspectors have access to undeclared facilities as well as setting procedures for verifying the absence of undeclared nuclear material and activities.[96] Similarly, questions arose regarding Iraq's nuclear program, further highlighting the issues that arise if the IAEA is unable to certify a state's submissions.

commitments; Annex II Sanctions related commitments; Annex II Attachments; Annex III Civil nuclear cooperation; Annex IV Joint Commission; and Annex V Implementation Plan. Vienna, July 14, 2015, http://eeas.europa.eu/statements-eeas/2015/150714_01_en.htm; Joint Statement by the IAEA Director General Yukiya Amano and the vice-president of the Islamic Republic of Iran, president of the Atomic Energy Organization of Iran, Ali Akbar Salehi and Road-map for the clarification of past and present outstanding issues regarding Iran's nuclear program, Vienna, July 14, 2015, www.iaea.org/newscenter/pressreleases/iaea-director-generals-statement-and-road-map-clarification-past-present-outstanding-issues-regarding-irans-nuclear-program.

[94] Note that the JPOA is a binding political accord rather than a legally binding agreement.

[95] SC Res 2231 (2015).

[96] "While EU, US, and UN sanctions were lifted on Implementation Day (January 16, 2016), following the verification by the IAEA that Iran has taken the actions specified in paragraphs 15.1–15.11 of Annex V of the Joint Comprehensive Plan of Action (JCPOA),* much work remains to be done by the seven States which have undertaken a special responsibility in the Joint Commission under the JCPOA and will be assisted by the IAEA. Iran's commitment to provisionally apply the Additional Protocol to its Comprehensive Safeguards Agreement and proceed with its ratification, and to fully implement the modified Code 3.1 of the Subsidiary Arrangements to its Safeguards Agreement (JCPOA, para. 13, in accordance with Annex I, para. 64) will be a relevant factor for preparing the Broader Conclusion that all nuclear material in Iran remains in peaceful activities (JCPOA, para. 34 iv), the actions to be taken by the EU and the US to terminate, or modify to effectuate the termination of, the remaining last tier of sanctions (Annex V, paras. 20 and 21),** and the final decision that the Security Council would no longer be seized of the Iran nuclear issue (Annex V, para. 24). The 'snap-back mechanism', introduced in the JCPOA, paras. 37–38, and confirmed by the Security Council acting under Article 41 of the UN Charter (SC Res 2231 (2015), paras. 11–13), ensures that previous sanctions re-apply in case of significant non-performance of commitments under the JCPOA."* Verification and Monitoring in the Islamic Republic of Iran in light of United Nations Security Council Resolution 2231 (2015), Report by the Director General (GOV/INF/2016/1, January 16, 2016). See also Tripartite Joint Statement of Intent Concerning the Arak Heavy Water Reactor Research Reactor Modernization Project under the Joint Comprehensive Plan of Action (October 18, 2015), http://energy.gov/articles/joint-statement-intent-concerning-arak-heavy-water-reactor-research-reactor-modernization; Official Document among E3/EU+3 and Iran for Collaboration in Furtherance of the Project for Modernization of the Reactor at Arak (November 2015), www.tehrantimes.com/index_View.asp?code=251036. The contractual framework for the modernization of the nuclear reactor at Arak, yet to be concluded between the China Atomic Energy Agency (CAEA) and the Department of Energy of the United States of America (DOE) on behalf of the E3/EU+3 Working Group, and the Atomic Energy Organization of Iran (AEOI) should further support implementation of the Accord.** Under a general reference to the JCPOA, the US Department of the Treasury's Office of Foreign Assets Control (OFAC) introduced national sanctions on January 17, 2016, targeting eleven entities and individuals involved in procurement on behalf of Iran's ballistic missile program, www.treasury.gov/press-center/press-releases/Pages/jl0322.aspx. See ILA Committee on Nuclear Weapons, Non-Proliferation and Contemporary International Law: Third Report: Legal Issues of Verification of Nuclear Non-Proliferation Commitments (Johannesburg, 2016), at p. 11. See www.ila-hq.org/en/committees/index.cfm/cid/1025.

Lessons Regarding Verification: Iran 153

Participation in the Iran Accord[97] was terminated by US President Donald Trump in May 2018,[98] despite the concerns of other countries and the EU, further demonstrating the complexity in agreeing and adhering to verification standards.[99] Iran's nuclear enrichment and conversion activities are under constant surveillance.[100] In a press statement Secretary of State Mike Pompeo stated:

> As we exit the Iran deal, we will be working with our allies to find a real, comprehensive, and lasting solution to the Iranian threat. We have a shared interest with our allies in Europe and around the world to prevent Iran from ever developing a nuclear weapon. But our effort is broader than just the nuclear threat and we will be working together with partners to eliminate the threat of Iran's ballistic missile program; to stop its terrorist activities worldwide; and to block its menacing activity across the Middle East and beyond. As we build this global effort, sanctions will go into full effect and will remind the Iranian regime of the diplomatic and economic isolation that results from its reckless and malign activity.[101]

Since that time, the United States has re-imposed a wide-ranging series of sanctions aimed at restricting the activities of companies that engage in certain commercial activities in Iran.[102] The aim is to make Iran capitulate so the United States can negotiate a deal more in line with President Trump's objectives.

On July 16, 2018, the Islamic Republic of Iran (Iran) filed proceedings before the ICJ against the United States alleging, *inter alia*, violations of the Treaty of Amity, Economic Relations, and Consular Rights between Iran and the United States of America, an agreement signed in Tehran on August 15, 1955 and entered into force on June 16, 1957.[103] In short, on October 3, 2018, the ICJ found in favor of Iran, unanimously, finding that:

---

[97] Joint Comprehensive Plan of Action (JCPOA).

[98] See www.state.gov/secretary/remarks/2018/05/281938.htm.

[99] See Declaration by US President Trump, terminating the United States' participation in the Joint Comprehensive Plan of Action (JCPOA) with Iran and re-imposing sanctions lifted under the deal (May 8, 2018), www.whitehouse.gov/briefings-statements/president-donald-j-trump-ending-united-states-participation-unacceptable-iran-deal/. See also press release "European Commission acts to protect the interests of EU companies investing in Iran as part of the EU's continued commitment to the Joint Comprehensive Plan of Action" (May 18, 2018), http://europa.eu/rapid/press-release_IP-18-3861_en.htm; International Association of Lawyers Against Nuclear Arms (IALANA), "Security Council Resolution 2231 and the JCPOA: Next Steps" (June 24, 2018), https://leroymoore .wordpress.com/2018/06/25/security-council-resolution-2231-and-the-jcpoa-next-steps/. Chair's statement following the May 25, 2018 meeting of the Joint Commission of the Joint Comprehensive Plan of Action, https://eeas.europa.eu/headquarters/headquarters-homepage/45227/chairs-statement-following-25-may-2018-meeting-joint-commission-joint-comprehensive-plan_en. Statement from the Joint Commission of the Joint Comprehensive Plan of Action, Vienna, July 6, 2018, https://eeas .europa.eu/headquarters/headquarters-homepage/48076/statement-joint-commission-joint-compre hensive-plan-action_en.

[100] Nuclear Threat Initiative, "Iran" (May 2018) online: www.nti.org/learn/countries/iran/nuclear/.

[101] See https://mr.usembassy.gov/on-president-trumps-decision-to-withdraw-from-the-jcpoa/.

[102] See Iran Sanctions www.state.gov/e/eb/tfs/spi/iran/index.htm.

[103] At p. 2. See https://assets.documentcloud.org/documents/4953320/175-20181003-ORD-01-00-En.pdf.

154   *Treaty Safeguards, Verification and Implementation*

The United States of America, in accordance with its obligations under the 1955 Treaty of Amity, Economic Relations, and Consular Rights, shall remove, by means of its choosing, any impediments arising from the measures announced on 8 May 2018 to the free exportation to the territory of the Islamic Republic of Iran of (i) medicines and medical devices; (ii) foodstuffs and agricultural commodities; and (iii) spare parts, equipment and associated services (including warranty, maintenance, repair services and inspections) necessary for the safety of civil aviation.[104]

Accordingly, the US Secretary of State Mike Pompeo announced that the United States would withdraw from the Treaty of Amity with Iran.[105] Such political difficulties regarding both the negotiation and the interpretation of Iraq's obligations pertaining to its nuclear program exemplify the need to have very clear objectives, as well as defined verification targets up front, and point to the importance of a strong verification regime. South Africa, in contrast, provides an example of leadership in disarmament in that it developed and dismantled nuclear weapons.[106,107]

---

[104] At p. 28. https://assets.documentcloud.org/documents/4953320/175-20181003-ORD-01-00-En.pdf. Also: "(2) Unanimously, The United States of America shall ensure that licences and necessary authorizations are granted and that payments and other transfers of funds are not subject to any restriction in so far as they relate to the goods and services referred to in point (1); (3) Unanimously, Both Parties shall refrain from any action which might aggravate or extend the dispute before the Court or make it more difficult to resolve."

[105] The US to end Treaty of Amity with Iran after ICJ ruling. See www.bbc.com/news/world-middle-east -45741270.

[106] See: Liberman, P. (2001). "The Rise and Fall of the South African Bomb." *International Security*, 26 (2), 45–86. doi: 10.1162/016228801753191132; Purkitt, H. E. and Burgess, S. F. (2005). *South Africa's Weapons of Mass Destruction*. Bloomington: Indiana University Press; and van Wyk, M. (2009). "Sunset Over Atomic Apartheid: United States – South African Nuclear Relations, 1981–93." *Cold War History*, 10(1), 51–79. doi: 10.1080/14682740902764569. This case is particularly complex: Narang V., *Nuclear Strategy in the Modern Era: Regional Powers and International Conflict.* Princeton University Press, 2014 draws in his chapter on South Africa (pp. 207–222) on interesting sources including: President F. W. de Klerk, Address to Special Joint Session of Parliament (March 25, 1993), reprinted in *De Klerk Discloses Nuclear Capability to Parliament*, FBIS-AFR-93-056; de Villiers J. W., Jardine R., Reiss M., "Why South Africa Gave up the Bomb," 72 no. 5 *Foreign Affairs* (November/December 1993), 98–109; Reiss M, *Bridled Ambition: Why Countries Constrain their Nuclear Capabilities*, Baltimore: John Hopkins University Press, 1995; Purkitt H. E., Burgess S. F., "South Africa's Nuclear Strategy," in Yoshihara T., Holmes J. R. (eds.), *Strategy in the Second Nuclear Age: Power, Ambition, and the Ultimate Weapon*, Washington, DC: Georgetown University Press, 2012. He makes the argument that in the Cold War there was a strong belief that even though the United States was sanctioning the apartheid regime, it would intervene in case of communist aggression against South Africa, and even more so to prevent nuclear proliferation in the region, a belief that was modeled on what was held to be the underlying reason for Israel's nuclear posture since the 1973 Yom Kippur War. South Africa's decision to dismantle its nuclear weapons in 1993 was certainly influenced by the fact that Russian intervention was no longer a realistic threat, but US support against any (other) aggression would be facilitated by South Africa's accession to the NPT.

[107] See also Yolandi Meyer, "An African/South African Reflection on Denuclearisation," in Black-Branch/Fleck (eds.), *Nuclear Non-Proliferation in International Law*, Vol. V (Asser Press/ Springer, 2020).

LESSONS FROM THE CHEMICAL AND BIOLOGICAL CONVENTION VERIFICATIONS

The Chemical Weapons Convention[108] verification regime provides further lessons to assist with the analysis of the TPNW. Experience under the Biological Weapons Convention[109] is different, as verification provisions are not expressly included in the latter Convention, so that verification issues remain problematic. Whereas there has generally been much progress on a global front in relation to chemical and biological fields, progress regarding nuclear verification remains slow. Hence, the frustration and impatience of humanitarian groups and civil society organizations is understandable. It seems that verification after ratification is likely to become complicated.

Reference to other conventions related to weapons of mass destruction such as the Chemical Weapons Convention or the Biological Weapons Convention may assist with this analysis.[110] In the case of the Biological Weapons Convention there have been eight review conferences and the efforts of an ad hoc working group to assist with implementation. Daryl Kimball, executive director of the Arms Control Association states:

> The treaty regime mandates that states-parties consult with one another and cooperate, bilaterally or multilaterally, to solve compliance concerns. It also allows states-parties to lodge a complaint with the UN Security Council if they believe other member states are violating the convention. The Security Council can investigate complaints, but this power has never been invoked. Security Council voting rules give China, France, Russia, the United Kingdom, and the United States veto power over Security Council decisions, including those to conduct BWC investigations.[111]

Trevor Findlay notes "At first blush, the outlook for cooperative, multilateral verification of compliance with the 1972 Biological Weapons Convention (BWC) looks grim."[112] The Chemical Weapons Convention features a comparably more complete regime, including a verification mechanism and an international organization supporting its mandate. Even still, recent verification disputes have been

---

[108] Convention on the Prohibition of the Development, Production, Stockpiling and Use of Chemical Weapons and on Their Destruction (January 13, 1993), www.opcw.org/chemical-weapons-convention/.

[109] Convention on the Prohibition of the Development, Production and Stockpiling of Bacteriological (Biological) and Toxin Weapons and on Their Destruction (April 10, 1972), www.unog.ch /80256EE600585943/(httpPages)/04FBBDD6315AC720C1257180004B1B2F?OpenDocument.

[110] "Why Nuclear Weapon Ban Treaty Is Unlikely to Fulfil Its Promise," Michal Onderco. See www .tandfonline.com/doi/full/10.1080/23340460.2017.1409082.

[111] The Biological Weapons Convention (BWC) At a Glance Daryl Kimball. (Factsheet updated September 2018.) See www.armscontrol.org/factsheets/bwc.

[112] Trevor Findlay (2006). Verification and the BWC: Last Gasp or Signs of Life? Retrieved from www .armscontrol.org/act/2006_09/BWCVerification. See also: Kahn, L. H. (2011). "The Biological Weapons Convention: Proceeding Without a Verification Protocol." Retrieved from http://thebulle tin.org/biological-weapons-convention-proceeding-without-verification-protocol.

156   *Treaty Safeguards, Verification and Implementation*

highlighted at meetings of both the executive council and the Conference of State Parties. For example, "[r]eports by diplomats of stalled meetings and weeks-long delays over the use of chemical weapons in Syria became commonplace. Despite having completed the destruction of all the declared chemical weapons material in the country in January 2016, the reports of the use of chemical weapons in Syria continue to emerge."[113]

Verification is an area requiring in-depth and specific oversight, not vague references. This is why the TPNW would be much improved if it included further verification oversight under subsequent protocols. Procedures and objectives of verification must undergo continuous scrutiny which goes hand in hand with cooperative action in this complex area.[114] What might assist further for nuclear compliance is the universalization of existing legally binding instruments such as the Convention on the Physical Protection of Nuclear Material (CPPNM)[115] and the Nuclear Terrorism Convention (ICSANT).[116] Reference to these would have strengthened the regulatory framework, as well as enhancing global security regarding these matters, not only making the TPNW stronger but advancing security in this area more broadly. Other existing mechanisms for nonproliferation such as the Global Initiative to Combat Global Terrorism (GICNT)[117] and the Proliferation Security Initiative (PSI) need to be strengthened with legally binding commitments and not simply policy aspirations amongst a coalition of the willing.[118]

THE INTERNATIONAL ATOMIC ENERGY AGENCY SAFEGUARDS SYSTEM AND THE PROHIBITION TREATY

The main objective of the TPNW is to eliminate nuclear weapons. At the heart of this lies the regulation of nuclear capacity. The primary organization monitoring nuclear safety is the International Atomic Energy Agency (IAEA). Historical

---

[113] "Why Nuclear Weapon Ban Treaty Is Unlikely to Fulfil Its Promise." See Michal Onderco, www .tandfonline.com/doi/full/10.1080/23340460.2017.1409082. See Malsin, J. (2016). *Assad's Regime Is Still Using Chemical Weapons in Syria.* Retrieved from http://time.com/4492670/syria-chemical-weapon-aleppo-assad-regime/.

[114] See Recommendation D 11, Fourth Report of the Committee on Nuclear Weapons, Non-Proliferation and Contemporary International Law of the International Law Association at p. 28. See www.ila-hq.org/index.php/committees.

[115] Convention on the Physical Protection of Nuclear Material – CPPNM – (November 1, 1979), 1456 UNTS 125, entered into force on February 8, 1987, amended on July 8, 2005 (amendment entered into force on April 8, 2016), INFCIRC/274/Rev 1, www.iaea.org/Publications/Documents/Conventions/ cppnm.html, www.iaea.org/About/Policy/GC/GC49/Documents/gc49inf-6.pdf.

[116] International Convention for the Suppression of Acts of Nuclear Terrorism (Nuclear Terrorism Convention – ICSANT) (April 13, 2005), 2445 UNTS 89, http://untreaty.un.org/cod/avl/ha/icsant/ icsant.html.

[117] See www.gicnt.org.

[118] See Jonathan Black-Branch, "Nuclear Terrorism by States and Non-State Actors: Global Responses to Threats to Military and Human Security in International Law." *Journal of Conflict & Security Law* (2017) pp. 1–48. Oxford University Press.

perspectives help us fully to understand nuclear developments and the roles of respective institutions and organizations against the backdrop of agreeing the TPNW. One of the biggest challenges facing the world today is the ability to harness energy. Societies depend on energy sources and it is safe to say their relative wealth, economic prosperity and social development is partly linked to their ability to provide affordable energy supplies. Many diplomatic relations between countries are interconnected with energy-related trade. Indeed, many conflicts and environmental concerns are inextricably linked to energy exploitation.

Post-World War II the development of nuclear energy was viewed by many as a panacea that could transform the world. Hence reference to its use for peaceful purposes was included in the NPT as an "inalienable right,"[119] with both supporters and opponents of such inclusion.[120] Its benefits and opportunities quickly captured the imaginations of most governments, whereby a state could harvest energy in what was heralded as an effective and efficient method. In order to assist such endeavors, the IAEA was created in 1953 under US President Eisenhower's "Atoms for Peace" initiative,[121] with the organization's governing Statute[122] entering into force in 1957. Note that this was an entire decade before the Nuclear Non-Proliferation Treaty (NPT)[123] was agreed upon, and sixty years before the most recent TPNW came about. Nuclear energy is not an inherent right, but rather deemed to be in the national interest to have peaceful uses of nuclear energy. A general "right to energy" would be seen to go beyond peaceful uses of nuclear energy.[124]

Issues of energy aside, and indeed a state's right to energy,[125] the NPT sought to address rising concerns regarding the development and proliferation of nuclear

[119] Article IV of the NPT States: "1. Nothing in this Treaty shall be interpreted as affecting the inalienable right of all the Parties to the Treaty to develop research, production and use of nuclear energy for peaceful purposes without discrimination and in conformity with Articles I and II of this Treaty."

[120] See "The 'Inalienable Right' to Peaceful Nuclear Power: A Recipe for Chaos," Alice Slater pp. 57–63 in *At the Nuclear Precipice: Catastrophe or Transformation?* Richard Falk and David Krieger (eds.), Palgrave Macmillan, 2008.

[121] See Address by Mr. Dwight D. Eisenhower, President of the United States of America, to the 470th Plenary Meeting of the United Nations General Assembly, www.iaea.org/about/history/atoms-for-peace-speech. The idea of an international organization in charge of the control of atomic energy dates back from before 1953 though; see UNGA A/RES/1(I)(1946), Acheson Lilienthal Report (March 16, 1946), www.learnworld.com/ZNW/LWText.Acheson-Lilienthal.html, Baruch Plan (1946), www.atomicarchive.com/Docs/Deterrence/BaruchPlan.shtml.

[122] Statute of the International Atomic Energy Agency – IAEA Statute – (October 26, 1956, amended 1963, 1973, 1989, and 1999), www.iaea.org/about/about-statute.

[123] Agreed in 1968 and coming into force in 1970. Treaty on the Non-Proliferation of Nuclear Weapons (July 1, 1968) 729 *UNTS* 161.

[124] See "The Right to Develop Research, Production and Use of Nuclear Energy for Peaceful Purposes: Shortcomings and Loopholes in Legal Regulation," Dieter Fleck, in Black-Branch/Fleck (eds.), *Nuclear Non-Proliferation in International Law*, Vol. III (Asser Press/Springer, 2016) at 529–531.

[125] Article IV of the NPT States: "1. Nothing in this Treaty shall be interpreted as affecting the inalienable right of all the Parties to the Treaty to develop research, production and use of nuclear energy for peaceful purposes without discrimination and in conformity with Articles I and II of this Treaty."

Treaty Safeguards, Verification and Implementation

weapons for defense and military purposes. Conversely, the IAEA seeks to accelerate and enlarge the contribution of atomic energy toward peace, health and prosperity throughout the world while ensuring that its assistance is not used to further military purposes under its supervision or control.[126] In order to achieve its objectives, the Agency is authorized "to establish and administer safeguards designed to ensure that special fissionable and other materials, services, equipment, facilities and information made available by the Agency or at its request or under its supervision or control are not used in such a way as to further any military purpose."[127] Such efforts in no way interfere with the objectives of the TPNW. Then, one must ask whether the IAEA Statute as it stands is sufficient to verify implementation of the TPNW. As it stands, the IAEA is authorized "to apply safeguards, at the request of the parties, to any bilateral or multilateral arrangement, or at the request of a State, to any of that State's activities in the field of atomic energy." These aims may well be seen as complementing the objectives of the TPNW, as opposed to conflicting with them. Individual countries may request further IAEA oversight and adopt higher standards than the international minimum required by the Agency, in order to be compliant with their obligations under Article III of the NPT.[128]

With this in mind, one sees that the IAEA safeguards system is a central feature of the Agency's activities, as well as the assistance, services and supplies it provides to Member States.[129] Notably, the IAEA played an instrumental role as a forum for exchange during NPT negotiations, and thereafter its board of governors adapted both in size and composition in order to accommodate the Agency's evolving role and functions under the NPT.[130] The same cooperation cannot be observed regarding the TPNW, however, which simply makes reference to the existing regime without any concrete details, as discussed earlier in this chapter. The safeguards provision listed under Article 3 of the TPNW could have required each state party to go further than the bare "minimum" standards. The TPNW offered a valuable opportunity to address outstanding concerns regarding IAEA supervisory powers, but this was not acted upon and was therefore perhaps a missed opportunity. Addressing these concerns could have strengthened the TPNW regarding contentious issues relating to IAEA jurisdiction over safety issues, as well as dual-use materials and verification matters.

The main issue here is that under the NPT, different standards of verification apply to non-NWS and NWS, whereas under Article 4 of the TPNW, a state that

---

[126] Article II of the IAEA Statute.

[127] Article III.A.5 of the IAEA Statute.

[128] See wwwupdate.un.org/disarmament/WMD/Nuclear/NPTtext.shtml.

[129] Laura Rockwood, "The Treaty on the Non-Proliferation of Nuclear Weapons (NPT) and the IAEA Safeguards Agreements," in Geir Ulfstein (ed.), *Making Treaties Work. Human Rights, Environment and Arms Control* (Cambridge University Press, 2007) 301–323; see also Rockwood, *Legal Framework for IAEA Safeguards* (Vienna: IAEA, 2013).

[130] Mohamed I. Shaker, *The Nuclear Nonproliferation Treaty: Origin and Implementation 1959–1979*, 3 vols. (London/Rome/New York: Oceana, 1980), Vol. 1, 67, 362–368.

"owned, possessed or controlled nuclear weapons" must still conclude a safeguards agreement, sufficient to enable the IAEA to provide credible assurance of the non-diversion of declared nuclear material from peaceful activities and the absence of undeclared nuclear material in the state. Furthermore, it is unclear as to what extent the TPNW's provisions apply to "umbrella states" which form security relationships for NWS. Questions remain as to whether it would suffice for them to have an Additional Protocol under INFCIRC/540, although not all aspects of their involvement in nuclear planning and nuclear participation are covered here. The discussion that follows will point out some additional missed opportunities with respect to the IAEA.

Verification and Dual-Use Issues

In addition to these verification standards, the second pillar of the NPT guarantees the inalienable right of all states parties to nuclear energy for peaceful purposes, including to develop research and to produce and use of nuclear energy.[131] Indeed, "[t]he right to peaceful use of nuclear energy is conditioned by an obligation to accept verification and control of full compliance with non-proliferation agreements and to implement the obligations under Security Council Resolutions 1540 (2004) and 2325 (2016)."[132] Each non-nuclear weapon NPT state party must accept and comply with IAEA safeguards. To date, 191 parties[133] have joined the Treaty, including the five NWS, demonstrating the significance of the Treaty globally in terms of its credibility as the cornerstone of nuclear issues. As referred to in Articles 3 and 4 of the TPNW, general standards for NPT implementation are provided in the IAEA's INFCIRC/153. Notably, the IAEA has developed a Model Additional Protocol to the comprehensive safeguards agreements that non-NWS are to conclude in accordance with their Article III obligation of the NPT.[134] Note that this is

---

[131] Pursuant to: "Article III 1. Each non-nuclear-weapon State Party to the Treaty undertakes to accept safeguards, as set forth in an agreement to be negotiated and concluded with the International Atomic Energy Agency in accordance with the Statute of the International Atomic Energy Agency and the Agency's safeguards system, for the exclusive purpose of verification of the fulfilment of its obligations assumed under this Treaty with a view to preventing diversion of nuclear energy from peaceful uses to nuclear weapons or other nuclear explosive devices. Procedures for the safeguards required by this Article shall be followed with respect to source or special fissionable material whether it is being produced, processed or used in any principal nuclear facility or is outside any such facility. The safeguards required by this Article shall be applied on all source or special fissionable material in all peaceful nuclear activities within the territory of such State, under its jurisdiction, or carried out under its control anywhere."

[132] See Conclusion B 2, *Fourth Report* of the Committee on Nuclear Weapons, Non-Proliferation and Contemporary International Law of the International Law Association at p. 25. See www.ila-hq.org/index.php/committees.

[133] See http://disarmament.un.org/treaties/t/npt.

[134] IAEA, Model Protocol Additional to the Agreement(s) between State(s) and the International Atomic Energy Agency for the Application of Safeguards, INFCIRC/540 (Corr.), as of December 1, 1998,

160 *Treaty Safeguards, Verification and Implementation*

not a strict legal obligation, SC Res 1887 (2009) notwithstanding.[135] It must be noted that many states have no more than an INFCIRC/113 agreement.[136]

Verification is at the heart of IAEA activities and the dual-use issue regarding nuclear materials and the many steps leading to nuclear weapons certainly further complicate verification matters. In this context, a question needing clarification is whether, and under what conditions, enrichment/reprocessing may be considered for peaceful uses.[137] Michal Onderco reiterates Albert Wohlstetter's basic argument about "getting the bomb while not quite breaking the rules."[138] It seems that a country can get very close to having a nuclear weapon capability without actually building a nuclear weapon. This continues to pose international and regional challenges, making the dual-use nature of the process leading to the nuclear weapons difficult to verify.[139]

In relation to this long-standing problem, further oversight could have been enshrined in the TPNW for those states ratifying the Treaty, requiring them to adhere to stricter conditions under the auspices of the IAEA and hence setting higher standards and conditions regarding enrichment/reprocessing for peaceful use. Although some states continue to worry about potential intrusions on their national sovereignty,[140] without clear legal authority and direction extended to the IAEA on such matters, dual-use concerns are likely to continue to trouble the international community. Togzhan Kassenova points to an example of such resistance. Brazil, as one of the main forces behind the nuclear weapons ban, resists the IAEA Additional Protocol because of protection of national sovereignty and the country's nuclear expertise, which developed within a framework of a nuclear program under the military's auspices.[141] Article 3(2) of the TPNW specifies that "[e]ach State Party to which Article 4, paragraph 1 or 2, does not apply shall,[142] at a minimum, maintain its International Atomic Energy Agency safeguards obligations in force at the time of entry into force of this Treaty,

---

www.iaea.org/Publications/Documents/Infcircs/1997/infcirc540c.pdf. See SC Res 1887 (2009), para. 15 b.

[135] See https://digitallibrary.un.org/record/665529?ln=en.
[136] See www.iaea.org/publications/documents/infcircs?page=80.
[137] See Terms and Conditions of Peaceful Uses of Nuclear Energy, Fourth Report of the Committee on Nuclear Weapons, Non-Proliferation and Contemporary International Law of the International Law Association at para. 7, p.5. See .www.ila-hq.org/index.php/committees.
[138] See Onderco n. 143. Albert Wohlstetter. (1976). "Spreading the Bomb without Quite Breaking the Rules," *Foreign Policy*, 25, 88–94. doi: 10.2307/1148025.
[139] Matthew Fuhrmann. (2012).*Atomic Assistance: How "Atoms for Peace" Programs Cause Nuclear Insecurity*. Ithaca, NY: Cornell University Press.
[140] Sarah E. Kreps. (2018) "The Institutional Design of Arms Control Agreements," *Foreign Policy Analysis*, 14(1), 127–147.
[141] Kassenova, T. (2014). *Brazil's Nuclear Kaleidoscope: An Evolving Identity*. Washington, DC: Carnegie Endowment for International Peace, as cited from "Why Nuclear Weapon Ban Treaty Is Unlikely to Fulfil Its Promise," Michal Onderco. See www.tandfonline.com/doi/full/10.1080/23340460.2017.1409082.
[142] Article 4 referring to those moving toward the total elimination of nuclear weapons.

without prejudice to any additional relevant instruments that it may adopt in the future."[143]

Most states parties to the NPT adhere to high standards, but significant questions nevertheless remain regarding full and verifiable compliance with IAEA requirements and how to achieve this aim. There is no doubt that regulating the use of nuclear energy is complicated by varying and competing interpretations regarding the role of the IAEA. Admittedly, a very small minority of states question the Agency's actual legal authority over its nuclear program in respect of the Additional Protocol. This fact highlights potential and continued challenges regarding the TPNW, particularly when so many states refused to participate in negotiating or signing the TPNW in the first place. Clarification on these points would have been prudent for both setting out clear jurisdiction for the IAEA in conjunction with the NPT as well as demonstrating absolute commitment to settling dual-use concerns. It could also effectively have addressed issues that might well serve to jeopardize the very objective of the Treaty – complete [and verifiable] disarmament. That is to say that disarmament must be verifiable. States must adhere to requirements in a clear and unambiguous manner, carried out by an independent authority such as the IAEA. With the current state of affairs, varying interpretations remain creating confusion and a lack of clarity. Without addressing this confusion and attaining clarity, achieving the goals of the TPNW may well be thwarted. Verifiable disarmament, which is currently lacking under the NPT, and IAEA legal architecture needs tightening, as does the need to address oversight for non-state actors. Linking the TPNW to this endeavor could have set clear roles regarding states and standards.

Jonathan Herbach notes that while the NPT is the "cornerstone of the legal regime concerning nuclear weapons," there are fundamental weaknesses in its very structure, and it fails to account for the non-state acquisition of nuclear material.[144] "Unlike in the case of the Biological Weapons Convention and the Chemical Weapons Convention ... the NPT codifies a stratified system in which certain States ... retain their nuclear weapons ... while others commit to foregoing such weapons."[145] The NPT lacks universality and fails to "adequately address the

---

[143] See also "Why Nuclear Weapon Ban Treaty Is Unlikely to Fulfil Its Promise," Michal Onderco. See www.tandfonline.com/doi/full/10.1080/23340460.2017.1409082. See also: Michael Onderco (2016). *Iran's Nuclear Program and the Global South: The Foreign Policy of India, Brazil, and South Africa.* Basingstoke: Palgrave; and Matias Spektor (2010, June 18–19). "Uncovering the Sources of Nuclear Behavior: Brazil." Paper presented at the uncovering the sources of nuclear behavior: Historical dimensions of nuclear proliferation, Zurich.

[144] Jonathan Herbach, "The Evolution of Legal Approaches to Controlling Nuclear and Radiological Weapons and Combating the Threat of Nuclear Terrorism," Terry D. Gill et al., in *Yearbook of International Humanitarian Law* (Asser Press, 2014) at 54.

[145] Jonathan Herbach, "Reinforcing the Three Pillars: How Nuclear Security Efforts Underwrite the Strength of the Non-Proliferation Regime," online: http://belfercenter.ksg.harvard.edu/files/JDHerbach.pdf at 1.

threat of nuclear terrorism perpetrated by non-State actors."[146] Given the relatively recent nature of such developments no such considerations were included in the NPT which at the time was concerned primarily with state-actors. Herbach suggests that a "nuclear security framework" could address these weaknesses and so "contribute to the effectiveness of the NPT regime."[147] Given this, one might question why the TPNW simply makes tenuous references to existing international infrastructure, rather than seeking to address legal shortcomings in relation to nonproliferation and strengthening the verification regime in relation to the NPT and the role of the IAEA regarding both states and non-state actors, alike. Again, the brevity in the negotiating period did not allow for such considerations. For credibility and effectiveness, the TPNW should address these practical real-life modern concerns. Given that the text is already adopted, it could now be done by a Protocol to the TPNW.

A recurring theme surfaces. By focusing on efficiency in negotiating the TPNW, both in terms of its time frame and its actual result, the process may have sacrificed effectiveness. The simple ban process may in the end not be so simple. All the same, it is now necessary to address such deficiencies whereby many options remain open.

A COMPETENT INTERNATIONAL AUTHORITY: AUTHORITY TO DISARM AND DISMANTLE

The TPNW makes express reference to a competent international authority designated by states parties to assume responsibility for verification of the submissions about disarmament. It does not, however, provide further detail as to the nature of that body or whether it might be an existing organization such as the IAEA. If that is the intention, despite the IAEA's extensive, and indeed, unsurpassed expertise in nuclear matters, it may not have sufficient expertise in weapon dismantlement and disarmament verification as it currently stands.[148] VERTIC, the London-based verification group, indicates that if it were to accept the challenge, to verify complete nuclear disarmament, the IAEA would have to increase its capacity, including manpower, and expertise, and their powers would have to increase substantially.[149] At this time, it is not abundantly clear as to whether member states would be in favor of such a development.[150] Again, clarity in the TPNW would have assisted in this regard and allowed states to expressly agree to

---

[146] Ibid.
[147] Ibid.
[148] Wolfsthal, J. (2017). *Second Time Is Not a Charm for the Nuclear Ban Treaty*. Retrieved from www.armscontrolwonk.com/archive/1203455/second-time-is-not-a-charm-for-the-nuclear-ban-treaty/.
[149] VERTIC. (2015a). *The IAEA and Nuclear Disarmament Verification: A Primer*. See www.vertic.org/media/assets/Publications/VM11%20WEB.pdf.
[150] Ibid.

A Competent International Authority

any enlargement of such power in this domain as it pertains to verification authority under the TPNW.[151]

The TPNW and the Role and Authority of the IAEA

In relation to the TPNW, one must bear in mind that the verification process should provide meaningful information about a state's compliance or indeed its

---

[151] In relation to the IAEA mandate and a "completeness" approach there was contentious debate regarding the Agency's mandate and authority regarding paragraph 2 INFCIRC/153 (Corr.). It involved whether it should be read as implying that the IAEA is actually authorized to verify the absence of "undeclared" nuclear activities in the state subject to safeguards under Comprehensive Safeguard Agreements (CSAs), specifically, whether there is "completeness" of the declarations made by the state on the extent of its nuclear activities. Indeed, this was examined in-depth at the 2014 Cologne conference. (See also: Black-Branch/Fleck (eds.), *op. cit.* Vol. II Chapters 2 (Tariq Rauf), 3 (Pierre-Emmanuel Dupont), 4 (Laura Rockwood and Larry Johnson), 5 (Masahiko Asada), 8 (Gerald Kirchner and Stefan Oeter), and 11 (Barry Kellman).) The Safeguards Legal Framework provides that under a comprehensive safeguards agreement, the IAEA has both the right and the obligation to ensure that safeguards are applied regarding "all" nuclear material within the territory, or under its jurisdiction or control, "for the exclusive purpose of verifying that such material is not diverted to nuclear weapons or other nuclear explosive devices." (Safeguards Legal Framework. www.iaea.org/topics/safeguards-agreements.) The role of the IAEA in relation to the "completeness" of state declarations to that effect discussed in the Third ILA Report (*Third Report* of the Committee on Nuclear Weapons, Non-Proliferation and Contemporary International Law of the International Law Association at p. 4. See www.ila-hq.org/index.php/committees). There was perceived to be a gap between the IAEA mandate and its authority. On one hand, a textual approach examining the context, object and purpose of CSAs, taking into account the *travaux préparatoires*, provides support to the "completeness" argument so that it could be assumed that this embodies a correct interpretation of the disputed provision. This position is weakened, however, by the consideration of other relevant elements: at the time of the entry into force of the NPT and of the negotiation of the INFCIRC/153 safeguards system. At least until the 1990s there was no shared understanding on the now disputed interpretation of para. 2 of INFCIRC/153. The various decisions of the IAEA board of governors between 1992 and 95 that are often invoked as supporting the "completeness" argument did not in fact embody a common unequivocal endorsement by the board. Disagreements on interpretation have persisted to this date, with a few states expressing reservations on the "completeness" argument; subsequent agreement or subsequent practice that would confirm the "completeness" argument could not be identified; hence an authority of the IAEA to verify the completeness of declarations of states could only derive, practically and also legally, from the application of an Additional Protocol. (See Pierre-Emmanuel Dupont, "Interpretation of Nuclear Safeguards Commitments: The Role of Subsequent Agreement and Practice," *op. cit.*, Chapter 3.) On the other hand, proponents of a "completeness" approach would counter these arguments by saying that even without an Additional Protocol, the IAEA is fully authorized to verify the completeness of States' declarations based on a plain reading in good faith in accordance with the ordinary meaning to be given to the terms of the NPT, which was agreed a decade after the IAEA came into being. The IAEA Statute and the respective safeguards agreements within their context, and in the light of their object and purpose, clearly demonstrate both the right and the obligation of the Agency to verify the non-diversion of the declared nuclear material and moreover the absence of undeclared nuclear material and activities. This has been supported by the very context of these agreements in the light of their object and purpose and the circumstances of their conclusion; the negotiation history further confirms this interpretation, as do subsequent agreements and the practices of the parties to those agreements, as reflected in the documents adopted by the states parties to the NPT in their quinquennial review conferences, the decisions of the IAEA policy-making organs, and the consistent practice of the IAEA, at least since the early 1980s. (See Laura Rockwood and Larry Johnson, "Verification of Correctness and Completeness in the Implementation of IAEA Safeguards: the law and practice," *op. cit.*, Chapter 4.)

non-compliance with NPT obligations, taking into account the possibility of concealment methods.[152] TPNW verification requires the consideration of relevant activities which include reporting by a state; on-site inspection measurement data and observations; taking of samples; measurement from installed instrumentation (on-site or networks); outputs of surveillance devices; satellite imagery; publicly available information; and third-party information. This invariably includes national technical means and cyber applications independently examined and assessed by the Agency. The IAEA must then analyze such information and data and in a timely fashion whereby any anomalies or inconsistencies must be scrutinized and investigated and, where possible, resolved, with a view to drawing unbiased and technically accurate conclusions which are independent and verifiable.

In order to meet these requirements, the TPNW verification system should fulfill basic minimum standards, including that: (1) its *system design* should provide for a timely, high-confidence capability to detect all plausible means of evading treaty obligations and all means of concealing evasion; (2) the *information* collected for this purpose should be "meaningful" in that it is necessary and sufficient for the performance of the mandate and its use should be transparent to Member States. All such information should be authenticated; (3) appropriate procedures should ensure professional *data analysis*, internal consistency, data authentication and transparency to Member States; (4) *questions and inconsistencies* should be investigated; (5) *results* should be evaluated and interpreted in a technically sound manner.[153] Specific reference to this oversight reveals what some may consider a missed opportunity in the negotiations and drafting of the TPNW. That said, an Additional Protocol could be devised and approved for these purposes.

Future Treaty Developments – Additional Protocols

In light of the above discussion there may be scope for future treaty development. Note that any such moves would be the domain of the board of governors acting in accordance with the IAEA Statute. While the IAEA did not participate in the negotiations of the TPNW, it has a built-in mechanism to allow for amendments and additions. Article 8, notably, requires states parties to "meet regularly" and where necessary to take decisions in respect of matters regarding the application or implementation of the Treaty.[154] The first meeting of states parties is to be convened within one year of the Treaty's entry into force.[155] This requirement is aimed at actions for

---

[152] Third Report of the Committee on Nuclear Weapons, Non-Proliferation and Contemporary International Law of the International Law Association at p. 4. See www.ila-hq.org/index.php /committees.
[153] Ibid.
[154] Article 8(1). See http://undocs.org/A/CONF.229/2017/8.
[155] Article 8(2). See http://undocs.org/A/CONF.229/2017/8.

A Competent International Authority 165

providing further measures for nuclear disarmament, including both the status of implementation[156] and verification measures for the time-bound and irreversible elimination of nuclear-weapon programs.[157] Explicitly built into this section is the option of additional protocols to the TPNW.[158]

Article 10 provides for future amendments at any time after its entry into force.[159] Nothing in the Treaty prevents the states parties from addressing some of the areas of concern addressed throughout this discussion. The parties would be free to consider any development that might complement or enhance achieving the over-arching aims or objectives of the TPNW – the elimination of nuclear weapons. It must be noted that when parties amend the Treaty pursuant to Article 10, final amendments will only apply to those parties who choose to ratify such amendments. This could potentially create two groups of parties, those adhering to the original terms of the Treaty and those accepting and adopting the changes.

Following basic procedures, amendments require the text of a proposed amendment to be communicated to the secretary-general of the United Nations, for circulation to all states parties, seeking their views and if receptive, the proposal will be considered when they next convene.[160] Amendments require a positive vote of a majority of two-thirds of the states parties at which point the depositary will communicate any adopted amendment to all states parties.[161] It will enter into force for each state party that accepted the amendment ninety days following the deposit of their respective instruments of ratification or acceptance.[162] These provisions invariably leave open future developments to address some of the concerns and criticisms leveled by many involved in arms control. There is no question that the fundamental goal of proponents of the TPNW was to achieve a result – a Treaty. These built-in clauses also provide an opportunity to fine tune and develop its scope.

---

[156] Article 8(1)(a).

[157] Article 8(1)(b).

[158] Article 8(1)(b).

[159] "Article 10 Amendments 1. At any time after the entry into force of this Treaty, any State Party may propose amendments to the Treaty. The text of a proposed amendment shall be communicated to the Secretary-General of the United Nations, who shall circulate it to all States Parties and shall seek their views on whether to consider the proposal. If a majority of the States Parties notify the Secretary-General of the United Nations no later than 90 days after its circulation that they support further consideration of the proposal, the proposal shall be considered at the next meeting of States Parties or review conference, whichever comes first. 2. A meeting of States Parties or a review conference may agree upon amendments which shall be adopted by a positive vote of a majority of two thirds of the States Parties. The Depositary shall communicate any adopted amendment to all States Parties. 3. The amendment shall enter into force for each State Party that deposits its instrument of ratification or acceptance of the amendment 90 days following the deposit of such instruments of ratification or acceptance by a majority of the States Parties at the time of adoption. Thereafter, it shall enter into force for any other State Party 90 days following the deposit of its instrument of ratification or acceptance of the amendment."

[160] Article 10(1).

[161] Article 10(2).

[162] Article 10(3).

CONCLUSIONS

The basic concept of the TPNW was to take "a simple-ban" approach, whereby it explicitly prohibits nuclear weapons outright. This humanitarian disarmament method of agreeing a treaty allowed for the parties to come together and to agree the text of a treaty to eliminate nuclear weapons within a short period of time. As a result of this strategy, the TPNW does not contain elaborate provisions for safeguards, verification and enforcement, which would inevitably have required a much longer negotiating period. By design, it lacks complex details regarding verification mechanisms and monitoring or surveillance systems. The TPNW requires a simple reporting mechanism whereby states self-assess and report, working under a competent international authority and adhering to established IAEA safeguards.

At first glance this approach may seem naïve, as it effectively assumes that those committed to banning nuclear weapons will follow their word and abide by their commitments, therefore not requiring elaborate verification, monitoring and enforcement mechanisms. But for those committed to a world without nuclear weapons the treaty itself has been achieved. After all, it could be said that the treaty dove-tails well with existing infrastructure under the IAEA and allows scope for further development in this regard.

Nevertheless, at present the complete lack of safeguards and verification raises serious concerns regarding its implementation and enforcement. Safeguards, in particular, could have been added not simply to complement or rely on the IAEA process, but also to enhance them. The negotiating process under the treaty provided a ripe opportunity to address long-standing contentious issues pertaining to correctness of conduct and verification completeness. It was an opportunity to allocate clear and unambiguous authority to the IAEA regarding tangible outcomes and measurable outputs as well as setting benchmarks of achievement, including stipulating metrics of compliance and practicalities such as on-site visits. Further oversight relating to the non-diversion of nuclear material from declared peaceful activities – correctness of conduct – and the absence of undeclared nuclear activities – completeness – may have been agreed, or at least attempted. There could have been deeper legal oversight under the emerging irreversible expectations under the TPNW in relation to the IAEA. Furthermore, there could have been discussion with potential formal links between the TPNW and the NPT in relation to the oversight it extends to the IAEA regarding nuclear materials for peaceful purposes under Article III and the working mandate of the IAEA. Although they are two different treaties, creating separate legal orders, they could have been linked via a special bilateral relationship between a state party to the TPNW and the IAEA, or perhaps under a new Additional Protocol.

It could have served to clarify outstanding points of legal contention as well as to strengthen the role of the Agency in this important area regarding safeguards,

Conclusions 167

verification and compliance. The limited elaboration of the role of IAEA resulted in a missed opportunity which would have added extra assurances of achieving the main objective of the Treaty toward the elimination of nuclear weapons under both complete as well as verifiable disarmament by states ratifying it.

Critics point to the safeguard and verification deficiencies as short-comings of the TPNW, especially since it will inadvertently rely on the IAEA without having expressly involved the organization in their deliberations. The TPNW could be criticized as a missed opportunity to have strengthened the existing safeguards with enhanced legal authority and regulatory frameworks regarding verification.

Despite the concerns raised by critics, supporters of the TPNW would argue that at least there is a now treaty prohibiting nuclear weapons and that, in and of itself, this is an important milestone toward disarmament and safeguarding against nuclear war. This author contends that a world without nuclear weapons would be a safer one in which individuals have nuclear peace, living without nuclear fear. Despite its apparent shortcomings regarding effective oversight, the simple ban approach served to achieve the TPNW, which is a positive step toward nuclear peace and freedom from nuclear fear.

7

Nuclear Deterrence Policies and the Prohibition Treaty: Disarmament Considerations

> It is my fervent goal and hope ... that we will some day no longer have to rely on nuclear weapons to deter aggression and assure world peace. To that end the United States is now engaged in a serious and sustained effort to negotiate major reductions in levels of offensive nuclear weapons with the ultimate goal of eliminating these weapons from the face of the earth.
>
> *Ronald Reagan, October 20, 1986*[1]

Advocates of the Treaty on the Prohibition of Nuclear Weapons (TPNW) invariably view nuclear weapons as a threat to international peace and security. The ideals presented by the humanitarian disarmament movement challenge conventional nuclear deterrence policies and defense doctrines currently held by the nuclear-weapon states and their allies. An aim of the TPNW is to challenge basic deterrence assumptions with the intention of advancing normative change by delegitimizing nuclear weapons and changing how they are perceived throughout the world. The position of some states that nuclear weapons provide a military deterrence for overall global security and protection against war is under increasing scrutiny and now there is an actual treaty – the TPNW – opposing this position.

This chapter analyzes deterrence polices in a contemporary context, looking at the newly emerging position advanced through international humanitarian activism. It explores how nuclear weapons have traditionally been promoted as effective deterrents by nuclear-weapon states and organizations such as NATO, examining various challenges to this hitherto accepted defense doctrine. Discussion focuses on the relationship between the TPNW and NATO and umbrella states under today's humanitarian movement.

NUCLEAR WEAPONS AND THE THEORY OF DETERRENCE

Nuclear Weapons and Deterrence

Despite the end of the Cold War in the 1990s, the pervading attitude under nuclear deterrence continues to dominate the defense doctrines of nuclear-armed states and

---

[1] See www.thereaganvision.org/quotes/.

their allies. Supporters of the TPNW contend that this is unacceptable in a modern context. Humanitarian arguments question the status quo advocating that nuclear deterrence is an outdated concept that amounts to nothing more than an extension of Cold War-style defense strategies. Again, as per the NPT,[2] the so-called "Big Five" states[3] may possess nuclear weapons.[4] In essence, they claim that these weapons protect peace through deterrence. Many other states are protected by the United States either as a part of NATO or another alliance under what is commonly known as "Umbrella States," with NATO or the United States extending their nuclear umbrella protection over their allies.[5] A state can become an umbrella state via direct alliance with a nuclear-armed state, or by becoming a member of a treaty-formed organization.[6]

NATO was founded in 1949 with three of the Big Five states (the United Kingdom, France and the United States) as founding members[7] and nuclear weapons were subsequently adopted as part of its defense strategy as a deterrent.[8] A "policy of deterrence"[9] was adopted by all nuclear-weapon states during the early years of the Cold War, wherein fear of nuclear attack from either the USSR or the United States was cited as reason enough not to go to war. Other arrangements exist through the Russian Federation under the Collective Security Treaty Organization (CSTO), as well as the Shanghai Cooperation Organisation (SCO).

Deterrence

Deterrence is "the action of discouraging an action or event through instilling doubt or fear of the consequences."[10] The theory of deterrence is not applied solely within the context of nuclear weapons. For example, in criminal law sentencing the "theory of deterrence is the fear of punishment will cause potential wrongdoers to act within the parameters of the law,"[11] in order to induce legal compliance, hence, changing a behavior toward a desired outcome. Some jurisdictions employ capital punish-

---

[2] Treaty on the Non-Proliferation of Nuclear Weapons (July 1, 1968) 729 *UNTS* 161.
[3] China, France, the Russian Federation, the United Kingdom and the United States.
[4] Edward Ifft, "A Challenge to Nuclear Deterrence" (March 2017), online: *Arms Control Association*: www.armscontrol.org/act/2017–03/features/challenge-nuclear-deterrence#note01.
[5] International Law and Policy Institute, "Nuclear Umbrellas and Umbrella States" (last modified April 22, 2016), online: *International Law and Policy Institute*: nwp.ilpi.org/?p=1221.
[6] Ibid.
[7] North Atlantic Treaty (1949-08-24) 34 *UNTS* 243.
[8] Michael S. Gerson, "Conventional Deterrence in the Second Nuclear Age" (2009) 39:3 *Parameters: US Army War College* 32 at 34. See also Patrick Morgan, *Deterrence Now* (Cambridge: Cambridge University Press, 2003) at 25.
[9] *Legality of the Threat or Use of Nuclear Weapons*, Advisory Opinion, ICJ Reports 1996, p. 226, para. 67
[10] The Oxford English Dictionary, 2nd ed., *sub verbo* "deterrence."
[11] *R. v. Melnyk* [1997] 8 WWR 589, [1997] SJ No. 392 at 40.

ment – the death penalty – as a deterrent to more serious crimes such as murder.[12] From a state's military defense standpoint, deterrence is "the threat of force intended to convince a potential aggressor not to undertake a particular action because the costs will be unacceptable or the probability of success extremely low."[13] After states began obtaining nuclear weapons in the mid-to-late 1940s, nuclear weapons were inducted in their defense strategies. With the goal of preventing nuclear conflict, states undertook "the development and rigorous analysis of deterrence as a discrete strategic concept" for nuclear weapons.[14] Thus, nuclear "[d]eterrence theory was developed against the backdrop of the Cold War nuclear arms race and focused on the prevention of nuclear conflict."[15] During this period, "deterrence became synonymous with nuclear weapons [and] assumed an increasingly important role in the development of military strategy."[16] Nuclear deterrence is a defense strategy to warn states that nuclear weapons may be used against them, where the nuclear-armed states conditionally promise to deploy them in the event of an act of aggression or threat to, or breach of peace.[17] This is done with the intention of achieving a desired outcome: preventing military conflict or aggression; threatening nuclear aggression to prevent aggression.

Deterrence and the Threat of Nuclear Weapons under Article 1: An Absolute Clause

Article 1(d) of the TPNW prohibits the "use" or to "threaten to use nuclear weapons or other nuclear explosive devices."[18] This clause forms an important component of the purpose and object of the Treaty, but its inclusion was not straightforward. This wording only came about as a result of strenuous urging on the part of numerous states and civil society groups. Indeed, it did not appear in earlier drafts of May 22 and June 27, 2017 and was finally introduced by the working group on Article 1 into the text of June 30 where proposed amendments introduced "threaten to use,"[19]

---

[12] Note that the right to life and the prohibition from torture or cruel, inhuman or degrading treatment or punishment are protected under the Universal Declaration of Human Rights, 1948.

[13] Michael S. Gerson, "Conventional Deterrence in the Second Nuclear Age" (2009) 39:3 Parameters: US Army War College 32 at 34.

[14] Ibid.

[15] Ibid.

[16] Ibid.

[17] See Brian Angelo Lee, "Preventative War, Deterrent Retaliation, and Retrospective Disproportionality" (2009) Vol. 2009:2, Brigham Young University LR 253 at 258; and Brian Drummond, "Is the United Kingdom Nuclear Deterrence Policy Unlawful" (2009) Vol. 11, NZYB Int'l L 107 at 117.

[18] See https://undocs.org/A/CONF.229/2017/8 (1)(d) "Use or threaten to use nuclear weapons or other nuclear explosive devices."

[19] See https://s3.amazonaws.com/unoda-web/wp-content/uploads/2017/06/Preamble-Article-1– 21_compilation_-SA-proposal_29-June.docx (June 29, 2017) (by Argentina and Iran).

"threat to use,"[20] "threat of use,"[21] or "threat of nuclear weapons use"[22] with the expression "threaten to use."[23,24]

Hayashi points out that the resistance to the idea of explicitly prohibiting threatened use of nuclear weapons was on the ground that it was encompassed by the broader prohibition on threatened use of armed force. He notes Austria's fear, similar to that of Mexico, Sweden and Switzerland.[25] Specifically, Austria stated:

> We do not believe that explicitly prohibiting the threat of use, the scope of which is subject to differing interpretation. There is already a general prohibition on the threat of use of (armed) force in the UN Charter. In incorporating a specific prohibition of the threat of use of nuclear weapons, we could be seen as calling into question the validity of that more general norm.[26]

In that regard Hayashi argues that "a more specific rule found in one instrument does not necessarily compromise a more general rule found in another instrument."[27] Furthermore, he notes that "the validity of a pre-existing norm – 'already' is the word used by Austria – does not really depend on the non-articulation of a subsequent norm ... It is exceedingly unlikely that the Charter prohibition on threat of force will suffer because Article 1(d) of the TPNW prohibits threats of nuclear weapons use."[28]

As for the term "use" of nuclear weapons or other nuclear explosive devices this is quite clear. Each state party undertakes never, under any circumstances, to use nuclear weapons or devices, regardless of the circumstances. This is an absolute clause requiring it to be taken at its highest meaning and interpreted in its strictest sense. It would be clear when, and if, a party used a nuclear weapon or an explosive device. In so doing they would be in breach of their treaty obligations. What may

---

[20] See ibid. (by Cuba and Thailand).

[21] See ibid. (by Egypt, Fiji and Guatemala).

[22] See ibid. (by Kazakhstan).

[23] See https://undocs.org/A/CONF.229/2017/8 (1)(d).

[24] See *Nuclear Ban Daily*, Vol. 2, No. 11 (July 3, 2017). As noted in: N Hayashi, "Is the Nuclear Weapons Ban Treaty Accessible to Umbrella States?," in Black-Branch/Fleck (eds.), *Nuclear Non-Proliferation in International Law*, Vol. IV (Asser Press/Springer, 2019), 377–394.

[25] Quoted from: N Hayashi, "Is the Nuclear Weapons Ban Treaty Accessible to Umbrella States?," in Black-Branch/ Fleck (eds.), *Nuclear Non-Proliferation in International Law*, Vol. IV (Asser Press/ Springer, 2019), at p. 380. See *Nuclear Ban Daily*, Vol. 1, No. 4 (March 30, 2017) (citing Austria, Mexico, Sweden and Switzerland); *Nuclear Ban Daily*, Vol. 2, No. 3 (June 19, 2017) (citing Switzerland).

[26] Statement made on March 29, 2017, reportedly by Hajnoczi himself (*Nuclear Ban Daily*, Vol. 1, No. 4 (March 30, 2017)). As quoted at p. 380 of N Hayashi, "Is the Nuclear Weapons Ban Treaty Accessible to Umbrella States?," in Black-Branch /Fleck (eds.), *Nuclear Non-Proliferation in International Law*, Vol. IV (Asser Press/Springer, 2019), 377–394.

[27] See N Hayashi, "Is the Nuclear Weapons Ban Treaty Accessible to Umbrella States?," in Black-Branch /Fleck (eds.), *Nuclear Non-Proliferation in International Law*, Vol. IV (Asser Press/Springer, 2019), at p. 380 – 377–394.

[28] See N Hayashi, "Is the Nuclear Weapons Ban Treaty Accessible to Umbrella States?," in Black-Branch / Fleck (eds.), *Nuclear Non-Proliferation in International Law*, Vol. IV (Asser Press/Springer, 2019), at p. 381 – 377–394.

172   *Deterrence Policies and the Prohibition Treaty*

draw more attention, requiring further analysis is the phrase "threaten to use nuclear weapons or other nuclear explosive devices." What is a threat within this context? Moreover, does this refer to nuclear deterrence? Is deterrence a form of "threat"?

In this context, is a threat a mere off-the cuff comment between two leaders? Or, is it a leader's unilateral declaration regarding its defense doctrine? In January 2006, in a high-profile speech updating military officers on France's strategic doctrine, French President Jacques Chirac, "threatened to use nuclear weapons against any state that supported terrorism against his country or considered using weapons of mass destruction."[29] Mr. Chirac stated: "The leaders of states who use terrorist means against us, as well as those who would consider using, in one way or another, weapons of mass destruction, must understand that they would lay themselves open to a firm and adapted response on our part,. ... This response could be a conventional one. It could also be of a different kind."[30]

It was well accepted that President Chirac's speech was aimed at preventing rogue states from sponsoring terrorists, rather 1980s-style antics of the Soviet era. It is safe to say his words were meant as a warning and not a threat. All the same, this warning that nuclear weapons could be used against terrorist states put him more in line with the controversial nuclear posture of the United States which was unveiled in 2002, also listing nuclear arms as a credible deterrent to rogue states armed with non-conventional weapons.[31] This begs the question as to whether there is a difference between a threat and a warning, or whether they are strategically the same? It may be that a warning is more open-ended and all pervasive, whereas a threat is more focused and specific. This begs a further question as to whether one has more legal significance than the other. After all, Mr. Chirac's comments were specific in actions – use of nuclear weapons – but were more general in scope – against any state that supported terrorism. A threat must be more specific both in action and scope – to use nuclear weapons against a specific, named state. The fine tuning between actions and scope aside, the main purpose was to deter would-be terrorist states from propagating terrorist acts in France. It was meant as a deterrent whereby nobody could say for sure whether France would have deployed nuclear weapons in reaction to terrorist activities against it. To do so would be sheer speculation, and begs the question as to whether France might have been militarily involved in states where ISIS was active, as a response to the ISIS-instigated terrorist acts in Paris etc.

What remains to be determined is whether nuclear deterrence is an actual "threat" within the meaning of Article 1. There are two ways of looking at this issue. An immediate response may be: No: nuclear deterrence is not a threat within the

---

[29]   France delivers nuclear threat. John Thornhill and Peter Spiegel in January 20, 2006 *Financial Times*: www.ft.com/content/e805e2d4-88e6-11da-94a6-0000779e2340. See also www.spiegel.de/international/chirac-warns-terrorists-france-has-nuclear-retaliation-option-a-396191.html.

[30]   Quoted from: "France Delivers Nuclear Threat," John Thornhill and Peter Spiegel in January 20, 2006 *Financial Times*: www.ft.com/content/e805e2d4-88e6-11da-94a6-0000779e2340.

[31]   Ibid.

meaning of Article 1 of the TPNW. The term was included in the Treaty within a broader global context, whereby nuclear deterrence is a modern reality that is taken for granted. Indeed, the ICJ in its 1996 Advisory Opinion acknowledged that deterrence is a "fact" in the global context. Yet, the ICJ refrained from scrutinizing this "fact" under legal terms. There is an understanding that this is a political reality; that Article 1 of the TPNW itself will not change. Why would nation states negotiate a treaty with which several states are unable and unwilling to comply? Its inclusion could not have been intended to cover nuclear deterrence, therefore, "threaten to use nuclear weapons or other nuclear explosive devices"[32] does not include deterrence.

This author would argue differently. It is meant to cover nuclear deterrence. In the context of the TPNW, nuclear deterrence would indeed be perceived as a threat within the intended scope of the treaty. It is all-inclusive and intended to be covered. After all, the main intention of the TPNW is to rid the world of nuclear weapons and the threat of their use has dominated the international political debate in defense circles for decades. Under a strict interpretation, this author cannot see how there could be any other interpretation, other than an absolute requirement. To allow a state to threaten the use of nuclear weapons through a deterrence policy would defeat the intent of the Treaty which is to be nuclear-weapons free. Upon joining the TPNW, under their own national sovereignty, contracting parties would have agreed to curtail their respective powers in regard to nuclear deterrence. To do otherwise, a state would either not ratify the TPNW in the first place or have to withdraw from the Treaty which would require it to give notice to take effect twelve months after the date of the receipt of the notification.[33] In the exercise of its own sovereign will, a state party will have bound itself to an absolute prohibition of nuclear threats, which include deterrence. Had the intention been to simply limit "use," then the wording would have been different.

Is deterrence a threat? Yes, deterrence is an all-pervasive threat which cannot be seen in any other light. Deterrence could be viewed as a warning, but then a warning is not to ward off unwanted behaviors unless there are consequences and actions to follow. It seems clear that deterrence, be it a warning or a promise, is a threat that cannot be dressed up in any other language. If it were not a threat, then it would be a mere idea of little consequence. It is not meant as a request that is also permissive, as in "please do not," but it is coercive and commanding in nature, as in "you must

---

[32] See https://undocs.org/A/CONF.229/2017/8 (1)(d) "Use or threaten to use nuclear weapons or other nuclear explosive devices."

[33] Article 17 Duration and withdrawal "1. This Treaty shall be of unlimited duration. 2. Each State Party shall, in exercising its national sovereignty, have the right to withdraw from this Treaty if it decides that extraordinary events related to the subject matter of the Treaty have jeopardized the supreme interests of its country. It shall give notice of such withdrawal to the Depositary. Such notice shall include a statement of the extraordinary events that it regards as having jeopardized its supreme interests. 3. Such withdrawal shall only take effect 12 months after the date of the receipt of the notification of withdrawal by the Depositary. If, however, on the expiry of that 12-month period, the withdrawing State Party is a party to an armed conflict, the State Party shall continue to be bound by the obligations of this Treaty and of any additional protocols until it is no longer party to an armed conflict." See https://undocs.org/A/CONF.229/2017/8.

174 *Deterrence Policies and the Prohibition Treaty*

not do – or else." Whether or not the state in question actually fulfills the threat is a completely different issue. As long as the promise of its intention – use – is present then it is a threat which is now prohibited under Article 1.

Those relying on nuclear deterrence cannot have it both ways. They cannot be seen as gaining the benefit from an overarching promise, a threat to do something – to use force (having potentially horrific consequences for those affected by their actions) – without bearing the burden of being seen as exerting coercive messages to achieve an objective. To this end, deterrence is meant to encompass a threat within the meaning of Article 1.

One may ask why a nation state would ratify a prohibition treaty regarding which several states are unable and unwilling to comply. It is because such nuclear activities are deemed inappropriate by those supporting the TPNW. Nuclear weapons are no longer acceptable in the view of some humanitarian groups. On the one hand, some argue that the law has to be realistic. To negotiate a law that is unacceptable and unenforceable by many states is unrealistic and sets it up for failure. On the other hand, law can set higher objectives as well, raising accepted standards of international behaviors toward higher goals. Local laws often criminalize behaviors that are common and known to occur, such as drug trafficking. The law does not mold itself to the activities of the offenders but to the ideals and aspirations of the intended outcome. As far removed as this argument may seem, the NPT does require "cessation of the nuclear arms race at an early date" and "complete disarmament under strict and effective international control."[34] As unrealistic as these outcomes may seem to some, states parties to the NPT have agreed to them and the TPNW is simply reaffirming long-standing international obligations.

That is not to ignore the reality that nuclear deterrence is in fact a way of life for nuclear-weapon states and their allies, but it does not mean that the status quo should prevail forever without any progress toward the intended outcomes of Article VI of the NPT. While some might say that the TPNW is flawed and unrealistic, as it is better to have a treaty to which many states adhere, supporters of the TPNW would argue that it is better to strive toward higher goals than to accept lower standards that do not match those agreed in the NPT. Of course, this begs the question as to what happens if these higher standards do not correspond to generally accepted norms of many states. Should a treaty not reflect an objective reality at the time it was concluded? Evidently, in this case the framers of the TPNW felt not. They wish to change norms and have nuclear standards evolve. Indeed, they reflect the emerging will of many states and civil society organizations, as well as citizens of the world.

Effectively, Article 1(1)(d) means that states parties will not be entitled to threaten to use nuclear weapons under any circumstances, even if they fulfill other aspects of international law allowing them lawful self-defense under *jus ad bellum*. Whilst threatening to use force is generally unlawful, under *jus ad bellum*,[35] it can also be

---

[34] Article VI. See www.un.org/disarmament/wmd/nuclear/npt/text/.
[35] See, e.g., *Legality of the Threat or Use of Nuclear Weapons, Advisory Opinion*, ICJ Reports 1996, p. 226, para. 105(2)(C) ("A threat ... of force ... that is contrary to Article 2, paragraph 4 ... and that fails to meet all the requirements of Article 51, is unlawful"); Grimal 2012, at 145–146, 153.

Nuclear Weapons and the Theory of Deterrence 175

lawful, in self-defense and if the necessity and proportionality requirements are fulfilled. That said, states signatories to the TPNW have to be prepared to jettison any recourse to threatening to use nuclear force if they adopt the TPNW, regardless of whether they may have the right to do so, or be justifiable in doing so under general international law. Becoming party to the TPNW is a form of special club to which they would be bound unless they withdrew.[36]

The UN Security Council has authority to apply lawful use of force under *jus ad bellum* in accordance with its Chapter VII powers.[37] Under Article 39 of the UN Charter, the Security Council shall determine the existence of any threat to the peace, breach of the peace, or act of aggression.[38] In that regard, Article 1(1)(d) could in no way be seen as either trumping or taking precedence over such powers. The Security Council (SC) has the sole discretion to decide what constitutes a threat to the peace. That said, there is nothing stopping individual states from having their own heightened set of standards as to what constitutes a threat to the peace in their view, so long as they comply with international law as well as with any resolutions advanced by the SC.

The ICJ found that there is no specific authorization of the threat or use of nuclear weapons or any other weapon in international customary and treaty law. Nor is there a prohibition against nuclear weapons in international customary and treaty law. The "General Assembly resolutions affirming the illegality of nuclear weapons" were evidence of an emerging "customary international law prohibiting the use of nuclear weapons," however, the practice of deterrence resulting in a "substantial number of negative votes and abstentions to the resolutions" led the ICJ to determine that there was no *opinio juris* prohibiting nuclear weapons. Accordingly, the ICJ concluded:

> It follows from the above-mentioned requirements that the threat or use of nuclear weapons would generally be contrary to the rules of international law applicable in armed conflict, and in particular the principles and rules of humanitarian law; However, in view of the current state of international law, and of the elements of fact at its disposal, the Court cannot conclude definitively whether the threat or use of nuclear weapons would be lawful or unlawful in an extreme circumstance of self-defence, in which the very survival of a State would be at stake.[39]

So, what does this mean for the TPNW? The UN Charter, ICJ jurisprudence and customary practice do not expressly prohibit the threat of use of force, whereas the TPNW now does. In examining the preamble of the TPNW along with the various

---

[36] Under Article 17 Duration and withdrawal. https://undocs.org/A/CONF.229/2017/8.

[37] See http://legal.un.org/repertory/art39.shtml.

[38] "The Security Council shall determine the existence of any threat to the peace, breach of the peace, or act of aggression and shall make recommendations, or decide what measures shall be taken in accordance with Articles 41 and 42, to maintain or restore international peace and security." See http://legal.un.org/repertory/art39.shtml.

[39] ICJ, *Legality of the Threat or Use of Nuclear Weapons*, Advisory Opinion of July 8, 1996 (General Assembly Opinion), *ICJ Reports* (1996), 226, 35 *ILM* (1996), at para. 105(2)(E).

176   *Deterrence Policies and the Prohibition Treaty*

clauses under Article 1, it is difficult to conclude how the TPNW could otherwise not have intended to include deterrence as a threat. Its tone is emphatic and absolute. Each state party undertakes "never under any circumstances" to use them or threaten to use them. It would seem to this author that having nuclear weapons for deterrence purposes is a form of "use" as well as a "threat" to employ them. Subparagraph 1(1)(a) notes the wide range of prohibitions regarding "nuclear weapons or other nuclear explosive devices." Article 1(1)(b) and (c) prohibits parties to "transfer" or "receive" either "directly or indirectly." Article 1(1)(e) requires parties never to "assist, encourage or induce, in any way, anyone to engage in" any prohibited activity; whereas, subparagraph (f) states that parties should not "seek or receive any assistance, in any way, from anyone to engage in" any prohibited nuclear activity. From these clear messages, nuclear threats must invariably include deterrence. It would seem odd to carve out one exception, especially one that is at the heart of promoting the development, modernization and stationing of nuclear weapons and devices, which is the focal point of the prohibition. Participants in the Working Group insisted on having the threat of use of nuclear weapons and devices included in the final draft of the TPNW. They persisted until it was prohibited under Article 1, even though the president had not included it in the first two drafts. It is hardly likely that they did not see nuclear deterrence as a threat to nuclear peace. They are more determined than ever on changing perceptions through stigmatization until governments reconsider their respective positions on not just the "use" of nuclear weapons, but also nuclear deterrence.

Collective Deterrence and the Inception of NATO

"Collective deterrence" was adopted by states at the international level prior to the development of nuclear weapons.[40] For example, the formation of the League of Nations was "meant to provide deterrence by the entire membership against any member thinking about attacking another."[41] In the early years of the development of nuclear weapons, nuclear-weapon states and their allies adopted the "collective deterrence" strategy via international defense treaties. In the West, the North Atlantic Treaty[42] founded the North Atlantic Treaty Organization (NATO) in 1949. NATO is a political and military alliance dedicated to the defense of its member countries.[43] NATO was founded upon, and remains committed to, collective defense where an attack against one of its members is considered as an attack against all members.[44] Three of its members are nuclear-armed states. NATO adopted nuclear weapons into its defense strategy as deterrents. "From the mid-1960s onward, NATO relied on

---

[40]   Patrick Morgan, *Deterrence Now* (Cambridge: Cambridge University Press, 2003) at 7.
[41]   Ibid.
[42]   North Atlantic Treaty (1949-08-24) 34 *UNTS* 243.
[43]   What is NATO? See www.nato.int/nato-welcome/index.html.
[44]   Article 5, North Atlantic Treaty (1949-08-24) 34 *UNTS* 243. See also What is NATO, 2.2 Collective Defence: www.nato.int/nato-welcome/index.html.

conventional power, backed by the threat of nuclear escalation, to deter any conventional assault on Europe by the numerically superior Warsaw Pact, and relied on nuclear weapons to deter nuclear attacks."[45]

NATO's Current Defense Strategy for Nuclear Weapons

NATO notes that its nuclear policy is based on its 2010 Strategic Concept and the 2012 Deterrence and Defence Posture Review.[46] The bulk of NATO's current defense strategy resembles the "policy of deterrence"[47] adopted by states during the Cold War. Specifically, these documents emphasize that NATO remains a nuclear alliance dedicated to the defense of its member states against attack.[48] Its policies are such that the security of its members is dependent upon the "strategic nuclear forces of the Alliance, particularly those of the United States; the independent strategic nuclear forces of the United Kingdom and France, which have a deterrent role."[49] Thus, "[d]eterrence, based on an appropriate mix of nuclear and conventional capabilities, remains a core element of [its] overall strategy."[50] But NATO also emphasizes that "the circumstances in which any use of nuclear weapons might have to be contemplated are extremely remote."[51]

LEGAL AND POLITICAL RAMIFICATIONS FOR NATO MEMBERS, UMBRELLA AND OTHER STATES UNDER THE TPNW

"As long as nuclear weapons exist, NATO will remain a nuclear alliance."[52] This standpoint, found in NATO's 2010 Strategic Concept, indicates that any member signing the 2017 TPNW would not be likely to remain a member thereafter. While

[45] Michael S. Gerson, "Conventional Deterrence in the Second Nuclear Age" (2009) 39:3 *Parameters: US Army War College* 32 at 34. See also Patrick Morgan, *Deterrence Now* (Cambridge: Cambridge University Press, 2003) at 25.

[46] NATO, "NATO's Nuclear Deterrence Policy and Forces" (May 17, 2018), online: *North Atlantic Treaty Organization*: www.nato.int/cps/em/natohq/topics_50068.htm.

[47] *Legality of the Threat or Use of Nuclear Weapons*, Advisory Opinion, ICJ Reports 1996, p. 226, para. 67.

[48] Section 16, NATO "Strategic Concept for the Defence and Security of the Members of the North Atlantic Treaty Organization" (November 19, 2010), online: *North Atlantic Treaty Organization*: www .nato.int/cps/em/natohq/official_texts_68580.htm?selectedLocale=en.

[49] Section 17–18, NATO "Strategic Concept for the Defence and Security of the Members of the North Atlantic Treaty Organization" (November 19, 2010), online: *North Atlantic Treaty Organization*: www .nato.int/cps/em/natohq/official_texts_68580.htm?selectedLocale=en.

[50] Section 17, NATO "Strategic Concept for the Defence and Security of the Members of the North Atlantic Treaty Organization" (November 19, 2010), online: *North Atlantic Treaty Organization*: www .nato.int/cps/em/natohq/official_texts_68580.htm?selectedLocale=en.

[51] Chicago Summit Declaration 2012, May 20, 2012. See www.nato.int/cps/su/natohq/official_ texts_87593.htm.

[52] Section 17, NATO "Strategic Concept for the Defence and Security of the Members of the North Atlantic Treaty Organization" (November 19, 2010), online: *North Atlantic Treaty Organization*, www .nato.int/cps/em/natohq/official_texts_68580.htm?selectedLocale=en.

178 *Deterrence Policies and the Prohibition Treaty*

NATO is "resolved to . . . create the conditions for a world without nuclear weapons in accordance with the goals of the Nuclear Non-Proliferation Treaty,"[53] each of its members agrees to "ensure the broadest possible participation of Allies in collective defence planning on nuclear roles, in peacetime basing of nuclear forces, and in command, control and consultation arrangements."[54] In the beginning, it appears the implications for a state signing the TPNW may differ, depending on whether a particular country allows nuclear weapons to be based in their sovereign soil. For those that do, the requirement would be to remove them within a set period of time. For those that do not have nuclear weapons stationed within their jurisdiction, it is much more straightforward. For either state, at present their relationship with NATO would either have to be severed or dramatically realigned as discussed below.

TPNW Implications for NATO States Basing Nuclear Weapons

Currently, NATO has arranged for US nuclear weapons to be based in five NATO countries: Belgium, Germany, Italy, the Netherlands and Turkey.[55] Separate from the TPNW, prima facie, this may also seem to violate Articles I and II of the NPT which prohibit nuclear-weapon states from transferring nuclear weapons to a non-nuclear-weapon state and non-nuclear-weapon states from receiving the transfer of nuclear weapons from nuclear-weapon states.[56] Note, a "transfer" would go beyond stationing with the consent of the receiving state. NATO is adamant, however, that "US nuclear weapons based in Europe are in the sole possession and under constant and complete custody and control of the United States"[57] thus, not violating the NPT. That is to say, NATO takes the view that from a technical, a practical and a legal standpoint, nuclear weapons have not been transferred to these respective host states which are non-nuclear-weapon states; and the non-nuclear-weapon states in question have not received the transfer of nuclear weapons from a nuclear-weapon state. Hence, there is no breach of Articles I or II of the NPT. Accepting this position, the five host states are not in breach of their obligations under the NPT, nor is the United States in breach of its obligation in having transferred them.

But if Belgium, Germany, Italy, the Netherlands, or Turkey were to sign the TPNW, strictly speaking they would be required to ensure that the United States

---

[53] Section 24, NATO "2012 Deterrence and Defence Posture Review" (May 20, 2012), online: *North Atlantic Treaty Organization*: www.nato.int/cps/en/natohq/official_texts_87597.htm.

[54] Section 19, NATO "Strategic Concept for the Defence and Security of the Members of the North Atlantic Treaty Organization" (November 19, 2010), online: *North Atlantic Treaty Organization* www.nato.int/cps/em/natohq/official_texts_68580.htm?selectedLocale=en.

[55] Robert Norris and Hans Kristensen, "US Tactical Nuclear Weapons in Europe, 2011" (2011) 67:1 *Bulletin of the Atomic Scientists* 64 at 65.

[56] Articles I and II, Treaty on the Non-Proliferation of Nuclear Weapons (July 1 1968) 729 *UNTS* 161.

[57] NATO, "NATO's Positions Regarding Nuclear Non-Proliferation, Arms Control and Disarmament and Related Issues" (October 22, 2009) at 3, online (pdf): *North Atlantic Treaty Organization* www.nato.int/nato_static/assets/pdf/pdf_topics/20091022_NATO_Position_on_nuclear_nonproliferation-eng.pdf.

Legal and Political Ramifications under the TPNW

removes the nuclear weapons from their sovereign territory as Article I of the TPNW prohibits the storage, stationing and installation of nuclear weapons in a signatory's sovereign land.[58] In this regard, there is little doubt that such a request would result in their receiving push-back from NATO headquarters as well as its fellow NATO Member States. Removing nuclear weapons would invariably affect NATO's defense position. Despite this potential backlash, the TPNW signatory state would still, in theory, at least in the first instance be a member of NATO. This leads to the question of whether such a state, which currently does host nuclear weapons, would be able to remain a NATO member if it were to adopt the TPNW. On the face of it, it would seem not.[59] That said, NATO countries are likely to come under increasing political pressure from their citizens to justify their respective national nuclear deterrence policies.

At present, there seems to be no breach of Articles I or II of the NPT, as the weapons in question are under the US control. Strictly speaking the same could not be argued regarding Article I of the TPNW.[60] Perhaps similarly the state in question is neither deemed to have received the weapons in question, nor have such weapons been transferred to it in the same manner as is currently argued under the NPT. After all, as it is an acceptable for one treaty (i.e., the NPT), it should also be acceptable for the TPNW. Article 1(1)(g) TPNW prohibits any stationing, installation or deployment of any nuclear weapons or other nuclear explosive devices in its territory or at any place under its jurisdiction or control. Alternatively, a new signatory state to the TPNW could decide to relinquish its respective military territory on which the weapons are stationed, to the sovereign authority of the nuclear-weapon state controlling such weapons (i.e., the United States). Admittedly, this would be highly unlikely and indeed unacceptable for any ally. Hypothetically speaking, the state in question would have to relinquish sovereignty over the area in question in order not to have weapons stationed on its soil or within its jurisdiction. Notably, European NATO allies that have given their consent to the stationing of US nuclear weapons would insist that they have not given up their sovereignty and are unlikely to do so under any circumstance, especially to join the TPNW. If they did relinquish sovereignty, however, they could argue there is no breach, as strictly speaking no such weapons are stationed within their sovereign territory as required by Article I of the TPNW.[61]

Thus, from a technical standpoint, no nuclear weapons have been transferred to the non-nuclear-weapon state and accordingly the non-nuclear-weapon state has not received the transfer of nuclear weapons from the nuclear-weapon state. Moreover,

---

[58] Article 1, Treaty on the Prohibition of Nuclear Weapons, A/CONF.229/2017/8.
[59] See N. Hayashi, "Is the Nuclear Weapons Ban Treaty Accessible to Umbrella States?," in Black-Branch/Fleck (eds.), *Nuclear Non-Proliferation in International Law*, Vol. IV (Asser Press/Springer, 2019), 377–394.
[60] Article 1, Treaty on the Prohibition of Nuclear Weapons, A/CONF.229/2017/8.
[61] Ibid.

it does not have weapons stationed on its soil or within its jurisdiction, as it is deemed to have relinquished sovereignty over the area in question. Again, here there would be no breach of Articles I or II of the NPT and strictly speaking no such weapons are stationed within the state's sovereign territory as required by Article I of the TPNW.[62]

A realistic question is whether a state party to the TPNW would still enjoy protection under the nuclear umbrella. It would seem that they could not have an official arrangement, per se. As to whether they could accept, if offered assistance, it would seem that parties to the TPNW should object to any such assistance.

As has become apparent, such arguments are unlikely to garner much support from committed supporters of the TPNW. *De jure* arguments aside as to whether the state in question is actually legally compliant, that state is *de facto* supporting and promoting nuclear weapons and would not be deemed to be in full compliance with the spirit of the TPNW, strictly speaking. The acquiescence of sovereignty over sections of a state's territory in order to circumvent the reality of stationing nuclear weapons on its soil, demonstrates a clear and direct passing of control indicating that such matters are expressly within a state's legal authority and that it has made a direct decision to use nuclear weapons for the purposes of defense. By relinquishing sovereignty, in order to comply with Article 1, they would use creative compliance techniques that violate both the spirit of the TPNW, as well as the letter of the law itself.

The usefulness of such a discussion may be called into question, because at first blush, the answer appears obvious. Why would a state want to explore such protracted exercises in considering such positions? Simply put, the answer is that many of the NATO states are full-participatory democracies in which governments answer to their respective electorates and are often reactive to the political climate of the day. As the groundswell of support for the TPNW grows, some current NATO governments may face political challenges to their nuclear defense positions. This may force them to entertain methods of creative compliance in order to advance democratic will whilst maintaining the status quo in regard to their nuclear defense doctrines. With this in mind, there is some evidence that such creative maneuvering, as explored above, may be on the political radar of some Western democracies that are likely to face political pressure from civil society organizations and individual citizens alike to adopt the TPNW. While public opinion may reflect an important part of political decision making, it is hardly indicative of government positions when addressing issues of external security and cooperation within the relevant alliance. That said, for a state to station nuclear weapons on its soil would not be compatible with Article 1 of the TPNW. Regardless, of the technical aspects of possession, per se, such a state would be, in effect, relying on nuclear weapons for purposes of defense and deterrence.

[62] Ibid.

Implications for NATO States Not Basing Nuclear Weapons

Some NATO members are positioned differently from others, given they do not all have nuclear weapons stationed within their territories as with the five allied states mentioned above.[63] Indeed, NATO employs a defense strategy which utilizes both conventional and nuclear weapons.[64] An argument may be that it might be possible for a state signing the TPNW to maintain its NATO membership by contributing conventional weapons and alternative forces without reliance on nuclear. This might also be an option for a state such as Australia which does not have US nuclear weapons on its territory, but has joined the Treaty of Rarotonga, benefiting from its Article 5 (which allows cooperation with the US Navy).

In examining whether or not NATO states without nuclear weapons could adopt the TPNW, as they do not harbor such weapons, the conclusion must be that they cannot. Again, as long as NATO is a nuclear alliance it would seem unlikely that NATO membership would fall within the spirit of the TPNW, regardless of the real or actual physical presence of weapons on their soil. NATO membership would be in contravention of TPNW obligations for states with, or without, nuclear weapons stationed or stored within their jurisdiction. The legal commitment to "a nuclear alliance"[65] likely precludes membership of the TPNW as Member States agree to the nuclear defense doctrines, *de jure* and/or *de facto*. Even if NATO does not have weapons stationed within a state's territory and it allowed the state to ratify the TPNW, again, the fact that they are in a defense alliance which ultimately relies on nuclear weapons for defense and deterrence purposes would be against the intention and integrity of the TPNW. That is to say their military security would be based on nuclear capabilities, whether used or not.

While NATO membership seems incompatible with accession to the TPNW, it does seem to be clear that the TPNW would not allow a state to be a member of NATO. Note that under the Washington Treaty, NATO is not given a right to expel a member state. That said, one must bear in mind that NATO promotes nuclear deterrence and is irrefutably a nuclear alliance[66] which is willing to utilize nuclear weapons to defend its Member States.[67] Specifically, "NATO does not follow either

---

[63] Belgium, Germany, Italy, the Netherlands and Turkey. See Robert Norris and Hans Kristensen, "US Tactical Nuclear Weapons in Europe, 2011" (2011) 67:1 *Bulletin of the Atomic Scientists* 64 at 65.

[64] Section 17, NATO "Strategic Concept for the Defence and Security of the Members of the North Atlantic Treaty Organization" (November 19, 2010), online: *North Atlantic Treaty Organization* www.nato.int/cps/em/natohq/official_texts_68580.htm?selectedLocale=en.

[65] Ibid.

[66] Ibid.

[67] NATO, "NATO's Positions Regarding Nuclear Non-Proliferation, Arms Control and Disarmament and Related Issues" (October 22, 2009) at 4, online (pdf): *North Atlantic Treaty Organization* www.nato.int/nato_static/assets/pdf/pdf_topics/20091022_NATO_Position_on_nuclear_nonproliferation-eng.pdf.

182   *Deterrence Policies and the Prohibition Treaty*

a nuclear First-Use or No-First-Use policy. The Alliance does not determine in advance how it would react to aggression. It leaves this question open, to be decided as and when such a situation materialized."[68] Article 1(f) of the TPNW prohibits signatory states from seeking or receiving any assistance, "in any way, from anyone to engage in any activity prohibited to a State Party under this Treaty."[69] Threatening to use and using nuclear weapons is prohibited under Article 1(d) of the TPNW.[70] NATO and the five nuclear-weapon states all continue to utilize a "policy of deterrence"[71] for their nuclear-weapon defense strategy. A key component of a deterrence strategy is the "concept of a retaliatory threat"[72] which means NATO and the Big Five are acting contrary to TPNW Article 1(f). It could be argued that by being an Umbrella State any member of NATO is requesting a nuclear-weapon state to threaten the use of nuclear weapons also on its behalf. This is in direct contravention of TPNW Article 1(f). Furthermore, if the situation arose where a nuclear-armed state used nuclear weapons to protect an Umbrella State, the protected state would be in contravention of TPNW Article 1(f) for receiving assistance. Therefore, as long as NATO is a nuclear alliance, it would seem that any member that wants to accede to the TPNW must leave NATO. This is also true for Australia.

Implications for Any Umbrella State Signing the TPNW

If an Umbrella State becomes a signatory to the TPNW it would seem that it must also void its umbrella agreement. Again, although technically speaking they may not be in possession of nuclear weapons, per se, they are still relying on nuclear weapons for defense and deterrence purposes. In the case of Umbrella States linked to US-NATO protection, they are not members of NATO, and therefore have different legal and defense obligations to their respective allies. Consequently, they are positioned differently from NATO countries, whether or not they have nuclear weapons, conventional weapons or both stationed within their respective territories. Note as well that Armenia and Belarus are Umbrella States vis-à-vis the Russian Federation. The argument could be made that it may be possible for a state signing the TPNW to maintain its *umbrella* status by contributing conventional weapons and alternative forces without reliance on protection by nuclear weapons.

Umbrella States without nuclear weapons seemingly could not adopt the TPNW. Perhaps no nuclear weapons have been transferred to them and consequently they have not received the transfer of nuclear weapons, hence, no apparent breach of the NPT or Article I of the TPNW.[73] Again, it would seem unlikely that umbrella status

---

[68] Ibid.

[69] Article 1, Treaty on the Prohibition of Nuclear Weapons, A/CONF.229/2017/8.

[70] Ibid.

[71] *Legality of the Threat or Use of Nuclear Weapons*, Advisory Opinion, ICJ Reports 1996, p. 226, para. 67.

[72] Patrick Morgan, *Deterrence Now* (Cambridge: Cambridge University Press, 2003) at 13.

[73] Article 1, Treaty on the Prohibition of Nuclear Weapons, A/CONF.229/2017/8.

would fall within the spirit of the TPNW, despite their not actually stationing nuclear weapons on their soil in express contravention of TPNW. The respective umbrella commitment to NATO or the Russian Federation most likely precludes membership of the TPNW, again as with NATO states, where members expressly agree to the nuclear defense doctrines. Even if NATO did not position nuclear weapons within a state's territory and allowed that state to ratify the TPNW, the fact that NATO relies on nuclear weapons for defense and deterrence purposes would be contrary to the intention and integrity of the TPNW.

While it is unclear how NATO would react if one of its members were to accede to the TPNW, what does come clear is that the TPNW would prohibit it, because NATO[74] uses nuclear weapons to defend its Member States.[75] As discussed, Article 1 (f) of the TPNW prohibits signatory states from seeking or receiving "any assistance, in any way, from anyone to engage in any activity prohibited to a State Party under this Treaty"[76] and threatening to use and using nuclear weapons is prohibited under Article 1(d) of the TPNW.[77] Furthermore, if the situation arose where a nuclear-armed state used nuclear weapons to protect an Umbrella State or fellow NATO member, the protected state would be in contravention of TPNW Article 1(f) for receiving assistance.

Additionally, it would seem that nuclear umbrella arrangements wherein there are no weapons stationed on the soil may still be in contravention of Article 1(1)(e) which prohibits a state to "assist, encourage or induce prohibited activities."[78] It would seem that a state party could not remain in a nuclear umbrella arrangement as it would be seen to be encouraging or inducing such activities. Therefore, if an Umbrella State becomes a signatory it must void its umbrella agreement.

FORCING NUCLEAR DISARMAMENT IN NATO AND UMBRELLA STATES?

Shortly after NATO was formed, US nuclear weapons were stationed in Europe.[79] NATO's concern about the numerical superiority of the Warsaw Pact's conventional military forces prompted the United States to send droves of nuclear weapons to

---

[74] Section 17, NATO "Strategic Concept for the Defence and Security of the Members of the North Atlantic Treaty Organization" (November 19, 2010), online: *North Atlantic Treaty Organization* www .nato.int/cps/em/natohq/official_texts_68580.htm?selectedLocale=en.

[75] NATO, "NATO's Positions Regarding Nuclear Non-Proliferation, Arms Control and Disarmament and Related Issues" (October 22, 2009) at 4, online (pdf): *North Atlantic Treaty Organization* www .nato.int/nato_static/assets/pdf/pdf_topics/20091022_NATO_Position_on_nuclear_nonproliferation-eng.pdf.

[76] Article 1, Treaty on the Prohibition of Nuclear Weapons, A/CONF.229/2017/8.

[77] Ibid.

[78] Article 1(1)(e) "Assist, encourage or induce, in any way, anyone to engage in any activity prohibited to a State Party under this Treaty." See https://undocs.org/A/CONF.229/2017/8.

[79] Beatrice Heuser and Kristan Stoddart (2017) Difficult Europeans: NATO and Tactical/Non-strategic Nuclear Weapons in the Cold War, Diplomacy & Statecraft, 28:3, 454–476 at 457.

184 Deterrence Policies and the Prohibition Treaty

Europe. According to Heuser and Stoddart, "[b]y early 1961, approximately 3,900 American nuclear weapons were on European soil; by May 1965, the figure had grown to 5,950; by September 1966 around 7,000; and by 1968, where it peaked, 7,161."[80]

The 1987 INF Treaty[81] signed between the United States and the Soviet Union called for both countries to eliminate and permanently give up their nuclear and conventional ground-launched ballistic and cruise missiles with ranges of 500 to 5,500 kilometers (310 to 3,400 miles) as well as to partake in extensive on-site inspections for verification purposes. Not covered by the Treaty were air- or sea-launched weapons, including the American Tomahawk and Russian Kalibr cruise missiles that are launched from ships, submarines or airplanes, which could fly similar distances. Between the United States and the Soviet Union as many as 2,692 missiles were destroyed by the Treaty's implementation deadline of June 1, 1991.[82] By 1991, with the INF and after several nuclear disarmament agreements being implemented between the United States and the Soviet Union, there were approximately 2,000 American nuclear weapons stationed in Europe.[83] Since peaking in 1968, the number of nuclear weapons stationed in Europe by the United States has slowly diminished to the approximately 200 located in Europe today.[84] As the INF Treaty has now been terminated, it will be interesting to see whether such numbers will change.

As mentioned above, US nuclear weapons are based in five NATO countries: Belgium, Germany, Italy, the Netherlands and Turkey.[85] NATO and its Member States remain firm that the nuclear weapons based in Europe are under the "sole possession" and "complete custody and control" of the United States[86] thus, not violating NPT Articles I and II. Proponents of the TPNW would argue that the action of stationing of nuclear weapons sets a dangerous international precedent.

[80]   Ibid. at 455.
[81]   Treaty on the Elimination of Intermediate-Range and Shorter-Range Missiles. See www.state.gov/t/avc/trty/102360.htm
[82]   Note that in December 2018, US Secretary of State Michael Pompeo gave Russian President Vladimir Putin sixty days to return to full compliance of INF obligations or the US would also cease to honor its terms. On February 2, 2019, President Putin announced that Russia, too, would suspend the INF and start work on creating new weapons and delivery systems.
[83]   Andrew Futter (2011) "NATO, Ballistic Missile Defense and the Future of US Tactical Nuclear Weapons in Europe" European Security, 20:4, 547–562 at 550.
[84]   Tom Sauer and Bob van der Zwaan, "US Tactical Nuclear Weapons in Europe after NATO's Lisbon Summit: Why Their Withdrawal Is Desirable and Feasible" (2012) 26:1 International Relations 78–100 at 83.
[85]   Robert Norris and Hans Kristensen, "US tactical nuclear weapons in Europe, 2011" (2011) 67:1 Bulletin of the Atomic Scientists 64 at 65. See also Tom Sauer and Bob van der Zwaan, "US Tactical Nuclear Weapons in Europe after NATO's Lisbon Summit: Why Their Withdrawal Is Desirable and Feasible" (2012) 26:1 International Relations 78–100 at 83.
[86]   NATO, "NATO's Positions Regarding Nuclear Non-Proliferation, Arms Control and Disarmament and Related Issues" (October 22, 2009) at 3, online (pdf): North Atlantic Treaty Organization www.nato.int/nato_static/assets/pdf/pdf_topics/20091022_NATO_Position_on_nuclear_nonproliferation-eng.pdf.

NATO's practice of positioning nuclear weapons in host nations establishes that non-NATO nuclear-weapon states can also station such weapons in host nations, increasing the number of nations with nuclear weapons which expressly goes against the principles of nonproliferation.[87] Although the host countries may not technically own the weapons, per se, their presence serves to enlarge – proliferate – the number of states in which such devices are stationed amounting to what could be called de facto nuclear proliferation.

As discussed in Chapter 5, in order for a state to be bound by a prohibition against nuclear weapons under customary international law two main conditions must be fulfilled. The acts concerned must amount to a settled practice, as evidenced by both a belief that this practice is obligatory by the existence of a rule of law requiring it and their exercising the practice in question.[88] With this in mind, it is worth exploring the actual position and the actions of the five nuclear-weapon-harboring states regarding their respective State practice.

The Netherlands

As the Netherlands was the only NATO state that participated in the Treaty negotiations and was also the only state that voted against its adoption, it can clearly be seen as persistently objecting to the prohibitions established by the TPNW. Thus, the doctrine of persistent objector appears to apply to the Netherlands as its objection occurred during the formation of the Treaty and before any norm has been established and especially prior to the crystallization of any form of customary practice or behavior in question. Therefore, any status of emerging norms under the Treaty requiring nations harboring nuclear weapons to remove them from their jurisdiction would not apply to the Netherlands.[89]

Germany

Over the past seven decades, Germany appears to have become more and more reluctant to host nuclear weapons within its sovereign territory, yet it has been a host nation since the 1950s. Several statements and actions taken by Germany's leaders provide evidence of an ambiguous relationship between the state's official position

---

[87] Mohamed ElBaradei, "Five Steps Towards Abolishing Nuclear Weapons," *Süddeutsche Zeitung*, February 4, 2009 as cited in Tom Sauer and Bob van der Zwaan, "US Tactical Nuclear Weapons in Europe after NATO's Lisbon Summit: Why Their Withdrawal Is Desirable and Feasible" (2012) 26:1 *International Relations* 78–100 at 85.

[88] See *Continental Shelf (Libyan Arab Jamahiriya/Malta)*, Judgment, ICJ Reports 1985, p. 13. The material of customary international law, as noted by the ICJ in the *Continental Shelf (Libya/Malta)* case, is to be sought for "primarily in the actual practice and opinio juris of States" [para. 27]. www.icj-cij.org/files/case-related/68/068–19840321-JUD-01-00-EN.pdf.

[89] For further discussion on European attitudes on nuclear disarmament see www.ecfr.eu/specials/scorecard/eyes_tight_shut_european_attitudes_towards_nuclear_deterrence

186 *Deterrence Policies and the Prohibition Treaty*

and the hosting of nuclear weapons on its soil. When nuclear weapons were first deployed to Europe, some authors argue that Chancellor Konrad Adenauer of West Germany, as it then was, was not fully in favor of hosting nuclear weapons with the range to reach the Soviet Union, as it then was.[90] Note that this is disputable. No treaty was concluded, not even formal minutes taken on the "deal" between John Foster Dulles and Konrad Adenauer in 1956. There is no evidence as to whether the reach of weapons to be stationed was an issue at this time.

Later, long-range nuclear weapons were deployed in Germany by the United States from 1962 to 1969. During the height of the Cold War, from 1965 to the mid-1980s, West German strategists "feared that having only American-based strategic nuclear or battlefield nuclear weapons for use against Warsaw Pact forces that had already penetrated NATO territory – and thus on NATO territory, that is in West Germany, but also Norway, Turkey and Greece – signalled the existence of a 'firebreak' between the United States and especially German soil."[91] Thus, German strategists argued for a full spectrum of ranged nuclear weapons. This argument was adopted by West German Chancellor Helmut Schmidt in his 1977 lecture to the London security community. He argued for the nuclear arsenal stationed in Western Germany to be updated in order for there to be a balance of forces.[92] The public saw through this argument, as there was equality of forces if the French and British were included in the count.[93] Regardless, the nuclear arsenal in Germany was updated, shorter-range nuclear weapons were eliminated altogether, and the remaining nuclear arsenal was slowly reduced over the next fifteen years as the United States and the Soviet Union initiated several disarmament agreements.[94]

---

[90] Thomas Risse-Kappen, "Déjà vu: Deployment of Nuclear Weapons in West Germany – Historical Controversies," *Bulletin of Peace Proposals*, 14/4 (1983), 327–336 as cited in Beatrice Heuser and Kristan Stoddart (2017) "Difficult Europeans: NATO and Tactical/Non-strategic Nuclear Weapons in the Cold War," *Diplomacy & Statecraft*, 28:3, 454–476 at 457.

[91] Ibid. at 458.

[92] Helmut Schmidt, "The 1977 Alastair Buchan Memorial Lecture," Survival, 20/1 (1978), 4–5 as cited in Beatrice Heuser and Kristan Stoddart (2017) "Difficult Europeans: NATO and Tactical/Non-strategic Nuclear Weapons in the Cold War," *Diplomacy & Statecraft*, 28:3, 454–476 at 458. On the speech, see Kristina Spohr-Readman, "Conflict and Co-operation in intra-Alliance Nuclear Politics: Western Europe, America and the Genesis of NATO's Dual-Track Decision, 1977–1979," *Journal of Cold War Studies*, 13/2 (2011), 40–41.

[93] K.-Peter Stratmann, "Das 'eurostrategische' Kräfteverhältnis. Zweifelhafte Bewertungen als Folge der Anwendung unterschiedlicher Kriterien," *Europa Archiv*, 36/13 (1981), 387–398 describes the difficulties created by this approach. Cf. Lt. Gen. Hans Hinrichs, "Warum Nachrüstung statt Umrüstung?," *Europäische Wehrkunde*, 31/12 (1982), 48; Gerhard Wettig, "Das Problem des militärischen Gleichgewichts," *Aussenpolitik*, 33/4 (1982), 337–345. For examples of this argument being used, see Chapter 4B; Hoimar von Ditfurth, "Real ist nur die eigene Angst," *Der Spiegel* (June 6, 1983), 52 ff. as cited in Beatrice Heuser and Kristan Stoddart (2017) "Difficult Europeans: NATO and Tactical/Non-strategic Nuclear Weapons in the Cold War," *Diplomacy & Statecraft*, 28:3, 454–476 at 458.

[94] Andrew Futter (2011) "NATO, Ballistic Missile Defense and the Future of US Tactical Nuclear Weapons in Europe," *European Security*, 20:4, 547–562 at 549. See also Oliver Meier, "News Analysis: An End to US Tactical Nuclear Weapons in Europe?" (2006) *Arms Control Today*, Vol. 36, No. 6 (July/August 2006), 37–40 at 37.

After the collapse of the Soviet Union and the end of the Cold War, nuclear weapons remained in the Western part of Germany. "US and European officials readily acknowledge that they have held on to the weapons for predominantly political rather than military reasons."[95] In 1999, NATO acknowledged that relations with Russia had improved such that nuclear weapons were no longer necessary in Europe but still decided nuclear weapons should remain there to maintain the political solidarity of the Alliance.[96] Andrew Flutter observes that "In May 2005, a resolution was introduced into the German Bundestag (parliament) [by the German Free Democrats' opposition party] calling on the German government to work 'towards the withdrawal of US tactical nuclear weapons on German soil.'"[97] Without the backing of the majority government, the Christian Democrats, this resolution had little effect. In 2006, many were hopeful that the replacement of Germany's nuclear-capable aircraft, the Tornado, with the Eurofighter would result in the removal of nuclear weapons from Germany as the Eurofighter was not certified to carry nuclear weapons. The end of life expectancy for the Tornados was 2015 but the Eurofighter had already come into production. But the Christian Democrats, decided to delay rather than solve the issue by keeping the Tornados past their life expectancy, possibly up to the year 2020. All three opposition parties in the German parliament were opposed to this and "introduced resolutions calling for a complete end to Germany's involvement in nuclear sharing and a withdrawal of US tactical nuclear weapons from German territory."[98] The Christian Democrats rejected the idea of basing a decision on Germany's future involvement in nuclear sharing on the phasing out of the Tornado. "Instead, it should be a political judgment whether nuclear sharing is still up to date or not."[99] Public opinion polls conducted in 2006 revealed antinuclear sentiment was prevalent in Germany, at 70.5 percent. These polls also revealed that approximately 60 percent of the population of Germany did not know nuclear weapons were deployed in their country.[100]

In 2007, scientists realized that the United States had removed approximately 130 nuclear weapons from Ramstein air force base in Germany, some time within the preceding two years. This left approximately twenty nuclear weapons still in Germany.[101] Reactions from German politicians differed. "Karl-Theodor zu

---

[95] Oliver Meier, "News Analysis: An End to US Tactical Nuclear Weapons in Europe?" (2006) *Arms Control Today*, Vol. 36, No. 6 (July/August 2006), 37–40 at 37.

[96] Ibid.

[97] Andrew Futter (2011) "NATO, Ballistic Missile Defense and the Future of US Tactical Nuclear Weapons in Europe" *European Security*, 20:4, 547–562 at 551. See also Oliver Meier, "Belgium, Germany Question US Tactical Nuclear Weapons in Europe" (June 1 2005), online: *Arms Control Today*: www.armscontrol.org/print/1818.

[98] Oliver Meier, "News Analysis: An End to US Tactical Nuclear Weapons in Europe?" (2006) *Arms Control Today*, Vol. 36, No. 6 (July/August 2006), 37–40 at 38.

[99] Ibid.

[100] Ibid, at 40.

[101] Ibid. at 32.

188   *Deterrence Policies and the Prohibition Treaty*

Guttenberg, arms control spokesperson for the Christian Democrats, [said] a partial withdrawal of US nuclear weapons would not contribute necessarily 'to departure of others, such as Iran, from their nuclear ambitions.'"[102] "Uta Zapf, Social Democrat and chair of the Bundestag's subcommittee on disarmament, arms control and non-proliferation, [said] the withdrawal of nuclear weapons from Ramstein is good news but 'by itself does not signify a change in policy' because US nuclear weapons remain deployed at Büchel and in five other European countries."[103] Opposition parties continued to call for the removal of nuclear weapons in Germany.

Flutter recounts that "In April 2009, the new German coalition government [made] the 'withdrawal of remaining nuclear weapons from Germany, both within NATO and vis-à-vis our American allies . . .' a key part of their policy program. This represented the first time that a NATO member government had 'publicly promoted the removal of US nuclear weapons from its territory.'"[104] Implementing this policy proved difficult for Germany. Sauer and van der Swaan describe what happened thus:

> In February 2010 a joint letter was sent by Belgium, Germany, Luxemburg, the Netherlands and Norway . . . to NATO's Secretary-General Anders Rasmussen, asking him to put the issue on the agenda of the informal NATO meeting of Ministers of Foreign Affairs in Tallinn in April 2010. But at a press conference in Tallinn on 22 April, Rasmussen suggested that US tactical nuclear weapons should remain in Europe: "My personal opinion is that the stationing of US nuclear weapons in Europe is part of deterrence to be taken seriously."[105]

This setback was followed by another in 2012 when it was time for Germany to make a final decision whether to retire the Tornado aircraft in 2015 or extend their service to 2020.[106] The government, following the decision of their counterparts in 2006, decided to delay rather than to resolve the issue by keeping the Tornados past their life expectancy, up to the year 2020. When the TPNW was introduced to the United Nations, Germany and all other NATO states, except the Netherlands, chose not to participate in the negotiations.

---

[102] Ibid. at 33.

[103] Ibid.

[104] Andrew Futter (2011) "NATO, ballistic missile defense and the future of US Tactical Nuclear Weapons in Europe" *European Security*, 20:4, 547–562 at 551. See also Oliver Meier, "German Nuclear Stance Stirs Debate" (December 2009), online: *Arms Control Today* www.armscontrol.org /act/2009_12/GermanNuclearStance.

[105] Tom Sauer and Bob van der Zwaan, "US Tactical Nuclear Weapons in Europe after NATO's Lisbon Summit: Why Their Withdrawal Is Desirable and Feasible" (2012) *International Relations*, Vol. 26(1) 78–100 at 82. See also "US Urged to Remove Tactical Nukes in Europe," *NTI Global Security Newswire*, April 22, 2010.

[106] Andrew Futter (2011) "NATO, Ballistic Missile Defense and the Future of US Tactical Nuclear Weapons in Europe," *European Security*, 20:4, 547–562 at 555. See also Oliver Meier, "German Nuclear Stance Stirs Debate" (December 2009), online: *Arms Control Today* www.armscontrol.org /act/2009_12/GermanNuclearStance.

There is no doubt that Germany would not be bound by the TPNW but when considering its past positions and the potential influence of public opinion, repeated parliamentary actions, policy implementation and interactions with NATO there is an ever-looming position that nuclear weapons should be removed from Germany. That said, the decisions of the German government to continue delaying the date when Germany's aircraft can no longer carry nuclear weapons and its decision to not participate in the TPNW negotiations indicates that at least for the moment there is a political gain to be had by not challenging the status quo. Germany's nuclear power phase-out "Atomausstieg" started in 2000. In 2011 – after Fukushima – implementation was accelerated to be achieved by 2022. Whether advocates of humanitarian disarmament can mobilize such idealism to the opposition to nuclear weapons and challenges to security considerations and concerns related to the humanitarian impact of nuclear armament remains to be seen. But even if this may be case, such decision would rather be based on policy considerations and could hardly be said to reflect *opinio juris*.

Belgium

Since the end of the Cold War, Belgium's hosting of nuclear weapons has been somewhat controversial. Nevertheless, the Belgian government has not decided to have them removed. Oliver Meier writes that "In April 2005, the Belgian Senate unanimously passed a resolution calling on the Belgian government to take an initiative in NATO to review its nuclear doctrine and to initiate the gradual withdrawal of US tactical nuclear from Belgium territory."[107] In 2010, Belgium was party to the joint letter[108] addressed to NATO's Secretary-General regarding the removal of nuclear weapons as an agenda of its meeting in Tallinn in April 2010.[109] "A national protest meeting was organized on October 20, 2013, and the government agreed on a resolution asking for withdrawal in April 2015."[110] This progress was hindered by the Belgian government, which – like Germany – decided to delay rather than resolve the issue by keeping their nuclear capable F-16 aircraft past their life expectancy, up to the year 2020.[111]

---

[107] Oliver Meier, "News Analysis: An End to US Tactical Nuclear Weapons in Europe?" (2006) *Arms Control Today*, Vol. 36, No. 6 (July/August 2006), 37–40 at 39.

[108] Along with Germany, Luxemburg, the Netherlands and Norway.

[109] Tom Sauer and Bob van der Zwaan, "US Tactical Nuclear Weapons in Europe after NATO's Lisbon Summit: Why Their Withdrawal Is Desirable and Feasible" (2012) *International Relations*, Vol. 26(1) 78–100 at 82. See also "US Urged to Remove Tactical Nukes in Europe," *NTI Global Security Newswire*, April 22, 2010.

[110] Mustafa Kibaroglu and Tom Sauer, "Mr. Trump, Post Nuclear Ban Treaty, NATO's Nuclear Weapons in Europe Are Obsolete" (2017) *Insight Turkey* Vol. 19, No. 3, 23–33 at 32.

[111] Oliver Meier, "News Analysis: An End to US Tactical Nuclear Weapons in Europe?" (2006) *Arms Control Today*, Vol. 36, No. 6 (July/August 2006), 37–40 at 39. See also Andrew Futter (2011) "NATO, Ballistic Missile Defense and the Future of US Tactical Nuclear Weapons in Europe," *European Security*, 20:4, 547–562 at 555.

190   *Deterrence Policies and the Prohibition Treaty*

The security of nuclear weapons hosted in Belgium has repeatedly been undermined, providing an excellent reason for the Belgian government to request their removal but it has not done so. For example, in 2001, "Nisar Trabelsi – born in Tunisia, raised in Belgium, and radicalized by his al-Qaeda brothers in the Afghanistan-Pakistan region – reportedly had concrete plans to blow up the Kleine Brogel air base where the US tactical nuclear weapons in Belgium are stored. Luckily, this terrorist plot was thwarted and Trabelsi was taken into custody."[112] "In January 2010 peace activists climbed over the fence of the Kleine Brogel Air Base, walked around for more than an hour without meeting any hindrance, reached the nuclear-weapons storage bunkers, videotaped them, exited through the entrance to the base and succeeded in smuggling out the videotape and posting it on the internet."[113] A similar intrusion had occurred in November 2009. A Belgian defense official insisted that the activists "never, ever got anywhere near a sensitive area," and that it would be "another cup of tea" if they approached "sensitive areas."[114] "Later on, Belgium experienced nuclear terrorism incidents similar to that envisioned by Trabelsi, including sabotage at the Doel 4 nuclear reactor on August 4, 2014, and a surveillance incident in November 2015 that may have led to the kidnapping of a high-level nuclear expert by those who are responsible for the Paris and Brussels terrorist attacks."[115]

While some Belgians feel that in spite of the various security instances nuclear weapons should not be hosted in their country, at present the Belgian government has decided not to remove the nuclear weapons, delaying the date when Belgium's aircraft can no longer carry nuclear weapons. The government's further decision not to participate in the TPNW negotiations demonstrated a continuance of the existing state of affairs regarding their nuclear defense policy. Only time will tell whether political momentum will grow under the TPNW movement.

Turkey

Turkey shows few signs of wanting nuclear weapons removed from its sovereign territory. A 2006 survey on the question of nuclear weapons deployments revealed

---

[112] Mustafa Kibaroglu and Tom Sauer, "Mr. Trump, Post Nuclear Ban Treaty, NATO's Nuclear Weapons in Europe Are Obsolete" (2017) *Insight Turkey* Vol. 19, No. 3, 23–33 at 27. See also Tom Sauer and Bob van der Zwaan, "US Tactical Nuclear Weapons in Europe after NATO's Lisbon Summit: Why Their Withdrawal Is Desirable and Feasible" (2012) *International Relations*, Vol. 26(1) 78–100 at 87.

[113] Tom Sauer and Bob van der Zwaan, "US Tactical Nuclear Weapons in Europe after NATO's Lisbon Summit: Why Their Withdrawal Is Desirable and Feasible" (2012) *International Relations*, Vol. 26(1) 78–100 at 87. See also Robert Norris and Hans Kristensen, "US Tactical Nuclear Weapons in Europe, 2011" (2011) 67:1 *Bulletin of the Atomic Scientists* 64 at 68.

[114] Robert Norris and Hans Kristensen, "US Tactical Nuclear Weapons in Europe, 2011" (2011) 67:1 *Bulletin of the Atomic Scientists* 64 at 68.

[115] Mustafa Kibaroglu and Tom Sauer, "Mr. Trump, Post Nuclear Ban Treaty, NATO's Nuclear Weapons in Europe are Obsolete" (2017) *Insight Turkey* Vol. 19, No. 3, 23–33 at 27–28. See also Simon Lunn, Isabelle Williams and Steve Andreasen, "NATO's Nuclear Future: Deter, Reassure, Engage?" (2016) Nuclear Threat Initiative, online: www.nti.org/media/documents/NATOs_Nuclear_Future_FINAL.pdf.

that almost two-thirds of the populations in all nuclear weapons host nations except Turkey want Europe to be free of nuclear weapons.[116] Unlike Germany, the Netherlands and Belgium, Turkey has embraced upgrading its nuclear-capable aircraft. Starting in 2015, Turkey has been replacing its F-16s with Joint Strike Fighters (JSFs). It was intended that by 2025, Turkey would have 100 JSFs, capable of carrying nuclear weapons.[117] It remains to be seen whether this will proceed under President Trump. All of the nuclear weapons, approximately sixty to seventy,[118] stationed in Turkey are at the Incirlik base close to the Syrian border.[119] "In March 2016, the Pentagon reportedly ordered military families out of southern Turkey, primarily from Incirlik Air Base, due to ISIS-related security concerns."[120] Then in July 2016, "the Turkish military commander of the base, was involved in the coup attempt, and reportedly refused to allow a US combat aircraft to land during the episode. At the same time, he allowed Turkish military aircraft to play an active role during the attempted coup."[121] The Turkish commanding officer at Incirlik was then arrested for his alleged role in the Turkish coup plot.[122] Following this incident, Turkey did not request the removal of nuclear weapons from its territory or participate in the negotiations of the TPNW. Accordingly, there appears to be no traction against the hosting of nuclear weapons in Turkey, making it difficult to see a change of circumstances in the near future regarding this position.

Italy

Italy hosts approximately seventy nuclear weapons[123] and its Tornado aircraft are scheduled to be fully replaced by 2025. Public opinion polls conducted in 2006 revealed antinuclear sentiment was prevalent in Italy, at 71.5 percent. In 2006, however, Italy committed to upgrading its Tornados to JSFs, ignoring the calls of members within the coalition party to "cancel Italian participation in the JSF [and

---

[116] Oliver Meier, "News Analysis: An End to US Tactical Nuclear Weapons in Europe?" (2006) *Arms Control Today*, Vol. 36, No. 6 (July/August 2006), 37–40 at 40.

[117] Robert Norris and Hans Kristensen, "US Tactical Nuclear Weapons in Europe, 2011" (2011) 67:1 *Bulletin of the Atomic Scientists* 64 at 70.

[118] Tom Sauer and Bob van der Zwaan, "US Tactical Nuclear Weapons in Europe after NATO's Lisbon Summit: Why Their Withdrawal Is Desirable and Feasible" (2012) *International Relations*, Vol. 26(1) 78–100 at 83.

[119] Mustafa Kibaroglu and Tom Sauer, "Mr. Trump, Post Nuclear Ban Treaty, NATO's Nuclear Weapons in Europe Are Obsolete" (2017) *Insight Turkey* Vol. 19, No. 3, 23–33 at 28.

[120] Steve, "Rethinking NATO's Tactical Nuclear Weapons" (2017) *Survival: Global Politics and Strategy*, 59:5, 47–53 at 49.

[121] Mustafa Kibaroğlu and Tom Sauer, "Mr. Trump, Post Nuclear Ban Treaty, NATO's Nuclear Weapons in Europe Are Obsolete" (2017) *Insight Turkey* Vol. 19, No. 3, 23–33 at 28.

[122] Steve Andreasen, "Rethinking NATO's Tactical Nuclear Weapons" (2017) *Survival: Global Politics and Strategy*, 59:5, 47–53 at 50.

[123] Tom Sauer and Bob van der Zwaan, "US Tactical Nuclear Weapons in Europe after NATO's Lisbon Summit: Why Their Withdrawal Is Desirable and Feasible" (2012) *International Relations*, Vol. 26(1) 78–100 at 83.

192   *Deterrence Policies and the Prohibition Treaty*

instead] initiate discussions on nuclear sharing 'with a view to free our country from nuclear weapons.'"[124] By 2025, Italy will have 131 JSFs capable of carrying nuclear weapons.[125] Italy has not requested the removal of nuclear weapons from its territory or participated in the negotiations of the TPNW, instead it is upgrading its nuclear capable aircraft. As a result, it is difficult to argue any change is on the horizon regarding Italy's nuclear defense doctrine or its intention to be bound by the TPNW.

Australia

Australia is an umbrella state and cooperates with NATO. For example, it is one of the top non-NATO contributors of troops to NATO-led efforts in Afghanistan. In this regard, NATO and Australia are strengthening relations to address shared security challenges.[126] They have been engaged in dialogue and cooperation for many decades, expanding a security reach beyond the Euro-Atlantic area in an arrangement commonly referred to as "partners across the globe."[127] Together, in a joint political declaration in June 2012, they signaled their commitment to strengthening cooperation and since February 2013, their work continues to advance the Individual Partnership and Cooperative Programme.[128] They aim to work together more closely on crisis and conflict management as well as to protect the rules-based international order, promote mutual understanding of global security issues, and enhance interoperability between NATO and Australia.[129] In addition, along with the United States and New Zealand, they are party to ANZUS, the Australia, New Zealand, United States of America Security Treaty.[130] Australia is a member of the Rarotonga Treaty.[131]

Australia did not participate in the TPNW negotiations. The Government of Australia officially opposed the TPNW being one of some thirty-five nations to vote against the UN General Assembly Resolution 71/258 of December 23, 2016[132] to negotiate the TPNW, later publicly announcing its intention to boycott treaty

---

[124] Oliver Meier, "News Analysis: An End to US Tactical Nuclear Weapons in Europe?" (2006) *Arms Control Today*, Vol. 36, No. 6 (July/August 2006), 37–40 at 38.
[125] Robert Norris and Hans Kristensen, "US Tactical Nuclear Weapons in Europe, 2011" (2011) 67:1 *Bulletin of the Atomic Scientists* 64 at 69.
[126] See www.nato.int/cps/en/natohq/topics_48899.htm.
[127] Ibid.
[128] Ibid.
[129] Ibid.
[130] Security Treaty between Australia, New Zealand and the United States of America (ANZUS Treaty), adopted September 1, 1951, entered into force April 29, 1952.
[131] South Pacific Nuclear Free Zone Treaty (Treaty of Rarotonga) and Protocols thereto (August 6, 1985), 1676 *UNTS* 326.
[132] "Taking forward Multilateral Nuclear Disarmament Negotiations," UN General Assembly Resolution 71/258, A/RES/71/258, December 23, 2016. See http://undocs.org/A/RES/71/258.

negotiations citing its long-standing position that the TPNW would not offer a practical path to effective disarmament or enhanced security.[133]

As emphatic as this position would seem, there is a strong support, particularly within the Labor Party, to sign the TPNW. An article published by the International Human Rights Clinic in the Human Rights Program at Harvard Law School reports that an Ipsos public opinion poll released in November 2018, found some 78.9 percent of the public supported Australia joining the TPNW, with 82.7 percent of Labor voters saying they would support a future Labor government joining the TPNW.[134] Indeed, the Labor Party, had incorporated its support for the negotiations for a global treaty prohibiting nuclear weapons into its 2015 National Platform.[135] Moreover, the local councils of both Melbourne and Sydney have endorsed the International Campaign to Abolish Nuclear Weapons (ICAN) Cities Appeal, declaring that they "firmly believe that [their] residents have the right to live in a world free from this threat," and calling on the Australian government to join the TPNW.[136]

While popular public opinion hardly dictates government security policy, it does reflect an important part of political decision making, particularly in a participatory democracy such as in Australia. At present, Australia does not have US nuclear weapons on its territory, but rather in its territorial waters from time to time. Even if it decided to accede to the TPNW, it would have to address compliance issues under Article 1(1)(e).

Japan

Japan has a security treaty with the United States aimed at mutual cooperation and security between the two countries and their concern for international peace and security in the Far East.[137] In addition, NATO and Japan are currently strengthening relations to address shared security challenges.[138] Since the early 1990s, they have been engaged in dialogue and cooperation. Japan is one of a range of countries participating beyond the Euro-Atlantic area, in a relationship that is referred to as "partners across the globe." In a joint political declaration signed in April 2013 they

[133] Ben Doherty, "Australia to Boycott Global Summit on Treaty to Ban Nuclear Weapons," *Guardian*, February 16, 2017, www.theguardian.com/world/2017/feb/17/australia-to-boycott-global-summit-on-treaty-to-bannuclear-weapons.

[134] See Australia and the Treaty on the Prohibition of Nuclear Weapons December 2018. International Human Rights Clinic, Human Rights Program, Harvard Law School at p. 2. See http://hrp .law.harvard.edu/wp-content/uploads/2018/12/Australia-TPNW-12-12-18-FINAL.pdf.

[135] Ibid.

[136] See Australia and the Treaty on the Prohibition of Nuclear Weapons December 2018. International Human Rights Clinic, Human Rights Program, Harvard Law School at p. 2. See http://hrp .law.harvard.edu/wp-content/uploads/2018/12/Australia-TPNW-12-12-18-FINAL.pdf.

[137] Treaty of Mutual Cooperation and Security between Japan and the United States of America, January 19, 1960. This follows an earlier treaty of 1951. See www.mofa.go.jp/region/n-america/us/ q&a/ref/1.html.

[138] See www.nato.int/cps/en/natohq/topics_50336.htm.

signaled their commitment to strengthening cooperation, and since 2014 they have been involved in the Individual Partnership and Cooperation Programme, as well as engaging in practical cooperation in areas such as cyber defense, maritime security, nonproliferation, defense science and technology, and women, peace and security.[139]

Japan holds a unique position in that it is the only country in the world in which atomic weapons were detonated as a strategic tactic to achieve military capitulation. The bombings of Hiroshima and Nagasaki in 1945 left the country to face the horror of war first-hand and to live with the devastating aftermath. Ironically, Japan has embraced nuclear technology and is again facing the disturbing consequences of nuclear fall-out having experienced the tragic melt down of Fukushima Daiichi.[140] No country has faced similar nuclear hardship in the way Japan has. Consequently, it would be safe to conclude that the Japanese have a complicated relationship with nuclear matters.

Commemorating the seventy-third anniversary of the US bombing, the Mayor of Hiroshima announced its Peace Declaration, pledging to do everything in its power to achieve lasting world peace and the abolition of nuclear weapons.[141] In so doing he called on,

> the Japanese government to manifest the magnificent pacifism of the Japanese Constitution in the movement toward the entry into force of the Treaty on the Prohibition of Nuclear Weapons by playing its proper role, leading the international community toward dialogue and cooperation for a world without nuclear weapons. In addition, I hereby demand an expansion of the black rain areas along with greater concern and improved assistance for the many people suffering the mental and physical effects of radiation, especially the *hibakusha*, whose average age is now over 82.[142]

The Declaration contends that:

> Nuclear deterrence and nuclear umbrellas flaunt the destructive power of nuclear weapons and seek to maintain international order by generating fear in rival countries. This approach to guaranteeing long-term security is inherently unstable and extremely dangerous. [accordingly] World leaders must have this reality etched in their hearts as they negotiate in good faith the elimination of nuclear arsenals, which is a legal obligation under the Nuclear Non-Proliferation Treaty. Furthermore, they

---

[139] See www.nato.int/cps/en/natohq/topics_50336.htm.

[140] On March 11, 2011, following a major earthquake, a fifteen-meter tsunami disabled the power supply and cooling of three Fukushima Daiichi reactors, causing a nuclear accident. See Fukushima Daiichi Accident. See www.world-nuclear.org/information-library/safety-and-security/safety-of-plants/fukushima-accident.aspx.

[141] City of Hiroshima Peace Declaration, announced by MATSUI Kazumi, the Mayor of the City of Hiroshima. See www.city.hiroshima.lg.jp/www/contents/1343890585401/index.html.

[142] Ibid.

Forcing Nuclear Disarmament? 195

must strive to make the Treaty on the Prohibition of Nuclear Weapons a milestone along the path to a nuclear-weapon-free world.[143]

In contrast, Prime Minister Shinzo Abe also marked the seventy-third anniversary of the bombings of Hiroshima and Nagasaki, reiterating the government's firm opposition to joining the TPNW.[144] Japan has security concerns in the region and relies on the nuclear umbrella of the United States and NATO. The official Japanese position is that Japan remains committed to the NPT process and according to the Diplomatic Bluebook 2017,

> Japan has been engaged in various diplomatic efforts to achieve a world free of nuclear weapons. The Treaty on the Non-proliferation of Nuclear Weapons (NPT) is the cornerstone of the international nuclear disarmament and non-proliferation regime. Under a principle of coming up with realistic and practical proposals to maintain and strengthen the NPT regime, Japan has been making concrete contributions through frameworks such as the G7 and the Non-proliferation and Disarmament Initiative (NPDI), a group consisting of 12 non-nuclear-weapon States.[145]

On the one hand the Japanese people understand the devastating force of such weapons and technology; on the other hand, the government feels they should embrace weapons in order to protect them from possible threats in the region. That said, while the government maintains its stance against the TPNW with Shinzo Abe insisting that "the treaty is unrealistic,"[146] at the same time the civil society seems to be resisting his position.

Republic of Korea – South Korea

In October 1953 the United States signed a Mutual Defense Treaty with the Republic of Korea, "desiring to . . . defend themselves against external armed attack so that no potential aggressor could be under the illusion that either of them stands alone in the Pacific area."[147] The United States deployed nuclear weapons on the Korean Peninsula between 1958 and 1991, removing them as a part of a post-Cold

---

[143] Ibid.
[144] Japan Holds Firm Against Nuclear Ban Treaty on Anniversary of Nuclear Bombings – Shinzo Abe insists that the treaty is unrealistic, but civil society is pushing back. Andrew Hurst *The Diplomat* August 18, 2018. See https://thediplomat.com/2018/08/japan-holds-firm-against-nuclear-ban-treaty-on-anniversary-of-nuclear-bombings/.
[145] Diplomatic Bluebook 2017, Chapter 3, Japan's Foreign Policy to Promote National and Worldwide Interests, Disarmament, Non-proliferation and the Peaceful Uses of Nuclear Energy.
[146] Japan Holds Firm Against Nuclear Ban Treaty on Anniversary of Nuclear Bombings – Shinzo Abe insists that the treaty is unrealistic, but civil society is pushing back. Andrew Hurst, *The Diplomat* August 18, 2018. See https://thediplomat.com/2018/08/japan-holds-firm-against-nuclear-ban-treaty-on-anniversary-of-nuclear-bombings/.
[147] Mutual Defense Treaty Between the United States and the Republic of Korea; October 1, 1953. See http://avalon.law.yale.edu/20th_century/kor001.asp.

War change in its nuclear position.[148] "The only warheads remaining in the US stockpile that could be deployed on the Korean Peninsula are B61 bombs."[149] Under the 1953 Mutual Defense Treaty, the United States remains committed to defending South Korea and to employing nuclear weapons, if necessary, in that defense.[150]

Along with US support, NATO and the Republic of Korea are currently strengthening relations to address shared security challenges in the Korean Peninsula, having been engaged in dialogue and cooperation since 2005.[151] South Korea is one of the range of countries beyond the Euro-Atlantic area under the "partners across the globe."[152] Since 2012, work has been done through the Individual Partnership and Cooperation Programme, which was renewed in November 2017.[153] The Individual Partnership and Cooperation Programme lays out objectives between different parties, providing a communication framework for dialogue and cooperation between them.

Needless, to say South Korea's fate and future is highly influenced by its blood relative and northern neighbor, the Democratic People's Republic of North Korea (DPRK). North Korea withdrew from the NPT on March 12, 1993,[154] and has since embarked on a nuclear weapons program developing nuclear weapons and missile technology and boasting of its successes. Most worrying for South Korea as well as for Japan and other countries far beyond the Korean Peninsula is the DPRK's threatening tone regarding its deployment tactics. Despite various announcements regarding the "complete denuclearization of the Korean Peninsula,"[155] South Korea feels it

---

[148]   Congressional Research Service Report. Redeploying US Nuclear Weapons to South Korea: Background and Implications in Brief. Amy F. Woolf and Emma Chanlett-Avery. September 14, 2017. See https://fas .org/sgp/crs/nuke/R44950.pdf.

[149]   See Redeploying US Nuclear Weapons to South Korea: Background and Implications in Brief. Amy F. Woolf and Emma Chanlett-Avery. September 14, 2017. See https://fas.org/sgp/crs/nuke/R44950 .pdf.

[150]   See Redeploying US Nuclear Weapons to South Korea: Background and Implications in Brief. Amy F. Woolf and Emma Chanlett-Avery. September 14, 2017. See https://fas.org/sgp/crs/nuke/R44950 .pdf.

[151]   See www.nato.int/cps/en/natohq/topics_50098.htm.

[152]   Ibid.

[153]   Ibid.

[154]   Whilst the withdrawal was suspended on June 11, 1993, on January 10, 2003 the DPRK declared an "immediate effectuation of its withdrawal from the NPT," see www.atomicarchive.com/Docs/ Deterrence/DPRKNPTstatement.shtml. The Security Council has requested the Democratic People's Republic of Korea to retract its withdrawal and abandon all nuclear weapons and existing nuclear programs in a complete, verifiable and irreversible manner, see SC Res 1695 (2006), 1718 (2006), 1874 (2009), 2050 (2012), 2087 (2013), 2094 (2013), 2270 (2016), 2276 (2016), 2321 (2016), 2345 (2017), 2356 (2017), 2371 (2017), 2375 (2017), 2397 (2017) and 2407 (2018). Additional sanctions have been enacted at national level, see the US North Korea Sanctions and Policy Enhancement Act of 2016, PL 114–122, H.R.757, 130 Stat. 93. See also Black-Branch for a technical discussion regarding the official notice lifting the suspension on January 10 where there was no clear statement provided for reinstating the withdrawal notice. Nuclear Terrorism by States and Non-State Actors: Global Responses to Threats to Military and Human Security in International Law. *Journal of Conflict & Security Law (2017)* at p. 7. Oxford University Press.

[155]   Joint Statement of President Donald J. Trump of the United States of America and Chairman Kim Jong Un of the Democratic People's Republic of Korea at the Singapore Summit, www

Forcing Nuclear Disarmament? 197

can take no chances and must be in a state of preparedness for nuclear threats as well as potential attacks. Consequently, it firmly favors a nuclear deterrence option. In an article published in the *Washington Post* in September 2017 it was reported that: "Still, 60 percent of South Koreans in theory support nuclear weapons for their country, according to Gallup Korea. A poll by YTN, a cable news channel, in August [2017] found that 68 percent of respondents supported redeploying tactical nuclear weapons to South Korea."[156] Despite efforts on the part of President Trump to open talks on the denuclearization of the Korean Peninsula, the current nuclear position of North Korea[157] continues to render South Korea vulnerable from a military perspective making the TPNW seem far from a viable option at this point in time. The diplomatic challenges are formidable. The political challenges would be problematic in convincing South Koreans to give up nuclear deterrence and accede to the TPNW.

Switzerland

Switzerland assumes a position of permanent neutrality.[158] "Switzerland shares the objective of a world without nuclear weapons. A strong commitment to nuclear disarmament and non-proliferation is therefore part of the country's foreign and security policy."[159] It also maintains a permanent Mission to NATO in Brussels, which is responsible for safeguarding Swiss interests within NATO.[160] It plays an active role in promoting positive relations between itself and NATO under the Partnership for Peace (PfP). It follows the military policy developments within the alliance and represents Switzerland on individual committees and promotes foreign policy initiatives relevant to Switzerland within NATO and participates in the interdepartmental working group for security policy, helping to shape and formulate international security policy.[161] Actively cooperating in several important areas, including the development and maintenance of capabilities of the Swiss armed

---

.whitehouse.gov/briefings-statements/joint-statement-president-donald-j-trump-united-states-america-chairman-kim-jong-un-democratic-peoples-republic-korea-singapore-summit/.

[156] More than ever, South Koreans want their own nuclear weapons. Michelle Ye Hee Lee September 13, 2017. See www.washingtonpost.com/news/worldviews/wp/2017/09/13/most-south-koreans-dont-think-the-north-will-start-a-war-but-they-still-want-their-own-nuclear-weapons/?utm_term=.945a40a7c4fo.

[157] See the North Korean Nuclear Challenge: Military Options and Issues for Congress Kathleen J. McInnis, Andrew Feickert, Mark E. Manyin, Steven A. Hildreth, Mary Beth D. Nikitin and Emma Chanlett. November 6, 2017. See https://fas.org/sgp/crs/nuke/R44994.pdf.

[158] See Daniel Rietiker "Why Swiss Neutrality Is No Obstacle to Joining the Treaty on the Prohibition of Nuclear Weapons (TPNW)," https://safna.org/2018/10/22/why-swiss-neutrality-is-no-obstacle-to-joining-the-treaty-on-the-prohibition-of-nuclear-weapons-tpnw/ (October 22, 2018).

[159] See www.eda.admin.ch/dam/eda/en/documents/aussenpolitik/sicherheitspolitik/2018-bericht-arbeitsgruppe-uno-TPNW_en.pdf at p. 1.

[160] See www.eda.admin.ch/eda/en/home/aussenpolitik/internationale_organisationen/nato/ch-mission-nato.html.

[161] Ibid.

forces they work with NATO and other partner countries in multinational peace-support operations.[162]

NATO notes its respect for Switzerland's neutrality, highlighting the importance of Swiss cooperation in key practical areas.[163] It deems Switzerland a long-standing and valued partner, noting bilateral cooperation in the Partnership for Peace (PfP) program and its becoming a member of the Euro-Atlantic Partnership Council (EAPC) in 1997. They also cooperate under the country's Individual Partnership and Cooperation Programme (IPCP).[164]

Christian Nünlist highlights Switzerland's emerging relationship with NATO and how it has developed significantly since 1949 from its official policy of armed neutrality and strict distance from the Western military alliance to the 1990s, when Switzerland introduced its new strategy of "security through cooperation" and joined NATO's Partnership for Peace (PfP) initiative. He notes that since 1999, Switzerland has contributed a military contingent (Swisscoy) to the NATO-led peacekeeping mission in Kosovo and that its cautious partnership with the Western alliance has become an accepted normality, even though full NATO membership remains a political taboo.[165]

Switzerland was one of the few Western democracies that participated in the TPNW negotiations. Indeed, it voted for the adoption of the TPNW in July 2017, reaffirming its commitment to nuclear disarmament.[166] A subsequent report, how-ever, raised concerns that ratifying the TPNW would create disagreement amongst countries in the region, adversely affecting its position.[167] Examining the foreign and security policy dimensions, the report noted that Switzerland's position must be considered against the backdrop of a changing foreign and security policy environ-ment, wherein nuclear weapons are both a factor of security as well as of uncertainty:

> In an environment shaped by rivalries and tensions, the role of nuclear weapons is once again gaining importance. They continue to act as a deterrent, in particular to prevent direct armed conflicts between major powers. However, nuclear weapons also involve risks, for example a nuclear exchange as a result of misperceptions. And as long as nuclear weapons exist, Switzerland still runs the risk of being affected by the direct or indirect consequences of a nuclear confrontation. In principle, nuclear disarmament is therefore in the security interests of a non-nuclear-weapon state such as Switzerland. However, it is important to prevent uncoordinated or one-

---

[162] Switzerland's cooperation with NATO includes: building capabilities and interoperability; support for NATO-led operations and missions; and Wider cooperation. See www.nato.int/cps/en/natohq/topics_52129.htm.

[163] See www.nato.int/cps/en/natohq/topics_52129.htm.

[164] Ibid.

[165] See Christian Nünlist, "Switzerland and NATO: From Non-Relationship to Cautious Partner," pp. 181–210 in The European Neutrals and NATO, ed. Andrew Cottey (2017).

[166] See www.reachingcriticalwill.org/images/documents/Disarmament-fora/nuclear-weapon-ban/documents/voting-record.pdf.

[167] See www.eda.admin.ch/dam/eda/en/documents/aussenpolitik/sicherheitspolitik/2018-bericht-arbeitsgruppe-uno-TPNW_en.pdf.

sided disarmament leading to greater instability and a heightened risk of military confrontations. Numerous global challenges still need to be overcome in order to guarantee security and stability in a world without nuclear weapons.[168]

Another concern noted in the report related to nuclear deterrence. "As the declared goal of the TPNW is to delegitimize nuclear weapons, TPNW membership would have to be combined with a firm stance against the nuclear deterrence doctrine (e.g. in the context of meetings of states parties). Switzerland would pursue a position in clear opposition to the nuclear weapon states and their allies, although it has always advocated disarmament with and not against these states."[169] Indeed the report concluded that in light of various considerations, "the working group concludes that from today's perspective, for Switzerland the arguments against an accession to the TPNW outweigh the potential opportunities of an accession."[170]

In June 2018, the Swiss National Council adopted Motion 17.4241encouraging the Federal Council to sign the TPNW without delay. To the dismay of many, the Federal Council announced in August 2018 that Switzerland would not sign the TPNW "at this juncture." It is said that the Swiss government was contemplating the "option" of forming an alliance as a nuclear umbrella state. By signing the TPNW Switzerland would, in extreme cases of self-defense "reduce its freedom of action and abandon the option of explicitly placing itself under a nuclear umbrella within the framework" of self-defense alliances "not least with nuclear weapon states or their allies."[171] Needless to say, these moves were followed by public backlash against the government's decision to adopt a wait-and-see approach to the TPNW.

In December 2018, the Council of States of the Swiss Federal Assembly joined the National Council in passing Motion 17.4241 and calling on the Swiss government to sign the TPNW and submit it to Parliament for ratification without delay.[172] It seems that Switzerland is committed to a world without nuclear weapons. In the words of the report: "It shares the objective of a world without nuclear weapons and continues to be engaged in favor of nuclear disarmament."[173] Although the report itself did not recommend going quite that far, it seems that the voice of the people does and Switzerland has.

---

[168] See www.eda.admin.ch/dam/eda/en/documents/aussenpolitik/sicherheitspolitik/2018-bericht-arbeitsgruppe-uno-TPNW_en.pdf at p. 6.

[169] Ibid. at p. 6.

[170] Ibid. at p. 10.

[171] Quoted from www.thelocal.ch/20180816/switzerland-will-not-sign-treaty-banning-nuclear-bombs-for-now.

[172] "Le Conseil fédéral est invité à signer au plus vite le traité sur l'interdiction des armes nucléaires et à le soumettre sans tarder à la ratification du Parlement." See www.parlament.ch/en/ratsbetrieb/suche-curia-vista/geschaeft?AffairId=20174241.

[173] See www.eda.admin.ch/dam/eda/en/documents/aussenpolitik/sicherheitspolitik/2018-bericht-arbeitsgruppe-uno-TPNW_en.pdf at p. 10.

NATO, UMBRELLA AND OTHER STATES

NATO has an extensive reach around the world having entered into a variety of security arrangements with a broad range of countries. The degree to which any of these states will be receptive to the TPNW remains to be seen. Current indications are not hopeful amongst NATO and umbrella States. But one must bear in mind that there is always a difference between official government positions on such matters and the changing wishes and aspirations of individual citizens at the ballot box regarding what they expect from their governing politicians. There remains a solid set of states firmly opposing the Treaty, and reaffirming their position on nuclear deterrence. For Italy and Turkey there is little evidence of a change in policies regarding their respective nuclear defense and deterrence policies. The Netherlands are persistent objectors of the TPNW. With regard to Germany and Belgium, however, parliamentary resolutions to remove nuclear weapons and the joint letter sent to NATO indicate that there is some political discussion that these states do not necessarily want nuclear weapons any longer within their respective territory. Based on the action of extending the life of nuclear capable aircraft in these states, one sees that such is not necessarily based on their military doctrine and their belief that such weapons are appropriate mechanisms for defense purposes, but based purely on their political posturing within the NATO alliance. There is belief among many people and politicians alike that nuclear weapons should not be hosted by Germany and Belgium, so the decision of these nations to acquire new nuclear capable aircraft will be a huge factor in determining future defense positions within these prominent locations within Western Europe. Even if US warheads were to be removed from these countries, there is no evidence that they would take a position different from those NATO states that accept the nuclear umbrella without hosting these weapons on their soil.

OTHER ARRANGEMENTS: THE CSTO AND SCO

It should be noted that there are other cooperative arrangements through the Russian Federation under the Collective Security Treaty Organization (CSTO) and the Shanghai Cooperation Organisation (SCO).

Collective Security Treaty Organization

The Russian Federation, under the Collective Security Treaty Organization (CSTO), consists of a loose military alliance between Russia, Belarus, Armenia, Kazakhstan, Kyrgyzstan, Tajikistan and Uzbekistan.[174] Keaney notes, "Originally pitched as the 'Eastern NATO,' the CSTO has failed to become a significant factor

---

[174] Russia: The Nuclear Umbrella and the CSTO. See https://worldview.stratfor.com/article/russia-nuclear-umbrella-and-csto.

for the security of its member states. That does not mean that the CSTO does not have its uses."[175]

Shanghai Cooperation Organisation

The Shanghai Cooperation Organisation (SCO) was announced in June 2001 as a permanent intergovernmental international organization. It was preceded by the Shanghai Five mechanism. The Shanghai Cooperation Organisation Charter was signed in June 2002, entering into force on September 19, 2003. Its main goals are to strengthen "mutual trust and neighbourliness" through effective cooperation in politics, trade, the economy, etc. as well as to make joint efforts to maintain and ensure peace, security and stability in the region while moving toward "the establishment of a democratic, fair and rational new international political and economic order."[176] The SCO comprises eight member states: the Republic of India, the Republic of Kazakhstan, the People's Republic of China, the Kyrgyz Republic, the Islamic Republic of Pakistan, the Russian Federation, the Republic of Tajikistan and the Republic of Uzbekistan. It has four observer states, the Islamic Republic of Afghanistan, the Republic of Belarus, the Islamic Republic of Iran and the Republic of Mongolia, and six dialogue partners, namely the Republic of Azerbaijan, the Republic of Armenia, the Kingdom of Cambodia, the Federal Democratic Republic of Nepal, the Republic of Turkey and the Democratic Socialist Republic of Sri Lanka. China boycotted the TPNW negotiations but abstained from commencing Treaty negotiation in the UN General Assembly.[177]

ANALYSIS AND CONCLUSIONS

The TPNW has divided the world, whereby being a party to the TPNW and subscribing to nuclear deterrence are mutually exclusive endeavors. A state cannot advance both aims simultaneously. Advocates of the TPNW, who promote humanitarian disarmament, challenge nuclear deterrence policies and defense doctrines stating that nuclear deterrence threatens peace. They seek to challenge traditional deterrents advanced by nuclear-weapon states and organizations such as NATO, rejecting their accepted defense doctrine. Nevertheless, the adoption of TPNW has left the United States, NATO, and its umbrella allies unaffected, thus demonstrating continued support around the world for continued nuclear deterrence policies.

---

[175] John Keaney, CSTO: A Military Pact to Defend Russian Influence (2017) www.americansecuritypro ject.org/csto-a-military-pact-to-defend-russian-influence/. See also Richard Weitz, Assessing the Collective Security Treaty Organization: Capabilities and Vulnerabilities. See www.hsdl.org/? abstract&did=817793.

[176] See http://eng.sectsco.org/about_sco/.

[177] China and the Nuclear Weapons Prohibition Treaty (September 2017) by Tong Zhao and Raymond Wang: https://carnegietsinghua.org/2017/09/21/china-and-nuclear-weapons-prohibition-treaty-pub -73488.

Simply put, proponents of the TPNW would contend that five nuclear-weapon states are keeping the world safe by holding the world hostage under their current deterrence and defense policies. Nuclear-weapon states maintain that they can protect humanity by holding such weapons, but they deny them to other states. In this way the whole world is kept safe by the threat of nuclear war. They proffer that their possession of nuclear weapons deters other countries from acquiring them or using them in a similar way that the death penalty deters murder or the threat of prison deters crime and serves to protect the public. This is a consequentialist argument, that if the five NWS possess nuclear weapons the world will be safe. The argument follows that keeping the world safe is good, therefore the five NWS ought to possess nuclear weapons for the good of the world.

Some may say that the strategy of deterrence seems to have worked. In theory, any state could buy a nuclear warhead and use it, but this has not yet happened. The extent to which this is attributable to deterrence and to the fear of retribution if it were to be used remains debatable. That aside, the nuclear states, however, are under increased legal and political scrutiny, under changing international expectations influenced by international activists who maintain that deterrence may actually threaten global and regional security. It does *not* protect it. Nuclear weapons that have traditionally been promoted as effective deterrents by nuclear-weapon states and organizations such as NATO, are no longer deemed acceptable. This perception has become of paramount importance. The seeming lack of influence by those opposing nuclear deterrence and armament policies at NPT Review Conferences has moved them to take matters into their own hands. Consequently, they are adopting a different approach, imposing a new agenda that not only delegitimizes the threat of use of nuclear weapons as aggressive and inappropriate under emerging international humanitarian law standards but also stigmatizes the act of owning such weapons, presenting it as a threat to peace contrary to emerging contemporary norms and the global good. In taking this position, they highlight that there is an absence of clear and progressive leadership regarding disarmament wanting to effectively implement obligations under Article VI of the NPT. Indeed, the TPNW demonstrates that a large number of states, representing a large percentage of the world's population feel that this consequentialist argument of deterrence is no longer acceptable. Even if one accepts the consequentialist argument, nuclear weapons are clearly no longer the best way to keep the world safe. They now pose a greater danger and risk that outweighs any potential benefits of possessing them, especially with some non-nuclear-weapon states aspiring to acquire them. Disarmament is now accepted by a growing segment of the public as the best way to promote peace, foster security and to keep the world safe – not by outmoded defense doctrines and deterrence policies.

Whether the implementation of the TPNW will lead to changes in how nuclear weapons are perceived and utilized around the world, from a defense and security

Analysis and Conclusions 203

perspective, remains to be seen. What seems certain, however, is that in the immediate future there will be no change amongst states continuing to maintain and advance their nuclear positions. The only point of agreement is that the TPNW has led to an ever-widening chasm between those who adopt a comprehensive ban on nuclear weapons and those who oppose it in favor of nuclear deterrence.

8

Nuclear Defense Doctrines: Disarmament and Emerging Humanitarian Concerns

A nuclear war cannot be won and must never be fought. The only value in our two nations possessing nuclear weapons is to make sure they will never be used. But then would it not be better to do away with them entirely?

Ronald Reagan, 1984 State of the Union Address[1]

Although disarmament is required under Article VI of the NPT, there seems to be little movement toward this end.[2] Indeed, a recent review of various nuclear defense doctrines in nuclear-armed states reveals the opposite, with clear evidence of nuclear renewal policies, raising questions amid mounting humanitarian pressures and developments. In an attempt to move disarmament efforts forward, the Marshall Islands raised vital questions in the International Court of Justice regarding long-standing questions on disarmament and negotiations toward a treaty to cease the arms race pursuant to Article VI of the NPT.[3] The Court, however, ruled for the respondents who challenged the Court's jurisdiction on the grounds that there was no justiciable dispute between them and the Marshall Islands, based on the absence of knowledge of a dispute. In so doing, the Court did not address issues relating to obligations to negotiate a nuclear cessation treaty and to disarm. Many had hoped that the case would assist in exerting pressure on nuclear-armed states toward disarmament efforts pursuant to Article VI of the NPT.[4]

This Court action was soon followed by the adoption of the TPNW in 2017 highlighting a growing humanitarian disarmament movement. Treaty supporters

[1] See www.thereaganvision.org/quotes/.
[2] See D. Fleck, "Legal Aspects of Nuclear Weapons Doctrines"; and J. L. Black-Branch "Precarious Peace: Nuclear Deterrence and Defence Doctrines of Nuclear-Weapon States in the Post-Cold War Era," in Black-Branch/ Fleck (eds.), *Nuclear Non-Proliferation in International Law*, Vol. V (Asser Press/Springer, 2020).
[3] Obligations concerning Negotiations relating to Cessation of the Nuclear Arms Race and to Nuclear Disarmament (*Marshall Islands* v. *United Kingdom*). See www.icj-cij.org/en/case/160/summaries.
[4] See "International Obligations Concerning Disarmament and the Cessation of the Nuclear Arms Race: Justiciability over Justice in the Marshall Islands Cases at the International Court of Justice," *Journal of Conflict & Security Law* (2019) Vol. 24, Issue 3, Autumn 2019, pp. 449–472. Oxford University Press.

advocate against national defense policies based on nuclear arms, arguing that the use of nuclear weapons would constitute a serious breach of international humanitarian law (IHL). For starters, the main premise of the TPNW is to rid the world of nuclear weapons, effectively eliminating them as a central feature of a state's defense platform. Based on humanitarian principles, the Treaty focuses on the destructive impact, emphasizing the harm to individuals and the environment caused by the use or testing of nuclear weapons. Specifically, Article 6 requires victim assistance and environmental remediation, calling on state parties to adequately provide "age – and gender-sensitive assistance, without discrimination, including medical care, rehabilitation and psychological support, as well as provide for their social and economic inclusion."[5] Such Treaty requirements stand in stark contrast to many state nuclear defense doctrines.

Moreover, strategic defense concerns mount over the recent INF developments, as outlined in Chapter 7, raising serious concerns that there may be a renewed arms race in which nuclear capacity is stockpiled instead of decreased. Again, in 1987, the United States and the Union of Soviet Socialist Republics (Russia) signed the Treaty on the Elimination of Intermediate-Range and Shorter-Range Missiles, commonly referred to as the INF (Intermediate-Range Nuclear Forces) Treaty.[6] The leaders of the two nuclear superpowers, inspired hope in the world with this important bilateral agreement, requiring the destruction of ground-launched ballistic and cruise missiles with ranges of between 500 and 5,500 kilometers (310 to 3,400 miles), their launchers and associated support structures and support equipment. Despite impressive progress with as many as 2,692 missiles destroyed by June 1, 1991, some thirty years on, however, it would seem that the spirit of this agreement is no longer intact. Both the United States and Russia have officially withdrawn from the agreement and are formulating plans to develop new weapons meant to be prohibited under the INF. Dieter Fleck notes that all five nuclear powers, as well as other states possessing nuclear weapons, are currently updating and renewing their nuclear defense stock.[7]

Proponents of the TPNW point to actions such as nuclear renewals and the withdrawal from the INF Treaty as evidence of a lack of commitment to these nations' respective obligations under the NPT, highlighting the need for increasing scrutiny and pressure to reassess their defense doctrines. They challenge military defense based on nuclear weapons arguing that in a modern-day context the very existence of nuclear defense doctrines serves as a "threat of force" under Article 2(4) of the UN Charter, or even as a "threat to the peace," a "breach of the peace," or an "act of aggression" as per Article 39 of the Charter. Moreover, the use of nuclear force would be incompatible with many aspects of humanitarian law under

---

[5] See https://undocs.org/A/CONF.229/2017/8.

[6] See www.state.gov/t/avc/trty/102360.htm.

[7] D. Fleck, "Legal Aspects of Nuclear Weapons Doctrines," in Black-Branch/Fleck (eds.), *Nuclear Non-Proliferation in International Law*, Vol. V (Asser Press/Springer, 2020).

206 *Nuclear Defense Doctrines*

emerging normative practice serving to outlaw nuclear force completely. Discussion in this chapter focuses on defense under Cold War-style doctrines in light of developments under the TPNW,[8] examining new expectations for a world without nuclear weapons under the following framework:

(1) The Threat of Force and the ICJ Advisory Opinion
  (a) Nuclear Weapons and the UN Charter
  (b) Deterrence, the Prohibition of Threats to Use Force, and Acts of Aggression
  (c) UN Resolutions
  (d) *Jus ad Bellum* and *Jus in Bello.*
(2) The Implementation of the TPNW and Its Potential for Change as to How Nuclear Weapons Are Perceived and Utilized Around the World
  (a) The Treaty on the Prevention of Nuclear Weapons and *Nuclear Weapons* Advisory Opinion
  (b) Recent Developments under International Human Rights Law
  (c) Torture, cruel or inhuman treatment under International Humanitarian Law
  (d) Nuclear Weapons, International Humanitarian Law, and the TPNW.
(3) Conclusions

THE THREAT OF FORCE AND THE ICJ ADVISORY OPINION

In the *Legality of the Threat or Use of Nuclear Weapons*[9] the International Court of Justice rendered its Advisory Opinion relating to the question from the General Assembly:[10] "Is the threat or use of nuclear weapons in any circumstance permitted under international law?" In the matter the Court[11] found that applicable law was that relating to the use of force, in the United Nations Charter, and the law applicable in armed conflict, together with any specific treaties on nuclear weapons that the Court might find relevant.[12] The Court then considered the question of the legality or illegality of the use of nuclear weapons in the light of the provisions of the Charter relating to the threat or use of force, deciding that any threat or use of nuclear weapons that is contrary to Article 2(4) of the UN Charter, and fails to meet requirements under Article 51, would be unlawful. An exercise of self-defense would be subject to the test of being proportional to the armed attack and the necessity in responding to it. In so doing, the Court observed that those provisions applied to any use of force, regardless of the type of weapons employed.

---

[8] Treaty on the Prohibition of Nuclear Weapons, A/CONF.229/2017/8.
[9] ICJ, *Legality of the Threat or Use of Nuclear Weapons*, Advisory Opinion of July 8, 1996 (General Assembly Request), *ICJ Reports* (1996), 226, 35 *ILM* (1996).
[10] Resolution 49/75K adopted on December 15, 1994.
[11] Having concluded that it had jurisdiction to render an opinion on the question.
[12] See www.icj-cij.org/en/case/95.

The Threat of Force and the ICJ Advisory Opinion   207

In that regard, it stated that the principle of proportionality might not in itself exclude the use of nuclear weapons in self-defense in all circumstances. At the same time, however, in order to be lawful, a use of force that was proportionate under the law of self-defense had to meet the requirements of the law applicable in armed conflict, including, in particular, the principles and rules of international humanitarian law. It highlighted that the notions of a "threat" and "use" of force within the meaning of Article 2(4),of the Charter stood together in the sense that if the use of force itself in a given case was illegal – for whatever reason – the threat to use such force would likewise be illegal.[13] Marco Roscini suggests that a threat does not necessarily need to materialize into the actual exertion of force and should be differentiated from planning and preparation. The distinguishing factor between planning and preparation actions and threat of force actions "is the intention to put abusive pressure on the victim state without a predetermined decision to use force."[14] Needless to say, it can be a delicate judgment to determine what crosses the threshold into being a threat because intention and predetermined decisions are hard to verify.[15]

The ICJ examined the law applicable in situations of armed conflict from a customary and conventional law perspective, concluding that the use of nuclear weapons could not be seen as specifically prohibited on the basis of that law, nor did it find any specific prohibition of the use of nuclear weapons in the treaties that expressly prohibited the use of certain weapons of mass destruction.[16]

> 56. ... it does not seem to the Court that the use of nuclear weapons can be regarded as specifically prohibited on the basis of the ... provisions of the Second Hague Declaration of 1899, the Regulations annexed to the Hague Convention IV of 1907 or the 1925 Geneva Protocol.
>
> 57. The pattern until now has been for weapons of mass destruction to be declared illegal by specific instruments ... The Court does not find any specific prohibition of recourse to nuclear weapons in treaties expressly prohibiting the use of certain weapons of mass destruction.
>
> 58. In the last two decades, a great many negotiations have been conducted regarding nuclear weapons; they have not resulted in a treaty of general prohibition of the same kind as for bacteriological and chemical weapons ...
>
> 62. The Court notes that the treaties dealing exclusively with acquisition, manufacture, possession, deployment and testing of nuclear weapons, without specifically addressing their threat or use, certainly point to an increasing concern in the international community with these weapons; the Court concludes from this that these treaties could therefore be seen as foreshadowing a future general prohibition

---

[13] Ibid.

[14] Marco Roscini, "Threats of Armed Force and Contemporary International Law" (2007) 54:2 *Netherlands International Law Review* 229–277 at 231.

[15] Roscini, ibid.

[16] See www.icj-cij.org/en/case/95.

208   *Nuclear Defense Doctrines*

of the use of such weapons, but that they do not constitute such a prohibition by themselves . . .[17]

The TPNW highlights an interesting turning question with regard to this point. For the first time there is a treaty prohibiting nuclear weapons making both their possession and their use illegal. This demonstrates a developing body of law, treaty law as well as humanitarian principles against these weapons and their use for those adopting and ratifying the TPNW. If a weapon is illegal, then its use is also illegal regardless of the reasons for deploying it. There will be a growing number of states in which these weapons will be illegal. It may be that one state's international commitments cannot be used by to bind or force another state to comply, but there is no doubt that supporters will exert pressure to persuade non-party states to adopt the TPNW. Given the groundswell of support for the TPNW, the nuclear-armed states are a relatively small albeit powerful bloc. Again, 122 states adopted the TPNW in July 2017 at the UN General Assembly demonstrating the powerful array of support for it and making the nuclear-armed states look old, outdated and out of touch with the general populace in a modern world. Call it a generational shift or people simply fed up with inertia and perceived reluctance under the NPT process, whatever the reason, times are changing and future judgments of the ICJ may not be so conservative in its reading of normative developments.

In examining customary international law to determine whether a prohibition of the threat or use of nuclear weapons as such flowed from that source of law, the ICJ in its *Advisory Opinion*, noted that the members of the international community were profoundly divided on the matter of whether non-recourse to nuclear weapons over the past fifty years constituted the expression of an *opinio juris*. Consequently, it was not able to find that there was such an *opinio juris*.

> 67. [The Court notes that] the Members of the international community are profoundly divided on the matter of whether non-recourse to nuclear weapons over the past fifty years constitutes the expression of an *opinio juris*. Under these circumstances the Court does not consider itself able to find that there is such an *opinio juris*.
>
> 68. According to certain States, the important series of General Assembly resolutions, beginning with resolution 1653 (XVI) of 24 November 1961, that deal with nuclear weapons and that affirm, with consistent regularity, the illegality of nuclear weapons, signify the existence of a rule of international customary law which prohibits recourse to those weapons. According to other States, however, the resolutions in question have no binding character on their own account and are not declaratory of any customary rule of prohibition of nuclear weapons; some of these States have also pointed out that this series of resolutions not only did not meet with the approval of all of the nuclear-weapon States but of many other States as well.

---

[17] ICJ, *Nuclear Weapons*, paras. 56–73. See www.icj-cij.org/files/case-related/95/7497.pdf.

The Threat of Force and the ICJ Advisory Opinion

70. The Court notes that General Assembly resolutions, even if they are not binding, may sometimes have normative value. They can, in certain circumstances, provide evidence important for establishing the existence of a rule or the emergence of an *opinio juris*. To establish whether this is true of a given General Assembly resolution, it is necessary to look at its content and the conditions of its adoption; it is also necessary to see whether an *opinio juris* exists as to its normative character. Or a series of resolutions may show the gradual evolution of the *opinio juris* required for the establishment of a new rule.

The Court also addressed the question of whether recourse to nuclear weapons ought to be considered illegal in light of the principles and rules of international humanitarian law applicable in armed conflict[18] and of the law of neutrality.[19] In doing so it emphasized two cardinal principles: the first of which is aimed at the distinction between combatants and non-combatants. States must never make civilians the object of attack and must consequently never use weapons that are incapable of distinguishing between civilian and military targets. Secondly, unnecessary suffering should not be caused to combatants. It follows that states do not have unlimited freedom of choice in the weapons they use; "it is accordingly prohibited to use weapons causing them such harm or uselessly aggravating their suffering."[20]

Both arguments are explored later in this chapter but suffice it to say that the use of nuclear force is unlikely to distinguish between a combatant and a non-combatant. The attacks in Hiroshima and Nagasaki in 1945 amply demonstrate that nuclear blasts do not discriminate between military or civilian objects. Nuclear testing as in the case of the Marshall Islands also demonstrates the point that civilians are not exempted from the effects of a nuclear fallout. Aside from whether or not the state is intending to make civilians the object of an attack, they know that in using such weapons innocent civilians will be caught in the cross-fire and will suffer ill-effects, if not death. In other words, these weapons are not able to distinguish between civilian populations and military targets and consequently proponents of the TPNW would say that nuclear weapons must never be used. In addition, there is little doubt that such weapons cause unnecessary suffering to both combatants and non-combatants going against humanitarian principles as demonstrated in the previously cited examples in Japan and the Marshall Islands.

The Court in 1996 recognized that states do not have unlimited freedom of choice in the weapons they use.[21] It referred to the Martens Clause, according to which civilians and combatants remained under the protection and authority of the principles of international law derived from established custom, the principles of humanity and the dictates of public conscience.[22] One would think that such

[18] At paras. 74–87. See www.icj-cij.org/files/case-related/95/7497.pdf.
[19] At paras. 88–89. See www.icj-cij.org/files/case-related/95/7497.pdf.
[20] At paras. 74–87. See www.icj-cij.org/files/case-related/95/7497.pdf.
[21] Ibid.
[22] Ibid. Note the important dissenting opinions by Judge Weeramantry and by Judge Shahabuddeen.

210   *Nuclear Defense Doctrines*

principles remain today, have been reiterated and indeed strengthened under the TPNW, which demonstrates a growing movement to further enforce such principles.

In 1996 the Court indicated that, although the applicability to nuclear weapons of the principles and rules of humanitarian law and of the principle of neutrality was not in dispute, the conclusions to be drawn from it were all the same controversial.[23] In that regard the Court pointed out that, in view of the unique characteristics of nuclear weapons, their use seemed scarcely reconcilable with respect for the requirements of the law applicable in armed conflict. But, in its conclusions on the applicability of international humanitarian law in armed conflict and the law of neutrality the Court stated:

> 90. Although the applicability of the principles and rules of humanitarian law and of the principle of neutrality to nuclear weapons is hardly disputed, the conclusions to be drawn from this applicability are, on the other hand, controversial.
>
> 91. According to one point of view, the fact that recourse to nuclear weapons is subject to and regulated by the law of armed conflict does not necessarily mean that such recourse is as such prohibited . . .
>
> 92. Another view holds that recourse to nuclear weapons could never be compatible with the principles and rules of humanitarian law and is therefore prohibited . . .
>
> 93. A similar view has been expressed with respect to the effects of the principle of neutrality . . .
>
> 95. . . . In view of the unique characteristics of nuclear weapons . . . the use of such weapons in fact seems scarcely reconcilable with respect for such requirements. Nevertheless, the Court considers that it does not have sufficient elements to enable it to conclude with certainty that the use of nuclear weapons would necessarily be at variance with the principles and rules of law applicable in armed conflict in any circumstance.
>
> 97. Accordingly, in view of the present state of international law viewed as a whole, as examined above by the Court, and of the elements of fact at its disposal, the Court is led to observe that it cannot reach a definitive conclusion as to the legality or illegality of the use of nuclear weapons by a State in an extreme circumstance of self-defense, in which its very survival would be at stake.[24]

An added feature of the ICJ ruling was its view regarding the obligation of the states parties to the NPT to pursue in good faith the requirement to conclude negotiations leading to nuclear disarmament in all its aspects under strict and effective international control. The NPT stipulates this under Article VI and the Court reiterated the obligation raising it to what might be perceived as a positive duty. The fact that it is stipulated in the NPT means it is a duty of the respective states parties both

---

[23] At paras. 90–97. See www.icj-cij.org/files/case-related/95/7497.pdf.
[24] Ibid.

The Threat of Force and the ICJ Advisory Opinion

individually and collectively to honor this. The Court recognized this obligation reminding all states of their respective duties.

Currently, NATO and its allies insist that the "role of nuclear weapons in NATO's strategy fully conforms with international law."[25] This position is predicated upon the 1996 International Court of Justice *Advisory Opinion*.[26] In its *Opinion* the Court concluded that any threat or use of nuclear weapons that is contrary to Article 2(4), of the UN Charter would be unlawful if it fails to meet the self-defense requirements under Article 51 of the Charter. Neither customary nor conventional international law provide a specific authorization, or any comprehensive and universal prohibition of the threat of use or use of nuclear weapons. Furthermore, the Court could not conclude definitively – as mentioned with a 7:7 vote – whether the threat or use of nuclear weapons would be lawful or unlawful in an extreme circumstance of self-defense.[27]

The Court made these conclusions over two decades ago and prior to the adoption of the TPNW at the UN General Assembly. To summarize the main position, the starting point is that the use of force is prohibited under Article 2(4) of the Charter. Article 51 of the Charter, however, specifies that force can be used lawfully for self-defense purposes. In its deliberations, the Court noted the existence of the policy of nuclear deterrence as a "fact," but as to whether a policy of nuclear deterrence is an actual threat contrary to Article 2 (4) would depend on whether the exercise of self-defense measures are proportionate to the armed attack and are deemed necessary in responding to the attack.[28] Under the principle of proportionality, the use of nuclear weapons in self-defense might not in all circumstances result in the unlawful use of nuclear weapons. That said, however, the Court found that the use must meet the requirements of the law applicable in armed conflict, especially international humanitarian law.

Turning to international humanitarian law, the ICJ found there "exists no specific authorisation of the threat or use of nuclear weapons or any other weapon in international customary and treaty law."[29] There also did not exist a prohibition of

---

[25] NATO, "NATO's Positions Regarding Nuclear Non-Proliferation, Arms Control and Disarmament and Related Issues" (October 22, 2009) at 4, online (pdf): *North Atlantic Treaty Organization*, see www .nato.int/nato_static /assets/pdf/pdf_topics/20091022_NATO_Position_on_nuclear_nonproliferation-eng.pdf.

[26] ICJ, *Legality of the Threat or Use of Nuclear Weapons*, Advisory Opinion of July 8, 1996 (General Assembly Opinion), *ICJ Reports* (1996), 226, 35 *ILM* (1996).

[27] See NATO, "NATO's Positions Regarding Nuclear Non-Proliferation, Arms Control and Disarmament and Related Issues" (October 22, 2009) at 4, online (pdf): *North Atlantic Treaty Organization*, see www .nato.int/nato_static /assets/pdf/pdf_topics/20091022_NATO_Position_on_nuclear_nonproliferation-eng.pdf.

[28] See International Law Association, Nuclear Weapons, Non-Proliferation and Contemporary International Law, Second Report: Legal Aspects of Nuclear Disarmament (2014) at 6.

[29] Sofia Björk, *Use the Force? An Analysis of the Effect of the TPN on the Legality or Illegality of Nuclear Weapons* (LLM Thesis, Lund University, Faculty of Law, 2018), see lup.lub.lu.se/student-papers /record/8940779 at 13.

nuclear weapons in international customary and treaty law at that time. In that regard, there was not an *opinio juris* prohibiting nuclear weapons at the time of the Advisory Opinion. Therefore, based on the above points, the ICJ concluded that the threat or use of nuclear weapons would generally be contrary to the rules of international law applicable in armed conflict and, in particular, the principles and rules of humanitarian law. That said, in view of the then current state of international law, and taking into consideration the elements of facts at its disposal, the Court could not conclude definitively whether the threat or use of nuclear weapons would be lawful or unlawful in an extreme circumstance of self-defense, in which the very survival of a state would be at stake.[30]

The ICJ concluded that the answer to the question posed by the General Assembly had to be found principally in *jus ad bellum* and *jus in bello*, both of which were designed to deal with the use of weapons, including nuclear weapons, in armed conflict. Answering the main questions of the GA in the negative, the Court's *Opinion* is important in several respects. Firstly, it reaffirms that the use of nuclear weapons is subject to international humanitarian law. Even though states had not contested this in the respective submissions, it had frequently been challenged by various commentators and by at least one state in the past. This unequivocally established the point.[31] Secondly, the Court's assessment of the United Nations Charter makes clear that modern *jus ad bellum* is not concerned solely with whether the initial resort to force is lawful; it also has implications for the subsequent conduct of hostilities. Finally, while other areas of international law may have a bearing on armed conflict, the *Opinion* clearly rejects arguments that the detailed *lex specialis*, which has been developed over the years to deal with the conduct of hostilities, can be circumvented by reference to general provisions of environmental or human rights law.[32]

Nuclear Weapons and the UN Charter

In applying *jus ad bellum* to the use of nuclear weapons, the ICJ reached the unanimous conclusion that: "A threat or use of force by means of nuclear weapons that is contrary to Article 2, paragraph 4, of the Charter of the United Nations and that fails to meet all the requirements of Article 5 1 is unlawful." In relation to this, it is important to bear in mind that Article 2(4) and Article 51 make no reference to any specific type of weapons, be they nuclear or otherwise. When the Charter was concluded in 1945, the threat was immediately prevalent and led to the very first

---

[30] ICJ, *Legality of the Threat or Use of Nuclear Weapons*, Advisory Opinion of July 8, 1996 (General Assembly Opinion), *ICJ Reports* (1996), 226, 35 *ILM* (1996), at para. 105(2)(E).

[31] See the Advisory Opinion on nuclear weapons and the contribution of the International Court to international humanitarian law by Christopher Greenwood, February 28, 1997 Article, *International Review of the Red Cross*, No. 316 at p. 68.

[32] Ibid.

The Threat of Force and the ICJ Advisory Opinion

GA Res 1 (I) of January 24, 1946 some fifty years later when this ICJ heard the arguments. Moreover, the Court reaffirmed that any right of self-defense was subject to the requirement of proportionality, apparently accepting that the need to ensure that a use of force in self-defense was proportionate had implications for the degree of force and, consequently, for the type of weaponry which a state might use lawfully.[33]

Furthermore, in determining whether the use of a particular weapon in a given case would be lawful, it would be necessary to comply with international humanitarian law; international humanitarian law applies likewise for the attacking and the defending party. Notably, the Court did not state that the use of nuclear weapons could never be a proportionate measure of self-defense.[34] If the threat or use of nuclear weapons could be lawful in an extreme situation of self-defense, it would be proportional, i.e., not incompatible with international humanitarian law.

Deterrence, the Prohibition of Threats to Use Force and Acts of Aggression

To date, there is little state practice on the prohibition of threats to use force under international law.[35] In the *Nicaragua* Case,[36] the ICJ stated that "... in international law there are no rules, other than such rules which may be accepted by the State concerned, by treaty or otherwise, whereby the level of armaments of a sovereign State can be limited, and this principle is valid for all States without exception." Under contemporary norms and standards, the use of force is generally guided by the principles of *jus ad bellum* and *jus ad bello*. Note that since World War I there has been a general prohibition against war. In 1919, the Covenant of the League of Nations and again, in 1928, the Treaty of Paris (the Briand-Kellogg Pact) sought to outlaw war.[37] This stance was confirmed in the United Nations Charter in 1945. The UN Charter extends a general prohibition to both the "threat ... of force" as well as the "use of force" under Article 2(4). Such prohibitions are reiterated in many international treaties, most notably articulated in the Protocols additional to nuclear-weapon-free-zone treaties.[38]

---

[33] Ibid. at p. 70.

[34] Opinion, paras. 42–43.

[35] Second Report of the Committee on Nuclear Weapons, Non-Proliferation and Contemporary International Law, Second Report: Legal Aspects of Nuclear Disarmament (Washington, DC 2014), at p. 2. See www.ila-hq.org/en/committees/index.cfm/cid/1025.

[36] ICJ, *Military and Paramilitary Activities in and against Nicaragua (Nicaragua v. United States)*, Judgment, June 27, 1986, Merits, ICJ Reports 1986, para. 269.

[37] "What Are jus ad bellum and jus in bello? By the International Committee of the Red Cross" (2015), online: www.icrc.org/en/document/what-are-jus-ad-bellum-and-jus-bello-0.

[38] Treaty for the Prohibition of Nuclear Weapons in Latin America and the Caribbean – Treaty of Tlatelolco (February 14, 1967), 634 *UNTS* 326; South Pacific Nuclear Free Zone Treaty (Treaty of Rarotonga) and Protocols thereto (August 6, 1985), 1676 *UNTS* 326; Treaty on the South-East Asia Nuclear Weapon Free Zone – Treaty of Bangkok (December 15, 1995), 1981 *UNTS* 129; African

Specifically, Article 2 of the Charter requires that its Members act in accordance with the principles of "sovereign equality of all its Members";[39] fulfilling their obligations in "good faith";[40] as well as settling "their international disputes by peaceful means in such a manner that international peace and security, and justice, are not endangered."[41] Moreover, Article 2(4) requires that: "All Members shall refrain in their international relations from the threat or use of force against the territorial integrity or political independence of any state, or in any other manner inconsistent with the Purposes of the United Nations."[42]

Again, in the *Legality of the Threat or Use of Nuclear Weapons* case, the Court noted the existence of the policy of nuclear deterrence as a fact, but the issue of whether a nuclear deterrence doctrine possesses an actual threat contrary to Article 2(4) would depend on whether its self-defense measures were proportionate to the armed attack and necessary in responding to the attack.[43] Under the rule of proportionality, the use of nuclear weapons in self-defense might, in some circumstances, constitute unlawful use.[44] The use of a nuclear weapon might be deemed appropriate in terms of acting proportionately in an extreme case of self-defense, whereas in other situations it may not. In other words, according to the ruling, it is not the character of nuclear weapons, per se, but the margin of utility in self-defense that is called into question here.[45]

Specifically, Article 51 recognizes the inherent right to self-defense stating that, "Nothing in the present Charter shall impair the inherent right of individual or collective self-defense if an armed attack occurs against a Member of the United Nations, until the Security Council has taken measures necessary to maintain international peace and security ..."[46] Note, however, there are qualifications placed on the right such as "if an armed attack occurs" and that measures taken by members in the exercise of self-defense "shall be immediately reported to the Security Council and shall not in any way affect the authority and responsibility of

---

Nuclear-Weapon-Free Zone Treaty – Treaty of Pelindaba (April 11, 1996), 35 *ILM* 698; Treaty on a Nuclear-Weapon-Free Zone in Central Asia – Semipalatinsk Treaty (September 8, 2006). See also Declaration by Mongolia of its nuclear-weapon-free status (September 25, 1992), and the Law of Mongolia on its Nuclear-Weapon-Free Status which entered into force on February 3, 2000, www.nti.org/treaties-and-regimes/nuclear-weapon-free-status-mongolia/, and was recognized by UNGA Res 55/33 S (November 20, 2000).

[39] Article 2(1). See www.un.org/en/sections/un-charter/un-charter-full-text/index.html.
[40] Article 2(2). See www.un.org/en/sections/un-charter/un-charter-full-text/index.html.
[41] Article 2(3). See www.un.org/en/sections/un-charter/un-charter-full-text/index.html.
[42] Article 2(4). See www.un.org/en/sections/un-charter/un-charter-full-text/index.html.
[43] See International Law Association, Nuclear Weapons, Non-Proliferation and Contemporary International Law, "Second Report: Legal Aspects of Nuclear Disarmament" (2014) at 6.
[44] The Court also stated that the use must meet the requirements of the law applicable in armed conflict, especially international humanitarian law.
[45] See also Limits on the Use of Nuclear Weapons Under the International Law of Self-Defence, Andrew Clapham. See www.unog.ch/80256EDD006B8954/(httpAssets)/F3646C889F657E65C1257B8700574243/$file/Andrew+Clapham.pdf.
[46] See www.un.org/en/sections/un-charter/un-charter-full-text/index.html.

The Threat of Force and the ICJ Advisory Opinion   215

the Security Council under the present Charter to take at any time such action as it deems necessary in order to maintain or restore international peace and security."[47] Notably, both advocates for and against nuclear weapons agree that the international law rules of distinction between military objectives and civilians, proportionality and necessity apply to nuclear weapons, noting that the rule of distinction would render it unlawful to use weapons wherein the likely or foreseeable effects could not distinguish between military and civilian objects. In *Nicaragua v. United States of America* the ICJ found that in the exercise of self-defense only measures proportional to the armed attack and necessary in responding to the attack are lawful.[48] Under proportionality it would be unlawful to use nuclear weapons whereby the probable effects upon combatant or non-combatant persons or objects are likely be disproportionate to the value of the military objective. And, the rule of necessity would make it unlawful to use weapons involving a level of force that is disproportionate, that is not necessary in the circumstances to achieve the overall military objective.

Needless to say, using "low-yield" nuclear warheads invariably influences both potential indiscriminate effects, as well as arguments regarding proportionality and also increasing the likelihood that nuclear weapons will be deployed.[49]

While the ICJ in the *Legality of the Threat or Use of Nuclear Weapons* case did not reach a definite conclusion on the lawfulness of the use or threat of use of nuclear weapons, President Mohammed Bedjaoui[50] emphasized that "licence" cannot be deduced from this. States having nuclear weapons must ensure that nuclear deterrence is not directed against the purposes of the United Nations, and must be used only as a last resort and in an extreme situation of self-defense and only against an armed attack in which the issue of the very survival of the state is at stake. Moreover, the Charter assigns primary responsibility to the Security Council regarding peace and security and Article 51 recognizes its "authority and responsibility ... to take at any time such action as it deems necessary in order to maintain or restore international peace and security." Effectively, the possession of weapons lies within the domestic jurisdiction of states, subject to international legal commitments and

[47] Ibid.
[48] *The Military and Paramilitary Activities in and against Nicaragua*, ICJ Reports 1986, p. 14, at para. 176.
[49] Thomas Gaulkin says the 2018 Nuclear Posture Review reaffirmed the Trump administration's commitment to the broad modernization of the nuclear weapons. It also introduced two new weapons, one of which is the W76-2. Gaulkin notes: "That so-called 'low-yield' nuclear warhead may soon be carried on some or all of the 14 active US Navy nuclear ballistic submarines that form one leg of the nuclear deterrence triad (the two other legs being US Air Force bombers and ground-launched intercontinental ballistic missiles). Former Secretary of Defense Mattis told Congress last year, 'I don't think there is any such thing as a "tactical nuclear weapon." Any nuclear weapon used any time is a strategic game-changer.' And a long list of experts, including the chairman of the House Armed Services Committee, say these kinds of 'small' warheads increase the likelihood that nuclear weapons will be used – and full-scale nuclear war will follow." Say WHAT? – A case of low-yield nuclear thinking. February 14, 2019. https://thebulletin.org/2019/02/say-what-a-case-of-low-yield-nuclear-thinking/?utm_source=Bulletin%20Newsletter&utm_medium=iContact%20email&utm_campaign=FebSayWhat_02142019.
[50] In para. 14 of his Declaration.

216   *Nuclear Defense Doctrines*

obligations as well as ultimate oversight by the Security Council.[51] So, in principle, nuclear-weapon states may use nuclear weapons as part of their deterrence policy as long as they are complying in good faith with their NPT obligations, as well as any other international requirements. Again, in noting the existence of the policy of nuclear deterrence as a fact, the ICJ in examining whether a nuclear deterrence position may actually constitute a threat contrary to Article 2(4) UN Charter, the Court noted that it "depends on whether the particular use of force envisaged would be directed against the territorial integrity or political independence of a state, or against the Purposes of the United Nations or whether, in the event that it were intended as a means of defense, it would necessarily violate the principles of necessity and proportionality." Effectively, the Court found it necessary to evaluate such a nuclear threat both under the *jus ad bellum* and the *jus in bello*. Furthermore, the Court stated that "if the use of force itself in a given case is illegal – for whatever reason – the threat to use such force will likewise be illegal" adding that the use of nuclear weapons "in fact seems scarcely reconcilable" with the principle of distinction between civilian objects and military objectives and the prohibition of unnecessary suffering.[52]

UN Resolutions

The ICJ in the *Legality of the Threat or Use of Nuclear Weapons* case noted that the Security Council, in Resolution 984 (1995), welcomed security assurances given by the nuclear-weapon states, the implication of which was that not all uses of nuclear weapons would violate the Charter's provisions on the use of force.[53] In the UN resolution,[54] the General Assembly stressed the belief that the only assurance against the threat of nuclear war would be the complete elimination of nuclear weapons.[55] The General Assembly noted that the Fourth Review Conference of the Parties to the Treaty on the Non-Proliferation of Nuclear Weapons left the need of progress toward the complete elimination of nuclear weapons.[56] The General Assembly resolution[57] "declared that the use of nuclear weapons would be a violation of the

---

[51] See Second Report of the Committee on Nuclear Weapons, Non-Proliferation and Contemporary International Law, Second Report: Legal Aspects of Nuclear Disarmament (Washington, DC 2014), at p. 2. See www.ila-hq.org/en/committees/index.cfm/cid/1025.)

[52] ICJ, ibid., paras. 47 and 95. For a more detailed legal assessment see D. Fleck, "Nuclear Weapons," Chapter 16, in Rain Liivoja/Tim McCormack (eds.), *Routledge Handbook of the Law of Armed Conflict* (Routledge, 2014).

[53] See Christopher Greenwood, "The Advisory Opinion on nuclear weapons and the contribution of the International Court to international humanitarian law," No. 316 International Review of the Red Cross (1997), at p. 70.

[54] Regarding general and complete disarmament (A/RES/49/75 K).

[55] "Convinced that the complete elimination of nuclear weapons is the only guarantee against the threat of nuclear war." A/RES/49/75 K. See www.un.org/documents/ga/res/49/a49r075.htm.

[56] See www.un.org/documents/ga/res/49/a49r075.htm.

[57] Making reference to its previous resolutions: Resolutions 1653 (XVI) of November 24 1961, 33/71 B of December 14, 1978, 34/83 G of December 11, 1979, 35/152 D of December 12, 1980, 36/92 I of December 9, 1981, 45/59 B of December 4, 1990 and 46/37 D of December 6, 1991.

Charter and a crime against humanity."[58] States in favor of nuclear weapons use the security assurances made by the Security Council, such as in Resolutions 255 (1968) and 984 (1995) in relation to the NPT as an argument for the legality of the use of nuclear weapons. For example, in regard to measures to safeguard non-nuclear-weapon states parties to the treaty on the non-proliferation of nuclear weapons, Resolution 255 (1968) reaffirmed "the inherent right, recognized under Article 51 of the Charter, of individual and collective self-defense if an armed attack occurs against a Member of the United Nations, until the Security Council has taken measures necessary to maintain international peace and security."[59] Also, Resolution 984 (1995) reaffirmed the inherent right under Article 51 for "individual and collective self-defense if an armed attack occurs ..."[60]

The ICJ in the *Legality of the Threat or Use of Nuclear Weapons* case rejected an argument to the effect that the resolutions adopted by the United Nations General Assembly on the subject of nuclear weapons reflected a customary law prohibition.[61] As the Court points out from the case, while resolutions of the General Assembly could constitute authoritative declarations of custom, these did not. The essence of customary international law is, of course, the actual practice and *opinio juris* of states,[62] and "the General Assembly resolutions fell short of establishing that *opinio juris*, as well as being at odds with the practice of a significant number of States."[63]

The UN Charter further prohibits "threats to the peace, breaches of the peace, and acts of aggression" under Article 39.[64] Authority is granted to the Security Council to exert its powers under Chapter VII, including "measures" (sanctions) under Article 41,[65] or the use of force under Article 42, should it consider that measures provided for in Article 41 would be inadequate or have proved to be inadequate in relation to such threats and breaches of the peace, or acts of

---

[58] See www.un.org/documents/ga/res/49/a49r075.htm.

[59] See repository.un.org/handle/11176/76037.

[60] At para. 9. See https://documents-dds-ny.un.org/doc/UNDOC/GEN/N95/106/06/PDF/N9510606 .pdf?OpenElement.

[61] See the Advisory Opinion on nuclear weapons and the contribution of the International Court to international humanitarian law by Christopher Greenwood, February 28, 1997 Article, *International Review of the Red Cross*, No. 316 at p. 71.

[62] Opinion, para. 64.

[63] See also Greenwood, *loc. cit.*, at p. 71.

[64] Article 39 states that "The Security Council shall determine the existence of any threat to the peace, breach of the peace, or act of aggression and shall make recommendations, or decide what measures shall be taken in accordance with Articles 41 and 42, to maintain or restore international peace and security." See http://legal.un.org/repertory/art39.shtml.

[65] Article 41 states: "The Security Council may decide what measures not involving the use of armed force are to be employed to give effect to its decisions, and it may call upon the Members of the United Nations to apply such measures. These may include complete or partial interruption of economic relations and of rail, sea, air, postal, telegraphic, radio, and other means of communication, and the severance of diplomatic relations." See http://legal.un.org/repertory/art41.shtml.

218 *Nuclear Defense Doctrines*

aggression.[66] In that light, it could be argued that not only the use of aggressive force, but also the threat of aggressive force is prohibited by *jus cogens*.[67] A case in point would be the US attacks against Hiroshima and Nagasaki in 1945. Note, however, Marc Weller emphasizes that "international law still supports the 'realist' doctrine of nuclear deterrence through arms control agreements. It accepts that wars may occur by providing for rules of warfare and humanitarian law."[68]

One must recall that, at the time, the ICJ judges were evenly split on this issue by seven votes to seven, with President Bedjaoui's casting the vote in favor.[69] It followed from the above-mentioned requirements that the threat or use of nuclear weapons would generally be contrary to the rules of international law applicable in armed conflict, and in particular the principles and rules of humanitarian law. In view of the state of international law, and of the elements of fact at its disposal, however, the Court could conclude definitively whether the threat or use of nuclear weapons would be lawful or unlawful in an extreme circumstance of self-defense, in which the very survival of a state would be at stake.[70] Questions arise as to how objective

[66] Article 42 states: "Should the Security Council consider that measures provided for in Article 41would be inadequate or have proved to be inadequate, it may take such action by air, sea, or land forces as may be necessary to maintain or restore international peace and security. Such action may include demonstrations, blockade, and other operations by air, sea, or land forces of Members of the United Nations." See http://legal.un.org/repertory/art42.shtml.

[67] Albrecht Randelzhofer/Oliver Dörr, Art. 2(4), MN 42 in Bruno Simma, et al. (eds.), *The Charter of the United Nations* 3rd ed. (Oxford University Press, 2012). Observe that the definition of a threat of force has received far less consideration in legal writings than that of the "use of force." But see Romana Sadurska, "Threats of Force," 82 (1988) *AJIL.* 239–268; Matthew A. Myers, "Deterrence and the Threat of Force Ban: Does the UN Charter Prohibit Some Military Exercises?," 162 (1999) *Military Law Review* 132–169; Marco Roscini, "Threats of Armed Force and Contemporary International Law" (2007) *Netherlands International Law Review* 229–277, at 243–258, 276–277; Nikolas Stürchler, *The Threat of Force In International Law* 218–251 (Cambridge University Press, 2007); Michael Wood, "Use of force, Prohibition of Threat," *MPEPIL*; James A. Green and Francis Grimal, "The Threat of Force as an Action in Self-Defense Under International Law" 44 (2011) *Vanderbilt Journal of Transnational Law,* 285–329; Francis Grimal, *Threats of Force: International Law and Strategy* (London and New York: Routledge, 2013). There may still be "a high degree of tolerance towards mere threats of force," as Randelzhofer/Dörr, id, suggest. But this does not apply to any threat with weapons of mass destruction.

[68] Marc Weller (ed.), *The Oxford Handbook of the Use of Force in International Law* (Oxford University Press, 2015), at pp. 32–33.

[69] By seven votes to seven, decided by the President's casting vote. In favor: President Bedjaoui; Judges Ranjeva, Herczegh, Shi, Fleischhauer, Vereshchetin, Ferrari Bravo; and Against: Vice-President Schwebel; Judges Oda, Guillaume, Shahabuddeen, Weeramantry, Koroma, Higgins.

[70] ICJ, ibid., paras. 95–97, 105(2)E. The fact that this finding was, and still is, extremely controversial, both inside the Court and in legal literature – see e.g. Laurence Boisson de Chazournes and Phillipe Sands (eds.),*International Law, the International Court of Justice and Nuclear Weapons* (Cambridge University Press, 1999); Ved P. Nanda and David Krieger, *Nuclear Weapons and the World Court* (Ardsley NY, Transnational Publishers, 1998); and more recently Daniel Thürer, "The Legality of the Threat or Use of Nuclear Weapons: The ICJ Advisory Opinion Reconsidered," inaugural speech, Geneva Academy of International Humanitarian Law (October 20, 2011), see www .geneva-academy.ch/docs/events/Adh-Geneva-inaugural-speech-2011-2012-Prof-Thuerer.pdf, at 8–17; John Borrie and Tim Caughley, *Viewing Nuclear Weapons through a Humanitarian Lens* (eds.), UNIDIR 2013, see www.unidir.org/files/publications/pdfs/viewing-nuclear-weapons-through-a-humani

The Threat of Force and the ICJ Advisory Opinion 219

such an assessment is likely to be in weighing and evaluating factors under such considerations in attempting to reach a sound and measured decision under extreme circumstances, especially in the broader context where the nuclear-weapon state sees nuclear deterrence as a legitimate position and nuclear defense as a viable option for its protection.

Judge Jiuyong Shi stated: "In my view, 'nuclear deterrence' is an instrument of policy which certain nuclear-weapon States use in their relations with other States and which is said to prevent the outbreak of a massive armed conflict or war, and to maintain peace and security among nations." One can debate that the policy of deterrence is just that, a policy, and therefore has no legal standpoint in the formation of a customary rule but should rather be an object regulated by law.[71] Judge Ferrari Bravo stated that a precise and specific rule prohibiting nuclear weapons does not yet exist. To this end, the policy of deterrence is lacking legal validity and force, and while being a legal practice of nuclear-weapon states and their allies, the policy of deterrence cannot be considered a legal practice which could be the basis of an international custom. Judge Ferrari Bravo stated "The theory of deterrence, to which the Advisory Opinion makes no more than passing reference (para. 96), would have merited further consideration. I have already said that, in my view, the idea of nuclear deterrence has no legal validity and I would add that the theory of deterrence, while creating a practice of nuclear-weapon States and their allies, is not able to create a legal practice which could serve as the basis for the creation of an international custom."[72] Judge Guillaume, in contrast, maintained that the Court ought to have explicitly recognized the legality of the policy of deterrence, particularly when it comes to the defense of the fundamental interests of states, as this has been the practice of a significant section of the international community for several years.[73] Agreeing with Judge Guillaume was Judge Fleischhauer who maintained that the policy of deterrence is based on the right of self-defense, and that the reservations to the treaties of Tlatelolco and Rarotonga as well as the lack of objections to these treaties indicate a practice which must be regarded as legal state practice.[74]

The Court was also "divided on the matter of whether non-recourse to nuclear weapons over the past fifty years constitutes the expression of an *opinio juris*."[75] The ICJ did not address the problem of "empty" or "unserious" threats which has become more visible in the meantime. The decision clearly requires putting strict limits on

---

tarian-lens-en-601.pdf – shall not be discussed in any detail here, as those controversies are fully part of the prevailing realities of nuclear deterrence and cannot remove the obligation under Art. VI NPT.

[71] Advisory Opinion, Declaration of Judge Shi, p. 277. See www.icj-cij.org/files/case-related/95/095-19960708-ADV-01-03-EN.pdf.

[72] At p. 284. Advisory Opinion, Declaration of Judge Ferrari Bravo, pp. 283–284. www.icj-cij.org/files/case-related/95/095-19960708-ADV-01-05-EN.pdf.

[73] Advisory Opinion, Separate Opinion of Judge Guillaume, pp. 290–291. See www.icj-cij.org/files/case-related/95/095-19960708-ADV-01-06-EN.pdf.

[74] Advisory Opinion, Separate Opinion of Judge Fleischhauer, pp. 307–309. See www.icj-cij.org/files/case-related/95/095-19960708-ADV-01-08-EN.pdf.

[75] ICJ, ibid., para. 67.

strategies of nuclear-weapon states to ensure that these are weapons of last resort for a victimized state to exercise its right of self-defense. In this context, it should also be considered that a policy of deterrence from nuclear attack as the "sole purpose" of nuclear weapons may be considered as further raising the threshold for nuclear weapons even beyond the policy of "no first use" of nuclear weapons[76] which was of certain influence during the Cold War.[77] In this context, recent technological developments in nuclear weapons and devices as well as their means of delivery deserve consideration. While precision guidance of delivery vehicles and systems as well as precision calibration of effectors may have undergone one or more innovation cycles since the end of the Cold War, and this development includes substrategic nuclear weapons, possible consequences for military operations need to be evaluated. Technological innovations may lead to the avoidance of casualties, but they might also lead to developments that could render the use of nuclear weapons more probable. Such issues must be balanced in light of the *jus ad bellum* and the *jus in bello*.

The ICJ 7:7 vote on the lawfulness of the threat or use of nuclear weapons in an extreme circumstance of self-defense demonstrates the narrow margin on this point. A future reassessment in light of the TPNW might render a different decision in the face of the growing body of support through this Treaty and the chorus of humanitarian principles in limiting the use of weapons generally. Developments regarding land mines, cluster munitions and chemical weapons, can hardly be ignored in examining whether any weapons with such a magnitude of blast and destructive force could be deemed appropriate within the context of the modern battlefield whereby the assured outcome would be tragic. At the same time in today's defense climate, it is questionable from a military and strategic point of view. It might be argued by NWS that land mines, cluster munitions and chemical weapons, are not essential for modern defense strategies; nuclear weapons are, as long as nuclear weapons exist.

Jus ad Bellum *and* Jus in Bello

The ICJ clearly drew a distinction between *jus ad bellum*[78] and *jus in bello*.[79] Its consideration on use vs. threat of use (para. 47) belongs to the former. By way of background, the principle of *jus ad bellum* refers to the conditions under which states may resort to war or to the use of armed force in general.[80] It may be thought of

---

[76] See Scott D. Sagan, "The Case for No First Use" (2009, June–July) *Survival*; Morton H. Halperin, Bruno Tetrais, Keith B. Pane, K. Subrahmanyam, Scott D. Sagan, "The Case for No First Use: An Exchange" (2009, October–November) *Survival*.

[77] See Josef Goldblat, Arms Control. A *Guide to Negotiations and Agreements* (Sage 1994), 197–199.

[78] Paras. 37–50.

[79] Paras. 51 and 74.

[80] "What Are jus ad bellum and jus in bello? By the International Committee of the Red Cross" (2015), online: see www.icrc.org/en/document/what-are-jus-ad-bellum-and-jus-in-bello-o.

as "law on the use of force" or *jus contra bellum* – law on the prevention of war – addressing the legitimate and illegitimate causes and the prevention of conflict.[81] The prohibition against the use of force amongst states and the exceptions to it, that is., self-defense and UN authorization for the use of force, set out in the UN Charter of 1945, form the core ingredients of *jus ad bellum*. Effectively, *jus ad bellum* sets out criteria to go to war with parameters for limiting justifications for going to war or entering into armed conflict. Questions of whether nuclear deterrence policies in and of themselves could constitute a threat that sets the conditions for war remain to be explored in the contemporary context of emerging humanitarian law. Whether North Korea's acquisition of nuclear arms, for example, could justify the use of force remains to be explored. If the United States were to rely on anticipatory self-defense in light of various threats it would certainly provoke much condemnation and cries of illegal action, especially if it were to use nuclear strikes in its operations. It is unlikely in today's climate that the United States could drop bombs on Hiroshima and Nagasaki, as it did in 1945, without facing heightened scrutiny. Indeed, they say that the purpose of nuclear deterrence is to ensure that nuclear weapons will not be used.

Jus in bello regulates the conduct of parties engaged in an armed conflict and may be thought of as the law in war, seeking to limit human suffering by protecting and assisting victims in conflict. It does this through the body of international humanitarian law (IHL) that protects victims irrespective of which side they fall on and regulates the behavior of fighting parties in terms of the humanitarian impact of their actions, regardless of fault or justifications.[82] Notably, IHL is taken to be synonymous with *jus in bello*, seeking to minimize suffering in armed conflicts, especially by protecting and assisting all victims of armed conflict to the greatest extent possible.[83] In that regard "IHL applies to the belligerent parties irrespective of the reasons for the conflict or the justness of the causes for which they are fighting . . . [It] is intended to protect victims of armed conflicts regardless of party affiliation. That is why *jus in bello* must remain independent of *jus ad bellum*."[84]

Effectively, *jus in bello* sets out acceptable behaviors in war and standards of conduct during conflict. It focuses on legitimate conduct in the unavoidable event that a state finds itself embroiled in armed conflict or military intervention. Using nuclear weapons during any conflict must be assessed in accordance with these emerging principles. It is likely that using nuclear weapons, as was done in Hiroshima and Nagasaki, would amount to prohibited behavior in a modern-day context. But the role of nuclear weapons in current strategies is different and more complex. The examination of whether a war was *just* was looked at separately from

---

[81] See "Towards a New European Security Strategy? Assessing the Impact of Changes in the Global Security Environment," online: see www.europarl.europa.eu/RegData/etudes/STUD/2015/534989/ EXPO_STU(2015)534989_EN.pdf.

[82] Ibid.

[83] "What Are jus ad bellum and jus in bello? By the International Committee of the Red Cross" (2015), online: see www.icrc.org/en/document/what-are-jus-ad-bellum-and-jus-bello-0.

[84] Ibid.

222   *Nuclear Defense Doctrines*

the examination of the conduct of warfare, hence the distinction between *jus ad bellum* and *jus in bello*.[85] *Jus in bello* rights and obligations apply irrespective of the parties' conviction as to whether the war is being fought for a just or unjust cause. This bifurcation was reflected in textual codifications of legal norms, specifically, the Hague Conventions[86] and Geneva Conventions[87] governing the conduct of warfare; whereas the Kellogg-Briand Pact[88] addressed the lawfulness of war itself. Needless to say, this normative conception of war has evolved over time with the distinction between a *just* war and the lawful waging of war eventually merging. This conceptual change emerged near the end of World War II with the adoption of the London Agreement[89] which established the Nuremberg War Crimes Tribunal, and under the adoption of the Charter of the United Nations.[90] Note that Nuremberg did not create, but confirmed this conviction – as per the principle *nullum crimen sine lege* – "no crime without law."[91] This Agreement and the Charter addressed

[85] See R. Lagoni, "Comments: Methods or Means of Warfare, Belligerent Reprisals, and the Principle of Proportionality," in I. F. Dekker and H. H. G. Post (eds.), *The Gulf War of 1980–1988* (The Hague: T. M.C. Asser Instituut, 1992) 115 at 118–119.

[86] Hague Convention (IV) Respecting the Laws and Customs of War on Land, with Annex of Regulations, October 18, 1907, T.S. No. 539, 1 Bevans 631, 36 Stat. 2277 (entered into force January 26, 1910) (hereinafter Hague Convention (IV)); Hague Convention (V) respecting the Rights and Duties of Neutral Powers and Persons in Case of War on Land, October 18, 1907, 205 Consol. T.S. 299 (entered into force January 26, 1910); Hague Convention (VI) relative to the Status of Enemy Merchant Ships at the Outbreak of Hostilities, October 18, 1970, 205 Consol. T.S. 305 (entered into force January 26, 1910); Hague Convention (VII) relative to the Conversion of Merchant-Ships into War-Ships, October 18, 1907, 205 Consol. T.S. 319 (entered into force January 26, 1910); Hague Convention (VIII) Relative to the Laying of Automatic Submarine Contact Mines, October 18, 1907, 205 Consol. T.S. 331 (entered into force January 26, 1910).

[87] Geneva Convention for the Amelioration of the Condition of the Wounded and Sick in Armed Forces in the Field, August 12, 1949, 75 UNTS 31 (entered into force October 21, 1950); Geneva Convention for the Amelioration of the Condition of Wounded, Sick and Shipwrecked Members of Armed Forces at Sea, August 12, 1949, 75 UNTS 85 (entered into force October 21, 1950); Geneva Convention relative to the Treatment of Prisoners of War, August 12, 1949, 75 UNTS 135, 6 UST 3316. TIAS No. 3364 (entered into force October 21, 1950); Geneva Convention Relative to the Protection of Civilian Persons in Time of War, August 12, 1949, 75 UNTS 287, 6 UST 3516, TIAS No. 3365 (entered into force October 21, 1950) (hereinafter Fourth Geneva Convention); Protocol Additional to the Geneva Conventions of August 12, 1949, and Relating to the Protection of Victims of International Armed Conflicts (Protocol I), December 7, 1978, 16 ILM 1391, (entered into force December 7, 1978) (hereinafter Geneva Convention-Protocol I); Protocol Additional to the Geneva Conventions of August 12, 1949, and Relating to the Protection of Victims of Non-International Armed Conflicts (Protocol II), June 8, 1977, 16 ILM1442 (entered into force December 7, 1978) (hereinafter Geneva Convention-Protocol II).

[88] Treaty Providing for the Renunciation of War as an Instrument of National Policy, August 27, 1928, LNTS 57, 46 Stat. 2343, T.S. No. 796, 2 Bevans 732 (entered into force for the United States July 24, 1929).

[89] Agreement for the Prosecution and Punishment of the Major War Criminals of the European Axis, and Charter of the International Military Tribunal, August 8, 1945, 82 UNTS 280, 59 Stat. 1544 (entered into force August 8, 1945) (hereinafter London Charter).

[90] See www.un.org/en/charter-united-nations/.

[91] The principle exists in criminal law and international criminal law in that a person will not or should not face criminal punishment except for an act that was criminalized by law before the act in question was performed. It may also be referred to as the legality principle and is often interchangeable with

The Threat of Force and the ICJ Advisory Opinion 223

both crimes against peace and war crimes in the same instrument, and more recently, the Rome Statute establishing the International Criminal Court.[92] IHL or the *jus in bello* imposes a set of principles regarding the protection of civilians during war and the need for proportionality when force is employed. In particular, the Geneva Conventions,[93] comprising four treaties and three additional protocols set out basic standards and international legal requirements for humanitarian treatment during hostilities. *Jus ad bellum*, by contrast, is often thought of from the perspective of the proper authority and public declaration. In this regard, intervention is to be waged under a legitimate or the right authority, which is usually rooted in the sovereign state and not insurgent or terrorist groups, for example. Intervention should be based on a just cause or have a right intention and should not be based on narrowly defined state-political interests but aimed at restoring the peace. The right to protect has been viewed as falling under such category. Indeed, such bases have been challenged under the Bush doctrines of anticipatory and pre-emptive self-defense. Another relevant consideration is the probability of success and whether the aim is achievable and effectively at what cost in terms of civilian populations. This is equally relevant with regard to nuclear attacks.

The rule of proportionality has to factor into consideration, intervention and methods employed during a conflict. The force and means exerted must be

---

"*nullum poena sine lege*," which translates to "no punishment without law." See www.law.cornell.edu /wex/nullum_crimen_sine_lege.

[92] Rome Statute of the International Criminal Court, July 17, 1998, Article 5, UN Doc. A/CONF.183 /9 [hereinafter ICC Statute]. See F. F. Martin et al., *International Human Rights Law & Practice: Cases, Treaties and Materials* (The Hague: Kluwer Law International, 1997) for a discussion of cases adjudicated by international human rights and war crimes tribunals. "Although war crimes and crimes against peace remain two different *crimes*, it does not necessarily follow that *jus in bello* and *jus ad bellum* cannot be integrated and unified insofar as the use of force is concerned, as this article will demonstrate. Furthermore, it is important to note that the law of armed conflict (and especially its criminal aspects) has not had the opportunity to develop as much as international human rights law because international human rights law has been interpreted by numerous global and regional tribunals, unlike the law of armed conflict. There is a substantially greater number of international human rights cases that have flushed out the international law governing armed conflict than cases decided by international criminal tribunals, and many of these human rights cases addressed the use of force in armed conflict."

[93] Convention (I) for the Amelioration of the Condition of the Wounded and Sick in Armed Forces in the Field. Geneva, August 12, 1949 (196 states parties); Convention (II) for the Amelioration of the Condition of Wounded, Sick and Shipwrecked Members of Armed Forces at Sea. Geneva, August 12, 1949 (196 states parties); Convention (III) relative to the Treatment of Prisoners of War. Geneva, August 12, 1949 (196 states parties); Convention (IV) relative to the Protection of Civilian Persons in Time of War. Geneva, August 12, 1949 (196 states parties); Protocol Additional to the Geneva Conventions of August 12, 1949, and relating to the Protection of Victims of International Armed Conflicts (Protocol I), June 8, 1977 (174 states parties, 3 states signatories); Protocol Additional to the Geneva Conventions of August 12, 1949, and relating to the Protection of Victims of Non-International Armed Conflicts (Protocol II), June 8, 1977 (168 states parties, 3 states signatories); and Protocol additional to the Geneva Conventions of August 12, 1949, and relating to the Adoption of an Additional Distinctive Emblem (Protocol III), December 8, 2005 (75 states parties, 21 states signatories). See www.icrc.org/en/war-and-law/treaties-customary-law/geneva-conventions.

proportionate to the military objective, which is particularly relevant to a discussion regarding the employment of nuclear force. In exerting such force, issues of collateral damage must be assessed in relation to a justifiable measure. The use of a powerful blast may well be deemed disproportionate and excessive by reasonably objective standards. The question is whether the excessive effects caused by the blast and the subsequent radiation, including heat, blast, electromagnetic pulse and radiation effects[94] would be considered excessive and disproportionate. In addition, international humanitarian law stipulates that weapons may not be used if they cause unnecessary suffering or superfluous injury to combatants. The 1868 St Petersburg Declaration sought to limit weapons "which uselessly aggravate the suffering of disabled men or render their death inevitable."[95] Moreover, the IV Hague Convention of 1907 prohibited the use of "arms, projectiles, or material calculated to cause unnecessary suffering."[96] In particular, Additional Protocol I to the Geneva Conventions 1977 states: "It is prohibited to employ weapons, projectiles and material and methods of warfare of a nature to cause superfluous injury or unnecessary suffering."[97] While this rule is primarily intended to protect combatants during conflict, civilians also benefit indirectly from such protections.[98] Notably, in its *Advisory Opinion* the ICJ highlighted that this is one of the most fundamental rules of IHL, and that it was directly relevant to nuclear weapons.[99]

In addition, armed intervention must be waged as a last resort in that all peaceful means must have been exhausted before such a measure is implemented and especially where there is the deployment of nuclear weapons. The ICJ, in its consideration on use versus the threat of use concluded: "In short, if it is to be lawful, the declared readiness of a State to use force must be a use of force that is in conformity with the Charter."[100] Additionally, "if the use of force itself in a given case is illegal – for whatever reason – the threat to use such force will likewise be illegal."[101] The Court emphasized that the use of nuclear weapons "in fact seems

---

[94] Charles J. Moxley, John Burroughs and Jonathan Granoff, "Nuclear Weapons and Compliance with International Humanitarian Law and the Nuclear Non-Proliferation Treaty" (2011) 34:4 *Fordham Intl LJ* 595 at 642.

[95] *Legality of the Threat or Use of Nuclear Weapons*, Advisory Opinion, [1996] ICJ Rep 226 at para. 77.

[96] Convention (IV) respecting the Laws and Customs of War on Land and its annex: Regulations concerning the Laws and Customs of War on Land, October 18, 1907, the Hague art. 23(e).

[97] Protocol Additional to the Geneva Conventions of August 12, 1949, and relating to the Protection of Victims of International Armed Conflicts (Protocol I), June 8, 1977, 1125 UNTS 3 art. 35(2).

[98] Louis Maresca and Eleanor Mitchell, "The Human Costs and Legal Consequences of Nuclear Weapons Under International Humanitarian Law" (2015) 97:899, *Intl Rev of the Red Cross* 621 at 637.

[99] *Legality of the Threat or Use of Nuclear Weapons*, Advisory Opinion, [1996] ICJ Rep. 226 at 638.

[100] Para. 47.

[101] ICJ, ibid., paras. 47 and 95. For a more detailed legal assessment see D. Fleck, "Nuclear Weapons," Chapter 16, in Rain Liivoja/Tim McCormack (eds.), *Routledge Handbook of the Law of Armed Conflict* (Routledge, 2014).

scarcely reconcilable" with the principle of distinction between civilian objects and military objectives and the prohibition of unnecessary suffering.[102] Given the progress under international humanitarian law, it is likely that a Court would issue an even stronger rebuke regarding the use of such weapons, depending of course on the strength and size of the weapon deployed.

An aspect of nuclear weapons worth noting is the sheer destructive force which invariably distinguishes them from conventional weapons. Hence, applying the laws of war to the potential use of nuclear weapons proves to be difficult.[103] Nevertheless, all nuclear-weapon states, including the United States, maintain that the same laws of war governing the use of conventional weapons, in general also apply to nuclear weapons, including the principles of proportionality and distinction.[104] Note that new rules introduced under the Additional Protocol were intended to apply to conventional weapons, irrespective of any other rules of international law applicable to other types of weapons, and consequently they do not influence, regulate, or prohibit the use of nuclear weapons, per se.[105]

Indeed, the Protocol Additional to the Geneva Conventions of 12 August 1949, and Relating to the Protection of Victims of International Armed Conflicts (Protocol I) (hereinafter Geneva Conventions – Protocol I or API) addresses the use of force against combatants in relation to *jus in bello*. Article 35 states: "It is prohibited to employ weapons, projectiles and material and methods of warfare of a nature to cause superfluous injury or unnecessary suffering." This Rule requires a balancing test during conflict, with suffering and injury that is "unnecessary" or "superfluous" measured against the weapons and force used during conflict. Such deliberations require deeper enquiry. It would seem that the unpredictability of the level and degree of injury remains hypothetical. A precautionary approach would be that no use is the safest.

Notably, the ICJ articulated the status of the law at that time, wherein the TPNW has added another important dimension to the ever-emerging practice amongst states around the world. The following discussion will examine such developments.

---

[102] ICJ, ibid., paras. 47 and 95. For a more detailed legal assessment, see D. Fleck, "Nuclear Weapons," Chapter 16, in Rain Liivoja/Tim McCormack (eds.), *Routledge Handbook of the Law of Armed Conflict* (Routledge, 2014).

[103] See Christopher Vail, "The Legality of Nuclear Weapons for Use and Deterrence," 48 *Geo. J. Int'l L.* 839 (2017).

[104] See US Department of Defense, Law of War Manuel 393 (2015).

[105] See the "nuclear weapons clause," UK *Manual of the Law of Armed Conflict* (Oxford University Press, 2004), para. 6.17; see also the Letter from Department of State Legal Adviser, John B. Bellinger III, and Department of Defense General Counsel, William J. Haynes II, to the President of the International Committee of the Red Cross (ICRC) Dr. Jakob Kellenberger, November 3, 2006, in *International Legal Materials* (2007), 514–531 and 866 *International Review of the Red Cross* (2007), 443–471, see www.icrc.org/en/international-review/article/us-government-response-international-committee-red-cross-study.

226 *Nuclear Defense Doctrines*

THE IMPLEMENTATION OF THE TPNW AND ITS POTENTIAL FOR CHANGE AS TO HOW NUCLEAR WEAPONS ARE PERCEIVED AND UTILIZED AROUND THE WORLD

The TPNW highlights a growing collective determination by many states that nuclear deterrence under global security and defense umbrellas is viewed as a threat to peace and security. The position is definitively emerging whereby civil society organizations, individual citizens and countries alike are demanding a reconsideration of defense doctrines based on nuclear deterrence. They are calling for an outright ban on nuclear weapons under any circumstances. Many states see the continued retention and modernization of nuclear weapons as not only unacceptable, but actually imperiling peace. For example, R. M. Marty M. Natalegawa, minister for foreign affairs of Indonesia, speaking on behalf of the Non-Aligned Movement, stated at the 2010 NPT Review Conference, that,

> 40 years after the [NPT] Treaty's entry into force and 20 years after the end of the cold war, the world was still at a critical juncture … It was unacceptable that nuclear-weapon States and those remaining outside the NPT continued to retain and even modernize their nuclear arsenals, imperilling the regional and international peace and security, in particular, in the Middle East. That was a dangerous and destabilizing trend of vertical proliferation. It also constituted non-compliance by the nuclear-weapon States with their article VI obligations. Moreover, as long as some States possessed those weapons, there would always be a tendency for others to seek to possess them.[106]

As discussed in previous chapters, under the adoption and successive implementation of the TPNW, the defense strategy of any signatory countries can no longer include nuclear weapons as the Treaty specifically prohibits the use, development, storage, stationing and installation of nuclear weapons in a signatory's sovereign land.[107] This raises a number of questions regarding potentially evolving normative behavior and obligations for various states, especially for those that adopt the TPNW, and their relationship with those that do not. The introduction of the TPNW marks a dramatic shift under international law as to how the world perceives nuclear weapons and most notably how many non-NATO states and civil society organizations wish to approach nuclear defense doctrines from this point forward. Upon the fiftieth ratification, the TPNW comes into force,[108] altering the international legal landscape with the intent to disrupt the status quo in this important

---

[106] Statement by H. E. Dr. R. M. Marty M. Natalegawa, Minister of Foreign Affairs of the Republic of Indonesia on behalf of the Non-Aligned Movement, to the NPT before the 2010 Review Conference (May 3, 2010). See DC/3226 "You Are Here Not Simply to Avoid a Nuclear Nightmare," Secretary-General Tells Nuclear Non-Proliferation Treaty Review, "But to Build a Safer World for All," see www.un.org/press/en/2010/dc3226.doc.htm and www.un.org/en/conf/npt/2010/statements/pdf/nam_en.pdf, p. 3.

[107] Article 1, Treaty on the Prohibition of Nuclear Weapons, A/CONF.229/2017/8.

[108] Article 15.1, Treaty on the Prohibition of Nuclear Weapons, A/CONF.229/2017/8.

The TPNW and Its Potential for Change

area regarding law, diplomacy and defense policies. The implementation of the TPNW requires a major reassessment of well-accepted military positions, as well as reopening long-standing divides such as whether under the TPNW the possession or use of nuclear weapons would be considered a "threat of force" under Article 2(4) of the UN Charter, or an act of aggression under Article 39.[109] Effectively, the TPNW now prohibits both the threat and the use of nuclear weapons making it illegal for those who ratify the treaty.

The Treaty on the Prevention of Nuclear Weapons and the Nuclear Weapons Advisory Opinion

With the inception of the TPNW, the decision on the *Legality of the Threat or Use of Nuclear Weapons* determined today might be quite different. In light of the various humanitarian developments that have arisen since 1996, including the TPNW, it certainly would be argued differently. The issue of whether the use of nuclear weapons would be either lawful or unlawful in an extreme circumstance of self-defense (Article 51) pursuant to Article 2(4) would be irrelevant if nuclear weapons were deemed illegal. The *Lotus* principle highlights that legality or illegality stems from explicit prohibitions, and as the Court in the *Advisory Opinion* concluded, traditionally the illegality of weapons of mass destruction has taken place through treaties of prohibition. That is to say, the use of nuclear weapons may be on the way to becoming illegal even when used in self-defense. In order for this to happen, the TPNW would have to be accepted as a law-making treaty in order to be binding within this context.

Law-making treaties are treaties which lay down general rules and are applicable to the international community generally, as opposed to ordinary treaties merely binding between the parties.[110] In order for a treaty to have a law-making effect, special attention needs to be given to the number of parties to the treaty, the general acceptance of the rules by states and sometimes the declaratory character of the provisions (i.e., the universal form of an obligation).[111] Examples of treaties of this kind are the Hague Regulations of 1899 and 1907, and the 1925 Geneva Protocol, and, more recently, the United Nations Convention on the Law of the Sea (UNCLOS). An important characteristic of law-making treaties is a large number of ratifications to these treaties. *The Encyclopedia Dictionary of International Law* notes that,

> [T]reaties concluded for the purpose of laying down general rules of conduct among a considerable number of States ... may be termed "law-making" treaties ... In a sense the distinction between law-making treaties and other of

---

[109] Charter of the United Nations, 59 Stat. 1031; TS 993; 3 Bevans 1153. See N. Stürchler, *The Threat of Force in International Law* (Cambridge University Press, 2007).

[110] Jennings and Watts, p. 32; Crawford, p. 31; Clapham, pp. 55–56.

[111] Ibid.

treaties is merely one of convenience. In principle, all treaties are law-making inasmuch as they lay down rules of conduct which the parties are bound to observe as law. However, relatively extensive participation in a treaty, coupled with a subject matter of general significance and stipulations which accord with the general sense of the international community, do establish for treaties an influence far beyond the limits of formal participation in them. These factors give such a treaty something of the complexion of a legislative instrument, and assist the acceptance of the treaty's provisions as customary international law in addition to their contractual value for the parties.[112]

It seems likely that the TPNW will eventually have large numbers of ratifications. But questions remain as to what constitutes a "considerable number" of states as long as there remain states that persistently object to the rules. Questions for TPNW supporters arise as to how this ever could apply to treaties rejected by certain states. Presently, the five NPT nuclear-states show no desire to become signatories to the treaty. Could TPNW states create rules binding others – absent a practical possibility? Will TPNW states try to deny the right to self-defense to other states facing overwhelming conventional armament by an aggressor state? TPNW supporters may hope they can eventually do so.

Despite the fact that nuclear-weapon states are non-parties, as well as persistent objectors, as the TPNW comes into force and is fully implemented by state parties to it, calls to revisit issues from the *Legality of the Threat or Use of Nuclear Weapons Advisory Opinion* are likely to be brought forward. Should that occur, the ICJ would face evidence from General Assembly resolutions along with the TPNW, itself, regarding emerging customary international law prohibiting nuclear weapons. As discussed in Chapter 2, in 2015 the UNGA Resolution 70/33 established a working group to address concrete effective measures and legal provisions for maintaining a nuclear-free world.[113] The working group presented a report in 2016 recommending a legally binding instrument;[114] followed by the UNGA resolution of November 2016 calling upon "States participating in the conference to make their best endeavours to conclude as soon as possible a legally binding instrument to prohibit nuclear weapons, leading towards their total elimination ..."[115] This led directly to the draft text of the TPNW and its subsequent successful adoption in July 2017. Again, the ICJ would likely be asked to determine whether these General Assembly resolutions relating to the legality of nuclear weapons along with a binding TPNW, signed and ratified by a substantial number of States representing a large percentage of the world's population, represents emerging customary international law prohibiting nuclear weapons.

[112] *Perry and Grant Encyclopedia Dictionary of International Law* (third ed.) John P. Grand and J. Craig Barker (Oxford University Press, 2009), at pp. 337–338.

[113] Para. 1. GA Resolution 70/33. See http://undocs.org/A/RES/70/33.

[114] See www.unidir.org/files/publications/pdfs/the-2016-open-ended-working-group-en-660.pdf.

[115] Para. 12. United Nations. (2016). *General and Complete Disarmament: Taking forward Multilateral Nuclear Disarmament Negotiations* (A/C.1/71/L.41).

The TPNW and Its Potential for Change 229

Such developments will draw security assurances into question. With the adoption of the NPT the Security Council welcomed "the intention expressed by certain states that they will provide support and immediate assistance, in accordance with the Charter, to any non-nuclear-weapon State Party to the Treaty on the Non-Proliferation of Nuclear Weapons that is a victim of an act or an object of a threat of aggression in which nuclear weapons are used."[116] These "positive assurances" need review in light of the TPNW. Non-first use policies result in negative security guarantees which are also extended to non-nuclear weapon states under security alliances. A first-use of nuclear weapons is not excluded by eight states, the United States, the United Kingdom, France and Russia, Pakistan, India, North Korea and Israel. Only China has undertaken "not to be the first to use nuclear weapons at any time or under any circumstances."[117]

Again, referring to Article VI of the NPT, the ICJ notes states' obligations in relation to their respective duties. Arguably, this gives credence to the TPNW in three ways. Firstly, it demonstrates a positive duty to disarm under strict and effective control. Secondly, states parties have not expressly rejected this stipulation declared by the Court. Thirdly, their continued statements of their commitments to disarmament reinforce a position accepting disarmament. In essence, their obligation under Article VI, along with the Court's pronouncement, in conjunction with their own continued statements of their commitments to disarmament demonstrate an overall obligation to disarm, and surely such an obligation must be even more pressing in light of the developments under the TPNW.

It would seem that the TPNW cannot be construed as establishing *opinio juris* through its adoption by some 122 states at the General Assembly, or as a declaration of state practice, as it remains at odds with the practice of a number of states, including those expressing their continued need of nuclear weapons for defense and deterrence purposes at this point in time. That said, whether the ICJ today would accept the existence of the policy of nuclear deterrence as a fact under emerging norms remains to be answered. The TPNW transforms it into an "issue." While it may be accepted that nuclear-weapon states do "in fact" have nuclear weapons; the acceptability of this position, however, may be questioned in light of the TPNW. This is increasingly problematic in the absence an apparent legitimate attempt or meaningful intension to negotiate a disarmament treaty either in good faith or in a timely manner, as per Article VI of the NPT. Some would take the view that the five permanent members of the UN Security Council (the United States, the United Kingdom, China, Russia and France), which all possess nuclear

---

[116] SC Res 255 (1968), para. 2.

[117] UN Doc S/1995/265, para. 1. While in the most recent Chinese White Paper on Defence (2013). The Diversified Employment of China's Armed Forces (Beijing, April 2013), news.xinhuanet.com/english/china/2013-04/16/c_132312681.htm. This commitment has not been reaffirmed (as nuclear issues have not been addressed explicitly in this document), no-first-use of nuclear weapons remains stated Chinese policy.

230 *Nuclear Defense Doctrines*

arms under the terms of the NPT, are not fulfilling their full obligations under Article VI of that Treaty. It requires nuclear disarmament and agreement on a treaty to that effect under strict and effective international control. The obvious emerging "fact" is recalcitrance on their part in fulfilling their legal obligations under Article VI.

Recent Developments under International Human Rights Law

Emerging principles expressed in the TPNW, as discussed throughout the working group sessions and explored in Chapter 2, would surely play into any analysis and *jus ad bellum* considerations. Although both the *jus ad bellum* and the *jus in bello* have not changed since 1996, there are a number of considerations worth noting in today's context. For example, in regard to nuclear and other weapons of mass destruction, in October 2018 the UN Human Rights Committee adopted a new general comment on the right to life pursuant to Article 6[118] of the *International Covenant on Civil and Political Rights*.[119] Of relevance to this discussion, its opening sentence reads: "The threat or use of weapons of mass destruction, in particular nuclear weapons, which are indiscriminate in effect and are of a nature to cause destruction of human life on a catastrophic scale is incompatible with respect for the right to life and may amount to a crime under international law." The comment goes on to note that "States parties must take all necessary measures to stop the proliferation of weapons of mass destruction, including ... to refrain from developing ... and using them, [as well as] to destroy existing stockpiles ... all in accordance with their international obligations."[120]

[118] The Committee notes that, "Article 6 recognizes and protects the right to life of all human beings. It is the supreme right from which no derogation is permitted even in situations of armed conflict and other public emergencies which threatens the life of the nation." At para. 2.

[119] Human Rights Committee General Comment No. 36 (2018) on Article 6 of the International Covenant on Civil and Political Rights, on the right to life. See https://tbinternet.ohchr.org /Treaties/CCPR/Shared%20Documents/1_Global/CCPR_C_GC_36_8785_E.pdf. For background on the general comment, see Office of the High Representative for Human Rights: see www .ohchr.org/EN/NewsEvents/Pages/DisplayNews.aspx?NewsID=23797&LangID=E

[120] Specifically, para. 66 states in full: "The threat or use of weapons of mass destruction, in particular nuclear weapons, which are indiscriminate in effect and are of a nature to cause destruction of human life on a catastrophic scale is incompatible with respect for the right to life and may amount to a crime under international law. States parties must take all necessary measures to stop the proliferation of weapons of mass destruction, including measures to prevent their acquisition by non-state actors, to refrain from developing, producing, testing, acquiring, stockpiling, selling, transferring and using them, to destroy existing stockpiles, and to take adequate measures of protection against accidental use, all in accordance with their international obligations. They must also respect their international obligations to pursue in good faith negotiations in order to achieve the aim of nuclear disarmament under strict and effective international control. and to afford adequate reparation to victims whose right to life has been or is being adversely affected by the testing or use of weapons of mass destruction, in accordance with principles of international responsibility." See Treaty on the Non-Proliferation of Nuclear Weapons, July 1, 1968, 729 UNTS 161; Comprehensive Test Ban Treaty, September 10, 1996, Treaty on the Prohibition of Nuclear Weapons, July 7, 2017 (not yet in force); Convention on the Prohibition of the Development, Production and Stockpiling of Bacteriological (Biological) and Toxin Weapons and on their Destruction, April 10, 1972, 1015 UNTS 163;

The significance of this comment cannot be ignored. First and foremost, the Human Rights Committee (HRC) remarks that the mere threat, and not exclusively the use, of such weapons would be incompatible with the right to life under Article 6. This stand is consistent with a central feature of the TPNW as listed under Article 1(d), which sets out to prohibit state parties from both using and threatening to use nuclear weapons. Daniel Rietiker points out that: "Both clauses are powerful statements against the threat of nuclear weapons. In view of the centrality of threat to now decades-old reliance on nuclear weapons in military and security postures, they will be significant tools in delegitimizing 'nuclear deterrence' as contrary to international law as well as common sense in view of the immense risks involved."[121]

Torture, Cruel or Inhuman Treatment under International Humanitarian Law

International humanitarian law, as it pertains to *jus ad bellum* is relevant to armed conflicts, be they international or non-international in nature. The ICRC highlights that the prohibition of torture was already recognized in the Lieber Code, under Article 16,[122] further noting that Article 6(b) of the Charter of the International Military Tribunal at Nuremberg included "ill-treatment" of civilians and prisoners of war as a war crime.[123] Common Article 3 of the Geneva Conventions prohibits "cruel treatment and torture" and "outrages upon personal dignity, in particular humiliating and degrading treatment" of civilians and persons *hors de combat*.[124] The concept of torture will be discussed in greater detail in Chapter 12, but suffice it to say at this point that military defense doctrines must consider such issues in relation to their use of nuclear weapons under appropriate *jus ad bellum* requirements.

Nuclear Weapons, International Humanitarian Law and the TPNW

It could be argued that the TPNW further illustrates that nuclear weapons may violate *jus ad bellum*. There is no doubt that this is not a simple conclusion. Legal scholars are divided as to whether using nuclear weapons is illegal under international law. On the one hand, the disastrous health conditions and physical effects inflicted upon victims of nuclear attacks render their use incompatible with modern-

---

Convention on the Prohibition of the Development, Production, Stockpiling and Use of Chemical Weapons and on Their Destruction, September 3, 1992, 1974 UNTS 45. [274] General Comment 14, para. 7. Cf. Legality of the Threat or Use of Nuclear Weapons, 1996 ICJ 226, 267. [275] Concluding Observations: France (2015), para. 21.

[121]   Threat and use of nuclear weapons contrary to right to life, says UN Human Rights Committee. See https://safna.org/2018/11/07/threat-and-use-of-nuclear-weapons-contrary-to-right-to-life-says-un-human-rights-committee/; Rietiker.

[122]   Lieber Code, Article 16 (cited in Vol. II, Ch. 32, § 1010).

[123]   IMT Charter (Nuremberg), Article 6(b) (ibid., § 982).

[124]   Geneva Conventions, common Article 3 (ibid., § 984). As quoted from: https://ihl-databases.icrc.org /customary-ihl/eng/docs/v1_rul_rule90.

232   *Nuclear Defense Doctrines*

day humanitarian principles of customary international law. Some argue that the military advantage would never outweigh the indiscriminate and uncontrollable humanitarian implications caused by the spread of radiation. Poignantly, the indiscriminate aspect alone may be seen to violate *jus ad bellum*. Arguably, there are more precise tactical weapons which are more discriminate in focus, but even the most strategic nuclear weapons used in conflict have indiscriminate adverse effects.

Perhaps the TPNW complicates the current position moving further toward a position that nuclear weapons violate *jus ad bellum* requirements. In discussing the legality of nuclear weapons and how the laws of war would apply, theoretically, it could be argued that the use of nuclear weapons would be a violation of IHL due to the restrictions of proportionality and the distinction in international law between the types of weapons that states use.[125] The principles of proportionality and distinction come from customary international law and have been confirmed by Additional Protocol I of the Geneva Conventions, which came into effect in 1977. The term distinction refers to an indiscriminate attack that could be construed to include a weapon that causes a disproportionate amount of injury to civilians.[126] Article 51 of Additional Protocol I to the Geneva Conventions states and further specifies the proportionality rule.[127]

---

[125] See Elliott L. Meyrowitz, *Prohibition of Nuclear Weapons: The Relevance of International Law* (Dobbs Ferry, New York: Transnational Publishers Inc 1990).

[126] Article 48 provides the Basic rule: "In order to ensure respect for and protection of the civilian population and civilian objects, the Parties to the conflict shall at all times distinguish between the civilian population and combatants and between civilian objects and military objectives and accordingly shall direct their operations only against military objectives." https://ihl-databases.icrc .org/applic/ihl/ihl.nsf/Article.xsp?action=openDocument&documentId=8A9E7E14C63C7F30C12563 CD0051DC5C. Note as well that under Article 4(1) of the draft Additional Protocol II submitted by the ICRC to the CDDH provided: "In order to ensure respect for the civilian population, the parties to the conflict ... shall make a distinction between the civilian population and combatants." This proposal was amended and adopted by consensus in Committee III of the CDDH. The approved text provided: "In order to ensure respect and protection for the civilian population ... the Parties to the conflict shall at all times distinguish between the civilian population and combatants." It was later deleted in the plenary, because it failed to obtain the necessary two-thirds majority (thirty-six in favor, nineteen against and thirty-six abstentions). The preamble to the 1997 Ottawa Convention on Anti-Personnel Mines, states parties based their agreement on various principles of IHL, including "the principle that a distinction must be made between civilians and combatants." In addition, the preamble to the 2008 Convention on Cluster Munitions, states parties based their agreement on the prohibition of the use, development, production, stockpiling, retention or transfer of cluster munitions on various principles of IHL, including "the rule ... that the parties to a conflict shall at all times distinguish between the civilian population and combatants." See https://ihl-databases.icrc.org/customary-ihl/eng/ docs/v2_rul_rule1.

[127] "Protection of the civilian population 1. The civilian population and individual civilians shall enjoy general protection against dangers arising from military operations. To give effect to this protection, the following rules, which are additional to other applicable rules of international law, shall be observed in all circumstances. 2. The civilian population as such, as well as individual civilians, shall not be the object of attack. Acts or threats of violence the primary purpose of which is to spread terror among the civilian population are prohibited. 3. Civilians shall enjoy the protection afforded by this Section, unless and for such time as they take a direct part in hostilities. 4. Indiscriminate attacks are prohibited. Indiscriminate attacks are: (a) those which are not directed at a specific military objective; (b) those which employ

The TPNW and Its Potential for Change 233

In relation to the 1996 Court consideration as to whether the use of nuclear weapons could ever be compatible with international humanitarian law, Greenwood notes that "it is here that its answer becomes particularly enigmatic."[128] Accordingly, the ICJ held unanimously that "[a] threat or use of nuclear weapons should also be compatible with the requirements of the international law applicable in armed conflict, particularly those of the principles and rules of international humanitarian law, as well as with specific obligations under treaties and other undertakings which expressly deal with nuclear weapons."[129] This, of course, was in addition to complying with provisions of the UN Charter regarding the use of force. With this in mind, proponents of the TPNW will invariably seize the opportunity to argue that the TPNW advances international humanitarian law, and that the use of nuclear weapons is now explicitly prohibited and incompatible. Others may not enthusiastically embrace this perspective, and although they acknowledge the evolution of principles and approaches to international law, in that regard, IHL has not changed since 1996. At the time, in examining whether there was a prohibition of nuclear weapons in international humanitarian law, the Court found that no specific and comprehensive prohibition existed, either in customary or conventional law. In reviewing relevant treaties which served to limit the possession, testing and deployment of nuclear weapons, such as those within nuclear-weapon-free zones (i.e., the 1967 Treaty of Tlatelolco),[130] the Court held that those treaties, too, did not amount to a comprehensive prohibition of the use of nuclear weapons as a matter of existing international law.[131] Specifically,

a method or means of combat which cannot be directed at a specific military objective; or (c) those which employ a method or means of combat the effects of which cannot be limited as required by this Protocol; and consequently, in each such case, are of a nature to strike military objectives and civilians or civilian objects without distinction. 5. Among others, the following types of attacks are to be considered as indiscriminate: (a) an attack by bombardment by any methods or means which treats as a single military objective a number of clearly separated and distinct military objectives located in a city, town, village or other area containing a similar concentration of civilians or civilian objects; and (b) an attack which may be expected to cause incidental loss of civilian life, injury to civilians, damage to civilian objects, or a combination thereof, which would be excessive in relation to the concrete and direct military advantage anticipated. 6. Attacks against the civilian population or civilians by way of reprisals are prohibited. 7. The presence or movements of the civilian population or individual civilians shall not be used to render certain points or areas immune from military operations, in particular in attempts to shield military objectives from attacks or to shield, favor or impede military operations. The Parties to the conflict shall not direct the movement of the civilian population or individual civilians in order to attempt to shield military objectives from attacks or to shield military operations. 8. Any violation of these prohibitions shall not release the Parties to the conflict from their legal obligations with respect to the civilian population and civilians, including the obligation to take the precautionary measures provided for in Article 57." https://ihl-databases.icrc.org/applic/ihl/ihl.nsf/Article.xsp?action=openDocument&documentId=4BEB D9920AE0AEAEC12563CD0051DC9E.

[128] See The Advisory Opinion on nuclear weapons and the contribution of the International Court to international humanitarian law by Christopher Greenwood, February 28, 1997 Article, *International Review of the Red Cross*, No. 316 at p. 70.

[129] At para. 2D.

[130] Treaty for the Prohibition of Nuclear Weapons in Latin America and the Caribbean – Treaty of Tlatelolco (February 14, 1967), 634 *UNTS* 326.

[131] Opinion, paras. 58–63.

234 *Nuclear Defense Doctrines*

a number of States have undertaken not to use nuclear weapons in specific zones (Latin America; the South Pacific) or against certain other States (non-nuclear-weapon States which are parties to the Treaty on the Non-Proliferation of Nuclear Weapons)

. . .

nevertheless, even within this framework, the nuclear weapon States have reserved the right to use nuclear weapons in certain circumstances.[132]

So, while some instruments may restrict the use of nuclear weapons in certain regions, there is no instrument that specifically prohibits nuclear weapons.[133] That said, the adoption of the TPNW may be argued as emblematic of changing views, whereby some might argue that there has been change over the past twenty years and the adoption of the TPNW represents such an evolution, marking distinct changes and calling for a reassessment of such positions.

CONCLUSIONS

It would seem that existing international law under the UN Charter, ICJ jurisprudence and customary state practice does not expressly prohibit the threat of use under military nuclear doctrines. That said, the TPNW now does so. Indeed, there are mounting claims that nuclear weapons should be declared illegal, outright.

Amid this seemingly intractable debate, there is growing support for the belief that the use of nuclear weapons would constitute a serious breach of international humanitarian law. Moreover, there is traction behind the opinion that the threat of nuclear weapons under deterrence policies could be perceived as a "threat of force" under Article 2(4) and a "threat to the peace," as per Article 39 of the UN Charter. Veiled threats aside, arguably first-use policies and promises of force not only serve to threaten global and regional security, but are a "breach of the peace, or [even an] act of aggression" under Article 39 of the Charter in today's context. Such emerging positions challenge the status quo regarding hitherto accepted deterrence policies.

It would seem that the world is divided into two different spheres, one that allows nuclear weapons, including threats of which deterrence is included, and another that does not allow such threats and feels they should be abolished. Indeed, the gap seems to be widening with no apparent bridge to unite the two camps. That said, the dichotomy demonstrates the mobilization of a different way of thinking about nuclear issues generally and deterrence and defense doctrines in particular. Just as those who argued to have the threat of use of nuclear weapons and devices included in the TPNW persisted until it was prohibited under Article 1, they now feel they will persist in changing hearts and minds through persuasion and stigmatization until

---

[132] At paras. 49–73. See www.icj-cij.org/files/case-related/95/7497.pdf.
[133] At paras. 52–63.

governments either accept or are forced by their citizens to reconsider their respective positions and find new ways forward regarding their nuclear deterrence policies.

It remains to be seen how the TPNW, which marks a shift in how the world perceives and approaches nuclear weapons, will develop globally as it pertains to the possession or use of nuclear weapons as well as a "threat of force" under Article 2(4) of the UN Charter,[134] and how it will influence normative behavior. That said, developments under the TPNW seem to mandate fresh thinking and new challenges to security orthodoxy amid emerging new trends. Nuclear states say that their defense doctrines protect global security. Supporters of the TPNW say these doctrines threaten it. Activists are looking to their roots to support their cause. They are turning to the very humanitarian principles on which the TPNW is based to argue that nuclear weapons should be declared illegal under emerging customary international humanitarian law; the standards and principles on which the TPNW is founded.

---

[134] Charter of the United Nations, 59 Stat. 1031; TS 993; 3 Bevans 1153.

9

Competition, Fragmentation and Polarization: A Bifurcated International Legal Infrastructure Regarding the Nuclear Architecture and Regulation?

THE TPNW: UNITING DIVISION

Nothing about developing and implementing a treaty on the prohibition of nuclear weapons is easy. While supporters of the TPNW undoubtedly claim a victory in its coming into being, its opponents note its shortcomings warning of the adverse and dire consequences. The degree to which such concerns will materialize remains to be seen. What is certain, however, is that the adoption of the TPNW has marked the beginning of a new schism in the international community. The word schism is appropriate in this context, loosely defined as "a split or division between strongly opposed sections or parties, caused by differences in opinion or belief."[1] It is not the case that such a definition was tailored to the negotiations surrounding the TPNW. Nevertheless it seems to apply aptly to the current context.

There is no doubt that various positions relating to nuclear weapons have prevailed since World War II, with many conflicting views over such delicate matters and strong divisions manifesting themselves. The Treaty negotiations and the quest for signatures and accessions has taken this to a whole new level, however. From the start of these developments, various parties staked their claim, transforming what should have been an opportunity to move toward disarmament, a goal that the overwhelming majority of states said they wanted. Instead, the process was marred by political posturing and mired in divisive language. Few issues have divided the international community in the same manner, and to the same extent. Indeed, the situation has deteriorated into a massive rupture dividing the family of nations into two distinct camps: those for the Treaty on the Prohibition of Nuclear Weapons and those against it. Suffice it to say, there is a new playing field in the global community pitting nuclear-aligned states firmly against non-nuclear aligned states.

In the wake of key states refusing to participate in the negotiations, agreement on the final text or the adoption of the treaty at the General Assembly, the world is left to

---

[1] English Oxford Living Dictionaries. See https://en.oxforddictionaries.com/definition/schism. Its origin from "Late Middle English and from Old French scisme, via ecclesiastical Latin from Greek skhisma 'cleft', from skhizein 'to split,'" may more aptly describe the current situation.

decipher the consequences and long-term ramifications of this acrimonious episode that has led to an intractable division. This problem is especially acute amid treaty skeptics' concerns regarding its wording and its uncertain relationship to existing nonproliferation treaties, commitments and other obligations.[2] Unless both sides of the TPNW argument take leadership to bridge the gulf between these two camps, there is likely to be further polarization before unity on nuclear disarmament matters.

THE TPNW IN THE INTERNATIONAL CONTEXT

While the TPNW does not intend to prejudice existing international agreements or obligations undertaken by states parties, important questions remain regarding its future and the existing legal order under international nuclear law. As will be discussed in this chapter, some fear that the TPNW may serve to challenge existing international legal infrastructure by establishing a different set of legal norms and expectations that may fragment an already divided global community. Furthermore, it is thought that the Treaty may challenge the nonproliferation and disarmament framework, serving to disrupt current nuclear legal authority and organizational architecture. Discussion in this chapter will explore matters regarding the TPNW and: (1) the NPT; (2) the IAEA; (3) the CTBTO; (4) approaches regarding terrorism by non-state actors; (5) NATO and its umbrella states; and (6) the nuclear-weapon-free zones (NWFZ). Moreover, this chapter examines the degree to which the TPNW may serve to fragment existing structures, forging its own international legal infrastructure regarding nuclear disarmament and nuclear nonproliferation law. Discussion concludes by calling on all states on both sides of the divide to come together to provide clarity, close the gaps in regulation, and work together toward increased legal certainty rather than persisting in uncertainty and ambiguity, which invariably fosters competing regimes that polarize an area which requires a harmonious approach and not division.

TWO CAMPS: RESOLUTE STATES AND STALWART STATES

The 2017 TPNW has essentially split the international community into two firm camps: those states that will ratify the Treaty, either now or will accede to it in the future, and those that will not. These may be referred to as the resolute states and the stalwart states. Unlike other arms control treaties inspired by humanitarian concerns such as the Anti-Personnel Mine Ban Convention (1997) or the Cluster Munitions Convention (2008), which were greeted with more mixed receptions, and involved somewhat different factors in deciding whether to ratify, the TPNW is more emphatic with states resolutely for the Treaty or stalwartly against it. Unlike these other developments, state reactions to the TPNW come across as black or white,

[2] See Alicia Sandres-Zakre, "Ban Talks Advance with Treaty Draft" (June 2017) *Arms Control Today*, online: www.armscontrol.org/act/2017–06/news/ban-talks-advance-treaty-draft.

with no gray area. These two positions are increasingly intractable with growing polarization between the two camps.

On one hand, the countries affirming their support for the TPNW, the resolute states, are strongly committed to the goal of nuclear disarmament and see the Treaty as the means of achieving this outcome. Roughly speaking, they fall into one of the following three categories: (1) the absolutist resolute states, consisting of states fully committed to nuclear disarmament without conditions or reservations in an absolute sense; (2) morally conscientious resolute states, which are states having reservations but taking the overall view that their commitment to disarmament should prevail and override any doubts; (3) resolute political states – politically conscientious resolute states, which have apprehensions or political doubts about joining the Treaty but whose citizens ask or demand that they reconsider their respective position and follow the political will of the people and agree to commit to disarmament.

Both absolutist resolute and morally conscientious resolute states see the overall objective of nuclear disarmament as the central goal that needs to moved forward in a progressive and successive manner, specifically, that it is time to take collective action on this long-neglected and seemingly abandoned goal under Article VI of the NPT. Some see the intransigence and outright failure on the part of the nuclear-weapon states to proceed with this matter in a meaningful and constructive manner as a central motivator for their taking control of the disarmament agenda. The politically conscientious resolute category is guided by the democratic will of the electorate. As the governing regime in power, the political establishment may not wish to adopt the TPNW, but they may be compelled to reconsider because of general popular support amongst their electorates.

On the other hand, countries opposing the Treaty, the stalwart states, are adamant in their resistance against this development, feeling that it undermines the existing international legal framework and current regulatory nuclear infrastructure (e.g., under the IAEA and the NPT Review Conferences). The word stalwart is defined as: "loyal, reliable, and hard-working."[3] Most of these states regard themselves as such, committed to the status quo, and the existing international framework under the NPT and the IAEA. They expound the importance of working within the current nuclear architecture and moving progressively toward nuclear disarmament within the existing nuclear framework. Stalwart states consist of five main groups: (1) militant stalwart states[4] (i.e., the five nuclear-weapon-states); (2) militarily joined

---

[3] English Oxford Living Dictionaries. See https://en.oxforddictionaries.com/definition/stalwart. Note that synonyms include: staunch, loyal, faithful, committed, devoted, dedicated, dependable, reliable, steady, constant, trusty, hard-working, vigorous, stable, firm, steadfast, redoubtable, resolute, unswerving, unwavering, unhesitating, unfaltering. Antonyms include: disloyal, unfaithful, unreliable. See https://en.oxforddictionaries.com/thesaurus/stalwart.

[4] It should be noted that these states take the position of nuclear deterrence; to avoid war. Hence, the word "militant" in this context refers to an active position to defend.

stalwart states consisting of NATO members;[5] (3) militarily aligned stalwart states consisting of nuclear umbrella states that are not part of NATO, per se; (4) militarily unaligned stalwart states which consist of non-NATO, non-umbrella, states against the prohibition treaty; and (5) regressive stalwart states which consist of states possessing nuclear weapons or wishing to do so against the terms of the Treaty. While a line may be firmly drawn between the resolute and stalwart camps, within the stalwart states, there is a major distinction between some of them regarding their varying nuclear positions and resistance to the TPNW.

Aside from their commitment to the status quo, the existing international architecture and their opposition to the Treaty, the stalwarts are sub-divided into two main factions: the progressive stalwarts and the resistant stalwarts. Progressive stalwarts consist of the first four categories listed above, specifically: (1) militant stalwart states; (2) militarily joined stalwart states; (3) militarily aligned stalwart states; and (4) militarily unaligned stalwart states. By and large, the progressive stalwart states see themselves as committed to the existing international systems and processes without the need for the TPNW. They express their commitment to nonproliferation and general nuclear disarmament by insisting on adherence to the NPT framework as a means and mechanism of achieving the ultimate goal of disarmament under appropriate prudent and successive steps. They consist of both nuclear-weapon states (NWS) and non-nuclear-weapon states (Non-NWS). Indeed, with the Non-NWS, there are several which are differently placed geographically and with regard to their military defense capabilities, but all subscribe to similar defense doctrines and strategies based on deterrence.

Firstly, the militant stalwart states consist of the five NWS under Articles I and IX(3), second sentence of the NPT,[6] which are also the only permanent members of the United Nations Security Council.[7] They play a pivotal role in UN matters relating to international peace and security. They participate in the quinquennial – five-yearly – NPT Review Conference and maintain that they are committed to collective security.

The second collection of states in this wider group, militarily joined stalwart states are NATO[8] members[9] who expressly belong to and participate in governance and

---

5   Non-nuclear-weapon states as defined under Article II of the NPT. For this purpose, non-nuclear-weapon state members of NATO are classified as distinct from umbrella states. Needless to say, there are similarities between groups (2) and (3).

6   See wwwupdate.un.org/disarmament/WMD/Nuclear/NPTtext.shtml.

7   Article 23 (1) UN Charter.

8   NATO was formed by twelve founding members, under the Washington Treaty, or North Atlantic Treaty which was signed in Washington, DC on April 4, 1949. The Treaty forms the basis of the North Atlantic Treaty Organization, or what is known as NATO. See www.nato.int/cps/en/natolive/topics_67656.htm. For a copy of the Official Text of the Treaty, see www.nato.int/cps/en/natohq/official_texts_17120.htm.

9   The following countries belong to NATO, indicating the year they joined: Albania (2009); Belgium (1949); Bulgaria (2004); Canada (1949); Croatia (2009); Czech Republic (1999); Denmark (1949); Estonia (2004); France (1949); Germany (1955); Greece (1952); Hungary (1999); Iceland (1949); Italy

Competition, Fragmentation and Polarization

military exercises under the organization.[10] Membership of this alliance requires them to adhere to a collective military defense policy,[11] in which decisions are reached by consensus.[12]

The third group, militarily aligned stalwart states are referred to as "nuclear umbrella" states,[13] a term which generally refers to military cooperation between a non-NWS and a nuclear-weapon state or states, whereby military protection is accorded to that country under its protective umbrella, including nuclear protection, as discussed in Chapter 7. Such arrangement may or may not be officially documented or publicly known. Although nuclear umbrellas are usually declared, they are not always "explicitly declared."[14] As defined by the former International Law and Policy Institute,

> nuclear umbrellas are rooted in military and diplomatic *practices*. A "nuclear umbrella," is *a security arrangement under which the participating states consent to or acquiesce the potential use of nuclear weapons in their defence.* The related concept of "extended nuclear deterrence" may be understood as the *intended effect* of a nuclear umbrella. A *"nuclear umbrella state" is a state without nuclear weapons under the supposed protection of the nuclear weapons of another state.*[15]

(1949); Latvia (2004); Lithuania (2004); Luxembourg (1949); Montenegro (2017); Netherlands (1949); Norway (1949); Poland (1999); Portugal (1949); Romania (2004); Slovakia (2004); Slovenia (2004); Spain (1982); Turkey (1952); United Kingdom (1949); and the United States (1949). See www.nato.int/nato-welcome/index.html.

[10] NATO sees itself as a political and military alliance, stating: "Security in our daily lives is key to our well-being. NATO's purpose is to guarantee the freedom and security of its members through political and military means. Political NATO promotes democratic values and enables members to consult and cooperate on defence and security-related issues to solve problems, build trust and, in the long run, prevent conflict. Military NATO is committed to the peaceful resolution of disputes. If diplomatic efforts fail, it has the military power to undertake crisis-management operations. These are carried out under the collective defence clause of NATO's founding treaty – Article 5 of the Washington Treaty or under a United Nations mandate, alone or in cooperation with other countries and international organisations." See www.nato.int/nato-welcome/index.html.

[11] Collective Defence: "NATO is committed to the principle that an attack against one or several of its members is considered as an attack against all. This is the principle of collective defence, which is enshrined in Article 5 of the Washington Treaty. So far, Article 5 has been invoked once – in response to the 9/11 terrorist attacks in the United States in 2001." See www.nato.int/nato-welcome/index.html.

[12] Decisions and Consultations: "Every day, member countries consult and take decisions on security issues at all levels and in a variety of fields. A 'NATO decision' is the expression of the collective will of all 29 member countries since all decisions are taken by consensus. Hundreds of officials, as well as civilian and military experts, come to NATO Headquarters each day to exchange information, share ideas and help prepare decisions when needed, in cooperation with national delegations and the staff at NATO Headquarters." See www.nato.int/nato-welcome/index.html. For more information on consensus and decision making at NATO. See www.nato.int/cps/en/natolive/topics_49178.htm.

[13] The English Oxford Living Dictionaries define it as: "the supposed protection gained from an alliance with a country possessing nuclear weapons." See https://en.oxforddictionaries.com/definition/us/nuclear_umbrella.

[14] "Nuclear Umbrella States: A Brief Introduction to the Concept of Nuclear Umbrella States," Nutshell Paper No. 4/2011 by the International Law and Policy Institute. See http://nwp.ilpi.org/wp-content/uploads/2015/03/NP04-11-UmbrellaStates.pdf.

[15] Nuclear umbrellas and umbrella states, by the International Law and Policy Institute. See http://nwp.ilpi.org/?p=1221. Note that the International Law and Policy Institute (ILPI) closed on June 30, 2017.

Unlike NATO states, per se, they seem to be given the same military protection as that of an alliance member, without being a part of the governance structure.

The fourth category in the stalwart camp, militarily unaligned stalwart states, includes countries that are neither members of NATO[16] nor on the face of it under shelter of nuclear umbrella protection, or under a private, undisclosed, arrangement. These states have chosen not to ratify the TPNW based on their own sovereign processes and have decided not to adhere to the TPNW at this stage.

Together, this broad collection of four groups consisting of nuclear-weapon states and non-nuclear-weapon states are opposed to acceding to the TPNW and perhaps even its ratification by any other state. For the most part, the stalwart states are rooted in the existing international nuclear-regulatory architecture and are committed to these processes. Whilst not agreeing to be bound by the TPNW, they affirm their commitment to complete and verifiable disarmament as required by Article VI of the NPT and highlighted by the ICJ in its 1996 *Advisory Opinion*. They openly acknowledge criticism and deficiencies of the current system but feel the existing infrastructure is the best method of achieving progress toward nonproliferation and disarmament. Needless to say, as discussed in Chapter 7, nuclear deterrence is at the heart of their concerns, seeing it as a central plank of their defense policies, without which they would consider themselves to be vulnerable to attack and potentially forced to submit to either aggressive state or non-state actors. They are loyal to the existing system, but realistic regarding humanitarian concerns.

The fifth group of stalwarts, what one might refer to as regressive stalwart states, are loyal to their position and the opposition to the TPNW for fundamentally different reasons. They prefer the status quo because arguably it allows them to maintain their stance on owning or aspiring to acquire nuclear weapons and failure to comply with many generally accepted requirements pertaining to nuclear regulation. While sharing a common goal with their contemporaries for voting purposes, against the TPNW and its non-realization, in reality their interests in opposing the TPNW are somewhat different. Many of the regressivists differ from the four sets of countries named above who subscribe to the NPT and its processes, in that they have either not ratified the NPT, or not fully committed to it, and do not necessarily wish to submit to its full implementation.

---

[16] Note that NATO has enlargement opportunities whereby NATO membership is generally open to "any other European state in a position to further the principles of this Treaty and to contribute to the security of the North Atlantic area." Note that aspiring states must be invited to accede to the NATO Treaty. NATO also has what it calls the Membership Action Plan where it helps aspiring members to prepare for membership and meet key requirements by providing practical advice and targeted assistance. See www.nato.int/nato-welcome/index.html.

Competition, Fragmentation and Polarization

Two Categories of States

Resolute States – For the TPNW	Stalwart States – Against the TPNW

Sub-Categories of States

Resolute States:	Stalwart States:
Absolutists resolute	Militant stalwart states
Morally conscientious resolute	Militarily joined stalwart states
Resolute political	Militarily aligned stalwart states
	Militarily unaligned stalwart states
	Regressive stalwart states

Characteristics of States

Resolute States	Characteristics: For the TPNW
Absolutist resolute states	Fully committed to disarmament without conditions or reservations.
Morally conscientious resolute states	Have reservations but overall committed to disarmament which overrides any doubts.
Resolute political states: Politically conscientious resolute states	Have political apprehensions but their citizens have forced them to reconsider their position and commit to disarmament.

Stalwart States	Characteristics: Against the TPNW
Militant stalwart states	The five nuclear-weapon-states, China, France, Russia, UK and US. Who adhere to defense doctrines based on nuclear deterrence.
Militarily joined stalwart states	NATO members, part of the military alliance with shared military protection accorded under nuclear deterrence and defense doctrines.
Militarily aligned stalwart states	Nuclear umbrella states seeking military cooperation with military protection accorded under a protective nuclear umbrella.
Militarily unaligned stalwart states	Non-NATO, non-umbrella, states against the Prohibition Treaty and unaligned to any overt protection system.
Regressive stalwart states	States possessing nuclear weapons or wishing to do so against the terms of the Treaty and fail to adhere to other nuclear commitments.

STALEMATE BETWEEN RESOLUTE AND STALWART STATES

The current stalemate and intransigence between the two sides of the TPNW divide raises much concern. Contrary to abating, the divide between the resolute and stalwart states appears to be widening. The stalwart states have expressed the view that the TPNW is naïve and underdeveloped, while the resolute states have taken the moral high-ground on this issue and presume that history will be on their side. They are resolute in their humanitarian focus which they feel will prevail over what they see as outdated military defense doctrines based on deterrence.

A fear of this author regarding the international community is that the growing divide between the two camps could in effect work to the advantage of rogue elements and states harboring nuclear ambitions and non-state actors seeking destruction. This rift creates a global level of uncertainty and chaos that could allow states and entities pursuing nefarious activities to lie low and avoid pressure to ratify the NPT or to adhere to safeguards under the IAEA. They may seize this opportunity of disagreement over the TPNW to their advantage, with the effect of intensifying proliferation matters. In addition, such divisive discussions distract from efforts to gain support for the CTBT.

At this time, there needs to be more clarity on nuclear nonproliferation issues so that more states do not acquire nuclear weapons and explosive devices. Gaps in regulation need to be narrowed and closed so that terrorists and non-state actors do not slip through the cracks and acquire nuclear materials. This precarious period requires all states and parties to work toward more legal certainty in this area, rather than further uncertainty and polarization. To avoid further polarizing the debate, states desiring nuclear prohibition must find a harmonious approach.

Along these lines, another danger of the TPNW is that it will shift the focus and efforts of current treaties away from existing debates, pressures and movement in the direction of disarmament, toward pressures to sign the TPNW. This treaty has evidently changed the emphasis of the nuclear conversation, because it calls for a complete ban and stigmatizes nuclear weapons, meaning nuclear states are left arguing about, and defending the importance of, their nuclear stance as deterrence instead of working toward disarmament as they are obliged to do under Article VI of the NPT. The NWS are entrenching their positions and their hold on nuclear weapons. We now have treaties that may be competing and contradictory in some respects and inconsistent or redundant in other respects.

Before the TPNW, the NWS were aligned with the NPT and the CTBT, but now we have activists and states pushing the focus to signing the TPNW. This competing demand for loyalty may create fragmentation in the international legal nuclear infrastructure, creating a space for non-nuclear-weapon states that currently possess nuclear weapons to use this opportunity to develop nuclear weapons beyond the immediate attention of the international community as mentioned above. States not complying with the NPT may capitalize on this perceived division and nuclear

244   *Competition, Fragmentation and Polarization*

schism for their own gains; that is, to create nuclear weapons, knowing they are not in the spotlight or under scrutiny as the two camps air their disagreements. Next, this discussion will explore the specific relationships between the TPNW with other legal instruments and parties, in an effort to identify areas of potential fragmentation.

The Non-Proliferation Treaty and Fragmentation?

Critics of the TPNW are concerned that it might undermine the authority of the NPT, effectively fragmenting the international community between two differing loyalties. There are concerns that it might undermine the NPT and its verification system of International Atomic Energy Agency (IAEA) safeguards. Entering into force in 1970, the NPT commits the nuclear-weapon states to disarmament but is not an outright ban on possession, per se. The NPT is intended to be a progressive instrument toward incremental disarmament, as non-nuclear-weapon NPT states are to forego nuclear weapons and place nuclear materials and facilities under international safeguards.[17] The NPT states that nothing in it "affects the right of any group of States to conclude regional treaties in order to assure the total absence of nuclear weapons in their respective territories."[18] That said, some commentators express concern regarding the TPNW's wording and its relationship to other treaties.[19] As noted in Chapter 4, questions remain regarding the relationship of the TPNW to the NPT. Although the TPNW recognizes in its preamble that the full and effective implementation of the NPT plays a vital role in promoting international peace and security and that the NPT serves as the cornerstone of the nuclear disarmament and nonproliferation regime,[20] no express reference to it has been made in the text of the articles. Indeed, it might be argued that the absence of such substantive references allows for differing standards that may be reduced under the TPNW. Critics aside, indeed some governments fear that the TPNW may fragment international law as a result of its ambiguity regarding the inter-relationship between the TPNW and the NPT.

The Permanent Representative of Switzerland to the Conference on Disarmament, for example, in her letter of explanation of vote in signing the Treaty in July 2017, outlined Swiss concerns stating: "the treaty is deficient in the sense that some of its provisions are not effectively verifiable. This constitutes a departure from the principle that we have all agreed to in the NPT framework that nuclear disarmament should be both irreversible and verifiable."[21] This concern was

---

[17]   The Nuclear Ban Treaty: An Overview July 10, 2017 (IN10731) CRS Insight. See https://fas.org/sgp/crs/nuke/IN10731.pdf.

[18]   Article VII. See wwwupdate.un.org/disarmament/WMD/Nuclear/NPTtext.shtml.

[19]   See Alicia Sandres-Zakre, "Ban Talks Advance with Treaty Draft" (June 2017) *Arms Control Today*, online: www.armscontrol.org/act/2017-06/news/ban-talks-advance-treaty-draft.

[20]   See http://undocs.org/A/CONF.229/2017/8.

[21]   United Nations Conference to Negotiate a Legally Binding Instrument to Prohibit Nuclear Weapons Explanation of Vote New York, July 7, 2017 H. E. Ms. Sabrina Dallafior Permanent Representative of

mentioned earlier, but for the purposes of this discussion, it must be noted that different standards of verification could formulate between the requirements of the TPNW and the NPT causing a fragmentation on such issues, especially at a time where more harmony and unity is called for. Switzerland also noted concern regarding "risks for existing norms, instruments and fora" stating that "treaty provisions could also challenge the centrality of the NPT."[22] Again, other than in the preamble, there was no mention of the NPT in the main text with no articles reinforcing its role or authority within this sphere. One would have thought that the supposed "cornerstone" of disarmament law deserves explicit reference in this context.

Notably, in its explanatory letter, Switzerland also reaffirmed the NPT as "the cornerstone of the nuclear disarmament and non-proliferation regime."[23] In discussing the TPNW's interaction with other treaties and fora,[24] Switzerland noted that the NPT is the "key instrument in the nuclear disarmament and non-proliferation architecture, as well as the foundation of an international order ... [and that] The continued and uncontested existence of the NPT is pivotal to the achievement of a world without nuclear weapons."[25] The report notes Switzerland's relative isolation on many of these issues throughout the TPNW's negotiations, highlighting its efforts to "endeavour to negotiate an agreement that preserves and reinforces the added value of the NPT."[26] The negotiators' seeming lack of interest in prioritizing the NPT reinforces concerns that, in effect, there could be fragmentation in nuclear treaty law. Moreover, such an "objective was only partially achieved ... [in that] the centrality of the NPT could not be more firmly enshrined in the treaty text (apart from a hard-won mention in the preamble stating that it is the cornerstone of the nuclear non-proliferation and disarmament regime)."[27]

Switzerland adds that while "it was not possible to prevent the regular meetings of state parties in the TPNW format being able to negotiate additional (also legally binding) nuclear disarmament measures ... future meetings of states parties will show whether this treaty will allow constructive interaction between the various agreements, or whether established processes, such as the NPT review process, will be duplicated, encouraging fragmentation and further polarisation."[28] In that regard, "[i]n the absence of clear statements in the treaty text, it will only be possible to assess the interplay between the TPNW and the NPT/CTBT in the medium term.

Switzerland to the Conference on Disarmament. See https://s3.amazonaws.com/unoda-web/wp-content/uploads/2017/07/Swiss-Explanation-of-Vote2.pdf.

[22] Ibid.

[23] Ibid.

[24] In its Report of the Working Group to Analyse the Treaty on the Prohibition of Nuclear Weapons June 30, 2018 – English translation from the German original version. See www.eda.admin.ch/dam/eda/en/documents/aussenpolitik/sicherheitspolitik/2018-bericht-arbeitsgruppe-uno-TPNW_en.pdf, at p. 3.

[25] Ibid.

[26] Ibid.

[27] Ibid.

[28] Ibid.

246 *Competition, Fragmentation and Polarization*

Indicators of the treaties' relationship will be future NPT, CTBT and TPNW conferences, as well as developments in the relevant UN bodies."[29]

The Netherlands has expressed similar frustrations, calling the TPNW "a recipe for competition and fragmentation when our efforts on disarmament should be concentrated."[30] The Netherlands suggests the TPNW failed to "strengthen and complement the NPT," and says it "would be unable to sign up to any instrument that is incompatible with our NATO obligations, that contains inadequate verification provisions or that undermines the Non-Proliferation Treaty."[31]

These statements from the Swiss and Dutch governments point to the TPNW's potential to fragment international law, particularly through its unclear relationship with the NPT. Such ambiguity is sure to create concern at a time when the global community strives for more certainty on these important matters.

International Atomic Energy Agency

As discussed in Chapter 6 on safeguards and verification, Articles 3[32] and 4[33] of the TPNW make express reference to the role of the International Atomic Energy

---

[29] Ibid.

[30] Explanation of vote of the Netherlands on text of Nuclear Ban Treaty. See https://s3.amazonaws.com/unoda-web/wp-content/uploads/2017/07/Netherlands-EoV-Nuclear-Ban-Treaty.pdf.

[31] Ibid.

[32] "Article 3 Safeguards 1. Each State Party to which Article 4, paragraph 1 or 2, does not apply shall, at a minimum, maintain its International Atomic Energy Agency safeguards obligations in force at the time of entry into force of this Treaty, without prejudice to any additional relevant instruments that it may adopt in the future. 2. Each State Party to which Article 4, paragraph 1 or 2, does not apply that has not yet done so shall conclude with the International Atomic Energy Agency and bring into force a comprehensive safeguards agreement (INFCIRC/153 (Corrected)). Negotiation of such agreement shall commence within 180 days from the entry into force of this Treaty for that State Party. The agreement shall enter into force no later than 18 months from the entry into force of this Treaty for that State Party. Each State Party shall thereafter maintain such obligations, without prejudice to any additional relevant instruments that it may adopt in the future."

[33] Article 4: Towards the total elimination of nuclear weapons "1. Each State Party that after 7 July 2017 owned, possessed or controlled nuclear weapons or other nuclear explosive devices and eliminated its nuclear-weapon program, including the elimination or irreversible conversion of all nuclear weapons-related facilities, prior to the entry into force of this Treaty for it, shall cooperate with the competent international authority designated pursuant to paragraph 6 of this Article for the purpose of verifying the irreversible elimination of its nuclear-weapon programme. The competent international authority shall report to the States Parties. Such a State Party shall conclude a safeguards agreement with the International Atomic Energy Agency sufficient to provide credible assurance of the non-diversion of declared nuclear material from peaceful nuclear activities and of the absence of undeclared nuclear material or activities in that State Party as a whole. Negotiation of such agreement shall commence within 180 days from the entry into force of this Treaty for that State Party. The agreement shall enter into force no later than 18 months from the entry into force of this Treaty for that State Party. That State Party shall thereafter, at a minimum, maintain these safeguards obligations, without prejudice to any additional relevant instruments that it may adopt in the future. 2. Notwithstanding Article 1 (a), each State Party that owns, possesses or controls nuclear weapons or other nuclear explosive devices shall immediately remove them from operational status, and destroy them as soon as possible but not later than a deadline to be determined by the first meeting of States

Agency regarding safeguard obligations. As mentioned previously, there are unanswered questions regarding the link between the IAEA and the TPNW itself. Instead of clarifying the role of the IAEA, the open language of the TPNW may actually have opened a gap between the two, effectively creating ambiguity and uncertainty regarding verification efforts. Article 8 of the TPNW requires the states parties to "meet regularly in order to consider ... [and to decide on] ... measures for the verified, time-bound and irreversible elimination of nuclear-weapon programmes."[34] This enforcement clause may allay certain fears in that the states parties will deal with verification and enforcement issues. That said, it may also heighten concerns that two verification regimes could emerge, causing disjuncture and competing interpretations in this important area.

A bifurcation of inspection roles, for example, could evolve which may effectively duplicate or split important safety and security measures by establishing separate and disconnected regimes in an area which requires unity in both purpose and process, rather than ambiguity and uncertainty. Countries might then feel they are meeting

Parties, in accordance with a legally binding, time-bound plan for the verified and irreversible elimination of that State Party's nuclear-weapon programme, including the elimination or irreversible conversion of all nuclear-weapons-related facilities. The State Party, no later than 60 days after the entry into force of this Treaty for that State Party, shall submit this plan to the States Parties or to a competent international authority designated by the States Parties. The plan shall then be negotiated with the competent international authority, which shall submit it to the subsequent meeting of States Parties or review conference, whichever comes first, for approval in accordance with its rules of procedure. 3. A State Party to which paragraph 2 above applies shall conclude a safeguards agreement with the International Atomic Energy Agency sufficient to provide credible assurance of the non-diversion of declared nuclear material from peaceful nuclear activities and of the absence of undeclared nuclear material or activities in the State as a whole. Negotiation of such agreement shall commence no later than the date upon which implementation of the plan referred to in paragraph 2 is completed. The agreement shall enter into force no later than 18 months after the date of initiation of negotiations. That State Party shall thereafter, at a minimum, maintain these safeguards obligations, without prejudice to any additional relevant instruments that it may adopt in the future. Following the entry into force of the agreement referred to in this paragraph, the State Party shall submit to the Secretary-General of the United Nations a final declaration that it has fulfilled its obligations under this Article. 4. Notwithstanding Article 1 (b) and (g), each State Party that has any nuclear weapons or other nuclear explosive devices in its territory or in any place under its jurisdiction or control that are owned, possessed or controlled by another State shall ensure the prompt removal of such weapons, as soon as possible but not later than a deadline to be determined by the first meeting of States Parties. Upon the removal of such weapons or other explosive devices, that State Party shall submit to the Secretary-General of the United Nations a declaration that it has fulfilled its obligations under this Article. 5. Each State Party to which this Article applies shall submit a report to each meeting of States Parties and each review conference on the progress made towards the implementation of its obligations under this Article, until such time as they are fulfilled. 6. The States Parties shall designate a competent international authority or authorities to negotiate and verify the irreversible elimination of nuclear-weapons programmes, including the elimination or irreversible conversion of all nuclear weapons-related facilities in accordance with paragraphs 1, 2 and 3 of this Article. In the event that such a designation has not been made prior to the entry into force of this Treaty for a State Party to which paragraph 1 or 2 of this Article applies, the Secretary-General of the United Nations shall convene an extraordinary meeting of States Parties to take any decisions that may be required."

[34] Article 8(1)(b). See http://undocs.org/A/CONF.229/2017/8.

248   *Competition, Fragmentation and Polarization*

their obligations under the TPNW while bypassing or challenging the role of the IAEA; or they may refuse to allow the organization to develop a deeper involvement in their territory or to agree future additional protocols or arrangements.

Some states feel that the lack of concrete measures in the TPNW itself threatens its credibility as an arms control treaty. The Netherlands, for one, stated it would be unable to sign up to any instrument that, *inter alia*, "contains inadequate verification provisions."[35] The Dutch statement adds that "the draft is, in essence, not verifiable. This harms its credibility … Moreover, the draft contains a safeguards standard that even in this day is not sufficient for the IAEA to draw a conclusion about the absence of undeclared nuclear activities. It will certainly not provide the kind of assurances needed toward a nuclear free world."[36] Switzerland also expressed its reservations on this front, stating that: "Provisions related to IAEA safeguards might erode efforts to strengthen standards in this domain. Besides, tasks given to the Meeting of States Parties could duplicate or even contradict efforts undertaken in other fora."[37] Again, these statements show the TPNW's lack of clarity regarding the IAEA opening the door for a fragmented international legal standards and systems throughout the global community.

Clarifying, Confirming and Expanding the Role of the IAEA

As discussed in Chapter 6, negotiations regarding the TPNW may have been an opportunity to clarify and confirm an expanding role of the IAEA regarding nuclear oversight. Alicia Sandres-Zakre points out that, "The text [of the TPNW] does not call for states-parties to adopt the stricter verification requirements embodied in the International Atomic Energy Agency (IAEA) Additional Protocol which some states, such as Sweden and Switzerland, advocated for in March [2017]."[38] As discussed in Chapter 6, the IAEA is the principal international organization responsible for monitoring nuclear safety. In that regard, over the years, questions about the extent and reach of the Agency's power and authority have been raised in relation to state jurisdiction and sovereignty. Negotiating the TPNW may have provided an opportunity to clarify and indeed actually expand the role of the IAEA, through Additional Protocols or bilateral agreements, to tighten gaps and strengthen enforcement mechanisms for states planning to ratify the TPNW. That is, to set stricter criteria for those states acceding to the TPNW; those who are committed to complete disarmament and therefore would be willing to agree to higher standards and stricter

---

[35] Explanation of vote of the Netherlands on text of Nuclear Ban Treaty. See https://s3.amazonaws.com/unoda-web/wp-content/uploads/2017/07/Netherlands-EoV-Nuclear-Ban-Treaty.pdf.

[36] Ibid.

[37] United Nations Conference to Negotiate a Legally Binding Instrument to Prohibit Nuclear Weapons Explanation of Vote New York, July 7, 2017 H. E. Ms. Sabrina Dallafior Permanent Representative of Switzerland to the Conference on Disarmament. See https://s3.amazonaws.com/unoda-web/wp-content/uploads/2017/07/Swiss-Explanation-of-Vote2.pdf.

[38] See Alicia Sandres-Zakre, "Ban Talks Advance with Treaty Draft" (June 2017) *Arms Control Today*, online: www.armscontrol.org/act/2017-06/news/ban-talks-advance-treaty-draft.

Stalemate between Resolute and Stalwart States 249

and tighter regulations rather than accepting the current arrangement, especially in light of criticisms regarding varied interpretations.

At present, under the NPT, the non-nuclear-weapon states parties must conclude safeguards agreements with the IAEA.[39] To that effect, the IAEA developed INFCIRC/153 (Corr.), which serves as the basis of Comprehensive Safeguards Agreements (CSAs).[40] Specifically, paragraph 2 provides that:

> The Agreement should provide for the Agency's right and obligation to ensure that safeguards will be applied, in accordance with the terms of the Agreement, on all source or special fissionable material in all peaceful nuclear activities within the territory of the State, under its jurisdiction or carried out under its control anywhere, for the exclusive purpose of verifying that such material is not diverted to nuclear weapons or other nuclear explosive devices.[41]

The intent and scope of this obligation has been confirmed by the IAEA board of governors.[42] This firstly, authorizes and secondly, requires the IAEA to verify the non-diversion of nuclear material from declared activities (i.e., correctness) as well as to verify the absence of undeclared nuclear activities in a state (i.e., completeness of national reports).[43] Notably,[44] reporting obligations apply even in cases of the use of nuclear material in a non-proscribed military activity (i.e., for non-explosive military purposes, such as nuclear naval propulsion and space propulsion).[45] This

---

[39] Article III.1 NPT.

[40] IAEA, The Structure and Content of Agreements Between the Agency and States required in connection with the Treaty on the Non-Proliferation of Nuclear Weapons, INFCIRC/153 (Corr.) (June 1972). See www.iaea.org/sites/default/files/publications/documents/infcircs/1972/infcirc153.pdf.

[41] The Agreement should provide for the Agency's right and obligation to ensure that safeguards will be applied, in accordance with the terms of the Agreement, on all source or special fissionable material in all peaceful nuclear activities within the territory of the State, under its jurisdiction or carried out under its control anywhere, for the exclusive purpose of verifying that such material is not diverted to nuclear weapons or other nuclear explosive devices.

[42] It has confirmed on numerous occasions, since as early as 1992.

[43] IAEA Report GOV/2013/6 (February 21, 2013), n. 61. See www.iaea.org/Publications/Documents/Board/2013/gov2013-6.pdf. The correctness and completeness argument has also been discussed in other contexts, see e.g. document GC (39)/17, Strengthening the Effectiveness and improving the Efficiency of the Safeguards System, Report by the Director General to the General Conference, August 22, 1995. See www.iaea.org/About/Policy/GC/GC39/GC39Documents/English/gc39-17_en.pdf., para. 5: "The problem of undeclared activities was highlighted in Iraq, but was not unknown. Indeed, the need for the safeguards system to provide assurances regarding both the correctness and the completeness of a State's nuclear material declarations was considered by the drafters of the INFCIRC/153 (Corr.), the basis for comprehensive safeguards agreements. The scope of INFCIRC/153 was not limited to the nuclear material actually declared by the State; it also includes that which should be declared. However, the system such as it had developed up to the Iraqi case, had limited capability to deal with completeness. This was the result of practical, rather than legal, considerations."

[44] As highlighted in the Third ILA Report of the Committee on Nuclear Weapons, Non-Proliferation and Contemporary International Law of the International Law Association at p. 4. See www.ila-hq.org/index.php/committees.

[45] See paragraph 14 of INFCIRC/153/Corr., stating *inter alia*: "The Agreement should provide that if the State intends to exercise its discretion to use *nuclear material* which is required to be safeguarded thereunder in a nuclear activity which does not require the application of safeguards under the

obligation invariably applies for material containing uranium or thorium, which has not yet reached the stage of the nuclear fuel cycle where it is suitable for fuel fabrication or isotopic enrichment, and is directly or indirectly exported to a non-nuclear-weapon state, or also when it is imported to that State.[46]

In this regard, the IAEA has developed a state-level approach regarding safeguards implementation resulting from the Agency's focus on strengthening the effectiveness and efficiency of the overall safeguards system.[47] Arguments as to whether the IAEA has acted *ultra vires* (i.e., beyond its legal and administrative discretionary powers), by assuming its authority to verify the completeness of states' declarations in conducting verification activities,[48] have heightened the need to develop treaty law in this area. States must unequivocally undertake to inform, and to accept inspector access, regarding all aspects of the nuclear fuel cycle within their respective territories and under their jurisdictional control and reach. That is, they must accept and

Agreement, the following procedures will apply: (a) The State shall inform the Agency of the activity, making it clear: (i) That the use of the *nuclear material* in a non-proscribed military activity will not be in conflict with an undertaking the State may have given and in respect of which Agency safeguards apply, that the *nuclear material* will be used only in a peaceful nuclear activity; and (ii) That during the period of non-application of safeguards the *nuclear material* will not be used for the production of nuclear weapons or other nuclear explosive devices."

[46] See paragraph 34 of INFCIRC/153/Corr., stating: "The Agreement should provide that: (a) When any material containing uranium or thorium which has not reached the stage of the nuclear fuel cycle described in sub-paragraph (c) below is directly or indirectly exported to a non-nuclear-weapon State, the State shall inform the Agency of its quantity, composition and destination, unless the material is exported for specifically non-nuclear purposes; (b) When any material containing uranium or thorium which has not reached the stage of the nuclear fuel cycle described in sub-paragraph (c) below is imported, the State shall inform the Agency of its quantity and composition, unless the material is imported for specifically non-nuclear purposes; and (c) When any *nuclear material* of a composition and purity suitable for fuel fabrication or for being isotopically enriched leaves the plant or the process stage in which it has been produced, or when such *nuclear material*, or any other *nuclear material* produced at a later stage in the nuclear fuel cycle, is imported into the State, the *nuclear material* shall become subject to the other safeguards procedures specified in the Agreement."

[47] See IAEA reports on the State-Level Concept (SLC): Document GOV/2013/38, https://armscontrol law.files.wordpress.com/2012/06/state-level-safeguards-concept-report-august-2013.pdf: 12. The term "State-Level Concept" was first introduced to the board of governors in the Safeguards Implementation Report (SIR) for 2004 to describe safeguards implementation that is based on state-level approaches developed using safeguards objectives common to all states with CSAs and taking state-specific factors into account. 21 As the SIR for 2004 noted, the state-level concept was being implemented for states with integrated safeguards and would be extended to all other States with CSAs; Document GOV/2014/41, https://armscontrollaw.files.wordpress.com/2014/09/iaea-state-level-safeguards-document-august-2014.pdf. The SLC refers to the general notion of implementing safeguards in a manner that considers a state's nuclear and nuclear-related activities and capabilities as a whole, within the scope of the state's safeguards agreement. See also Laura Rockwood, "The IAEA's State-Level Concept and the Law of Unintended Consequences," in *Arms Control Today* (September 2014), www.armscontrol.org/act/2014_09/Features/. "So entered into the lexicon of safeguards the state-level concept, simply another way of referring to the agency's practice, well established by then, of evaluating all safeguards-relevant information about a state as a whole and, where possible, tailoring safeguards to fit the state concerned."

[48] See the three rounds of discussion between Daniel H. Joyner, Christopher A. Ford and Andreas Persbo, *Bulletin of the Atomic Scientists*, October, November and December 2012, http://thebulletin.org/iran-and-bomb-legal-standards-iaea-o.

expressly agree that the IAEA has the ultimate and definitive authority to verify the completeness of states' declarations regarding such materials. Reference to this important area could have been addressed and clarified in the TPNW, but it was not.

The IAEA developed the Model Additional Protocol (AP) to the agreements concluded between states and the Agency. In light of the various practical limitations of verifying completeness under INFCIRC/153 safeguards agreements,[49] the application of safeguards was developed to strengthen the IAEA's ability to verify completeness. To that end, in 2009 the Security Council called upon all non-nuclear-weapon states parties to the NPT to sign, ratify and implement the AP.[50] The Model Additional Protocol focuses on measures for strengthening the effectiveness and improving the efficiency of IAEA safeguards which could not be implemented under the legal authority of safeguards agreements.[51]

First approved by the IAEA board of governors in 1997, the Agency uses the AP for negotiating and concluding additional protocols and other legally binding agreements: (1) with states and other parties to comprehensive safeguards agreements, containing all of the measures provided for in this document as the standard; (2) with nuclear-weapon states, incorporating those measures from this document that each such state has identified as capable of contributing to the nonproliferation and efficiency aims of the Model AP when implemented with regard to that state, and as consistent with that state's obligations under Article I of the NPT; and (3) with other states that are prepared to accept measures provided for in this document in pursuance of safeguards effectiveness and efficiency objectives.[52] Generally speaking, this has been a successful undertaking with the IAEA reporting in 2015 that safeguards were applied in 181 states (including Taiwan and China) with some 173 of these having comprehensive safeguards agreements in place.[53] By 2016, AP were in force in 129 States (up two from the 2015 numbers).[54] That said, a number of states are not yet using the Model AP and have reached no agreement on its "compulsory" adoption.[55] Compliance issues regarding nuclear energy for peaceful purposes under the NPT continue to raise concerns related to dual-use of nuclear capability for both energy and weapons; hence highlighting the importance of moving such compliance issues forward under the TPNW. A future protocol to the Treaty may serve to assist in this regard.

Today, a significant number of states are yet to comply with the above request, begging the question as to whether these same states would actually comply with the

---

[49] IAEA, Model Protocol Additional to the Agreement(s) between State(s) and the International Atomic Energy Agency for the Application of Safeguards, INFCIRC/540 (Corr.) (September 1997).
[50] SC Res 1887 (2009), paras. 15b and 19.
[51] See www.iaea.org/topics/safeguards-agreements.
[52] IAEA Safeguards Glossary 2001 Edition, para. 1.15.
[53] See www.iaea.org/topics/safeguards-in-practice.
[54] See www.iaea.org/sites/default/files/sg_infographic.pdf.
[55] For example, during 2015, safeguards were not implemented in the Democratic People's Republic of Korea.

Competition, Fragmentation and Polarization

TPNW requirements or simply use the TPNW to confuse the discussion by creating the appearance of nuclear compliance, but in reality, dragging out the process and delaying full AP adherence. This is particularly concerning when there remains outstanding work toward the universal acceptance of the AP.[56] The TPNW provides a tremendous opportunity to move this matter forward by requiring acceptance of the AP international standard as the minimum under Articles 3 and 4. Indeed, if states are truly committed to the universality of the TPNW, would it not follow that they agree the highest of verification standards?

Forum Shopping under the TPNW

Some concerns have been raised relating to potential forum shopping under the TPNW which may serve to polarize the international community and possibly fragment nuclear compliance efforts. Prior to the adoption of the TPNW, Adam Mount and Richard Nephew warned that states may decide to withdraw from the NPT in order to sign onto the TPNW.[57] The authors note that in a legal context[58] the term usually "refers to an attempt by one party involved in litigation to find the most favourable jurisdiction in which to contest a case."[59] They clarify their usage, to "mean that a state might purposefully sign on to a simple ban treaty that lacks non-proliferation safeguards in order to avoid the more burdensome NPT requirements for international monitoring and transparency, which might allow them latitude to withdraw from the NPT."[60] If electing to withdraw from the NPT, it would be interesting to see what reasons a contracting party would provide for its withdrawal.

Supporters of the TPNW deny that it would lead to lower standards, or in any way serve to jeopardize the goals of the NPT. Indeed, they contend that the TPNW would assist the nonproliferation process, as well as enhancing nuclear-disarmament efforts. Mount and Nephew say that "good intention is not sufficient to ensure the

---

[56] See Conclusion of Additional Protocols: Status as of December 31, 2014, www.iaea.org/safeguards/documents/AP_status_list.pdf; www.iaea.org/safeguards/documents/sir_table.pdf; Masahiko Asada, "The NPT and the IAEA Additional Protocol," in Black-Branch/Fleck (eds.), *op. cit.* Vol. II, Chapter 5.

[57] See Adam Mount and Richard Nephew, "A Nuclear Weapons Ban Should First Do No Harm to the NPT," *The Bulletin of the Atomic Scientists*, March 7, 2017. Online: www.frstrategie.org/publications/notes/a-treaty-banning-nuclear-weapons-diversion-or-breakthrough-08-2017 and https://thebulletin.org/2017/03/a-nuclear-weapons-ban-should-first-do-no-harm-to-the-npt/ and: The Nuclear Forum Shop (Nuclear Ban Treaty Challenges And Prospects) September 30, 2017, Qura tul ain Hafeez. See http://southasiajournal.net/the-nuclear-forum-shop-nuclear-ban-treaty-challenges-and-prospects/.

[58] See "Forum Shopping before International Tribunals: (Real) Concerns, (Im)Possible Solutions," Joost Pauwelyn and Luiz Eduardo Salles, *Cornell International Law Journal*, Vol. 42 Issue 1 Winter 2009 Article 4.

[59] Adam Mount and Richard Nephew, "A Nuclear Weapons Ban Should First Do No Harm to the NPT," *The Bulletin of the Atomic Scientists*, March 7, 2017. Online: www.frstrategie.org/publications/notes/a-treaty-banning-nuclear-weapons-diversion-or-breakthrough-08-2017 and https://thebulletin.org/2017/03/a-nuclear-weapons-ban-should-first-do-no-harm-to-the-npt/</u.

[60] Ibid.

ban treaty's complementarity with the existing NPT regime."[61] Like other critics, they note that the absence of specific provisions in support of the NPT, could "inadvertently do it substantial harm by creating an opportunity for nuclear aspirants to 'forum-shop.'"[62] They state:

> Unless the text of the ban treaty explicitly forecloses this kind of behavior, a state that is party to both the NPT and the ban might perceive an additional opportunity: to withdraw from the NPT but mitigate some of the resulting political or military backlash by arguing that its membership in the ban treaty was sufficient to uphold its non-proliferation obligations. That state may appeal to other non-nuclear weapon states over unfair treatment under the NPT and argue that its fidelity to a looser, unenforced nuclear weapon ban treaty is sufficient to address international concerns about its activities.[63]

Notably the final text of the TPNW did not explicitly address such concerns. States parties nevertheless would be required to follow IAEA safeguards under the TPNW. Article 3 requires adherence to IAEA safeguards, at a minimum.[64] Article 4 requires states that owned nuclear weapons to conclude a safeguards agreement with the IAEA in order "to provide credible assurance of the non-diversion of declared nuclear material from peaceful nuclear activities and of the absence of undeclared nuclear material or activities."[65] That said, these relate to standards today but if IAEA standards increase they would not necessarily have to adhere to the higher agreed standards.

Preparatory Commission for the Comprehensive Nuclear Test-Ban Preparatory Organization (CTBTO)[66]

The preamble of the TPNW recognizes "the vital importance of the Comprehensive Nuclear-Test-Ban Treaty and its verification regime as a core element of the nuclear disarmament and non-proliferation regime."[67] Critics of the TPNW, however, express general concern regarding verification systems and their relationship with the emerging role of the Comprehensive Nuclear Test-Ban Treaty Organization in relation to monitoring for Security Council enforcement purposes. In stating its reservations, Switzerland noted that some of the Treaty's provisions "bear risks for existing norms, instruments and fora. For instance, the generic reference to nuclear testing could undermine the CTBT norm as well as efforts for its early entry into force."[68]

---

[61] Ibid.
[62] Ibid.
[63] Ibid.
[64] See Article 3 Safeguards. See https://undocs.org/A/CONF.229/2017/8.
[65] See Article 4. See https://undocs.org/A/CONF.229/2017/8.
[66] See www.ctbto.org/the-treaty/.
[67] See http://undocs.org/A/CONF.229/2017/8.
[68] United Nations Conference to Negotiate a Legally Binding Instrument to Prohibit Nuclear Weapons Explanation of Vote New York, July 7, 2017 H. E. Ms. Sabrina Dallafior Permanent Representative of

254   *Competition, Fragmentation and Polarization*

As noted in Chapter 4 on legal congruence, the prohibition on testing proved to be one of the most controversial elements in negotiating the TPNW, resulting in disagreement amongst the parties so as to not undermine the final ratifications of the Comprehensive Nuclear Test Ban Treaty along with the long-awaited Test Ban Organization's coming into force.[69] As a consequence of these discussions, specific reference to the CTBT was noted in the preamble, which recognizes the CTBT's vital importance as well as noting "its verification regime as a core element of the nuclear disarmament and non-proliferation regime"[70] within the global community. Indeed, the TPNW draws on wording from the CTBT regarding the prohibition on testing as highlighted above. The text fails, however, to address the relationship between these two treaties regarding compliance with prohibiting the testing of nuclear weapons as it has done with regard to the NPT. Additionally, it does not specify that adherence to the CTBT would be a requirement, upon the CTBT's coming into force, for ensuring compliance with a prohibition on nuclear weapons testing.[71]

Insisting on more specific reference to the CTBT may have been inappropriate at this point, at least until it comes into force as a legally binding set of obligations. For all intents and purposes, the Comprehensive Nuclear Test-Ban Preparatory Organization (CTBTO)[72] is, however, presently operating as a fully fledged organization with monitoring systems in place. To that end, it is concerning that the prohibition against the testing of nuclear weapons under the TPNW does *not* include an express reference to the CTBT's International Monitoring System (IMS), which consists of a global network of sensors to detect nuclear explosions. Critics may also question the decision to replicate the CTBT, by explicitly banning nuclear testing, without expressly referencing the IMS. Arguably, this position could serve to undermine the CTBT.[73] Or, in due course it may serve to fragment the international community.

As mentioned previously, countries including Mexico, the Netherlands, Sweden and Switzerland, voiced concerns that the TPNW may actually harm the CTBT. Switzerland made an attempt, supported by the Netherlands and Sweden, to include the phrase "in accordance with the CTBT" to the wording

---

Switzerland to the Conference on Disarmament. See https://s3.amazonaws.com/unoda-web/wp-content/uploads/2017/07/Swiss-Explanation-of-Vote2.pdf.

[69] See Gaukhar M. 2017, "Nuclear Weapons Treaty, Negotiation and Beyond" (2017), *Arms Control Today*, online: www.armscontrol.org/act/2017-09/features/nuclear-weapons-prohibition-treaty-negotiations-beyond.

[70] "Recognizing the vital importance of the Comprehensive Nuclear-Test-Ban Treaty and its verification regime as a core element of the nuclear disarmament and non-proliferation regime." Preamble at: http://undocs.org/A/CONF.229/2017/8.

[71] See William C. Potter (2017) "Disarmament Diplomacy and the Nuclear Ban Treaty," *Survival*, 59:4, 75–108, DOI: 10.1080/00396338.2017.1349786.

[72] See www.ctbto.org/the-treaty/.

[73] See Alicia Sandres-Zakre 2017, "Ban Talks Advance with Treaty Draft," *Arms Control Today*, online: www.armscontrol.org/act/2017-06/news/ban-talks-advance-treaty-draft.

on testing.[74] Other countries, including Algeria, Cuba and Iran, tried to broaden the scope of the testing prohibition, to "fix" perceived loopholes in the CTBT, arguing for a specific reference to subcritical tests and computer simulations, and objecting to the use of the CTBT formulation prohibiting "any nuclear test explosion or any other nuclear explosion."[75]

A compromise devised by President Whyte Gómez was to include "test" among the core prohibitions under Article 1(a), so that states parties would undertake "never under any circumstances to . . . test . . . nuclear weapons or other nuclear explosive devices." Nevertheless, this broad formulation did not fully satisfy either side of the debate. States such as Cuba, Iran and Nigeria announced that they would interpret the text as encompassing "all forms" of nuclear testing, including subcritical tests, although that does not constitute an agreed interpretation of the treaty conference. The broader interpretation means little in practical terms because there is no verification in place for subcritical testing and computer simulations, and the nuclear-armed states are openly refusing to join the TPNW. Yet, this inconsistency could exacerbate the criticism that the TPNW reinterprets or otherwise undermines existing instruments.[76,77] It could result in two variations of interpretation on this matter, driving a further wedge between an increasingly divided global community.

Verification Issues under the Preparatory Commission for the Comprehensive Nuclear Test-Ban Treaty Organization[78]

On the face of it, the CTBT remains in flux with its status unenforceable as treaty law. That said, despite the CTBT not having been ratified by the requisite states and therefore languishing in abeyance without having entered into legal force, the work of the CTBTO plays a vital role in nuclear security, a role that will hopefully assume increasing prominence, upon the long-anticipated ratification of the CTBT. In this regard, fear that the TPNW may thwart the relevance of the CTBT or hinder the work of the CTBTO has surfaced. Given the important verification role the organization assumes, and to fully grasp the concerns expressed by the various states mentioned above, it is important to understand the relevance of the CTBTO within its broader historical context as well as its role in scientific monitoring and nuclear surveillance.

---

[74] See "Compilation of Amendments Received from States on the Revised Draft Submitted by the President Dated June 30, 2017; A/CONF.229/2017/CRP.1/Rev.1," June 30, 2017, https://s3.amazonaws.com/unoda-web/wp-content/uploads/2017/06/CRP1_rev1_compilation_30-June-1-2_8pm.docx.

[75] See Gaukhar M. 2017, "Nuclear Weapons Treaty, Negotiation and Beyond" (2017), *Arms Control Today*, online: www.armscontrol.org/act/2017-09/features/nuclear-weapons-prohibition-treaty-negotiations-beyond.

[76] See: Gaukhar, id.

[77] Documents generally referred to are: A/CONF.229/2017/CRP.1/Rev.1, June 30, 2017 and A/CONF.229/2017/CRP.1/Rev.1, June 29, 2017.

[78] See www.ctbto.org/the-treaty/.

256 *Competition, Fragmentation and Polarization*

Throughout the Cold War period, various attempts were made to conclude a comprehensive test ban treaty. These years were characterized by the stark realities of realpolitik within geostrategic policy making, during which time, deep distrust and insecurity was prevalent. The era was marked by many scientific and technical disagreements over verification methods, which in part stymied the successful conclusion of a comprehensive test ban treaty. As a direct result of such fear, the Swedish Defense Research Institute (SDRI) proposed creating a Group of Scientific Experts (GSE) to study the technical aspects of monitoring nuclear explosions in the early 1970s. In this unprecedented move, the Conference on Disarmament made the decision to grant the GSE a long-term mandate to study these issues.[79]

Given that political progress had been slow during the Cold War, the GSE was able to design and test technical features of the seismic monitoring system.[80] Some thirty to forty countries met regularly in Geneva to conduct practical, hands-on work, which helped to build confidence in the system and to reinforce the global nature of the verification regime.[81] The GSE's work effectively served as "one big training exercise."[82] Through global training courses, GSE members acquired and expanded their knowledge of four relevant technologies: (1) seismic, (2) hydroacoustic, (3) infrasound and (4) radionuclide, and also supported each other on how to incorporate them into a global nuclear explosion detection system.[83] As a result, the GSE had several decades of study through which to understand enforcement and monitoring mechanisms, which assisted in building momentum and confidence toward a comprehensive treaty and organization to supervise compliance.

Against this backdrop, in January 1994 the Conference on Disarmament[84] began negotiating a comprehensive nuclear test ban treaty under an ad hoc committee aiming to develop effective enforcement and monitoring systems under an international treaty.[85] In June 1996 a final draft treaty was presented to the Conference on Disarmament with an overwhelming majority of Member States expressing their readiness to support the draft treaty, which was adopted by the General Assembly and opened for signature in September 1996.[86] The Treaty requires states parties to

[79] Ibid.
[80] Ibid.
[81] Ibid.
[82] Ibid.
[83] Ibid.
[84] See www.un.org/disarmament/wmd/nuclear/ctbt/. The Conference was "established in 1979 as the single multilateral disarmament negotiating forum of the international community, following the first Special Session on Disarmament (SSOD I) of the United Nations General Assembly held in 1978. The Director-General of UNOG is the Secretary-General of the Conference on Disarmament as well as the Personal Representative of the UN Secretary-General to the CD." See www.unog.ch/80256EE600585943/(httpHomepages)/6A03113D1857348E80256F04006755F6?OpenDocument.
[85] Two working groups were established on February 16, 1994. Working group 1 was to address issues of verification, while working group 2 would consider legal and institutional aspects of the Treaty. See www.ctbto.org/the-treaty/1993-1996-treaty-negotiations/1993-95-prelude-and-formal-negotiations/.
[86] By resolution A/RES/50/245 Comprehensive Nuclear-Test-Ban Treaty. See www.undocs.org/A/RES/50/245.

Stalemate between Resolute and Stalwart States   257

undertake "not to carry out any nuclear weapon test explosion or any other nuclear explosion, and to prohibit and prevent any such nuclear explosion at any place under its jurisdiction or control."[87] In addition, Parties are "to refrain from causing, encouraging, or in any way participating in the carrying out of any nuclear weapon test explosion or any other nuclear explosion" and to establish an international test monitoring and verification system.[88] The Treaty will enter into force 180 days after the ratification of some forty-four specific states,[89] the majority of whom have done so.[90] Nevertheless, important nuclear players are yet to ratify it.

The CTBT seeks "to take further effective measures toward nuclear disarmament and against the proliferation of nuclear weapons in all its aspects,"[91] emphasizing "the need for continued systematic and progressive efforts to reduce nuclear weapons globally, with the ultimate goal of eliminating those weapons, and of general and complete disarmament under strict and effective international control."[92] To achieve effective measures of nuclear disarmament and nonproliferation, efforts are to focus on "constraining the development and qualitative improvement of nuclear weapons and ending the development of advanced new types of nuclear weapons."[93] Central to it, all parties are prohibited from conducting "any nuclear weapon test explosion or any other nuclear explosion."[94]

Comprehensive Monitoring and Verification under the CTBTO

Monitoring is a central feature of the CTBT. The monitoring of nuclear activities takes place through the Comprehensive Test Ban Treaty Organization,[95] created under the Treaty and consisting of a conference of states parties, an executive council, and a technical secretariat based in Vienna, which will implement and enforce the Treaty as well as providing a forum for consultation and cooperation. As mentioned in Chapter 4, the technical secretariat will implement verification procedures of the CTBT, supervise the operation of the international monitoring

---

[87] Article I. Comprehensive Nuclear-Test-Ban Treaty.
[88] Article II. Comprehensive Nuclear-Test-Ban Treaty.
[89] As per Article XIV, listed in Annex 2.
[90] Algeria, Argentina, Australia, Austria, Bangladesh, Belgium, Brazil, Bulgaria, Canada, Chile, Colombia, Democratic Republic of the Congo, Finland, France, Germany, Hungary, Indonesia, Italy, Japan, Mexico, Netherlands, Norway, Peru, Poland, Romania, Republic of Korea, Russian Federation, Slovakia, South Africa, Spain, Sweden, Switzerland, Turkey, Ukraine, United Kingdom of Great Britain and Northern Ireland and Vietnam. China, Democratic People's Republic of Korea, Egypt, India, Iran (Islamic Republic of), Israel, Pakistan and the United States of America have not yet ratified the treaty, as required under Article XIV. For a data sheet regarding signatures and ratifications, see Daryl Kimball, *The Status of the Comprehensive Test Ban Treaty: Signatories and Ratifiers*, online: www.armscontrol.org/factsheets/ctbtsig.
[91] See http://ctbto.org/fileadmin/content/treaty/treaty_text.pdf.
[92] Ibid.
[93] Ibid.
[94] As per Article I.
[95] Article II.

258 *Competition, Fragmentation and Polarization*

system, receive, process, analyze and report on the data collected, manage the International Data Centre,[96] and be involved in on-site inspections.[97] The verification protocol specifies compliance measures under the Treaty,[98] consisting of four main elements: (1) the international monitoring system; (2) consultation and clarification; (3) on-site inspections; and (4) confidence-building measures.[99]

The International Data Centre

The International Data Centre is a key part of the CTBTO's monitoring role. All data collected by the monitoring system is to be transferred to the International Data Centre for storage and processing. Effectively, the Centre will screen out non-nuclear events and provide states with relevant summaries of information collected by the monitoring system, and provide relevant raw and processed data.[100]

The International Monitoring System

The primary purpose of the International Monitoring System under the CTBT is to detect and identify any specific activity that has been prohibited under Article I of the CTBT. This monitoring system will include a network of fifty primary and 120 auxiliary seismic stations strategically positioned around the world for both comprehensive reach and efficient monitoring. These stations will be designed to distinguish between actual nuclear explosions and natural occurrences such as earthquakes. The monitoring system will also include some eighty radionuclide stations and sixteen radionuclide laboratories to detect radioactive particles released during a nuclear test. Additionally, sixty infrasound and eleven hydroacoustic

---

[96] "All the data collected by the monitoring system will be transferred to the international data center for storage and processing. The center will screen out non-nuclear events and provide states with summaries of information picked up by the monitoring system, as well as providing raw and processed data." See www.ucsusa.org/nuclear-weapons/us-nuclear-weapons-policy/comprehensive-test-ban-treaty.html#bf-toc-4.

[97] For On-Site Inspection, see On-Site Inspections Under the Comprehensive Nuclear-Test-Ban Treaty1 (Edward Ifft), online: http://aip.scitation.org/doi/pdf/10.1063/1.5009217. See also: Reviews of the Comprehensive Nuclear-Test-Ban Treaty and US security AIP Conference Proceedings 1898, 030001 (2017); 10.1063/1.5009216; A new era of nuclear test verification AIP Conference Proceedings 1898, 030004 (2017); 10.1063/1.5009219; The future of US-Russia nuclear arms control AIP Conference Proceedings 1898, 020001 (2017); 10.1063/1.5009206; Alert status of nuclear weapons AIP Conference Proceedings 1898, 020003 (2017); 10.1063/1.5009208 Unmaking the bomb: Verifying limits on the stockpiles of nuclear weapons AIP Conference Proceedings 1898, 020006 (2017); 10.1063/1.5009211 Lab-to-Lab Cooperative Threat Reduction AIP Conference Proceedings 1898, 020010 (2017); 10.1063/1.5009215.

[98] Article IV.

[99] See www.ucsusa.org/nuclear-weapons/us-nuclear-weapons-policy/comprehensive-test-ban-treaty.html#bf-toc-4.

[100] Ibid.

Stalemate between Resolute and Stalwart States   259

stations will be used to detect the sound of a nuclear explosion conducted either underground or under water.[101]

The CTBTO's Processes for Consultation and Clarification

Furthermore, there is a consultation and clarification process that is designed to encourage state parties to resolve any possible violations before requesting an on-site inspection. In this regard, either a state or the executive council can request clarification on such matters. States requesting such clarification must explain any perceived violation, or the occurrence of any ambiguous event, within a forty-eight-hour period.[102]

On-Site Inspections by the CTBTO

In the event that consultation and clarification fail to resolve an ambiguity or issue raised, each state has the right to request an on-site inspection. An inspection request must be based on information that has been collected from the monitoring system or from some national technical means of verification, such as satellites. A request cannot be based on information collected through any nefarious activity including espionage. The material request must be specific in terms of the state to be inspected, the geographical coordinates, the estimated depth, the area to be inspected and the environment and time of the event. It must also include all evidence on which the request is based, including the identity of the observer (if possible), and the results of the consultation and clarification process. The executive council will decide on the request for an inspection within ninety-six hours of receiving it. However, an inspection will only be authorized if a minimum of thirty of the council's fifty-one members agrees to it.

In terms of the logistics, an inspection team will arrive at the state in question within six days of the request. The team may request to conduct drilling during the inspection, which must be approved by a majority (twenty-six) of council members. Normally, an inspection should not take longer than sixty days, but it may be extended by up to seventy days with express council approval if necessary to do so. If the executive council rejects the inspection request and finds it to be unnecessary, or if the inspection is canceled for the same reasons, the council may discipline the requesting state. Such admonishment may include requiring the state to pay the costs of inspection preparations as well as moving to suspend the state's right to request future inspections and to serve on the council.[103]

[101] Ibid.
[102] Ibid.
[103] Ibid.

Confidence-Building Measures

In order to encourage and to promote compliance, the verification procedure also includes confidence-building measures. Hoping to reduce the number of ambiguous events, each state will voluntarily notify the technical secretariat of any chemical explosion of 300 tons for more. In addition, states can help to calibrate monitoring stations.[104]

The Role of the Comprehensive Nuclear Test-Ban Preparatory Commission

Established in November 1996, following the adoption of the Comprehensive Nuclear-Test-Ban Treaty, the Comprehensive Nuclear Test-Ban Treaty Organization Preparatory Commission is an international organization established by the states signatories to the Treaty to prepare for the Treaty's entry into force. The Preparatory Commission is taking the necessary preparations for the effective implementation of the CTBT, including establishing a global verification regime. This regime consists of a plenary body composed of all states signatories to the Treaty and a Provisional Technical Secretariat, providing a forum for both consultation and cooperation among Member States. Notably, a relationship agreement between the United Nations and the CTBTO was adopted in 2000 by the General Assembly.[105]

The NPT aims to prohibit non-nuclear-weapon states from acquiring nuclear weapons, and binds its five parties possessing nuclear weapons to eliminate them under Article VI. Meanwhile, the CTBT prohibits its parties from testing them. Both treaties, together, constitute an international regime for nonproliferation, disarmament, and international security.[106] The CTBT verification regime is unprecedented in its global reach, as noted in the United Nations Security Council Resolution 2310 of 2016, which urges states toward the complete construction of the IMS facilities and to transmit data to the International Data Center. Completion of the IMS will achieve both a political and scientific benchmark for the CTBT. The CTBTO also supports the Resolution's call on states to refrain from conducting any nuclear weapon test explosion and to maintain their moratoria on testing.[107]

The Preparatory Commission's Working Group on verification issues has noted how the GSE has contributed to the success of the CTBT,[108] in that throughout the Cold War, the GSE was able to develop the seismic monitoring system, as mentioned earlier.[109] The regular meetings in Geneva assisted with building confidence in the system and establishing a verification regime,[110] and contributed to training GSE

[104] Ibid.
[105] Resolution A/RES/54/280.
[106] See www.ctbto.org/
[107] Ibid.
[108] Ibid.
[109] Ibid.
[110] Ibid.

members in the main technological areas[111] regarding nuclear explosion detection systems.[112] As a result of the GSE and several decades of study, the CTBTO was able to form a solid foundation for when the treaty finally comes into force.

In contrast, the TPNW did not benefit from a preparatory committee such as the GSE. Once it comes into effect, it will therefore be lacking a sufficient enforcement and monitoring mechanism. This demonstrates how the CTBT is a more comprehensive and functionally sound document comparatively.[113] Moreover, it highlights how the two systems could complement each other, instead of raising fears that they may compete.

In this light, the CTBTO sees itself as instrumental in meeting the obligation of Article VI of the NPT: To pursue measures toward the cessation of the nuclear arms race and disarmament. Today, more than twenty years after the opening for signature of the CTBT, with 168 ratifications (April 23, 2020) and most of its International Monitoring System (IMS) installed, it has established almost universal support and a global norm against nuclear weapon test explosions with strong international support.[114] Indeed, the CTBT has been reaffirmed through multiple UN General Assembly resolutions and UN Security Council resolutions, such as the aforementioned Resolution 2310, which reaffirmed the widespread global support for the CTBT, reinforced the norm against testing, expressed strong support for the work of the CTBTO, and recognized that the state signatories of the CTBT are obliged not to take any action contrary to the object and purpose of the treaty, including by conducting nuclear test explosions.[115] Some would say that the TPNW serves to *reinforce* the CTBT and especially the non-testing norm, emphasizing that states parties may not "test" nuclear weapons or devices.[116] Others, however, point out the TPNW's potential for fragmentation in the international regime. Switzerland, for one, points out its concern that "[the CTBT], which is regrettably still not in force, could not be given greater consideration in the treaty text."[117]

Now that the Preparatory Commission has been in operation for over two decades, there is a strong foundation for the CTBT's entry into force. This role of the CTBT and the Preparatory Commission were largely overlooked in the final text of the TPNW, which also lacks a similar type of preparatory committee. Many of the concerns expressed in this discussion ultimately demonstrate the potential for uncertain and potentially competing legal regimes in this area of disarmament law. There are fears that the focus may stray from the value and importance of the

---

[111] Namely, seismic, hydroacoustic, infrasound and radionuclide.

[112] See www.ctbto.org/.

[113] Ibid.

[114] Ibid.

[115] See www.armscontrol.org/pressroom/2017-09/civil-society-leaders-renew-action-bring-ctbt-into-force.

[116] Ibid.

[117] In its Report of the Working Group to Analyse the Treaty on the Prohibition of Nuclear Weapons, June 30, 2018 – English translation from the German original version. See www.eda.admin.ch/dam/eda/en/documents/aussenpolitik/sicherheitspolitik/2018-bericht-arbeitsgruppe-uno-TPNW_en.pdf, at p. 3.

262 Competition, Fragmentation and Polarization

CTBT and the importance of gaining ratification by the outstanding states in order for it to come into full force as soon as possible.

Horizontal Nonproliferation and Vertical Nonproliferation of Non-State Actors

Until relatively recently, nuclear concerns related mainly to the domain of the nation state, as fissile material and technical knowledge was assumed to be under direct state control. Consequently, the activities of non-state actors seemed less problematic in their acquiring nuclear materials. Recent terrorist activities, however, have ignited concern that terrorist groups and non-state actors may seek nuclear and radioactive materials, for nefarious purposes.[118]

While the NPT is the main regulatory framework, in conjunction with a safeguards system under the responsibility of the IAEA regarding compliance issues, together they have limited enforcement capacity. The current NPT-IAEA framework lacks appropriate authority, posing a global challenge in regulating and preventing non-state actors from gaining access to nuclear materials. Addressing such vertical nonproliferation has become a major source of worry – one which may have been prudent to address directly in the TPNW.

A Global survey regarding the implementation of Security Council Resolution 1373 (2001) concluded: "The terrorist threat is evolving rapidly. It has also become more diverse, challenging and complex, partly because of the considerable financial resources flowing to certain terrorist organizations from the proceeds of transnational organized crime ... Some terrorist groups control vast territories and harbour aspirations to establish State-like structures."[119]

Following this, the UNGA adopted a comprehensive counterterrorism strategy with a view to developing legal and operational frameworks aimed at suppressing terrorist networks and strengthening capacity building and to improve control over materials for weapons of mass destruction, including nuclear.[120]

On the one hand, a lack of reference in the TPNW to combating such challenges means there would be seen to be no room for fragmentation or polarization. On the other hand, the treatment of non-state actors within the nuclear realm requires a coordinated and harmonious effort. Several commentators, including

---

[118] See www-ns.iaea.org/downloads/security/nuclear-security-plan2014-2017.pdf.

[119] Global survey of the implementation by Member States of Security Council resolution 1373 (2001). S/2016/49 at par. 11 and 12. See www.un.org/ga/search/view_doc.asp?symbol=S/2016/49&referer=/english/&Lang=E.

[120] UN Doc A/RES/60/288 (September 20, 2006). This strategy was reaffirmed in 2012, reiterating that, "international cooperation and any measures taken by Member States to prevent and combat terrorism must fully comply with their obligations under international law, including the Charter of the United Nations, in particular the purposes and principles thereof, and relevant international conventions and protocols, in particular human rights law, refugee law and international humanitarian law." UN Doc A/RES/66/282 (July 12, 2012).

this author,[121] have noted the need for proactive measures in order to address the serious threat of nuclear materials making their way into the hands of non-state actors, including terrorist groups.

The TPNW focuses primarily on measures against horizontal nonproliferation and disarmament, aiming to eliminate states from possessing, acquiring or developing nuclear weapons. Increasingly problematic is the question of how to stop non-state actors from acquiring nuclear weapons or materials to develop and potentially detonate or threaten to detonate a nuclear device. Leaving such a task solely to the efforts (i.e., the goodwill), of the nation state, without additional overarching safeguards may be remiss. The international response to any nuclear threats from non-state actors requires consistency, and it would be an unsettling position to have any sort of legal regimes lacking coordination in this area. The Security Council has addressed these issues under a series of resolutions and specifically Resolution 1540.

Resolution 1540: Suppressing the Activities of Terrorist Non-State Actors

Security Council Resolution 1540 (2004) was adopted in an attempt to fill gaps and address deficiencies in national legislation.[122] The resolution calls on all states to adopt and enforce appropriate effective laws aimed at prohibiting non-state actors from manufacturing, acquiring, possessing, developing, transporting, transferring or using nuclear weapons for terrorist purposes. They must establish domestic controls aimed at preventing the proliferation of nuclear weapons, and establish appropriate controls over such related material.[123] States are also required to implement a wide range of accountancy and control measures, including, physical protection measures; border controls; measures to detect, deter, prevent and combat illicit trafficking; and import and export control measures.[124]

In addition, 1540 requires all states to refrain from providing any form of support to non-state actors[125] that attempt to develop, acquire, manufacture, possess, transport, transfer or use nuclear, chemical or biological weapons and their means of

---

[121]   Black-Branch, Jonathan. "Nuclear Terrorism by States and Non-State Actors: Global Responses to Threats to Military and Human Security in International Law," in *Journal of Conflict and Security Law*, Vol. 22, Issue 2, July 1, 2017, pp. 201–248, https://doi-org.uml.idm.oclc.org/10.1093/jcsl/krx004.

[122]   See Jones, Scott. "Resolution 1540: Universalizing Export Control Standards?" *Arms Control Today*, Washington 36.4 (May 2006): 18–22.

[123]   For the purpose of Resolution 1540, Related materials refers to "materials, equipment and technology covered by relevant multilateral treaties and arrangements, or included on national control lists, which could be used for the design, development, production or use of nuclear, chemical and biological weapons and their means of delivery" (S/RES/1540 (2004)).

[124]   Resolution 1540 (2004) S/RES/1540 (2004).

[125]   For the purpose of Resolution 1540, a non-state actor is defined as an "individual or entity, not acting under the lawful authority of any State in conducting activities which come within the scope of this resolution" (S/RES/1540 (2004)).

delivery.[126] Additionally, states must adopt and enforce appropriate and effective laws regarding such activities in relation to nuclear, chemical or biological weapons,[127] and must enforce effective domestic controls to prevent the proliferation of nuclear, chemical, or biological weapons, including the development of effective measures to account for and secure such items in production, use, storage or transport;[128] develop effective physical protection measures;[129] and ensure there are effective border controls and law enforcement efforts to detect, deter, prevent and combat the illicit trafficking and brokering in such items.[130] In this regard, states must also establish, develop, review and maintain appropriate effective national export and trans-shipment controls over such items and enforce appropriate criminal or civil penalties for violations of such export control laws and regulations.[131]

Differing Legal Regimes with Respect to Non-State Actors

The preamble of the TPNW makes reference to the first resolution of the General Assembly of the United Nations, adopted on January 24, 1946, and generically notes subsequent resolutions calling for the elimination of nuclear weapons.[132] It does not, however, make any explicit reference to UNSC Resolution 1540 in the main body of the text with its substantive provisions. Aside from 1540, there is the United Nations Comprehensive Counter-Terrorism Strategy as well as other SC measures under Resolutions 1373, 1887 and 2325. The IAEA also drew-up a Nuclear Security Plan. After the TPNW's entry into force there may be disputes with a state affected by certain verification activities on the proper conduct or the assessment of such activities. Irrespective of whether such state will be party to the TPNW or not, there will be hardly any successful dispute settlement except by international cooperation. Any verification activities conducted by the CTBTO Preparatory Commission are based on a shared interest of participating states. Again, international responses to nuclear threats by non-state actors require a consistent and harmonious approach and not a piecemeal patchwork quilt of good intentions that remain unenforceable under disconnected and seemingly competing legal regimes. It may have been prudent to make reference to 1540, providing built-in complementary enforcement requirements or delegating powers to authoritative powers able to assist.

---

[126] Article 1 Security Council Resolution 1540 (2004). For the purpose of Resolution 1540, Means of delivery refers to "missiles, rockets and other unmanned systems capable of delivering nuclear, chemical, or biological weapons, that are specially designed for such use" (S/RES/1540 (2004)).

[127] Article 2 Security Council Resolution 1540 (2004).

[128] Article 3(a) Security Council Resolution 1540 (2004).

[129] Article 3(b) Security Council Resolution 1540 (2004).

[130] Article 3(c) Security Council Resolution 1540 (2004).

[131] Article 3(d) Security Council Resolution 1540 (2004).

[132] See https://undocs.org/A/CONF.229/2017/8.

NATO and Umbrella States

Another area of discrepancy is the contrasting views between the proponents of the TPNW and some stalwart states. As noted in prior chapters, there are well-established international obligations requiring states parties to pursue nuclear disarmament. The move toward nuclear disarmament was not only an important policy aspiration of the UN General Assembly since its first resolution of January 1946,[133] but also a long-standing legal obligation under Article VI of the NPT. This obligation has become something of a sore point in the international community. The failure to achieve the objective has, at least in part, led to the high level of support for the TPNW. While some have interpreted the obligation to mean an outright ban of nuclear weapons under an actual treaty, others justify it as incorporating effective measures in their defense doctrines such as a "no first-use" policy.[134] Whether it is a binding treaty or simply a series of legal instruments supporting disarmament efforts, the challenge today is that NATO and its allies now have the TPNW to contend with whilst considering their respective disarmament obligations. While the TPNW is thought to be an appropriate development by some, unfortunately, others perceive it as actually increasing the gaps between states instead of filling them.

It cannot be ignored that the adoption of the TPNW "reflected the frustration of many non-nuclear weapon states that the nuclear weapon states were not taking seriously their obligation under the NPT to pursue nuclear disarmament."[135] The resolute states described above acknowledged that the TPNW "would have no immediate impact on existing nuclear arsenals," but highlight that its long-term normative impact "would serve to delegitimize and stigmatize nuclear weapons and thereby contribute to achieving the ultimate goal of nuclear disarmament."[136] At the same time, as the Stockholm International Peace Research Institute observes, "there was a recognition during 2017 that the relationship between the TPNW, the NPT and related agreements would have to be defined over time in order to prevent the fragmentation of nuclear disarmament efforts."[137] So, while the TPNW was viewed by the resolute states as being a positive step toward disarmament as required by Article VI of the NPT, others could argue that it is in fact making disarmament more difficult to achieve by fragmenting and polarizing the international community – particularly NATO states – hence complicating international nuclear legal commitments.

These frustrations are evident within segments of the global community, particularly in the post-TPNW statements of some NATO members and umbrella states.

---

[133] UNGA Res. 1(I) of January 24, 1946; see also UNGA Res. 192 (III) of November 19, 1948.
[134] See Treasa Dunworth, "Pursuing 'effective measures' Relating to Nuclear Disarmament: Ways of Making a Legal Obligation a Reality," 97 (899) *International Review of the Red Cross* (2016), 601–619.
[135] See www.sipri.org/yearbook/2018/07.
[136] Ibid.
[137] Ibid.

Switzerland, for example, in its letter of explanation expressed its "regret" that it had not been possible to have a "more inclusive negotiation process." It notes "key concerns of States who had question marks about this negotiating process, whether they finally took part in it or not, were for the most part not taken into account." Moreover, Switzerland points out that a number of treaty provisions "lack clarity" which "may give rise to different legal interpretations and therefore create some confusion and uncertainties." Indeed, Switzerland itself in its letter raised issues of the "effectiveness of the treaty" as well as potential "universalization" concerns, concluding that it sees risks that the TPNW may "weaken existing norms and agreements and create parallel processes and structures which may further contribute to polarization rather than reduce it." A subsequent statement by Switzerland's Working Group to analyze the TPNW notes:

> [t]he NPT is the key instrument in the nuclear disarmament and non-proliferation architecture, as well as the foundation of an international order that is supported by Switzerland. The continued and uncontested existence of the NPT is pivotal to the achievement of a world without nuclear weapons ... In the TPNW negotiations, Switzerland therefore endeavoured to negotiate an agreement that preserves and reinforces the added value of the NPT. This objective was only partially achieved.[138]

It should be noted that this apparent fragmentation is more of an ideological one than an actual undermining of the validity of the NPT. Article 18 of the TPNW addresses the relationship between treaties, stating that "the implementation of this Treaty shall not prejudice obligations undertaken by States Parties with regard to existing international agreements, to which they are party, where those obligations are consistent with the Treaty."[139] The issue is that many states have not accepted their Article VI NPT obligations to be entirely consistent with the TPNW's more progressive view, which in turn has created further tension and polarization within the international community, making one of the true purposes of the NPT – disarmament – more difficult to achieve. What is needed is more legal certainty in this area, rather than what may be perceived as competing regimes that serve to polarize states in an area that, again, requires unity and working together in harmony.

NUCLEAR-WEAPON-FREE ZONES

Other areas raising questions of harmony is that of the relationship between states parties to nuclear-weapon-free zone treaties and their respective non-party counterparts with whom they have agreements. A nuclear-weapon-free zone, is defined as any zone recognized as such by the General Assembly, which

---

[138] See www.eda.admin.ch/dam/eda/en/documents/aussenpolitik/sicherheitspolitik/2018-bericht-arbeits gruppe-uno-TPNW_en.pdf.

[139] Article 18 of http://undocs.org/A/CONF.229/2017/8.

Nuclear-Weapon-Free Zones 267

any group of States, in the free exercise of their sovereignty, has established by virtue of a treaty or convention whereby:

(a) The statute of total absence of nuclear weapons to which the zone shall be subject, including the procedure for the delimitation of the zone, is defined;
(b) An international system of verification and control is established to guarantee compliance with the obligations deriving from that statute.[140]

The relationship between existing nuclear-weapon-free zones and the TPNW is yet to be developed. The TPNW may actually create a unique nuclear-weapons-free zone of its own, effectively creating a quasi-bipolar nuclear world between those in a TPNW-nuclear-free zone and those that are not. The NPT and treaties on nuclear-weapon-free zones require the exclusive use of IAEA safeguards from their states parties, creating a possible conflict between these unique obligations and those of the TPNW.[141] Examined firstly is what is meant by an NWFZ, followed by an overview of the relevant obligations that arise from the TPNW, comparing them to, and contrasting them with, existing NWFZ treaty obligations. Also explored is how these differing sets of obligations might conflict with, or perhaps reinforce, one another. The section concludes that on the one hand, the TPNW has the potential to strengthen NWFZs, as they could help to promote the implementation and ratification of the TPNW. On the other hand, the TPNW's strict obligations could cause severe division between NNWS and NWS, thus resulting in the breakdown of the complex legal framework created by NWFZs and ultimately disrupting an otherwise functioning relationship.

How Nuclear-Weapon-Free Zones Work

An NWFZ is a region in which member states have formally agreed through a treaty not to stockpile, acquire, deploy, or test nuclear weapons within territories, waters or airspace.[142] All members of these zones must agree only to use nuclear energy for peaceful purposes, which must be supervised by the IAEA and any agency established by the NWFZ treaty.[143] Additionally, all NWFZ treaties must be of indefinite duration

---

[140] As per UN General Assembly Resolution 3472B of 1975.
[141] Treaty for the Prohibition of Nuclear Weapons in Latin America and the Caribbean – Treaty of Tlatelolco (February 14, 1967), 634 UNTS 326; South Pacific Nuclear Free Zone Treaty (Treaty of Rarotonga) and Protocols thereto (August 6, 1985), 1676 UNTS 326; Treaty on the South-East Asia Nuclear-Weapon-Free Zone – Treaty of Bangkok (December 15, 1995), 1981 UNTS 129; African Nuclear-Weapon-Free Zone Treaty – Treaty of Pelindaba (April 11, 1996), 35 ILM 698; Treaty on a Nuclear-Weapon-Free Zone in Central Asia – Semipalatinsk Treaty (September 8, 2006). See also Declaration by Mongolia of its nuclear-weapon-free status (September 25, 1992), and the Law of Mongolia on its Nuclear-Weapon-Free Status which entered into force on February 3, 2000, www.nti.org/treaties-and-regimes/nuclear-weapon-free-status-mongolia/, and was recognized by UNGA Res 55/33 S (November 20, 2000).
[142] Paul J. Magnarella, "Attempts to Reduce and Eliminate Nuclear Weapons through the Nuclear Non-Proliferation Treaty and the Creation of Nuclear-Weapon-Free Zones" (2008) 33:4 Peace & Change at 511.
[143] Ibid.

268 *Competition, Fragmentation and Polarization*

and cannot be ratified with reservations.[144] NWFZs serve many purposes, but they are primarily in place to increase security in the relevant region and reduce the space in which nuclear weapons are permitted. Therefore, by establishing NWFZs, states can both increase security and make further progress toward the goal of global disarmament.

Most NWFZ treaties contain at least one protocol, which may be signed and ratified by the five NWS listed under the Non-Proliferation Treaty.[145] These protocols ask NWS to respect the status of the zone and not to *use* nuclear weapons or *threaten* to use nuclear weapons against states that are party to the treaty.[146] These types of agreements are often referred to as negative security assurances.[147] Once ratified by an NWS, that state agrees to the following criteria: (1) not to use or threaten to use nuclear weapons against members within the NWFZ; (2) not to test or assist in the testing of nuclear weapons within the NWFZ; and (3) not to engage in an act that would constitute a violation of the NWFZ treaty.[148]

Today, there are five recognized NWFZ treaties and three other treaties of interest to this discussion and all of them have officially come into force. The treaties are as follows: (1) the Treaty of Tlatelolco 1967 (Latin America and the Caribbean NWFZ); (2) the Treaty of Rarotonga 1985 (South Pacific NWFZ); (3) the Treaty of Bangkok 1995 (Southeast Asia NWFZ); (4) the Treaty of Pelindaba 1996 (African NWFZ); (5) the Treaty on an NWFZ in Central Asia 2006 (Central Asian NWFZ); (6) The Outer Space Treaty 1967; (7) the Antarctic Treaty 1959; and (8) the Seabed Arms Control Treaty 1971.[149] Note that these NWFZs have a unique relationship with the NPT. They can be seen as a means to accomplish the goals of global disarmament, nonproliferation, and using nuclear energy for peaceful purposes.

THE TPNW

The TPNW may be seen as a large-scale NWFZ treaty in its own right. In terms of relevant obligations the TPNW affirms existing and future nuclear-weapon-free zones as consistent with and in support of the TPNW's goal of disarmament in its preamble,

> Reaffirming the conviction that the establishment of the internationally recognized nuclear-weapon-free zones on the basis of arrangements freely arrived at among the

---

[144] Ibid.

[145] *The Non-Proliferation Treaty*, July 1, 1968 (entered into force March 9, 1970). See www.un.org/disarmament/wmd/nuclear/npt/text.

[146] Kelsey Davenport, "Nuclear-Weapon-Free Zones (NWFZ) at a Glance" (2017) 47:6 Arms Control Association. See www.armscontrol.org/factsheets/nwfz.

[147] Ibid.

[148] "Nuclear-Weapons-Free Zones: Comparative Chart," Inventory of International Nonproliferation Organizations and Regimes, Center for Nonproliferation Studies, Last Updated April 30, 2018. See www.nti.org/media/pdfs/apmnwfzc_vlZojvV.pdf?_=1525129530 (accessed on May 27, 2018).

[149] UNODA, "Nuclear-Weapon-Free Zones" (accessed May 27, 2018), online: www.un.org/disarmament/wmd/nuclear/nwfz/.

The TPNW 269

States of the region concerned enhances global and regional peace and security, strengthens the nuclear non-proliferation regime and contributes toward realizing the objective of nuclear disarmament.[150]

Similar to most NWFZ treaties, Article 1 of the TPNW, stipulates that states should never: develop, test, produce, manufacture, otherwise acquire, possess, stockpile, transfer, receive the transfer of or control over, use, threaten to use, assist, allow any stationing, installation, or deployment of nuclear weapons or other nuclear explosive devices within their territory or at any place under their jurisdiction or control or to encourage or induce anyone to do any of the above activities.[151]

As harmonious as this may seem, the TPNW may strengthen, conflict with, or indeed weaken existing NWFZ treaties. Each will be explained in brief in order to set the stage for further analysis. First, the Treaty of Tlatelolco (Treaty for the Prohibition of Nuclear Weapons in Latin America and the Caribbean ("LANWFZ")) is an NWFZ that protects certain regions within Mexico, the Caribbean, Central America and South America and has been signed and ratified by thirty-three different states.[152] The treaty creates obligations for each contracting party to prohibit and prevent the testing, use, manufacturing, production, acquisition, receipt, storage, installation or deployment of nuclear weapons and to refrain from engaging in, encouraging or authorizing, directly or indirectly, or in any way participating in the above activities.[153] The treaty is also subject to IAEA safeguards and violations are reported to the UN Security Council, the UN General Assembly and the IAEA.[154] This treaty does contain one provision, under Article 18, that allows for explosions of nuclear devices for peaceful purposes as long as the party is transparent about the nature, purpose and effects.[155] However, it should be noted that this controversial provision has been nullified by NPT and CTBT provisions. Finally, all five NWS have signed and ratified the treaty and have agreed that all of their territories in the treaty region are parties to the treaty. NWS have also agreed not to violate the treaty or use or threaten to use nuclear weapons against treaty parties, thus offering negative security assurances to all states within the NWFZ.[156]

---

[150] The TPNW preamble.

[151] Article 1, TPNW.

[152] The thirty-three states are: Antigua and Barbuda, Argentina, Bahamas, Barbados, Belize, Bolivia, Brazil, Chile, Colombia, Costa Rica, Cuba, Dominica, Dominican Republic, Ecuador, El Salvador, Grenada, Guatemala, Guyana, Haiti, Honduras, Jamaica, Mexico, Nicaragua, Panama, Paraguay, Peru, St. Kitts and Nevis, St. Lucia, St. Vincent and the Grenadines, Suriname, Trinidad and Tobago, Uruguay, Venezuela. Treaty for the Prohibition of Nuclear Weapons in Latin America and the Caribbean (LANWFZ) (Tlatelolco Treaty) Nuclear Threat Initiative, online: www.nti.org/learn/treaties-and-regimes/treaty-prohibition-nuclear-weapons-latin-america-and-caribbean-lanwfz-tlatelolco-treaty/. Last Updated: April 30, 2018 (NTI, Tlatelolco).

[153] Treaty For the Prohibition of Nuclear Weapons in Latin America and the Caribbean: Treaty of Tlatelolco, S/Inf. 652 Rev. 3 January 29, 2002, Art. 1

[154] NTI, Tlatelolco.

[155] Treaty of Tlatelolco, Art. 18.

[156] NTI, Tlatelolco.

270   *Competition, Fragmentation and Polarization*

The Treaty of Rarotonga (South Pacific Nuclear Free Zone ("SPNFZ")) has thirteen full members; Australia, New Zealand and the South Pacific Forum.[157] The obligations are mostly identical to LANWFZ, but it contains additional obligations not to provide sources or special fissionable materials or equipment to any NNWS or NWS unless subject to safeguards agreements. Further,

> States Parties are also obligated to prevent in the territory of States Parties the stationing of any nuclear explosive device; to prevent the testing of any nuclear explosive device; not to dump radioactive wastes and other radioactive matter at sea, anywhere within the SPNFZ, and to prevent the dumping of radioactive wastes and other radioactive matter by anyone in the territorial sea of the States Parties.

The Bangkok Treaty (Southeast Asian Nuclear-Weapon-Free-Zone Treaty ("SEANWFZ")) protects parts of Southeast Asia, which consists of ten eligible countries.[158] Most of the obligations are also identical to the LANWFZ. However, unlike the LANWFZ this treaty also states that no fissile material or related equipment shall be provided to NWS or NNWS unless under NPT and IAEA regulations. Similar to the SPNFZ, the SEANWFZ treaty prohibits the dumping or storage of radioactive materials. The enforcement of the obligations under the treaty shares similarities to that found under the LANWFZ. Namely, this treaty also requires the sharing of reports and the use of IAEA safeguards.[159] However, it differs in the sense that it has a fact-finding mandate.

The Bangkok Treaty does contain several provisions that differ from other NWFZs. Under the treaty, state parties can allow peaceful safeguarded nuclear programs.[160] Additionally, the treaty allows states to decide for themselves whether or not they should allow for passage of nuclear weapons through their territories.[161] These provisions are unique in the sense that they do permit nuclear weapons, as long as they meet the requirements of a peaceful safeguarded nuclear program. Furthermore, the treaty is unique in the sense that nuclear weapons can be transported on the territories to which it applies, which is usually completely prohibited under NWFZ treaties. The treaty, which contains one protocol stating that no NWS shall violate the provisions of the treaty, has not been signed by any NWS.[162] There is also a negative security assurance provision, which states that no NWS shall use or threaten to use nuclear weapons against any state party to the treaty.

The Treaty of Pelindaba (African NWFZ) has forty member states in Africa and island states. Its prohibitions are also mostly identical to the LANWFZ, but it also

---

[157] See www.nti.org/learn/treaties-and-regimes/south-pacific-nuclear-free-zone-spnfz-treaty-rarotonga/.
[158] Parties: Brunei Darussalam, Cambodia, Indonesia, Laos, Malaysia, Myanmar, Philippines, Singapore, Thailand, and Vietnam, Southeast Asian Nuclear-Weapon-Free Zone (SEANWFZ) Treaty (Bangkok Treaty). Last Updated: April 30, 2018, online: www.nti.org/learn/treaties-and-regimes/southeast-asian-nuclear-weapon-free-zone-seanwfz-treaty-bangkok-treaty/.
[159] Ibid.
[160] Ibid.
[161] Ibid.
[162] See www.nti.org/learn/treaties-and-regimes/southeast-asian-nuclear-weapon-free-zone-seanwfz-treaty-bangkok-treaty/.

The TPNW   271

prohibits research on nuclear explosive devices and "mandates reversal of nuclear capabilities according to IAEA procedures; mandates IAEA physical protection procedures; prohibits armed attack of nuclear installations."[163] It also contains three protocols: "Protocol I calls on the NWS not to use or threaten to use a nuclear explosive device against any Party to the Treaty and any territory within the Pelindaba NWFZ," which all NWS have signed and ratified.[164] "Protocol II calls on the NWS not to test or assist or encourage the testing of any nuclear explosive device anywhere within the Pelindaba NWFZ," [165] which all NWS have signed and ratified. "Protocol III calls on each Party, with respect to the territories for which it is *de jure* or *de facto* internationally responsible and situated within the Pelindaba NWFZ, to apply to the provisions of the Treaty." [166]

The Central Asian Nuclear-Weapon-Free Zone ("CANWFZ") is an NWFZ that includes five Central Asian nations. It entered into force March 21, 2009.[167] This treaty contains a strict and comprehensive list of prohibitions, which includes the following. First, the treaty prohibits the research, development, manufacturing, stockpiling, acquisition, possession, testing, or control over any nuclear weapon or other nuclear explosive device.[168] Furthermore, the treaty prohibits the assistance and encouragement of any of the above acts.[169] The treaty mandates export controls, which requires that member states must not provide any special fissionable material or related equipment to any NNWS that has not concluded an IAEA comprehensive safeguards agreement and Additional Protocol.[170] Lastly, the treaty requires that IAEA physical protection procedures and standards expressed in the Convention on Physical Protection of Nuclear Material be satisfied.[171] The treaty obligations are enforced by states exchanging reports amongst each other and all states party to the treaty must comply with IAEA safeguards.[172]

Relative to other NWFZ treaties the CANWFZ contains significant differences in its provisions. For one, the treaty requires that an Additional Protocol be signed within eighteen months after entry into force.[173] Secondly, it allows each state party

[163] Nuclear-Weapons-Free Zones: Comparative Chart, Inventory of International Nonproliferation Organizations and Regimes Center for Nonproliferation Studies, Last Updated April 30, 2018 (NWFZ Chart).

[164] NTI.org, African Nuclear-Weapon-Free Zone (ANWFZ) Treaty (Pelindaba Treaty). See James Martin Center for Nonproliferation Studies at the Middlebury Institute of International Studies at Monterey.

[165] See www.nti.org/learn/treaties-and-regimes/african-nuclear-weapon-free-zone-anwfz-treaty-pelin daba-treaty/.

[166] Ibid.

[167] NWFZ Chart.

[168] See www.nti.org/learn/treaties-and-regimes/central-asia-nuclear-weapon-free-zone-canwz/.

[169] Ibid.

[170] Ibid.

[171] Ibid.

[172] Ibid.

[173] Ibid.

to the treaty to determine for itself whether or not it should allow transit of nuclear weapons through its airspace or ports.[174] Additionally, it bans the import of radio-active waste from outside the zone.[175] Lastly, similar to the TPNW, it requires that parties to the treaty assist in the environmental rehabilitation of territories contam-inated as result of past activities related to the development, production, or storage of nuclear weapons or other nuclear explosive devices.[176] The Protocols under this treaty are identical to those under the Bangkok Treaty. However, all NWS have signed on to the Protocol.

The Antarctic Treaty is an NWFZ that now protects the Antarctic region includ-ing ice shelves. Originally signed on December 1, 1959, it has now been signed by fifty-three nations.[177] The treaty prohibits any military use of the Antarctic, peaceful and non-peaceful nuclear explosions, and all forms of nuclear waste storage.[178] Designated observers enforce these prohibitions and have authority to inspect any ships and aircraft in port and inspect all regions within the Antarctic.[179] This treaty differs from other NWFZs in that it does not use IAEA safeguarding for enforcement and verification, most likely because the Antarctic Treaty predates the entry into force of the NPT. It also does not contain any special protocols and thus no negative security assurances by the NWS.

The Outer Space Treaty (Treaty on Principles Governing the Activities of States in the Exploration and Use of Outer Space, including the Moon and Other Celestial Bodies) entered into force on October 10, 1967 and currently has 107 states parties (January 3, 2019). Article IV states:

> States Parties to the Treaty undertake not to place in orbit around the earth any objects carrying *nuclear weapons* or any other kinds of weapons of mass destruction, install such weapons on celestial bodies, or station such weapons in outer space in any other manner.
>
> The moon and other celestial bodies shall be used by all States Parties to the Treaty exclusively for peaceful purposes. The establishment of military bases, installations and fortifications, the testing of any type of weapons and the conduct of military manoeuvres on celestial bodies shall be forbidden. The use of military personnel for scientific research or for any other peaceful purposes shall not be prohibited. The use of any equipment or facility necessary for peaceful exploration of the moon and other celestial bodies shall also not be prohibited.[180]

---

[174] Ibid.

[175] Ibid.

[176] Ibid.

[177] NWFZ Chart. See also, The Antarctic Treaty, December 1, 1959 (entered into force June 23, 1961), online: Secretariat of the Antarctic Treaty. See www.ats.aq/e/ats.htm.

[178] Ibid.

[179] NWFZ Chart.

[180] Treaty on Principles Governing the Activities of States in the Exploration and Use of Outer Space, including the Moon and Other Celestial Bodies, online: http://disarmament.un.org/treaties/t/outer_space/text, accessed December 17, 2018.

This treaty prohibits states parties from sending nuclear weapons into space or stationing them on the moon or other planets and stars, thus creating a nuclear free outer space.

The Seabed Arms Control Treaty (Treaty on the Prohibition of the Emplacement of Nuclear Weapons and Other Weapons of Mass Destruction on the Sea-Bed and the Ocean Floor and in the Subsoil Thereof, entered into force on May 18, 1972 and has ninety-five states parties). Article I(1) states:

> The States Parties to this Treaty undertake not to emplant or emplace on the sea-bed and the ocean floor and in the subsoil thereof beyond the outer limit of a sea-bed zone, as defined in article II, any nuclear weapons or any other types of weapons of mass destruction as well as structures, launching installations or any other facilities specifically designed for storing, testing or using such weapons.[181]

This treaty essentially prohibits any state party from using the ocean floor or seabed to launch, or station nuclear weapons.

HOW THE TPNW AND NWFZS MIGHT INTERACT

In comparing and contrasting the NWFZs with the TPNW, we begin to see how this delicate relationship could either be enhanced, effectively advancing the objectives of the various zones, or diminished, serving to jeopardize unique agreements effectively damaging delicate working relationships. Reference is made to an article written by Michael Hamel-Green where he outlines potential implications of the TPNW for existing and proposed nuclear-weapon-free zones.[182] NWFZs emerged in part as a response among non-nuclear-weapon states to the NPT's lack of legally binding negative security assurances, which assure them "against the use or threat of use of nuclear weapons against them."[183] Indeed, the network of non-nuclear states already parties to NWFZs were also the most influential protagonists of the TPNW.[184] Hamel-Green argues that even if the TPNW were to be universally adopted and implemented, NWFZs would still need to play a key role in regional zone measures to "complement central measures of verification, compliance; to create regional security forums and governance pursuing cooperative security rather than arms racing; and to address the need for linkage to wider zonal bans on all kinds of weapons of mass destruction."[185]

---

[181] Treaty on the Prohibition of the Emplacement of Nuclear Weapons and Other Weapons of Mass Destruction on the Sea-Bed and the Ocean Floor and in the Subsoil Thereof, online: http://disarmament.un.org/treaties/t/sea_bed/text, accessed December 17, 2018.

[182] Michael Hamel-Green, "The Implications of the 2017 UN Nuclear Prohibition Treaty for Existing and Proposed Nuclear-Weapon-Free Zones," *Global Change, Peace & Security*, 30:2 (2018), 209–232.

[183] Hamel-Green at 212.

[184] Hamel-Green at 213.

[185] Green at 213.

274   *Competition, Fragmentation and Polarization*

There is no doubt that NWFZs will help put pressure on states to join the TPNW and, given the absence of NWS participation in the treaty, NWFZs may be the best way to "secure legally binding negative security guarantees" and could help move the TPNW toward universal accession and ratification.[186] Indeed, NWFZs have the potential to address both specific regional needs and almost universal adherence by NWS as demonstrated by various nuclear-free zone arrangements under the Tlatelolco Treaty, the Treaty of Rarotonga, the Treaty of Pelindaba, the Treaty on a Nuclear-Weapon-Free Zone in Central Asia, and the Nuclear-Weapon-Free Status of Mongolia, all of which have special protocols and negative security assurances from a majority of the NWS.[187] Thus, it is safe to say that at a regional level, NWFZs contribute "to furthering the process of delegitimization of nuclear weapons, and progressively reducing the number of regional sites of nuclear confrontation."[188] Moreover, they have proven to be more successful than the TPNW has been in gaining NWS support.[189]

Regarding the implications of the TPNW for existing NWFZs, a number of noteworthy points arise. For starters, Article 1(d) of the TPNW goes further than the legal obligations enlisted under most NWFZs, which focus primarily on preventing use or threats *by or against member states*, by unconditionally prohibiting all possible use or threat of use of nuclear weapons.[190] Hamel-Green notes that of the five main NWFZs, only the Bangkok Treaty contains a protocol that explicitly prevents "external nuclear weapon states from utilizing zone territory to use or threaten to use nuclear weapons against countries outside the zone," which explains "why the P5 NWS have so far refused to sign or ratify the Protocol."[191] The Tlatelolco Treaty can also be interpreted as prohibiting NWS from using zone members' territory for use or threats.[192] In contrast, the TPNW prevents all NWS from using any state party territory to use or threaten to use nuclear weapons against other countries, which would conflict with almost all other NWFZ treaties that theoretically allow, or more specifically do not explicitly prohibit, NWS to use a zone member's territory for use or threats against a non-member state.

The strict and unconditional prohibition of use and threats under Article 1(d) of the TPNW, would also conflict with some NWFZ members who rely on extended nuclear deterrence as part of their national defense strategy.[193] Umbrella states may

---

[186]   Green at 214.
[187]   NWFZ Chart.
[188]   Green at 216.
[189]   Green at 216.
[190]   Green 217.
[191]   Green 217.
[192]   Green at 217: "from a legal standpoint, Protocol II Article 1 obligates NWS to 'fully' respect 'in all its express aims and provisions' the 'statute of denuclearization of Latin America in respect or warlike purposes', within the boundaries of the zone under Article 4 of the main treaty provisions including not only zone state land territory but also international waters bounded by a zone geographic frame within defined latitudes and longitudes (now applicable since all relevant regional states have signed and ratified the Treaty)."
[193]   Green at 218.

be unduly affected as discussed in earlier in the book. Australia, which is a member of the Rarotonga Treaty NWFZ, for example, relies on US nuclear capabilities as a deterrent against nuclear threats against it and the treaty itself does not clearly prohibit this reliance.[194] It would seem that the TPNW would prohibit this reliance as it would violate both the spirit and purpose of the treaty which is to ban nuclear weapons and to eliminate them from existence. Relying on nuclear weapons for defense purposes would contradict the purpose of the TPNW and undermine its intentions.

The Central Asia Treaty also has no explicit prohibition against relying on extended nuclear deterrence.[195] Since relying on another state to use or threaten to use nuclear weapons on one's behalf would be a direct violation of Article 1(d) of the TPNW, Australia and any other state relying on extended nuclear deterrence would have to change their defense policies in order to sign and ratify the TPNW.

Given its nature, the TPNW imposes additional and stronger obligations including not to control, assist or receive assistance. Article 1(b) provides a ban on the "transfer to any recipient of or control over such weapons … directly or indirectly," and under 1(c) directs states not to "receive … the control over nuclear weapons or other nuclear explosive devices directly or indirectly."[196] Article 1(e) and (f) prohibits parties from assisting, receiving assistance, encouraging or inducing anyone to engage in any activity prohibited in the Treaty.[197] These articles imply that parties to the TPNW are compelled to not allow their territory to be used for the control of nuclear weapons. Again, along these lines Australia would be barred from joining the TPNW while hosting the US C3I in the Pine Gap and North West Cape bases, which are used to alert US nuclear weapon forces of missile launches and to assist in attack preparation, targeting and missile defense, since they would be deemed to be assisting a NWS to have control over nuclear weapons and playing a pivotal role in the use and threat of use nuclear weapons.[198] Articles 1(b), (c), (e) and (f) would also impose additional or stronger obligations on parties to the Rarotonga Treaty and the Pelindaba Treaty which do not explicitly prohibit providing or receiving assistance through control over nuclear weapons.[199]

Implementation and Compliance Requirements for the NWFZ and the TPNW

Article 5 of the TPNW requires each state party to "adopt the necessary measures to implement its obligations under this Treaty" and "take all appropriate legal,

---

[194] Australian Government, 2017 Foreign Policy White Paper, www.fpwhitepaper.gov.au/foreign-policy-white-paper, 84 (accessed December 3, 2017) in Green 218.

[195] Green at 219.

[196] See Green at 219.

[197] TPNW Art. 1(e).

[198] Green at 220.

[199] Green at 222.

276   Competition, Fragmentation and Polarization

administrative and other measures, including the imposition of penal sanctions, to prevent and suppress any activity prohibited to a state party under this Treaty undertaken by persons or on territory under its jurisdiction or control."[200] As noted earlier, the main problem with many NWFZ treaties is that most states parties have not incorporated them into their national legislation. Thus, states that are party to existing NWFZ and the TPNW would be required to incorporate into their domestic laws existing NWFZ obligations consistent with the TPNW and additional obligations that go beyond the NWFZ treaty.[201] This requirement could be a barrier for states that are operating on the notion of good faith in their fulfillment of their NWFZ obligations and want to maintain the status quo.

Finally, under the TPNW Articles 6 and 7 require states parties to provide victim assistance, environmental remediation and assistance to parties affected by testing or use of nuclear weapons. Presently, only one NWFZ partially addresses remedial obligations, the CANWFZ which requires parties to assist with "environmental rehabilitation of territories contaminated as a result of past activities related to the development, production or storage of nuclear weapons."[202] There is no mention in that treaty, however, or any other NWFZ treaty, of assistance to radiation victims of past nuclear-weapon-related activities.[203] This is significant since states parties to the South Pacific Rarotonga Treaty and the Treaty of Pelindaba have been victims of nuclear weapons testing conducted by the United States from 1946 to 1962, the United Kingdom from 1952 to 1958, and France from 1966 to 1996.[204]

The TPNW would impose additional obligations, with financial implications, on parties to repair environmental damage and to provide medical care for past victims within their respective jurisdiction, which could also prove to be a barrier for states who have large numbers of people in need of costly medical assistance. This requirement could also be a barrier to the United States, the United Kingdom and France who have used and tested nuclear weapons within NWFZs and thus would likely be held liable for massive costs relating to remediation.

THE TPNW CREATES A NEW NWFZ

Looking at the larger picture, when comparing the existing NWFZs with the obligations of the TPNW, one can see that once the TPNW enters into force it will give rise to

[200]   TPNW Article 5.1, 5.2.
[201]   Green at 222.
[202]   Green at 223.
[203]   Ibid.
[204]   For accounts of the impact of Pacific nuclear testing on victims and the environment, see Tilman A. Ruff, "The Humanitarian Impact and Implications of Nuclear Test Explosions in the Pacific Region," *International Review of the Red Cross* 97, no. 899 (2015): 775–813; Nic Maclellan, *Grappling with the Bomb: Britain's Pacific H-Bomb Tests* (Canberra: Australian National University Press, 2017); Nic Maclellan and Jean Chesneaux, *After Mururoa: France in the South Pacific* (Melbourne: Ocean Press, 1998), cited in Green at 224, n. 57.

The TPNW Creates a New NWFZ 277

an extensive nuclear-weapon-free zone within every state that ratifies it. It will form a patchwork quilt of sorts across the globe, albeit with many holes representing non-member states. There are advantages and disadvantages to this additional legal framework being superimposed onto the legal framework of existing NWFZs. The main advantages are that the TPNW aspires to move the world closer to global disarmament than the existing framework has been capable of achieving. It will require states parties to renounce extended nuclear deterrence, to stop assisting NWS, and to explicitly discontinue the use of their territories for control of nuclear weapons. This will make it more difficult for NWS to continue developing and advancing their nuclear programs in these areas and will inhibit their communication, command and control systems that rely on satellites and warning or control systems located in other states' territories. In this way it will move the world closer to global disarmament, from a land mass perspective.

Nevertheless, the disadvantages are significant. The obligations of the TPNW are very strict and inflexible. In that regard, forcing further requirements as mandated under the TPNW may threaten to alter existing relationships that non-nuclear states who are currently party to NWFZs have carefully built up with the P5 NWS over the years. They have developed important arrangements in a delicate area of law, defense and diplomacy. Tinkering with theses precarious treaty frameworks may have adverse consequences in not only breaking this tenuous relationship, but also retracting the valuable progress that has been made to date regarding nuclear nonproliferation and disarmament.

The NWFZs have been uniquely successful in gaining NWS support and ratification. If these same NWFZ states now become party to the TPNW and start implementing the additional obligations into their national laws, they will likely be forced to revise or add to the existing NWFZ treaties in so far as they are inconsistent with the obligations of the TPNW.[205] This may prove to be nearly impossible, given the strict requirements and restrictions the TPNW imposes on NWS. If NNWS states attempt to implement the TPNW obligations, the NWS will either withdraw from the existing NWFZ treaties, creating more instability, or refuse to accept the revisions, which may force the NNWS to withdraw either from the NWFZ treaty or from the TPNW. What will emerge is nothing less than a bipolar nuclear world where, on the one hand, parties to the TPNW and an NWFZ will be trying to implement their obligations, and on the other hand, those same parties will be trying to maintain relationships with the NWS. If the NWFZ legal framework breaks down, and the NWS continue to resist the TPNW, the world may be left with further entrenchment of the expanding division along with an even more volatile and

[205] Treaty on the Prohibition of Nuclear Weapons, A/CONF.229/2017/8 Article 18: "The implementation of this Treaty shall not prejudice obligations undertaken by States Parties with regard to existing international agreements, to which they are party, where those obligations are consistent with the Treaty."

278 *Competition, Fragmentation and Polarization*

fragmented nuclear world that is sharply divided and moving away from, rather than toward, global disarmament.

CONCLUSION

The international community seems to have been split into two firm camps regarding the TPNW. The resolute states committed to humanitarian disarmament are actively moving toward the complete elimination of nuclear weapons based on their moral and political stands and in doing so advocating support for the TPNW and shunning those who do not. Stalwart states resist the adoption of the TPNW contending that it is unrealistic and undermines the existing disarmament architecture. There are fears that this rift may lead to competition within the global disarmament sphere, leading to differing sets of legal norms and expectations that may serve to fragment an already divided global community. This widening gulf could result in a polarized nuclear world between the resolute states and stalwart states. In that regard, many states express frustration, with some already calling the TPNW "a recipe for competition and fragmentation."[206] They believe the TPNW may undermine the NPT as the cornerstone of disarmament. In addition, it may deflect states away from supporting the CTBT, seeking their own TPNW verification framework. It is feared that some states may seek to bypass existing architecture in favor of a new regime under the TPNW. Rogue states and those less keen on supporting any nuclear regulations may capitalize on this nuclear schism for their own nefarious ends.

While it is difficult to predict exactly what will evolve, the ever-increasing divergence is sure to alter states' relationships, most particularly in relation to the NPT, the IAEA, the CTBT/CTBTO, NATO, the Security Council and NWFZs. This raises substantial concern regarding the interplay of the TPNW and these important international instruments and institutions. It may be difficult to achieve unity and cohesiveness under emerging competing international legal regimes, effectively undermining overall progress on nuclear nonproliferation and disarmament matters. As a practical step, perhaps stalwart states could be invited to participate in the forthcoming Meeting of States Parties under Article 8 TPNW.

In sum, the international community is divided between resolute states that will ratify the TPNW and stalwart states that will not. Resolute states subscribe to humanitarian disarmament moving toward the banning of nuclear weapons. Stalwart states resist the TPNW feeling it thwarts existing disarmament efforts. Indeed, the current stalemate between the two sides heightens concern in a sensitive area, wherein this divide seems to be widening. One side feels the TPNW is

---

[206] Explanation of vote of the Netherlands on text of Nuclear Ban Treaty. See https://s3.amazonaws .com/unoda-web/wp-content/uploads/2017/07/Netherlands-EoV-Nuclear-Ban-Treaty.pdf.

underdeveloped, failing to address the nuclear reality, with the other arguing that today's nuclear dilemma requires a bold approach, assuming the moral high ground.

A common theme is that most agree that disarmament should be the ultimate goal and claim to be committed to that end. What is needed now is a new attempt to bring both sides back to the table. What may be helpful is to advance informal consultation mechanisms aimed at de-escalating the tension that has arisen and bridging the divide that has formed with a growing gulf between the parties. A truce of sorts might go a long way at this point whereby agreement on a mutually verifiable nuclear disarmament strategy is formulated, including an incrementalist phase-in plan of states to the TPNW, taking into consideration the *erga omnes* nature of their respective obligations. A process of this nature must include both nuclear-armed states and non-nuclear-weapon states, in order to turn competing positions into shared loyalties, fragmentation into unity and polarization into common ground. After all a bifurcated international legal infrastructure regulating nuclear arms within the global security architecture is in no state's interest.

10

Stigmatization-Action and Changing Global Perceptions to Delegitimize and Eliminate Nuclear Weapons

STIGMATIZATION AND MORAL TRACTION

Civil society organizations and proponents of disarmament feel they are on the right side of history and morality in advocating for the elimination of nuclear weapons. They see growing support on a global scale to ban the testing and use of nuclear weapons or explosive devices under any circumstances. As this movement gains traction, supporters of the TPNW are mobilizing to hasten the pace of nuclear abolition in an absolutist form. They are actively working to change how individuals and states view nuclear weapons with the ultimate goal of universal disarmament through an active campaign of stigmatization and delegitimization.

Although both nuclear-weapon states and several non-nuclear states say they will not become party to the TPNW, its supporters seem undeterred. This is a moral crusade. Their main strategy is not necessarily to build consensus and find ways to guarantee arms control under conventional or incrementalist approaches. They are convinced that the time for promising slow progressive reduction of nuclear arms has passed and that it is now time for decisive action aimed at discrediting and delegitimizing nuclear weapons – to discredit them morally via human rights and humanitarian discourse and through direct stigmatization-action. Whilst there is no question that universal Treaty ratification may not be realistic now, or even in the immediate future, the stigmatization movement is under way to delegitimize the perception of nuclear weapons on a global front. It hopes that such ambitions may well move international society into a new way of viewing and classifying these weapons. There is a worldwide global movement afoot to delegitimize them as horrific weapons of war that threaten international peace and security. The purpose of this chapter is to explore how civil society is working toward the successive elimination of nuclear weapons through stigmatization-action aimed at complete denuclearization. It will advance an understanding of how some states, civil society groups and other influences are attempting to alter the nuclear status quo in order to change the disarmament discourse within diplomatic relations and international affairs. It highlights various voices and perspectives regarding this emerging schism

Stigmatizing Nuclear Weapons

in the international community between nuclear abolitionists and nuclear-armed states and their allies, ultimately calling for collective action toward addressing the growing divide between states supporting the TPNW and those opposing it.

STIGMATIZING NUCLEAR WEAPONS

The concept of stigmatization may not be familiar to most lawyers. Moreover, it may not seem as an obvious strategy for changing international law. So, what is stigmatization and how does it work? The following discussion focuses on existing research on stigmatization and how it may affect change in relation to nuclear weapons under the TPNW. Leading sociologist, Erving Goffman published a ground-breaking work on stigmatization.[1] Through social interaction, Goffman examined the role of stigma, advancing significant understandings regarding social stigma and its effects on those experiencing it. His work has had a significant influence on approaching strategic interaction within game theory and its role in a wider societal setting.

Goffman defines stigma as "the process by which the reaction of others spoils normal identity."[2] Stigma may be negative or indeed positive leading to stereotyping and labeling. For example, some may see a stigma attached to wealth or perceived privilege. Although singled out as different – stigmatized – it does not necessarily disadvantage these individuals or classes. Despite negative overtones, overall there may be positive associations rather than negative ones. The stigma simply differentiates them in an overall positive manner, as opposed to disadvantaging them. Negative stigma, however, serves to disadvantage. It has an overall negative impact that is meant to isolate and discredit in a manner that does not serve the interests of those affected.

Mitsuru Kurosawa[3] has written a comprehensive account of stigmatization. He uses the Oxford definition of stigmatize, meaning: "to set a stigma upon; to make with a sign of disgrace or infamy; to 'brand'; esp. to call by a disgraceful or reproachful name; to characterize by a term implying severe censure or condemnation."[4] Applying stigma to nuclear weapons, Kurosawa points to Nina Tannenwald's research on the development of "nuclear taboo," highlighting that, "[t]he antinuclear weapon movement contributed to the formation of a taboo in three ways: by shifting the discourse on nuclear weapons, by engaging in moral consciousness-raising, and by mobilizing public support in favor of nuclear restraint."[5]

Kurosawa also quotes Joelien Pretorius' comments on the current TPNW:

---

[1] Erving Goffman. "Stigma and Social Identity," *Stigma: Notes on the Management of Spoiled Identity* (Prentice-Hall, 1963).

[2] Steven S. Sharfstein, "Status of Stigma," 2012, *Psychiatric Services* 2012 63:10, 953. See Erving Goffman, "Stigma and Social Identity," *Stigma: Notes on the Management of Spoiled Identity* (Prentice-Hall, 1963).

[3] From Osaka Jogakuin University.

[4] Simpson and Weiner 1989, XVI, 691 as quoted from Mitsuru Kurosawa (2018) "Stigmatizing and Delegitimizing Nuclear Weapons," *Journal for Peace and Nuclear Disarmament*, 1:1, 32–48, 35.

[5] At p. 22.

282 Stigmatization of Nuclear Weapons

To stigmatize means to brand something (or someone) disgraceful, odious, and worthy of disapproval, after stating, I don't see a ban treaty as a tool that can force nuclear-armed states to give up their nuclear weapons. Rather, it's a tool that can stigmatize nuclear weapons and more deeply entrench the taboo against their use – creating the conditions for disarmament.[6]

For the purposes of this discussion nuclear stigmatization is meant to discredit, devalue, scorn, shame and shun. In the context of the TPNW, civil society activities are intended to devalue nuclear weapons based on their negative humanitarian impact and the effect they have on individuals and the health of society;[7] to discredit nations that own, or rely on, nuclear weapons highlighting their destructive force; to scorn countries who support the existence of nuclear weapons and devices; to be seen as hampering world peace; to shame those supporting their production, testing and use, arguing that they make the world unsafe and unsecure; to shun those who threaten their use and use them for deterrence or defense purposes in any capacity, in any way, shape or form and under any circumstances, highlighting the overall negative effect and adverse impact they have on individuals, communities and the health of the world at large. Indeed, it is safe to say that some advocates go further and actually want to ostracize states possessing, or aiming to possess, nuclear weapons (e.g., North Korea) – to expel them from normal diplomatic relations and international affairs; to cut, or limit, ties.

Marianne Hanson argues that in order to make progress toward eliminating nuclear weapons it is necessary to first reverse the normalization of nuclear weapons

---

[6] Pretorius 2017 as quoted from Kurosawa 2018, 36.

[7] The World Health Organization (WHO) Constitution (1946) envisages "... the highest attainable standard of health as a fundamental right of every human being." "Health is a state of complete physical, mental and social well-being and not merely the absence of disease or infirmity." See www .who.int/news-room/fact-sheets/detail/human-rights-and-health. It is broader than health care, which focuses primarily on problems and managing health-related conditions such as diabetes, hypertension and heart disease; or delivered to people suffering acute, chronic or degenerative conditions. Health as a policy outcome is more proactive and preventative in nature, addressing nutrition, and lifestyle choices, including a safe environment, clean air, water, sanitation and reproductive health. It promotes wellness and mindfulness. It is a "resource for everyday life, not [simply] the objective of living. Health is a positive concept emphasizing social and personal resources, as well as physical capacities." In 1986, the WHO advanced this definition under the Ottawa Charter for Health Promotion, www.who.int/healthpromotion/conferences/previous/ottawa/en/. It is a human right protected under the International Covenant on Economic, Social and Cultural Rights Adopted and opened for signature, ratification and accession by General Assembly Resolution 2200A (XXI) of December 16, 1966 entry into force January 3, 1976, in accordance with Article 27 (which holds the status of both treaty and customary law) needing to be protected and advanced. Article 12(1), enlists the right "to the enjoyment of the highest attainable standard of physical and mental health," whereby states should take "steps to achieve the full realization of this right shall include those necessary for: (a) The provision for the reduction of the stillbirth-rate and of infant mortality and for the healthy development of the child; (b) The improvement of all aspects of environmental and industrial hygiene; (c) The prevention, treatment and control of epidemic, endemic, occupational and other diseases; (d) The creation of conditions which would assure to all medical service and medical attention in the event of sickness."

Stigmatizing Nuclear Weapons 283

that began in 1945, which was achieved by leaders and strategists within the nuclear states.[8] She defines normalization as,

the creation of the state of affairs where possession of these weapons came to be constructed by their owners as "natural" and almost without question. This involved cultivating, over time, a faith in nuclear weapons, and presenting it to the layperson as an inevitable and indeed necessary development, notwithstanding the unprecedented nature of atomic weapons ... I refer to the myriad of bureaucratic and strategic everyday practices in nuclear-weapon states since 1945 which have built upon the belief that these weapons, even as they are to be greatly feared, are nevertheless to be accepted, indeed desired – at least for the nuclear-weapon states ... Thus, normalizing can be seen as the amelioration or even defusing of nuclear anxieties and the implicit conferring of a sense of everyday legitimacy (Ungar, 1992, p. 9) onto the "fact" of nuclear strategy.[9]

She argues that normalization was achieved by, "'nuclear forgetting' where a 'sustained governmental effort to downplay atomic dangers' (p. 16) meant that the realities of nuclear destruction were largely occluded."[10]

Beatrice Fihn, the executive director of ICAN provides a comprehensive overview as to how the TPNW will work to stigmatize nuclear weapons:

Past experience in the development of international norms strongly suggests a ban treaty would affect the behaviour even of states that do not join. A treaty prohibiting nuclear weapons without the signature of nuclear-armed states does not, in and of itself, constitute disarmament. But it directly challenges the acceptability of nuclear-weapon use and possession by any state under any circumstances, thereby providing further impetus for concrete legal, political and normative measures to eliminate nuclear weapons.[11]

Fihn points out that other nuclear-related treaties, such as the Comprehensive Nuclear Test- Ban Treaty (CTBT) and the NPT, have not achieved nuclear disarmament, noting, however, that "they have provided the impetus for making progress."[12] She stresses that, "prohibition delegitimising nuclear weapons" will "significantly contribute to a strengthened norm against the weapons, at a time when the world desperately needs it."[13] Thus, the last paragraph of the preamble of the TPNW emphasizes the importance of harnessing the public conscience in order to further the principles of humanity. This has been accomplished mostly by efforts made by the UN, IRC, the Red Crescent Movement, government and non-

---

[8] Marianne Hanson (2018) "Normalizing Zero Nuclear Weapons: The Humanitarian Road to the Prohibition Treaty," *Contemporary Security Policy*, 39:3, 464–486 at 466.
[9] Ibid.
[10] Ibid.
[11] Fihn 2017, "The Logic of Banning Nuclear Weapons," *Survival*, Vol. 59 No. 1, February–March 2017 pp. 43–50, 45.
[12] Ibid.
[13] Ibid.

284 *Stigmatization of Nuclear Weapons*

governmental organizations, religious leaders, parliamentarians, academics and the *hibakusha* (Hiroshima/Nagasaki survivors)[14] to stigmatize and delegitimize nuclear weapons.

NUCLEAR WEAPONS: STIGMATIZE, DELIGITIMIZE, ELIMINATE

Tillman Ruff, co-chair of ICAN and co-president of International Physicians for the Prevention of Nuclear War (IPPNW), argues that the TPNW is using the proven path of "'stigmatise – prohibit – eliminate' which is working for the treaties addressing all the other major types of inhumane, indiscriminate weapons."[15] Many echo the view that the nuclear ban treaty is following in the footsteps of other weapons treaties each of which were driven by humanitarian concerns. Marianne Hanson agrees that the TPNW has followed the same process as other disarmament projects stating:

> (for instance the campaigns to ban landmines, chemical weapons, and biological weapons) advocates have sought to employ a three-staged process: *first*, to stigmatize the weapon by publicizing its inhumane effects; *next*, to delegitimize the weapon through a legal ruling against its manufacture, possession and use; and *third*, to eliminate the weapon from the arsenals of states, over a period of time. We can see that in the above cases, weapons have been reduced and eliminated only after the first two phases have been completed. That is, a clear legal ruling on the acceptability of a particular weapon has been essential in the long-term process of moving away from a pattern where such weapons were widely possessed and used. These same steps are now being applied to nuclear weapons.[16]

Many of the negotiators of the TPNW have been working on stigmatization of nuclear weapons for a long time and it has taken many forms: (1) scientific research and presentations; (2) activism both inside and outside government institutions driven by civil society movements and nuclear survivors; (3) legal and philosophical research, debates and advocacy, utilizing social media and press coverage, and generally raising greater awareness of the dangers of nuclear weapons. Finally, (4) organizations and citizens are pressuring banks and corporations toward economic divestment of nuclear weapons. This author would also add (5) corporate social responsibility (CSR) to this list of potential influences in this developing area.

Scientific Research

One of the most important tools in stigmatizing nuclear weapons is conducting scientific research and presenting studies to public, academic, legal and political

---

[14] Treaty on the Prohibition of Nuclear Weapons, A/CONF.229/2017/8.
[15] Ruff 2018, 8.
[16] Hanson 2018, 464–465.

Stigmatize, Deligitimize, Eliminate 285

audiences exposing the potential consequences of the use of nuclear weapons. This has been an important method used by concerned citizens to protest against nuclear weapons since the invention of the atom bomb.

A few notable works written during the Cold War and published around 1985 particularly stand out. *Nuclear Winter* by Owen Greene et al. gives a detailed analysis of the how the explosions, fires and smoke of a nuclear war would lower temperature, change the climate of the Earth, cause plants and animals to become extinct, destroy harvests and advanced agriculture which would bring famine and starvation, cause the collapse of medical and public health services and the spread of disease, and could potentially cause human extinction.[17] This book references a famous group of scientists known as TTAPS; R. P. Turco, O. B. Toon, T. P. Ackerman, J. B. Pollack and Carl Sagan who published a well-known article called "Nuclear Winter: Global Consequences of Multiple Nuclear Explosions" published in *Science* and reproduced in *Scientific American* in 1983 and 1984. Other works focused on exploring the philosophical issues that arise from the scientific research such as, *Nuclear Ethics* (1986), *Thinking About Nuclear Weapons: Analyses and Prescriptions* (1985), *Nuclear War: Philosophical Perspectives* (1985), all of which include reference to scientific studies about the effects of nuclear weapons as well as moral and philosophical responses to those studies. Paul Meyer and Tom Sauer also point out the role of physicians during the end of the Cold War,

> NGOs such as International Physicians for the Prevention of Nuclear War (which received the Nobel Peace Prize in 1985) were at the forefront of establishing a new global movement that came to be known as the International Campaign to Abolish Nuclear Weapons (ICAN). Today encompassing more than 400 NGOs from over 100 states, ICAN was the recipient of the 2017 Nobel Peace Prize for its advocacy and lobbying efforts on behalf of the ban treaty.[18]

They go on to explain how the new "Humanitarian Initiative" that created the TPNW has also begun successfully to stigmatize nuclear weapons by drawing the public's attention to the horrific consequences of using nuclear weapons by getting scientists to,

> present updated studies on the phenomenon of "nuclear winter" for example, . . . One updated study was based on a scenario of a "limited" nuclear war between India and Pakistan involving the use of 100 nuclear weapons. The study found that even such a restricted nuclear exchange would directly kill 30 million people and imperil hundreds of millions more by lowering the earth's temperature and thereby contributing to crop failures. Other experts demonstrated the virtual certainty of killing large numbers of civilians even in the case of a single nuclear weapon

---

[17] See Owen Green, Ian Percival and Irene Ridge, *Nuclear Winter: The Evidence and the Risks* (Cambridge, Polity Press 1985), 1–7.
[18] Paul Meyer and Tom Sauer, "The Nuclear Ban Treaty: A Sign of Global Impatience," *Survival Global Politics and Strategy*, Vol. 60, Issue 2, 2018, 61–72 at 64.

286   *Stigmatization of Nuclear Weapons*

targeting a military installation. This analysis reinforced the view that any conceivable use of nuclear weapons would contradict international humanitarian law, with its principles of proportionality, discrimination and precaution.[19]

Indeed, a UK-based NGO called "Article 36" that works with ICAN to prevent harm caused by weapons of war, collaborated with Scientists for Global Responsibility to produce a report that analyzes the expected consequences of a nuclear attack on Manchester, which they presented to the UK Parliament in 2013.[20]

Another recent use of scientific research on nuclear weapons to raise awareness is the online "NUKEMAP" created by Alex Wellerstein, an historian of science and nuclear weapons and a professor at the Stevens Institute of Technology. Using this interactive map, one can drag a marker over any city in the world, enter the yield of the nuclear weapon measured in kilotons or select a preset from a list of every nuclear explosion, nuclear test and warhead known to exist. The user can also decide between an air burst or surface explosion and then click the "Detonate" button which provides a visual map of everything from estimated fatalities, injuries, air blast radius and ionizing radiation to burns, measuring the humanitarian impact including hospitals, schools and places of worship that would be destroyed.[21] The site says that on August 1, 2018 people have detonated 153.7 million nuclear explosion simulations. This is one effective way of giving curious individuals a visual representation, simulation, of the effects of nuclear war. Of course, maps and statistics are no replacement for hearing, seeing and feeling the effects first hand and scientific studies and predictions remain outside of the subjective experience of victims. For this reason, scientific studies must be supplemented by listening to survivors and victims of nuclear war or nuclear testing.

Modern research projects such as the extensive and thorough (296 pages) 2008 work by Barbara Rose Johnston and Holly Barker called the "Rongelap Report," which explores the effects of nuclear weapons testing, helps to raise awareness not only of the effects of nuclear weapons use, but also the consequences for the Indigenous Marshallese people from 1946–1958 in the name of science and national security.[22] The authors of that work effectively combined the scientific data, photography and eye-witness accounts of the victims who were evicted from their homes, moved to another island and had nuclear ash rain down on them without warning. The United States then treated the Marshallese people as scientific experiments used by the government who did not treat their radiation, instead, they observed the effects of radiation and subjected them to humiliating tests. This report spawned

---

[19]   Meyer and Sauer 2018, 65–66.

[20]   See www.article36.org/nuclear-weapons/new-research-highlights-consequences-of-nuclear-weapon-use/. For the full report see www.article36.org/wp-content/uploads/2013/02/ManchesterDetonation.pdf.

[21]   To try the NUKEMAP go to https://nuclearsecrecy.com/nukemap/. Also see Wellerstein's blog: http://blog.nuclearsecrecy.com.

[22]   *Consequential Damages of Nuclear War: The Rongelap Report*, Barbara Rose Johnston and Holly M. Barker (Left Coast Press, 2008).

numerous academic articles and helped fuel the lawsuits launched by "Nuclear Zero," a worldwide group of concerned lawyers, on behalf of the Marshall Islands against China, DPRK, France, Israel, Pakistan, India, the Russian Federation and the United Kingdom for failing to fulfill their nuclear disarmament obligations under the NPT.[23] ICAN has also been using scientific research to bolster their arguments and raise awareness since they began their campaign against nuclear weapons in 2007.[24]

Clearly, many lay people, scholars, scientists and lawyers have been deeply concerned about the possibility of nuclear war since the creation of the atomic bomb. A key difference between the scientific research used by antinuclear activists from 1945 to the end of the Cold War and the current humanitarian initiative is that the former was never successful in attempting to change the mindset of national leaders and military strategists, nor were they able to gather the support and unity of states (122) toward banning such weapons, as the creators of the TPNW have been able to. It is safe to say that the current humanitarian movement is unique and employs a different strategy to earlier activist movements and has been able to use scientific studies to inform its philosophical and moral convictions, transforming its ideas into action to get political leaders, states, the UNGA, and hundreds of civil society groups on board, the efforts of which seem to be gaining momentum, enhanced by a new era of social media.

Activism by Civil Society Movements, Survivors and Victims

Civil society activists in support of the TPNW have been successful in influencing government policy and have paved the way for other organizations to exert public pressure on governments. Pax, for example, a peace movement in the Netherlands was part of efforts to successfully pressurize the Dutch government to attend the treaty negotiations. In this regard Meyer and Suaer state:

> Indeed, official policy in the Netherlands has already been influenced by civil-society activism. Pax, the main peace movement in that country, successfully collected 40,000 signatures on a 2016 petition against nuclear weapons. That achievement led automatically to a debate on the subject being held in the Dutch parliament on 28 April 2016. The four-hour debate was attended by the Dutch minister of foreign affairs, Bert Koenders, and resulted in motions calling

[23] See "International Obligations Concerning Disarmament and the Cessation of the Nuclear Arms Race: Justiciability over Justice in the Marshall Islands Cases at the International Court of Justice," *Journal of Conflict & Security Law* (2019) Vol. 24, Issue 3, Autumn 2019, pp. 1–21. Oxford University Press.

[24] See Catastrophic Human Harm, ICAN, 2015, www.icanw.org/wp-content/uploads/2012/08/CHH-Booklet-WEB-2015.pdf; Unspeakable Suffering – the humanitarian impact of nuclear weapons, 2013, Reaching Critical Will of the Women's International League for Peace and Freedom, Geneva, www.icanw.org/wp-content/uploads/2012/08/Unspeakable.pdf. Also see ICAN website for a list of all publications they use to raise awareness: www.icanw.org/resources/publications/.

288 *Stigmatization of Nuclear Weapons*

upon the Dutch government to at least attend the ban-treaty negotiations. (These motions received the approval of both opposition and governmental parties.) Despite enormous pressure from the US, the UK and France, as well as other allies, Dutch diplomats did attend, and contribute to, the negotiations – though, as noted, the Netherlands was the only delegation to vote against the treaty.[25]

Moreover, Meyer and Suaer argue that this treaty will continue to progress the disarmament cause. It will

> demonstrably strengthen the global norm against nuclear weapons, thereby increasing the stigma for states that continue to possess them. It is possible that as support for the treaty grows, new societal and political debates about the future of nuclear weapons will emerge within the nuclear-weapons and allied states themselves, especially the five basing states for NATO's nuclear forces in Europe ... Meanwhile, eminent members of society in many non-nuclear NATO member states have spoken in favour of their governments adopting a positive stance towards the treaty. Once it enters into force, pressure will grow on at least some of these governments (to possibly include Belgium, Canada, Germany, the Netherlands and Norway) to sign the treaty or align their security policies with its goals.[26]

They also point out that the effects of the ban treaty are already being felt by the United Kingdom where the expensive renewal of the Trident nuclear deterrent has triggered a societal debate.

Meyer and Sauer point out that many Scottish politicians are against the retention of nuclear weapons, reflecting in part the fact that the only British nuclear base is less than sixty-five kilometers from Glasgow. Former Labour Party leader Jeremy Corbyn is a lifelong member of the Campaign for Nuclear Disarmament, and attended the 2014 Vienna Conference on the Humanitarian Impact of Nuclear Weapons. Many of his followers are fervent critics of nuclear weapons. When Labour Party leader, he declared that if he became prime minister he would never push the "nuclear button," although the official party line (reflecting the influence of labor unions and Members of Parliament) is still in favor of Trident renewal. "The Greens are against and Liberal Democrats are also lukewarm about maintaining nuclear weapons and have suggested a recessed nuclear deterrent instead. This leaves only the Conservative Party fully in favor of renewing Trident. The entry into force of the ban treaty may help the many advocates of nuclear disarmament in the United Kingdom to make their point even more vehemently."[27]

Many people, especially among the young, are becoming strong critics of nuclear weapons in part because of a growing presence of antinuclear campaigning on social media, online news and blogs. They will be the next generation of voters, policy makers, political leaders and lawyers who will shape the nuclear debates of the

---

[25] Meyer and Sauer 2018, 68.
[26] Ibid.
[27] Meyer and Sauer, 68–69.

future. ICAN has done incredible amounts of work to raise awareness and get citizens and leaders to sign petitions, and were instrumental drivers and framers of the TPNW. They have also utilized social media, with the ICAN twitter account having some 28,000 followers and regularly post updates on progress toward the elimination of nuclear weapons. ICAN and PAX recently commissioned a poll that found that people in Belgium, Germany, Italy and the Netherlands overwhelmingly want their governments to join the TPNW.[28]

Such developments mark important positions that governments will find difficult to ignore when reassessing their respective nuclear deterrence policies and defense doctrines.

In their totality, the survey results show a clear rejection of nuclear weapons by those Europeans who are on the frontline of any nuclear attack – those hosting US weapons on their soil. More than simply demonstrating a "not in my back yard" mentality, Europeans are even more strongly in favor of a blanket ban of all nuclear weapons worldwide than they are against simply removing the weapons from their own soil.[29]

Beatrice Fihn highlights that this reflects public opinion in all four host nations who are strongly in favor of their country signing the TPNW. She notes that support for signing is most outspoken in Germany and Italy, where in Germany 71 percent want the government to sign the TPNW and in Italy 72 percent of the population are in favor of the TPNW. In Belgium 66 percent of the population want the government to sign and in the Netherlands, 66 percent of respondents are in favor of signing.[30] Finn notes that across all those surveyed, "people were highly interested in supporting divestment from nuclear weapons producers – with significant majorities in all four countries."[31] Moreover, in Belgium 68 percent of the population does not want financial institutions to invest in nuclear weapons, while in the Netherlands, 71 percent of public opinion is against financial institutions investing in nuclear weapons. In Germany and Italy respectively 72 and 78 percent of respondents think it is not proper to invest in nuclear weapons.[32]

Again, the International Committee of the Red Cross and the Red Crescent Movement are mentioned in the preamble of the TPNW as essential players in changing the public conscience. It is noteworthy that these are credible organizations whose voice reaches deep into the hearts and souls of many people worldwide. They also worked with Switzerland to include a reference to "catastrophic humanitarian consequences" of the use of nuclear weapons in the final document of the

---

[28] Susi Snyder quotes Beatrice Fihn. See https://nonukes.nl/vast-majority-of-europeans-reject-us-nuclear-weapon-on-own-soil/.

[29] Ibid.

[30] Ibid.

[31] Ibid.

[32] Ibid.

2010 NPT Review Conference.[33] It was the Red Cross and the Red Crescent that assisted with the resolution in 2011 which included a four-year action plan toward the prohibition and elimination of nuclear weapons that was implemented and broadcast by each of their 189 national societies.[34] Mr. Peter Maurer, the president of the International Committee of the Red Cross has appealed to states, global leaders and citizens to reduce and eventually eliminate the risk of nuclear weapon use, to meet their obligations under the NPT, CTBT and to join the 2017 TPNW.[35]

The *hibakusha* – the survivors of Hiroshima and Nagasaki – have also contributed to delegitimizing, humanizing the effects and stigmatizing nuclear weapons by telling their stories online, through the Hiroshima Museum, and by speaking at international conferences, courts and at activist events.[36] Evidence of their influence is found in the TPNW which again explicitly mentions the *hibakusha* in the preamble and recognizes their efforts in shaping the public conscience, "Mindful of the unacceptable suffering of and harm caused to the victims of the use of nuclear weapons (hibakusha), as well as of those affected by the testing of nuclear weapons."[37]

Their influence can also be seen during the Cold War. Joseph S. Nye Jr., the author of *Nuclear Ethics* (1986), wrote his book in part because of his visit to the Hiroshima Museum where the Japanese guide was also a survivor. The guide admitted that Japan would have done what the United States had done if they had the bomb first, but he could not understand why so many innocent people had to die.[38] On July 7, 2017 Hiroshima survivor Setsuko Thurlow delivered a passionate call to action at the United Nations during the adoption of the TPNW.[39] Setsuko was also present at the International Conference on the Humanitarian Impact of Nuclear Weapons in Nayarit, Mexico.

Survivors from the Marshall Islands Nuclear Tests have also shared experiences and stories to raise awareness of the negative impacts of nuclear weapons testing.[40] The eyewitness accounts of suffering caused by nuclear weapons use and testing has been a powerful force added to the humanitarian initiative. It has helped awaken the international public conscience by connecting a voice and human face to what was once mainly viewed as an issue of national security.

[33] Meyer and Suaer, 64.
[34] See www.icanw.org/campaign-news/red-cross-and-red-crescent-reconfirms-commitment-to-a-nuclear-ban/.
[35] See www.icrc.org/en/document/nuclear-weapons-averting-global-catastrophe.
[36] See the YouTube videos of Hibakusha Stories that have been shared and tweeted recently on August 6, 2018 for the 73rd Anniversary of the bombing of Hiroshima and Nagasaki: https://youtu.be/oJWtd4Pleok and www.youtube.com/watch?v=Ko7i71kULaM.
[37] A/CONF.229/2017/8.
[38] Nye, *Nuclear Ethics* (New York, The Free Press, 1986).
[39] See this short animated film produced by ICAN of Setsuko's call to action: www.youtube.com/watch?time_continue=2&v=i9c6_qobMko.
[40] See "Consequential Damages of Nuclear War: The Rongelap Report," by Barbara Rose Johnston and Holly M. Barker (Left Coast Press, 2008).

Stigmatize, Deligitimize, Eliminate 291

Shifting from a "Nuclearist" to a "Non-Nuclearist" Worldview through Legal and Philosophical Research and Advocacy

"Nuclear Zero" – a group of lawyers using legal action to pressure states to fulfill their obligations under the NPT, worked with the Marshall Islands to file nine law suits against all of the states known to have nuclear weapons. The lawyers involved in the lawsuits belonged to the "Association of Lawyers Against Nuclear Arms" and "Lawyers Committee on Nuclear Policy." They gained support from numerous organizations, world leaders and Nobel Laureates and have secured 5,095,237 signatures for a petition calling on "nuclear weapon nations to urgently fulfill their moral duty and legal obligation to begin negotiations for complete nuclear disarmament."[41]

Advocacy and strong voices against nuclear weapons have also come from within the courts. International Court of Justice Judges Weeramantry and Cançado Trindade, in particular, have been the most notable and recent critics. Judge Cançado Trindade's eighty-eight-page dissenting opinion on the *Marshall Islands* v. *United Kingdom* case is an extensive, profound and passionate rebuke on the decision of the Court. In that case, the Marshall Islands claim that the United Kingdom has breached both treaty and customary obligations to pursue negotiations to cease the nuclear arms race and to pursue negotiations toward nuclear disarmament.[42] Cançado not only explains his reasons for disagreeing with the judgment, he also provides a detailed account of the foundations of his own position on the subject of nuclear disarmament. Trindade has also written an important contribution, "International Law for Humankind: Towards a New *Jus Gentium*," in which he voices his disappointment with the decisions of the ICJ regarding nuclear weapons. Firstly, he criticizes the decisions in the *Nuclear Tests* (1974 and 1995) cases in which Australia and New Zealand called on France to stop nuclear weapons testing in the South Pacific. He argues that the Court missed the opportunity to clarify the law on nuclear testing, but instead refused to give a decision because they wrongly decided there was no legal dispute between the parties. He is also strongly against the decision in the Advisory Opinion of 1996 on the *Legality of the Threat or Use of Nuclear Weapons*. By leaving open the option for states to use nuclear weapons in an "extreme circumstance of self-defence in which the very survival of the state would be at stake," the Court did not follow the principles of proportionality and discrimination between combatants and non-combatants during armed conflict, which are "intransgressible" principles of International Humanitarian Law.[43] Trindade does not mince words, his criticism is sharp and clear,

[41] See http://nuclearzero.org/petition.
[42] *Marshall Islands* v. *United Kingdom* ICJ, October 5, 2016, para. 1.
[43] A. A. Cançado Trindade, *International Law for Humankind: Towards a New Jus Gentium* (Leiden: Martinus Nijhoff Publishers, 2010), pp. 416–418.

292   *Stigmatization of Nuclear Weapons*

It was in Hiroshima and Nagasaki that the limitless insanity of man heralded the arrival of a new era, the nuclear one (with the detonation of the atomic bombs in Hiroshima 06.08.1945 and in Nagasaki on 09.08.1945), which, after six decades, – having permeated the whole cold war period, – remains a stalemate which continues to threaten the future of humankind. Ever since the outcry of humankind began to echo around the world as to the pressing need for International Law to outlaw all weapons of mass destruction, starting with nuclear weapons: this is the task which still remains before us today. Endeavors towards general and complete disarmament, in their distinct aspects, have indeed been permeated with basic considerations of humanity.[44]

Judge Weeramantry has also signaled his opposition to the use and threat of nuclear weapons in the ICJ Advisory Opinion of 1996 on the *Legality of the Threat or Use of Nuclear Weapons*, by voting against the proposition that there is no comprehensive and universal prohibition of the threat or use of nuclear weapons and he voted against the view of the Court that states could use nuclear weapons in extreme circumstance of self-defense, in which the survival of a state would be at stake.[45] He also voices strong opposition to nuclear weapons testing in the *Nuclear Tests* case (1995) where he argues that the court should have made a decision and declared the illegality of both atmospheric and underground nuclear tests, given relevant legal principles and the scientific studies that showed the potential harms caused to the environment and human beings if the water or seabed became contaminated by radioactive material.[46]

Legal Scholars John Finnis and John Burroughs have written extensively on the moral and philosophical issues surrounding the threat and use of nuclear weapons. Finnis wrote "Nuclear Deterrence, Morality and Realism" in 1987 to address the doctrine of nuclear deterrence during the Cold War. Finnis presents a forceful and logical argument against deterrence because it violates fundamental moral and legal principles. Most importantly he argues that deterrence violates the norm against killing and intending to kill innocent civilians and non-combatants. Burroughs published a book in response the *Advisory Opinion* called "The (Il)legality of Threat and Use of Nuclear Weapons" in 1997, which raised legal and moral issues of the law governing modern nuclear weapons. Each of these works articulate and perhaps help shape the views surrounding nuclear weapons of legal scholars, legal philosophers, international lawyers and judges alike.

Such arguments are essential for contributing to the dialogue amongst legal scholars, international organizations and courts because they gather together various pieces of expertise including scientific research, the humanitarian impact, legal precedents, treaties, principles, moral principles and philosophical arguments into

---

[44] Trindade 2010, 401.
[45] Legality of the Threat or Use of Nuclear Weapons, Advisory Opinion, ICJ Reports 1996, p. 226, para. 105.
[46] Dissent of Judge Weeramantry for Nuclear Test Case 1995, at 71.

Stigmatize, Deligitimize, Eliminate 293

coherent and comprehensive reasons for questioning the nuclear weapons status quo. Indeed, such arguments serve to influence the views of national leaders and in turn government defense policies. Together they form a puzzle-style picture that nuclear deterrence is not pleasant. Ray Acheson explains how this shift is happening.

> These conversations themselves have an impact on the *status quo*. The process to ban the bomb has, more than any other disarmament initiative before it, exposed the cognitive dissonance of "nuclear deterrence," illuminating its corrupt self-serving rationale and its influence over international affairs. Those engaged in banning nuclear weapons took away the veil of legitimacy and authority of the nuclear-armed states – dismantling their arguments, disrupting their narratives, and ultimately standing up to their projection of power.[47]

Aside from the influence on shaping the debate, Acheson sees how the TPNW will continue to shape these legal, moral and philosophical discussions, effectively having a snow-ball effect on creating an impetus to changing the current deterrence approach argued by nuclear-weapon states: "With the TPNW now firmly on the table, debates about the ban and about nuclear weapons are only increasing. This means new opportunities for public discussion about the nature of nuclear weapons, about the policies and practices that sustain them and put the world at risk, and about alternatives for global security."[48]

Acheson feels that such public awareness and discourse will in turn place governments under pressure to reconsider their respective positions on nuclear weapons.

> In this context, the tension between many governments' stated commitment to achieving a nuclear weapon free world and their actual policies that support the maintenance of these weapons is becoming clearer and more public. Several countries, such as Norway, Italy, Sweden, and Switzerland, are undertaking investigations into the legal and political implications of joining the TPNW. Some government officials already seem to be struggling with the dissonance between their current policies and their own rhetoric.

Such may result in national governments having to make tough decisions in relation to their respective sovereign security doctrines and may force them to reconsider their long-standing relations with international partners and organizations such as NATO:

> The Norwegian prime minister, for example, said in an interview with Norwegian Broadcasting Service (NRK Dagsrevyen) that while Norway supports the North Atlantic Treaty Organization (NATO)'s strategic doctrine, which includes nuclear weapons, Norway itself does not have a policy of being under a nuclear umbrella. Attempting to dissociate Norway from the use of nuclear weapons, she nevertheless

---

[47] Ray Acheson (2018) "Impacts of the Nuclear Ban: How Outlawing Nuclear Weapons Is Changing the World," *Global Change, Peace & Security*, DOI: 10.1080/14781158.2018.1465907. Acheson 2018, 2–3.
[48] Ibid.

294   *Stigmatization of Nuclear Weapons*

admitted that Norway supported NATO having and being willing to use nuclear weapons, including in "defence" of Norway.[49]

It seems that the TPNW will place some governments in delicate positions, forcing them to manage a precarious balancing act between their internal relations and their external affairs.

> This kind of intellectual wrestling with the reality of being complicit within the system of nuclear "deterrence" – the practice and policies which put the world at risk of annihilation – is a product of the stigmatization process. Stigmatizing nuclear weapons is proving to be essential – and rather straightforward. There is already a baseline from which to further undermine the justifications for these weapons. Even the countries that declare nuclear weapons essential for their security already respond with righteous indignation and economic sanctions against any new country that is suspected of developing a nuclear weapon capacity. If a North Korean or Iranian bomb is so awful that anything is justified to stop it, how is an American or Russian bomb any different? If we are afraid of nuclear weapons in Trump's hands, aren't we really afraid of nuclear weapons altogether? Regardless of which country or leader uses these weapons, the results will be the same. This is what it means to stigmatize the weapons, rather than those that wield them.[50]

Many hope the TPNW is set to change the nuclear narrative regarding the moral basis from which we view deterrence. From a philosophical perspective, it paints a picture that stigmatizes weapons changing the focus of the discussion by reframing the discourse and opening a different dialogue. Nuclear deterrence is not about defense security assurances; it is about military dominance and insecurity. The Treaty creates an option, an alternative, a choice – the option to legally accept the TPNW, an alternative to deterrence and a choice that delegitimizes nuclear weapons, rejecting the status quo and forcing states to reassess and realign military security policy for a safer world that is no longer dependent on strategic nuclear dominance.

Economic Divestment

PAX, a peace movement in the Netherlands and central member of ICAN launched a campaign report called "Don't Bank on the Bomb: A Global Report on the Financing of Nuclear Weapons Producers," which reviews the financing of the nuclear weapons industry by global financial institutions. The report effectively "names and shames those that are still okay with trying to make a profit from producing nuclear weapons."[51] They also produced a "hall of fame" for institutions

---

[49]   Acheson 2018, 2–3.
[50]   Ibid.
[51]   See www.ethicalconsumer.org/ethicalreports/ethical-finance/ethicalbanking/dontbankonthebomb .aspx.

that have a policy that exclude all types of investments in nuclear weapons companies. The "hall of shame" lists 288 institutions that do not have any policies prohibiting investments in nuclear weapons.[52] Making this report public and using it as a strategic tool of social pressure to further stigmatize investing in nuclear weapons and to pressure companies to develop strong policies that restrict nuclear investments can have a powerful effect. Most corporations, investment firms and banks depend a great deal on their reputation in the local and international community, so they would have a keen interest in avoiding the "hall of shame."

Beatrice Fihn comments on how effective this report and divest campaigns can be,

> The annual Don't Bank on the Bomb report tracks financial institutions and their investments in nuclear-weapons production. The report notes that a treaty prohibiting nuclear weapons would significantly impact investment decisions. Divestment campaigns are effective tools for stimulating change on the business side of weapons production. The bans on landmines and cluster munitions were followed by divestment and removal of funds available for companies involved in such production. In August 2016, Textron – the last US-based producer of sensor-fused cluster munitions – announced it would cease production. The company cited a decline in orders and "the current political climate" as motivation, an indication that the cluster-munition convention constitutes a global norm and that the stigma associated with cluster bombs is growing. One financial analyst also noted that ceasing production of cluster munitions could allow the company to gain access to funds from potential investors that had previously avoided them.[53]

Paul Meyer and Tom Sauer argue that the TPNW will put more pressure on private sector firms to exercise caution and be more careful about their funding in connection with nuclear weapons industry.

> Nevertheless, the treaty's advocates, while harbouring no delusion that the nuclear-weapons states will radically change course in the short term, believe that it sets in motion two forces that may eventually serve to alter the behaviour of these states and their allies. The first of these is the way the treaty may encourage enhanced restraint by private-sector firms (especially banks and investment funds) with respect to their exposure to the nuclear-weapons industry.[54]

Today more than ever, reputation and situational awareness are vital for companies and financial institutions alike. Meyer and Sauer state:

> In an age of ethical investing, banks and investment funds care about their reputation. Once nuclear weapons are declared illegal, many financial institutions will think twice before funding or investing in firms that are doing business in the

---

[52] See www.dontbankonthebomb.com/wp-content/uploads/2018/03/2018_Report.pdf.

[53] Fihn B. 2017, "The Logic of Banning Nuclear Weapons," *Survival* Vol. 59 No. 1, February–March 2017, pp. 43–50, 46.

[54] Meyer and Sauer, 67.

nuclear-weapons sector. Indeed, a large Norwegian pension fund changed its policy even before the treaty was agreed, and a Dutch pension fund followed suit shortly afterwards. It is possible that many more banks will come under pressure to do likewise, which would in turn cause problems for nuclear-weapons-related businesses. This could have implications for state policy.[55]

Acheson provides an account of how that divestment is already working:

> Another product of the stigmatization process is economic divestment. One of the key aspirations for the nuclear ban was that it could prohibit the financial investment in nuclear weapon production and maintenance. While this does not appear as a specific prohibition in the TPNW, it is included in the prohibition on assisting, encouraging or inducing anyone to engage in any activity prohibited by the Treaty.
>
> In practical terms, this means that states parties to the TPNW would need to withdraw any government money (such as pension funds) from companies that produce nuclear weapons. It also means that banks, pension funds and other financial institutions will face pressure to withdraw their money from such companies. In this way, the nuclear ban is likely to have a significant impact on nuclear weapon modernization programmes and financial investments in nuclear weapons, delivery systems, and related infrastructure.[56]

Acheson highlights that companies get and remain involved in the nuclear weapons business because it yields them significant income with low financial risk or investment. She points out:

> The work and relationships with governments involved in nuclear weapons facilitate other profitable activities, e.g. in the development and marketing of nuclear power stations, in physical security, or in surveillance, intelligence, and counter-proliferation. The prohibition on "assistance" with prohibited acts has a material impact on the corporations involved in the production of nuclear weapons. It helps to undermine these companies' rationale for being involved with the nuclear weapons business. For nuclear warheads per se, only a fairly small number of companies are involved, but many of these companies greatly value their wider international business.
>
> The divestment campaign accompanying the treaty banning cluster munitions has been successful in affecting the financial interests of corporations producing these weapon systems and related components. Even within countries that have not joined the Convention on Cluster Munitions, companies have ceased production on these illegal weapons. For example, the last company producing cluster munitions in the United States, Textron, announced in August 2016 that it would no longer produce these weapons. The US government has not allotted funds for cluster munition production since 2007, even though it did not join the Convention adopted in 2006.

---

[55] Ibid.
[56] Ray Acheson (2018), 3–5.

Many investment firms and pension funds are already divesting from nuclear weapons – including in those countries that have not yet joined the TPNW. The Norwegian government announced it will exclude investments in BAE Systems, AECOM, Fluror Corp, Huntington Ingalls Industries and Honeywell because of these companies' involvement in the production of key components for nuclear weapons. The largest Dutch pension fund, the civil servants fund Stichting Pensioenfonds (ABP), has decided to end its investments in producers of nuclear weapons. The pension fund recognizes that the TPNW was decisive in its decision.[57]

Economic divestment puts pressure on governments, private enterprise, corporations and banks to consider carefully their policies and practices regarding nuclear weapons funding, investment, or even connections. Organizations like "Don't Bank on the Bomb" are also signaling to individual consumers which corporations and banks do not have strict policies for not funding nuclear weapons. As the humanitarian movement grows and pricks the international public conscience, money will begin to talk to those who are listening, but it will stop talking to those who ignore this powerful non-nuclear wind blowing across our world.

Business and Corporate Social Responsibility

In line with the growth of social conscience generally, today there is an increased awareness on corporate social responsibility (CSR) and the reputation of companies requiring a distinct approach regarding business and labor standards. CSR[58] focuses primarily on business activities seeking to make business account for its practices in four main areas: (1) compliance with human rights norms and legal instruments[59] as well as not being complicit in such abuses;[60] (2) working conditions and labor standards;[61] (3) taking a precautionary approach to the environment;[62] and (4)

---

[57] Ray Acheson (2018), 3–5.

[58] See The Ten Principles of the UN Global Compact. See www.unglobalcompact.org/what-is-gc /mission/principles.

[59] Based on the principles articulated in the UN Declaration of Human Rights (1948) (see www .ohchr.org/EN/UDHR/Documents/UDHR_Translations/eng.pdf), the International Covenant on Civil and Political Rights (1966) (see https://treaties.un.org/doc/publication/unts/volume%20999/ volume-999-i-14668-english.pdf) and the International Covenant on Economic, Social and Cultural Rights (1966) (see www.ohchr.org/documents/professionalinterest/cescr.pdf).

[60] Human Rights "Principle 1: Businesses should support and respect the protection of internationally proclaimed human rights; and Principle 2: make sure that they are not complicit in human rights abuses." See www.unglobalcompact.org/what-is-gc/mission/principles.

[61] Labour "Principle 3: Businesses should uphold the freedom of association and the effective recognition of the right to collective bargaining; Principle 4: the elimination of all forms of forced and compulsory labour; Principle 5: the effective abolition of child labour; and Principle 6: the elimination of discrimination in respect of employment and occupation." See www.unglobalcompact.org /what-is-gc/mission/principles.

[62] Environment "Principle 7: Businesses should support a precautionary approach to environmental challenges; Principle 8: undertake initiatives to promote greater environmental responsibility; and

addressing issues of corruption within the business context.[63] Uranium mines, nuclear power plants and weapons manufacturers largely operate as private enterprises to which CSR principles apply.

Effectively, CSR requires a comprehensive and holistic focus on business activities, standards of performance in respecting and actively promoting human rights, labor, environmental and anticorruption principles. It endeavors to achieve social impact by addressing real problems, usually having an impact at a grassroots level in localized communities, addressing marginalized and disadvantaged individuals whilst promoting corporate responsibility and tackling "wicked-problems"[64] facing humanity today. This represents a growing focus in which the business sector moves toward social innovation, taking progressive steps to ameliorate socio-economic conditions, while advancing social justice and employing social capital to improve human inequality, address environmental challenges and rethink traditional approaches by acting in a proactive manner. Needless to say, uranium mines, nuclear power stations and weapons manufacturers will increasingly face challenges to apply CSR principles as a part of their corporate strategy and part of their business model and supply chain.

TPNW Analysis: Challenging Social Norms Globally toward Change

The TPNW itself is already gaining international attention from activists, governments, lawyers, legal scholars and citizens around the globe. Its creators hope it will challenge current perceptions and act as a catalyst for changing world views regarding nuclear weapons so that they are no longer seen or accepted as normal. As Hanson writes about the treaty, while it may seem that such

> ... developments are largely declaratory, and do not suggest an immediate change in the behavior or policies of the nuclear-weapon states, they do carry the potential to recast significantly the nuclear weapons' debate and to shift the characterization of nuclear weapons away from being "normal," toward one where they are seen as inhumane, morally unacceptable, and ultimately as abnormal elements of international relations.[65]

She feels that such a movement will potentially, over time make the elimination of nuclear weapons, the "new normal" despite currently being resisted by nuclear states.[66]

Discussing the potential, impact of the nuclear ban treaty, and how outlawing nuclear weapons is set to change the world, Acheson feels that in addition to

---

Principle 9: encourage the development and diffusion of environmentally friendly technologies." See www.unglobalcompact.org/what-is-gc/mission/principles.

[63] Anti-Corruption "Principle 10: Businesses should work against corruption in all its forms, including extortion and bribery." See www.unglobalcompact.org/what-is-gc/mission/principles.

[64] First defined by design theorists Horst Rittel and Melvin Webber who introduced the term "wicked problem." See www.stonybrook.edu/commcms/wicked-problem/about/What-is-a-wicked-problem.

[65] Hanson 2018, 465.

[66] Ibid.

economic divestment, as mentioned earlier, the intention is that the nuclear ban also enables an ideological divestment from deterrence as well as other arguments used to justify the maintenance and possession of nuclear weapons. She contends that it also exposes and challenges "patriarchal tactics used to suppress the perspectives and agency of anyone who might challenge those in a dominant position."[67] Indeed such intentions may have already generated concern amongst the nuclear establishment:

> Outlawing nuclear weapons in an international agreement that the nuclear-armed states did not negotiate has created much consternation in the political, diplomatic and academic spheres. Scepticism about the utility of the TPNW has been greatly encouraged by the nine countries that possess nuclear weapons: China, France, India, Israel, Pakistan, North Korea, Russia, United Kingdom and United States.[68]

Moreover, some of the US allies relying on security assurances with nuclear weapons "have also contributed to the embittered naysaying about the ban."[69] Acheson emphasizes that the perception of such "extended nuclear deterrence" is based on a myth.[70] Arguments against prohibition and maintaining the nuclear status quo generally assert that "the proponents of the ban do not understand the security concerns of countries with nuclear weapons – that they are naive, irrational, irresponsible, impractical and even emotional."[71]

The ban, is largely driven by governments from the global south, including almost all in Africa, Latin America, the Caribbean and Southeast Asia together with a cross-regional "core group" consisting of Austria, Brazil, Ireland, Mexico, Nigeria and South Africa, along with others such as Costa Rica, Jamaica, Malaysia, New Zealand and Thailand.[72] These states persevered in their endeavors despite strong opposition from the nuclear states and NATO allies. Acheson feels that, when governments possessing or supporting nuclear weapons accuse such supportive countries and civil society groups of "being naive, irrational, irresponsible and emotional, it comes across both as racist and patriarchal."[73] She challenges assertions made by "dominant" nuclear states as usually "unjustified, misinformed, and rooted in a material or political commitment to [maintain] the status quo." Acheson contends that those most negatively affected by such "dominant discourse" are "women, indigenous peoples, the poor, [and] inhabitants of the areas in which the weapons are stored,"[74] as well as tested as in the case of the Marshall Islands or potentially used.

---

[67] Acheson 2018, 5–7.
[68] Ibid.
[69] Ibid.
[70] Ibid.
[71] Ibid.
[72] Ibid.
[73] Ibid.
[74] Ibid.

The rejection of their perspectives and the dismissal of voices of those most affected, as "emotional" is "highly gendered,"[75] both in its intention and effect.

> When those flexing their "masculinity" want to demonstrate or reinforce their power and dominance, they try to make others seem small and marginalized by accusing them of being emotional, overwrought, irrational or impractical. Women have experienced this technique of dismissal and denigration for as long as gender hierarchies have existed. The denial of reason in one's "opponent" is destabilizing. It is an attempt to take away the ground on which the other stands, projecting illusions about what is real, what makes sense, or what is rational. It means putting self as subject and the other as object, eliminating their sense of and capacity for agency.

Acheson points out that many of the movers of the treaty are from what may be seen as the marginalized, oppressed and the non-white world. They are seeking to challenge the status quo:

> Women and LGBTQIA people are leaders in the current anti-nuclear movement, challenging the normative discourses that traditionally allow certain perspectives to be heard. Women also played a leading role amongst the diplomats in the process to ban nuclear weapons, with some delegations to the negotiations even being comprised solely of women. People of colour also played a leading role in the nuclear ban. The process was galvanized and led by the nonwhite world, both in terms of governments and civil society. ICAN campaigners from Brazil to Kenya to the Philippines were instrumental in advocacy while most of the governments involved in the process are also from the global south. Indigenous nuclear weapon test survivors from Australia and the Marshall Islands gave testimony during negotiations alongside Japanese atomic bomb survivors.[76]

Acheson argues that nuclear weapon policy has, "long been recognized as racist and colonial."[77] To that end, the goal of banning nuclear weapons means "taking a stand against these policies, [and] working together at the United Nations where all countries are supposed to have an equal say."[78] After all, the UN Charter recognizes "sovereign equality" of states.[79]

---

[75] Ibid.

[76] Ibid.

[77] See, for example, Vincent J. Intondi, *African Americans Against the Bomb: Nuclear Weapon, Colonialism, and the Black Freedom Movement* (Stanford, CA: Stanford University Press, 2015); and Kjølv Egeland, "UK Nukes: Why the World Is Asking Britain to Disarm," *New Internationalist*, October 26, 2016, https://newint.org/contributors/kjolv-egeland.

[78] Acheson 2018, 7.

[79] Article 2(1)–(5) "The Organization and its Members, in pursuit of the Purposes stated in Article 1, shall act in accordance with the following Principles. 1. The Organization is based on the principle of the sovereign equality of all its Members. 2. All Members, in order to ensure to all of them the rights and benefits resulting from membership, shall fulfil in good faith the obligations assumed by them in accordance with the present Charter. 3. All Members shall settle their international disputes by peaceful means in such a manner that international peace and security, and justice, are not

Stigmatize, Deligitimize, Eliminate

It is recognized that the TPNW will not achieve immediate and visible impact of universality. As with many social justice issues, laws prohibiting a given activity or mandating new behaviors cannot and "will not fix everything straight away."[80] Indeed, Acheson highlights that any gains made are to be "assaulted by push back from those who fear loss of their privilege and power."[81] Nevertheless, despite an apparent recalcitrance on the part of dominant nuclear states, campaigners remain undeterred and "things do [and will] change."[82] The nuclear ban must be seen in "the context of resistance to injustice, inequality and oppression; and in the context of making meaningful change through acts of courage."[83] Offered to the world is "an act of resistance and hope; an example of creating change in the face of powerful opposition."[84] "Regardless of whatever else the nuclear ban brings from here, this in itself has incredible significance."[85]

Amid the debate over the merits of nuclear deterrence and state dominance, one cannot lose sight of the fact that the nuclear ban is about people and the future of humanity. It,

> ... is not just the reason or rationality of those supporting the prohibition and elimination of nuclear weapons that is denied by the nuclear-armed states. It is also the lived experience of everyone who has ever suffered from a nuclear explosion, or mining of nuclear material, or dumping of nuclear waste.[86]

Realigning and changing the nuclear status quo requires challenging existing assumptions and cultural norms that are deeply embedded in the social construction of military defense and the presumed rational reality presented by nuclear-weapon states and their allies.

> Objectification of others and control of "reality" are integral to patriarchy, as they are to concepts like "nuclear deterrence" and "geostrategic stability" as a mechanism to maintain the current global hierarchy. The nuclear-armed states resisted the development of the humanitarian discourse because it focuses on what nuclear weapons actually do to human bodies, to societies, to the planet. Such evidence undermines the abstraction of nuclear weapons as deterrents or protectors,

---

endangered. 4. All Members shall refrain in their international relations from the threat or use of force against the territorial integrity or political independence of any state, or in any other manner inconsistent with the Purposes of the United Nations. 5. All Members shall give the United Nations every assistance in any action it takes in accordance with the present Charter, and shall refrain from giving assistance to any state against which the United Nations is taking preventive or enforcement action." See http://legal.un.org/repertory/art2.shtml.

[80] Acheson 2018, 7–8.
[81] Ibid.
[82] Ibid.
[83] Ibid.
[84] Ibid.
[85] Ibid.
[86] Ibid.

302 *Stigmatization of Nuclear Weapons*

and refocuses attention on the fact that they are tools of genocide, slaughter, extinction.[87]

Acheson criticizes this position highlighting the need to challenge defense assumptions:

> Within this patriarchal construct of the world order, disarmament seems impossible – like a utopian vision of a world that cannot exist because, the argument goes, there will always be those who want to retain or develop the capacity to wield massive, unfathomable levels of violence over others, and therefore the "rational" actors need to retain the weapons for protection against the irrational others. The refusal by the nuclear-armed states to constructively engage with the humanitarian discourse represents an acceptance of human beings intentionally put in harm's way – as objects, viewed within an abstract calculus of casualty figures. It stands in stark contrast to the concepts and laws of human rights and dignity and poses a serious challenge to global justice.[88]

It is essential we rethink modern politics within an interdependent world in order to move toward establishing shared and common values. The current approach based on "the notion that states, as coherent units, must always be at odds with one another, seeking an 'accommodation' of their differences rather than collectively pursuing a world in which mutual interdependence and cooperation could guide behaviour through an integrated set of common interests, needs and obligations, considerations that characterize human security, distinguishing it from state centred notions of security."[89] After all, policy decisions are based on nothing more than "conceptions of power imbued with mistrust, threat, fear and violence," advocating that such policies do not permit any other form of international engagement or relationship between citizens and states.[90] Moreover, they dismiss other alternatives as utopian and unrealistic, including those characteristic of feminist and human security-based approaches.[91]

Again, such a dismissal is seen to be rooted in patriarchy and unhelpful in pursuing a progressive perspective. Instead, they defend and maintain the status quo based on nuclear fear. "[C]linging to the established theory of 'realism' limits the range of acceptable responses to the nuclear ban treaty and accurate analyses of its potential or actual impacts. It also limits the ability of the theory's advocates and adherents from confronting the challenges that nuclear weapons pose to security and stability, at national and international levels."[92]

The TPNW is emblematic of both challenge and change, whereby we are in the midst of a paradigm shift regarding how we perceive and accept nuclear weapon

[87] Ibid.
[88] Ibid.
[89] Ibid.
[90] Ibid.
[91] Ibid.
[92] Ibid.

Conclusions: Stigmatize, Delegitimize, Eliminate 303

theory and practice. It must be recognized that it "took courage for states negotiating and signing the TPNW to stand up to the nuclear-armed states."[93] They have acted against the powerful, maintaining the courage of their convictions – courage that was denied to many of them "repeatedly by those entrenched in the dominant discourse of realism and international relations theory."[94] "Undertaken by a collective partnership of civil society and diplomatic actors in the face of strong opposition by the nuclear-armed states and some of their nuclear-supportive allies, the process to ban the bomb has confronted structures of power within international relations."[95] The nuclear world has entered into unchartered waters, in which it requires new approaches under this newly emerging nuclear reality.

CONCLUSIONS: STIGMATIZE, DELEGITIMIZE, ELIMINATE

There is little doubt that the TPNW sets out to change the nuclear dialogue in the international community. Challenges to the status quo are set to realign thinking amid a growing movement to change conventional wisdom regarding the place and importance of nuclear weapons within a contemporary context. The discussion throughout this chapter explored various ways in which a range of players are seeking to mobilize a re-thinking in order to stigmatize nuclear weapons by sensitizing leaders, governments and citizens alike to their adverse effects. It explores the idea that stigmatization may take many forms in order to act as a powerful force that will help propel the international community toward delegitimizing such weapons with a view to eventually eliminating them.

The TPNW is not necessarily intended to build consensus and find ways to guarantee nuclear arms control under incrementalist approaches. The time for promising a slow progressive reduction of nuclear arms has passed. It is now time for decisive action to delegitimize nuclear weapons on a global front. While the five NPT nuclear-weapon states call for "an incremental, step-by-step approach,"[96] those supporting the Treaty want a bolder and more progressive approach. The TPNW challenges the world to eliminate them through human rights and humanitarian discourse and stigmatization, and to reassess their need as a deterrent. Whilst there is no question that full universalization may not currently be on the cards, and the immediate impact is difficult to measure, the stigmatization movement is firmly afoot to delegitimize nuclear weapons on a global scale. In the long-term, it seems that such ambitions may well move global society into changing perceptions cumulating into new ways of looking at weapons and their role in defense doctrines. There

[93] Ibid.
[94] Ibid.
[95] Ibid.
[96] P-5, Statement by China, France, Russian Federation, United Kingdom and the United States to the 2015 Treaty on the Non-Proliferation of Nuclear Weapons Review Conference (New York: May 2015), www.un.org/en/conf/npt/2015/statements/pdf/P5_en.pdf accessed March 12 2017.

304   *Stigmatization of Nuclear Weapons*

is a worldwide universal movement in motion to delegitimize them as horrific weapons of war that threaten international peace and security reversing arguments that may be seen as inherently offensive for global security. In the end it would seem that the move to stigmatize nuclear weapons may have an important impact on emerging social norms. Attempts to delegitimize such weapons are building momentum in order to reduce, if not completely eliminate them globally.

A CALL TO ACTION TO OVERCOME THE GROWING SCHISM

Despite the different views and positions between the NWS and the NNWS, this author would argue that there is a pressing and increasingly urgent need to overcome this growing schism between the various camps. The discussion in this chapter and previously in Chapter 2, setting the background and historical context leading to the Treaty and Chapter 3, regarding the humanitarian movement behind the TPNW, aimed to develop an understanding of the position of various states, civil society groups and individuals and their commitment to its objectives. To address the growing division on nuclear disarmament positions, it is best to understand its nature and why it exists to hopefully move beyond the growing schism in a productive fashion, on a global front.

The TPNW is the first of its kind to ban nuclear weapons outright. Given the growing force behind it, and its overall objective, to advance humanitarian approaches to disarmament, it would be unhelpful to disregard it completely. The Treaty has come about partly as a result of ignoring such needs amid growing discontent over the lack of progress on disarmament, as required under Article VI of the NPT. Notably, it was adopted by nearly two-thirds of UN Member States, calling for significant changes to conventional armament under a unique legal framework.

It may be tempting for NWS and their allies to ignore the Treaty, given their opposition to it and the fact that they are unlikely to be legally bound by it under international law. This author feels that it would be more prudent to work on bridging the divide rather than exacerbating it; to work on moving forward in a constructive and progressive manner rather than being obstinate and potentially making matters even more divisive. The nine states with nuclear weapons, Russia, the United States, China, France and the United Kingdom, states parties to the NPT, as well as non-NPT states, India, Pakistan, Israel and North Korea, would be wise to open dialogue with those intending to accede to the TPNW.

In looking forward, states opposing the Treaty should not adopt a spiteful or dismissive attitude, seeking to punish or ignore those wanting to accede to it. It does not mean they have to embrace the Treaty, per se, but they should not develop a negative disposition toward it, pitting "us" against "them" in a haves versus have nots environment wherein some states have nuclear weapons and others do not.

Conflict surrounding these issues is not going to resolve itself; division on such matters is not going to go away.

It needs open and progressive dialogue, addressing these matters in a responsible and decisive manner, to bridge the growing gulf between the various positions. In so doing, all states must recognize their common disarmament obligations and shared responsibilities, *erga omnes*.

11

Toward Neo-Universalism: Toward a New Reality in International Law?

What we need is Star Peace and not Star Wars.

Mikhail Gorbachev

The TPNW was welcomed at the UN General Assembly, under the participation of a wide range of humanitarian groups and civil society organizations, supported by a groundswell of nations around the world. The Treaty firmly implants new law into the international legal landscape for states who wish to ratify it, sowing the seeds of potentially new normative behavior within the global community more generally. Indeed, the TPNW purports to strive for universality, raising significant questions regarding its ambitions in achieving legal unity within the wider international legal order. The dedication to the spirit of the Treaty cannot be ignored, nor can the optimism to ban nuclear weapons. That said, however, Treaty negotiations and its general reception lack firm endorsement from many relevant players in this area. Important states, including the five nuclear-weapon-states under the NPT, are diametrically opposed to the Treaty. Moreover, many non-nuclear-weapon states openly defy its central focus at this point, aimed at the total elimination of nuclear weapons in their defense policy, questioning the Treaty's utility as a credible contribution to developing international humanitarian law and legal norms.

Despite the pessimism of nuclear-weapon states and those saying they will neither become party to the TPNW, nor be bound by it under customary law, and consequently that the status quo will prevail, as discussed throughout this book, proponents of the TPNW are mobilizing in pursuit of collective action. They intend to change perceptions of nuclear weapons, and in doing so they are appealing to new forms of universal values indicating that the current nuclear posture may not reign supreme. This chapter seeks to examine how the TPNW will sow the seeds of new normative behavior under the guidance of humanitarianism within the global context. Whether or not states currently consent to the Treaty, there is at present an emerging hope toward universality, contributing to

306

a new post-Cold War era in nonproliferation discourse and direct action. The very existence of the Treaty banning nuclear weapons and explosive devices, in effect, creates normative pressure on nuclear-weapon states to reconsider their respective nuclear armament position which will invariably reinforce a new sense of universalism thus contributing to a new reality on a global front.

INTRODUCTION

There appear to be two separate but causally connected changes happening in the international community. Firstly, the goals of the TPNW are gaining increasing universal acceptance by many around the world. Civil support for the idea of a non-nuclear world seems to be growing rapidly and not showing signs of abating. Secondly, the very basis or grounds for the TPNW demonstrate a shift in the dominant theory of international law from pragmatism – whatever works is true and best – and legal and political realism – we must deal with reality as it is, not as we want it to be – toward universalism, which appeals to certain universal norms or ethical imperatives that every state is bound by, regardless of whether the state agrees to be bound or not. Needless to say, universalism, too, is based on interests and realistic assessments.

TOWARD UNIVERSAL ACCEPTANCE OF A NON-NUCLEAR WORLD

The global support from political leaders, citizens and civil society groups for the goals of the TPNW demonstrates the growth toward universal acceptance of a non-nuclear world. The Treaty is aiming for universality but as it stands today, it is unlikely to become customary international law; it is not likely to reach the status of universal law any time soon. Separate from whether it actually gains universality legally speaking, the non-nuclear ideas and goals of the treaty are moving toward a form of universalism, (i.e., universal acceptance). Those advocating against nuclear weapons are therefore changing the discourse of individuals and states, sowing the seeds of universalism and thus making the argument for universality. This is a sociological revolution challenging the legitimacy of the nuclear platform and changing the isomorphic sphere. Although different from other developments, such as civil rights, Black Lives Matter, antiwar or equality movements, both are driven by citizens voicing opposition and acting based on a deep conviction of what is right and wrong. One of two things happen when citizens become mobilized and motivated by a single issue; the state can either act or react. That is, it can respond proactively or exercise damage control; explode or implode. If citizens mobilize around the cause of eradicating nuclear weapons, governments could eventually be forced by their citizens to reassess their respective positions and perhaps give up their

308 Toward Neo-Universalism

nuclear weapons through a process of legislative reform led by parliamentary representatives or face potential civil disobedience and resistance. Such rebellion could come in the form of non-cooperation with government agencies, boycotting corporations and banks that are associated with nuclear weapons and their financing, public protests, or de-selecting leaders who refuse to listen to democratic voices. Members of ICAN suggest that fierce resistance to nuclear weapons means,

> ... disrupting the dominant narratives about nuclear weapons as tools of "safety" and "security" and "peace" ...
> ... connecting with other movements and initiatives for social change. Gun violence, climate change, racial justice, indigenous rights, diversity in political life – all of these and so much more are relevant for challenging nuclear weapons ...
> ... working locally with city or municipal council members to divest public funds from nuclear-weapons production ...
> ... educating legislators, parliamentarians, politicians, and other government officials about nuclear weapons and about the nuclear ban ...
> ... going to the sites of nuclear violence – sites of their use and testing, as well as their sites of production and manufacture, sites of uranium mining and waste dumping, sites of their assembly or their deployment. It means interrupting the daily work at the sites, distributing information about the humanitarian impacts of nuclear weapons and about the prohibition treaty, speaking with local communities and workers, and building connections among people.[1]

To date, the Treaty has already demonstrated a massive shift toward a non-nuclear world. Some 122 out of 193 countries under the UN have voted in favor of adopting the TPNW.[2] These countries represent nearly two-thirds of the world's leaders and approximately 3 billion people, 40 percent of the world's population.[3] Given the significance of being the first arms control treaty to ban nuclear weapons it is worth naming the states specifically in order to emphasize their sheer number. They are: Afghanistan, Algeria, Angola, Antigua & Barbuda, Argentina, Austria, Azerbaijan, Bahamas, Bahrain, Bangladesh, Belize, Benin, Bhutan, Bolivia, Botswana, Brazil, Brunei, Burkina Faso, Burundi, Cape Verde, Cambodia, Chad, Chile, Colombia, Congo, Costa Rica, Côte d'Ivoire, Cuba, Cyprus, Djibouti, Dominican Republic, DRC (Congo), Ecuador, Egypt, El Salvador, Equatorial Guinea, Eritrea, Ethiopia, Fiji, Gabon, Gambia, Ghana, Grenada, Guatemala, Guinea-Bissau, Guyana, Haiti, Holy See, Honduras, Indonesia, Iran, Iraq, Ireland, Jamaica, Jordan, Kazakhstan, Kenya, Kiribati, Kuwait, Laos, Lebanon, Lesotho, Liberia, Liechtenstein,

---

[1] Ray Acheson, Loreta Castro, Beatrice Fihn, Linnet Ngayu and Carlos Umaña, "Rebuilding the Antinuclear Movement," The Nation, online: www.thenation.com/article/rebuilding-antinuclear-movement/.

[2] Note that this total does not include the Holy See and the State of Palestine which are non-member observer states.

[3] The 2018 population statistics are from http://worldpopulationreview.com.

Public and Government Support for Disarmament 309

Madagascar, Malawi, Malaysia, Malta, Marshall Islands, Mauritania, Mauritius, Mexico, Moldova, Mongolia, Morocco, Mozambique, Myanmar, Namibia, Nepal, New Zealand, Nigeria, Oman, Palau, Palestine, Panama, Papua New Guinea, Paraguay, Peru, Philippines, Qatar, Saint Kitts & Nevis, Saint Lucia, Saint Vincent & the Grenadines, Samoa, San Marino, São Tomé & Principe, Saudi Arabia, Senegal, Seychelles, Sierra Leone, Solomon Islands, South Africa, Sri Lanka, Sudan, Suriname, Sweden, Switzerland, Tanzania, Thailand, Timor-Leste, Togo, Tonga, Trinidad & Tobago, Tunisia, Uganda, United Arab Emirates, Uruguay, Vanuatu, Venezuela, Vietnam, Yemen and Zimbabwe.[4]

As discussed in Chapter 2, in leading up to Treaty negotiations, in 2016 the UN Open-ended Working Group on Nuclear Disarmament (OEWG) adopted a recommendation calling on the UNGA to "convene a conference in 2017, open to all states, with the participation and contribution of international organizations and civil society, to negotiate a legally-binding instrument to prohibit nuclear weapons, leading towards their total elimination."[5] This recommendation received widespread support from fifty-four African states, ten South East Asian states, thirty-three states from Latin America and the Caribbean and a number of states from Asia, the Pacific and Europe. Only twenty-four states did not agree with the recommendation and instead recommended a slower progressive multilateral approach to nuclear disarmament.[6] In 2015, 120 states adopted the "Humanitarian Pledge for the Prohibition and Elimination of Nuclear Weapons" (Resolution 70/48).[7]

PUBLIC AND GOVERNMENT SUPPORT FOR DISARMAMENT

Most governments claim to want disarmament in some form or other. Some states want to achieve it through conventional arms control methods; not via the TPNW, per se. They support disarmament in principle, but in practice they want it done via the exiting nuclear infrastructure under the NPT process as well as by other arms controls measures such as the CTBT or negotiating a Fissile Material Cut-off Treaty. Despite their position, the adoption of the TPNW at the UN General Assembly in July 2017, nevertheless illustrates a groundswell of governmental support throughout the international community for the elimination of nuclear weapons through the implementation of the TPNW. Moreover, there seems to be growing momentum for the TPNW, even in some countries that did not sign the Treaty or participate in its negotiations. In many of these non-participant countries there is a divide between the government's position and that of the citizens themselves. Even in the most

---

[4] ICAN, Positions on the Treaty, see www.icanw.org/why-a-ban/positions/.
[5] UN Doc A/71/371, at 9, see https://documents-dds-ny.un.org/doc/UNDOC/GEN/N16/276/39/PDF/N1627639.pdf?OpenElement.
[6] UN Doc A/71/371, at 6.
[7] UN Doc A/RES/70/48. Online: see www.un.org/en/ga/search/view_doc.asp?symbol=A/RES/70/48.

310   *Toward Neo-Universalism*

recalcitrant countries opposing the Treaty, there is a vocal base wanting to adopt the Treaty despite the national governments' stance to the contrary.

STATE SUPPORT FOR THE TPNW

Polls done in various countries support trends with those without nuclear weapons accounting for the highest percentage of those strongly in favor of an international agreement for eliminating all nuclear weapon within a set time period; restricting all other countries from developing them; and close monitoring to ensure they were following the agreement.[8] According to reports from the World Publics on Eliminating All Nuclear Weapons, the countries with the highest percentage of people that support the elimination of all nuclear weapons are Argentina at 85 percent, Mexico at 70 percent and Kenya at 68 percent.[9] The following discussion focuses primarily on some of the countries that did not vote to adopt the TPNW in 2017 examining their respective positions on disarmament.

NUCLEAR-WEAPON STATES

Amongst the NWS countries there is a range of different policies and attitudes to nuclear weapons with many citizens increasingly voicing their concern over nuclear deterrence. The World Publics study indicated that the five nuclear weapons states also have a significant percentage of people that support the elimination of all nuclear weapons with China at 60 percent, France at 58 percent, Britain at 55 percent, United States at 39 percent and Russia at 38 percent.[10]

The United States of America

Notably, the World Publics study placed the United States at a low level of support for the elimination of all nuclear at 39 percent, with Russia at the lowest level with 38 percent support.[11] Various surveys regarding attitudes concerning nuclear weapons reveal different statistics in what at first may seem like contradictory results. Within the United States, which has been the most powerful and vocal opponent of the TPNW from the beginning, forty-five prominent organizations have also partnered with ICAN.[12] A 2010 CNN Opinion poll indicated that 36 percent of Americans are very worried about the possibility of nuclear war and 73 percent believe that the United States should sign a treaty with Russia to reduce the number

---

[8]   World Publics on Eliminating All Nuclear Weapons December 9, 2008, www.nuclearfiles.org/menu/library/opinion-polls/nuclear-weapons/world-publics-eliminating-nukes-2008.pdf.
[9]   Ibid.
[10] Ibid.
[11] Ibid.
[12] Partner organizations, see www.icanw.org/campaign/partner-organizations/.

of nuclear weapons in each country.[13] Another poll conducted in 2010 by GfK Roper Public Affairs & Media shows that 62 percent of Americans believe that no countries should be allowed to have nuclear weapons.[14] On the contrary, one Stanford study conducted in July 2015, suggests that a majority of Americans would still "approve of using nuclear weapons first against the civilian population of a non-nuclear-armed adversary [if provoked], even killing 2 million Iranian civilians, if they believed that such use would save the lives of 20,000 U.S. soldiers."[15] Sagan argues that one explanation for this majority support is the belief in retribution and the ability to assign blame to foreign civilians "because they had not overthrown their government."[16]

This data contradicts the argument of many scholars who suggest that there is a "nuclear taboo" among the US general public. Researchers such as Nina Tannenwald, Steven Pinker, Neta Crawford and Ward Thomas have pointed to various polls on nuclear weapons first-use action and opinions on the atomic bombs used against Japan to suggest that most people in the United States now think it is immoral to use nuclear weapons first and to kill large numbers of innocent civilians with nuclear weapons.[17] Sagan argues that this is not the case, the study shows that Americans, "appear to be willing both to support the use of whatever weaponry is deemed most effective militarily and to kill foreign civilians on a massive scale whenever such attacks are considered useful to defend critical US national security interests and protect the lives of significant numbers of US military personnel."[18]

The apparent paradox might be explained by the phrasing and focus of the questions in the opinion polls; the same person could consistently believe that the United States should not have dropped the bombs on Japan in 1945 and that ideally no countries should have nuclear weapons, while still holding that their own country would be justified in using nuclear weapons in order to protect its citizens. What is troubling with this reasoning is that if this public opinion is accurate, it contradicts IHL principles of necessity, proportionality and non-combatant immunity which places legal restrictions on a state's military actions during times of war. Indeed, in January 2020 President Trump announced that the United States may strike back in a "disproportionate manner" against Iran if it attacked American people or targets,

---

[13] CNN/Opinion Research Corporation Poll. Dec. 17–19, 2010. N=1,008 adults nationwide. Margin of error ± 3. See www.pollingreport.com/defense.htm.

[14] AP-GfK Poll conducted by GfK Roper Public Affairs & Media, November 3–8, 2010. N=1,000 adults nationwide. Margin of error ± 4.1. online: www.pollingreport.com/defense.htm.

[15] Clifton B. Parker, August 8, 2017 Public opinion unlikely to curb a US president's use of nuclear weapons in war, Stanford scholar finds, online: https://news.stanford.edu/2017/08/08/americans-weigh -nuclear-war/. (Parker C.2017) The full study can be found in: Scott D. Sagan and Benjamin A. Valentino, "Revisiting Hiroshima in Iran: What Americans Really Think about Using Nuclear Weapons and Killing Noncombatants," *International Security*, Vol. 42, Issue 1, Summer 2017, pp. 41–79, online: www.mitpressjournals.org/doi/full/10.1162/ISEC_a_00284 (Sagan S. and Valentino A).

[16] Parker C. 2017.

[17] Sagan S. and Valentino A. at 44.

[18] Ibid.

312   *Toward Neo-Universalism*

following the targeted execution of the Iranian high-level military figure Qassem Soleimani.[19]

The poll, again taken prior to this event, seems to support that an act of self-defense can go beyond what is proportionate to the threat and what is necessary to stop the threat. In addition, citizens see no problem with using weapons and military strategies that do not discriminate between civilians or non-combatants and combatants. Note as well, that the United States, has the strongest nuclear capacity in the world, so many taking such polls may view nuclear war as happening somewhere else, believing that US nuclear weapons would protect them from hostile nations. They may have an unrealistic view thinking that nuclear war would not affect them directly. That said, citizens in other nations that border nuclear weapon states, or are in states that are being threatened with nuclear weapons, have a very different perspective and thus a different view on the use of nuclear weapons.

United Kingdom

Again, the World Publics study indicated 55 percent British support the elimination of all nuclear weapons.[20] The power of civil society to influence government policies and the development of nuclear weapon has also been demonstrated in the past in places such as Berkshire in England, where in 1958 demonstrators marched between London and the Atomic Weapons Research Establishment at Aldermaston in Berkshire. Subsequently, in 1982, some 30,000 women protested and in 1983, 70,000 protestors formed a human chain between Greenham and Aldermaston protesting against a government decision to allow American cruise missiles to be held at the US base in Berkshire.[21] David Fairhall, author of *Common Ground: The Story of Greenham*, argues that the Greenham women "dragged discussion of nuclear weapons out of the dark world of SS20s and CTBTs [comprehensive nuclear-test-ban treaties], all those acronyms and technical details, and forced people to discuss them in plain language. And that meant they had to be discussed in the House of Commons."[22]

Reports from an adviser to Ronald Reagan suggests that they borrowed the "zero option" slogan straight from the protestors' banners.[23] The protestors helped form the Campaign for Nuclear Disarmament (CND) and, in 1980, European Nuclear

---

[19]   See www.independent.co.uk/news/world/americas/us-politics/iran-news-war-us-trump-strike-back-twitter-latest-a9271476.html.

[20]   Ibid. World Publics on Eliminating All Nuclear Weapons December 9, 2008, www.nuclearfiles.org /menu/library/opinion-polls/nuclear-weapons/world-publics-eliminating-nukes-2008.pdf.

[21]   Zoe Williams, September 6, 2017, *The Guardian*, "No more nukes? Why anti-nuclear protests need an urgent revival," www.theguardian.com/world/2017/sep/06/no-more-nukes-anti-nuclear-protests-cnd-greenham-common.

[22]   Ibid.

[23]   Ibid.

Nuclear-Weapon States 313

Disarmament, which shaped the public discourse on nuclear weapons and helped popularize the idea that peace and human rights were inseparable.[24]

In 2016, the Campaign for Nuclear Disarmament led a demonstration of over 60,000 people against the modernization of Trident, the British nuclear weapons system. The central message of the protest was: "Nuclear weapons are no deterrent. Trident does nothing to protect us on the brink of nuclear war: on the contrary it will make us a target."[25]

Today, the UK government's official stance is that it supports nuclear disarmament, advocating that it should take place through multilateral negotiations governed in accordance with the NPT and not the TPNW.

China

Despite some skepticism over the accuracy of the results, China showed an astonishing 60 percent popular support for the elimination of all nuclear weapons – the highest figure amongst NPT nuclear-armed states, followed by France at 58 percent, according to the World Publics survey.[26] While China boycotted the Treaty negotiations, it has been noted as "the most responsive of the five NWS towards the NWPT."[27] Specifically, China was the only one of the five permanent Security Council states that did not vote against starting the NWPT negotiation in the UN General Assembly. It abstained. Prior to the adoption of the TPNW, in a speech at the United Nations in Geneva following a landmark address at the World Economic Forum in Davos, Chinese President Xi Jinping called for a world without nuclear weapons and urged a multilateral system based on equality among nations large and small. President Xi stated: "Nuclear weapons should be completely prohibited and destroyed over time to make the world free of nuclear weapons."[28] That said, this comes at a time when China is continuing "to modernize its nuclear weapon delivery systems and is slowly increasing the size of its nuclear arsenal."[29] Moreover, there are increasing worries regarding China's military ambitions, particularly with its increasing presence in the South China Sea.[30]

[24] Ibid.
[25] Kate Hudson, September 8, 2017, "We Must Ramp Up Protest if We Are to Avoid Nuclear War," www.theguardian.com/world/2017/sep/08/we-must-ramp-up-protest-if-we-are-to-avoid-nuclear-war.
[26] Ibid. World Publics on Eliminating All Nuclear Weapons December 9, 2008, www.nuclearfiles.org/menu/library/opinion-polls/nuclear-weapons/world-publics-eliminating-nukes-2008.pdf.
[27] China and the Nuclear Weapons Prohibition Treaty (September 2017) by Tong Zhao and Raymond Wang. See https://carnegietsinghua.org/2017/09/21/china-and-nuclear-weapons-prohibition-treaty-pub-73488.
[28] "China's Xi Calls for a World Without Nuclear Weapons," *South China Morning Post*, January 19, 2017. See www.scmp.com/news/china/diplomacy-defence/article/2063383/chinas-xi-calls-world-without-nuclear-weapons.
[29] SPIRI as quoted from: Rajat Pandit Pakistan remains ahead in nuclear warheads but India confident of its deterrence capability June 18, 2018. See http://timesofindia.indiatimes.com/articleshow/64641056.cms?utm_source=contentofinterest&utm_medium=text&utm_campaign=cppst.
[30] See www.scmp.com/news/china/diplomacy/article/3042999/beijing-unlikely-back-down-over-south-china-sea-despite.

314 *Toward Neo-Universalism*

Russia

Russia accounted for the lowest population percentage of the NWS supporting the elimination of all nuclear weapons at 38 percent.[31] There is undoubtedly concern mounting at government levels with the growth of NATO over the past decades and the geopolitical position of China as a strong economic force. The degree to which this effects public opinion is difficult to measure, especially in light of recent concerns regarding protests and developments in Crimea and Ukraine.

France

France is openly in favor of nuclear disarmament, but only if the wider global security environment improves. It shows 58 percent support the elimination of all nuclear weapons.[32] At present it advances a minimal deterrence policy under which the government describes its vision as "pragmatic and progressive." Its Strategic Review highlights that disarmament "ought to be built gradually" under the framework of a realistic process of arms control and confidence-building, to achieve "strategic stability and shared security."[33] That said, the World Publics study indicated impressive support for disarmament,[34] especially for a NWS and a permanent member of the Security Council.

NUCLEAR-ARMED STATES

It is fitting at this point to turn to other nuclear-armed states, namely non-NWS under the NPT that possess weapons. They seem to see their future best protected under a policy of nuclear deterrence, showing a range of different attitudes to nuclear weapons.

North Korea

North Korea continues to defy pleas from the international community to halt its nuclear program. Despite a barrage of UN and individual state sanctions as well as various attempts by US President Donald Trump to move matters forward, North Korea still continues with its nuclear threats and tests. It is difficult to judge for certain how the population as a whole actually feels about the nation's nuclear position, as there is a lack of credible methods of assessing their views on these matters.

---

[31] Ibid. World Publics on Eliminating All Nuclear Weapons December 9, 2008. See www .nuclearfiles.org/menu/library/opinion-polls/nuclear-weapons/world-publics-eliminating-nukes-2008 .pdf.

[32] Ibid.

[33] Ibid. at p. 23.

[34] Ibid.

Nuclear-Armed States

That said, given the economic conditions reported and the daily challenges facing many people at the grassroots level, by all accounts it would seem their needs are based much more on survival in terms of nutrition and sustenance as opposed to existential nuclear threats. Needless to say, the elimination of the nuclear position would assist in allowing sanctions to be lifted, most likely alleviating some of these problems and serving to improve living standards as well as to establish friendly relations with their neighbors and to normalize trade opportunities. So, ironically, the nuclear threat that is claimed by leader Kim Jung-un to benefit the North Korean people is actually holding the nation back from achieving political stability, as well as limiting economic prosperity and social empowerment.

India

India first tested nuclear weapons in 1974, becoming the sixth country to detonate a nuclear device.[35] In a recent article "Rapidly expanding nuclear arsenals in Pakistan and India portend regional and global catastrophe,"[36] the authors document the growth in strength of these nation's nuclear program. They note that unless there is substantial provocation, neither Pakistan nor India is likely to initiate a nuclear conflict. India has a no first use of nuclear weapons policy, except in response to an attack with biological or chemical weapons. Amid tensions in 2019, however, there may be an appetite to revisit this two decades' old policy. For the first time since 1971, India bombed mainland Pakistan in retaliation after a Pakistan-based terrorist group supported a suicide bombing in Kashmir killing at least forty Indian paramilitary soldiers.[37] In August 2019, India's Defense Minister Rajnath Singh suggested that India may re-evaluate its "no first use of nuclear weapons."[38] He stated, "What happens in the future depends on the circumstances."[39]

Defense Minister Singh boasts "India attaining the status of a responsible nuclear nation is a matter of national pride."[40] In a study assessing Indian attitudes to nuclear issues, Aditi Malhotra echoes this statement contending, that "[o]verall, the public is

---

[35] See https://armscontrolcenter.org/indias-nuclear-capabilities/. See also: https://fas.org/nuke/guide/india/nuke/.

[36] Owen B. Toon, Charles G. Bardeen, Alan Robock, Lili Xia, Hans Kristensen, Matthew McKinzie, R. J. Peterson, Cheryl S. Harrison, Nicole S. Lovenduski, and Richard P. Turco. Rapidly expanding nuclear arsenals in Pakistan and India portend regional and global catastrophe. Science Advances, October 2, 2019: Vol. 5, no. 10, eaay5478 DOI: 10.1126/sciadv.aay5478.

[37] Caitlin Talmadge, "Are Nuclear Weapons Keeping the India-Pakistan Crisis from Escalating – or Making It More Dangerous?" March 5, 2019. See www.washingtonpost.com/politics/2019/03/05/are-nuclear-weapons-keeping-india-pakistan-crisis-escalating-or-making-it-more-dangerous/.

[38] Christopher Clary and Vipin Narang, Why India Wants to Break Its Decades-Old Nuclear Pledge, August 22, 2019, www.bbc.com/news/world-asia-india-49354185.

[39] Abigail Stowe-Thurston Added Ambiguity Over India's No First Use Policy Is Cause for Concern August 22, 2019. See https://armscontrolcenter.org/why-india-and-pakistan-should-both-have-no-first-use-policies/.

[40] Christopher Clary and Vipin Narang, Why India Wants to Break Its Decades-Old Nuclear Pledge August 22, 2019 www.bbc.com/news/world-asia-india-49354185.

316 *Toward Neo-Universalism*

considered supportive of the Indian nuclear weapons program. It is viewed as a symbol of the country's technological progress, self-confidence, and international prestige."[41] Malhotra notes that the combined growing energy needs and a call for decreased carbon emissions has resulted in greater investment and dependence on the nuclear sector.[42]

Despite this pride, however, there appears to be an important nuance in these positions. Nuclear technology aside, in relation to nuclear weapons, the Indian public sees them as political weapons, which will not be used for fighting a war.[43] Although 79 percent of the survey respondents believed that nuclear weapons were important for India to achieve its goals, when questioned about "what Indian foreign policy should be trying to achieve," some 92 percent considered "helping to prevent the spread of nuclear weapons" to be important, out of which 63 percent considered it "very important."[44] So, it seems that while nuclear weapons may be a source of pride in terms of reaffirming India's place from a modern scientific perspective, the people may not agree with the actual use of nuclear weapons from that of a military policy perspective. Those who may do so are undoubtedly influenced by fears of a Pakistani threat.

Pakistan

Like India, Pakistan is also continuing to develop and expand its nuclear arsenals.[45] "India and Pakistan are both expanding their nuclear weapon stockpiles as well as developing new land, sea and air-based missile delivery systems."[46] As reported in the *Times of India*, with the current strength of its nuclear program, Pakistan remains ahead in nuclear warheads, but India is confident of its deterrence capabilities.[47] Again, Pakistan is unlikely to initiate a nuclear conflict, declaring that it would only use nuclear weapons to stop an invasion by conventional means or if attacked by nuclear weapons.[48]

---

[41] Assessing Indian Nuclear Attitudes, Aditi Malhotra (2016) at p. 3. www.stimson.org/sites/default/files/ file-attachments/Assessing%20Indian%20Nuclear%20Attitudes%20-%20Final.pdf.

[42] Ibid. at p. 5.

[43] Ibid. at p. 3.

[44] Ibid. at p. 15.

[45] Owen B. Toon, Charles G. Bardeen, Alan Robock, Lili Xia, Hans Kristensen, Matthew McKinzie, R. J. Peterson, Cheryl S. Harrison, Nicole S. Lovenduski, and Richard P. Turco. "Rapidly Expanding Nuclear Arsenals in Pakistan and India Portend Regional and Global Catastrophe." *Science Advances* October 2, 2019: Vol. 5, No. 10, eaay5478 DOI: 10.1126/sciadv.aay5478.

[46] SPIRI as quoted from Rajat Pandit, Pakistan remains ahead in nuclear warheads but India confident of its deterrence capability, June 18, 2018. See http://timesofindia.indiatimes.com/articleshow/ 64641056.cms?utm_source=contentofinterest&utm_medium=text&utm_campaign=cppst.

[47] Rajat Pandit, Pakistan remains ahead in nuclear warheads but India confident of its deterrence capability, June 18, 2018. http://timesofindia.indiatimes.com/articleshow/64641056.cms? utm_source=contentofinterest&utm_medium=text&utm_campaign=cppst.

[48] Owen B. Toon, Charles G. Bardeen, Alan Robock, Lili Xia, Hans Kristensen, Matthew McKinzie, R. J. Peterson, Cheryl S. Harrison, Nicole S. Lovenduski, and Richard P. Turco. "Rapidly Expanding

Pakistan contends that the testing of atomic bombs by India eliminated chances of a nuclear weapons-free South Asia and that it was forced to test nuclear weapons in 1998 due to "hostile posturing" by India.[49] Speaking on the twentieth anniversary of its nuclear testing which took place in May 1998, Foreign Office spokesman Mohammad Faisal stated: "Pakistan was forced to take that decision as a response, in self-defense, to the nuclear tests and accompanying hostile posturing by its neighbor. These developments unfortunately put an end to the prospect for keeping South Asia free of nuclear weapons – an objective which Pakistan had actively pursued."[50] Whether that amounts to the government being willing to reverse its nuclear program if sufficient confidence measures could be put in place with India remains open, but on the face of it the government line seems to be that they were compelled to enter the nuclear arms race due to perceived threats by India and it continues to maintain this nuclear policy position as a result of the perceived threat.

India and Pakistan: Dream of a Nuclear-Weapon-Free Zone in South Asia

It appears that India has a nuclear presence, despite a comprehensive citizens' approval rating for such a position and Pakistan has one because of perceived security threats to its national political interests and territorial integrity. With this, there may be signs that hard-line nuclear posturing does not garner broader popular consensus, hence begging the question of appetite for denuclearization in support of Pakistan's dream of a nuclear-weapon-free zone in South Asia. Other countries within the broader region, namely Kazakhstan have followed a program of denuclearization, as has Ukraine.

NON-NUCLEAR-WEAPON STATES THAT RELINQUISHED NUCLEAR WEAPONS

Amid the concern of nuclear escalation, the world has also witnessed several success stories – states that inherited nuclear weapons following the dissolution of the former Soviet Union have voluntarily decommissioned their arsenals. Other nations have jettisoned their pursuit of a nuclear program, abandoning a nuclear military policy in favor of weapons-free status as will be discussed.

NUCLEAR-WEAPON-FREE KAZAKHSTAN, UKRAINE AND BELARUS

The dissolution of the Soviet Union in late 1991 resulted in four new states hosting nuclear weapons: Russia, Belarus, Kazakhstan and Ukraine. Despite potential for

---

Nuclear Arsenals in Pakistan and India Portend Regional and Global Catastrophe," *Science Advances* October 2, 2019: Vol. 5, No. 10, eaay5478 DOI: 10.1126/sciadv.aay5478.

[49] Was forced to test nukes in 1998 due to "hostile posturing" http://timesofindia.indiatimes.com/articleshow/64345362.cms?utm_source=contentofinterest&utm_medium=text&utm_campaign=cppst.

[50] Ibid.

318 *Toward Neo-Universalism*

chaos and nuclear disorder following the collapse of the Union, the transition went relatively smoothly. All of the former Soviet states had agreed in the Minsk Agreement on December 8, 1991 and the Alma-ata Declaration on December 21, 1991, that Russia, operating through the CIS and Strategic Forces, would take over de facto responsibility for the nuclear arms, and inherit both the permanent Security Council seat and the title of NWS within the meaning of the NPT.[51] While central to the smooth transition from being part of the Soviet Union to sovereign states, these agreements could not function alone to ensure the implementation of START I and accordingly Ukraine, Kazakhstan and Belarus acceded to the NPT as non-nuclear weapon states (NNWS).

Kazakhstan

In 1991 Kazakhstan possessed the fourth largest arsenal of nuclear weapons and voluntarily relinquished them.[52] Demonstrating its further commitment to disarmament, Kazakhstan signed the TPNW in March 2018 and has subsequently deposited the ratification instrument with the UN Secretariat in August 2019. In order to emphasize the importance of this exercise and the symbolism of the event, it held the signing ceremony on August 29, which is the International Day against Nuclear Tests.[53] It was on that day in 1949 that the first Soviet atomic bomb was tested on Kazakh soil, at the Semipalatinsk nuclear test site; and on that day in 1991 Kazakhstan's then-President Nursultan Nazarbayev signed the decree closing the test site. Thus, for Kazakhstan, approving the TPNW seems a natural choice; moreover, Kazakhstan's participation serves to strengthen the position of the TPNW for it has gone the full circle of having been a nuclear-armed State in which testing occurred to now being one of TPNW Member States with complete disarmament.

Despite Kazakhstan's disarmament efforts and its recent ratification of the TPNW, its true commitment to the total elimination of nuclear weapons has been questioned, however, because of its indirect association with nuclear weapon-related activities as a member of the Moscow-led Collective Security Treaty Organization (CSTO),[54] which relies on nuclear deterrence from the Russian Federation.[55] Moreover, it has allowed Russia, to carry out missile defense testing on its territory, which would be in clear violation of provisions 1(a) and (e) of the TPNW and could be

---

[51] International Atomic Energy Agency, "INFCIRC/397" (January 9, 1992), online: *International Atomic Energy Agency Circular* www.iaea.org/publications/documents/infcircs (perma.cc/7G4G-ST76); "The End Of The Soviet Union; Text of Accords by Former Soviet Republics Setting Up a Commonwealth," *New York Times* (December 23, 1991) 00010 (*Alma-ata Declaration*); Helen Fedor, *Belarus and Moldova Country Studies*, 1st ed. (Washington DC: Library of Congress, 1995) at 191–194 (The Minsk Agreement).

[52] See www.nti.org/learn/countries/kazakhstan/nuclear/.

[53] Dauren Aben, "Kazakhstan and the Nuclear Ban Treaty: It's Complicated," *The Diplomat.* December 1, 2019. See https://thediplomat.com/2019/11/kazakhstan-and-the-nuclear-ban-treaty-its-complicated/.

[54] See https://en.odkb-csto.org/.

[55] Ibid.

Africa: A Nuclear-Weapon-Free Zone 319

seen as undermining a central aim of the Treaty. That said, Kazakhstan professes to be committed to disarmament and its practical actions in ridding itself of its nuclear arsenals, and its recent ratification of the TPNW demonstrate such intentions.

Ukraine

Hosting the third largest nuclear weapons stockpile,[56] on December 5, 1994 Ukraine acceded to the NPT under a memorandum with Russia, Britain and the United States which was to provide Ukraine with security assurances in connection with its accession to the NPT as a non-nuclear weapon state. Essentially, Ukraine agreed to the removal of all nuclear weapons from its soil in exchange for assurances that Russia would respect its sovereignty.[57] Needless to say, events in recent years regarding Crimea have destroyed this promise, creating insecurity in the region. Nevertheless, Ukraine remains a success story in nuclear disarmament.

Belarus

With the collapse of the Soviet Union in 1991, Belarus de facto inherited some eighty-one single warhead missiles stationed on its territory and in May 1992, it acceded to the NPT. Belarus subsequently transferred its tactical warheads to the Russian Federation by May 1993, with the completion of transferring strategic warheads by November 1996.[58] There is no information readily available regarding attitudes to nuclear disarmament, but again, it is an example of another state that has adopted this position.

AFRICA: A NUCLEAR-WEAPON-FREE ZONE

South Africa, Niger and Namibia are amongst the top uranium exporters in the world and it is found in abundance in many other African states, including the Central African Republic, Botswana, Democratic Republic of the Congo and Angola. Despite the vast wealth of resources and potential for nuclear proliferation, Africa as a continent is committed to disarmament and is free from nuclear weapons.[59] In 1996 the continent adopted the African Nuclear-Weapon-Free Zone Treaty – the Pelindaba Treaty – firmly establishing its commitment to nonproliferation of nuclear arms and as a continent free of such weapons. Moreover, African countries seem firmly committed to the TPNW demonstrating their overwhelming endorsement in July 2017 and commitment to the ratification process.

[56] See www.armscontrol.org/factsheets/Ukraine-Nuclear-Weapons.
[57] Kateryna Oliynyk, "The Destruction of Ukraine's Nuclear Arsenal," January 9, 2019. See www .rferl.org/a/the-destruction-of-ukraines-nuclear-arsenal/29699706.html.
[58] See www.nti.org/analysis/articles/belarus-nuclear-disarmament/.
[59] Yolandi Meyer, "Lessons from South Africa's Voluntary Denuclearisation Process and the African Continent's Position on Nuclear Weapons," in J. L. Black-Branch and D. Fleck (eds.), Nuclear Non-Proliferation in International Law, Vol. V (2020) https://doi.org/10.1007/978-94-6265-347-4_9.

South Africa

South Africa's nuclear history is somewhat distinctive. Indeed, it had built six nuclear warheads before renouncing its weapons program in 1991.[60] Central to its decision to denuclearize was the hope of improving its international standing and relations with other states.[61] While perhaps its motives were not all that honorable, its decision was key, ensuring that the entire African continent was to become nuclear weapons free. South Africa is a rare example of a country voluntarily decommissioning its nuclear weapons program.

In March 1993, F. W. de Klerk, the former state president, informed South African Parliament that the country had embarked on the development of a limited nuclear deterrent in the 1970s and 1980s and confirmed that such deterrent had been dismantled fully in order to accede to the NPT in July 1991, and it subsequently concluded a Comprehensive Safeguards Agreement with the IAEA in September 1991.[62] Today there is no real debate on nuclear weapons and the country as well as the continent co-exist peacefully in an African nuclear-weapon-free zone.

Brazil

Brazil has one of the largest uranium reserves in the world that could potentially meet all of its nuclear fuel needs with its domestically-enriched uranium.[63] During the time of the military regime throughout the 1970s and 1980s, Brazil had a clandestine nuclear weapons program which was subsequently dismantled in the 1990s, following the country's move to civilian rule. Despite its extensive civil nuclear program, with expansion plans afoot, following civilian rule, it curtailed its ballistic missile program and ended a nuclear and missile rivalry with its neighbor Argentina harboring no armament ambitions.[64]

Argentina

Some sixty years of political and military rivalry between Argentina and Brazil has come to shape both its politics and national identity.[65] Needless to say, factoring

---

[60] See www.nti.org/learn/countries/south-africa/nuclear/.

[61] De Villiers et al. 1993, 102; "Why One President Gave Up His Country's Nukes" *The Atlantic* (Interview with President FW de Klerk by Uri Friedman, September 9, 2017), see www.theatlantic.com/international/archive/2017/09/north-korea-south-africa/539265/.

[62] Waldo Stumpf. Birth and Death of the South African Nuclear Weapons Programme, see https://fas.org/nuke/guide/rsa/nuke/stumpf.htm.

[63] See www.nti.org/learn/countries/brazil/.

[64] Ibid.

[65] Sharon Squassoni and Dadid Fite, Brazil's Nuclear History, see www.armscontrol.org/act/2005-10/brazils-nuclear-history.

Non-Nuclear-Weapon States Living in Nuclear Fear 321

nuclear matters into the equation could have been a recipe for disaster.[66] That said, on the contrary, this is a success story in a world where there were mounting fears of nuclear proliferation and hostile threats. It goes without saying that in the period between the 1960s to the early 1990s, Argentina's nuclear program raised much concern. Despite this, however, Argentina has never actually produced nuclear weapons, dismantling its ballistic missile program in the early 1990s.

In 1991, along with Brazil, Argentina entered into an agreement to use nuclear energy solely for peaceful uses and both countries have adopted the NPT as NNWS. They adhere to safeguards applied in both countries by the Brazilian-Argentine Agency for Accounting and Control of Nuclear Materials (ABACC) and the International Atomic Energy Agency (IAEA) under the Quadripartite Safeguards Agreement. The ABACC is modeled after the European Atomic Energy Community, particularly in relation to IAEA inspections.[67]

LATIN AMERICA AND THE CARIBBEAN: A NUCLEAR-WEAPON-FREE ZONE

Notably, both Argentina and Brazil have now acceded to the Treaty of Tlatelolco (or Treaty for the Prohibition of Nuclear Weapons in Latin America and the Caribbean).[68] The success of their efforts demonstrates how even political and military rivals can achieve denuclearliaztion. This can be done through confidence building and developing compliance mechanisms. Parties can enter into bilateral agreements and work in conjunction with the IAEA regarding monitoring, supervision and enforcement measures.

NON-NUCLEAR-WEAPON-STATES LIVING IN NUCLEAR FEAR

It is fitting at this point to turn the focus to NNWS some of which live in fear under nuclear threats, as well as nations that may have suffered from the effects of nuclear weapons testing, development, or their use. One sees that NNWS countries show a range of different policies and attitudes to nuclear weapons with many citizens

[66] Mariana Monteiro de Matos, "The Unclassic Match Between Brazil and Argentina: Past and Present of the Nuclear-Weapon-Free Zone in Latin America and the Caribbean," in J. L. Black-Branch and D. Fleck (eds.), *Nuclear Non-Proliferation in International Law*, Vol. V (2020). See https://doi.org/10 .1007/978-94-6265-347-4_9.

[67] Argentina and Brazil signed a bilateral agreement (in Guadalajara, July 1991) establishing the Brazilian-Argentine Agency for Accounting and Control of Nuclear Materials (ABACC). Argentina, Brazil, ABACC, and the IAEA subsequently signed the Quadripartite Safeguards Agreement later that year – entering into force in March 1994. See IAEA, INFCIRC/435, March 1994. Sharon Squassoni and Dadid Fite Brazil's Nuclear History. See www.armscontrol.org /act/2005-10/brazils-nuclear-history. See also José Goldemberg, Carlos Feu Alvim and Olga Y Mafra, "The Denuclearization of Brazil and Argentina," *Journal for Peace and Nuclear Disarmament*, Vol. 1, 2018 – Issue 2, pp 383–403. See https://doi.org/10.1080/25751654.2018.1479129.

[68] See www.nti.org/learn/countries/argentina/.

voicing concern over nuclear deterrence and a seeming recalcitrance on disarmament.

Japan

Research shows that there is growing antinuclear activism in Japan, where protests against nuclear power and nuclear weapons were organized by citizens in public spaces after the 2011 Fukushima Daiichi Nuclear Power Plant[69] meltdown following the earthquake.[70] That said, the government position firmly favors strategic military reassurances for protection in an increasingly volatile area of the world with more threats from North Korean and fear of attack.

South Korea

In September 2017 protestors in Seoul, South Korea demonstrated against the deployment and expansion of the US Terminal High Altitude Area Defense (THAAD) missile defense system. Their message was also clear, "deploying more weapons, conducting more military drills, and intensifying the war of words could soon tip the balance in favour of a real nuclear war that would kill millions."[71] From mid 2017 to April 2018 protestors blocked the only road to the site of the THAAD, forcing US military to use helicopters to shuttle in fuel, food and other supplies.[72] On April 23, 2018, thousands of riot police were sent to remove around 200 protestors.

South Korean Catholics have also been a strong voice in helping make people aware of the issues with nuclear weapons and nuclear power. It came as good news to South Korean activists when South Korea's new President Moon Jae-in pledged to cut back on the government's plans to expand the nuclear power industry.[73] Civil society has mobilized in the past and they are

---

[69] "Following a major earthquake, a fifteen-meter tsunami disabled the power supply and cooling of three Fukushima Daiichi reactors, causing a nuclear accident on March 11, 2011. All three cores largely melted in the first three days. The accident was rated 7 on the INES scale, due to high radioactive releases over days four to six, eventually a total of some 940 PBq (I-131 eq). Four reactors were written off due to damage in the accident – 2719 MWe net." See www.world-nuclear.org /information-library/safety-and-security/safety-of-plants/fukushima-accident.aspx.

[70] See http://asaa.asn.au/anti-nuclear-movement-street-politics-japan-fukushima/.

[71] Ibid. Kate Hudson, September 8, 2017, We must ramp up protest if we are to avoid nuclear war, www .theguardian.com/world/2017/sep/08/we-must-ramp-up-protest-if-we-are-to-avoid-nuclear-war. Also see www.reuters.com/article/us-northkorea-missiles-thaad/south-korean-protesters-denounce -u-s-anti-missile-system-ahead-of-north-south-summit-idUSKBN1HU101.

[72] Haejin Choi, Jane Chung and Cynthia Kim, Reuters, World News, April 23, 2018, www.reuters.com /article/us-northkorea-missiles-thaad/south-korean-protesters-denounce-u-s-anti-missile-system-ahead -of-north-south-summit-idUSKBN1HU101.

[73] Matthew Bell, May 2017, PRI's The World, South Korean Catholics take the lead in protesting against nuclear power, www.pri.org/stories/2017-05-11/south-korean-catholics-take-lead-protesting-against- nuclear-power.

mobilized now with a new efficiency, efficacy and unity and it remains to be seen what they are capable of when they are powered by hope of freedom from nuclear fear.

What the history of antinuclear movements and the current shift in civil society and state leaders demonstrates is growth of a conviction that a non-nuclear world is an increasingly attractive option. As these movements gain momentum and the attention of the media, they begin to change the discussions in communities, at home, around board rooms and within seats of power in governments and among decision makers. It is hoped that eventually an historically minority view seems set to become an overwhelming majority, whereby state leaders will be forced to reconcile their nuclear political positions and look for other more sustainable and less dangerous methods of maintaining peace and security.

Korean Peninsula: Denuclearization

At present the dream of a denuclearized Korean Peninsula seems a forlorn hope. That said, the example of Argentina and Brazil serves as an inspiration for bilateral partnership between North and South Korean and the region. Whilst many would say that this is highly unlikely because of the vast political differences between the two, this author contends that it is a matter of achieving the right political opportunity to identify an effective political incentive in order to fill this gap. As in the case of South Africa, perhaps the governing regime at the time moved away from armament for the wrong reasons, that is a perceived political advantage in external relations with other states, but in the end, it did the right thing. It achieved the right result; eliminating its nuclear weapons program. Perhaps North Korean may act in a similar way.

Two points emerge from this. South Africa moved to denuclearize because it thought that the rest of the world wanted this, which indicates that there is a universal value to disarming. Perhaps North Korean will recognize this same value. A second point is that, by and large, the people in this region would benefit from disarmament and therefore most likely want it. After all, there is a big difference between agreeing to a nation's having nuclear weapons, out of fear of military attack and their use as a deterrent, and agreeing that nuclear weapons are a good thing in the abstract. It would seem that, given a blank slate, most people would not want nuclear weapons, in the first place. Brazil and Argentina serve to illustrate this point, as do the tens of countries that have entered into nuclear-weapon-free zones. At the risk of sounding like a naïve optimist, a denuclearized Korean Peninsula may not be as far-fetched as it may seem at the moment and can be achieved under specific bilateral agreements based on the right political incentives, such as trade and social and economic development.

324 *Toward Neo-Universalism*

EU MEMBER STATES

Most European countries neither participated in the negotiations for the TPNW, nor voted for its adoption in 2017. What stands out is the reaction of many of these states to the TPNW. Many governments that are generally perceived as progressive countries that support the architecture of a rules-based order under an international framework seem firmly opposed to the Treaty. A comprehensive study by the European Council on Foreign Relations finds that, despite varying views, most EU Member States have two things in common. Firstly, nearly all of them share an official commitment to reducing nuclear weapons, with only three of the Member States[74] having reservations about the goal of nuclear disarmament; all the while many of these countries remain within NATO. Secondly, "nuclear weapons have little salience in the public imagination."[75]

That said, there is a range of different attitudes to nuclear weapons with many citizens increasingly voicing concern over nuclear deterrence with calls for disarmament. Indeed, EU countries hold a spectrum of positions regarding nuclear arms ranging from being fully committed to such weapons to determined abolitionists, depending on governmental and citizens' attitudes.[76] While various European citizens strongly favor nuclear disarmament and the total elimination of nuclear weapons, the European Council report notes that many EU governments take a realist view, maintaining the military status quo regarding nuclear deterrence. Many strongly support the universal adoption and entry into force of the Comprehensive Nuclear Test Ban Treaty, as well as being favorable to negotiations on the Fissile Material Cutoff Treaty. That aside, in some instances in states that do not support the TPNW, there is a divergence between official government position and popular support.

EUROPEAN NON-NWS NATO MEMBERS

France and the United Kingdom are NWS, invariably taking an official position favoring the nuclear deterrent whilst maintaining their commitment to disarmament under the NPT. Other states such as Poland and Romania are strong supporters of US and NATO-led nuclear policies based mainly on their fear of Russia and consequently their desire for security assurances. The majority – sixteen – of EU Member States are NATO members bound by its policy on nuclear deterrence and following its position regarding the TPNW, dismissing it as unrealistic and potentially damaging to the NPT. That said, the European Council on Foreign Relations report notes that some of these same EU states exhibit differing degrees of conviction, taking either a pragmatist or conformist view. Of these, the pragmatists,

---

[74] Including the United Kingdom which was an EU Member State at the time of the survey.

[75] Manuel Lafont Rapnouil, Tara Varma and Nick Witney, "Eyes Tight Shut: European Attitudes Toward Nuclear Deterrence," European Council on Foreign Relations (December 2018) at p. 3. See www.ecfr.eu/page/-/ECFR_275_NUCLEAR_WEAPONS_FLASH_SCORECARD_update.pdf.

[76] Ibid. at p. 3.

Other EU NATO States   325

consisting of eastern European countries Estonia, Lithuania, Latvia, Bulgaria and the Czech Republic, share to varying degrees, a matter-of-fact acceptance of the importance of the nuclear component in NATO's strategy, largely due to their distrust of Russia.

Czech Republic

The Czech Republic, for example, was strongly opposed to the TPNW feeling it challenges transatlantic ties and NATO and wishing to focus on the NPT regime.[77]

Belgium and Italy

Belgium and Italy also take a pragmatic stand with both harboring US nuclear weapons under their NATO commitments.[78] The Foreign Relations report notes Belgium as taking a pragmatic view regarding nuclear deterrence. That said, the report notes that while, Belgians do not seem to feel that nuclear issues are of major concern, during the Euromissile crisis large demonstrations against the deployment of US nuclear weapons took place on Belgian soil which led the government to postpone their installation.[79]

OTHER EU NATO STATES

Other NATO states in the EU seem less concerned with nuclear threats but conform to deterrence under NATO as "the easiest and most advantageous course" of action.[80] These include Croatia, Slovakia, Slovenia, Hungary, Greece, Denmark, Luxembourg, Spain and Portugal with each country having its distinct national attitudes toward deterrence and disarmament.[81] In some of these countries there seems to be a political disconnect between government policy and the attitudes of their respective citizens. While the official line of the state might be that of nuclear deterrence, the wishes of their citizens at a grassroots popular support level may not be so.

Croatia

Croatia does not appear to be worried about nuclear issues, per se, but is nonetheless concerned by Russian activities in the Balkans.[82] Hence, it looks at deterrence from

---

[77]   Ibid. at p. 19.
[78]   Ibid. at p. 6.
[79]   Ibid. at p. 15.
[80]   Ibid. at p. 6.
[81]   Ibid. at p. 6.
[82]   Ibid. at p. 6.

326   *Toward Neo-Universalism*

a pragmatic perspective and is not inclined to challenge NATO policy on such matters.

Denmark

The report highlights that Denmark does not generally view nuclear threats as important as other security threats. While political parties profess to favor nuclear disarmament, no governing party has made significant moves toward this end. It mostly favors US and Russian reductions in strategic weapons. Moreover, Denmark believes that the European Union should take action against the nuclear programs in both Iran and North Korea. While a majority seem to oppose the TPNW, pacifist and left–red/green alliance *Enhedslisten* argued that Denmark should support any attempt to limit nuclear weapons.[83]

ANTI-NUCLEAR EU MEMBERS

Other countries are more openly opposed in their stand on nuclear armaments. EU countries that are not members of NATO such as Ireland and Austria define themselves as antinuclear and were amongst those celebrated with the "Arms Control Person(s) of the Year" in 2017 for their efforts in securing the TPNW.[84]

Austria

Austria, in particular, stands out as uniquely placed compared to various other EU states. In its 2018 report, the European Council on Foreign Relations notes Austria's unique position as being a neutral country; a non-NATO member, as well as being a strong proponent of nuclear abolition. In what may be viewed as an extraordinary move, it has signed and ratified the TPNW, being the first EU Member State to have done so. It is a rare European example where government and public opinion are largely aligned regarding nuclear weapons policy.

Indeed, Austria participated in international-level efforts regarding the humanitarian consequences of nuclear weapons, as discussed in Chapter 2. Austria was the pioneer of a document that became a humanitarian pledge signed by 127 countries in 2014 moving on to co-sponsor UN General Assembly Resolution 71/258 in December 2016, leading to the TPNW.[85] Austria is aligned with and coordinates closely with a few like-minded countries such as the Nordic states, as well as non-EU members, Norway and Switzerland. Austria has been very active on this front, having

---

[83] Ibid. at p. 20.

[84] See www.armscontrol.org/pressroom/2018-01/acpoy-2017-winner.

[85] Manuel Lafont Rapnouil, Tara Varma and Nick Witney, "Eyes Tight Shut: European Attitudes Toward Nuclear Deterrence," European Council on Foreign Relations (December 2018) at p. 14. See www.ecfr.eu/page/-/ECFR_275_NUCLEAR_WEAPONS_FLASH_SCORECARD_update.pdf.

Anti-nuclear EU Members 327

ratified the TPNW in May 2019, and has been a vocal and avid supporter of the abolitionist agenda, holding the view that banning and condemning such weapons can lead to halting their proliferation.[86]

Ireland

Ireland takes a pro-disarmament stance with one of its main foreign policies being to achieve a world free of nuclear weapons in addition to promoting disarmament.[87] In 2017, the Irish UN disarmament delegation along with Austria and their counterparts from Brazil, Mexico, New Zealand and South Africa received the "Arms Control Person(s) of the Year" in recognition of their efforts in securing the TPNW.[88] The Irish public generally take a negative view of the use of military force including toward nuclear weapons. The government has long supported disarmament and nuclear nonproliferation, a principled stand equally shared by all political parties for more than sixty years.[89]

Malta and Cyprus

Although not as activist in their approach as Austria and Ireland, Malta and Cyprus are also non-aligned, with no reference to nuclear deterrence in their respective defense policies and have voted in favor of the TPNW in the General Assembly.

Finland

Finland is more nuanced in its stand in that although also non-aligned, over time it has drawn closer ties to NATO despite the fact that deterrence remains peripheral to its overall defense strategy. The European Council report concludes that to some extent, "Finland could be considered in a category of its own, based on the fact that it is so resolutely self-contained."[90] During the Cold War Finland consistently promoted nuclear arms control and nonproliferation, actively advancing the concept of a Nordic nuclear-weapon-free zone. It is also an active supporter of the NPT and CTBT, but not so keen on the TPNW expressing fears that it could weaken existing agreements, including the NPT, which it sees as the cornerstone of its nuclear

---

[86] Ibid. at p. 4.
[87] Ibid. at p. 4.
[88] As well as Ambassador Elayne Whyte Gómez of Costa Rica. See www.armscontrol.org/pressroom/2018-01/acpoy-2017-winner.
[89] Manuel Lafont Rapnouil, Tara Varma and Nick Witney, Eyes Tight Shut: European Attitudes Towards Nuclear Deterrence. European Council on Foreign Relations (December 2018) at p. 27. See www.ecfr.eu/page/-/ECFR_275_NUCLEAR_WEAPONS_FLASH_SCORECARD_update .pdf.
[90] Ibid. at p. 4.

328   *Toward Neo-Universalism*

policy.[91] But again, overall, it is safe to say that Finland is by and large opposed to nuclear weapons, with a proclivity toward disarmament.

AMBIVALENT EU STATES

Other EU states are not so secure in their stands of either being resolutely in favor of deterrence or opposed to it. They are conflicted, with a seemingly widening divide between government line and citizen participation.

Sweden

Historically neutral, Sweden was one of the few EU states to vote in favor of the TPNW. The European Council on Foreign Relations notes that Sweden, like the Netherlands and Germany are conflicted with a growing divide between government policy and wider public, with civil society groups actively opposing nuclear weapons. In the case of Sweden, there are growing worries about Russia resulting in their increasing defense cooperation with the United States and NATO. This has clashed with what the report calls its cherished "peace" tradition and has resulted in an open split within the government over its signing of the TPNW.[92]

The Netherlands

As noted earlier, PAX, an NGO supported by citizens, social organizations and churches in the Netherlands, collected over 45,000 signatures in the "Sign Against Nuclear Weapons" citizen's initiative which forced debate in the House of Representatives resulting in a reluctant Dutch government participating in the negotiations for the TPNW. Some citizens of the Netherlands have voiced concern about the twenty American nuclear warheads being stored in a Dutch Air Base.[93] PAX was also involved in organizing protests and demonstrations at BNP Paribas offices in seventy-four countries. BNP Paribas is a bank that has provided more than $8 billion USD in financing to nuclear-weapons-producing companies since 2014 and also invests in companies that "produce key components for the French, British, Indian and American nuclear weapon arsenals."[94] The protesters aimed to raise public awareness about BNP's investments and financing of nuclear weapons. They also called on the bank to increase transparency about who they are investing with, to fix their policy restricting investments in companies associated with the production

[91]   Ibid. at p. 22.
[92]   Ibid. at p. 4.
[93]   PAX, "40,000 People Have Signed Against Nukes," online: www.paxforpeace.nl/stay-informed/news/ 40-000-people-have-signed-against-nukes.
[94]   Pax Christi, "Pax Christi International Joins Actions Around the World to Push BNP Paribas to Stop Investing in Nuclear Weapons," September 26, 2018, online: www.paxchristi.net/news/pax-christi-international-joins-actions-around-world-push-bnp-paribas-stop-investing-nuclear.

of nuclear weapons, and to refer to the TPNW instead of the NPT, so that they no longer invest in any nuclear-weapon-associated company anywhere or offer investments in those companies as a product to their clients.[95] Although the government participated in TPNW negotiations, it remains opposed to it, despite its vocal citizens. How long the government can ignore public sentiment against such weapons remains to be seen.

Germany

The European Council on Foreign Relations report lists Germany as a conflicted state. That is one which "exhibits a strong divergence" between the views of the general public and that of the political establishment. It notes that, unlike in the Netherlands where the public exerts significant influence over the government on this issue, the same cannot be said for Germany.[96] While nuclear disarmament and nonproliferation are at the core of German policy, the report notes that it is apparent that the government opposed the TPNW, in direct contrast to popular opposition to nuclear weapons, resulting in political discussions taking place behind the scenes and the government taking such nuclear decisions removed from popular opinion. There was notable public moral repugnance toward all weapons, with the vast majority of Germans being in favor of worldwide nuclear disarmament and the total abolition of nuclear weapons. In 2017, some two-thirds of Germans wanted US nuclear weapons stationed in the country removed by the government, and more than 70 percent wanted it to sign the TPNW.[97]

OTHER STATES

Other states not favoring the TPNW also face mounting pressures amongst their electorates to consider disarmament action and meaningful change in attitudes toward discouraging proliferation.

Canada

Canada has traditionally taken a lead in humanitarian progress in weapons, peacekeeping efforts and advancing the settlement of disputes via open dialogue and peaceful means. Indeed, it was a leading country in banning antipersonnel land mines[98] and has ratified the Cluster Munitions Convention.[99] It did not, however,

---

[95] Nobel Winners Urge BNP Paribas to End Support for Nuclear Weapons, September 26, 2018, www.paxforpeace.nl/stay-informed/news/nobel-winners-urge-bnp-paribas-to-end-support-for-nuclear-weapons.
[96] Ibid. at p. 24.
[97] Ibid. at p. 24.
[98] See www.icbl.org/en-gb/the-treaty/treaty-in-detail/treaty-text.aspx.
[99] See https://laws-lois.justice.gc.ca/eng/acts/P-24.8/page-1.html.

330   *Toward Neo-Universalism*

participate in the TPNW negotiations.[100] Senator MacPhedran contends that this is out of character with Canada's global image and represents a clear departure from its past practice on such matters.[101] Foreign Minister Chrystia Freeland's press secretary, insisted nonetheless, "Canada remains firmly committed to concrete steps towards global nuclear disarmament and nonproliferation."[102] Thirteen Canadian members of Parliament have signed a parliamentary pledge for the Treaty[103] and seventeen Canadian organizations, political parties and religious denominations are listed as partners of ICAN, the coalition that spearheaded negotiations for the Treaty. The Canadian public and experts have also voiced overwhelming support for the elimination of nuclear weapons and many groups have urged Canada to sign and ratify the 2017 TPNW.[104]

A Hiroshima survivor Setsuko Thurlow, who is now a resident of Canada, voiced public disappointment and criticism of the government's refusal to sign or even participate in the negotiations for the Treaty.[105] Her comment, contrasted with those of the government which demonstrate the divergence between the political views and hers. Prime Minister Trudeau said the Treaty negotiations were well meaning but ineffective. "There can be all sorts of people talking about nuclear disarmament, but if they do not actually have nuclear arms, it is sort of useless to have them around, talking."[106] Ms. Thurlow said not signing it means "a lack of courage, for economic purpose or some other excuses, to ignore and neglect the well-being and security of

---

[100] The PM called the TPNW "sort of useless." Marie-Danielle Smith, October 26, 2017, "'Astonishing': Justin Trudeau criticized for not congratulating Nobel Peace Prize winners, keeping Canada out of nuclear treaty," *National Post*, https://nationalpost.com/news/politics/astonishing-justin-trudeau-criti cized-for-not-congratulating-nobel-peace-prize-winners-keeping-canada-out-of-nuclear-treaty.

[101] Marilou McPhedran, "Why Was Canada Not in the Room for the Nuclear Ban Treaty?," in Black-Branch and Fleck (eds.) *Nuclear Non-Proliferation in International Law: Vol. IV Human Perspectives on the Development and Use of Nuclear Energy* (Asser Press/Springer, 2019), 355–375.

[102] Marie-Danielle Smith, October 26, 2017, "'Astonishing': Justin Trudeau Criticized for Not Congratulating Nobel Peace Prize Winners, Keeping Canada out of Nuclear Treaty," *National Post*, https://nationalpost .com/news/politics/astonishing-justin-trudeau-criticized-for-not-congratulating-nobel-peace-prize-winners-keeping-canada-out-of-nuclear-treaty.

[103] ICAN Parliamentary Pledge, www.icanw.org/projects/pledge/.

[104] "Canada's failure to step up for last week's nuclear weapons ban was criticized from many corners. 'It's shocking that Canada is not going to participate,' asserted former Canadian ambassador for disarmament, Douglas Roche back in March. Paul Meyer, another former Canadian ambassador for disarmament described Canada's absence as 'pathetic.' Project Ploughshares' executive director Cesar Jaramillo considered it a hypocritical contradiction of the Trudeau government's stated commitment to multilateralism." Thomas Woodley, "Canada Is Now a Hawk on Nuclear Arms," July 13, 2017, Huffington Post Canada: The Blog. Online: www.huffingtonpost.ca/thomas-woodley /canada-nuclear-arms_a_23028119/.

[105] Laura Stone, October 27, 2017, Canada focused on "concrete measures" to ban nuclear weapons, Trudeau says, The Globe and Mail, www.theglobeandmail.com/news/politics/canada-focused-on-concrete-measures-to-ban-nuclear-weapons-trudeau-says/article36753598/.

[106] Laura Stone, October 26, Canadian woman who survived Hiroshima bombing urges change of heart from Trudeau, The Globe and Mail, https://beta.theglobeandmail.com/news/national/canadian-woman-who-survived-hiroshima-bombing-urges-change-of-heart-from-trudeau/article36725770/.

Other States 331

Canadian people."[107] She contends that "The Prime Minister seems to willfully ignore the fact that the majority of Canadians want a world without nuclear weapons . . . As a living witness to Hiroshima, I beseech Justin Trudeau to change course."[108]

According to a 2007 opinion poll, 88 percent of Canadians believe that nuclear weapons make the world a more dangerous place and only 6 percent say it creates a safer world.[109] Further, nine in ten Canadians strongly (73 percent), or moderately (15 percent), support the elimination of all nuclear weapons.[110] The possible next step is for the public to mobilize toward no longer depending on nuclear weapons for keeping the peace; to make adherence to American deterrence and membership in NATO an election issue and have the government to reconsider its stand on nuclear weapons.

Australia

Given Australia's geographic location it is removed from NATO but in light of its isolation and security concerns, it is increasingly engaged with US and NATO activities. Hence, its position seems far removed from giving up or challenging a nuclear deterrence option with its friends and allies. Australian citizens, however, appear to have different views from those of its government. It seems that more and more people are calling for disarmament and question the government position on such matters. It may well be that the electorate may call the government to account for this increasing divergence between governmental rule and popular support.

New Zealand as Nuclear-Weapon-Free Zone

New Zealand has a unique history in terms of nuclear capacity. In 1984, under Prime Minister David Lange, New Zealand barred nuclear-powered or nuclear-armed ships from entering its territorial waters or using its ports. Further, on June 8, 1987, the nation's Parliament passed into law the New Zealand Nuclear Free Zone, Disarmament, and Arms Control Act establishing it as a nuclear-free zone in which it is forbidden to manufacture, acquire, possess or have any control over any nuclear or biological weapon. It covers the nation's entire jurisdiction, including airspace and ocean territory up to the twelve-nautical mile limit (app. 22.2 km), prohibiting the entry of nuclear-powered ships as well as the dumping of radioactive waste. The Act does not, however, prohibit nuclear power plants, research facilities,

---

[107] Ibid. Laura Stone, October 26.
[108] Ibid.
[109] The Canada's World Poll, Environics Institute, Nuclear Weapons and Disarmament, www .environicsinstitute.org/docs/default-source/project-documents/canada-s-world-survey/nuclear-weapons-and-disarmament.pdf?sfvrsn=e76d56bb_2.
[110] Ibid.

the use of radioactive isotopes, or other land-based nuclear activities. Although having had nuclear power for a brief period between 1969 and 1976, from an early stage, New Zealanders were invariably determined to carve out their own path and set their destiny in relation to nuclear matters. The roots of nuclear-free movement emerged in the 1960s with a push for an independent, ethical foreign policy, which had partly grown out of opposition to the Vietnam War, and concerns regarding environmentalism to preserve New Zealand as a green unspoilt land.[111]

The Act was passed in the aftermath of the mid-1980s nuclear ships stand-off between New Zealand and the United States with the US government suspending its ANZUS obligations to New Zealand. In a largely symbolic act, the US Congress retaliated with the Broomfield Act, downgrading New Zealand's status from ally to friend. Labour Prime Minister David Lange's response was that if the cost of New Zealand's nuclear-free status was the end of the ANZUS security alliance, this was a "price we are prepared to pay."

In terms of New Zealanders' commitment to disarmament, in 1989, 52 per cent indicated that they would rather break their defense ties than admit nuclear-armed ships to their harbors; by 1990, even the national opposition had signed up to antinuclearism.[112] Consequently, today, New Zealand remains amongst the strongest antinuclear movement in the world.

PUBLIC AND GOVERNMENT SUPPORT FOR DISARMAMENT

While the antinuclear movement against NWS security assurances is not new, such sentiment in Africa, Latin America and Asia appear to be increasing. It seems that countries on these continents and throughout these nations are ignited with a new sense of urgency that has been in alignment with the TPNW. Antinuclear positions amongst citizens in European countries and those nations opposing the Treaty, however, are generally mixed, at times with marked differences between governments and citizens themselves. Many Central and Eastern European countries continue to feel the long shadow of Russia, which complicates their decision making regarding the balance between their free conscious on the one hand wanting disarmament, with existential security fears on the other needing deterrence. Despite any ambivalence, however, there is a growing awareness and there appears to be a general increase in support for the TPNW, but more especially disarmament as a desired outcome, with increasing numbers of people having the same sense of urgency as their contemporaries on other continents.

Many European citizens strongly favor nuclear disarmament and the total elimination of nuclear weapons. That said, the European Council on Foreign Relations report notes that most EU governments take a pragmatic or conformist view

---

[111] See https://nzhistory.govt.nz/new-zealand-becomes-nuclear-free.
[112] Ibid.

maintaining the status quo regarding nuclear deterrence. Although many nations may strongly support the universal adoption and entry into force of the Comprehensive Nuclear Test Ban Treaty and are favorable to negotiations on the Fissile Material Cut-off Treaty, the TPNW seems to be a step too far at the moment.

A SHIFT FROM REALISM TO UNIVERSALISM?

The shift from realism to universalism amongst several states and global civil society organizations can be seen most clearly in the words of the preamble of the TPNW. Universalist thinking has also emerged in the arguments made by the supporters of the Treaty. The realist arguments are most clearly seen in nuclear weapons policies of the NWS, responses by the NWS to the Treaty and legal scholars defending the existing regime.

Firstly is the need to define the various terms, realism, consequentialism and universalism as they are used within the context of this discussion regarding international law. Simply put, realism is the view that the global community must deal with the international situation as it is and not as one would necessarily want it to be. In trying to determine how to act or deal with a conflict, disagreement, problem or dispute one must operate on what is known from the past and what can be reasonably predicted about the future regarding the behavior of states and their leaders. In doing so, one also must consider the potential consequences of various actions on a national and international scale.

Universalism is the view that "the rules of international law apply to all states."[113] In other words, the binding authority of international law does not depend on consent or acknowledgment of any state, instead its authority transcends human opinion. It may be described as,

> By "universal extension," and thus the universalism of international law, we thus mean that it is this model for the generation and application of rules that has been extended throughout the entire planet in a universal manner, with its sets of general and special rules and their respective fields of application, with its primary and secondary rules, and with the principle of reciprocity functioning as the internal motor driving its implementation.[114]

Universalism can be seen as a form of deontology which determines the moral right or wrong of an action based on basic objective rules that exist independent of human subjective opinion. The literature cites various forms of universalism, but for the purposes of this discussion it is distinguished from consequentialism, relativism, constructivism, or contractarianism. For the

---

[113] Bradford and Posner, 7.

[114] Emmanuelle Jouannet, "Universalism and Imperialism: The True-False Paradox of International Law?" *EJIL* (2007), Vol. 18 No. 3, 379–407. *The European Journal of International Law*, Vol. 18 No. 3 © EJIL 2007 at 385–386.

334   *Toward Neo-Universalism*

purposes of this discussion, relativism means that a law's validity is dependent on the circumstances or opinions of each state or person. It also contrasts with constructivism which says that laws are mere human constructs created by the mind or the society and imposed on a specific group within a particular social context, with no anchor in an objective non-mental source. Thus, according to constructivism, laws are valid only in so far as they come from one's own mind or from one's society.

Contractarianism is the view that a law is valid only in so far as it is freely and rationally agreed upon or consented to by two or more parties or states. The main idea is that two parties mutually agree to restrict some action of their own in order to acquire a mutual benefit that they could not gain otherwise on their own.

Consequentialism is the view that an action is morally blameworthy or praiseworthy in so far as its consequences or ends promote a certain goal, the ends justify the means.

Secondly, one must examine the nuclear weapons policies and doctrines of the United States, Russia, France, Britain and China and how they have responded to the TPNW. To begin with, consider the arguments embedded in the Joint Press Statement from the US Permanent Representative to the UN following the adoption of the TPNW on July 7, 2017:

> This initiative clearly disregards the realities of the international security environment. Accession to the ban treaty *is incompatible with the policy of nuclear deterrence, which has been essential to keeping the peace in Europe and North Asia for over 70 years*. A purported ban on nuclear weapons that *does not address the security concerns that continue to make nuclear deterrence necessary cannot result in the elimination of a single nuclear weapon and will not enhance any country's security, nor international peace and security*. It will do the exact opposite by creating even more divisions at a time when the world needs to remain united in the face of growing threats, including those from the DPRK's ongoing proliferation efforts. This treaty offers no solution to the grave threat posed by North Korea's nuclear program, *nor does it address other security challenges that make nuclear deterrence necessary*. A ban treaty also risks *undermining the existing international security architecture which contributes to the maintenance of international peace and security*.
>
> We reiterate in this regard our continued commitment to the Treaty on the Non-Proliferation of Nuclear Weapons (NPT) and reaffirm our determination to safeguard and further promote its authority, universality and effectiveness. Working towards the shared goal of nuclear disarmament and general and complete disarmament must be done in a way that *promotes international peace and security, and strategic stability, based on the principle of increased and undiminished security for all*.
>
> We all share a common responsibility to *protect and strengthen our collective security system in order to further promote international peace, stability and security*.[115]

---

[115]   See https://usun.state.gov/remarks/7892.

A Shift from Realism to Universalism?

One cannot help but notice how many times the words security, deterrence and necessary are mentioned. This response to the Treaty sees it as a threat to the existing "international security architecture." The reasons listed for rejecting the treaty have little to do with the humanitarian concerns. It sees the threat of using nuclear weapons as necessary to keep the peace. What it assumes is that peace requires the deadly threat of annihilation because other states may not be trusted.[116] It assumes the Hobbesian state of nature where every state and person looks only for their own self-interest and who must and will ensure that they minimize any risks to themselves and exploit any potential weakness in the other. This position is clearly supported by the nuclear weapons defense doctrines advanced by nuclear-weapon states and NATO allies. They individually look to their own interest and in so doing enter into strategic alliances, based on individual self-interest. Could it not be said, however, that the TPNW is in and of itself also in their self-interest and the overall collective interest of the world and all humanity?

Thirdly, one must look at recent legal scholarship on arguments for nuclear deterrence which has been discussed in greater detail earlier in this work. Sir Michael Quinlan's book, *Thinking About Nuclear Weapons*, contains some arguments for deterrence based on realism. In his work he explains that "deterrence arises from basic and permanent facts about behaviour." The relevant facts determine how we respond to each other in our relationships. He explains:

> In deciding how to act, people customarily seek, whether consciously or not, to take into account the probable consequences of what they do. They refrain from action whose bad consequences for them seem likely to outweigh the good ones. And we exploit these universal realities as one means of helping to influence others against taking action that would be unwelcome to us, by putting clearly before them the prospect that the action will prompt a response that will leave them worse off than if they had not taken it.[117]

Quinlan combines consequentialism and Hobbesian realist assumptions about human nature to explain how most humans act and that fact determines how we *ought* to act. That is, he assumes that all humans and states operate solely on self-interest, distinct from regional or global interests. How should they not? Note that states do not necessarily have "friends," but interests. Even security guarantees to other states serve national interests. Quinlan goes on to explain how this view is applied to nuclear weapons:

> in the face of the vast new destructive power only virtually impermeable protection would be good enough, and such a standard was simply not attainable. So the prevention of war became imperative; and given that there could be no realistic expectation, amid the world's tensions during decades following World War II, that

---

[116] Note that confidence-building measures are certainly not excluded under NATO strategy.

[117] Quinlan M., *Thinking About Nuclear Weapons Principles Problems, Prospects*, (Oxford: Oxford University Press, 2009), at 20.

336   *Toward Neo-Universalism*

political and diplomatic processes alone could be relied upon for that, deterrence had to step forward. ... The world faced both necessity and possibility ... of unmistakably convincing anyone, however unprincipled or sanguine, who might have been minded to initiate war with an advanced power on crucial issue that doing so could not possibly on any calculus, yield net benefit.[118]

Quinlan also uses a realist argument to defend the NPT. He writes, "In the circumstances of the cold war it would have been fantasy to expect the US and the Soviet Union to abandon their armories."[119] He concludes that this is still true now. Since, it is still a fantasy to expect NWS to give up their nuclear weapons, NNWS have to ask themselves,

> whether they would prefer a discriminatory NPT or none. They have answered overwhelmingly in favor of the NPT. More states have acceded to this treaty than to any other in history because of their own interest and benefit, not as a favour to the nuclear powers, with only three abstentions India, Israel and Pakistan, and one declared withdrawal (North Korea) ... The NPT offers assurance that even amid possible stresses and strains they need not worry about or provide for local or regional nuclear-arms competition among themselves.[120]

His argument appears to rest on certain assumptions about human and state behavior – that one should not trust another state not to exploit another state's weakness thus we must operate with maximum protection of our own interests and only compromise on what can be reasonably guaranteed or predicted. Indeed, this author would argue that the opposite may well move the world forward, wherein international relations are used as confidence-building measures which invariably serve national interests. Again, the TPNW is in the overall collective interest of the entire world and all of humanity.

Fourthly, while nuclear disarmament and humanitarian concerns have already been underlying arguments for the NPT, in examining the preamble of the TPNW, and the arguments made by the supporters of the Treaty, one sees how the premises of the argument have not only been reinforced, but presented differently. The grounds for nuclear disarmament are now presented as humanitarian concerns and a global public good; legal principles, shared responsibilities, ethical imperatives, moral considerations and universal norms. When one steps back to compare the realist arguments with these arguments, it becomes clear that the concept of universalism is gaining traction. But it is somewhat of a new version, a neo-universalism that is not as narrow as its older self which demanded specific theological bases. It is accessible to everyone who feels or embraces the reasons for morality from within. It is the common ground for all who are willing to unite in the quest for freedom from being held hostage by a weapon created by humans that has

---

[118]   Ibid. at 21.
[119]   Ibid. at 79.
[120]   Ibid. at 80.

exceeded our ability to control its destructive forces and effects by creating an atmosphere of nuclear fear. The relevant passages are:

> ... and emphasizing that these risks concern the security of all humanity, and that *all States share the responsibility* to prevent any use of nuclear weapons,
>
> *Acknowledging the ethical imperatives* for nuclear disarmament and the urgency of achieving and maintaining a nuclear-weapon-free world, which is a *global public good of the highest order*, serving both national and collective security interests,
>
> Reaffirming the need for *all States at all times to comply with applicable international law*, including international humanitarian law and international human rights law,
>
> *Basing themselves on the principles and rules of international humanitarian law*, in particular the principle that the right of parties to an armed conflict to choose methods or means of warfare is not unlimited, the rule of distinction, the prohibition against indiscriminate attacks, the rules on proportionality and precautions in attack, the prohibition on the use of weapons of a nature to cause superfluous injury or unnecessary suffering, and the rules for the protection of the natural environment,
>
> Considering that *any use of nuclear weapons would be contrary to the rules of international law applicable in armed conflict, in particular the principles and rules of international humanitarian law*,
>
> Reaffirming that *any use of nuclear weapons would also be abhorrent to the principles of humanity and the dictates of public conscience*,
>
> Stressing *the role of public conscience in the furthering of the principles of humanity* as evidenced by the call for the total elimination of nuclear weapons.[121]

First, the language in the preamble emphasizes that *all states* share responsibility, there is no mention of consenting to the jurisdiction or accepting the obligation to prevent the use of nuclear weapons.

Secondly, it acknowledges ethical imperatives for nuclear disarmament which is a global public good of the highest order. It does not argue for the ethical imperative, it simply recognizes it as already existing before the TPNW comes into force and on which it is predicated. It is grounded in the promotion of a global good, not a national good or a personal egocentric good, based on state self-interest alone. The highest order is one which transcends positive law, it is what gives this law binding authority. As discussed in Chapter 2, in 2008 then UN Secretary-General, Ban Ki-Moon unveiled a five-point proposal on nuclear disarmament.[122] In his speech to the East-West Institute Moon spoke of the "unique dangers" of nuclear weapons and that they "should never again be used

---

[121] UN Doc A/CONF.229/2017/8, Treaty on the Prohibition of Nuclear Weapons.

[122] Secretary-General's address to the East-West Institute entitled "The United Nations and security in a nuclear-weapon-free world," October 24, 2008. www.un.org/sg/en/content/sg/statement/2008-10-24/secretary-generals-address-east-west-institute-entitled-united. See also: The Secretary-General's five point proposal on nuclear disarmament "The United Nations and security in a nuclear-weapon-free world." See www.un.org/disarmament/wmd/nuclear/sg5point/.

338   *Toward Neo-Universalism*

because of their indiscriminate effects, their impact on the environment and their profound implications for regional and global security."[123] He noted the importance of addressing such security challenges "to promote global goods" and to provide "remedies to challenges that do not respect borders," emphasizing that a "world free of nuclear weapons would be a global public good of the highest order," and consequently the focus of his talk. "Even when not used, they [nuclear weapons] pose great risks."[124] Indeed, this seems to have been on the minds of the founders of the NPT, and now those of the TPNW with the hope of eliminating the "great risked" posed by their existence.

Thirdly, all states at all times must comply with international law, again no mention of consenting to jurisdiction, it applies to all regardless of one's acceptance of the law as valid or binding. *Fourthly*, it is based on principles and rules of IHL, and that any use of nuclear weapons would violate those rules and principles, even though the 1996 ICJ Opinion left it open for states to potentially justify the use or threat of nuclear weapons if the survival of the state is at stake. This declaration asserts a higher authority than the ICJ position and declares a corrected and universal interpretation and application of IHL.

Finally, it appeals to the principle of humanity and the dictates of public conscience, that the use of nuclear weapons would not only violate international law, it would also violate a higher principle that we must treat human beings as ends in themselves and not as mere means. It would also violate the conscience of the public, which is assumed to be a universal conviction that nuclear catastrophe death is an unacceptable evil.

With these considerations in mind, this author argues that the TPNW reinforces the notion of a neo-universalism that elevates nuclear weapons to a distinct status. It effectively reconfigures arguments supporting nuclear weapons as weapons for peace, as presented by supporters of nuclear deterrence doctrines, to see them as weapons of fear and shame – weapons that destroy peace and serve to instill fear. They go against the public good; against shared responsibilities, ethical imperatives, moral considerations and universal norms.

CONCLUSION: CHANGING THE STATUS QUO THROUGH NEO-UNIVERSALISM

Although the TPNW is striving for universality, unless it becomes a treaty adopted by all states or acquires customary status under international law it will not be recognized as universal law. All indications are that the TPNW is not likely to achieve universality either as treaty law or to attain *opinio juris* under emerging customary practice under international law. Despite this, however, there is no question that it

[123] Ibid.
[124] Ibid.

represents a so-called game-changer, a major disruptor, in the international community. Adopted in the UN General Assembly in July 2017 by 122 countries out of 193, as discussed it represents a vast range of countries and a major portion of the world's population. Moreover, there is growing interest and citizen support for the Treaty in countries that did not participate in its negotiations or vote in favor of it in the General Assembly. Numbers appear to be growing both in size as well as impact. Statistical data indicate that large numbers of people, and in some instances the majority of the population of some countries, want to be a part of the TPNW and favor abolishing nuclear weapons completely.

While the Treaty's aspiration for universality may not amount to *opinio juris* and state practice from a black letter, *de jure*, perspective, there is no doubt that there is an emerging movement toward a neo-universalism on a global front regarding nuclear disarmament. Regardless of legal universality, the ideas and goals of the treaty are gaining a sense of universalism, against nuclear weapons and their harmful effects. This development is changing the discourse amongst individuals and states alike. Despite legal universality, it is sowing the seeds of an emerging neo-universalism that inspires the possibility of a world without nuclear arms based on deep moral conviction regarding what is right and wrong. It seems that many citizens of the world are uniting in their opposition to nuclear weapons, despite some official government positions to the contrary.

Indeed, the TPNW appears to be both a consequence, and a product of, changing perspectives. Moreover, it seems that the Treaty will now in turn assist in ushering in further support toward achieving disarmament aims under this movement toward universal acceptance and maintenance of a non-nuclear world as increasingly advocated by both citizens and states alike. The TPNW will no doubt be used to argue shifting the grounds regarding international humanitarian law. It will be used to reconsider the international architecture governing nuclear weapons by appealing to universalist notions and making realism seem outdated, cold, calculated and divorced from the human conscience and the humanitarian consequences resulting from the destruction and harm caused by a nuclear war and testing as well as the fear posed by the very existence of these destructive weapons. It will attempt to shift the focus away from what is labeled *realistic* security based on fear and distrust amongst states to that of a universal peace maintained by concern for humanity and for the fundamental good of the international community as a whole. This will encourage the universal application of a newly emerging higher law of which nuclear weapons are no longer acceptable as a means of defense, regardless of how well-intended the defense doctrine of deterrence may be. It reveals nuclear weapons for what they really are: weapons of war that are contrary to overall global peace and stability.

12

Obligations *Erga Omnes*: The Missing Link for Nuclear Nonproliferation and Disarmament Compliance

The hard part is: how do we create an environment in which nuclear weapons – like slavery or genocide – are regarded as a taboo and a historical anomaly?

Dr. Mohamed ElBaradei, Nobel Lecture, 2005.[1]

One of the fundamental problems with the TPNW is that the five officially recognized nuclear-weapons states – Russia, the United States, China, France and the United Kingdom, collectively the NWS – and four other states who possess nuclear weapons – India, Pakistan, Israel and North Korea – have boycotted the Treaty negotiations and refused to sign or ratify it. Despite moves toward neo-universalism, this leaves an important gap in the TPNW legal framework, because it does not directly bind the NWS and it seems unlikely that these NWS will join the Treaty or be bound under *opinio juris*. One way to remedy this problem and fill the legal gap is to appeal to an existing set of legal obligations found in international jurisprudence to which NWS are already bound. Specifically, the International Court of Justice (ICJ) has highlighted that states owe obligations *erga omnes* – toward all – that derive from other international laws, legal principles and conventions. Examples of these obligations listed by the ICJ are ones that derive from the outlawing of acts of aggression, genocide, principles and rules concerning the basic rights of the human person, including protection from slavery and racial discrimination.[2]

These obligations do not require consent, agreement, ratification of a treaty or contractual relations between states, per se; they exist as universal norms applicable to all states and thus legally bind the international community as a whole to meet these obligations. While the ICJ has not yet explicitly acknowledged this type of obligations in relation to nuclear weapons, this author argues that international obligations extracted from case law and existing treaties, conventions, norms and practice imply that nuclear obligations also have this unique status. These

---

[1] Nobel Lecture, Oslo, December 10, 2005. See www.nobelprize.org/prizes/peace/2005/elbaradei/26138-mohamed-elbaradei-nobel-lecture-2005-2/.

[2] *Barcelona Traction, Light and Power Co. Ltd. (Belg. v. Spain)*, 1970 ICJ 3, 32 (February 5) at paras. 33–34.

obligations ought to be acknowledged in theory and practice among the international community and enforced in international fora, including judicial proceedings before courts. If they were to be acknowledged and upheld within this context, the playing field would be leveled and both nuclear and non-nuclear weapons states would be much more likely to work toward the common goal of disarmament and the elimination of nuclear weapons and explosive devices, as required under Article VI of the NPT. This discussion will outline a number of arguments advancing the position that every state has *nuclear* obligations *erga omnes* under public international law, that is, obligations to the international community, to disarm their nuclear weapons, not to develop or to proliferate respective nuclear arsenals. Consequently, they must use nuclear energy for peaceful purposes only: to protect citizens from nuclear testing, accidents and terrorism, and ultimately to rid the world of nuclear weapons through disarmament efforts.

In doing so, firstly examined is what is meant by obligations *erga omnes* and how the international community currently recognizes these existing obligations including how such *erga omnes* obligations apply to *nuclear* obligations. Subsequently, the discussion will draw the link between *erga omnes* and nuclear obligations to the goals of the TPNW and a binding legal framework to which NWS already adhere. In doing so it will attempt to answer the following questions:

(1) What are *erga omnes* obligations?
(2) Does the international community currently recognize any *erga omnes* obligations?
(3) Why are *nuclear* obligations effective *erga omnes*?
(4) How should the international community enforce nuclear obligations *erga omnes*?
(5) How do obligations *erga omnes* act as a link between the goals of the TPNW and a binding legal framework that NWS already adhere to?

WHAT ARE *ERGA OMNES* OBLIGATIONS?

The concept itself has been referenced over time by various scholars such as Theodor Meron,[3] but the ICJ first acknowledged the existence of, and defined, *erga omnes* obligations in the *Barcelona Traction* case in 1970.[4] Here, the ICJ's approach to obligations *erga omnes* was built upon this longstanding acceptance of humanitarian intervention. The *Barcelona Traction* case dealt with the question of whether Belgium had legal standing to claim reparations for damages to Belgian nationals and shareholders in a company that was incorporated in Canada, caused

---

[3] Theodor Meron, *War Crimes Law Comes of Age*, Oxford University Press 1998, at n. 5, p. 122.
[4] As observed by Stefan Kadelbach in "Chapter I: Jus Cogens, Obligations Erga Omnes and other Rules – The Identification of Fundamental Norms," in *The Fundamental Rules of the International Legal Order* (Christian Tomuschat and Jean-March. Thouvenin, eds.) (2006, Koninjlijke Brill NV, Leiden) at 22.

342   *Obligations* Erga Omnes

by alleged unlawful acts of the state of Spain. The Court denied Belgium's right to bring proceedings because for the purposes of diplomatic protection the company did not possess Belgian nationality,[5] however in *obiter dictum*, the Court distinguished diplomatic obligations owed to other individual states from obligations states owe to the international community as whole, which are obligations *erga omnes*. This case was the catalyst for vigorous academic and legal debate about what the ICJ meant and about what obligations should be considered *erga omnes* and what legal entities (state actors, individuals, or international organizations with legal personality) are to be included in the "international community as a whole."[6] The relevant passage, reproduced here, states:

> 33. When a State admits into its territory foreign investments or foreign nationals, whether natural or juristic persons, it is bound to extend to them the protection of the law and assumes obligations concerning the treatment to be afforded them. These obligations, however, are neither absolute nor unqualified. In particular, an essential distinction should be drawn *between the obligations of a State towards the international community as a whole, and those arising vis-a-vis another State in the field of diplomatic protection. By their very nature the former are the concern of all States. In view of the importance of the rights involved, all States can be held to have a legal interest in their protection; they are obligations erga omnes.*
>
> 34. Such obligations derive, for example, in contemporary international law, from the outlawing of acts of aggression, and of genocide, as also from the principles and rules concerning the basic rights of the human person, including protection from slavery and racial discrimination. Some of the corresponding rights of protection have entered into the body of general international law (Reservations to the Convention on the Prevention and Punishment of the Crime of Genocide, Advisory Opinion, ICJ Reports 1951, p. 23); others are conferred by international instruments of a universal or quasi-universal character.[7]

One should note the relevant passage the court refers to from the ICJ's Advisory Opinion on *Reservations to the Convention on the Prevention and Punishment of the Crime of Genocide*, which provides further insight into the nature of these obligations and from where they derive their authority:

---

[5] Christian J. Tams and Antonios Tzanakopoulos, "*Barcelona Traction* at 40: The ICJ as an Agent of Legal Development," *Leiden Journal of International Law*, 23 (2010), pp. 781–800 at p. 782.

[6] Erika de Wet, "Invoking Obligations Erga Omnes in the Twenty-First Century: Progressive Developments since Barcelona Traction," 38 *S. Afr. Y.B. Int'l L.* 1 (2013) at 2–5. See also: James Crawford, "Articles on Responsibility of States for Internationally Wrongful Acts," United Nations Audiovisual Library of International Law 2012 at p. 7: "As with the definition of international responsibility in article 1, also article 48 avoids restricting the scope of obligations owed *erga omnes* by limiting their beneficiaries to States alone. In this sense, the concept of international community relevant for article 48 implies that this community does not consist exclusively of States and includes other entities, for example the United Nations, the European Union, the International Committee of the Red Cross."

[7] *Barcelona Traction, Light and Power Co. Ltd. (Belg. v. Spain)*, 1970 ICJ 3, 32 (February 5) at para. 33–34.

The origins of the Convention show that it was the intention of the United Nations to condemn and punish genocide as "a crime under international law" involving a denial of the right of existence of entire human groups, *a denial which shocks the conscience of mankind and results in great losses to humanity, and which is contrary to moral law and to the spirit and aims of the United Nations* (Resolution 96 (1) of the General Assembly, December 11th 1946). *The first consequence arising from this conception is that the principles underlying the Convention are principles which are recognized by civilized nations as binding on States, even without any conventional obligation. A second consequence is the universal character both of the condemnation of genocide and of the cooperation required "in order to liberate mankind from such an odious scourge"* ...

The objects of such a convention must also be considered. The Convention was manifestly *adopted for a purely humanitarian and civilizing purpose.* It is indeed difficult to imagine a convention that might have this dual character to a greater degree, since its object on the one hand is to safeguard the very existence of certain human groups and on the other to confirm and endorse the most elementary principles of morality. *In such a convention the contracting States do not have any interests of their own; they merely have, one and all, a common interest, namely, the accomplishment of those high purposes which are the raison d'être of the convention.* Consequently, in a convention of this type one cannot speak of individual advantages or disadvantages to States, or of the maintenance of a perfect contractual balance between rights and duties. *The high ideals which inspired the Convention provide, by virtue of the common will of the parties, the foundation and measure of all its provisions* ...

The complete exclusion from the Convention of one or more States would not only restrict the scope of its application, but would detract from *the authority of the moral and humanitarian principles which are its basis.*[8]

The Court, in this Advisory Opinion, is pointing out the unique binding authority of the law against genocide, which derives not from a voluntary contract or even convention, but from the "conscience of mankind," "the moral law," as well as "humanitarian principles," "the common will of the parties" and the "spirit and aims of the United Nations."[9] The Convention is not about protecting the self-interest of states, it is to "safeguard the very existence of human groups . . . and endorse the most elementary principles of morality."[10] This goal is a single and common interest of all states and thus binds all states equally by its very nature. In one sense, the Court is saying that each state has a duty to prevent and punish genocide *not because they are a party to the Convention,* but rather, the Convention is the result or expression of a universal *moral* law against denying the right of existence of an entire human group. Since this moral law is aimed at preserving the fundamental good of human

---

[8] Reservations to the Convention on the Prevention and Punishment of the Crime of Genocide, Advisory Opinion, ICJ Reports 1951, at pp. 23–24.

[9] Ibid.

[10] Ibid.

344   *Obligations* Erga Omnes

existence and preventing the destruction of that good, states, or rather the human beings they are composed of, are bound by this law because it is found within their conscience. In the same way, obligations *erga omnes* are of a different order than contractual or conventional obligations because they derive their authority not from voluntary agreement but from moral convictions of human beings which have gained universal acknowledgment and are now expressed in fundamental principles and rules of law that are binding on everyone and all states.

Many other scholars have analyzed and defined the *erga omnes* concept in relation to international law. Maurizio Ragazzi, in his work *The Concept of International Obligations Erga Omnes* (1997), gives us one of the clearest definitions:

> The dictum in the *Barcelona Traction* case identifies two characteristic features of obligations *erga omnes*. The first one is *universality*, in the sense that obligations *erga omnes* are binding on all States without exception. The second one is *solidarity*, in the sense that every State is deemed to have a legal interest in their protection.[11]

Furthermore, Tams and Tzanakopoulos describe the *erga omnes* concept in four simple steps:

(i)   International law draws a distinction between the general rules governing the treatment of aliens, and a special set of rules protecting fundamental values.
(ii)   To this special set of rules protecting fundamental values applies a special regime of standing. The right to raise claims in response to violations is not restricted to the state of nationality (as it is under diplomatic protection).
(iii) Instead, certain fundamental values, being the concern of the international community as a whole, can and should be protected by each and every State. [Indeed, as it relates to nuclear, presently the question is not whether they can be protected but whether states have a duty, an obligation, to protect them.]
(iv)   Finally, these rights of protection do not have to be conferred expressly by treaty, but do (also) exist without a special written "empowerment" – and would then flow from general international law.[12]

Thus, under international law, obligations *erga omnes* are special duties that every state has toward all other states that derive from other areas of public international law including international humanitarian law, international criminal law, and rules and principles concerning human rights (international human rights law). They are reciprocal in that they always require every party involved to be simultaneously fulfilling the same duty to the other parties. Even if a state that is not directly injured, it is entitled to invoke the responsibility of another state and may be eligible to take lawful measures against that state to ensure cessation of the breach and reparation

---

[11]   Maurizio Ragazzi, *The Concept of International Obligations Erga Omnes* (Oxford: Oxford University Press, 1997) at 17.
[12]   Tams and Tzanakopoulos, *Barcelona Traction* at 40, at p. 792.

What Are Erga Omnes *Obligations?*   345

(Articles 48, 54 ARSIWA).[13] The same applies to international organizations that may also have a right to take such measures subject to their constituent documents and existing principles and rules of international law (Articles 49, 57 DARIO).[14] For example, hypothetically speaking, if genocide was being committed by a foreign country, every other State would have a duty to the international community (*erga omnes*) and a legal interest in, preventing and punishing genocide. So, if State A committed genocide in State B, State C has the duty to punish State A for perpetrating genocide and if State C has failed to do so, State D has a right to take action for its failure. All states have the right, but also the duty to punish for the crime of genocide.

At the same time, those who were victims of genocide would have the right *erga omnes* to be protected from genocide by the international community. These duties and rights are binding because genocide is abhorrent; a derogation from and a destruction of the fundamental good of human existence, and this conviction has been expressed by all states through an international law (the Convention) which holds the status of *jus cogens* which give rise to obligations *erga omnes*. "The term 'jus cogens' means 'the compelling law' and, as such, a *jus cogens* norm holds the highest hierarchical position among all other norms and principles. As a consequence of that standing, *jus cogens* norms are deemed to be 'peremptory' and non-derogable."[15] Thus, every state has a legal interest in taking appropriate actions to prevent and punish it, in enforcing legal consequences on other states for not fulfilling their duty to prevent and punish it, and in calling on other states to protect their right not to be subject to it.

Erga omnes obligations are distinct from other kinds of obligations because they are said to arise not from explicit bilateral or multilateral relations or clearly defined international treaties and law,[16] but from customary international law,

---

[13]   See Jochen A. Frowein, *loc. cit.*, para. 9; Crawford, *op. cit.*, 578–579; Jonathan Black-Branch, "Countermeasures to Ensure Compliance with Nuclear Non-Proliferation Obligations," in Black-Branch and Fleck (eds.), *Nuclear Non-Proliferation in International Law, Vol. II: Verification and Compliance* (Asser Press/Springer, 2016), 351–387, at 363.

[14]   Draft articles on the Responsibility of International Organizations for Internationally Wrongful Acts – DARIO – UN Doc A/66/10 (2011), *Yearbook of the International Law Commission*, 2011, Vol. II, Part Two.

[15]   M. Cherif Bassiouni, "International Crimes: Jus Cogens and Obligatio Erga Omnes," *Law and Contemporary Problems*, Vol. 59: No. 4, 63 at 67.

[16]   Dr. Hossein Sartipi, Dr. Ali Reza Hojatzadeh, "The Innovation in Concept of the Erga-Omnesisation of International Law," *International Journal of Humanities & Social Science Studies*, Vol. II, Issue II, September 2015, p. 189 at pp. 193–194: "In strictly bilateral legal relationships, when one state violates its obligations, the directly affected has a right to reparations (in its various forms) and may have recourse to countermeasures (as a means to include compliance with the obligation by the state in breach) and diplomatic and judicial dispute settlement. Not only does the state have standing before the court in such cases, but it may also make legal claims through any venue available. Notwithstanding this, not all obligations today fit in this category, which was peculiar of classical international law. Obligations erga omnes do not share this quality. On the contrary when one State violates them, it is most difficult, if not impossible, to find a directly affected state with legal interest, or legal legitimacy (otherwise known as standing or *locus standi*) to make claim in this regard. Hence, in

346   *Obligations* Erga Omnes

jus cogens[17] (peremptory norms), human rights principles, and even from fundamental values of the international community.[18] The *Barcelona Traction* decision also implies that these obligations arise out of a logical and practical necessity to protect states and natural persons from violations of other fundamental international laws. What ultimately becomes clear in the debate is that obligations *erga omnes* come from a unique source because of the nature and subject matter of the obligation.

DOES THE INTERNATIONAL COMMUNITY CURRENTLY RECOGNIZE ANY *ERGA OMNES* OBLIGATIONS?

Since the *Barcelona Traction* case in 1970, the ICJ has acknowledged the notion of obligations *erga omnes* and states have employed the concept in several advisory opinions and cases. These are worth noting in full to emphasize the actual and indeed growing body of discussion in judicial fora, including: the *South West Africa* cases (1962 and 1966);[19] *Northern Cameroons* (1963);[20] *United States Diplomatic and Consular Staff in Tehran* (1980);[21] *Nicaragua v. United States of America* (1986);[22] *Nicaragua v. Honduras* (1988);[23] *Case Concerning East Timor* (1995);[24] *Legality of the Threat or Use of Nuclear Weapons, Advisory Opinion* (1996);[25] *Bosnia Herzegovina v. Yugoslavia* (1996);[26] the *Legal Consequences of the Construction of a Wall in the Occupied Palestinian Territory, Advisory Opinion* (2004);[27] *Belgium v. Senegal* (2009);[28]

---

traditional view those objectively affected by those breaches (such as individuals whose human rights were violated) were left without remedy."

[17]   It should be noted that, while the two concepts often overlap, not all obligations *erga omnes* are *jus cogens*; see Ulf Linderfalk, "International Legal Hierarchy Revisited – The Status of Obligations Erga Omnes," *Nordic J of International Law* 80 (2011) 1–23 at p. 5: "whether a norm is part of the international jus cogens or not, when it expresses obligations erga omnes, it is hierarchically superior to all other norms of non-peremptory international law." Kadelbach, at 27, observes that the distinction between *jus cogens* and *erga omnes* is often not "clear-cut" as the two principles are driven by the same justification, and "the primary rules ... are basically the same."

[18]   Erika de Wet, n. 2 above at p. 7.

[19]   See *Preliminary Objections* (ICJ Reports, 1962, p. 319) and *Second Phase* (ICJ Reports, 1966, p. 6).

[20]   *Cameroon v. United Kingdom (Preliminary Objections)*, (ICJ Reports 1963, p. 15).

[21]   *United States of America v. Iran* (ICJ Reports, 1980, p. 3).

[22]   *Nicaragua v. United States of America*, Merits, ICJ Reports 1986, 14 et seq., (134, para. 267).

[23]   *Border and Transborder Armed Actions (Nicaragua v. Honduras), Jurisdiction and Admissibility* (ICJ Reports 1988, p. 69).

[24]   *Portugal v. Australia*. ICJ Reports 1995, 90 et seq., (102, para. 29): "Portugal's assertion that the right of peoples to self-determination ... has an erga omnes character, is irreproachable."

[25]   *Legality of the Threat or Use of Nuclear Weapons, advisory Opinion* (ICJ Reports 1996, p. 226).

[26]   *Bosnia Herzegovina v. Yugoslavia, Preliminary Objections* (ICJ Reports 1996, 595 et seq. 616).

[27]   *Legal Consequences of the Construction of a Wall in the Occupied Palestinian Territory, Advisory Opinion* (ICJ Reports 2004, p. 136).

[28]   *Questions relating to the Obligation to Prosecute or Extradite (Belgium v. Senegal) (Provisional Measures), Order of 28 May 2009*, available at www.icj-cij.org.

Unilateral Declaration of Independence in Respect of Kosovo, Advisory Opinion (2010);[29] *Costa Rica* v. *Nicaragua* (2015);[30] and in *Jadhav (India versus Pakistan)* (2017).[31]

In relation to nuclear weapons, the ICJ did not deny the existence of *erga omnes* obligations in the *Marshall Islands Cases* (2016) and in the *Nuclear Tests* cases brought by Australia and Zealand against France in 1974 and revived in 1995.[32] The ICJ, however, has not yet made a decision on the basis of a nuclear obligation *erga omnes*.[33] That does not mean it does not exist as an obligation, but merely that the ICJ has not yet recognized it under case law, per se. Indeed, the Court recognized the binding obligations under Article VI which serve to reaffirm these duties under the NPT.

Other international and national courts have also addressed and employed *erga omnes* arguments. The Inter-American Court of Human Rights case of *Blake* v. *Guatemala* (1999) made use of the concept to demonstrate how an original judgment went wrong.[34] The case focused on what is the proper measure of reparations in pecuniary and non-pecuniary damages that Guatemala owed to the victim's next of kin for the violation of Articles 5 and 8 of the American Convention on Human Rights as they relate to the victim's disappearance.[35]

The High Court of England and Wales acknowledged that the prohibition on torture is a rule *jus cogens* applied *erga omnes*. It stated: "It is beyond dispute that the fact that a rule, such as the prohibition on torture, has achieved the status of a rule of *jus cogens erga omnes* in customary law gives rise to certain special consequences in international law."[36] Moreover, the European Court of Human Rights stated in *Al-Adsani* v. *The United Kingdom*, that "the prohibition of torture imposes on States obligations *erga omnes*, that is, obligations owed toward all the other members of the international community."[37] In *Prosecutor* v. *Furundzija*, the International Criminal Tribunal for the Former Yugoslavia stated that a breach of an obligation *erga omnes* constitutes a breach of the corresponding right of all members of the international

---

[29] *Accordance with International Law of the Unilateral Declaration of Independence in Respect of Kosovo, Advisory Opinion* (ICJ Reports 2010, p. 403).

[30] *Dispute Concerning Maritime Delimitation in The Caribbean Sea and The Pacific Ocean (Costa Rica v. Nicaragua)* 2015 ICJ Counter Memorial at 3.24.

[31] *Jadhav (India versus Pakistan)* 2017, Concurring Opinion of Judge Cancado Trindade at para, 28.

[32] Marshall Islands Cases: *Marshall Islands* v. *UK*, Preliminary Objections, ICJ General List 2016 No.160; *Marshall Islands* v. *Pakistan*, ICJ General List 2016 No.159; *Marshall Islands* v. *India*, ICJ General List 2016 No. 158; *Nuclear Tests (New Zealand v. France) Case*, ICJ Reports 1995, p. 288.

[33] Erika de Wet at p. 3. See also: Karl Zemanek, "New Trends in the Enforcement of erga omnes Obligations," in J. A. Frowein and R. Wolfrum (eds.), *Max Planck Yearbook of United Nations Law*, 2000 Kluwer Law International at p. 11.

[34] *Case of Blake* v. *Guatemala*, Inter-American Court of Human Rights Judgment of January 22, 1999, (Reparations and Costs) at paras. 39, 40.

[35] See: https://opil.ouplaw.com/view/10.1093/law:ihrl/1431iachr99.case.1/law-ihrl-1431iachr99.

[36] *Mohamed, R (on the application of)* v. *Secretary of State for Foreign & Commonwealth Affairs (Rev 31–07-2009)* [2008] EWHC 2048 (Admin) (August 21, 2008) at para. 171.

[37] *Al-Adsani* v. *The United Kingdom* – 35763/97 [2001] ECHR 761 (November 21, 2001) at para. 151.

348   *Obligations* Erga Omnes

community.[38] These statements further demonstrate a growing application of *erga omnes* obligations.

The International Law Commission (ILC) has also acknowledged the existence of obligations toward the international community as a whole – *erga omnes* – or toward a group of states – *erga omnes partes* – in its Articles on Responsibility of States for Internationally Wrongful Acts (ARISWA).[39] These developments further illustrate that *erga omnes* obligations are applied in various national, regional and international fora as well as increasingly recognized and gaining traction among legal academics and international lawyers, and within national and international courts.

WHY ARE *NUCLEAR* OBLIGATIONS EFFECTIVE *ERGA OMNES*?

One of the newest proposed applications of *erga omnes* is to nuclear law and obligations arising from nuclear weapons treaties. We now turn to a number of novel arguments in support of nuclear obligations *erga omnes*, beginning with an explanation of obligations dealing with nuclear weapons and energy. The following section will explain that the obligations under the Non-Proliferation Treaty, bolstered by the right not to live in fear of torture, suggest that the concept of *erga omnes* apply to the nuclear realm. Once this has been established, the remainder of the section will make the case that extending *erga omnes* obligations to nuclear weapons to be consistent with other existing *erga omnes* obligations, and that an extension of these principles is a necessary development based on moral and philosophical principles as well as by drawing analogy to tort law.

Which Obligations? The Three Pillars of Nonproliferation Treaty

The NPT comprises three central pillars: (1) nonproliferation, (2) the use of nuclear energy for peaceful purposes and (3) disarmament. The *first* of these pillars requires nonproliferation of nuclear weapons, whereby non-nuclear-weapon states agree not to import, manufacture or otherwise acquire nuclear weapons or other nuclear explosive devices. Nuclear-weapon states (the United States, Russia, the United Kingdom, France and China), are obliged not to transfer nuclear weapons to non-nuclear-weapon States. The *second* pillar ensures the right of all parties to develop research, production and use of nuclear energy for peaceful purposes, and that each non-nuclear-weapon state party must accept and comply with International Atomic

---

[38] *Prosecutor* v. *Furundzija, International Criminal Tribunal for the Former Yugoslavia*, unreported, December 10, 1998, Case No. IT – 95–17/T 10 at para. 151.

[39] Erika de Wet at p. 3. The commentary on Articles 1, 12, 25, 30, 33, 40, 42, 48, 54 of the ARSIWA all refer to obligations and interests owed by states to the international community as a whole. See: "Draft articles on Responsibility of States for Internationally Wrongful Acts, with commentaries, 2001," Report of the International Law Commission on the work of its fifty-third session, United Nations, 2008.

Energy Agency (IAEA) safeguards. Finally, the *third* pillar requires disarmament in that all parties undertake "to pursue negotiations in good faith on effective measures relating to cessation of the nuclear arms race at an early date and to nuclear disarmament, and on a treaty on general and complete disarmament under strict and effective international control."[40] The NPT is an interdependent treaty. Although each pillar may entail separate duties, obligations and responsibilities, all three pillars remain interdependent for full compliance and implementation as an overall package.

Effectively, the first pillar of nonproliferation includes the obligations of non-nuclear-weapon states (NNWS) not to acquire or build nuclear weapons and of NWS not to share such weapons with any other state. Both sets of states parties – NWS and NNWS – have different responsibilities that lead to the same fundamental goal: nonproliferation of nuclear weapons. The second pillar gives all states the right to develop nuclear energy, under a corresponding obligation only to use and develop such energy for peaceful purposes, as well as to ensure that they meet the safeguards of the IAEA in doing so. The third pillar may seem more amorphous, indicating that parties have an obligation to work toward disarmament. While it does not prescribe a process, as such, it does describe a result – disarmament.

Given these obligations, why should one treat them as obligations toward the international community as a whole and not just toward the Parties of the NPT?

This author argues that the Non-Proliferation Treaty gives rise to obligations *erga omnes* in that it articulates long-standing and undisputable believes of states regarding nuclear weapons and corresponding obligations in the international community. It does not establish them, per se, but it recognizes (i.e., articulates) the inherent obligation that states at the time expressed into law (i.e., the NPT). The NWS have a right to develop nuclear energy for peaceful purposes. With this comes corresponding obligations not to proliferate, not to use nuclear energy for non-peaceful purposes, and to move toward disarmament.[41] Again, all three pillars of the NPT are interdependent.

---

[40] See Jonathan Black-Branch, "Due Diligence as a Legal Concept to Ensure Security and Safety of Peaceful Uses of Nuclear Energy as well as Non-proliferation and Disarmament Obligations," in Jonathan L. Black-Branch and Dieter Fleck (eds.) *Nuclear Non-Proliferation in International Law – Volume III Legal Aspects of the Use of Nuclear Energy for Peaceful Purposes* (The Hague: Asser Press, 2016) at 493–495.

[41] See Jonathan Black-Branch, "Due Diligence as a Legal Concept to Ensure Security and Safety of Peaceful Uses of Nuclear Energy as well as Non-proliferation and Disarmament Obligations," in Jonathan L. Black-Branch and Dieter Fleck (eds.) *Nuclear Non-Proliferation in International Law – Volume III Legal Aspects of the Use of Nuclear Energy for Peaceful Purposes* (The Hague: Asser Press, 2016), at p. 489: "The Treaty acknowledges that five states are legally recognized as nuclear-weapon states under international law, namely the United States, Russia, the United Kingdom, France and China. Article IX(3) states that, 'a nuclear weapon State is one which has manufactured and exploded a nuclear weapon or other nuclear explosive device prior to 1 January, 1967'. Consequently, all other States fall into the category of non-nuclear weapons states for the purpose of the Treaty and general international law. Effectively, the 'object' and 'purpose' of the Non-Proliferation Treaty is to allow the development of nuclear energy for peaceful purposes whilst prohibiting the development of nuclear weapons beyond the five nuclear-weapon States, and assuring that non-nuclear-weapon States do not acquire nuclear weapons or devices."

350 *Obligations* Erga Omnes

Moreover, at first blush it would seem that the NWS also have a right to possess nuclear weapons under the NPT. Upon examination, however, one sees that the NWS do not have the right to possess nuclear weapons, per se. They are allowed to hold them pending the full realization of Article VI requirements. Thus, it is not a right as such, but permission to hold them for a time limited period.

This author would argue that the NPT does not establish such rights but merely articulates *erga omnes* obligations that already existed and that NPT negotiators and states at the time believed themselves. Perhaps they did not label them as *erga onmes partes* obligations as such, but in effect they were behaving as though they were and treating nuclear arms and approaching their possession of nuclear weapons as such. After all, nuclear security issues were at the forefront of the minds of nation states since the launch of the United Nations with the very first resolution of the UN General Assembly being the "Establishment of a Commission to Deal with the Problems Raised by the Discovery of Atomic Energy," adopted on January 24, 1946, in London (Resolution 1(I))[42] in what the UN refers to as a "landmark" document.

The establishment of the IAEA and NPT negotiations highlight the urgency and the need to achieve agreement on a treaty before more states acquired nuclear arsenals, demonstrating the fact that at the time the international community held the belief that the proliferation and ownership of nuclear weapons was against the "interest" of all states and humanity at large. The strict line the NPT takes regarding nonproliferation and the hard cap on the number of NWS serves further to demonstrate the recognition of a morality against such destructive weapons. Moreover, since its coming into force over fifty years ago, there has been unrelenting outrage against other states (e.g., North Korea and Iran) acquiring such weapons, reinforcing the *erga onmes* nature of such obligations and highlighting a belief that the possession of such weapons is incompatible with the morality of the international community as a whole. Indeed, negotiators and signatories, including the NWS are quick to point out that the NPT was agreed for humanitarian reasons as well as strategic military purposes.

The development of nuclear technology has been matched by efforts on various levels to develop and apply a legal and regulatory framework throughout the international community. Despite the fact that strict monitoring processes and reporting requirements have been adopted, Article VI of the NPT still requires that, "Each of the Parties to the Treaty undertakes to pursue negotiations in good faith on effective measures relating to cessation of the nuclear arms race at an early date and to nuclear disarmament, and on a treaty on general and complete disarmament under strict and effective international control."

Indeed, this author contends that the Non-Proliferation Treaty enforcements are obligations *erga omnes* required by both individual state and collective responsibility. Issues relating to nuclear weapons and nonproliferation law form a distinct and unique area of law that should constitute a subject discipline in its own right, separate

---

[42] UN General Assembly Resolution 1(I) January 24, 1946. See https://undocs.org/en/A/RES/1(I).

from other fields of international law, and to be distinguished from conventional weapons law and international humanitarian law. As such, it is owed an extraordinary[43] form of due diligence regarding the application and enforcement of the Non-Proliferation Treaty's object and purpose. There is a need for a paradigm-shift in how states and international institutions approach, interpret and apply this nonproliferation law, and it should be regarded as a special domain of law requiring a unique approach, separate from other forms of law by its very nature.[44]

In essence, as was recognized during the negotiation of the NPT and ever since, nonproliferation and disarmament law is unique because of its very subject matter. The detonation of high-impact nuclear weapons is capable of causing large-scale death and destruction and of setting in motion a nuclear war that could cause worldwide death and destruction.[45] Nuclear weapons, nuclear technology and nuclear energy can be stolen, used for non-peaceful purposes and contribute to the proliferation of more nuclear weapons, all of which affect the security and safety of the international community, which includes every state and every person on earth. When one examines World War II, the Cold War and the threats uttered by US and North Korean leaders in recent times (e.g., 2018), it seems that states have always threatened to use nuclear weapons as *international* weapons (i.e., with other nations being the target). The only use of nuclear weapons in history was *international* warfare; the United States dropped atomic bombs on Hiroshima and Nagasaki in 1945. Thus, the targets of nuclear weapons and their impact are not confined within state borders and are not merely a domestic concern; they are by nature a concern of every state within range of a nuclear missile or accessible by plane.

Under the UN Charter Article 2, states have a duty to act in accordance with the principle of "sovereign equality," and to "settle their international disputes by peaceful means in such a manner that international peace and security and justice are not endangered."[46] The existence, use and threats to use nuclear weapons all

---

43 Extraordinary Diligence is defined as: "That extreme measure of care and caution which persons of unusual prudence and circumspection use for securing and preserving their own property or rights." *Black's Law Dictionary*, http://thelawdictionary.org/extraordinary-diligence.

44 Jonathan Black-Branch, "Opening Remarks to the Third Round Table (London) on Nuclear Weapons, Nuclear Energy and Non-Proliferation under International Law: Current Challenges and Evolving Norms" (February 14–15, 2013 Oxford and Cambridge Club), www.ila-hq.org/en/committees/index.cfm /cid/1025.

45 One Minuteman III ICBM can be armed with up to three nuclear warheads each with 300–500 kilotons of explosive power. To get a sense of how much damage one of these weapons can cause, 500 kilotons is forty-one times the size of the "Little Boy" bomb which destroyed Hiroshima killing at least 75,000 people and the United States has 450 nuclear armed operational Minuteman III missiles along other kinds of nuclear weapons. Tom Demerly, "US Tests Minuteman Missile Amid North Korean Tension and Proposed ICBM Upgrade," *The Aviationist* (August 4, 2017), Online: The Aviationist https://theaviationist.com/2017/08/04/u-s-tests-minuteman-missile-amid-north-korean-tension-and-proposed-icbm-upgrade/. Fat Man and Little Boy dropped on Nagasaki and Hiroshima were twenty-one and fifteen kilotons respectively. Atomic Heritage Foundation, online: www.atomicheritage.org/history/little-boy-and-fat-man.

46 UN Charter Article 2.

352 *Obligations* Erga Omnes

serve to undermine *international* peace and security and are the concern of the international community, thus the obligations arising from the NPT are *erga omnes;* toward the international community as a whole. When considering these threats to international peace and security, a case can clearly be made that the NPT's provisions on the use and possession of nuclear weapons are in line with the *erga omnes* criteria observed in the of *universality* and *solidarity* as observed in the *Barcelona Traction* case cited above. In terms of universality, obligations of disarmament and nonproliferation are binding on all states without exception due to the fact that any use of nuclear weapons concerns all states, and in terms of solidarity, every state has a legal interest in protection against nuclear weapons. Indeed, the paradox is that states possessing nuclear weapons, or wanting to possess them, cite security reasons (i.e., deterrence through their destructive nature) as the rationale for needing them in the first place (i.e., defense purposes). So, in their reasoning for wanting to own or acquire nuclear weapons, they ironically recognize how it is in no state's overall best interests to have them, inadvertently highlighting the *erga omnes* character of nuclear nonproliferation and disarmament obligations.

It also is fitting to discuss the status of such International Humanitarian Law and International Human Rights as it pertains to *jus ad bellum.* Rule 90 of the ICRC rules pertaining to customary humanitarian law, prohibits torture, cruel or inhuman treatment and outrages upon personal dignity, in particular humiliating and degrading treatment. To that end, the International Committee of the Red Cross (ICRC) notes that state practice establishes this rule as a norm of customary international law applicable in both international and non-international armed conflicts.[47] Hence, it would invariably apply within a nuclear context.

Outlining its relevance to armed conflicts, be they international or non-international in nature, the ICRC highlights that the prohibition of torture was already recognized in the Lieber Code, under Article 16.[48] Further, it notes that Article 6(b) of the Charter of the International Military Tribunal at Nuremberg included "ill-treatment" of civilians and prisoners of war as a war crime.[49] In the event of a nuclear detonation exposing either civilians or prisoners, the failure to provide adequate or appropriate medical treatment, for example, might well allege to constitute ill-treatment for the purposes of Article 6(b) within the context in question, based on the facts of the case in the given scenario.

Common Article 3 of the Geneva Conventions prohibits "cruel treatment and torture" and "outrages upon personal dignity, in particular humiliating and degrading treatment" of civilians and persons *hors de combat.*[50] Furthermore, torture and cruel treatment are also prohibited by other provisions of the four Geneva

---

[47] See https://ihl-databases.icrc.org/customary-ihl/eng/docs/v1_rul_rule90.
[48] Lieber Code, Article 16 (cited in Vol. II, Ch. 32, § 1010).
[49] IMT Charter (Nuremberg), Article 6(b) (ibid., § 982).
[50] Geneva Conventions, common Article 3 (ibid., § 984). As quoted from https://ihl-databases.icrc.org /customary-ihl/eng/docs/v1_rul_rule90.

Conventions.[51] Specifically, First Geneva Convention, Article 12, second paragraph, "torture";[52] Second Geneva Convention, Article 12, second paragraph, "torture";[53] Third Geneva Convention, Article 17, fourth paragraph, "physical or mental torture";[54] Article 87, third paragraph, "torture or cruelty";[55] and Article 89, "inhuman, brutal or dangerous" disciplinary punishment;[56] Fourth Geneva Convention, Article 32 lists "torture" and "other measures of brutality."[57] Further, "torture or inhuman treatment" and "wilfully causing great suffering or serious injury to body or health" would constitute grave breaches of the Geneva Conventions and are considered war crimes under the Statute of the International Criminal Court.[58] Whether, and the specific circumstances under which, torture or other specific claims listed above could be alleged, or argued, under the four Geneva Conventions remain to be proven within their respective circumstances based on the facts of the case within their particular context. That said, any military defense doctrine must consider such possibilities in relation to their intention to employ such weapons either as a first move or retaliatory action, under appropriate *jus ad bellum* requirements.

The ICRC note further that, the prohibition of torture and outrages upon personal dignity, and in particular humiliating and degrading treatment, is recognized as a fundamental guarantee for civilians and persons *hors de combat* by Additional Protocols I and II.[59] Could it be considered an outrage upon personal dignity to subject them to nuclear war? Or, even the fear of a nuclear war and hypothesizing its potential aftermath? With the implementation of the TPNW these and other related questions are increasingly likely to be raised within the broader international context pertaining to *jus ad bellum* considerations.

Moreover, the ICRC note that "[t]orture, cruel treatment and outrages upon personal dignity, in particular humiliating and degrading treatment, constitute war crimes in non-international armed conflicts under the Statutes of the International Criminal Court, of the International Criminal Tribunal for Rwanda and of the Special Court for Sierra Leone."[60] Additionally, the ICRC notes that the prohibition

---

[51] First Geneva Convention, Article 12, second paragraph ("torture") (ibid., § 985); Second Geneva Convention, Article 12, second paragraph ("torture") (ibid., § 986); Third Geneva Convention, Article 17, fourth paragraph ("physical or mental torture") (ibid., § 987), Article 87, third paragraph ("torture or cruelty") (ibid., § 988) and Article 89 ("inhuman, brutal or dangerous" disciplinary punishment) (ibid., § 989); Fourth Geneva Convention, Article 32 ("torture" and "other measures of brutality") (ibid., § 990).

[52] Ibid., § 985.

[53] Ibid., § 986.

[54] Ibid., § 987.

[55] Ibid., § 988.

[56] Ibid., § 989.

[57] Ibid., § 990.

[58] Taken from https://ihl-databases.icrc.org/customary-ihl/eng/docs/v1_rul_rule90.

[59] Ibid.

[60] Ibid.

of torture, cruel or inhuman treatment and outrages upon personal dignity are contained in numerous military manuals, the legislation of a large number of states as well as in international cases and allegations as such have been condemned by the UN Security Council, UN General Assembly and UN Commission on Human Rights, and by regional organizations including the ICRC, whether in international or non-international armed conflicts.[61]

NPT Obligations *Erga Omnes* Are about Protecting International Human Rights

Erga omnes obligations derive from *principles and rules* concerning basic human rights in relation to nuclear proliferation and the international nuclear arms race that would violate the protection of basic rights of the person. Thus, nuclear obligations of nonproliferation and disarmament can be also considered *erga omnes* obligations to protect human rights.

Several human rights are jeopardized by nuclear weapons, further confirming the *erga omnes* nature of the NPT obligations. Countries that participate in nuclear proliferation, development and a nuclear arms race *are* threatening basic rights of the person in the following ways. They violate Article 6(1) of the ICCPR: "[e]very human being has the inherent right to life. This right shall be protected by law."[62] The right to life cannot be protected by law or secured in a country that has nuclear weapons or is in constant danger of nuclear attack, thus the right has no backing by the state or the international community which is unable to control the consequences of nuclear war. Nuclear weapons also violate right to life, liberty and security of the person under Article 3 of the UDHR.[63] The security of the physical person cannot be said to be fully protected in a state that is in danger of nuclear attack. The "right of everyone to the enjoyment of the highest attainable standard of physical and mental health" under the Article 12 of ICESCR[64] is also threatened by nuclear weapons; a person living in constant fear of nuclear annihilation cannot be benefiting from their full mental health. Further, any civilian subjected to the effects of nuclear testing or left with the aftermath of a nuclear attack would most certainly not be able to exercise this right to physical health.[65] Article 12 also provides steps to

---

[61] See https://ihl-databases.icrc.org/customary-ihl/eng/docs/v1_rul_rule90.

[62] UN General Assembly, *International Covenant on Civil and Political Rights*, December 16, 1966, United Nations, Treaty Series, vol. 999, p. 171 at Art. 6.

[63] UN General Assembly, *Universal Declaration of Human Rights*, December 10, 1948, 217 A (III) at Article 3.

[64] UN General Assembly, *International Covenant on Economic, Social and Cultural Rights*, December 16, 1966, United Nations, Treaty Series, vol. 993, p. 3 at Article 12 [ICESCR].

[65] *Dissenting Opinion of Trindade in Marshall Islands* v. *UK* at para. 176. In its oral arguments of March 7, 2016, the Marshall Islands stated: "The Marshall Islands has a unique and devastating history with nuclear weapons. While it was designated as a Trust Territory by the United Nations, no fewer than 67 atomic and thermonuclear weapons were deliberately exploded as 'tests' in the Marshall Islands, by the United States ... Several islands in my country were vaporized and others are

Why Are Nuclear Obligations Effective Erga Omnes? 355

be taken by states to achieve the above goal; a state that is modernizing and testing nuclear weapons, not meeting safety standards for nuclear energy, or sharing nuclear weapons and technology with other states is not improving environmental hygiene and providing for the healthy development of the child.[66] Rights of civilians to be protected from murder, indiscriminate destruction of property under the *Geneva Conventions*[67] would also be violated by the use of nuclear weapons, which do not discriminate between innocent noncombatants and combatants.

As discussed in Chapter 8 on Defense, emerging principles under international law will surely inform such considerations. Although the nature of both the *jus ad* bellum and the *jus in bello* have not changed since 1996, a number of recent developments have transpired within today's context, including the UN Human Rights Committee adopting a new general comment on the right to life pursuant to Article 6[68] of the International Covenant on Civil and Political Rights.[69] In particular, "The threat or use of weapons of mass destruction, in particular nuclear weapons, which are indiscriminate in effect and are of a nature to cause destruction of human life on a catastrophic scale is incompatible with respect for the right to life and may amount to a crime under international law." Moreover, the parties ". . . must take all necessary measures to stop the proliferation of weapons of mass destruction, including . . . to refrain from developing . . . and using them, [as well as] to destroy existing stockpiles . . . all in accordance with their international obligations."[70]

---

estimated to remain uninhabitable for thousands of years. Many, many Marshallese died, suffered birth defects never before seen and battled cancers resulting from the contamination. Tragically the Marshall Islands thus bears eyewitness to the horrific and indiscriminate lethal capacity of these weapons, and the intergenerational and continuing effects that they perpetuate even 60 years later." One test in particular, called the "Bravo" test (in March 1954), was 1,000 times more powerful than the bombs dropped on Hiroshima and Nagasaki.

[66] ICESCR at Art. 12 2. The steps to be taken by the states parties to the present Covenant to achieve the full realization of this right shall include those necessary for:

    (a) the provision for the reduction of the stillbirth-rate and of infant mortality and for the healthy development of the child;

    (b) the improvement of all aspects of environmental and industrial hygiene;

    (c) the prevention, treatment and control of epidemic, endemic, occupational and other diseases;

    (d) the creation of conditions which would assure to all medical service and medical attention in the event of sickness.

[67] Geneva Convention Relative to the Protection of Civilian Persons in Time of War (Fourth Geneva Convention), August 12, 1949, 75 UNTS 287 at Article 3, 147.

[68] The Committee notes that, "Article 6 recognizes and protects the right to life of all human beings. It is the supreme right from which no derogation is permitted even in situations of armed conflict and other public emergencies which threatens the life of the nation." At para. 2.

[69] Human Rights Committee General Comment No. 36 (2018) on Article 6 of the International Covenant on Civil and Political Rights, on the right to life. See https://tbinternet.ohchr.org /Treaties/CCPR/Shared%20Documents/1_Global/CCPR_C_GC_36_8785_E.pdf. For background on the general comment, see Office of the High Representative for Human Rights: www.ohchr.org /EN/NewsEvents/Pages/DisplayNews.aspx?NewsID=23797&LangID=E.

[70] Specifically, para. 66 states in full: "The threat or use of weapons of mass destruction, in particular nuclear weapons, which are indiscriminate in effect and are of a nature to cause destruction of human life on a catastrophic scale is incompatible with respect for the right to life and may amount to a crime

356   *Obligations* Erga Omnes

Notably, the idea that the mere threat, and not just their use, would be incompatible with the right to life under Article 6 is consistent with the central premise the TPNW (Article I(d)).[71]

Indeed, as discussed in Chapters 3 and 10, there is a growing chorus of discussion highlighting that the delegitimization of nuclear deterrence is an essential component to achieving the global abolition of nuclear arms.[72] The HRC considers nuclear weapons as indiscriminate in effect, as well as of a nature to cause destruction of human life on a catastrophic scale and, therefore, incompatible with the right to life. Moreover, the ICJ, in its 1996 Advisory Opinion, highlighted that "[t]he destructive power of nuclear weapons cannot be contained in either space or time."[73]

Apart from the International Covenant on Civil and Political Rights, three of the five nuclear-weapon states (the United Kingdom, France and Russia) are also parties to the European Convention on Human Rights,[74] which guarantees the right to life under Article 2. In addition, the Convention prohibits torture under Article 3, which

> under international law. States parties must take all necessary measures to stop the proliferation of weapons of mass destruction, including measures to prevent their acquisition by non-state actors, to refrain from developing, producing, testing, acquiring, stockpiling, selling, transferring and using them, to destroy existing stockpiles, and to take adequate measures of protection against accidental use, all in accordance with their international obligations. They must also respect their international obligations to pursue in good faith negotiations in order to achieve the aim of nuclear disarmament under strict and effective international control and to afford adequate reparation to victims whose right to life has been or is being adversely affected by the testing or use of weapons of mass destruction, in accordance with principles of international responsibility." See Treaty on the Non-Proliferation of Nuclear Weapons, July 1, 1968, 729 UNTS 161; Comprehensive Test Ban Treaty, September 10, 1996, Treaty on the Prohibition of Nuclear Weapons, July 7, 2017 (not yet in force); Convention on the Prohibition of the Development, Production and Stockpiling of Bacteriological (Biological) and Toxin Weapons and on their Destruction, April 10, 1972, 1015 UNTS 163; Convention on the Prohibition of the Development, Production, Stockpiling and Use of Chemical Weapons and on their Destruction, September 3, 1992, 1974 UNTS 45. General Comment 14, para. 7. Cf. Legality of the Threat or Use of Nuclear Weapons, 1996 ICJ 226, 267. Concluding Observations: France (2015), para. 21.

[71] See Threat and use of nuclear weapons contrary to right to life, says UN Human Rights Committee, https://safna.org/2018/11/07/threat-and-use-of-nuclear-weapons-contrary-to-right-to-life-says-un-human-rights-committee/.

[72] See Bonnie Docherty (2018): "A 'Light for all Humanity': The Treaty on the Prohibition of Nuclear Weapons and the Progress of Humanitarian Disarmament," *Global Change, Peace & Security*, DOI: 10.1080/14781158.2018.1472075.

[73] ICJ, Advisory Opinion on the Legality of the Threat or Use of Nuclear Weapons, *ICJ Reports 1996*, § 35. Note that when the general comment was being developed, IALANA and Swiss Lawyers for Nuclear Disarmament made two submissions to the Human Rights Committee, authored by Daniel Rietiker and John Burroughs with input from Roger Clark and Emilie Gaillard: "Threat or Use of Weapons of Mass Destruction and the Right to Life: Follow-up Submissions to UN Human Rights Committee," IALANA and Swiss Lawyers for Nuclear Disarmament, October 5, 2017. Threat or Use of Weapons of Mass Destruction and the Right to Life – Comments and Proposal, September 7, 2016, https://safna.org/2016/09/08/the-incompatibility-of-wmd-to-the-right-to-life-article-6-iccpr-a-submission-to-the-un-human-rights-committee/.

[74] Convention for the Protection of Human Rights and Fundamental Freedoms, November 4, 1950, 213 UNTS 221, Eur. T.S. 5 (European Convention on Human Rights).

states: "No one shall be subjected to torture or to inhuman or degrading treatment or punishment." This provision is a non-derogable right that cannot be suspended under any circumstances. Specifically, Article 15 of the European Convention allows for the derogation of certain specific rights in times of emergency, of which the prohibition of torture is precluded.[75] In *Ireland* v. *United Kingdom*,[76] the European Court of Human Rights found that the United Kingdom's use of five techniques of interrogation on fourteen individuals amounted to "inhuman and degrading treatment" in breach of Article 3 of the European Convention on Human Rights.[77] It could be argued that the threat of nuclear weapons amounts to inhuman or degrading treatment or punishment, and potentially the use of nuclear weapons in their actual deployment is torturous.

The use of nuclear weapons would also violate Articles 35, 51, 54 of Protocol (1) additional to the Geneva Conventions; the use of weapons that "cause superfluous injury or unnecessary suffering," as well as means of warfare that "cause widespread, long-term, and severe damage to the natural environment" are prohibited.[78] The conventions also outlaw indiscriminate attacks on civilian populations and the destruction of food, water and other materials needed for survival. Most high-impact nuclear weapons would include attacks on civilian populations and would contaminate and destroy food and water sources for a considerable time after an explosion.[79] If the use of high impact nuclear weapons is prohibited because their

---

[75] Specifically, Article 15 stipulates "1. In time of war or other public emergency threatening the life of the nation any High Contracting Party may take measures derogating from its obligations under this Convention to the extent strictly required by the exigencies of the situation, provided that such measures are not inconsistent with its other obligations under international law. 14 15 2. No derogation from Article 2, except in respect of deaths resulting from lawful acts of war, or from Articles 3 [Prohibition Against Torture], 4 (paragraph 1) and 7 shall be made under this provision. 3. Any High Contracting Party availing itself of this right of derogation shall keep the Secretary General of the Council of Europe fully informed of the measures which it has taken and the reasons therefor. It shall also inform the Secretary General of the Council of Europe when such measures have ceased to operate and the provisions of the Convention are again being fully executed."

[76] See https://hudoc.echr.coe.int/eng#{%22itemid%22:[%22001-57506%22]}.

[77] Although it did not rise to the level of torture, recent documents reveal that the decision of the European Commission was that the techniques did, in fact, amount to torture, although the European Court did not agree with this finding (see *Ireland* v. *United Kingdom* (Revision)), 2018. See https://hudoc.echr.coe.int/eng#{%22itemid%22:[%22001-181585%22]}.

[78] Protocol Additional to the Geneva Conventions of August 12, 1949, and relating to the Protection of Victims of International Armed Conflicts (Protocol I), June 8, 1977, 1125 UNTS 3, at Articles 35, 51, 54.

[79] Dissenting Opinion of Trindade, *Marshall Islands* v. *UK* at para. 185: "As pointed out in the pleadings before the ICJ of late 1995, the use of nuclear weapons thus violates the right to life (and the right to health) of 'not only people currently living, but also of the unborn, of those to be born, of subsequent generations'. Is there anything quintessentially more cruel? To use nuclear weapons appears like condemning innocent persons to hell on earth, even before they are born. That seems to go even further than the Book of Genesis's story of the original sin. In reaction to such extreme cruelty, the consciousness of the rights inherent to the human person has always marked a central presence in endeavours towards complete nuclear disarmament." Also See Barbara Rose Johnston and Holly M. Barker, *Consequential Damages of Nuclear War: The Rongelap Report* (California: Left Coast Press, 2008), on the effects of nuclear testing on the people and environment of the Marshall Islands.

358   *Obligations* Erga Omnes

effects are so disproportionate and indiscriminate, and cause needless suffering and irreparable environmental damage, and make recovery nearly impossible, then the obligations to move toward disarmament, nonproliferation and only use nuclear energy for peaceful purposes ought to be included as the positive steps required to *prevent* violations of these Conventions, covenants and customary international laws. Such an approach would be consistent with existing *erga omnes* obligations.

Beyond international humanitarian law prohibiting torture, it should be noted that the prohibition of torture and cruel, inhuman or degrading treatment or punishment is to be found in general human rights treaties as well as in specific treaties that seek to prevent and punish these practices.[80] This prohibition is non-derogable under these instruments.[81] Article 7 of the International Covenant on Civil and Political Rights (ICCPR) stipulates that "No one shall be subjected to torture, or to cruel, inhuman degrading treatment or punishment."[82] Unlike some sets of right (e.g., the right to life), the prohibition is viewed as an absolute right, meaning that it cannot be deprived of violated under any circumstances even in times of armed conflict. Note that the prohibition from torture or cruel, inhuman or degrading treatment or punishment as well as the right to life are protected under the Universal Declaration of Human Rights,1948, along with under several other international instruments that ban the use of the death penalty.[83]

DEFINING TORTURE, INHUMAN TREATMENT, OUTRAGES UPON PERSONAL DIGNITY. One must consider whether, and the extent to which, *jus ad bellum* considerations might apply. In defining torture, the ICRC notes that the Elements of Crimes for the International Criminal Court provides that the war crime of torture consists of the infliction of "severe physical or mental pain or suffering" for purposes such as "obtaining information or a confession, punishment, intimidation or coercion or for any reason based on discrimination of any kind."[84] The Committee highlights that contrary to protections under human rights law, such as under Article 1 of the Convention against Torture, the Elements of Crimes for the International Criminal Court does not require that the requisite pain or suffering be inflicted "by or at the

---

[80]   As noted in the Convention against Torture; Inter-American Convention to Prevent and Punish Torture; and European Convention for the Prevention of Torture.

[81]   See https://ihl-databases.icrc.org/customary-ihl/eng/docs/v1_rul_rule90.

[82]   *International Covenant on Civil and Political Rights*, December 19, 1966, 999 UNTS 171, Article 7 (entered into force March 23, 1976, accession by Canada May 19, 1976).

[83]   The Second Optional Protocol to the International Covenant on Civil and Political Rights, aiming at the abolition of the death penalty; Protocol No. 6 to the European Convention on Human Rights, concerning the abolition of the death penalty; Protocol No. 13 to the European Convention on Human Rights, concerning the abolition of the death penalty in all circumstances; and the Protocol to the American Convention on Human Rights to Abolish the Death Penalty. See "Death Penalty," Martin Scheinin, *Max Planck Encyclopedia of Public International Law* (MPEPIL) December 2008.

[84]   Elements of Crimes for the ICC, Definition of torture as a war crime (ICC Statute, Article 8(2)(a)(ii) and (c)(i)).

Why Are Nuclear Obligations Effective Erga Omnes? 359

instigation of or with the consent or acquiescence of a public official or other person acting in an official capacity."

Under these requirements it may at first seem difficult to envisage a scenario that might involve nuclear. That said, the question of "punishment," "intimidation" or "coercion" or "for any reason based on discrimination of any kind," may raise questions within the nuclear context, particularly in light of the TPNW where it might be argued that any use or threat of such weapons is seen as punishment; to induce intimidation or to coerce compliance; or, indeed discriminatory based on nationality.

One sees the concept developing. The ICRC points out that in the cases of both *Delalić* and *Furundžija* in 1998, the International Criminal Tribunal for the former Yugoslavia considered the definition contained in Article 1 of the Convention against Torture to be part of customary international law applicable in armed conflict. In the subsequent case of *Kunarac* in 2001, the Tribunal concluded that "the definition of torture under international humanitarian law does not comprise the same elements as the definition of torture generally applied under human rights law." In particular, it held that "the presence of a state official or of any other authority-wielding person in the torture process is not necessary for the offence to be regarded as torture under international humanitarian law." The Tribunal defined torture as the intentional infliction, by act or omission, of severe pain or suffering, whether physical or mental, in order to obtain information or a confession, or to punish, intimidate or coerce the victim or a third person, or to discriminate on any ground, against the victim or a third person. Again, with this one sees a continual evolution of standards and their application within a given context.

The ICRC points out that the term "inhuman treatment" is also defined in the Elements of Crimes for the International Criminal Court where it is listed as the infliction of "severe physical or mental pain or suffering."[85] The key element that distinguishes inhuman treatment from torture, per se, is the absence of the requirement that the treatment in question be inflicted for a specific purpose. The International Criminal Tribunal for the former Yugoslavia, however, has employed a wider definition concluding that inhuman treatment "causes serious mental or physical suffering or injury or constitutes a serious attack on human dignity."[86] Note that the element of "a serious attack on human dignity" was not included in the definition of inhuman treatment under the Elements of Crimes for the International Criminal Court because the war crime of "outrages upon personal dignity" would suffice to cover such attacks.[87] The ICRC highlights that human rights bodies apply a definition which is similar to the that used in the Elements of Crimes for the

---

[85] Elements of Crimes for the ICC, Definition of inhuman treatment as a war crime (ICC Statute, Article 8(2)(a)(ii)).
[86] See ICTY, *Delalić case, Judgment and Kordić and Čerkez Case*, Judgment.
[87] See Knut Dörmann, Elements of War Crimes under the Rome Statute of the International Criminal Court: Sources and Commentary, Cambridge University Press, 2003, pp. 63–64.

360 *Obligations* Erga Omnes

International Criminal Court, where in their case law they stress the severity of the physical or mental pain or suffering.

The concept of "outrages upon personal dignity," as noted by the ICRC, is defined in the Elements of Crimes for the International Criminal Court as acts which humiliate, degrade or otherwise violate the dignity of a person to such a degree "as to be generally recognized as an outrage upon personal dignity." The Elements of Crimes also specifies that such degrading treatment can apply to dead persons, and that the victim in question need not be personally aware of the humiliation;[88] thus covering the deliberate humiliation of unconscious or mentally handicapped individuals. The Elements of Crimes also stress that the cultural background of the person needs to be taken into account, thereby covering treatment that is humiliating to someone of a particular nationality or religion, for example. The European Commission of Human Rights defines "degrading treatment" as treatment or punishment that "grossly humiliates the victim before others or drives the detainee to act against his/her will or conscience."[89]

TORTURE, INHUMAN TREATMENT, OUTRAGES UPON PERSONAL DIGNITY: NUCLEAR APPLICATION. In relation to nuclear matters, again freedom from torture is protected as an absolute right under both international humanitarian law and international human rights law, applying *jus ad bellum* considerations in times of armed conflict. Relevant to nuclear weapons, both an initial nuclear blast as well as the radioactive fallout must be considered in respect of the above discussion regarding torture, inhuman treatment, and outrages upon personal dignity. Radiation, "adversely affects the immune system so that the injured will not recover in the way they could have from weapons without this effect."[90] It not only causes more deaths, but it also prolongs suffering.[91] Radiation exposure also "damages DNA and causes death and severe health defects throughout the entire lives of survivors as well as their children."[92]

While examining more specific effects of nuclear weapons, individuals can be "rendered blind from looking at the initial flash, and those not killed may suffer horrific burns."[93] Stuart Casey-Maslen emphasizes the importance of sight noting that vision is the "most important sense, perhaps accounting for 90 percent or more of our sensory input."[94] He notes that "while other senses, such as hearing and touch,

---

[88] Elements of Crimes for the ICC, Definition of outrages upon personal dignity, in particular humiliating and degrading treatment, as a war crime (ICC Statute, Article 8(2)(b)(xxi) and (c)(ii)).

[89] European Commission of Human Rights, Greek case.

[90] Stuart Casey-Maslen, "The Use of Nuclear Weapons and Human Rights" (2015) 97 *Intl Rev Red Cross* 663 at 674.

[91] Ibid.

[92] Anthony J Colangelo, "Article: The Duty to Disobey Illegal Nuclear Strike Orders" (2018) 51 *Harv National Security J* 84.

[93] Stuart Casey-Maslen, "The Use of Nuclear Weapons and Human Rights" (2015) 97 *Intl Rev Red Cross* 663 at 674.

[94] Ibid.

may facilitate post-blindness adjustment to one's life experience, none of them can come close to replacing sight."[95]

In relation to burns caused by nuclear exposure, they "may go beyond third-degree burns, in which all layers of the skin are destroyed, to fourth-degree burns, in which the injury extends into both muscle and bone."[96] Both these type of burns have the possibility of death and also due to the extent of the injury they "place a huge burden on medical resources, often requiring specialist treatment."[97]

The health effects and the suffering caused by nuclear blasts were noted by Judge Koroma in his dissent in the ICJ's Nuclear Weapons Advisory where he stated that "Over 320,000 people who survived but were affected by radiation still suffer from various malignant tumours caused by radiation, including leukaemia, thyroid cancer, breast cancer, lung cancer, gastric cancer, cataracts and a variety of other after-effects. More than half a century after the disaster, they are still said to be undergoing medical examinations and treatment."[98]

Along with this direct injury to individuals, nuclear weapons also cause environmental damage which "may produce not only devastating environmental harm itself but also widespread famine and starvation."[99] Such health effects are inevitable and even "entirely predictable consequences from the use of a nuclear weapon." Given the suffering that is involved with these injuries, the use of nuclear weapons would most likely "amount to a violation of the right to humane treatment,"[100] as well as of torture and outrages upon personal dignity. Under today's standards, some would want any nuclear attack to be indictable before the ICC as a crime against humanity.

The Right Not to Live in Fear of Torture or Inhuman or Degrading Punishment: An Analogy from Case Law

This author's position that nuclear weapons are governed by obligations *erga omnes* is strengthened by a consideration of the nature of the mere *threat* of nuclear weapons. Individuals should have a right to not live in fear of punishment or threats of conduct, especially if they would amount to a violation of Article 3 of Europe's Convention on the Protection of Human Rights and Fundamental Freedoms which reads: "No one shall be subjected to torture or to inhuman or degrading treatment or punishment."[101] In the *Case of Campbell and Cosans v. The United Kingdom* (1982), two parents launched a complaint against state schools in Scotland because

---

[95]   Ibid.

[96]   Ibid.

[97]   Ibid.

[98]   *Legality of the Threat or Use of Nuclear Weapons Case*, Advisory Opinion, [1996] ICJ Rep. 66.

[99]   Anthony J Colangelo, "Article: The Duty to Disobey Illegal Nuclear Strike Orders" (2018) 51 *Harv National Security J* 84.

[100]   Stuart Casey-Maslen, "The Use of Nuclear Weapons and Human Rights" (2015) 97 *Intl Rev Red Cross* 663 at 674.

[101]   Convention on the Protection of Human Rights and Fundamental Freedoms, Article 3.

362 *Obligations* Erga Omnes

headmasters were permitted to use corporal punishment and had threatened to use it on one of the parents' sons. The European Court of Human Rights made the following illuminating statement:

> Neither Gordon Campbell nor Jeffrey Cosans was, in fact, strapped with the tawse. Accordingly, the Court does not in the present case have to consider under Article 3 (art. 3) an actual application of corporal punishment.
>
> However, the Court is of the opinion that, *provided it is sufficiently real and immediate, a mere threat of conduct prohibited by Article 3 (art. 3) may itself be in conflict with that provision. Thus, to threaten an individual with torture might in some circumstances constitute at least "inhuman treatment."*[102]

The Court is signaling that if threats of torture rise to the level of immediacy and reality such that a person undergoes humiliation or debasement of a certain minimum level of severity, those threats would be considered inhumane treatment and a violation of Article 3 of the Convention.

Applying this thinking to nuclear weapons, arguably, a country that is being threatened with a nuclear attack is being threatened with conduct that would clearly fall within the scope of this opinion regarding Article 3 of the Convention, but also other international treaties which establish the right to life, liberty and the security of the person. A nuclear attack may be seen as subjecting individuals attacked, to violations of their right to life or, if they were injured, to violations of their right not be subjected to inhumane treatment and torture. A nuclear explosion on a populated area intentionally caused by another state may potentially be argued as war crimes, crimes against humanity, or acts of genocide, depending on the context, as well as torture and perhaps inhumane treatment or torture of those left behind to deal with illness and suffering caused by nuclear fallout. Therefore, to *threaten* a state with this kind of torture and death would be in conflict with all treaties that prohibit the conduct of torture and indiscriminate killing of civilians. This serves to bolster the argument for nuclear obligations *erga omnes:* possessing, modernizing and threatening to use nuclear weapons could well be taken as a violation of international law because it is causing individual persons to live in fear that amounts to inhumane treatment.

Existing *Obligations* Erga Omnes *Are Comparable to Nuclear Obligations*

The universal obligations relating to nuclear weapons are also consistent with other recognized *erga omnes* obligations. *Barcelona Traction* provides a list of sources for obligations *erga omnes*, most of which are *jus cogens*, that is, non-derogable norms of international law. If states owe obligations *erga omnes* to protect people from crimes against humanity, slavery, torture and general protection of human rights this would include positive action to prevent these acts from happening. Let us take the

---

[102] *Case of Campbell and Cosans* v. *The United Kingdom* (1982) European Court of Human rights, at para. 25.

Convention against Torture and Other Cruel, Inhuman or Degrading Treatment or Punishment 1984 as an example that parallels nuclear obligations. The Convention states in Article 2: "Each State Party *shall take effective legislative, administrative, judicial or other measures to prevent acts of torture* in any territory under its jurisdiction." And in Article 11: "Each State Party shall keep under systematic review interrogation rules, instructions, methods and practices as well as arrangements for the custody and treatment of persons subjected to any form of arrest, detention or imprisonment in any territory under its jurisdiction, *with a view to preventing any cases of torture.*" Article 16 states: "Each State Party *shall undertake to prevent* in any territory under its jurisdiction other acts of cruel, inhuman or degrading treatment or punishment which do not amount to torture as defined in article I, when such acts are committed by or at the instigation of or with the consent or acquiescence of a public official or other person acting in an official capacity."

Each article includes the obligation to prevent certain actions, which means that failure to take action that prevents torture could be seen as legally equivalent to committing the act of torture. International case law also explains how states have an obligation not only not to violate human rights, but a duty to prevent violations from happening. Judge Cançado Trindade, writing about the right to information on consular assistance in the 2017 case of *Jadhav (India v. Pakistan)*, argues for preventive obligations:

> In cases of the kind, involving the fundamental human right to life, – I proceeded, – the Court, by means of provisional measures of protection, goes well beyond the simple search for a balance of the interests of the contending parties (which used to suffice in traditional international law); one is here safeguarding a fundamental human right, and this shows – I concluded – that "provisional measures cannot be restrictively interpreted," and they impose themselves, to the benefit of the persons concerned, as *"true jurisdictional guarantees of a preventive character that they are."* (paras. 13–14, 16 and 18)
>
> I also pondered that they are transformed into such jurisdictional guarantees by the proper consideration of their *constitutive elements of extreme gravity and urgency, and prevention of irreparable damage to persons* (para. 10), – even more cogently when the fundamental right to life is at stake. *Provisional measures of protection have an important role to play when the rights of the human person are also at stake*; developed mainly in contemporary international case-law, they have, however, been insufficiently studied in international legal doctrine to date.[103]

In his dissenting opinion on *Marshall Islands v. United Kingdom*,[104] Judge Trindade highlights the conclusions of the 2014 Vienna Conference on the need for preventative measures in nuclear obligations:

---

[103] *Jadha* v. *(India versus Pakistan)* 2017, Concurring Opinion of Judge Cancado Trindade at para. 22–23.
[104] *Marshall Islands* v. *UK*, Preliminary Objections, ICJ General List 2016 No. 160 at para 283. See www .icj-cij.org/files/case-related/160/160-20161005-JUD-01-06-EN.pdf.

364 *Obligations* Erga Omnes

the existence itself of nuclear weapons raises serious ethical questions, – well beyond legal discussions and interpretations, – which should be kept in mind. Several Delegations asserted that, in the interest of the survival of humankind, nuclear weapons must never be used again, under any circumstances. . . . no State or international organ could adequately address the immediate humanitarian emergency or long-term consequences caused by a nuclear weapon detonation in a populated area, nor provide adequate assistance to those affected. *The imperative of prevention as the only guarantee against the humanitarian consequences of nuclear weapons use is thus to be highlighted.* (Emphasis added)[105]

In a statement that further echoes the importance of preventive measures to protect human rights, Judge Weeramantry argues in his dissenting opinion of the Nuclear Tests Case 1995 (*New Zealand* v. *France*) regarding the environmental effects of nuclear tests: "[e]nvironmental measures *must anticipate, prevent and attack the causes of environmental degradation.* Where there are threats of serious or irreversible damage, lack of full scientific certainty should not be used as a reason for postponing measures *to prevent environmental degradation.*"[106] There are several other examples regarding these requirements.

The main point is that the obligations of the NPT *are preventative measures exactly analogous* to all other preventative measures and *erga omnes* obligations demanded by *jus cogens* prohibitions on torture, genocide, slavery, racial discrimination, acts of aggression or other crimes against humanity. The effects of the use of nuclear weapons are also analogous and potentially much worse in degree and wider in range than the effects of violating the prohibitions listed above. If the effects of a breach of the NPT obligations and the preventative measures required are analogous to other *erga omnes* obligations, then *one must conclude that the status of NPT obligations are also analogous* and thus ought to be obligations *erga omnes.* Now many would argue that the use of smaller, tactical nuclear weapons is different from larger more potent arms. The fact that there is a sliding scale is irrelevant, the technology behind such weapons and the devastating harm caused by them that lingers after the hostilities with radiation and other harmful effects renders them inappropriate, *erga omnes.* Just as torture is torture no matter how you phrase it, nuclear instills fear and does harm.

Moral Outrage Calls for New Developments in International Law as It Has in the Past

Today, in an age of fake news where the truth is often absent or at best distorted for political advantage, it might seem somewhat outdated to argue that legal obligations

---

[105] Dissenting Opinion of Trindade, *Marshall Islands* v. *UK* at para. 286.

[106] Request for an Examination of the Situation in Accordance with Paragraph 63 of the Court's Judgment of December 20, 1974 in the Nuclear Tests (*New Zealand* v. *France*) Case, ICJ Reports 1995, p. 288 at para. 342.

Why Are Nuclear Obligations Effective Erga Omnes? 365

are grounded in moral and philosophical principles or human conscience, but the founders of international law appealed to "the common law of mankind,"[107] "the laws of nature"[108] or the "common sentiments of humanity";[109] and judges in the international courts continue to make decisions based on common moral principles.[110]

Judge Cançado Trindade, for example, in his dissenting opinion in the *Kingdom Marshall Islands v. United Case* appealed to morality and human conscience stating:

> This is the position that I also uphold; in my own understanding, it is the *universal juridical conscience that is the ultimate material source of international law*. In my view, one cannot face the new challenges confronting the whole international community keeping in mind only State susceptibilities; such is the case with the obligation to render the world free of nuclear weapons, an imperative of *recta ratio* and not a derivative of the "will" of States. In effect, to keep hope alive it is necessary to bear always in mind humankind as a whole.[111]

Throughout the history of international law, new obligations, rights and duties have been proposed and codified as a result of moral outrage or conviction. Indeed, the concept of *erga omnes* finds its roots in the early recognition of the right of humanitarian intervention. Theodor Meron argues that the concept of *erga omnes* can be traced back to Grotius (1583–1645), Suárez (1548–1617) and Gentili (1552–1608).[112] Writing in *War Crimes Law Comes of Age* Theodor Meron notes:

> student[s] of the concept of *erga omnes* trace its antecedents to the early recognition of the humanitarian intervention, which we often attribute to Grotius . . . However, some of the other principal works on international law before the Peace of Westphalia (1648) reveal that the concept of community interests, and the modern right of humanitarian intervention it spawned, pre-Grotian, that it appeared in the writings of Suarez and figured prominently in those of its true progenitor, the earlier Gentili [1588].[113]

Meron explains that the "Grotian scholar Peter Haggenmacher traces antecedents of the principle of humanitarian intervention even further back, to the 'altruistic,' 13th century school of Pope Innocent IV and the Scholastic writers."[114]

Hugo Grotius in his *Prolegomena*, asserts the right to wage war in humanitarian causes, which can be seen as "an important precursor to the recognition in modern

---

[107] Seneca 4 BCE–65 CE.
[108] Grotius.
[109] Gentili.
[110] Meron at 125, n. 17, 127.
[111] See the Dissenting Opinion of Judge Cançado Trindade, in *Marshall Islands v. United Kingdom*, Preliminary Objections, Judgment, ICJ Reports 2016, at para. 115.
[112] Theodor Meron, *War Crimes Law Comes of Age* (Oxford: Oxford University Press, 1998) at 122.
[113] Ibid.
[114] Ibid.

366   *Obligations* Erga Omnes

international law of universal jurisdiction over such matters as genocide, war crimes and crimes against humanity."[115] Emphasizing a right of sovereigns to insist on the punishment of perpetrators, on account of injuries that excessively violate the law of nature or of nations,[116] Grotius writes:

> Sciendum quoque est reges & qui par regibus ius obtinent ius habere poenas poscendi non tantum ob iniurias in se aut subditos suos commissos, sed & ob eas quae ipsos peculiariter non tangent, sed in quibusuis personis ius naturae aut gentium immaniter violant.
>
> [Kings have the right to insist in punishment not only on account of injuries committed against themselves or their subjects, but also on account of injuries which do not directly affect them but excessively violate the law of nature or of nations in regard to any persons whatsoever.]
>
> The fact must also be recognized that kings, and those who possess rights equal to those kings, have the right of demanding punishments not only on account of injuries committed against themselves or their subjects, but also on account of injuries which do not directly affect them but excessively violate the law of nature or of nations in regard to any persons whatsoever ...
>
> Truly it is more honourable to avenge the wrongs of others rather than one's own.[117]

Francisco Suárez, a Spanish Jesuit scholar, was wary of giving an open-ended license for humanitarian intervention, but he accepted the right of a prince to intervene in another state if another prince "forcibly compelled his subjects to practice idolatry; but under any other circumstances, [such a ground] would not be a sufficient cause for war, unless the whole state should demand assistance against its sovereign."[118] Alberico Gentili "was an Italian Protestant who took refuge in England and became Regius Professor of Civil Law at Oxford in 1587."[119] Gentili wrote in "Of an Honourable Reason for waging war": "There remains now the one question concerning an honourable cause for waging war ... which is undertaken for no private reason of our own, but for the common interest and in behalf of others. Look you, *if men clearly sin against the laws of nature and of mankind*, I believe that any one whatsoever may check such men by force of arms"[120] (Emphasis mine).

In another passage Gentili almost explicitly spells out obligations *erga omnes* to make war on pirates in order to protect individuals:

> And if a war against pirates justly calls all men to arms because of love for our neighbour and the desire to live in peace, so also do the *general violation of the common law of humanity and wrong done to mankind*. Piracy is contrary to the law of

---

[115]   Ibid. at p. 124.
[116]   *De iure belli ac pacis* (1646), book II, chapter 20, para. XI.
[117]   Meron, above, n. 111, at p. 124.
[118]   Ibid. at p. 126.
[119]   Ibid.
[120]   2 A. Gentili, *De Jure Belli Libri Tres*, chs. XVI and XXV at 122 cited in Meron at p. 127.

Why Are Nuclear Obligations Effective Erga Omnes? 367

nations and the league of human society. Therefore war should be made against pirates by all men, because *in the violation of that law we are all injured*, and individual in turn can find their personal rights violated.[121]

These scholars of international law provide us with historical examples of legal obligations toward the human society arising from moral principles or norms.

If we examine the more recent history of the Geneva Conventions, we find the US lawyer Francis Lieber, who witnessed the horror of war and what was happening on the battlefield and was morally outraged. He raised awareness of the injustice happening and "drafted what he wanted to be statements of the law and customs of war" which later became the Geneva Conventions of 1949.[122] Brian Simpson describes Lieber's initial draft of the Lieber Code:

> The Lieber Code stated a fundamental principle: "Men who take up arms against one another in public war do not cease on that account to be moral beings, responsible to one another and to God." It laid down principles designed to reduce suffering by non-combatants, to limit reprisals, to provide for the humane treatment of prisoners and wounded, to regulate the use of flags of truce, and to limit the severity of measures taken under martial law. Versions of the Code were adopted by other armies, for example by Germany, and so it acquired an international charac-ter. In any case it purported to state international law, not American law. Lieber's *innovative attempt to express the demands of humanity* in legal form encouraged the powers to produce formal agreements (variously called Declarations, Conventions and Protocols) on aspects of the laws of war.[123]

Just as Lieber saw how "the ferocity of battle came to be greatly enhanced by the development of ever more fearful weaponry and the beginnings of the 'weapons of mass destruction'. [and] [t]he ability to kill and maim enemies and civilians alike 'progressed' in a remarkable way,"[124] and responded with a bold new document, this author sees the development of nuclear weapons as one of the most serious threats to human existence and thus boldly asserts that nuclear obligations are the concern of every state and every human being and must be raised to the status of *jus cogens* and *erga omnes*.[125] The contemporary nuclear situation is similarly a cause for moral outrage over the proliferation, development and threats to use deadly nuclear

---

[121] Meron, at p. 127.
[122] Whitman, J. and Perrigo, S. *The Geneva Conventions Under Assault*. (2010) London: Pluto Press at 20.
[123] Whitman at 20.
[124] Whitman at 19–20.
[125] Dissenting Opinion of Trindade on *Marshall Islands v. UK* 2016 at para. 167: "Thus, it was stated, for example, that the 'experience of the Marshallese people confirms that unnecessary suffering is an unavoidable consequence of the detonation of nuclear weapons'; the effects of nuclear weapons, by their nature, are widespread, adverse and indiscriminate, affecting also future generations. It was further stated that the 'horrifying evidence' of the use of atomic bombs in Hiroshima and Nagasaki, followed by the experience and the aftermath of the nuclear tests carried out in the region of the Pacific Island States in the 1950s and the 1960s, have alerted to 'the much graver risks to which mankind is exposed by the use of nuclear weapons.'"

weapons. Thus, the law must adapt and develop new obligations to protect human life. The great injustice of whole countries living in constant fear and danger of annihilation in the name of state sovereignty, security and deterrence must be addressed by raising the standard of accountability for states to meet their obligations that they owe to the world around them.

The main thrust of this moral argument is that when a new situation arises in the world that creates new dangers for human beings, the law needs to adapt accordingly. Nuclear weapons are a newer technology and yet they are not formally recognized under *jus cogens*, or *erga omnes* obligations, while genocide, torture and slavery have been. The law must fill this gap, due to the incredible danger that nuclear weapons pose to the international community. The ultimate goal is to put greater pressure on states to rid the world of nuclear weapons and thus leave one less way to commit omnicide.

Judge Trindade argues in his dissenting opinion on the *Marshall Islands v. United Kingdom*:

> For its part, the International Law Association (ILA) [Committee on Nuclear Weapons, Non-proliferation and Contemporary International Law], [126] in its more recent work (in 2014) on nuclear disarmament, after referring to Article VI of the NPT, was of the view that it was not only conventional, but also an evolving customary international obligation with an *erga omnes* character, affecting "the international community as a whole," and not only the States Parties to the NPT. It also referred to the "world-wide public opinion" pointing to "the catastrophic consequences for humankind of any use or detonation of nuclear weapons," and added that reliance on nuclear weapons for "deterrence" was thus unsustainable.
>
> 155. In its view, "nuclear" deterrence is not a global "umbrella," but rather a threat to international peace and security, and NWS are still far from implementing Article VI of the NPT. To the International Law Association, the provisions of Article VI are not limited to States Parties to the NPT, "they are part of customary international law or at least evolving custom"; they are valid *erga omnes*, as they affect "the international community as a whole," and not only a group of States or a particular State. Thus, as just seen, learned institutions in international law, such as the IDI and the ILA, have also sustained the prohibition in international law of all weapons of mass destruction, starting with nuclear weapons, the most devastating of all.
>
> 156. A single use of nuclear weapons, irrespective of the circumstances, may today ultimately mean the end of humankind itself. All weapons of mass destruction are illegal, and are prohibited: this is what ineluctably ensues from an international legal order of which the ultimate material source is the universal juridical conscience. This is the position I have consistently sustained along the years, including in a lecture I delivered at the University of Hiroshima, Japan, on 20.12.2004. I have done so in the line of jusnaturalist thinking, faithful to the lessons of the "founding

[126] See Black-Branch, J. L. and Fleck, D. (2014) Legal Aspects of Nuclear Disarmament. Report of the International Law Association. See www.ila-hq.org/en/committees/index.cfm/cid/1025.

Why Are Nuclear Obligations Effective Erga Omnes? 369

fathers" of the law of nations, keeping in mind not only States, but also peoples and individuals, and humankind as a whole.[127]

In a Nuclear World All States Are Neighbors: An Analogy with Tort Law

Obligations of nuclear disarmament, nonproliferation and nuclear security have an *erga omnes* character that are owed to the international community as a whole, not specifically to individual states or groups of states party to a particular treaty. This includes trans-frontier effects caused by nuclear damage and responsibility of an international nature. To that end, all aspects of the NPT – nonproliferation of nuclear weapons, peaceful and secure use of nuclear energy and nuclear disarmament – are interrelated, which in turn create rights and obligations for both nuclear-weapon states and non-nuclear-weapons states. Negligence claims in tort law give us a good guide for holding states accountable for wrongful acts. Lord Atkin explained the basis of negligence in his House of Lords decision, *Donoghue v. Stevenson*:

> The rule that you are to love your neighbour becomes in law you must not injure your neighbour; and the lawyer's question, Who is my neighbour? receives a restricted reply. You must take reasonable care to avoid acts or omissions which you can reasonably foresee would be likely to injure your neighbour. Who, then, in law, is my neighbour? The answer seems to be persons who are so closely and directly affected by my act that I ought reasonably to have them in contemplation as being affected when I am directing my mind to the acts or omissions which are called in question.[128]

The nature of nuclear weapons is such that all states are neighbors and are all within proximity of each other. Based on what we know about Hiroshima, Nagasaki and the nuclear tests on the Marshall Islands, if a state were to use a nuclear weapon, their neighbors would be harmed, and thus the harm is foreseeable.[129] The duty and standard of care that each nation owes to the international community is defined in the NPT, especially the obligation to disarm in Article VI. And, there are no good policy reasons not to hold states liable for failure to meet the goals of the NPT, because the safety and flourishing of the future of the human race trumps any policy considerations since even international policies must be for the benefit of all the citizens they affect. As such, the positive *erga omnes* obligations suggested above are in line with widely accepted tort law principles.

The main objection to this approach is that an obligation that binds states to disarm could at the same time compromise their right to self-defense and state

---

[127] Judge Trindade argues along similar lines in his dissenting opinion on the *Marshall Islands v. United Kingdom* at paras. 154–156. See www.icj-cij.org/files/case-related/158/158-20161005-JUD-01-06-EN.pdf.

[128] *McAlister (Donoghue) v. Stevenson* (1932), [1932] AC 562 (UKHL), per Lord Atkin (quoted in Fleming's The Law of Torts, p. 153); Klar, *Tort Law*, 4th ed. (Carswell, 2008), pp. 157–162.

[129] Dissenting Opinion of Trindade on *Marshall Islands v. UK* 2016 at para. 167.

370   *Obligations* Erga Omnes

sovereignty. To overcome this objection, one must accept that the obligations of nonproliferation and disarmament do not deny the right to self-defense, but rather limit it in order to protect fundamental international human rights to life, liberty and security of the person, etc. This view finds support with Judge Trindade who points to the United Nations Millennium Declaration (adopted by General Assembly's resolution 55/2 in 2000) which states:

> the determination "to eliminate the dangers posed by weapons of mass destruction" (para. II(8)), and, noticeably,
> "To strive for the elimination of weapons of mass destruction, particularly nuclear weapons, and to keep all options open for achieving this aim, including the possibility of convening an international conference to identify ways of eliminating nuclear dangers" (para. II(9)).
> 127. In addition to our responsibilities to our individual societies, – the UN Millennium Declaration added, –
> *"we have a collective responsibility* to uphold the principles of human dignity, equality and equity at the global level. (...) [W]e *have a duty therefore to all the world's people, especially the most vulnerable and, in particular, the children of the world, to whom the future belongs.*
> We reaffirm our commitment to the purposes and principles of the Charter of the United Nations, which have proved timeless and universal. Indeed, their relevance and capacity to inspire have increased, *as nations and peoples have become increasingly interconnected and interdependent"* (paras. I(2–3)).[130]

Once we accept that the international community has become through globalization, a community of neighbors all within relatively close proximity, especially in a nuclear world, we must also accept the duties that arise within these relationships and circumstances.

HOW SHOULD THE INTERNATIONAL COMMUNITY ENFORCE NUCLEAR OBLIGATIONS *ERGA OMNES*?

The main problem to overcome is enforcing obligations *erga omnes* on states that do not consent to the jurisdiction of the ICJ. The East Timor Case highlights the issue of consent:

> In the Court's view, Portugal's assertion that the right of peoples to self-determination, as it evolved from the Charter and from United Nations practice, has an *erga omnes* character, is irreproachable. The principle of self-determination of peoples has been recognized by the United Nations Charter and in the jurisprudence of the Court (see *Legal Consequences for States of the Continued Presence of South Africa in Namibia (South West Africa) notwithstanding Security Council Resolution 276 (1970), Advisory Opinion, ICJ Reports* 1971, pp. 31–32, paras. 52–53;

---

[130] *Marshall Islands* above n. 32 at paras. 126–127.

Why Are Nuclear Obligations Effective Erga Omnes? 371

Western Sahara, Advisory Opinion, ICJ Reports 1975, pp. 31–33, paras. 54–59); it is one of the essential principles of contemporary international law. *However, the Court considers that the erga omnes character of a norm and the rule of consent to jurisdiction are two different things.* Whatever the nature of the obligations invoked, the Court could not rule on the lawfulness of the conduct of a State when its judgment would imply an evaluation of the lawfulness of the conduct of another State which is not a party to the case. Where this is so, the Court cannot act, even if the obligation in question is an obligation *erga omnes*.

States are likely to resist the idea of obligations toward states or parties that they did not consent to or if they are not party to a treaty, tribunal or contract. The only way to make it over this hurdle is to convince the international community of the legal, moral, and practical importance of compliance with nuclear obligations, which is what this chapter sets out to do.

The *second* challenge is that if a state brings a complaint against another state on the grounds that an obligation has been breached, does the defendant state owe the obligation only to the state that brought the complaint or to the international community? If it is the international community, how would the courts create a remedy that addresses a multi-national duty?

The *third* challenge is how to define the corresponding rights *erga omnes* of the international community that arise from the obligations. Ragazzi explains this problem below:

> The Latin expression "erga omnes" means "towards all." The term "omnes" can have either a collective or a distributive connotation. (See Glare (ed.), Oxford Latin Dictionary (Oxford, 1982), pp. 1248–9 ("omnis").) As applied to the concept of obligations *erga omnes*, this double connotation raises the issue whether the international community as such can be bound by obligations erga omnes and be the bearer of the corresponding rights of protection.[131]

If each State owes a duty to the international community, can the international community also be a rights holder? Yes, if we conceive of the international community as a collection of individual States made up of individual persons, but the international community cannot be said to have an obligation or a right if we are denoting some new universal legal entity that is composed of every State and every human being in the world. This is because obligations and rights are relational; they require more than one party in order to mean anything. A community of a single person is not a community and it would be meaningless to say that person had rights or obligations. States exist only because human beings created a legal entity that could express a collective interest against other states. Thus, when we say that a State owes an obligation *erga omnes* (toward the international community) we are referring to the collective connotation because any violation of that obligation

---

[131] Maurizio Ragazzi, *The Concept of International Obligations Erga Omnes* (Oxford: Oxford University Press, 1997) at p. 1, n. 1.

372   *Obligations* Erga Omnes

simultaneously violates the obligation to everyone else in the international community. When we say that the international community has a right *erga omnes* to be protected from violations of nuclear law, we are referring to the distributive connotation because every member of the community has a right to be protected from any other individual state violating that right.

To help clarify how the collective connotation applies to obligations and the distributive connotation applies to rights, imagine a community consisting of three people A, B and C who each have dangerous weapons that could destroy the whole community. A has obligation toward the collective community (B and C) not to share or misuse those weapons and to eventually get rid of them. B and C each possess a right not to live in a community where A is misusing and building up weapons. At the same time B and C as individuals have obligations toward A to protect the corresponding right that A has, not to live in a community where B and C are sharing, misusing and building up their stockpile of dangerous weapons. Judge Weeramantry, in his dissent on the *East Timor* Case argues similarly that *erga omnes* obligations originate from *erga omnes* rights:

> The existence of a right is juristically incompatible with the absence of a corresponding duty. The correlativity of rights and duties, well established in law as in logic (see, especially, Hohfeld, Fundamental Legal Conceptions, 1923), means that *if the people of East Timor have a right erga omnes to self-determination, there is a duty lying upon all Member States to recognize that right.* To argue otherwise is to empty the right of its essential content and, thereby, to contradict the existence of the right itself.[132] (Emphasis added)

Based on this analysis, and the sections above, it becomes clear that the entire international community holds both rights and obligations in the international legal area of nuclear weapons.

Finally, how does one enforce compliance with obligations *erga omnes* with universal reciprocity of duties and rights that would exist between all states simultaneously? After all, these duties "go beyond the bilateral reparation scheme which applies in reciprocal legal relationships."[133] This challenge can be overcome with some helpful clarification. In a case where a state breaches an obligation and that breach also adversely affects a neighboring country, in order to clarify who the obligation is owed to, the ICJ could create separate remedies that address both the negative effect on the specific state and the enforcement of the obligation owed to the international community.

Karl Zemanek points out the distinct nature of standard setting conventions that create *erga omnes* obligations; they are not contractual obligations that come with substantive rights, rather they come only with right to request fulfillment of the commitments by all other parties. This kind of obligation conflicts with the principle

---

[132]   East Timor s. c.i at p. 209.
[133]   Kadelbach, at 26.

Why Are Nuclear Obligations Effective Erga Omnes? 373

of non-intervention which derives from state sovereignty which is the foundation of traditional international law.[134] Zemanek quotes Bruno Simma's explanation of *erga omnes* obligations are performed and enforced:

> When human rights are violated there simply exists no *directly* injured State because international human rights law does not protect States but rather human beings or groups directly. Consequently, the substantive obligations flowing from international human rights law are to be performed above all within the State bound by it, and not *vis-a-vis* other States. In such instances to adhere to the traditional bilateral paradigm and not to give other States or the organized international community the capacity to react to violations would lead to the result that these obligations remain unenforceable under general international law.
>
> The crucial aspect of *erga omnes* obligations is, therefore, the manner in which they may eventually be enforced.[135]

The unique nature of *erga omnes* obligations is that they are owed to every state and thus every and any state would have legal standing to bring a claim against another state for a breach. Were a state to breach an obligation, every other state or an organized group of states could also subject that state to countermeasures as way of enforcing compliance. The problem that could arise, is if a powerful or influential state did not cooperate with countermeasures or was simply not interested in enforcing the obligation or protecting the rights of other states who are less powerful. Would we then argue that the powerful state is breaching their duty to protect *erga omnes* rights? Who would hold them accountable and enforce their compliance? This is a challenge that will need to be addressed by the courts and states in the future, but this is not a reason to ignore the fact that extending *erga omnes* obligations to nuclear weapons would be both morally and legally consistent with other *erga omnes* obligations, as set out above.

As Tams and Tzanakopoulos argue, there is hope that the *erga omnes* concept is impacting international law and being used to build up state accountability and responsibility[136] to the international community:

> [E]ven without proper ICJ cases, the *erga omnes* concept has left its mark on international law. It has "developed apace" and "spilled over" into other areas of law, notably the law of state responsibility. The ILC's 2001 Articles (not binding in law, but formulated in close co-operation with governments) in particular take up the idea of "law enforcement in the public interest." Drawing on *Barcelona Traction*, Article 48 of the ILC's text recognizes the right of each state to invoke another state's responsibility if "the obligation breached is owed to the international community as a whole" (i.e. an obligation *erga omnes*). While Article 48 merely spells out the meaning of the Barcelona Traction dictum, that dictum has also been

---

[134] Zemanek at 9.
[135] Ibid. at p. 10.
[136] The idea of state responsibility is echoed by Kadelbach, where the author argues that "*Erga omnes* obligations ... have been considered so far, by and large, as a concept of State responsibility."

374   *Obligations* Erga Omnes

applied to justify other forms of law enforcement. Much of the debate has centered on the countermeasures – that is, coercive measures taken in response to serious and well-attested violations of obligations *erga omnes*. Whether such a right exists remains a matter for debate. The ILC seemed unable to expressly recognize it, and in its Article 54 left the matter open. However, practice suggests a more liberal approach. On frequent occasions, states have asserted a right to suspend treaties, freeze foreign assets, or impose embargoes in response to erga omnes breaches, against other states such as Zimbabwe, Belarus, Yugoslavia, South Africa, and so forth. Given this rather widespread practice, much suggests that the "erga omnes rationale" has modified the rules governing countermeasures.[137]

The hope is that the growing acknowledgment of the *erga omnes* concept in other areas of law will also spill over into nuclear law as leaders and courts begin to recognize the overwhelming human impetus and moral basis for enforcing disarmament, nonproliferation and peaceful use of nuclear energy by raising the status of these obligations to *erga omnes*. It is fitting to end with a quote from a champion of obligations *erga omnes* in the ICJ; Judge Cancado Trindade:

> the "great legacy of the juridical thinking of the second half of the XXth century, in my view, has been, by means of the emergence and evolution of the ILHR, the rescue of the human being as subject of the law of nations, endowed with international legal personality and capacity" (para. 10). This was due to the awakening of the *universal juridical conscience* (paras. 25 and 28), – the *recta ratio* inherent to humanity, – as the *ultimate material source* of the law of nations, standing well above the "will" of individual States. It was necessary, in our days, – I added, – "to stimulate this awakening of the *universal juridical conscience* to intensify the process of humanization of contemporary international law" (para. 25).[138]

HOW DO OBLIGATIONS *ERGA OMNES* ACT AS A LINK BETWEEN THE GOALS OF THE TPNW AND A BINDING LEGAL FRAMEWORK THAT NWS ALREADY ADHERE TO?

Although the nuclear-armed states do not support the TPNW, they are the missing link between implementation and universality of the TPNW. To fill that gap, proponents of the TPNW should appeal to obligations to which these and all states are already bound (i.e., commitments under Article VI of the NPT), as well as highlight that such requirements are not just treaty law, but also form *erga omnes* obligations. Again, *erga onmes* obligations are owed to the international community as a whole and not specifically to individual states or groups of states party to

[137] Christian J. Tams, Antonios Tzanakopoulos, "Barcelona Traction At 40: The ICJ As an Agent of Legal Development," *Leiden Journal of International Law*, 23 (2010), 781 at 793.

[138] Concurring Opinion in the IACtHR's complementary Advisory Opinion no. 18 on the *Juridical Condition and Rights of Undocumented Migrants* (of September 17, 2003) cited in *Jadhav (India versus Pakistan)* 2017, Concurring Opinion of Judge Cancado Trindade at para. 30.

a particular treaty as in the instance of the NPT. They should reframe the question to change the mindset of how nuclear-armed states view the problem and highlight their respective responsibilities in addressing it. If these states were to recognize that the Article VI obligations to disarm and not proliferate are obligations which they owe to the international community as whole, that must be fulfilled whether they are party to the NPT or not, they might be more open – and obliged – to pursuing the fulfillment of the goals of the TPNW. Moreover, they would be compelled to honor their obligations where it is incumbent on all states to hold them responsible and accountable.

The NWS rejected the TPNW because they see it as too restrictive and extreme, professing to prefer a more incrementalist approach to fulfilling disarmament requirements. Appealing to obligations *erga omnes* could be a way to reframe the problem and the understanding of the armed states to move toward global disarmament in a way that the TPNW has thus far been unable to. One might respond to this suggestion by arguing that obligations *erga omnes* will be just as powerless to make real progress toward the goals of the TPNW as the NPT itself because there are no measurable time lines for the obligations to disarm within the NPT.

This author would argue that the obligations have immediate urgency, given the constant and seemingly increasing threat that nuclear weapons pose to international peace and security as long as such weapons continue to exist and remain ready for use with renewal plans being implemented. A possible strategy for increasing pressure on states to respect these obligations is to impose countermeasures against those states failing to fulfill their obligations. Countermeasures may only be taken as a last resort, and in conformity with existing legal standards in relation to clearly defined issues.[139] While disputes should always be settled in a peaceful and cooperative manner, it remains within the domain of states acting individually or collectively to consider sanctions or countermeasures in order to bring about compliance if they are unable to reach a friendly and peaceful settlement as required under Article 2(3) and Chapter VI of the UN Charter.

It must be noted that even a state that has not been directly injured itself, is still entitled to invoke the responsibility of another state and may be eligible to take lawful measures against that state to ensure cessation of the breach and reparation as per Articles 48 and 54 ARSIWA;[140] as with international organizations, subject to

---

[139] See *Handbook on Nuclear Law*. Part V of the Handbook specifically deals with Non-Proliferation and Physical Protection (Chapter 12 on Safeguards, Chapter 13 on Export and Import Controls and Chapter 14 on Physical Protection).

[140] See Jochen A. Frowein, *loc. cit.*, para. 9; Crawford, *op. cit.*, 578–579; Jonathan Black-Branch, "Countermeasures to Ensure Compliance with Nuclear Non-Proliferation Obligations," in Black-Branch and Fleck (eds.), *Nuclear Non-Proliferation in International Law, Vol. II: Verification and Compliance* (Asser Press/Springer, 2016), 351–387, at 363.

376 *Obligations* Erga Omnes

their constitutions and existing principles and rules of international law, as per Articles 49 and 57 DARIO.[141]

It remains within the domain of states to revert to retortions, consisting of lawful acts or omissions such as export limitations, traffic controls, travel restrictions and criminal prosecution to ensure compliance with nonproliferation obligations. Such retortions or sanctions must be proportionate to their intended outcome, continuously scrutinized and terminated as soon as they have fulfilled their aim or objective. Again, there are also judicial strategies for increasing pressure on states to respect these obligations by commencing legal action based on obligations *erga omnes* against those states that are failing to fulfill their duties. Any of the above actions might very well be seen to link to the overarching goals regarding nuclear security, the nonproliferation of nuclear weapons and nuclear disarmament.

SUMMARY AND CONCLUSION

Noted in the *Barcelona Traction* case in 1970,[142] the ICJ highlighted, *obiter dictum*, obligations *erga omnes*. States owe them to the international community as whole; "toward all."[143] Derived from other international laws, legal principles and conventions they do not require consent, agreement, ratification of a treaty or any form of contractual relations as they exist as universal norms applicable to all states and as a result they legally bind the international community as a whole.

Although the court has not yet applied such obligations to nuclear weapons, this author contends that they do apply, and should be applied. That is, international nuclear disarmament and nonproliferation obligations are of an *erga omnes* nature. Moving forward, all states, individually and collectively owe it to themselves and others to actively and expressly enforce nuclear obligations *erga omnes*. Both nuclear-armed and non-nuclear-armed states must acknowledge their respective *erga omnes* obligations and work toward complete and verifiable disarmament as articulated under Article VI of the NPT. The international community as a whole must embrace *erga omnes* obligations and call for the elimination of nuclear weapons and explosive devices as a matter of urgency.

---

[141] Draft articles on the Responsibility of International Organizations for Internationally Wrongful Acts – DARIO – UN Doc A/66/10 (2011), *Yearbook of the International Law Commission*, 2011, Vol. II, Part Two.

[142] As observed by Stefan Kadelbach in "Chapter I: Jus Cogens, Obligations Erga Omnes and other Rules – The Identification of Fundamental Norms," in *The Fundamental Rules of the International Legal Order* (Christian Tomuschat and Jean-March. Thouvenin, eds.) (2006, Koninjlijke Brill NV, Leiden) at 22.

[143] *Barcelona Traction, Light and Power Co. Ltd. (Belg.* v. *Spain)*, 1970 ICJ 3, 32 (February 5) at para. 33–34.

13

The Treaty on the Prohibition of Nuclear Weapons within the Nuclear Nonproliferation and Security Architecture in International Law: From Grand Bargain to Grand Challenges with the Right to Nuclear Peace and Freedom from Nuclear Fear: Summaries and Conclusions

Our moral imperative is to work with all our powers for that day when the children of the world grow up without the fear of nuclear war.

Ronald Reagan[1]

TOWARD NEW APPROACHES TO OLD PROBLEMS

The TPNW represents an unprecedented departure from current practice in that it is the first multilateral treaty to ban nuclear weapons. It is supported by 122 nations, representing a sizable contingent of the world's population spanning various geographical divides. Although not celebrated by all nations, and vehemently opposed by nuclear-weapon states, its adoption at the UN General Assembly in July 2017 marks a fundamental departure from the status quo regarding armament matters. The primary purpose of this book was to examine the TPNW within the broader legal, diplomatic and political context in relation to the existing nuclear nonproliferation and disarmament framework in international law, exploring the influence of the Treaty from various perspectives and its potential impact on the nuclear architecture as it stands today. Surveying its historical development reveals many Treaty strengths and weaknesses some of which were identified during its historic negotiations, highlighting both opportunities and challenges that will carry into the Treaty's implementation (Chapter 2). The creators of the TPNW followed a similar approach to those taken under the land mines and cluster munitions treaties negotiations, focusing directly on reducing human suffering through the elimination of dangerous weapons. Looking carefully at the emerging humanitarian disarmament movement that drove the Treaty reveals the unique "process, purposes and provisions" of this movement that distinguishes it from traditional disarmament approaches (Chapter 3). In the process they gained significant worldwide support to achieve the

---

[1] From "Reagan's Secret War," Martin and Annelise Anderson www.thereaganvision.org/quotes/.

378 *From Grand Bargain to Grand Challenges*

first treaty of its kind. Presented in this chapter is a series of observations, conclusions and recommendations. In particular, it introduces two newly emerging concepts into the nuclear debate: the right to nuclear peace and freedom from nuclear fear as recently advanced under the Nuclear Declaration on the Right to Nuclear Peace and Freedom from Nuclear Fear 2018, as first advanced by ISLAND - International Society of Law and Nuclear Disarmament at a conference convened in Canada.

New *Direction in International Disarmament Law*

The TPNW is a novel treaty in the international community. Proponents see it as an innovative and long-overdue development to a seemingly intractable problem: nuclear arms and nuclear proliferation. Despite the various challenges, legal, political and diplomatic, the Treaty represents the dawn of a *new* era in the plight against nuclear weapons. Its adoption is seen as providing a much-needed impetus towards disarmament. Its creation emanates largely from a group of like-minded countries and civil society groups taking action against the backdrop of what they see as failings on a global front in the lack of discernible progress towards implementing Article VI disarmament obligations of the NPT. Disappointed with the absence of concrete measures throughout several NPT quintennial review cycles, many non-nuclear weapon states decided to take control of their own disarmament agenda, establishing the open-ended working group under the General Assembly to move "forward multilateral disarmament negotiations."[2]

Ultimately adopted in 2017 and currently open for signatures, the TPNW faces large-scale opposition by many influential states, including UN permanent Security Council members and those favoring nuclear deterrence, who see the Treaty as disruptive and unhelpful. They resisted its development and indeed continue to oppose its ratification and implementation as an international arms control treaty. Consequently, the Treaty is a unique development, in its origins, its perceived value and its outcome. Additionally, it is unique in its unity and its divisiveness. The combination and cluster of states supporting its shared vision is met by that of the diverse composition of states opposing it. The sheer number of states gathering together to support disarmament is unprecedented. Moreover, they represent a wide range of geographical locations as well as economic and political interests, consisting of developing nations, emerging economies and relatively wealthy middle powers hailing from both the global south and north. They all converge around a shared goal to eliminate nuclear weapons across the globe.

While proponents of the Treaty favor an outright ban following a simple ban approach, in opposition, is arguably an even more divided array of states, conglomerating together to stifle and thwart the actualization of this Treaty. Former Cold War enemies, as well as modern-day adversaries, and some considered rogue players

---

[2] A/RES/67/56 (2012), www.un.org/disarmament/wmd/nuclear/tpnw/.

Toward New Approaches to Old Problems 379

in the international community, form a commonality in their opposition to the TPNW. It must be noted, however, that their common opposition to the Treaty does not necessarily mean they have a shared view as to how to move forward regarding disarmament and nonproliferation matters. Indeed, they have a divergent range of different perspectives regarding nuclear arms control measures. For example, the five NPT nuclear-weapon states advocate "an incremental, step-by-step approach" as "the only practical option for making progress towards nuclear disarmament, while upholding global strategic security and stability,"[3] unlike some other states which seem to oppose both the Treaty and disarmament altogether.

As discussed in Chapter 2, former UN Secretary General Ban-Ki Moon proposed that nuclear-weapon states create a framework of separate mutually reinforcing instruments or a nuclear weapons convention with a strong system of verification that would ultimately lead to nuclear disarmament. This approach would involve nuclear-armed states. While the UN Working Group recognized that the best chance for reaching a world without nuclear weapons would be by involving all states that possess nuclear weapons, the final Treaty negotiations did not reflect this reality and nuclear-weapon states want nothing to do with it and openly oppose it. Amid such large-scale opposition by states, including nuclear-armed states resisting its implementation, one of the greatest challenges the Treaty now faces is how to convince them to accede to the Treaty and bring them into its regime to achieve universality.

Universality: Aspirational or a Forlorn Hope?

In the present climate, universal acceptance and ratification of the TPNW is unlikely, given the current stance amongst its opponents and objectors. As discussed in Chapter 5, as it stands, non-party states to the TPNW would not currently be bound under customary international law until all nuclear-armed states radically shift their current mindset regarding state practice. The Treaty clearly conflicts with the current nuclear deterrence doctrines of nuclear-armed states, NATO members and umbrella states. Moreover, as nuclear defense doctrines stand, the Treaty prohibits the use or threat of use of nuclear weapons which conflicts with ICJ jurisprudence and existing defense policies (Chapters 7 and 8). With this in mind, it has positive humanitarian implications. Specifically, it is hoped that it will strengthen norms governing *jus ad bellum* and *jus in bello* making it more difficult to legally justify any use of nuclear weapons to initiate war or to use during war. The Treaty may also challenge the nonproliferation and disarmament framework, serving to disrupt current nuclear legal authority and organizational architecture.

---

[3] P-5, Statement by China, France, Russian Federation, United Kingdom and the United States to the 2015 Treaty on the Nonproliferation of Nuclear Weapons Review Conference (New York: May 2015), www.un.org/en/conf/npt/2015/statements/pdf/P5_en.pdf accessed March 12, 2017.

380 *From Grand Bargain to Grand Challenges*

Humanitarian Nuclear Disarmament vs Traditional Disarmament

The humanitarian movement, resisting traditional disarmament approaches toward nuclear disarmament, has been effective in mobilizing civil society groups around the world in its drive to change the dialogue toward the adoption of the TPNW aimed at eliminating nuclear weapons. Under what may be described as humanitarian disarmament, it is aimed at refocusing the nuclear debate on preventing and remediating *human* suffering caused by nuclear weapons. It seeks to rival traditional disarmament approaches largely established and reinforced under the NPT 1968 nuclear framework, wherein states are said to control nuclear weapons in order to advance their own state security and political interests over the greater protection of individuals and tenants of peace.

As discussed in Chapter 3, in advocating change, they highlight the NPT as an example of traditional disarmament appealing to the protection of states' security interests rather than preventing or addressing the suffering of individuals as its primary concern. In contrast to the thrust of traditional disarmament found in the NPT, aimed at preventing nuclear war and protecting the security of states, humanitarian disarmament seeks to reduce human suffering through the elimination of nuclear weapons. To that end, the humanitarian disarmament provisions in the TPNW are unique in that they contain preventative obligations, remedial measures and obligations to cooperate with other states for its implementation. It contains dispute settlement provisions under Article 11. Moreover, the provisions include an outright – absolute – ban on nuclear weapons.

Despite not gaining the support of the NWS, a main impact of the TPNW is that it seeks to deny the five NWS's absolute control over the nuclear disarmament political and legal framework, leading some 122 states without nuclear weapons, civil societies and civilians who have been directly affected by nuclear weapons to set and advance their own agenda. Regardless of what various states and political leaders may think of the TPNW, the world cannot ignore this new reality. Issues of universality and legal enforcement aside, this development is moving forward and is a force to be reckoned with.

Legal Congruence with Treaty Law and Customary International Law

International treaty law requires that a state consent, sign and ratify a treaty in order to be legally bound by it. As discussed in Chapters 4 and 5, the NWS have made it very clear that they are not bound, and do not intend to be bound by it. NATO has directly criticized the Treaty for conflicting with existing nonproliferation and disarmament architecture including the NPT and the IAEA safeguards regime which supports it. NATO members and umbrella states would also be precluded from ratifying the Treaty because their reliance on nuclear deterrence does not concur with Articles 1 and 18 of the TPNW.

The ICJ Jurisprudence in the 1996 *Advisory Opinion* may also be at odds with Article 1 of the Treaty in that it did not declare whether the threat or use of nuclear weapons would be unlawful in a case where the survival of the state is at stake. The TPNW does not take such an agnostic position; clearly advancing a diametrically opposite stance against nuclear use and threats. Indeed, the lack of firm ICJ guidance to ban nuclear weapons has been one of the driving forces for many proponents of the TPNW and thus partly forms the basis of its origins.

States not party to the Treaty are not currently bound to it either by treaty law or by customary international law and will remain that way unless state practice and the sense of legal obligation radically changes amongst those states opposing the Treaty, namely NWS and some NNWS. The ICJ Advisory Opinion also declares that there is no customary prohibition or authorization of the threat or use of nuclear weapons. Universality is unlikely at this point.

Overall, the Treaty seems to be significantly incongruent with the existing legal framework governing nuclear weapons. That said, regardless of how one frames it, the nuclear status quo has been disrupted.

Safeguards, Verification and Fragmentation

Exploring the Treaty's legal congruence with existing treaty obligations highlights how the implementation of the Treaty could create serious conflict with some nuclear treaties and the organizations that implement them. The Treaty's safeguards, verification and implementation also contain major gaps and lack defined and achievable outcomes (as discussed in Chapters 6 and 9). The future of the Treaty will depend on how states parties address these issues.

Verification deficiencies of the TPNW include problems with states self-declaring whether they own or have eliminated their nuclear weapons, different requirements for different states, and not involving the IAEA in the negotiations. Moreover, it may have been a missed opportunity to strengthen existing safeguards through bilateral agreements or additional protocols under the auspices of the IAEA.

The Treaty will likely have difficulty developing a competent international authority with expertise, capacity and staff even if the authority was allocated to the IAEA, given the lack of clarity about their legal authority within the Treaty text. The "simple ban" approach of the TPNW may not be as simple, or achievable, as they hoped.

With further amendments or additional protocols, the Treaty could address the various challenges in developing a competent international authority allocating expertise, capacity and staff which would require clarity regarding any role of the IAEA as the principal legal authority.

The relationship between existing nuclear-weapon free zones (NWFZ) and the obligations of the TPNW reveals that NWFZ may serve to strengthen and further the goals of the Treaty and that it will likely create additional obligations on NWFZ states that will advance nuclear disarmament. That said, the TPNW also has the potential to disrupt NWFZ states' relationships with NWS and break down the complex legal framework between the parties of the many NWFZ Treaties (as discussed in Chapter 9).

In addition, the TPNW recognizes the importance of the CTBT but Article 1 contains a separate prohibition on nuclear testing which does not reference the CTBT International Monitoring System, and it makes no distinctions between NWS and NNWS, which could make it less effective in monitoring, verifying and enforcing compliance. Some states have also expressed concern that the TPNW will undermine and harm the CTBT and prevent or hinder its entry into force.

The TPNW also reaffirms the implementation of the NPT as the cornerstone of nuclear disarmament and declares that it does not affect the rights and obligations of states parties to the NPT. Some experts argue that the TPNW violates the rights of NWS to possess nuclear weapons under the NPT and that the Vienna Convention on the Law of Treaties implies that other treaties would take legal precedence over the TPNW which would frustrate the goals of the TPNW.

Closing various gaps in regulation toward more safeguards, enforcement measures and legal certainty is required to prevent polarization.

Deterrence and Defense

The TPNW clearly prohibits threats to use nuclear weapons which, this author argues, includes for deterrence purposes. This implies that the TPNW could be construed to be in direct conflict with the collective nuclear deterrence strategy of NATO, requiring states parties who aspire to accede to the TPNW and who are also NATO members or umbrella states either to sever their relationship or significantly alter it, depending on whether they possess or host nuclear weapons (as discussed in Chapters 7 and 8). At present, states currently hosting nuclear weapons show no sign of adopting the TPNW in the immediate or long-term future demonstrating the challenges that faces TPNW proponents aspiring toward universality and full elimination of such weapons.

Defense doctrines predicated on nuclear arms and the use of nuclear weapons would be contrary to the spirit and intent of the TPNW. However, some of the citizens of these states are voicing opposition to their hosting nuclear weapons and this could eventually influence their government's policy on nuclear weapons, forcing new developments in line with international humanitarian law.

Moreover, a future decision of the ICJ 1996 *Advisory Opinion* might decide differently today given the emerging shift in how many states are now against

Toward New Approaches to Old Problems 383

the use of nuclear weapons. Again, the Treaty also has important implications for international law under *jus ad bellum* and *jus in bello*, such that it may strengthen these norms and further restrictions on the use of nuclear weapons as reason to initiate war or to use during a war. The Treaty could also bolster norms that restrict the use of nuclear weapons under International Humanitarian Law.

Stigmatization and Universalism

Advancing the goals of the TPNW requires concerted efforts on the part of the various nations, civil society groups and citizens that drove the creation of the Treaty in the first place (as discussed in Chapters 10 and 11). They have effectively utilized many tools on a local and global scale to stigmatize nuclear weapons and move closer to a nuclear-free world under this monumental Treaty. Stigmatization may prove to be the most powerful tool Treaty supporters have to continue to change public opinion and pressure governments to adopt it. Proponents of the Treaty are successfully changing perceptions of nuclear weapons by appealing to a new form of universal values based on humanitarian interests, indicating that the current nuclear posture may not remain supreme.

Civil society groups are working toward the successive elimination of nuclear weapons through stigmatization-action aimed at complete denuclearization. Advocates of the Treaty employ scientific research, activism within and outside governmental institutions driven by civil society groups and nuclear survivors, legal and philosophical research and advocacy to their cause, including economic divestment of nuclear weapons. Their aim is to move citizens and states from a "nuclearist" stance to that of a "non-nuclearist" worldview. This shift is currently happening among lawyers, citizens, government leaders, corporations and banks, further contributing to the stigmatization of nuclear weapons with a view to their eventual elimination.

Aside from the goal of universality, there could be an opportunity to achieve universalism with the Treaty goals and aspirations. Many proponents of the Treaty are concentrating their efforts on mobilizing collective action in order to change perceptions of how nuclear weapons are perceived and valued both locally and globally. Effectively, they are appealing to a new form of universal values based on peace without nuclear fear. Consequently, a new form of universalism could change the current nuclear posture. The guise of nuclear disarmament humanitarianism may sow the seeds of new normative behavior within the global context ultimately contributing to an ideological shift from the current conventional armament stance based on realism to that of a humanitarian universalism that shuns nuclear defense doctrines and the weapons which anchor their very foundations.

384   *From Grand Bargain to Grand Challenges*

Whether or not states currently consent to the Treaty, at present there is an emerging move toward a united neo-universal understanding of the risks and perils that such weapons pose. Deterrence polices do nothing more than contribute to a new revisited, Cold War era. Nonproliferation discourse and direct action seeks to change accepted deterrence ideology. The very existence of the Treaty banning nuclear weapons and explosive devices, in effect, provides the impetus to open a whole new dialogue. Those opposing this stance will ultimately create normative pressure on nuclear-weapon states to reconsider their respective nuclear armament position which may reinforce a revived sense of neo-universalism thus creating a new reality on a global front, advocating against nuclear toward freedom from nuclear fear with nuclear peace.

FROM A PASSIVE TO AN ACTIVE ROLE FOR TPNW STATES

States adopting the TPNW will be legally compelled to implement and enforce Treaty provisions, moving into a new domain of international nuclear obligations and commitments. This will invariably alter their relations with states especially those who will not be Party to the Treaty, potentially having an impact on their diplomatic relations and affairs with these states; particularly the nuclear-armed states and their allies. In effect, the Treaty not only changes the status quo regarding the role of nuclear weapons in the military doctrines for those acceding to it, but it will likely go beyond this in terms of their respective broader political relations and cooperation with non-parties across the globe. Article 16 stipulates that there can be no reservations to it and Article 12, calls for universality, requiring states parties actively to encourage its adoption and accession by others not yet party to it. Given the central goal of eliminating nuclear weapons, it is difficult to see how a state party to the TPNW could ignore non-compliance by other states within the broader international context in their intergovernmental relations and diplomatic affairs. They would be required to address it and potentially take countermeasures.

The Treaty goes beyond the current position, including for previous arrangements such as those under nuclear-weapon-free zones (NWFZ).[4] At present, states maintain their sovereignty and, when under an NWFZ arrangement, they have agreed to a series of arrangements that effectively allow for differing nuclear positions, in accordance with the specific NWFZ agreement in question. Agreements vary and are relatively broad in scope, respecting different military positions between the nuclear-weapon-free-zone states and nuclear-armed states. The TPNW departs from the NWFZ arrangements and individual state positions

---

[4]   There are five such treaties in force: 1967 Treaty of Tlatelolco – Treaty for the Prohibition of Nuclear Weapons in Latin America and the Caribbean; 1985 Treaty of Rarotonga – South Pacific Nuclear Free Zone Treaty; 1995 Treaty of Bangkok – Treaty on the Southeast Asia Nuclear Weapon-Free Zone (SEANWFZ Treaty); 1996 Treaty of Pelindaba – African Nuclear-Weapon-Free Zone Treaty; and 2006 Treaty on a Nuclear-Weapon-Free Zone in Central Asia.

in two important ways. Firstly, states parties to the TPNW will now adhere to a new regime. The TPNW is one international Treaty that applies to all parties with no reservations or facility for special arrangements. By way of comparison, unlike NWFZ, which are multilateral regional arrangements, there is no room for variation based on individual circumstances or regional practicalities. The TPNW is a one-size-fits-all treaty applying equally and uniformly to all parties and to all regions and in all circumstances. There is no room for peculiarities, so no individual arrangements will be permitted.

Secondly, its aim is to eliminate nuclear weapons. Accordingly, under a strict interpretation, a party to the TPNW should not be tolerant of military positions that support nuclear weapons or devices, under any circumstances. This is relevant in that it does not accommodate different views on nuclear possession. Neither should it allow for broader military protection from nuclear-armed states. It seems that the Treaty departs from a passive approach currently taken by some non-nuclear states and echoed in their arrangements under NWFZs, wherein a non-nuclear state passively allows for there to be a different national nuclear defense policy between parties to the NWFZ treaties and the major armed-powers with whom they deal. Now, there will be a much stricter – active – approach that disallows this difference in military positions between the two camps. Moreover, the TPNW mandates open engagement for the elimination of nuclear weapons and the condemnation of military doctrines that support them.

From a Territorial Nuclear Approach to the Compound Nuclear Solution

This author contends that the Treaty departs from current practice from what might be viewed as a territorial-based approach regarding nuclear nonproliferation and disarmament policies, migrating to that of a compound – uniform – approach for those states acceding to the TPWW. At present, consistent with state sovereignty, each state decides its own position regarding nuclear matters, in conformity with the NPT and international law. A state could take one position regarding one state's nuclear military position and take a very different position regarding another state's nuclear position, hence taking a territorial model. It accepts that nuclear-weapon states under the NPT are viewed differently from others, allowing specific states to have a varying position. It allows that a non-nuclear-weapon state under the NPT can have weapons stationed or stored within their territory, as long as it is not under their control. For example, NATO countries such as the Netherlands host nuclear weapons under the direct control of the United States. That is to say, up to this point each country may decide how it views another's nuclear position whereby there may be variations from territory to territory. Again, this may be viewed as a territorial approach to nuclear weapons under which each state decides its own respective policy relating to who has or

386   *From Grand Bargain to Grand Challenges*

hosts nuclear weapons, in line with state sovereignty, the NPT, international law and its respective nuclear obligations such as NATO membership.

This approach permits each state to determine its respective stand on nuclear policy with some entering into collective NWFZ agreements on the one hand, or strategic military alliances based on nuclear deterrence on the other. Nuclear-armed states actively engage in their own activities under the auspices of the NPT regime. Non-nuclear states passively allow for different national nuclear defense policies amongst states.

This territorial nuclear approach will be altered for those states acceding to the TPNW. With its implementation, TPNW parties will be obliged to take a much stricter line which does not allow for a territorial or differential approach. They will have to take a compound nuclear approach whereby regardless of the territory in question, their policy is consistent and singular. That is, nuclear weapons are to be eliminated; their possession is unacceptable. Even if a state does not adopt the Treaty, it does not allow for a different political or military position as previously. Parties to the TPNW must not allow non-parties differential status, adopting a compound approach whereby regardless of the territory in question they advance and uphold a consistent position aimed at banning and eliminating nuclear weapons, forever. Again, they will now adhere to a new system, in a one-size-fits-all regime to eliminate nuclear weapons with no room for special arrangements or variations regardless of circumstances or practicalities, and under a strict interpretation that mandates banning nuclear weapons and questioning defense doctrines that support them.

Whereas, under current NPT arrangements, a nuclear-armed state could openly possess nuclear weapons. Now, states parties to the TPNW will be required to actively pursue a harder, stricter and tougher line on this. Their hitherto passive voice must now become active in text, tone and tactic. They cannot passively allow for, or accommodate, any nuclear weapons or device under any circumstances. Tactically, the Treaty is intolerant of nuclear weapons possession, taking a strict and active position against nuclear weapons. To that end, theoretically speaking, there should be no difference between NPT-recognized nuclear-weapon states and non-NPT-nuclear weapon states as far as possession is concerned. Under the TPNW no state should possess such weapons, under any circumstances. After all, under the TPNW they will be now working toward a compound nuclear solution under which nuclear weapons are to be eliminated everywhere with zero tolerance for non-compliance.

Asymmetric Nuclear Disarmament

The TPNW is the first treaty to ban nuclear weapons outright, receiving widespread support amongst a variety of states at its adoption at the UN General Assembly. The TPNW moves the world into asymmetric nuclear disarmament, realigning the nuclear status quo and altering the international nuclear architecture in the process. This paradigm shift effectively transforms the nuclear territorial model under the NPT to that of a compound nuclear solution, whereby states acceding to the TPNW will have to openly resist nuclear weapons ownership policies and defense doctrines regardless of which state owns them or under what circumstances (i.e., being a party to the NPT or otherwise). This paradigm shift changes the international disarmament landscape. It creates an asymmetric state of affairs where two universes will never converge, and will continually collide, caught in a state policy conflict as long as nuclear weapons continue to exist.

Decisive Action on Disarmament and Compliance with Article VI of the NPT

One of the purposes of this book was to focus on developing broader understandings of the background to the TPNW with a view to understanding how to move forward regarding these important matters where the survival of humanity, as we know it, may be at stake. It seems that at the heart of the matter is Article VI of the NPT. Compliance is a central issue. As long as there is little or no movement toward the full implementation of commitments under Article VI, the rift will continue; and indeed will grow.

As long as the matter of disarmament is not addressed by the NPT-recognized NWS, those opposing nuclear weapons will continue to take their own course of action, widening the gap between those who want disarmament and those who seem to oppose it. Moreover, other states that have acquired nuclear weapons, such as India, Pakistan, Israel and North Korea will continue on their nuclear track. In addition, more states will likely work toward such ends, including Iran. Other states are sure to follow suit, out of fear and posturing. With such proliferation comes escalation in terms of the number of states possessing nuclear weapons, placing more pressure on states to acquire them for both deterrence and defense purposes, as well as others entering into defense alliances for collective military security and protection. This in turn encourages proliferation and moves toward armament; not disarmament. Many will feel forced to enlarge their capacity and stockpile arms, potentially sparking a new arms race.

This author feels that the biggest risk to world peace today is nuclear proliferation which has been exacerbated by a lack of meaningful action toward implementing Article VI.

The NPT was agreed in 1968, over fifty years ago, coming into effect in 1970. The distinct lack of discernible progress in relation to Article VI has festered. Many feel it is ignored, or at best paid insincere lip service. Whether or not this is indeed the case, the perception has served to shape a very important reality. It has been a central feature in shaping and forming the TPNW. The best way forward would be for states pursuing nuclear ambitions to cease as a matter of urgency; those states who have acquired nuclear weapons outside of the NPT should disarm immediately. They

388 *From Grand Bargain to Grand Challenges*

should have their weapons decommissioned; dismantled in an open and transparent manner under international supervision. In order to inspire confidence for states to do so, NPT-recognized NWS should take steps toward disarmament as required by Article VI of the NPT. The TPNW provides an opportunity to renew such opportunities.

It is safe to say that the TPNW is viewed as a disruptive irritant to the nuclear-armed states – no understatement intended. That said, it may be an inconvenient truth, but it does represent an important call to action that the status quo cannot prevail. The world deserves better than to be stuck in this arms-flux, with humanity languishing in a state of nuclear-drift. The world needs disarmament and nonprolif-eration; not the opposite. Fulfilling the requirements of Article VI of the NPT is at the heart of the solution, one that was legally agreed over a half century ago.

THE NUCLEAR PARADOX

There is a nuclear paradox in the international community relating to approaches to disarmament and nuclear nonproliferation. Indeed, there are two sets of factors that come into play and interact in this increasingly complex nuclear scenario. Specifically, there are two forces that stand separately but are related and intercon-nected. The first set of factors relates to commitments to the NPT and compliance with nonproliferation and adherence to requirements under Article VI. The second set relates to the TPNW and state relationships amid these two seemingly competing approaches to achieving disarmament. One side favors disarmament through the NPT; the other calls for the full ratification and implementation of the TPNW. These are not mutually competing treaties and they can co-exist and be fulfilled simultaneously.[5]

Paradoxically the two sides: non-TPNW vs TPNW; have become both contradict-ory but also interdependent. Paradoxes combine two elements that are in direct opposition to one another, but at the same time these elements come to define one other as they become locked in a perpetual interplay.[6] Applying this to nuclear disarmament, it seems that there are two paradoxical elements that are in direct opposition to one another. The proponents of the TPNW and those opposing it. They have become locked in perpetual interplay seemingly without resolution. But at the same time their perceptions define one other, as they both profess to want the same thing: nuclear disarmament. In the terminology of paradox theory, they are

---

[5] Needless to say, there are states that say they want nuclear weapons only in reaction to the existence of nuclear weapons in other states and not an epistemological stance, per se.

[6] See Jonathan Schad and Pratima Bansal, "Seeing the Forest and the Trees: How a Systems Perspective Informs Paradox Research," *Journal of Management Studies* 55:8 December 2018 doi: 10.1111/joms.12398. Schad, J., Lewis, M. W., Raisch, S. and Smith, W. K. (2016). "Paradox Research in Management Science: Looking Back to Move Forward," *Academy of Management Annals*, 10, 5– 64 at p. 6.

The Nuclear Paradox

contradictory, but interdependent. As separate as they may seem at first, in that they are in direct competition with one another, in reality they are not.

That is, both sides say that they want nuclear proliferation to cease so that more states do not acquire nuclear weapons. The TPNW calls for disarmament now. The five NPT nuclear-weapon states argue for an incremental option for nuclear disarmament, during which period they uphold global strategic security and stability.[7]

Both sides claim they want meaningful and effective disarmament. This encompasses the nuclear paradox. As separate as they may seem at first, they are in direct competition with one another. They are locked in perpetual interplay seemingly without resolution. While "conventional" armament approaches would suggest the need to trade off these competing demands, paradox theory suggests that by reframing them that they are seen not as problems but rather as opportunities, these apparently contradictory pressures can help innovate and improve both social and commercial outcomes.

Nuclear Reciprocity

Although those for and against the TPNW seem to be diametrically opposing forces, in terms of approaches to disarmament, in reality they are locked in a perpetual interplay. They are interdependent in terms of both sides wishing to achieve their ultimate goals of disarmament. To that end, there is a need for nuclear reciprocity. They both require taking a reciprocal approach and working together and not losing sight of the overall end result – the elimination of nuclear weapons.

While locked in an intractable state, neither side is likely to achieve their end goal, ultimate disarmament. Neither side will move forward as they will continue to compete with one another; not generating the trust, confidence and goodwill required to do so. As separate camps they should move toward the full implementation of the commitments under the pillars of the NPT and doing so simultaneously. That is, non-nuclear-weapon states should not proliferate (i.e., acquire weapons); nuclear-weapon states should move toward disarming. Both goals must occur in tandem. They require a constant and mutual interplay; one is not going to happen without the other and they will spend their time and resources competing with one another, effectively creating more tension which undermines confidence, erodes trust and diminishes goodwill.

The more the global community drifts without any meaningful or effective disarmament as required under Article VI, the more likely it is that other states will seek to acquire nuclear weapons, in defiance of nonproliferation as

---

[7] P-5, Statement by China, France, Russian Federation, United Kingdom and the United States to the 2015 Treaty on the Nonproliferation of Nuclear Weapons Review Conference (New York: May 2015), www.un.org/en/conf/npt/2015/statements/pdf/P5_en.pdf accessed March 12, 2017.

390   *From Grand Bargain to Grand Challenges*

required under the NPT. The more that states such as Iran and North Korea proliferate, the less likely it is that the five NPT nuclear states will pursue serious or effective disarmament, relying on deterrence. The longer deterrence lasts, and more proliferation occurs, the more those advocating for the TPNW are out of alignment with those states opposing the TPNW. Consequently, one side mutually reinforces the other, at a time when they need a reciprocal intervention and trust building. If not, they may become locked in constant interplay seemingly without resolution. While "conventional" armament approaches would suggest the need to trade off these competing demands, paradox theory suggests that by reframing them that they are seen not as problems but rather as opportunities, these apparently contradictory pressures can actually help to innovate and improve outcomes for both sides. It is time to start talking and moving toward a solution instead of drifting listlessly in the silence of defiance. Indeed, *erga omnes* obligations as well as long-standing human rights principles support the right to peace and freedom from fear as advanced by the Nuclear Declaration on the Right to Nuclear Peace and Freedom from Nuclear Fear 2018.

Erga Omnes *Obligations*

In conjunction with shifting attitudes regarding nuclear weapons, other considerations remain to be explored relating to states' nuclear obligations. Given the current opposition and rejection of the TPNW by the NWS, there remains a missing link in the full implementation and universality of the ideals of the TPNW. In order to fill that gap, this author contends that NNWS should appeal to obligations to which the NWS are already bound and argues that such requirements are *erga omnes* obligations consistent with NPT commitments. NPT requirements to disarm and not proliferate are obligations they owe to the international community as whole, that must be fulfilled whether they are party to the Treaty, or not.

Many NWS reject the TPNW arguing that it is too restrictive and extreme. That said, these same states have obligations *erga omnes* to move toward global disarmament in a way that is not so removed from the ultimate intent of the TPNW. One might respond to this suggestion by arguing that *erga omnes* obligations will be just as powerless to make real progress toward the goals of the NPT itself because there are no measurable timelines for the obligation to disarm.

This author would contend that the obligations have immediate urgency given the constant threat that nuclear weapons pose to international peace and security as long as they continue to exist and remain ready for use under military deterrence policies and defense doctrines.

A significant gap between the NPT and the TPNW legal framework remains because it does not directly bind the NWS and it seems unlikely that these NWS will

The Nuclear Paradox   391

join the Treaty or be bound under *opinio juris*. That said, *erga omnes* obligations address this important problem (as discussed in Chapter 12). To remedy this problem and to fill the legal gap is to appeal to this existing set of legal obligations found in international jurisprudence to which NWS are already bound. Specifically, the International Court of Justice (ICJ) has highlighted that states owe obligations *erga omnes*, that is "toward all," that derive from other international laws, legal principles and conventions. Examples of these obligations listed by the ICJ are ones that derive from the outlawing of acts of aggression, genocide, principles and rules concerning the basic rights of the human person, including protection from slavery and racial discrimination.[8] Non-compliant states could face international legal challenges based on obligations *erga omnes* against those states that are failing to fulfill them, eventually asking the ICJ to recognize that nuclear obligations are analogous to obligations to prevent genocide, torture, slavery and thus hold the NWS accountable to disarmament and nonproliferation commitments and requirements.

Erga omnes obligations do not require consent, agreement, ratification of a treaty, or contractual relations between states, per se; they exist as universal norms applicable to all states and thus legally bind the international community as a whole to meet these obligations. While the court has not yet explicitly acknowledged this kind of obligation in relation to nuclear weapons, this author argues that international case law and existing treaties, conventions, norms and practice imply that nuclear obligations also hold this unique status. These obligations ought to be acknowledged in theory and practice among the international community and enforced in international fora, including courts. By acknowledging them, the playing field would be leveled and both nuclear and non-nuclear weapons states would be much more likely to work toward the common goal of disarmament and seek the elimination of nuclear weapons and explosive devices. States owe it to the international community as a whole: "toward all."

Consistent with the NPT, it is essential to note that every state has *nuclear* obligations *erga omnes* under public international law; specifically, obligations to the international community, to disarm their nuclear weapons and not to proliferate their respective nuclear arsenals. Consequently, they must use nuclear energy for peaceful purposes only, to protect citizens from nuclear testing, accidents and terrorism, and ultimately to rid the world of nuclear weapons through disarmament efforts (as per Article VI).

Notably, the link between *erga omnes* and nuclear obligations to the goals of the TPNW and within the binding legal framework of the NPT regime is firmly embedded in the existing nuclear legal architecture to which NWS are already obliged to adhere. To that end the following must transpire; the nine states armed with nuclear weapons both states parties to the NPT – Russia, the United States,

---

[8] *Barcelona Traction, Light and Power Co. Ltd. (Belgium v. Spain)*, 1970 ICJ 3, 32 (February 5) at paras. 33–34.

China, France and the UK – as well as non-NPT parties – India, Pakistan, Israel and North Korea – must explore and adhere to their international responsibilities.

In sum, while full legal compliance with the TPNW may at first seem unlikely, states may be convinced to comply with the spirit as well as many of the ideals advanced by the TPNW in accordance with the *erga omnes* – "toward all" – obligations. In the final analysis, beyond the TPNW, one must note that states have obligations under the NPT and comprehensive safeguards agreements of an *erga omnes* character. They owe a duty to cooperate in ensuring compliance with such obligations. To that end, a state may be eligible to take countermeasures against serious breaches of such obligations, even if the state itself is not directly injured, per se. Similarly, international organizations may have a right to take countermeasures subject to their constituent documents and existing principles and rules of international law. In doing so, they must bear in mind that any coercive measure may only be taken as a last resort and must be specifically aimed at bringing about compliance with an international nuclear obligation. They must be proportionate, temporary, cooperative in scope and cease once the desired action is achieved. Notably, *erga omnes* obligations are real and binding international obligations requiring due respect and enforcement under prudent attention toward full compliance in an appropriate and accountable manner.

HUMAN RIGHTS OBLIGATIONS TO PEACE AND FREEDOM FROM FEAR

All states, whether nuclear-armed or non-armed and relying on nuclear protection through alliances or umbrella protections must bear in mind their international obligations and move toward disarmament. What seems to have happened over the past fifty years is that states have become complacent, and/ or arrogant in their respective responsibilities in that they view the nuclear state of affairs as the acceptable status quo – their normality. They have become reliant on nuclear as their military choice, either because it is easy or because it projects power. Both reasons demonstrate why it must stop. Nuclear weapons may seem relatively easy to acquire once a state has uranium production for nuclear energy, with dual-use capacity. Given the military situation with other states owning them and some NNWS seeking to acquire them, it is convenient – easy – to justify having them in the first instance and keeping them forever. States consequently defend possessing nuclear weapons by simply pointing to the fact that others possess them as justification. Moreover, they feel that having nuclear weapons makes their state powerful. Once a state acquires nuclear military capacity, it makes it feel like it has come of age in the international community, standing shoulder to shoulder with other nuclear-armed states and therefore taken seriously; given deference. It becomes part of a powerful nuclear club.

Obligations to Peace and Freedom from Fear

Nuclear then becomes their normality and the starting point of any military discussions. With this in mind, nuclear-weapon states have failed to take decisive or progressive steps toward eliminating their arsenals in a meaningful manner. Consequently, there is no clear plan, or demonstrated commitment, to alter this nuclear position. Instead, nuclear-armed states appear to be unrelenting in their reliance on nuclear weapons.

It may be analogous to what is happening in the world regarding environmental issues and climate change. For a long time, there has been a lack of concerted action on the part of many states to take decisive steps and collective action toward reversing adverse environmental impact caused by modern expectations. States have become complacent. For far too long they have continued to do what they have always done, business as usual despite the serious warning signs and calls to redress the situation. Moreover, their harmful patterns of behavior are being replicated by economies around the world, further contributing to this major crisis. What seems to have happened over the years is that states have accepted a false sense of normality. Now, one can see that they have gone too far and for far too long, requiring drastic measures to be taken to address the devastation caused by such destructive practices.

Similarly, with nuclear, armed states have been moving in one direction for far too long – developing and renewing nuclear arsenals – with many thinking they can continue on this track for the foreseeable future, if not indefinitely. Other states are inadvertently encouraged to follow suit, again, because it seems an easy route toward ultimate military protection that will make them powerful. At this rate, it will not be until it is too late, or states have gone too far, before they realize the nuclear path is the wrong one; a destructive one. Like climate change, this situation requires immediate decisive action now, not once the world has passed the nuclear precipice. There is a need to re-align and to recognize human rights obligations to peace and freedom from fear.

The Nuclear Declaration 2018

It seems that the nuclear-armed states have become dependent on nuclear, whereby nuclear weapons form the focal point of their respective military doctrines. In so doing they are failing to address important international nuclear obligations, as well as broader human rights commitments. To that end, the participants and attendees at a conference on Regional Nuclear Nonproliferation and Disarmament: Controls, Defence and Diplomacy, passed the Nuclear Declaration on the Right to Nuclear Peace and Freedom from Nuclear Fear 2018[9] on September 21 marking the International Day of Peace in the year of the "Right to Peace" 2018. The Declaration was considered and reaffirmed at a follow-up conference a year later

---

[9] A copy is included at the end of this chapter.

in September 2019.[10] The preamble of the Declaration, *inter alia*, notes concern over "increasing nonproliferation, disarmament and security challenges," as well as, "nuclear safety and security from nuclear weapons and materials, including environmental and health effects" with the need to explore "options for preventing the development and spread of nuclear weapons and the means of their delivery" and "recognizing the role that countries and regions can individually and collectively play in steps leading to nuclear disarmament as called for in the Nuclear Nonproliferation Treaty 1968."[11]

The Nuclear Declaration is borne out of mounting human rights concerns as well as anxiety over state security within the broader disarmament context, whereby over the past decades there appears to have been little progress toward nuclear disarmament under the rubric of the NPT.[12] Reductions in nuclear arsenals have slowed since 2010, with some NWS endeavoring to expand their arsenals,[13] in line with significant modernization programs. Notably, NWS have embarked on modernizing, seemingly without any intention of actually achieving disarmament any time in the immediate or medium-term, if ever.[14]

To that end, the Nuclear Declaration advances the human right to nuclear peace and the freedom from nuclear fear[15] as expressed in the Seventh Pillar of the Declaration: "Every individual has the right to nuclear peace and freedom from the fear, and threat, of nuclear weapons and nuclear warfare."[16]

The Nuclear Declaration 2018 is unique in both its nature and scope as it focuses on the "human right to nuclear peace and freedom from nuclear fear,"[17] as a basic right and a fundamental freedom which forms the core foundation of the Declaration. It advances (1) nuclear peace and (2) freedom from nuclear fear. Moreover, its core objectives are concerned with both individual rights and

[10] *Harnessing the Winds of Change in a Shifting Nuclear World.* Conference organized by Dean of Law, Dr. Jonathan Black-Branch – September 29–30, 2019 in Winnipeg, Manitoba, Canada at the Canadian Museum for Human Rights. The conference examined problems regarding nuclear safety/security, nonproliferation and disarmament, which continue to raise important legal and policy debates within the global community. It considered the potentially harmful effect of issues arising out of these important matters making it imperative to consider further legal and diplomatic consequences requiring a paradigm shift in how we approach, interpret and apply this area of law.

[11] Winnipeg Declaration 2018, at Pillar 1-6.

[12] Daniel Rietiker and Manfred Mohr, *Treaty on the Prohibition of Nuclear Weapons: A Short Commentary Article by Article* (Berlin: International Association of Lawyers Against Nuclear Arms, 2018) at 4, online: www.ialana.info/wp-content/uploads/2018/04/Ban-Treaty-Commentary_April-2018 .pdf.

[13] Hans Kristensen and Robert Norris, "Slowing Nuclear Weapon Reductions and Endless Nuclear Weapon Modernizations: A Challenge to the NPT" (2014) 70:4 *Bulletin of the Atomic Scientists* 94 at 95–96, 106; see also James Martin Center for Nonproliferation Studies, "Nuclear Disarmament Resource Collection" (August 7, 2018), *Nuclear Threat Initiative* (Blog), online: www.nti.org/analysis/reports/nuclear-disarmament/.

[14] Ibid. at 96.

[15] Winnipeg Nuclear Declaration, at Pillars 7 and 13.

[16] Ibid. at Pillar 7.

[17] Ibid. at Pillars 7 and 13.

Obligations to Peace and Freedom from Fear

freedoms, as well as state security and the rights and responsibilities of states. In fact, it addresses both aspects taking a two-pronged approach focusing on (1) protecting individual rights and freedom (i.e., the right to peace and freedom from fear), while at the same time (2) promoting state security interests and societal well-being; highlighting the need to protect both the individual and the state, including its territorial integrity, its physical environment and its economic, political and social cohesion. It is undoubtedly within every state's security interests to be at peace and free from the fear of nuclear war or threats to its survival as a legal entity and a sovereign equal amongst the international community operating within the long-standing concept of comity of nations.[18]

This is no doubt affirmed by the underlying objective and intent of the NPT and especially encompassed within the intention of Article VI and reiterated in numerous UN Security Council and General Assembly resolutions as well as the UN Charter itself.

Right to Nuclear Peace

The right to nuclear peace is a new concept derived from long-standing principles joining two important concepts, peace with nuclear obligations. Specifically, individuals have the inherent right to nuclear peace. Again, such protections serve the interests of every state from a security perspective toward its survival as well as the overall well-being for individuals. While unique in its focus on nuclear; the right to peace is well established in international instruments. Indeed, to mark the recognition and the importance of the right to nuclear peace, the Nuclear Declaration was agreed on the annual International Day of Peace,[19] September 21, and in 2018, a year designated as International Year of Peace to commemorate the seventieth anniversary of the Universal Declaration of Human Rights from where the "Right to Peace" originates.

Peace forms a central mission of the UN. Reference to it is mentioned in the preamble of the UN Charter[20] and forms part of the first substantive article of its first chapter. Specifically,

---

[18] That is "an association of nations for their mutual benefit." www.lexico.com/en/definition/comity (Powered by Oxford). "The friendship and respect between countries shown by accepting each other's laws, political systems and customs." See https://dictionary.cambridge.org/dictionary/english/comity-of-nations.

[19] The International Day of Peace also known as "Peace Day" is observed globally each year on September 21. It was established in 1981 by a unanimous United Nations resolution, to provide a globally shared date "for all humanity to commit to Peace above all differences and to contribute to building a Culture of Peace." See https://internationaldayofpeace.org/. See also: Resolution 53/243 B. Programme of Action on a Culture of Peace. See www.un-documents.net/a53r243b.htm.

[20] "The Charter of the United Nations was signed on 26 June 1945, in San Francisco, at the conclusion of the United Nations Conference on International Organization, and came into force on 24 October 1945." See www.un.org/en/charter-united-nations/.

Chapter I – Article 1

The Purposes of the United Nations are:

To maintain international peace and security, and to that end: to take effective collective measures for the prevention and removal of threats to the peace, and for the suppression of acts of aggression or other breaches of the peace, and to bring about by peaceful means, and in conformity with the principles of justice and international law, adjustment or settlement of international disputes or situations which might lead to a breach of the peace.[21]

Indeed, Membership in the United Nations is open to all other peace-loving states which accept the obligations contained in the present Charter and, in the judgment of the Organization, are able and willing to carry out these obligations.[22] The principal organs of the UN, specifically the General Assembly has at the heart of its mandate, considerations relating to "any questions relating to the maintenance of international peace and security";[23] while the UN confers functions and powers on the Security Council "primary responsibility for the maintenance of international peace and security ..."[24] Furthermore, the Charter dedicates a whole chapter to Pacific Settlement of Disputes outlining specific powers, duties and responsibilities pertaining to the endangerment and maintenance of international peace, stipulating various means for resolving disputes by peaceful means.[25]

Peace is recognized in the Universal Declaration of Human Rights,[26] as well as the International Covenant on Civil and Political Rights,[27] and the International Covenant on Economic, Social and Cultural Rights.[28] The Universal Declaration of Human Rights,[29] recognizes that, the inherent dignity and the equal and inalienable rights of all members of the human family is the foundation of freedom, justice and peace in the world. The International Covenants also reiterate this recognition.[30]

---

[21] See www.un.org/en/charter-united-nations/.

[22] Chapter II, Article 4(1).

[23] Chapter IV, Article 11(2), see also Article 11(1) and (3).

[24] Chapter V, Article 24(1).

[25] Chapter VI.

[26] UNGA, 1948, 183rd Plen Mtg, UN Res 217A(III) preamble. See www.un.org/en/universal-declaration-human-rights/.

[27] International Covenant on Civil and Political Rights, December 19, 1966, 999 UNTS 171 preamble (entered into force March 23, 1976). See www.ohchr.org/en/professionalinterest/pages/ccpr.aspx.

[28] International Covenant on Economic, Social and Cultural Rights, December 16, 1966, 993 UNTS 3 preamble (entered into force January 3, 1976). See www.ohchr.org/en/professionalinterest/pages/cescr.aspx.

[29] UNGA, 1948, 183rd Plen Mtg, UN Res 217A(III) preamble. See www.un.org/en/universal-declaration-human-rights/.

[30] International Covenant on Civil and Political Rights, December 19, 1966, 999 UNTS 171 preamble (entered into force March 23, 1976). See www.ohchr.org/en/professionalinterest/pages/ccpr.aspx and International Covenant on Economic, Social and Cultural Rights, December 16, 1966, 993 UNTS 3 preamble (entered into force January 3, 1976). See www.ohchr.org/en/professionalinterest/pages/cescr.aspx.

In order to emphasize the importance of this right, the UN General Assembly approved the Declaration on the Right of Peoples to Peace,[31] in 1984,[32] as well as the Declaration on the Right of Peoples to Peace on December 19, 2016.[33]

The 1984 resolution begins by reaffirming that the principal aim of the United Nations is the maintenance of international peace and security which is a central point of interest to this discussion and the Nuclear Declaration. A focal aim of the United Nations, reinforced in the UN Charter, is to maintain peace. It has been discussed at length that nuclear-armed states say that the motivation behind possessing nuclear weapons is first and foremost for peace, that is for deterrence purposes. That said, these same states will entertain using them either for reactive military self-defense, or as a first-use policy if under a credible threat in an anticipatory manner. The fact that they will use them under any circumstances is a threat and therefore an affront to peace. Or, if used, is an actual departure form a state of peace and constitutes military force.

Indeed, the 1984 Declaration on the Right of Peoples to Peace expresses "the will and the aspirations of all peoples to eradicate war from the life of mankind and, above all, to avert a world-wide nuclear catastrophe."[34] The very mention of the term "nuclear catastrophe" highlights the need for peace, as this would have been adopted at the height of the Cold War. It also demonstrates the importance of recognizing the right to peace today. Making a direct and specific reference to "nuclear catastrophe," a point behind one of the principle objectives of the Nuclear Declaration of 2018, is to achieve this same objective, more than three decades on.

The 1984 Declaration highlights that life without war serves as the primary international prerequisite for well-being, state development and progress as well as being central to the full implementation of all other rights and fundamental human freedoms. It is predicated on the awareness that in this nuclear age the establishment of a lasting peace on Earth represents the primary condition for the preservation of human civilization and the survival of mankind. The Declaration on the Right of Peoples to Peace goes as far as to note that the maintenance of a peaceful life for peoples is the sacred duty of each state. The Nuclear Declaration reaffirms and promotes this duty, challenging governments to take action on disarmament and nuclear issues – to avoid reproducing history by avoiding long-standing international obligations.

Against this backdrop, the Declaration on the Right of Peoples to Peace "solemnly proclaims that the peoples of our planet have a sacred right to peace."[35] Such proclamation could never been more relevant than today. It is this quest for

---

[31] Declaration on the Right of Peoples to Peace, www.ohchr.org/EN/ProfessionalInterest/Pages/RightOfPeoplesToPeace.aspx.
[32] UN General Assembly Resolution 39/11 of 12 November 12, 1984. https://undocs.org/en/A/RES/39/11.
[33] Declaration on the Right of Peoples to Peace A/RES/71/189.
[34] Ibid.
[35] Provision 1. UN General Assembly Resolution 39/11 of November 12, 1984. https://undocs.org/en/A/RES/39/11.

a "sacred right to peace" that motivates many people and indeed this author and those focusing on the Nuclear Declaration. It is easy to dismiss people as being naïve or out of touch with the real world for harboring such idealistic aspirations. But, the reality is that perhaps those driving nuclear ambitions need to become grounded in today's reality; the reality of the threat that such weapons pose to humanity and the future of the planet. It is not time to dismiss arguments for peace as naïve and simplistic, but, time to take a step back and see the harm these weapons potentially cause and not wait until it is too late, as has been the case with climate change and environmental degradation.

The Declaration on the Right of Peoples to Peace "solemnly declares that the preservation of the right of peoples to peace and the promotion of its implementation constitute a fundamental obligation of each State."[36] Like the Nuclear Declaration it calls on states and others to take action toward this end. "National governments, regions and cooperative arrangements must take decisive steps to adopt measurable and enforceable actions, in an open and transparent manner, regarding nonproliferation and disarmament along with confidence-building and the peaceful settlement of disputes."[37]

The Declaration on the Right of Peoples to Peace emphasizes that the exercise of the right to peace demands that "the policies of States be directed toward the elimination of the threat of war, particularly nuclear war."[38] Surely even the most militant state advocating nuclear defense would not want nuclear war. Moreover, war violates the right to nuclear peace; the threat of war breaches our freedom from nuclear fear. Both are an affront to state security as well as to human dignity.

The Declaration on the Right of Peoples to Peace calls on all states and international organizations "to do their utmost to assist in implementing the right of peoples to peace" by adopting appropriate measures at both the national and international levels.[39] The Nuclear Declaration calls on "governments to actively support, advance and implement these 13 Pillars in respect to the Right to Nuclear Peace and Freedom from Nuclear Fear."[40]

Few could contest that one has the right to peace as it is interwoven throughout the UN Declaration on Human Rights and the 1966 International Covenants, which have been ratified by many states and form customary international law. Taking a step further, is it not right to extend this to the domain of nuclear peace as well? It is only logical that to have peace from

---

[36] Provision 2.
[37] Ninth Pillar.
[38] As well as the renunciation of the use of force in international relations and the settlement of international disputes by peaceful means on the basis of the Charter of the United Nations. Provision 3.
[39] Provision 4.
[40] Thirteenth Pillar.

Obligations to Peace and Freedom from Fear 399

a general perspective would also entail enlarging within the specific context of nuclear peace. After all, peace is peace, be it related to nuclear or other issues. It is only logical that the two go hand in hand.

While a fundamental aspect of the right to peace is concerned with individual rights, it goes without saying that such rights are within the security interests of the state as well, serving to benefit the state and to advance its rights as well as fostering broader duties and responsibilities amongst the community of nations.

Freedom from Nuclear Fear

Freedom from Nuclear Fear is a new concept based on a familiar premise. The new point is to add the nuclear dimension to long-standing positions against fear. The concept of a right to freedom from nuclear fear, in particular, is developed by this author for the Winnipeg conference and Nuclear Declaration. But, in looking at various commitments already prevalent in the international community, it should not be unfamiliar. It is a human right, that should be applicable and accorded to all individuals, world-wide. It is grounded in the idea that a person is entitled to live their life without the fear that they might be subjected to a nuclear attack, engendered either implicitly as a fear of nuclear-armed states and their supposedly passive possession through their respective deterrence and defense policies, or by an explicit active nuclear threat of use of such weapons designed to strike fear. Some argue that deterrence policies do not intend to create fear, per se, but they invariably do. Whether, designed to do so, or not, the outcome is fear. Individuals, as well as states, live in apprehension as a result of the existence of nuclear weapons. Separate from deterrence, outright express nuclear threats are by design meant to induce fear as a strategic ploy to achieve a desired outcome. The actual use of nuclear weapons, such as the dropping of the bombs on Hiroshima and Nagasaki went far beyond the intention to create fear. These bombings extended well beyond the horror and devastation caused by these blasts. They have indelibly seared into the human consciousness the permanent message that a state has done this horrific act, psychologically reinforcing that it could happen again so that many people live in fear of the possibility of nuclear attacks. Acts of terror, such as the September 11, 2001, bombing of the World Trade Center towers in New York, prompt fear and apprehension in the minds of ordinary citizens, especially those directly affected. The threat of nuclear detonation also does for many people, especially for those who survived, such as the *Hibakusha* in Japan. These are not simply irrational unfounded anxieties. They are based on real fears based on the realty of living in a nuclear-armed world in which states exert their military muscle through deterrence policies and threats of nuclear detonation. Moreover, drawing on Japan's experience where these weapons were used, serves to reinforce apprehension, fear and anxiety causing trauma for many people who live in the fear of detonation. Even for those not in open fear, per se, many are left

400   *From Grand Bargain to Grand Challenges*

feeling impotent to change the nuclear reality and psychologically submissive to these factors and apprehensive regarding this reality.

While fear has a new nuclear component to it, the concept of freedom from fear is not without precedent in international law. The idea of freedom from fear has long been part of international law, and has been espoused by the United Nations since its inception in 1945. Specifically, it appears in the preamble of the Universal Declaration of Human Rights,[41] as well as the International Covenant on Civil and Political Rights,[42] and the International Covenant on Economic, Social and Cultural Rights.[43] Specifically, the Universal Declaration states: "Whereas disregard and contempt for human rights have resulted in barbarous acts which have outraged the conscience of mankind, and the advent of a world in which human beings shall enjoy freedom of speech and belief and *freedom from fear* [emphasis added] and want has been proclaimed as the highest aspiration of the common people." Surely, there could be few areas demonstrating more of a "disregard and contempt for human rights" that would result "in barbarous acts" that would outrage "the conscience of mankind" than nuclear war and its aftermath. Even if one were to survive such an attack, the planet would be left reeling from the aftermath, both in terms of nuclear destruction as well as radioactive fallout from the nuclear blast. Moreover, financial and economic activities would be drastically altered, potentially throwing many regions throughout the world into chaos. This UN preamble calls for "the advent of a world in which human beings shall enjoy ... freedom from fear ..." That "freedom" should encompass living without the fear of nuclear aggression and threats; blasts and fallout; as well as, economic and social ramifications.

The International Covenant on Civil and Political Rights reinforces the UN Declaration recognizing freedom from fear in that, "... the ideal of free human beings enjoying civil and political freedom and freedom from fear and want can only be achieved if conditions are created whereby everyone may enjoy his civil and political rights..."[44] The International Covenant on Economic, Social and Cultural Rights reinforces these same principles referring specifically to one's enjoyment of economic, social and cultural rights in conjunction with civil and political rights.[45]

While freedom from fear as a concept has been consistently incorporated into these international instruments, it requires substantive enforcement as it relates to

---

[41] UNGA, 1948, 183rd Plen Mtg, UN Res 217A(III) preamble. See www.un.org/en/universal-declaration-human-rights/.

[42] International Covenant on Civil and Political Rights, December 19, 1966, 999 UNTS 171 preamble (entered into force March 23, 1976). See www.ohchr.org/en/professionalinterest/pages/ccpr.aspx.

[43] International Covenant on Economic, Social and Cultural Rights, December 16, 1966, 993 UNTS 3 preamble (entered into force January 3, 1976). See www.ohchr.org/en/professionalinterest/pages/cescr.aspx.

[44] International Covenant on Civil and Political Rights, December 19, 1966, 999 UNTS 171 preamble (entered into force March 23, 1976). See www.ohchr.org/en/professionalinterest/pages/ccpr.aspx.

[45] International Covenant on Economic, Social and Cultural Rights, December 16, 1966, 993 UNTS 3 preamble (entered into force January 3, 1976). See www.ohchr.org/en/professionalinterest/pages/cescr.aspx.

nuclear matters. Rather than simply being viewed as a broad conception meant to encapsulate the wider goals of international law and UN principles it requires development and elaboration within the disarmament context.

The right to freedom from nuclear fear advanced by this author builds on this long-standing but often over-looked concept, deriving from it a specific and, theoretically, enforceable right possessed by all individuals and invariably linked to their dignity as well as other rights including freedom from torture, inhuman or degrading treatment, or punishment. The concept should encapsulate an important principle relating to fear itself. It has potential to address the claim that effective deterrence does not actually envisage or promote nuclear weapon use, and may provide a basis for the assertion made by some that the mere possession is sufficient to constitute a threat contrary to Article 2(4) of the Charter of the United Nations. From this perspective, freedom from nuclear fear has the potential to open up new avenues in disarmament discussions, and to provide a fresh lens through which to consider these issues. The right to freedom from nuclear fear remains underdeveloped and ripe for advancement within the disarmament context. Its applicability to nuclear arms is apparent, but "nuclear fear" could also encapsulate other fear engendered by peaceful uses of nuclear, such as a fear of reactor meltdowns, or of contamination from uranium mining operations.

The definition of "fear" under this right is also important. There are several aspects to such a definition that must be considered, such as when the apprehension or anxieties over nuclear activities rise to the level of a fear, and to what extent, if any, such a fear must be reasonably held and indeed addressed.

As with the right to peace, the objective of freedom from fear is concerned with both individual freedoms and state security. While meant to protect individuals in their quest for human protections under international law, it also focuses on the rights and responsibilities of states in their relations amongst one another.

Nuclear Declaration Conclusions: Peace and Freedom from Fear

The Right to Nuclear Peace and Freedom from Nuclear Fear present new considerations for assessing obligations regarding nuclear nonproliferation and disarmament matters. In essence, they declare the existence of two separate but interdependent rights. While these rights are similar, they perform fundamentally different functions. The first is a "right to nuclear peace." This right provides individuals with a covenant against a nuclear war. While this may seem difficult to guarantee, steps toward disarmament and nonproliferation will inspire confidence that measures are being taken toward this end. The right to "freedom from nuclear fear" provides a promise against the fear that this outcome may come to pass. In this regard, actions speak louder than words and diplomatic efforts make a big difference; as do legally binding commitments. Again, while difficult to make absolute statements, progress in the direction of disarmament will strengthen belief that this is possible.

While these sets of rights are inextricably linked concepts, they are virtually opposite sides of the same coin. Thus, while it is possible to hold the latter right without holding the former, the two clearly operate more effectively in conjunction with one another and are, therefore, symbiotic.[46] Derived from long-standing principles in international law and joining important variables relating to peace and freedom from fear they also link human security, presenting a new impetus for addressing these important matters and taking clear and decisive action to this end. What is more, they also touch on the concerns raised by many states relating to these same protections and obligations as demonstrated in the TPNW as well as the NPT. The two-pronged approach focuses on protecting individual rights and freedom, while promoting state interests regarding security and territorial integrity concerns.

The intent and aims of these protections is best understood as part of the wider nuclear disarmament debate and characterized by its emphasis on the impact of nuclear on the rights of individuals, as well as its influence on conceptions of national security, defense and the rights, duties and responsibilities of states. The Nuclear Declaration stands apart from other pronouncements in that it brings to the disarmament discussion an entirely new way of framing obligations to disarm and work toward fulfilling long-standing nuclear obligations linked to both human rights and state security. The role that the right to nuclear peace and freedom from nuclear fear must play is central in the current debate; it must evolve in a substantive manner going forward as a new concept to drive nuclear disarmament in new directions. It cannot be seen in isolation or intended to diminish security or state sovereignty, but to the contrary, to say that both rights and state concerns are better secured under progressive disarmament developments wherein both individuals and states alike no longer live in nuclear fear. It provides a new focus amid the many setbacks currently plaguing disarmament and nonproliferation discussions. Indeed, it sets a goal to engage individual states and regional groups in moving toward disarmament, as set out in the NPT,[47] all the while addressing serious human rights imperatives and *erga omnes* obligations.

The framework of the Nuclear Declaration adopts a human lens in that nuclear issues should also be seen as human rights issues. It calls on states to work with each other as well as with individuals and regional arrangements and organizations to address these vital issues taking an all-encompassing approach based on the interdependence and interconnectedness of the three pillars of the NPT – disarmament, nonproliferation and the use of nuclear energy for peaceful purposes, all being singular and interdependent requirements.

---

[46] Defined as "involving interaction between two different organisms living in close physical association." See www.lexico.com/en/definition/symbiotic (Powered by Oxford).

[47] Pillars 5 and 6.

No doubt, it is important to recognize the effect of these rights in practice. A right to nuclear peace, held by every individual, effectively amounts to progressive steps toward a full prohibition on the use of nuclear weapons and testing. If every person has a right not to be subjected to nuclear violence, then it follows that there are no situations in which the use of nuclear weapons can be justified. Similarly, accepting that every individual holds a right to be free from nuclear fear necessarily prohibits nuclear weapons. Thus, adoption of the Nuclear Declaration indicates recognition of these two rights, and by extension, would represent a recognition that in due course nuclear weapons and devices should be unlawful within this context.

This author sees the importance of advocating nuclear disarmament and peace efforts against the backdrop of prospects of mounting armament. Rather than sounding like a naïve optimist, he is very aware of the importance of state security and adequate military protections and deterrents. For many people, at present it seems that nuclear is the most viable option, especially in light of mounting fears from proliferation in other states such as Iran and North Korea. That said, this becomes an intractable argument. The more states rely on nuclear weapons for security, the more they augment their arsenals in that direction and this effectively becomes the nuclear status quo. This creates downward spiral, a race to the bottom in which the only viable option on the table remains nuclear. That being the case, other states in turn endeavor to have nuclear capacity. This has been the case since the end of World War II. Indeed, it was this fear that led to the NPT which was struck as a "grand bargain" which recognized the right to nuclear energy for peaceful purposes on the proviso that non-nuclear states would never acquire them – nonproliferation – and those with nuclear-weapons would in time disarm, as per Article VI. It is now time to return to the premise, and the promise, of NPT discussions of more than a half century ago – to take decisive action and engage in collective discussions toward nuclear arms reduction with a view to disarmament. Denuclearization is the only option. Without it we will continue to wade through the quagmire of doubt mired in nuclear fear.

Nuclear fear manifests itself in subtle ways. Even citizens wanting peace, may advocate for nuclear weapons due to security concerns. If they fear other countries, they are likely to make decisions based on fear of these other states, rather than an objective alternative based on nuclear-free options. As long as we have nuclear fear, there will be no truly open discussion or viable alternatives. It takes a concerted effort on the part of all parties to move the agenda toward nuclear peace and freedom from nuclear fear. It takes brave leadership in this area to move in the right direction.

To meet these objectives of the Nuclear Declaration 2018 is acknowledging and protecting individual rights and freedoms, and at the same time respecting and promoting state security, rights and responsibilities. To take this two-pronged

404 *From Grand Bargain to Grand Challenges*

approach moves the world toward security interests for both the individual and the state, while calling for social cohesion and greater societal well-being – to promote the dignity, rights and freedoms of the individual, whilst preserving state integrity and its physical environment, economic and political interests. The right to nuclear peace and freedom from nuclear fear presents new avenues for exploring peace and stability for nuclear security and peace.

CONCLUSIONS AND RECOMMENDATIONS

The legal impact of the TPNW remains to be seen, but ongoing political fallout seems inevitable. Whether, and the degree to which, there will be any significant legal changes depends largely on state support to accede to the Treaty. Legalities aside, the reduction and elimination of nuclear weapons is a good thing politically for a peaceful and stable world. This is, of course, assuming that reduction is reciprocal and elimination is global and verifiable. Any traction toward actual disarmament depends largely on political and diplomatic moves. After all, it is within diplomatic reach to open discussions, and within political grasp to heal the divide. Such nuclear leadership is not just needed; more than ever it is imperative.

This author calls on states from both sides of the disarmament debate to work together toward legal clarity, addressing the gaps and inconsistencies, and avoiding a sharp divide among the international community in order to face nuclear challenges that require a shared and cooperative approach. A truce must be called to close the growing gap between supporters of the TPNW and those opposing it. This gulf must be bridged. While at first it may seem that both sides of the divide are in diametrically opposing camps, upon further examination, however, one sees that they actually have many similar nonproliferation goals and complementary nuclear obligations. Perhaps there could be a meeting of minds toward recognizing and reconciling differences of legal approach and interpretation.

Suggested below are a set of recommendations that are intended to bridge the gap between those acceding to the TPNW and those who do not, in the hope of working toward the right to nuclear peace and freedom from nuclear fear. It is intended to provide guidance regarding nuclear disarmament, nonproliferation and challenges posed by nuclear energy for peaceful purposes. As noted at the outset of this book, this author is in favor of any agreement or development that moves toward complete and verifiable nuclear disarmament. Any apparent criticisms are intended to be constructive and aimed at understanding outstanding gaps to be filled for full compliance with nuclear obligations either through the 2017 Treaty regime, or by other means within the existing and expanded infrastructure within the nuclear architecture. Hence, it is hoped that the following recommendations will be given due consideration and action will be taken accordingly. The results may not necessarily develop uniformity between the two camps and marry exact expectations, but it is hoped that it

Conclusions and Recommendations

will help to narrow the gaps and address outstanding differences between the various sides and at least build some consensus in this important area effecting international stability, peace and security.

Recommendations Toward International Nuclear Peace, Security and Global Stability

All states to the NPT, should conduct an audit regarding their state of compliance with nuclear nonproliferation and disarmament obligations in international law. A needs assessment should be carried out with a view to full compliance in a transparent and accountable manner. States that are not party to the NPT, should accede to it as a matter of urgency.

Nuclear Disarmament Recommendations

It goes without saying that nuclear warfare is one of the greatest threats to regional and international peace and security, as well as global stability. Many would include deterrence policies in this category. At the heart of this is the need for disarmament which entails adherence to, and the effective implementation of, Article VI of the NPT. This calls for successive and progressive, concrete and measurable steps toward realizing and actualizing the obligations outlined in Article VI which require parties to achieve: (1) the cessation of the nuclear arms race at an early date, (2) nuclear disarmament, and (3) general and complete disarmament. To this end, this requires: (1) negotiations, (2) to be pursued, (3) in good faith, and (4) the implementation of measures, (5) under: (a) strict, (b) effective and (c) international control. These legal nuclear obligations are valid *erga omnes*, as they affect the international community as a whole rather than a particular state or group of states. Moreover, as part of customary international law or at least evolving customary norms they are not limited to states parties to the NPT.

This requires states to take effective steps and accountable measures to end the nuclear arms race and to lower levels of armament with a view to elimination. Consequently, as stated above, states parties must pursue negotiations; they must do so in good faith; moving toward effective measures in order to achieve a precise result;[48] under a legal instrument; aimed to prohibit the use of nuclear weapons and to eliminate nuclear weapons; which is to be monitored under strict and effective international control; and to be done so under an accountable process and achieved within a determinable time frame.

Again, states that are not party to the NPT should accede to the Treaty as a matter of priority. In order to achieve nuclear security, cooperation is required between all states, including nuclear-armed and non-nuclear-weapon states.

To this end, to achieve disarmament:

---

[48] This requirement goes beyond a mere obligation of conducting but actually achieving.

From Grand Bargain to Grand Challenges

States must develop and implement verifiable nuclear disarmament measures built on confidence and transparent metrics regarding military defense policies and doctrines, anti-ballistic missile defense, force structures and alert levels.

States must terminate the production of weapons-usable fissile material except under appropriate international control.

States must not use outer space for military purposes.

States must accurately report information regarding their nuclear weapons and their alert status.

States must cooperate and share information regarding measures taken toward nuclear disarmament and nonproliferation.

Transparency regarding concerns about nuclear-armed states is required in order to establish open discussions toward accountability and to encourage confidence-building measures.

All states, including states acceding to the TPNW must be under strict legal obligations to refrain from using or threatening to use nuclear force.

Non-party states to the TPNW should also reconsider, with a view to refraining, from using or threatening to use nuclear force, noting the ICJ jurisprudence strictly limiting the threat or use of such weapons as a means of last resort in an extreme circumstance of self-defense in which the very survival of the state would be at stake.

Nuclear Nonproliferation Recommendations

Nuclear disarmament to prevent nuclear war is essential to reducing threats to international peace and security for global stability. Hand in hand with disarmament is nonproliferation and the safety and security of nuclear materials as used for peaceful purposes, or as part of military doctrines in nuclear-armed states.

In order to achieve this, there must be nonproliferation of nuclear weapons and other nuclear explosive devices, as well as effective control over materials, through legally binding instruments that are articulated (agreed), upheld and enforced.

In conjunction with respect and enforcement, these legally binding commitments must be politically cherished and not undermined in any way through negative rhetoric and fully endorsed and promoted through diplomatic and military channels. To this end, nonproliferation requires good practice in this area consisting of:

Adherence to comprehensive IAEA safeguards by states parties to the NPT and nuclear-weapon-free zones.[49]

---

[49] Treaty for the Prohibition of Nuclear Weapons in Latin America – Treaty of Tlatelolco (February 14, 1967) 634 UNTS 326; South Pacific Nuclear Free Zone Treaty – Rarotonga Treaty (August 6, 1985) 1676 UNTS 223; Treaty on the South-East Asia Nuclear Weapon Free Zone – Bangkok Treaty – (December 15, 1995) 1981 UNTS 129; African Nuclear-Weapon-Free Zone Treaty – Pelindaba Treaty (April 11, 1996) 35 ILM 698; Treaty on a Nuclear-Weapon-Free Zone in Central Asia – Semipalatinsk Treaty (September 8,

Conclusions and Recommendations 407

Verification of the correctness and completeness of declarations made by all states.

Assurances of the non-diversion of nuclear material from declared activities by all states.

Cooperation between states and the IAEA as per Article 3 INFCIRC/153 and Article 1 INFCIRC/540.[50]

Improving and adding bilateral safeguard agreements to augment and complement obligations pursuant to NPT and IAEA safeguards agreements, for all states, and in particular parties acceding to the TPNW.

Stricter international regulation and control is required over uranium enrichment and reprocessing of spent fuel under harmonized measures, in order to reduce proliferation risks relating to peaceful nuclear activities and civil use of nuclear-weapon-usable nuclear material.

Further *cooperation and control* relating to dual-use technology transfers in that they are complementary to effective nonproliferation.

Accession to the Comprehensive Nuclear Test Ban Treaty (CTBT)[51] by all states with an emphasis on the remaining eight of the specific forty-four states listed in Annex 2 of the CTBT),[52] namely: India, the Democratic People's Republic of Korea and Pakistan (that have not yet signed the Treaty) and China, Egypt, Iran, Israel and the United States (that have signed but not yet ratified it).

Implementation of compulsory nuclear-test-ban verification, in conjunction with the CTBT Preparatory Commission and continued cooperation, especially in regard to settling any disputes that may arise relating to interpretation and implementation of respective obligations.

Establish a central universal nuclear security regime, developed and elaborated upon under existing legally binding instruments, in order to strengthen nuclear security and transparency.

This work must complement and enhance existing regimes under the Convention on the Physical Protection of Nuclear Material (CPPNM),[53]

2006), www.opanal.org/NWFZ/CentralAsia/canwfz_en.htm. A treaty on a nuclear-weapon-free-zone in the region of the Middle East is subject of a long-standing proposal of the UN General Assembly and NPT Review Conferences, see www.fas.org/nuke/control/menwfz/index.html; Declaration by Mongolia of its nuclear-weapon-free status (September 25, 1992), and the Law of Mongolia on its Nuclear-Weapon-Free Status which entered into force on February 3, 2000, www.nti.org/treaties-and-regimes/nuclear-weapon-free-status-mongolia/, recognized by UNGA Res 55/33 S (November 20, 2000).

[50] IAEA, The Structure and Content of Agreements between the Agency and States Required in Connection with the Treaty on the Nonproliferation of Nuclear Weapons, INFCIRC/153 (Corr.), June 1972. IAEA, Model Protocol Additional to the Agreement(s) Between State(s) and the International Atomic Energy Agency for the Application of Safeguards, INFCIRC/540 (Corr.), September 1997. See SC Res 1887 (2009), para. 15.

[51] Comprehensive Nuclear-Test-Ban Treaty (CTBT), adopted by General Assembly Resolution 50/245 (September 10, 1996).

[52] Comprehensive Nuclear-Test-Ban Treaty (CTBT), adopted by General Assembly Resolution 50/245 (September 10, 1996).

[53] Convention on the Physical Protection of Nuclear Material (CPPNM), adopted on November 1, 1979, 1456 UNTS 125, entered into force on February 8, 1987.

408 *From Grand Bargain to Grand Challenges*

amended on July 8, 2005[54] and the International Convention for the Suppression of Acts of Nuclear Terrorism (ICSANT).[55]

To *maximize* nonproliferation controls and measures to ensure nuclear safety and security amid increasing terrorist concerns.

To *develop* legal oversight and strict law enforcement through criminal prosecution to ensure nuclear safety and security regarding nuclear terrorism.

Further *development and full implementation* of Security Council Resolutions 1540 (2004) and 2325 (2016) requirements to strengthen and enhance global nuclear security and reduce the risk of nuclear terrorism.

Use of Nuclear Energy for Peaceful Purposes Recommendations

The NPT recognizes the right to develop research into the production and use of nuclear energy for peaceful purposes, without discrimination. The TPNW does not specifically address or alter this position. This area requires national vigilance and international monitoring oversight regarding nuclear safety and security. Notably, with the benefits of peaceful uses of energy also come state responsibility to ensure nuclear security and nuclear safety, including a safe radioactive waste management and storage system. To that end, all states need to take a precautionary and proactive approach to environmental protection regarding all:

> nuclear and radioactive materials;
> nuclear and radioactive waste;
> nuclear and radioactive spillage;
> nuclear and radioactive fallout; and
> handling and storage of nuclear and radioactive waste.

States must:

Provide appropriate environmental remedial assistance to areas affected by any adverse nuclear effects.

Take a precautionary and proactive approach to protecting individuals.

Safeguard individuals from adverse nuclear effects.

Provide appropriate remedial assistance to those affected by any adverse nuclear effects of:

> nuclear and radioactive materials;
> nuclear and radioactive waste;
> nuclear and radioactive spillage;
> nuclear and radioactive fallout;
> as well as the storage of nuclear and radioactive waste.

---

[54] The amendment entered into force on April 8, 2016, see INFCIRC/274/Rev 1.

[55] International Convention for the Suppression of Acts of Nuclear Terrorism (ICSANT), adopted on April 13, 2005, 2445 UNTS 89.

Conclusions and Recommendations

409

Accept and fully implement verification and control in nonproliferation agreements.

Account for and clarify in a transparent manner enrichment and reprocessing activities for peaceful uses.

Work with the IAEA to fulfil its mandate as the central support for states in meeting their nuclear safety and security responsibilities.

Develop and implement global standards and regulations pertaining to storage, handling and disposal of radioactive waste, including developing and implementing common standards regarding:

technologies;
sustainable radioactive waste management;
early warning systems pertaining to nuclear waste and radioactive fallout.

Cooperation, Compliance and Enforcement of Nuclear Nonproliferation and Disarmament Obligations

State cooperation and dialogue is essential in order to develop existing, and to formulate new, legal agreements and diplomatic exchanges. The introduction of the TPNW presents a new avenue and opportunity toward disarmament and cooperation in this area. A variety of bilateral agreements could be adopted to strengthen and improve new and existing arrangements. The NPT remains the cornerstone of disarmament and nuclear nonproliferation architecture and consequently, any further developments should endeavor to complement, and or improve, NPT specifications and obligations in relation to furthering and enhancing disarmament commitments.

With this in mind it is essential to reiterate that the three pillars of the NPT – disarmament, nonproliferation and peaceful uses of nuclear energy – are inextricably linked and interrelated. Whilst the three pillars form separate obligations, each with its unique status within the nuclear legal framework, they are interconnected in the broader international nuclear legal framework and inextricably linked within any enforcement or compliance regime. Effective, progressive and verifiable control over nuclear armament is not likely to happen under any approach other than one that respects and accounts for this inter-dependability.

Within the scope of the nonproliferation and disarmament, there is now a template under the 2017 TPNW to re-assess current practices. Specifically, the Treaty serves as an important starting point for nuclear-armed states to open discussions toward implementing Article VI of the NPT. It provides a valuable mechanism for further cooperation toward movement in this important area with a view to addressing long-standing tensions in this area of international law requiring resolution. States must cooperate in the settlement of disputes related to nuclear

410   *From Grand Bargain to Grand Challenges*

nonproliferation, the use of nuclear energy for peaceful purposes and nuclear disarmament. Such an approach must respect existing international law, as well as implementing all UN Security Council and General Assembly resolutions and may involve regional or international organizations including incentives to encourage good practice.

Measures should support strict and effective export controls under open and transparent mechanisms.

States should adopt an open, transparent and progressive approach in their pursuit and implementation of verification objectives and procedures, to be monitored under continual scrutiny.

States must accept their primary responsibility for ensuring compliance and enforcement with their nuclear obligations.

Any State in dispute with, or taking action against, another state, either individually or collectively, must explore all applicable avenues to resolve outstanding issues peacefully and in accordance with international law and *droit de regard.*

Any enforcement of obligations must be through legal means, such as retortions. Sanctions and countermeasures must comply with international law and be used to resolve the dispute at hand in a proportionate manner to achieve their intended outcome. They should not seek to penalize, but to remedy the behaviors in question, and brought to an end as soon as they have fulfilled their purpose.

Final Conclusion: Advancing Nuclear Peace – Reducing Nuclear Fear

The TPNW is an important nuclear disarmament treaty which invariably raises questions in legal, political and diplomatic circles. Adopted by 122 states at the UN General Assembly in July 2017, it represents a clear departure from the nuclear status quo within the current international nuclear architecture. While the impact of the Treaty continues to play out, there is little doubt that the TPNW has and will continue to generate discussion around the world highlighting a variety of views, some heated, others more sanguine. This book has sought to explore the 2017 Treaty, examining it from many different perspectives, including its development, looking at its philosophical and sociological underpinnings and foundations; possible legal implications, pertaining to its real and potential impact within the broader global context for both states acceding to it as well as those opposing it; as well as its current and possible future effects on the international legal, institutional and diplomatic architecture governing nuclear disarmament and nonproliferation. In so doing, the work explores the Treaty's potential for good within the current international environment, noting deficiencies of the TPNW, including its effects on international relations under the new global humanitarian movement and future development in the area of nuclear disarmament and nonproliferation law.

One can only resolve a conflict if one has first taken the time and effort to understand why it exists and carefully examine arguments from both sides in their

Conclusions and Recommendations   411

strongest form. If Treaty proponents and objectors did this, they might, over time, come to a shared understanding necessary to move beyond the current stalemate in our nuclear-charged world.

The TPNW is the first treaty to ban nuclear weapons outright, advancing humanitarian approaches to disarmament. It is supported by the vast majority of UN Member States, representing a wide range of social, cultural and political realities across the globe. The Treaty calls for a major change to the conventional armament approach, enlisting new obligations within a different legal framework and developing its own distinct legal regime. For states acceding to the Treaty, it requires a paradigm shift regarding defense policies and the legality of nuclear weapons within their respective jurisdictions and beyond. It mandates a change of relations with states that are outside the Treaty's domain, potentially altering relations with nuclear-armed states and their allies. For states opposing the Treaty, it marks potential for a significant change in their relations with those states acceding to it.

A fundamental problem facing the TPNW is that the nine states with nuclear weapons openly oppose it. Both states parties to the NPT – Russia, the United States, China, France and the United Kingdom – as well as non-NPT parties – India, Pakistan, Israel and North Korea – oppose it outright, viewing it as an offensive and disruptive force. They refused to participate in Treaty negotiations and contend they will neither sign, nor ratify it. Moreover, they have important backing from other states through various agreements such as NATO and umbrella alliances. Consequently, it seems there is an important gulf between supporters of the TPNW and those opposing it. With this in mind, the dream of legally enforcing the Treaty seems more than remote; indeed, it seems non-existent. The TPNW does not directly bind the NWS and it seems highly unlikely that they would ever join the Treaty or be bound under customary international law, as it stands today. At present there appears to be an unbridgeable gap between the positions of both camps.

An aim of this book has been to focus on both a legal assessment, as well as developing a broader understanding of the nature of the emerging schism between those forcing disarmament and those resisting it. It seems that at the heart of the gap between the two camps is Article VI of the NPT. As long as there is little or no meaningful movement toward the implementation of commitments under Article VI, the rift will continue, and indeed will grow. The matter of disarmament must be addressed in a concrete, decisive and accountable manner. NWS under the NPT have both a political commitment and a legal duty to do so. In the absence of real or tangible action on this front, other states will continue to acquire nuclear weapons, or seek to do so.

In order to address this increasingly intractable problem, this author challenges all states on both sides of the divide to come together to provide legal clarity; to close the gaps in regulation; and to work together toward more legal certainty rather than persisting with uncertainty and ambiguity, which foster competing regimes that polarize an area that requires a harmonious approach – to work toward implementing the above recommendation in this chapter.

The TPNW itself represents a new mindset requiring different ways of interacting in this TPNW era. It provides a new opportunity to re-engage in nuclear disarmament matters regarding one of the most important issues facing humanity for global peace and security. It provides a fresh look and unique perspective from which to approach nuclear weapons and devices. Notably, all states must fulfill their nuclear legal obligations and commitments. They must adhere to transparency and accountability in fulfilling their respective nuclear commitments and requirements and do so in accordance with existing obligations under international humanitarian law, human rights law and environmental law.

Ignoring this Treaty development will not change its trajectory, but may only serve to exacerbate matters and strain relations, amongst would-be friends and allies. Refusing to participate in talks or negotiations will not assist broader tenets of peace and security; promote greater overall prosperity; or establish shared solutions. Such refusal will only serve to balkanize an already divided community, sowing the seeds for greater dissent, distrust and division. There is a fundamental difference between dialogue and division; openness and isolation; and problems and possibilities.

The TPNW requires a re-think, a fresh approach that would advance the interests of all humanity. It sets a marker of sorts to reframe and revise nuclear and military positions and assist to advance wider disarmament goals and improve legal and diplomatic stands regarding nuclear weapons and defense doctrines.

States must work together; they must not lose sight of the broader picture. All states, for or against the Treaty, should work together toward a shared future for all humanity toward implementing the right to nuclear peace and freedom from nuclear fear. Work toward common disarmament obligations and responsibilities, *erga omnes*.

After all, nuclear weapons do not protect peace. Nuclear weapons threaten peace and create fear.

NUCLEAR DECLARATION ON THE RIGHT TO NUCLEAR PEACE AND FREEDOM FROM NUCLEAR FEAR 2028

The Conference on Regional Nuclear Nonproliferation and Disarmament: Controls, Defence and Diplomacy, held September 20–21, 2018, organized by Dr. Jonathan L. Black-Branch at the Canadian Museum for Human Rights, Winnipeg, Manitoba, establishes and endorses 13 pillars, consisting of 6 premises and 7 principles, central to the Right to Nuclear Peace and Freedom from Nuclear Fear, RNP-FNF. The pillars correspond to the thirteen phases of the moon as described in a blessing given by an Indigenous Elder at the outset of the Conference.

First Pillar *Emphasizing* the human rights and fundamental freedoms of all individuals,

Second Pillar *Reaffirming* the dignity and worth of all individuals and Peoples,

Third Pillar *Considering* increasing nonproliferation, disarmament and security challenges,

Fourth Pillar *Concerned* about nuclear safety and security from nuclear weapons and materials, including environmental and health effects,

Fifth Pillar *Exploring* options for preventing the development and spread of nuclear weapons and the means of their delivery,

Sixth Pillar *Recognizing* the role that countries and regions can individually and collectively play in steps leading to nuclear disarmament as called for in the Nuclear Nonproliferation Treaty 1968,

Declare that,

Seventh Pillar Every individual has the right to nuclear peace and freedom from the fear, and threat, of nuclear weapons and nuclear warfare – nuclear fear.

Eighth Pillar Individuals shall participate in discussions and the development of nuclear disarmament policies, and they should accept this challenge.

Ninth Pillar National governments, regions and cooperative arrangements must take decisive steps to adopt measurable and enforceable actions, in an open and transparent manner, regarding nonproliferation and disarmament along with confidence-building and the peaceful settlement of disputes.

Tenth Pillar Nuclear defence policies and actions must not adversely affect civilian populations.

Eleventh Pillar Environmental and health effects of uranium mining, peaceful nuclear activities and radioactive waste management require stringent independent regulatory oversight, impact monitoring and remediation.

Twelfth Pillar Appropriate support and care must be provided to all individuals suffering the ill-effects of nuclear detonation, testing and damage from accidents or disasters.

Thirteenth Pillar We call on governments to actively support, advance and implement these 13 Pillars in respect to the Right to Nuclear Peace and Freedom from Nuclear Fear.

Agreed on the International Day of Peace in the year of the
"Right to Peace" 2018.

Index

Antarctic Treaty, 81, 268, 272

Bangkok Treaty, 81, 268–276
Barcelona Traction, 341–346
Belarus, 319
Biological weapons, 155–156, 263–264
Blix Commission, 19

Canada, 109–111, 329–331
Central Asian NWFZ, 271–272
Chemical weapons, 155–156, 220, 263–264
China, 150, 229, 313, 407
  Public Opinion on Nuclear Weapons,
    310
Civil society organizations, 11, 15, 46,
    287–290
Cold War, 11, 40, 47, 169, 186
Collective security, 28
Comprehensive Nuclear-Test-Ban Treaty, 13
Convention on Cluster Munitions, 50
CSTO, 7, 9, 169, 200, 318
CTBT, 36, 53

Delivery vehicles, 34–36, 220, 313, 394
Deterrence doctrine, 199, 214, 338, 379
Disarmament
  Humanitarian, 25, 46–73, 278–279
  Hybrid, 49
  Security, 49
  Traditional, 49
Dual use, 93, 159–162, 251, 392, 407

Education, 37
Enforcement, 64–70, 96, 135–151
  IAEA, 246–252
  Iran, 151–154
Erga omnes, xv, 9, 61, 64, 279, 305, 340–376,
    390–392, 405, 412

France, 314

Humanitarian
  Consequences, 37–39
  Disarmament. *See* disarmament
  Efforts, 11
  Pledge, 14

ICAN, xv, 4, 54, 193, 283–300, 308, 310, 330
ICJ, 40
  Advisory Opinion, 102–103, 106, 131–134,
    206–225
  Advisory Opinion, 1996, 13, 18, 29
ILA, 148
ILC, 133, 348, 373
International Campaign to Abolish Nuclear
    Weapons. *See* ICAN
International Day for the Total Elimination of
    Nuclear Weapons, 39
Iran, 79, 107, 126, 127, 403

Japan, 101, 193–197, 311, 322

Land Mine Ban Treaty, 50

Marshall Islands, 14, 50, 68, 204, 209, 287, 290, 291,
    309, 347, 363, 365, 369
MNWC, 13

Non-first use policy, 229
Normative behavior, 226, 235, 383
North Korea, 58, 77, 89, 103, 196, 323
NPT
  Article IV, 12, 67, 272
  Article VI, 14, 29, 52–59
  Review Conference
    1995, 113.1
    2000, 111.1, 111.2, 111.3

2010, 110.1, 110.2, 110.3
2015, 112.1
Nuclear fear, 8–10, 167, 302, 321–323, 337, 377–378,
383–384
Winnipeg Declaration, 393–405, 412–413
Nuclear waste, 408–409, 413
Nuclear Zero (Group), 291
NWFZ, 267–268

Outer Space Treaty, 81–83, 268, 272

Pelindaba Treaty, 81, 268, 270, 274–276
Plutonium, 94
Proliferation Security Initiative, 156
PTBT, 6, 75, 80

Radioactive Waste, 270, 272, 331
Rarotonga Treaty, 81, 181, 192, 219, 268, 270,
274–276
Red Cross, 42
Resolute states, 8, 237–238, 242–243, 265, 278–279
Resolution, 23
1653 (XVI), 208
67/409, 24
68/32, 26, 31
68/46, 44
69/41, 44
70/33, 88
71/258, 15, 45, 116, 138
71/371, 26, 39
96/41, 24
A/67/409, 44
A/70/33, 25

A/70/460, 44
Millennium, 16, 44, 370
S-10/2,16
Russia, 182–185, 314
CSTO, 201

Seabed Arms Control Treaty, 81, 83–85, 268, 273
Security Council, 215–219
Self-declaration, 139
Shanghai Cooperation Organisation, 7, 169, 201
SIPRI, 54
South Africa, 319–320, 323
Stalwart states, 8, 237–243, 265, 278–279
START, 32–33, 318
Stigma, 59, 280–304, 383
Sustainable development, 39

Terrorism, 19, 32, 61, 162, 172, 190, 237,
262–264, 391
Cyber, 39
Global Initiative to Combat Global Terrorism,
148, 156
Tlatelolco Treaty, 80, 89, 219, 233, 268, 269, 274, 321
Treaty on the Elimination of Intermediate-Range
and Shorter-Range Missiles, 135, 184, 205

Ukraine, 319
Uranium, 40, 78, 80, 93, 250, 319–320, 392, 407
Mining, 298, 308, 401, 413

Verification, 155–156
Vienna Humanitarian Impact of Nuclear
Weapons Conference, 14, 29, 89, 288, 363

CPSIA information can be obtained
at www.ICGtesting.com
Printed in the USA
LVHW011609030821
694401LV00006B/365